Methods of
Meta-Analysis

Methods of Meta-Analysis

Correcting Error and Bias in Research Findings

John E. Hunter
Frank L. Schmidt

SAGE PUBLICATIONS
The International Professional Publishers
Newbury Park   London   New Delhi

For information address:

SAGE Publications, Inc.
2455 Teller Road
Newbury Park, California 91320

SAGE Publications Ltd.
6 Bonhill Street
London EC2A 4PU
United Kingdom

SAGE Publications India Pvt. Ltd.
M-32 Market
Greater Kailash I
New Delhi 110 048 India

Printed in the United States of America

Library of Congress Cataloging-in-Publication Data

Hunter, John E. (John Edward), 1939-
    Methods of meta-analysis : correcting error and bias in research
findings / John E. Hunter, Frank L. Schmidt.
        p.   cm.
    Includes bibliographical references.
    ISBN 0-8039-3222-7. — ISBN 0-8039-3223-5 (pbk.)
    1. Social sciences — Statistical methods.   2. Meta-analysis.
I. Schmidt, Frank L.   II. Title.
HA29.H847   1990
300'.72—dc20
                                                        89-10766
                                                        CIP

91   92   93   94   15   14   13   12   11   10   9   8   7   6   5   4   3   2

Brief Contents

Contents

Preface

Scientists have known for centuries that a single study will not resolve a major issue. Indeed, a small sample study will not even resolve a minor issue. Thus, the foundation of science is the cumulation of knowledge from the results of many studies.

There are two steps to the cumulation of knowledge: (1) the cumulation of results across studies to establish facts, and (2) the formation of theories to organize the facts into a coherent and useful form. The focus of this book is on the first of these, the resolution of the basic facts from a set of studies that all bear on the same relationship. For many years this was not an important issue in the social sciences because the number of studies dealing with a given issue was small. But that time has passed. There are now hundreds of studies that have sought to measure the extent to which we can predict job performance in clerical work from cognitive ability, hundreds of studies that seek to measure the effect of psychotherapy, and so on.

With as many as a hundred or more studies on a relationship, one might think that there would be a resolution of the issue. Yet most review studies traditionally have not concluded with resolution, but with a call for more research on the question. This has been especially frustrating to organizations that fund research in the behavioral and social sciences. Many such organizations are now questioning the usefulness of research in the social sciences on just this ground. If research never resolves issues, then why spend millions of dollars on research?

In this book we will review all the methods that have been proposed for cumulating knowledge across studies, including the narrative review, counting statistically significant findings, and the averaging of quantitative outcome measures. Our critique will show that the narrative review has often worked poorly. We will note how significance counting can be done correctly in those limited conditions in which it is appropriate. Most of the book will be devoted to methods of averaging results across studies (as advocated by Glass, 1976, and Schmidt & Hunter, 1977). We will refer to the averaging methods as "meta-analysis" (we view the Glass procedure as only one such method). Most methods of meta-analysis have been concerned with one artifactual source of variation across studies: sampling error. Following the lead of work in personnel selection on "validity generalization," we will extend meta-analysis to consider two other major problems that create artifactual variation across studies: error of measurement, and range variation (restriction of range in personnel selection). We will also consider other artifacts, such as the effects of dichotomization of continuous variables, and errors in data.

The main focus of the book will be on methods of distinguishing between variance across studies due to artifacts (such as sampling error, error of measurement, and restriction in range) and variance across studies due to real moderator variables. We will also present a historical review of cumulation methods after the current methods have been described.

The Meta-Analysis Dilemma for Behavioral and Social Scientists

Meta-analysis is rapidly increasing in importance in the behavioral and social sciences, a development we predicted in our 1982 meta-analysis book. The increasing importance of meta-analysis and the reasons for it are discussed in Chapter 1. But most behavioral and social scientists will not need this presentation to be convinced; the evidence is in the journals they read. It is not merely the use of meta-analysis that has increased; the number of different techniques and methods in meta-analysis has also increased dramatically, particularly since some mathematical statisticians have turned their attention in this direction. The result has been a proliferation of complex and highly technical and statistical journal articles on proposed new techniques in meta-analysis. Books on meta-analysis that are equally forbidding have also been published. A survey of primary authors of reviews in *Psychological Bulletin* — a group that should be more familiar with meta-analysis than most of their colleagues — obtained the following responses to this question (Jackson, 1984):

How familiar are you with meta-analysis at this time?

1. Very familiar; I have used it.	12%
2. Fairly familiar; I could use it without much further study.	21%
3. Somewhat familiar; I know the basic principles.	35%
4. Not very familiar; I could not state the basic principles.	31%

Clearly, even many authors of research reviews are unfamiliar with meta-analysis. The percentage that is completely unfamiliar with even basic meta-analysis principles is almost certainly much larger than 31% in the social sciences in general.

These developments have placed many researchers and teachers of methodological courses in a difficult position: they need to know and understand meta-analysis to be effective in their work, yet they do not have the time, inclination, or sometimes the training, to plough through the highly technical material now available on meta-analysis. Many need to apply meta-analysis in their own research. But even those with no plans to apply meta-analysis must be familiar with it to understand the research literature in their fields. Today, it is a rare research literature that is still unaffected by applications of meta-analysis; it will be even less common in the future (see Chapter 1). Thus, the need for familiarity with meta-analysis is now almost universal. But with the "fuller development" of meta-analysis methods of recent years, many of the published articles, and many chapters and sections in books, are now devoted to elaboration and exploration of methods that are really of only statistical interest; that is, they are devoted to methods that, despite their statistical elegance, will rarely be used in reality, because better methods are available or because the data conditions required for their application are virtually never met. For those who are primarily researchers rather than methodologists, reading and evaluating such articles is probably not the best use of their time.

In this book we have attempted to sort the wheat from the chaff. We have made judgments about which meta-analysis methods are the most useful and informative for researchers in integrating research findings across studies. For these methods, we have attempted to present a simple, clear and thorough presentation. The goal is that the reader will not only understand but be able to apply these methods based on the material in this book. We have not attempted to be encyclopedic; we do not cover all meta-analysis methods in detail. In the case of those methods that are less informative or practical than other available methods, we present only a general conceptual description and references for further reading. Methods for the cumulation of p-values across studies are one such example. Our interest has been to spare the reader the difficult and time-consuming task of wading through complex statistical material that has little future applications value. We hope this will leave more of the reader's time and energy for the technical material that is truly useful.

In short, our goal has been to write a meta-analysis book that is (1) simply and clearly enough written that it is understandable by most researchers in the behavioral and social sciences, and (2) focused on the meta-analysis methods that we believe are the most useful and informative in integrating research, rather than exhaustively treating all methods, both trivial and important. Thus, this book attempts to provide a solution to the dilemma faced by many researchers today. To the extent that this purpose is achieved, this book will have been successful.

Brief History of this Book

Gene V. Glass published the first journal article on meta-analysis in 1976. In that article, he laid out the essential rationale and defined many of the basic features of meta-analysis as it is known and used today. He also coined the term "meta-analysis." Unaware of Glass's work, we developed our meta-analysis methods in 1975 and applied them to empirical data sets from personnel selection research. But, instead of submitting our report immediately for publication, we entered it in the James McKeen Cattell Research Design contest sponsored by Division 14 (The Society for Industrial and Organization Psychology) of the American Psychological Association. Although our development and initial applications of meta-analysis won the Cattell award for 1976, a one-year delay in publication resulted (Schmidt & Hunter, 1977). But Glass's (1976) article was not only first in time, it was also the first to emphasize meta-analysis as a fully general set of methods that should be applied to the integration of literatures in all areas of research. Although our article mentioned this as a possibility for the future, our major emphasis was on solving the problem of the apparent substantial variability of test validities in the personnel selection literature (see Chapter 4). However, we were aware of and discussed the potential of our methods for broader application. So when Lee J. Cronbach suggested to us in correspondence in early 1978 that our methods might be usefully generalized to research literatures in many different areas of the behavioral and social sciences, we had already begun to think about a possible book. That book was published in 1982 (Hunter, Schmidt, & Jackson, 1982). (Again, Glass was first; he and his associates published their book on meta-analysis in 1981 [Glass, McGaw & Smith, 1981]). Since then, the methods presented in our 1982 book have been widely applied, particularly in the industrial-organizational research literature (see Hunter & Hirsh, 1987), but also in other areas. However, our 1982 work was intended to be a short introductory book on meta-analysis; as a result, some potentially useful material was omitted. And since then there have been many new developments in meta-analysis methodology and numerous new applications of interest. As a result, we began to receive requests from colleagues and researchers for an expanded and updated treatment of meta-analysis. This book is our attempt to respond to that need.

Other Characteristics of this Book

There are six other characteristics of this book that should be mentioned.

First, this is the only meta-analysis book focused specifically on the areas of Industrial-Organizational (I/O) Psychology and Organizational Behavior (OB). Other books focus on research in other areas: social psychology (Rosenthal, 1984; Cooper, 1984) or research in education (Hedges & Olkin, 1985; Glass, et al., 1981). Wolf (1986) is a very short (56 pages) overview of meta-analysis. In keeping with this substantive emphasis, we have used examples from the I/O and OB research literatures.

Second, this book is different from other books on meta-analysis because of its presentation of methods unique to our approach to meta-analysis. Specifically, our methods allow one to determine how much of the variance in findings across studies is due to sampling error, measurement artifacts, and other artifacts, and to adjust for the effects of these artifacts, yielding an estimate of the true population variability of study outcomes. This true variance is often either remarkably small or zero, indicating that many of the apparent disagreements among different studies are illusory. Our methods also allow correction of correlations and study effect sizes for the attenuating effects of measurement error and other artifacts. The meta-analysis methods used to make these corrections are typically based on psychometric principles, and thus these methods can collectively be referred to as psychometric meta-analysis. There are no comparable methods in the Glass, McGaw, and Smith (1981), Rosenthal (1984), or Cooper (1984) books. This distinction is discussed by Bangert-Drowns (1986) in his review of meta-analysis methods. The Glass et al. (1982) method focuses on magnitudes of effect sizes, like our method, but does not correct the variance of effect sizes for variance produced by artifacts. Rosenthal (1984) focuses primarily on the cumulation of p-values (significance levels) across studies, with some emphasis on mean effect sizes, but very little emphasis at all on the variance of effect sizes. Cooper (1984) focuses primarily on methods for locating and organizing primary studies and has only a limited treatment of statistical methods of combining results across studies. His statistical methods are similar to those of Rosenthal (1984). The Light and Pillemer (1984) book focuses heavily on the use of qualitative information in conjunction with meta-analysis methods that are similar to those of Glass and Rosenthal.

Third, this book examines in detail the severe distorting effects of statistical, measurement, and other methodological artifacts on the outcomes of the *individual* study. In addition to its contribution to the question of how best to combine findings across studies, this examination illustrates how untrustworthy empirical data in any study can be and usually are. In our judgment, there is a strong cult of overconfident empiricism in the behavioral and social sciences. There is an excessive faith in data as the source of scientific truths and an inadequate appreciation of how misleading most social science data are when accepted at face value and interpreted naively. The commonly held belief that research progress will be made if only we "let the data speak" is sadly erroneous. Because of the effects of the artifacts discussed in this book, it would be more accurate to say that data come to us encrypted, and to understand their meaning we must first break the code. One purpose of this book is to contribute to that process.

Fourth, we have attempted to write this book in a simple, direct and readable style. We believe there is a need for a book that can be read and understood by behavioral and social scientists who are not mathematical statisticians or even methodological specialists. The essential concepts in meta-analysis are not complex or difficult. We reject the position that to be correct and authoritative, discussions of meta-analysis must be written in the arcane language of mathematical statistics. Where appropriate and needed, we cite such references for further reading. More difficult statistical material (demonstration, proofs, and so on) has been put in special sections; those who are interested will find the detailed treatment there, while the average reader can skip over these materials. This book is intended to be a clear nontechnical presentation that makes important methodological tools available to a wider group of users. This was a deliberate choice. We recognize the dilemma in mode of presentation. Authors who present methodological material in highly complex technical language avoid the criticism that they are oversimplifying complex issues and questions. On the other hand, their presentations have little impact because they are not widely read; and when they are read, they are often misunderstood and misquoted. Authors who present matters in simpler, more direct language can communicate to a much wider audience; however, critics often charge that they have ignored many complexities and special cases. Also, there is among some an unfortunate tendency to believe that anything that can be communicated clearly in relatively nontechnical language must be unimportant and/or inherently too simple to be of much real scientific significance. We will take that chance.

However, none of this means that this book is a simplified presentation of methods that have appeared elsewhere earlier in less accessible form. This book is not a presentation of the existing literature. It contains much new and original material on meta-analysis methods — material that cannot be found in journals or in books (including our 1982 meta-analysis book). It also contains considerable new material of a conceptual (as opposed to methodological) nature.

A fifth feature of this book is the extensive use of examples to illustrate meta-analysis methods. To keep the examples simple and to avoid large data sets, the examples are usually based on hypothetical (but realistic) data.

Finally, we have included information on meta-analysis computer programs (in IBM BASIC) in Appendix 1. These are programs that we have written and used in some of our own research. These programs can be run on any IBM PC or clone. We have found these programs to be useful, and others who have used them have, too.

Organization of the Book

In normal science writing, historical review is presented first. However, in our case the historical review is very difficult for novices. In effect, the new methods can only be compared to earlier methods if the new methods are first understood. Therefore, we will first present the methods of psychometric meta-analysis in some detail. Later in the book (Chapter 11), we will present our review and critique of earlier methods.

In the course of conducting a meta-analysis, the steps would be as follows: (1) search for and gather studies, (2) extract and code information from the studies, and (3) apply meta-analysis to the information extracted. We will discuss all three steps, but not in their natural chronological order. The reason for this is that to know what is good or bad procedure in early steps, you must know what you are going to do in the third step. Thus, we will cover meta-analysis methods first, then return to issues of defining the study domain, deciding what to code, and writing up the meta-analysis report. Finally, we will go back one step further and present a list of recommendations for changes in publication practices for primary studies that we believe are necessary for optimal cumulation of results across studies.

ACKNOWLEDGMENTS

This book did not just appear out of a vacuum without assistance and stimulation from others. We would like to thank all of our colleagues and students whose persistent curiosity and questions about meta-analysis stimulated the development of many of the new ideas and methods in this book. We would also like to thank them for repeatedly urging us to write this new, expanded treatment of psychometric meta-analysis and for encouraging us to finish it once we had started. We hope they will be happy with the final product. We would like to thank our editors, Diane Foster and Deborah Laughton, for their patience, professionalism, and support. Finally, we would like to thank those who worked so hard and so skillfully and professionally on the preparation of the manuscript: Denise Davis, Kate Walters, and Irma Herring. And we would like to thank Phyllis Irwin for her skillful coordination of the whole complex process.

PART I

Introduction to Meta-Analysis

1 Integrating Research Findings Across Studies

Before we delve into an abstract discussion of methods, we would like to consider a concrete example. The next section presents a set of studies to be reviewed, then a sample narrative review, followed by a critique of this review. It has been our experience that personal experience with the problems of such a review greatly quickens the learning process.

General Problem and an Example

A major task in all areas of science is the development of theory. In many cases, the theorists have available the results of a number of previous studies on the subject of interest. Their first task is to find out what empirical relationships have been revealed in these studies so they can take them into account in theory construction. In developing an understanding of these relationships, it is often helpful in reviewing the studies to make up a table summarizing the findings of these studies. Table 1.1 shows such a summary table put together by a psychologist attempting to develop a theory of the relationship between job satisfaction and organizational commitment. In addition to the observed correlations and their sample sizes, the psychologist has recorded data on (1) sex, (2) organization size, (3) job level, (4) race, (5) age, and (6) geographical location. The researcher believes variables 1, 2, 3, and 4 may affect the extent to which job satisfaction gets translated into organizational commitment. The researcher has no hypotheses about variables 5 and 6, but has recorded them since they were often available.

As an exercise in integrating findings across studies and constructing theory, we would like you to spend a few minutes examining and interpreting the data in Table 1.1. We would like you to jot down the following:

1. the tentative conclusions you reached about the relationship between job satisfaction and organizational commitment and the variables that do and do not moderate that relation
2. an outline of your resulting theory of this relationship.

Table 1.1 Correlations Between Organizational Commitment and Job Satisfaction

Study	N	r	Sex	Size of Organization	White vs. Blue Collar	Race	Under vs. Over 30	North vs. South
(1)	20	.46*	F	S	WC	B	U	N
(2)	72	.32**	M	L	BC	Mixed	Mixed	N
(3)	29	.10	M	L	WC	W	O	N
(4)	30	.45**	M	L	WC	W	Mixed	N
(5)	71	.18	F	L	BC	W	O	N
(6)	62	.45**	F	S	BC	W	U	N
(7)	25	.56**	M	S	BC	Mixed	U	S
(8)	46	.41**	F	L	WC	W	Mixed	S
(9)	22	.55**	F	S	WC	B	U	N
(10)	69	.44**	F	S	BC	W	U	N
(11)	67	.34**	M	L	BC	W	Mixed	N
(12)	58	.33**	M	S	BC	W	U	N
(13)	23	.14	M	S	WC	B	O	S
(14)	20	.36	M	S	WC	W	Mixed	N
(15)	28	.54**	F	L	WC	W	Mixed	S
(16)	30	.22	M	S	BC	W	Mixed	S
(17)	69	.31**	F	L	BC	W	Mixed	N
(18)	59	.43**	F	L	BC	W	Mixed	N
(19)	19	.52*	M	S	BC	W	Mixed	S
(20)	44	−.10	M	S	WC	W	O	N
(21)	60	.44**	F	L	BC	Mixed	Mixed	N
(22)	23	.50**	F	S	WC	W	Mixed	S
(23)	19	−.02	M	S	WC	B	O	S
(24)	55	.32**	M	L	WC	W	Mixed	Unknown
(25)	19	.19	F	S	WC	B	O	N
(26)	26	.53**	F	S	BC	B	U	S
(27)	58	.30*	M	L	WC	W	Mixed	S
(28)	25	.26	M	S	WC	W	U	S
(29)	28	.09	F	S	BC	W	O	N
(30)	26	.31	F	S	WC	Mixed	U	S

*p < .05.
**p < .01.

A Typical Interpretation of the Example Data

The typical report on the findings shown in Table 1.1 would run like this: The correlation between occupational commitment and job satisfaction varies from study to study with a median value of .34 and a range of −.10 to .56. Although 19 out of 30 studies found a significant correlation, 11 of 30 studies found no relationship between commitment and satisfaction. Why are commitment and satisfaction correlated within some organizations and not within others?

Table 1.2 The Existence of Correlation Between Organizational Commitment and Job Satisfaction as Under Various Conditions Shown by the Studies in Table 1.1

	Sex				Organization Size		
	M	F			S	L	
Not Significant	7	4	11	Not Significant	9	2	11
Significant	8	11	19	Significant	9	10	19
	15	15	30		18	12	30
	$\chi^2 = 1.29$				$\chi^2 = 3.44$		

	Job Level				Race			
	WC	BC			W	B	Mix	
Not Significant	8	3	11	Not Significant	7	3	1	11
Significant	8	11	19	Significant	13	3	3	19
	16	14	30		20	6	4	30
	$\chi^2 = 2.62$				$\chi^2 = 1.64$			

	Age					Geographical Location		
	Young	Old	Mix			N	S	
Not Significant	2	7	2	11	Not Significant	6	5	11
Significant	7	0	12	19	Significant	11	7	18
	9	7	14	30		17	12	29
	$\chi^2 = 16.52$					$\chi^2 = .12$		

Table 1.2 presents a breakdown of the findings according to the features of the organization and the nature of the work population being studied. For example, for male work populations, commitment and satisfaction were correlated in eight studies and not correlated in seven (i.e., correlated in 53% of the studies), while for women there was a correlation in eleven of fifteen cases (or in 73% of the studies). Correlation was found in 83% of the large organizations, but in only 50% of the small organizations. Correlation was found in 79% of the blue-collar populations, but in only 50% of the white-collar populations. Correlation was found in 67% of the populations that were all white or mixed race, while correlations were

found in only 50% of those work populations that were all black. Correlation was found in 83% of the cases in which the work force was all under 30 or a mixture of younger and older workers, while not a single study with only older workers found a significant correlation. Finally, 65% of the studies done in the North found a correlation, while only 58% of the Southern studies found a correlation.

Each of the differences between work populations could be regarded as the basis for a hypothesis that there is an interaction between that characteristic and organizational commitment in the determination of job satisfaction. However, some caution must be urged since the only chi-square value that is significant in Table 1.2 is that for age. That is, the difference in the frequency of correlation between older and younger workers is significant (χ^2 = 16.52; df = 2; p < .01), while the other differences can only be regarded as trends.

If the studies done on older workers are removed, then significant correlation is found for 19 of the remaining 23 studies. If these 23 cases are examined for relationship to organizational characteristics, then all of the chi squares are nonsignificant. These results are shown in Table 1.3. However, the chi square for size of organization is very close (χ^2 = 3.72; 3.84 required). Within the 23 studies with younger or mixed-age work populations, all 10 correlations for large organizations were significant.

There are thirteen studies of younger or mixed-age work populations in small organizations. None of the chi-square values even approaches significance on this set of studies, although with thirteen cases the power of the chi-square test is low. These results are shown in Table 1.4. Within this group of studies, there is a tendency for correlation between organizational commitment and job satisfaction to be more likely found among women, among blue-collar workers, in all black work populations, and in the North.

Conclusion

Organizational commitment and job satisfaction are correlated in some organizational settings, but not in others. In work groups in which all workers are over thirty, the correlation between commitment and satisfaction was never significant. For young or mixed-age work populations, commitment and satisfaction are always correlated in large organizations. For young or mixed-age work populations in small organizations, correlation was found in nine of thirteen studies with no organizational feature capable of perfectly accounting for those cases in which correlation was not found.

Table 1.3 Analysis of Correlations from Studies Based on Younger or Mixed Age Subjects

	Sex				Organization Size		
	M	F			S	L	
Not Significant	3	1	4	Not Significant	4	0	4
Significant	8	11	19	Significant	9	10	19
	11	12	23		13	10	23

$$\chi^2 = 1.43 \qquad\qquad \chi^2 = 3.72$$

	Job Level				Race			
	WC	BC			W	B	Mix	
Not Significant	3	1	4	Not Significant	3	0	1	4
Significant	8	11	19	Significant	13	3	3	19
	11	12	23		16	3	4	23

$$\chi^2 = 1.43 \qquad\qquad \chi^2 = .81; \; df = 2$$

	Geographic Area		
	N	S	
Not Significant	1	3	4
Significant	11	7	18
	12	10	22

$$\chi^2 = 1.72$$

These findings are consistent with a model that assumes that organizational commitment grows over about a ten-year period to a maximum value at which it asymptotes. Among older workers, organizational commitment may be so uniformly high that there is no variation. Hence, among older workers there can be no correlation between commitment and job satisfaction. The finding for large organizations suggests that growth of commitment is slower there, thus generating a greater variance among workers of different ages within the younger group.

Table 1.4 Analysis of Correlations from Studies Based on Younger and Mixed Age Subjects in Small Organizations

	Sex				Job Level		
	M	F			WC	BC	
Not Significant	3	1	4	Not Significant	3	1	4
Significant	3	6	9	Significant	9	10	19
	6	7	13		13	10	23
	$\chi^2 = 1.93$				$\chi^2 = 1.93$		

	Race					Geographical Location		
	W	B	Mix			N	S	
Not Significant	3	0	1	4	Not Significant	1	3	4
Significant	5	3	1	9	Significant	4	4	8
	8	3	2	13		5	7	12
	$\chi^2 = 1.84$					$\chi^2 = .69$		

Critique of the Sample Review

The preceding review was conducted using standard review practices that characterize many review articles not only in psychology, but in sociology, education, and the rest of the social sciences as well. Yet every conclusion in the review is false. The data were constructed by a Monte Carlo run in which the population correlation was always assumed to be .33. After a sample size was randomly chosen from a distribution centering about 40, an observed correlation was chosen using the standard normal distribution for r with mean $\rho = .33$ and variance

$$\frac{(1 - \rho^2)^2}{N - 1}.$$

That is, the variation in results in Table 1.1 is entirely the result of sampling error. Each study is assumed to be conducted on small sample size and hence will generate an observed correlation that will depart by some random amount from the population value of .33. The size of the departure depends on sample size. Note that the largest and smallest values found in Table 1.1 are all from studies with very small samples. The larger sample size studies tend to be found in the central part of the range, i.e., they tend to show less of a random departure from .33.

The moderator effects appear to make sense, yet they are purely the results of chance. The values for the organizational characteristics were assigned to the studies randomly. The fact that one of the six was highly significant is due solely to capitalization on chance.

The crucial lesson to be learned from this exercise is this: "Conflicting results in the literature" may be entirely artifactual. The data in Table 1.1 were generated by using one artifact for generating false variation across studies, sampling error. There are other artifacts that are found in most sets of studies: Studies vary in terms of the quality of measurement in their scales; researchers make computational or computer errors; people make typographical errors in copying numbers from computer output or in copying numbers from handwritten tables onto manuscripts or in setting tables into print; people study variables in settings with greater or smaller ranges of individual differences, and so on. In our experience (to be described later), most of the interactions invented to account for differences in findings in different studies are nonexistent, i.e., they are apparitions composed of the ectoplasm of sampling error and other artifacts.

Problems with Statistical Significance Tests

In the data set given in Table 1.1, all population correlations are actually equal to .33. Of the 30 correlations, 19 were found to be statistically significant. But 11 of the 30 correlations were not significant. That is, the significance test gave the wrong answer 11 out of 30 times, an error rate of 37%. In oral presentation, many express shock that the error rate can be greater than 5%. The significance test was derived in response to the problem of sampling error, and many believe that the use of significance tests guarantees an error rate of 5% or less. This is just not true. Statisticians have pointed this out for many years; the possibility of high error rates is brought out in discussions of the "power" of statistical tests. However, statistics teachers are all well aware that this point is missed by most students. The 5% error rate is guaranteed only if the null hypothesis is true. If the null hypothesis is false, then the error rate can go as high as 95%.

Let us state this in more formal language. If the null hypothesis is true for the population and our sample data leads us to reject it, then we have made a Type I error. If the null hypothesis is false for the population and our sample data leads us to accept it, then we have made a Type II error. The statistical significance test is defined in such a way that Type I error rate is at most 5%. However the Type II error rate is left free to be as high as 95%. The question is which error rate applies to a given study. The answer is that the relevant error rate can only be known if we know whether the null hypothesis is true or false for that study. If we know that the null hypothesis is true, then we know that the significance test has an error rate of 5%. Of course, if we know that the null hypothesis is true and we still do a significance test, then we should be told to wear a dunce cap. If we know the null hypothesis to be true, then we can obtain a 0% error rate by ignoring the data. That is, there is a fundamental circularity to the significance test. If you do not know whether the null hypothesis is true or false, then you do not know whether the relevant error rate is the Type I error or the Type II, i.e., you do not know if your error rate is 5% or some value as high as 95%. There is only one way to guarantee a 5% error rate in all cases: abandon the significance test and use a confidence interval.

Consider our hypothetical example from Table 1.1. But let us simplify the example still further by assuming that the sample size is the same for all studies, say $N = 40$. The one-tailed significance test for a correlation coefficient is $\sqrt{N-1}\,r \geq 1.64$; in our case $\sqrt{39}\,r \geq 1.64$ or $r \geq .26$. If the population correlation is .33 and the sample size is 40, the mean of the sample correlation is .33, while the standard deviation is $(1 - \rho^2)/\sqrt{N-1} = (1 - .33^2)/\sqrt{39} = .14$. Thus, the probability that the observed correlation will be significant is the probability that the sample mean correlation will be greater than .26 when it has a mean of .33 and a standard deviation of .14.

$$P\{r \geq .26\} = P\left\{\frac{r - .33}{.14} \geq \frac{.26 - .33}{.14}\right\} = P\{z \geq -.50\} = .69$$

That is, if all studies were done with a sample size of 40, then a population correlation of .33 would mean an error rate of 31%.

Suppose that we alter the population correlation in our hypothetical example from .33 to .20. Then the probability that the observed correlation will be significant drops from .69 to

$$P\{r \geq .26\} = P\left\{z \geq \frac{.26 - .20}{.15} = .39\right\} = .35$$

That is, the error rate rises from 31% to 65%. In this realistic example, we see that the error rate can be over 50%. A two-to-one majority of the studies can find the correlation to be not significant despite the fact that the population correlation is always .20.

Error rates of over 50% have been shown to be the usual case in personnel selection research. Thus, reviewers who count the number of significant findings are prone to incorrectly conclude that a given procedure does not predict job performarce. Furthermore, as Hedges and Olkin (1980) point out, this situation wil only get worse as more studies are done. The reviewer will become ever more convinced that the majority of studies show no effect and that the effect thus does not exist.

If the null hypothesis were true in a set of studies, then the base rate for significance is not 50% but 5%. If more than one in twenty studies finds significance, then the null hypothesis must be false in some studies. We must then avoid an error made by some of the reviewers who know the 5% base rate. Given 35% significant findings, some have concluded that "Since 5% will be significant by chance, this means that the number of studies in which the null hypothesis is truly false is 35–5 = 30%." Our hypothetical example shows this reasoning to be false. If the population correlation is .20 in every study and the sample size is always 40, then there will be significant findings on only 35% of the studies even though the null hypothesis is false in all cases.

The typical use of significance test results leads to terrible errors in review studies. Most review studies falsely conclude that further research is needed to resolve the "conflicting results" in the literature. These errors in review studies can only be eliminated if errors in the interpretation of significance tests can be eliminated. Yet those of us who have been teaching power to generation after generation of graduate students have been unable to change the reasoning processes and the false belief in the 5% error rate (Sedlmeier & Gigerenzer, 1989). If there is an alternative analysis, then maybe it is time to abandon the significance test.

There are two alternatives to the significance test. At the level of review studies, there is meta-analysis. At the level of single studies, there is the confidence interval.

The Confidence Interval

Consider studies 17 and 30 from our hypothetical example in Table 1.1. Study 17, with $r = .31$ and $N = 69$, finds the correlation to be significant at the .01 level. Study 30, with $r = .31$ and $N = 26$, finds the correlation to be not significant. That is, two authors with an identical finding, $r = .31$, come to opposite conclusions. Author 17 concludes that organizational commitment is highly related to job satisfaction, while Author 30 concludes that they are independent. Thus, two studies with identical findings can lead to a review author claiming "conflicting results in the literature."

The conclusions are quite different if the results are interpreted with confidence intervals. Author 17 reports a finding of $r = .31$ with a 95% confidence interval of $.10 \leq \rho \leq .52$. Author 30 reports a finding of $r = .31$ with a 95% confidence interval of $-.04 \leq \rho \leq .66$. There is no conflict between these results; the two confidence intervals overlap substantially. On the other hand, the fact recorded by the significance test is still given in the two confidence intervals. Study 17 finds that $\rho = 0$ is not a reasonable possibility, while study 30 finds that $\rho = 0$ cannot be ruled out. Thus the two separate studies do not draw conclusions inconsistent with the significance test. But the two studies considered together lead to the correct conclusion if confidence intervals are used.

Consider now studies 26 and 30 from Table 1.1. Study 26 finds $r = .53$ with $N = 26$, which is significant at the .01 level. Study 30 finds $r = .31$ with $N = 26$, which is not significant. That is, we have two studies with the same sample size but apparently widely divergent results. Using significance tests, one would conclude that there must be some moderator that accounts for the difference. This conclusion is false.

Had the two studies used confidence intervals, the conclusion would be different. The confidence interval for study 26 is $.25 \leq \rho \leq .81$ and the confidence interval for study 30 is $-.04 \leq \rho \leq .66$. It is true that the confidence interval for study 30 includes $\rho = 0$, while the confidence interval for study 26 does not; this is the fact registered by the significance test. But the crucial thing is that the two confidence intervals show an overlap of $.25 \leq \rho \leq .66$. Thus, consideration of the two studies together leads to the correct conclusion that it is possible that both studies could imply the same value for the population correlation ρ. Indeed, the overlapping intervals include the correct value, $\rho = .33$.

Two studies with the same population value can have nonoverlapping confidence intervals, but this is a low probability event (about 5 percent). But then confidence intervals are not the optimal method for looking at results across studies; that distinction belongs to meta-analysis.

Confidence intervals work better than significance tests for two reasons. First, the interval is correctly centered on the observed value rather than on the hypothetical value of the null hypothesis. Second, it gives the author a correct image of the extent of uncertainty in small-subsample studies. It may be disconcerting to see a confidence interval as wide as $-.04 \leq \rho \leq .66$, but that is far superior to the frustration produced over the years by the false belief in "conflicting results."

Confidence intervals can be used to generate definitions for the phrase "small sample size." Suppose that we want the confidence interval for the correlation coefficient to define the correlation to the first digit, i.e., to have a width of $\pm .05$. Then, for small population correlations, the minimum sample size is approximately 1,538. In order that a sample size of 1,000 be sufficient, the population correlation must be at least .44. Thus, under this standard of accuracy, for correlational studies "small-sample size" includes all studies with less than a thousand persons and often extends higher yet.

There is a similar calculation for experimental studies. If the statistic used is the d statistic (by far the most frequent choice at this time), then small-effect sizes will be specified to their first digit only if the sample size is 3,076. If the effect size is larger, then the sample size must be even greater than 3,076. For example, if the difference between the population means is .3 standard deviations or more, then the minimum sample size to yield accuracy to within ± .05 of .30 is 6,216. Thus, given this standard of accuracy, for experimental studies, "small-sample size" begins with 3,000 and often extends well beyond that.

Confidence intervals give a correct picture of the extent of uncertainty that surrounds results computed from small-sample studies. However, the only way to eliminate uncertainty is to either run large-sample single studies or to combine results across many small-sample studies. Given the limited resources available to social scientists, this means that the only possible answer in most areas is meta-analysis.

Meta-Analysis

Is there a quantitative analysis that would have suggested that all the differences in Table 1.1 might stem from sampling error? Suppose we compute the variance of the correlations, weighting each by its sample size. The value we obtain is .02258 (SD = .150). We can also compute the variance expected solely on the bias of sampling error. The formula for the sampling error variance of each individual correlation r_i is $(1 - .331^2)^2/(N_i - 1)$, where .331 is the sample size weighted mean of the correlations in Table 1.1. If we weight each of these estimates by its sample size (as we did in the case of the observed variance), the formula for variance expected from sampling error is:

$$S_e^2 = \frac{\sum\limits_{i=1}^{i=30} \left[\dfrac{N_i (1 - .331^2)^2}{N_i - 1} \right]}{\Sigma N_i}$$

This value is .02058 (SD = .144). The ratio of variance expected from sampling error to actual (observed) variance is .02058/.02258 = .91. Thus, sampling error alone accounts for an estimated 91% of the observed variance in the correlations. The best conclusion is that the relation between job satisfaction and organizational commitment is constant across sexes, races, job levels, age, geographical locations, and size of organization. The best estimate of this observed value is .331 — the sample size weighted mean of the thirty correlations. Our analysis indicates that this relation holds across ages, sexes, races, geographical locations, job levels, and different-sized organizations. When people in oral presentations analyzed the data from these thirty studies qualitatively, different people came to different conclusions. In contrast, all researchers applying the quantitative method used here would (barring arithmetic errors) come to exactly the same conclusion.

For theoretical purposes, the value .331 is not the one we want, since it has been attenuated by unreliability in both measures. Suppose from information in the thirty studies, we estimate the average reliability of job satisfaction measures at .70 and the average reliability of organizational commitment measures at .60. Then the correlation between true scores on each measure is $.331/\sqrt{.70(.60)} = .51$.

In many research areas the complexity of the task of integrating findings across studies in a subjective or qualitative manner is much greater than the task presented by the data in Table 1.1 because the number of studies to be integrated is much greater than thirty. Traditional review procedures are inadequate to integrate conflicting findings across large numbers of studies. As Glass (1976, p. 4) has pointed out, the results of hundreds of studies "can no more be grasped in our traditional narrative discursive review than one can grasp the sense of 500 test scores without the aid of techniques for organizing, depicting and interpreting data." In such areas as the effects of class size on student learning, the relation of IQ to creativity, and the effects of psychotherapy on patients, literally hundreds of studies can accumulate over a period of only a few years. Glass (1976) has noted that such studies collectively contain much more information than we have been able to extract from them to date. He points out that because we have not exploited these gold mines of information, "We know much less than we have proven." What is needed are methods that will integrate results from existing studies to reveal patterns of relatively invariant underlying relations and causalities, the establishment of which will constitute general principles and cumulative knowledge.

At one time in the history of psychology and the social sciences, the pressing need was for more empirical studies examining the problem in question. In many areas of research, the need today is not additional empirical data but some means of making sense of the vast amounts of data that have been accumulated. Given the increasing number of areas within psychology and the other social sciences in which the number of available studies is quite large and the importance to theory development and practical problem solving of integrating conflicting findings to establish general knowledge, it is likely that methods for doing this will attain increasing importance in the future. Such methods can be built around statistical procedures that are already familiar to us. As Glass (1976, p. 6) has stated:

> Most of us were trained to analyze complex relationships among variables in the primary analysis of research data. But at the higher level, where variance, nonuniformity and uncertainty are no less evident, we too often substitute literary exposition for quantitative rigor. The proper integration of research requires the same statistical methods that are applied in primary data analysis.

Role of Meta-Analysis in the Behavioral and Social Sciences

In an invited address to the American Psychological Association Convention in 1970, then-Senator Fritz Mondale made the following statement:

> What I have not learned is what we should do about these problems. I had hoped to find research to support or to conclusively oppose my belief that quality integrated education is the most promising approach. But I have found very little conclusive evidence. For every study, statistical or theoretical, that contains a proposed solution or recommendation, there is always another, equally well documented, challenging the assumptions or conclusions of the first. No one seems to agree with anyone else's approach. But more distressing: no one seems to know what works. As a result I must confess, I stand with my colleagues confused and often disheartened.

Things were to get worse before they got better. By the middle or late seventies the behavioral and social sciences were in serious trouble in the United States. Large numbers of studies had accumulated on many questions that were important not only to theory development but also to social policy decisions. Results of different studies on the same question typically were conflicting. For example, are workers more productive when they are satisfied with their jobs? The studies did not agree. Do students learn more when class sizes are smaller? The studies did not agree. Does participative decision making in management work? Does job enlargement increase job satisfaction and output? Does psychotherapy really help people? The studies did not agree. The public and government officials were becoming increasingly disillusioned with the behavioral and social sciences, and it was becoming more and more difficult to obtain funding for research. Finally in 1981, David Stockman, then Director of the Federal Office of Management and Budget, proposed an 80% reduction in federal funding for research in the behavioral and social sciences. Such proposed cuts are typical trial balloons sent up to see how much political opposition they arouse. Even when proposed cuts are much smaller than a draconian 80%, constituencies can be counted on to come forward and protest the proposed cuts dramatically. This usually happens, and many behavioral and social scientists sat back and waited for it to happen. Nothing happened. The behavioral and social sciences, it turned out, had no constituency among the public. The public did not care (see "Cuts Raise New Social Science Query," 1981). Finally, out of desperation, the American Psychological Association took the lead in forming the Consortium of Social Science Associations to lobby against the proposed cuts. Although this super-association had some success in getting these cuts reduced (and even, in some areas, getting small increases in research funding in subsequent years), these developments should make us look carefully at how such a thing could happen.

The sequence of events that led to this state of affairs has been much the same in one research area after another. First, there is initial optimism about using social science research to answer socially important questions that arise. Do government sponsored job training programs work? We will do studies to find out. Does Headstart really help disadvantaged kids? The studies will tell us. Does integration increase the school achievement of black children? Research will provide the answer. Next, several studies on the question are conducted, but the results are conflicting. There is some disappointment that the question has not been answered, but policymakers — and people in general — are still optimistic. They, along with the researchers, conclude that more research is needed to identify the interactions (moderators) that have caused the conflicting findings. For example, perhaps whether job training works depends on the age and education of the trainees. Maybe smaller classes in the schools are beneficial only for lower IQ children. It is hypothesized that psychotherapy works for middle-class but not lower-class patients.

In the third phase, a large number of research studies are funded and conducted to test these moderator hypotheses. When they are completed, there is now a large body of studies, but instead of being resolved, the number of conflicts *increases*. The moderator hypotheses from the initial studies are not borne out. No one can make much sense out of the conflicting findings. Researchers conclude that the phenomenon that was selected for study in this particular case has turned out to be hopelessly complex, and turn to the investigation of another question, hoping that this time the question will turn out to be more tractable. Research sponsors, government officials, and the public become disenchanted and cynical. Research funding agencies cut money for research in this area and in related areas. After this cycle has been repeated enough times, social and behavioral scientists themselves become cynical about the value of their own work, and they publish articles expressing doubts about whether behavioral and social science research is capable *in principle* of developing cumulative knowledge and providing general answers to socially important questions (e.g., see Cronbach, 1975; Gergen, 1982; Meehl, 1978).

Clearly, at this point the need is not for more primary research studies, but for some means of making sense of the vast number of accumulated study findings. This is the purpose of meta-analysis. Applications to date have taken important steps in the direction of achieving this purpose, as the examples cited in this book illustrate. Applications of meta-analysis to accumulated research literatures have generally shown that our research findings are not nearly as conflicting as we had thought and that useful general conclusions can be drawn from past research. Cumulative knowledge is possible in the behavioral and social sciences after all. Socially important questions can be answered. Just as important, it means that scientific progress is possible. It means that cumulative understanding and progress in theory development is possible after all. It means that the behavioral and social sciences can attain the status of true sciences; they are not doomed forever to the status of pseudo-sciences, or even quasi-sciences. The gloom, cynicism, and even nihilism, that have enveloped many in the behavioral and social sciences is lifting. Young people starting out in the behavioral and social sciences today can hope for a much brighter future.

In fact, meta-analysis has even produced evidence that cumulativeness of research findings in the behavioral sciences is probably as great as in the physical sciences. We have long assumed that our research studies are less replicable than those in the physical sciences. Hedges (1987) used meta-analysis methods to examine variability of findings across studies in 13 research areas in particle physics and 13 research areas in psychology. Contrary to common belief, his findings showed that there was as much variability across studies in physics as in psychology. Furthermore, he found that the physical sciences used methods to combine findings across studies that were "essentially identical" to meta-analysis. The research literature in both areas — psychology and physics — yielded cumulative knowledge when meta-analysis was properly applied. He also found that researchers in the physical sciences (other areas as well as physics) much more frequently discarded extreme study findings (outliers) than is the case in the behavioral and social sciences. (The question of outliers is discussed in Chapter 5). In the particle physics area, roughly 40% of the available studies are omitted from meta-analysis for one reason or another (Hedges, 1987, p. 447). In the social sciences, it is rare for even the 10% of studies with the most extreme findings to be discarded. Hedges's major finding is that the frequency of conflicting research findings is probably no greater in the behavioral and social sciences than in the physical sciences. The fact that this finding has been so surprising to many social scientists points up the fact that we have long overestimated the consistency of research findings in the physical sciences. In the physical sciences also, no research question can be answered by a single study, and physical scientists must use meta-analysis to make sense of their research literature, just as we do. The same is true in medical research (Baum, Anish, Chalmers, Sacks, Smith, & Fagerstrom, 1981; Halvorsen, 1986).

Other changes have also been produced by meta-analysis. The relative status of reviews has changed dramatically. Journals that formerly published only primary studies and refused to publish reviews are now publishing meta-analytic reviews in large numbers. In the past, research reviews were based on the narrative-subjective method, and they had limited status and gained little credit for one in academic raises or promotions. Perhaps this was appropriate since such reviews rarely contributed to cumulative knowledge. The rewards went to those who did primary research. Not only is this no longer the case, but there has been a far more important development. Today, most discoveries and advances in cumulative knowledge are no longer being made by those who do primary research studies, but by those who use meta-analysis to discover the latent meaning of existing research literatures. A young behavioral or social scientist today with the needed training and skills can make major original discoveries and contributions without ever conducting a single primary research study — simply by mining the rich untapped veins of information in accumulated research literatures. This process is well under way today. The industrial-organizational psychology and organizational behavior research literatures — the ones with which we are most familiar — are rapidly being mined. The same is true in education, social psychology, and other areas.

The meta-analytic process of cleaning up and making sense of research literatures not only reveals the cumulative knowledge that is there, but also provides clearer directions about what the remaining research needs are. That is, we also learn what kinds of primary research studies are needed next. However, some have raised the concern that meta-analysis may be killing the motivation and incentive to conduct primary research studies. Meta-analysis has clearly shown that no single primary study can ever resolve an issue or answer a question. Research findings are inherently probabilistic (Taveggia, 1974), and, therefore, the results of any single study could have occurred by chance. Only meta-analytic integration of findings across studies can control chance and other artifacts and provide a foundation for conclusions. And yet meta-analysis is not possible unless the needed primary studies are conducted. In new research areas, this potential problem is not of much concern. The first study conducted on a question contains 100% of the available research information, the second contains roughly 50%, and so on. Thus, the early studies in any area have a certain status. But the 50th study contains only about 2% of the available information, and the 100th, about 1%. Will we have difficulty motivating researchers to conduct the 50th or 100th study? The answer will depend on the future reward system in the behavioral and social sciences. On the other hand, it should be noted that those who raise this question overlook a beneficial effect that meta-analysis is having: it is preventing the diversion of valuable research resources into truly unneeded research studies. Meta-analysis applications have revealed that there are questions on which additional research would waste scientifically and socially valuable resources. For example, as of 1980, 882 studies based on a total sample of 70,935 had been conducted relating measures of perceptual speed to the job performance of clerical workers. Based on these studies, our meta-analytic estimate of this correlation is .47 (SD = .22; Pearlman, Schmidt, & Hunter, 1980). For other abilities, there were often 200 to 300 cumulative studies. Clearly, further research on these relationships is not the best use of available resources.

Role of Meta-Analysis in Theory Development

The major task in the behavioral and social sciences, as in other sciences, is the development of theory. A good theory is simply a good explanation of the processes that actually take place in a phenomenon. For example, what actually happens when employees develop a high level of organizational commitment? Does job satisfaction develop first and then cause the development of commitment? If so, what causes job satisfaction to develop and how does it have an effect on commitment? How do higher levels of mental ability cause higher levels of job performance? Only by increasing job knowledge? Or also by directly improving problem solving on the job? The social scientist is essentially a detective; his or her job is to find out why and how things happen the way they do. But to construct theories, we must first know some of the basic facts, such as the empirical relations among variables. These relations are the building blocks of theory. For example, if we know there is a high and consistent population correlation between job satisfaction and organization commitment, this will send us in particular directions in developing our theory. If the correlation between these variables is very low and consistent, theory development will branch in different directions. If the relation is highly variable across organizations and settings, we will be encouraged to advance interactive or moderator-based theories. Meta-analysis provides these empirical building blocks for theory. Meta-analytic findings tell us what it is that needs to be explained by the theory. Meta-analysis has been criticized because it does not directly generate or develop theory (Guzzo, Jackson, & Katzell, 1986). This is like criticizing typewriters or word processors because they do not generate novels on their own. The results of meta-analysis are indispensable for theory construction; but theory construction itself is a creative process distinct from meta-analysis.

As implied in language used in our discussion, theories are causal explanations. The goal in every science is explanation, and explanation is always causal. In the behavioral and social sciences, the methods of path analysis (e.g., see Hunter & Gerbing, 1982) can be used to test causal theories when the data meet the assumptions of the method. The relationships revealed by meta-analysis — the empirical building blocks for theory — can be used in path analysis to test causal theories even when all the delineated relationships are observational rather than experimental. Experimentally determined relationships can also be entered into path analyses along with observationally based relations. It is only necessary to transform d values to correlations (see Chapter 7). Thus, path analyses can be "mixed." Path analysis can be a very powerful tool for narrowing down the number of theories that could possibly be consistent with the data, sometimes to a very small number, and sometimes to only one theory (Hunter, 1988). For an example, see Hunter (1983f). Every such reduction in the number of possible theories is an advance in understanding. In the introduction, we stated that it has now become a virtual necessity that every researcher understand meta-analysis. This may not yet be the case for path analysis, but it will become so in the future.

Increasing Use of Meta-Analysis

The use of meta-analysis has expanded dramatically in recent years. Guzzo, Jackson, and Katzell (1986) tabulated the number of journal articles and dissertations in *Psychological Abstracts* from 1967 to 1984 that were key worded as meta-analysis. No entries were found from 1967 to 1976; after this the rate of increase was rapid and consistent.

1977	1978	1979	1980	1981	1982	1983	1984
2	4	6	9	18	32	55	63

Lamb and Whitla (1983), in an extensive literature search, found a strong linear increase from 2 to 120 in the number of meta-analyses published each year from 1976 to 1982. The correlation between year and number of studies published was .85. An estimate that approximately 300 meta-analyses had been conducted (Kulik, 1984) was probably outdated by the time it was published. There have been over 500 applications of our meta-analysis methods alone in just the one area of the validity of personnel selection procedures; and applications have been made of these methods in many other areas in industrial-organizational psychology and organizational behavior (see Hunter & Hirsh, 1987), as well as in other areas such as medical research (Baum et al., 1981; Halvorsen, 1986) and finance (Coggin & Hunter, 1983, 1987; Dimson & Marsh, 1984; Ramamurti, 1989). The rapid growth of meta-analysis is likely to continue. In concluding his excellent review of meta-analysis methods, Bangert-Drowns (1986, p. 398) stated:

> Meta-analysis is not a fad. It is rooted in the fundamental values of the scientific enterprise: replicability, quantification, causal and correlational analysis. Valuable information is needlessly scattered in individual studies. The ability of social scientists to deliver generalizable answers to basic questions of policy is too serious a concern to allow us to treat research integration lightly. The potential benefits of meta-analysis method seem enormous.

Meta-Analysis in Industrial-Organizational Psychology

The methods in this book are general and can be applied to virtually any research literatures. However, from a substantive point of view, this book is oriented toward industrial-organizational (I/O) psychology, as we noted in the Preface. The most extensive and detailed application of meta-analysis in I/O psychology has been the study of the generalizability of the validities of employment selection procedures (Schmidt, 1988; Schmidt & Hunter, 1981). Most of the applications have been to employment tests of ability and aptitude, but other procedures, such as employment interviews (McDaniel, Whetzel, Schmidt, Hunter, Mauer, & Russell, 1988), assessment centers (Gaugler, Rosenthal, Thornton, & Bentson, 1987), and ratings of training and experience (McDaniel, Schmidt, & Hunter, 1988a) have also been studied. The findings have resulted in major changes in the field of personnel selection. Validity generalization research and its impact are discussed in Chapter 4.

The meta-analysis methods presented in this book have also been applied in other areas of I/O psychology and organizational behavior (OB).

Between 1978 and 1988, there have been approximately 45 such published applications. The following are some examples:

1. correlates of role conflict and role ambiguity (Fisher & Gittelson, 1983; Jackson & Schuler, 1985).
2. relation of job satisfaction to absenteeism (Hacket & Guion, 1985; Terborg & Lee, 1982).
3. relation between job performance and turnover (McEvoy & Cascio, 1987).
4. relation between job satisfaction and job performance (Iaffaldono & Muchinsky, 1985; Petty, McGee, & Cavender, 1984).
5. effects of nonselection organizational interventions on employee output and productivity (Guzzo, Jette, & Katzell, 1985).
6. effects of realistic job previews on employee turnover, performance and satisfaction (Premack & Wanous, 1985; McEvoy & Cascio, 1985).
7. evaluation of Fieldler's theory of leadership (Peters, Harthe, & Pohlmar, 1985).
8. accuracy of self-ratings of ability and skill (Mabe & West, 1982).

These applications have been to correlational and experimental literatures. Sufficient meta-analyses have been published in I/O psychology that a review of meta-analytic studies in this area has now been published. This lengthy review (Hunter & Hirsh, 1987) reflects the fact that this literature is now quite large. It is noteworthy that the review devotes considerable space to the development and presentation of theoretical propositions; this reflects the fact that the clarification of research literatures produced by meta-analysis provides a basis for theory development that previously did not exist. It is also noteworthy that the findings in one meta-analysis were often found to be theoretically relevant to the interpretation of the findings in other meta-analyses.

In view of the large number of meta-analyses now present in the I/O and OB literatures, some readers may wonder why the examples we use in this book to illustrate meta-analysis principles and methods do not employ data from those meta-analyses. The primary reason is that the amount of data (the number of correlations or d statistics) is usually so large as to result in cumbersome examples. For pedagogical reasons, we have generally employed examples consisting of small numbers of studies in which the data are hypothetical. As explained in the following chapters, meta-analyses based on such small numbers of studies would not ordinarily yield results that would be optimally stable. (We discuss second-order sampling error in Chapter 9.) However, such examples provide the means to simply and clearly illustrate the principles and methods of meta-analysis, and we believe this is the crucial consideration.

2 Study Artifacts and Their Impact on Study Outcomes

The goal of a meta-analysis of correlations is a description of the distribution of actual correlations between a given independent and a given dependent variable. If all studies were conducted perfectly, then the distribution of study correlations could be used directly to estimate the distribution of actual correlations. However, studies are never perfect. Thus, the relationship between study correlations and actual correlations is more complicated.

There are many dimensions along which studies fail to be perfect. Thus, there are many forms of error in study results. Each form of error has some impact on the results of a meta-analysis. Some errors can be corrected and some cannot. We will refer to study imperfections as "artifacts" to remind ourselves that errors in study results produced by study imperfections are artifactual or man-made errors and not properties of nature. In later chapters, we present formulas that correct for as many artifacts as possible. Correction of artifacts requires auxiliary information such as study sample sizes, study means and standard deviations, estimates of reliability, and so on.

The complexity of formulas depends on two things: (a) the extent of variation in artifacts and (2) the extent of variation in actual correlations. Formulas for meta-analysis would be simplest if artifacts were homogeneous across studies; i.e., if all studies had the same sample size, all had the same reliability for the independent and dependent variables, all had the same standard deviations, and so forth. If artifacts were homogeneous, then the primary calculations would all be simple averages and simple variances. In actuality, artifacts vary from study to study and, hence, more complicated weighted averages are necessary.

If there is variation in actual correlations, that variation must be caused by some aspect of studies that varies from one study to the next, i.e., a "moderator" variable. If the meta-analyst anticipates variation in actual correlations, then studies will be coded for aspects that are thought to be potential moderators. For example, studies can be coded as based on white-collar or blue-collar workers. If the variation in actual correlations is large, then the key question is this: "Is the moderator variable one of those identified as a potential moderator?" If the larger moderator variables are coded study aspects, the overall meta-analysis is not particularly important. The key meta-analyses will be those run on the moderator study subsets where the variation in actual correlations will be much smaller in magnitude (and perhaps zero).

Study Artifacts

We have identified 11 artifacts that alter the size of the study correlation in comparison to the actual correlation. These artifacts are listed in Table 2.1 along with typical substantive examples from the personnel selection research literature. The most damaging artifact in narrative reviews has been sampling error. Sampling error has been falsely interpreted as conflicting findings in almost every area of research in the social sciences. However, some of the other artifacts induce quantitative errors so large as to create qualitatively false conclusions (Hunter & Schmidt, 1987a, 1987b) or to greatly alter the practical implications of findings (Schmidt & Hunter, 1977; Schmidt & Hunter, 1981). This is especially important to consider when several artifacts work in conjunction.

Sampling Error

Sampling error affects the correlation coefficient additively and non-systematically. If the actual correlation is denoted ρ and the sample correlation r, then sampling error is added to the sample correlation in the formula

$$r = \rho + e.$$

The size of sampling error is primarily determined by sample size. Since the effect is unsystematic, the sampling error in a single correlation cannot be corrected. Sampling error and the corrections for it in meta-analysis are discussed in detail in Chapters 3, 4, 6, and 7.

Error of Measurement

Note that the distinction between artifacts 2 and 3 versus artifacts 8 and 9 in Table 2.1 represents the distinction between simple or unsystematic error of measurement versus systematic error (or departures from perfect construct validity). Simple error of measurement is the random measure-

Table 2.1 Study Artifacts That Alter the Value of Outcome Measures, with Examples from Personnel Research

---

1. Sampling error:
   Study validity will vary randomly from the population value because of sampling error.

2. Error of measurement in the dependent variable:
   Study validity will be systematically lower than true validity to the extent that job performance is measured with random error.

3. Error of measurement in the independent variable:
   Study validity for a test will systematically understate the validity of the ability measured since the test is not perfectly reliable.

4. Dichotomization of a continuous dependent variable:
   Turnover—the length of time that worker stays with the organization is often dichotomized into "more than . . ." or "less than . . ." where . . . is some arbitrarily chosen interval such as one year or six months.

5. Dichotomization of a continuous independent variable:
   Interviewers are often told to dichotomize their perceptions into "acceptable" versus "reject."

6. Range variation in the independent variable:
   Study validity will be systematically lower than true validity to the extent that hiring policy causes incumbents to have a lower variation in the predictor than is true of applicants.

7. Attrition artifacts: Range variation in the dependent variable:
   Study validity will be systematically lower than true validity to the extent that there is systematic attrition in workers on performance, as when good workers are promoted out of the population or when poor workers are fired for poor performance.

8. Deviation from perfect construct validity in the independent variable:
   Study validity will vary if the factor structure of the test differs from the usual structure of tests for the same trait.

9. Deviation from perfect construct validity in the dependent variable:
   Study validity will differ from true validity if the criterion is deficient or contaminated.

10. Reporting on transcriptional error:
    Reported study validities differ from actual study validities due to a variety of reporting problems: inaccuracy in coding data, computational errors, errors in reading computer output, typographical errors by secretaries or by printers. Note: These errors can be very large in magnitude.

11. Variance due to extraneous factors:
    Study validity will be systematically lower than true validity if incumbents differ in job experience at the time their performance is measured.

---

ment error assessed as unreliability of the measure. Error of measurement has a systematic multiplicative effect on the correlation. If we denote the actual correlation by ρ and the observed correlation by ρ_0, then

$$\rho_0 = a\rho$$

where a is the square root of the reliability. Since a is a number less than 1 in magnitude, the size of the correlation is systematically reduced by error of measurement. For a high reliability such as $r_{xx} = .81$ (a typical reliability of a test of general cognitive ability), the correlation is multiplied by $\sqrt{.81}$ or .90; i.e., reduced by 10%. For a low reliability of .36 (the average reliability of a supervisor global rating on a one-item rating scale), the correlation is multiplied by $\sqrt{.36}$ or .60, a reduction of 40%.

There is a separate effect for error of measurement in the independent variable and error of measurement in the dependent variable. Thus, for error in both variables — the usual case — we have

$$\rho_0 = ab\rho$$

where a is the square root of the reliability of the independent variable and b is the square root of the reliability of the dependent variable. For a test of general cognitive ability predicting the immediate supervisor's rating on a single global item, the correlation would be multiplied by $(.90)(.60) = .54$. That is nearly a 50% reduction.

Dichotomization

If a continuous variable is dichotomized, then the point biserial correlation for the new dichotomized variable will be less than the correlation for the continuous variable. If the regression is bivariate normal, the effect of dichotomizing one of the variables is given by

$$\rho_0 = a\rho$$

where a depends on the extremeness of the split induced by the dichotomization. Let P be the proportion in the "high" end of the split and $Q = 1 - P$ be the proportion in the "low" end of the split. Let c be the point in the normal distribution that divides the distribution into proportions P and Q. For example, $c = -1.28$ divides the distribution into the bottom 10% versus the top 90%. Let the normal ordinate at c be denoted $\phi(c)$. Then

$$a = \phi(c) / \sqrt{PQ} \ .$$

The smallest reduction in the correlation occurs for a median, or 50-50 split, where $a = .80$, a 20% reduction in the correlation.

If both variables are dichotomized, there is a double reduction in the correlation. The exact formula is more complicated than just the product of an "a" for the independent variable and a "b" for the dependent variable. The formula is that for the "tetrachoric" correlation. However, Hunter and Schmidt (in press) have shown that the double product is a very close approximation under the conditions in most current meta-analyses. Thus, the attenuation produced by double dichotomization is given by

$$\rho_0 = ab\rho.$$

If both variables are split 50-50, the correlation is attenuated by approximately

$$\rho_0 = (.80)(.80)\ \rho = .64\rho,$$

i.e., by 36%. For splits more extreme than 50-50, there is even greater attenuation. If one variable has a 90-10 split and the other variable has a 10-90 split, then the double product estimate of attenuation is

$$\rho_0 = (.59)(.59)\ \rho = .35\rho,$$

a 65% reduction in the correlation. If the actual correlation is greater than $\rho = .30$, then the reduction is even greater than that predicted by the double product formula (Hunter & Schmidt, in press).

Range Variation in the Independent Variable

Because the correlation is a standardized slope, its size depends on the extent of variation on the independent variable. At the extreme, in a population in which there is perfect homogeneity (no variance) on the independent variable, the correlation with any dependent variable will be zero. At the other extreme, if we fix the amount of error about the regression line and then consider populations in which people spread out farther and farther on the independent variable, the population correlations increase eventually to 1.00. If correlations from different studies are to be compared, then differences in the correlations due to differences in spread (variance) on the independent variable must be controlled. This is the problem of range variation on the independent variable.

The solution to range variation is to define a reference population and express all correlations in terms of that reference population. If the regression of dependent variable onto the independent variable is linear and homoscedastic (bivariate normality is a special case of this), then there is a formula (discussed in Chapter 3) that computes what the correlation in a given population would be if the standard deviation were the same as in the reference population. This same formula can be used in reverse to compute the effect of studying the correlation in a population with a standard deviation different from that in the reference population. The standard deviations can be compared by computing the ratio of standard deviations in the two groups. Let u be the ratio of the study population standard deviation divided by the reference group population. That is $u = SD_{study}/SD_{ref}$. Then the study population correlation is related to the reference group population by

$$\rho_0 = a\rho$$

where

$$a = u/[\ (u^2 - 1)\,\rho^2 + 1\ ]^{1/2}.$$

This expression for the multiplier contains the actual correlation ρ in the formula. In practice, it is the attenuated correlation ρ_0 that is observed. A very useful algebraic identity in terms of ρ_0 was derived by Callender and Osburn (1980):

$$a = [\ u^2 + \rho_0^2(1 - u^2)\ ]^{1/2}.$$

The multiplier a will be greater than 1.00 if the study standard deviation is larger than the reference standard deviation. The multiplier a will be less than 1.00 if the study standard deviation is smaller than the reference standard deviation.

There are two cases in which range variation appears in the empirical literature: (1) scientifically produced artificial variation and (2) variation that arises from situation constraints. Scientific variation can be produced by manipulation of the data. The most frequent of these infrequent cases are those in which the scientist creates an artificially high variation by deliberately excluding middle cases (Osburn, 1978). For example, a psychologist studying anxiety might use an anxiety test to preselect "High" or "Low" subjects to be in the top 10% or bottom 10%, respectively. The correlation between anxiety and the dependent variable calculated in such an experiment would be larger than the correlation in the original population. The increase in the correlation would be determined by the increase in the standard deviation of the independent variable. If the original population standard deviation were 1.00, then the standard deviation in a group composed of the top and bottom 10% would be 1.80. For this artificially inflated range variation, the multiplier would be

$$a = 1.80 / [(1.80^2 - 1) \rho^2 + 1]^{\frac{1}{2}} = 1.80 / [1 + 3.24 \rho^2]^{\frac{1}{2}}.$$

For example, if the reference correlation were .30, the multiplier would be 1.58 and the study correlation would be .48, a 58% increase in the correlation. In a small sample study, this increase in the study correlation would greatly increase the statistical power and, hence, make the significance test work much better. That is, the significance test would have higher statistical power to detect the correlation (Osburn, 1978).

If situational constraints cause the deviation in the standard deviation, then it is usually because subjects are selected into the situation by some factor that tends to block entry for subjects at one end or the other of the independent variable. That is, usually situation constraints tend to block either at the high end or the low end. In either case, the result is a study standard deviation that is lower than the reference standard deviation. Thus, in field studies the range variation is usually range restriction. For example, suppose that a football team measures the speed of applicants running the 40-yard dash. If only those in the top half were considered further, then the standard deviation among those considered would be only 60% as large as the standard deviation among all applicants. The applicant correlation between speed and performance would be reduced by the multiplier

$$a = .60 / [(.60^2 - 1) \rho^2 + 1]^{\frac{1}{2}} = .60 / [1 - .64 \rho^2]^{\frac{1}{2}}.$$

If the correlation were $\rho = .50$ for applicants, the multiplier would be .65, and the correlation among those considered would be reduced to

$$\rho_0 = a\rho = .65(.50) = .33,$$

a 34% reduction in the correlation.

Attrition Artifacts: Range Variation on the Dependent Variable

Range variation on the dependent variable is usually produced by attrition artifacts. For example, in personnel selection the study correlation is computed on current workers (i.e., incumbents) because data on job performance is available only on those hired. However, workers with poor performance are often fired or quit voluntarily. Those who participate in the study will be only those still on the job. This population will differ from applicants because of that attrition.

There is one special case of attrition artifacts that can be eliminated with statistical formulas, a case in which there is no situational constraint on the independent variable. If there is selection on the dependent variable, this will cause induced selection on any independent variable correlated with it. Assume that there is no selection other than this form of induced selection. In such a case, attrition artifacts can be treated statistically as range variation on the dependent variable. Statistically, the independent and dependent variables are symmetrically related to the correlation coefficient. The special case of attrition artifacts described above exactly reverses this symmetry. Thus, the formulas are the same, except that the standard deviation ratio u is defined by the dependent variable rather than the independent variable.

In personnel selection most studies are affected by both range restriction on the independent variable and by attrition artifacts on the dependent variable (in addition to firing poor performers, employers also promote good performers). However, at present there is no technology for dealing with range restriction and attrition artifacts simultaneously. The underlying mathematical problem is that selection on one variable changes the regression for the other variable in a complex way so that the regression is no longer linear and homoscedastic. For example, when there is selection on the predictor, then the regression of the predictor onto job performance is no longer linear and homoscedastic.

A new development related to this problem came to our attention as this book was being finished. Alexander, Carson, Alliger, and Carr (1987) proposed a very clever idea. They noted that after one has selected on the independent variable, the regression of the independent variable onto the dependent variable (the "reverse regression") is not linear and homoscedastic. Thus, the slope of that regression line will not remain the same when restriction is introduced on the dependent variable. But they conjectured that it might not change much. The same is true for homoscedasticity: The conditional variance will not remain exactly the same after the second truncation, but perhaps it doesn't change by much. If both changes are small, then assumption of no change would yield an approximation equation for correction of range restriction, which might be accurate enough for practical purposes. They derived their equation for a special case of double-range restriction: double truncation. That is, they assumed that the range restriction is caused by a double threshold: Any data point is lost if the independent variable is less than an x cutoff value or if the dependent variable is less than a y cutoff value. Thus, in the study population — what they call the "doubly truncated population" — the only people left are those for whom both variables are above the respective thresholds. In the case of personnel selection, this would correspond to a situation in which hiring was done using only the test and using it with a fixed threshold, and where termination from the job was based on a specific fixed performance level threshold. There is probably no actual selection situation that fits the double truncation model, but it is a good mathematical beginning point. Alexander et al. (1987) tested their correction approximation for various double truncation combinations. They varied each cutoff value independently from −2.0 standard deviations below the mean (which eliminates only the bottom 2.5% of cases) to +2.0 standard deviations (where 97.5% of cases are eliminated). They varied the untruncated population correlation from −.90 to +.90. They claimed to find exceedingly accurate results; however, their description of the results was logically contradictory. They said that (1) all results were within 1% of the actual correlation and (2) only 10% of results differed by more than .02 from the actual value. The inconsistency is this: The unattenuated correlation is a fraction and thus less than 1 in absolute value. To be within 1% of a number less than 1 is to be within .01 of that value. Thus, if all values had been within 1%, then all values would be within .01 of the actual value and no values would be off by .02 or more. At least one of these statements must be wrong. We used direct numerical integration to test their equation. We found that their statement that all values are within 1% is false. If the corrected correlation is rounded to two places, then only 5 to 6% of corrected correlations are within 1% of the actual correlation. On the other hand, the accuracy is quite good: 84% of values are within 3% of the correct value. The worst fit is for the population correlation of .50. For that value, the corrected correlations are as much as 6% too high in 8.6% of the combinations. The combinations where the fit is poorer are the combinations where there is high selection on both variables and where the two cutoff scores are about equal. This would be predicted by the fact that the formula works perfectly for range restriction on one variable only (it reduces to the Pearson range restriction formula presented earlier). The cases showing the greatest inaccuracy may not be very realistic. If the cutoff is +1.0 standard deviation above the mean for both variables, then the truncated population usually represents little more than 3% of the untruncated population. Elimination of 97% of the original population would probably rarely occur in real data.

The findings for absolute accuracy are even more promising. The Alexander et al. (1987) claim that only 10% of corrected correlations differ by more than .02 from the actual correlation is correct. In fact, if the corrected correlation is rounded to two places, the value is within .02 in 94% of cases. In no case was their formula off by more than .03. The poorest fit is for a population correlation of .60 where 17% of cases were off by .03. The cases of poor absolute fit were essentially the same as the cases with poor percentage fit: the cases of equally severe selection on both variables. Although the Alexander et al. formula is not as accurate as they thought, it is certainly accurate enough for practical purposes. The next question is: Does the formula remain accurate for the more realistic case of probabilistic selection? Our calculations indicate that the formula is even more accurate in the realistic case of probabilistic selection. This work is not yet complete, but we hope to have a paper written by the time this book is published. To correct for double-range restriction in meta-analysis, we need not only a correction formula but an attenuation formula as well. We have derived attenuation formulas at three levels of increasing accuracy of approximation, and we are testing them now. The attenuation formulas are not as accurate as the correction formula, but the error looks as if it will be small enough so that the meta-analysis will not be greatly affected. By the time this book is published, we expect to be able to present a full treatment of meta-analysis correcting for double-range restriction in the realistic case. Our belief is that the Alexander et al. contribution is a major breakthrough in this area.

Imperfect Construct Validity in the Independent Variable

This section is considerably longer than the other sections on study artifacts. In our judgment, however, this is unavoidable since it is essential to develop an understanding of how study outcomes are distorted by departures from perfect construct validity. This section and the following section are of necessity based on path analysis. We have tried to make the discussion as simple as possible, and we believe most readers will be able to follow it. Readers who have difficulty may want to skip ahead to the section entitled "Errors in the Data." However, we hope that such readers will return to these sections later when they no longer seem so difficult.

The independent variable used in a given study may suffer from either of two kinds of error of measurement: random error or systematic error. The effect of random error was discussed under the label "error of measurement." The extent to which a measure is free of random error is measured by the coefficient of reliability of that measure. This section will treat systematic error under the label "imperfect construct validity." The phrase "construct invalidity" would also be correct grammatically, but there are many who would react to the word "invalidity" in an absolute sense. That is, some would react to the word "invalidity" as if it meant "completely invalid" and would disregard the study. Actually, it is infrequent that a study independent variable is so construct-invalid that the study should be disregarded. Instead, imperfect construct validity may be dealt with adequately in any of three ways: (1) by using a statistical correction formula, (2) by treating variations in measurement strategy as a potential moderator variable, or (3) (for minor departures from perfect validity) by ignoring the imperfection. If the imperfection is ignored, then the study correlation is attenuated by an amount proportional to the quantitative departure from perfect validity. If there is variation across studies in the extent of construct validity and it is ignored, that variation contributes to uncontrolled artifact variation in the residual variance computed as the final step in meta-analysis. That is, ignored variation in construct validity would have the same appearance as a real moderator variable.

Construct validity is a quantitative question, not a qualitative distinction such as "valid" or "invalid"; it is a matter of degree. In most cases, construct validity can be quantified as a correlation coefficient, namely, the correlation between the variable intended and the variable as measured. We will define construct validity as the correlation between the intended independent variable and the actual independent variable used in the study when both variables are measured without random error. This definition is used to distinguish between the effects of random and systematic error. The error in the actual study used will be assessed by a correlation called the "operational quality" of the measure. The operational quality is determined in part by the extent of construct validity and in part by the reliability of the study variable.

The effect of systematic error on the correlation between independent and dependent variables depends not only on the extent of construct validity of the study independent variable, but on the qualitative structure of the causal relationships between the three variables: the intended or desired independent variable, the study independent variable, and the dependent variable. In certain cases, the effect of systematic error is simple: The correlation between independent and dependent variable is multiplied by the construct validity of the study independent variable. However, there are cases where this simple relationship does not hold. In such cases, the meta-analyst may not be able to use the study.

Consider an example in which we want to examine the relationship between general cognitive ability and performance in recreational activities. Since performance in recreational activities depends on learning, we hypothesize that people with high cognitive ability will perform better than average. We find a survey study of a large bowling league in which one of the variables is the bowling performance average. The study has no measure of general cognitive ability, but it does have a measure of amount of education. Suppose we use the education variable as an imperfect indicator for cognitive ability. In the language of econometrics, we use education as a "proxy variable" for ability. How good a proxy is amount of education for cognitive ability? One answer would be the correlation between education and ability. However, there are two other considerations that enter into this decision. First, there is the question of which correlation to use: the correlation between ability and actual education or the correlation between ability and the study measure of education. This is the issue of distinguishing between construct validity and reliability. Second, there is the issue of the relationship between the proxy variable and the dependent variable. For certain kinds of relationships, the effect of using a proxy variable is easily quantified and can be computed from the coefficient of construct validity. For other relationships, the effect may be much more complicated. In such complicated cases, use of the proxy variable may be problematic.

To show the distinction between systematic and random error of measurement, suppose that the study does not have a perfect measure of education. Whereas we would like a measure of the exact amount of education, the study recorded only the measure

$X = 0$ if the person did not finish high school

$X = 1$ if the person finished high school but not college

$X = 2$ if the person finished college.

There are then two kinds of error in the study variable. There is the systematic error produced by using education instead of ability and there is the random error produced by using an imperfect measure of education. This situation is illustrated in the path diagram in Figure 2.1.

In Figure 2.1, general cognitive ability is the independent variable that we wanted to measure. Thus the ability variable in the path diagram is implicitly assumed to be perfectly measured. Figure 2.1 shows an arrow from general cognitive ability to amount of education where amount of education is assumed to be perfectly measured. This represents the assumption that ability is one of the causal determinants of amount of education. If ability were the sole cause of differences in the amount of education, then ability and education would be perfectly correlated and there would be no problem in using education as a proxy for ability. In fact, the correlation between ability and education is only about .50, and there is thus a considerable discrepancy between the two measures. The size of the correlation between ability and education determines the size of the path coefficient from ability to education and, hence, measures the

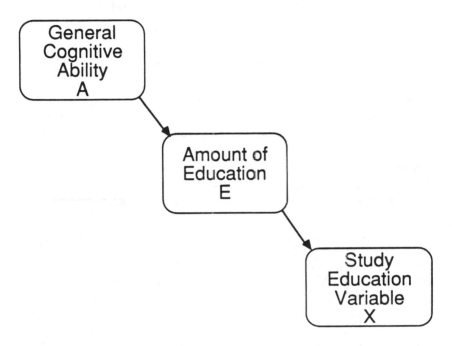

Figure 2.1 The Path Model Showing the Causal Nature of Imperfect Construct Validity in Using Education as a Proxy Variable for General Cognitive Ability

extent of systematic error in substituting education for ability. The correlation between ability and education where both are perfectly measured is the construct validity of education as a measure of ability. The construct validity of education as a measure of ability is the path coefficient in Figure 2.1.

Figure 2.1 also shows an arrow from amount of education to the study education variable X. Qualitatively, this arrow represents the introduction of random error into the measure of education. Quantitatively, the path coefficient measures the amount of random error. The path coefficient for this arrow is the correlation between actual amount of education and the study education measure. This correlation is less than 1.00 to the extent that the study measurement procedure introduces random error into the estimate of education. The square of the correlation between actual and estimated education is the reliability of the study measure of education.

The total discrepancy between the intended independent variable of ability and the study measure of education is measured by the correlation between the two. According to path analysis, the correlation between ability and the study measure of education is the product of the two path coefficients. That is,

$$r_{AX} = r_{AE} \, r_{EX} \, .$$

Let us define the phrase "the operational quality of the proxy variable" to be the correlation between the intended variable and the study proxy variable. Then we have shown that the operational quality is the product of two numbers: the construct validity of the proxy variable, r_{AE}, and the square root of the reliability of the proxy variable, $r_{EX} = \sqrt{r_{XX}}$.

The key semantic issue in the definition of the phrase "construct validity" is to choose between two correlations: the correlation between the intended variable and the proxy variable as perfectly measured, or the correlation between the intended variable and the study variable as measured with random error. The substantial and conceptual meaning of the phrase "construct validity" is represented by the correlation between intended and proxy variables measured without random error. Thus we label that correlation as "construct validity." On the other hand, the total impact of substitution depends also on the amount of random error in the study variable, and hence, we need a name for that correlation as well. The name used here is "operational quality." We can thus say that the operational quality of the study proxy variable depends on the construct validity of the proxy variable and the reliability of the study measure. In a simple case such as that of Figure 2.1, the operational quality is the product of construct validity and the square root of the reliability of the proxy measure.

We can now consider the main question: What is the effect of systematic error in the measure of cognitive ability on the observed correlation between ability and performance? This is answered by comparing two population correlations: the desired correlation between cognitive ability and performance versus the correlation between the study measure of education and performance. To answer this question we must know the causal relationship between education, ability, and performance. Consider the causal model shown in Figure 2.2.

Figure 2.2 shows an arrow from cognitive ability to bowling performance. This arrow represents the hypothesized effect of differences in learning ability on differences in performance. Figure 2.2 shows no causal arrow from education to performance. This corresponds to the assumption that the material learned in mastery of bowling does not depend on the specific material learned in school. Thus, among people matched on cognitive ability, there would be no correlation between amount of educa-

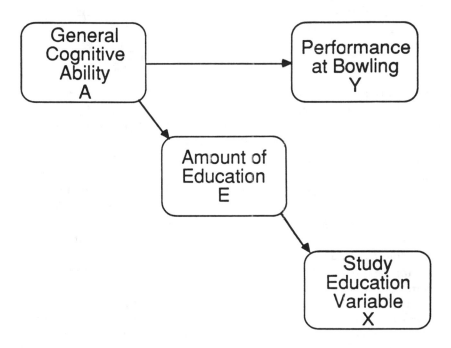

Figure 2.2 The Path Model Showing the Assumed Causal Structure of Ability, Education, and Performance

tion and performance at bowling. According to this path model, ability is a common causal antecedent to both performance and education. Therefore, the correlation between the study education variable X and the performance measure Y is the product

$$r_{XY} = r_{AE} \, r_{EX} \, r_{AY} \, .$$

Thus, the desired population correlation r_{AY} is multiplied by two other correlations: the construct validity of education as a measure of ability, r_{AE}, and the square root of the reliability of the study education measure, r_{EX}. Denote the product of these two correlations by a. That is, define a by

$$a = r_{AE} \, r_{EX} \, .$$

Then a is the operational quality of the study independent variable as a measure of cognitive ability. The desired population correlation r_{AY} is related to the study population r_{XY} by the equation

$$r_{XY} = a\ r_{AY} .$$

Since a is a fraction, this is an attenuation formula. The observed correlation is attenuated by the factor a. That is, the lower the operational quality of the study independent variable, the greater the attenuation of the study correlation between independent and dependent variables.

The total attenuation of the effect size is given by the net attenuation factor, which is the operational quality of the study independent variable. However, this net attenuation factor is itself the product of two other attenuation factors. One factor is the square root of the study variable reliability. This is the familiar attenuation factor for random error of measurement. The second factor is the construct validity of the study variable as a measure of the intended independent variable. Thus, one factor measures the effect of random error while the second factor measures the effect of systematic error.

The previous example shows that under certain conditions the effect of systematic error on the study effect size is to multiply the desired population effect size by the operational quality of the study proxy variable. A second example will show that this simple formula does not always work. Finally, we will present a third example, which shows a different causal structure for which the same simple attenuation formula can be used.

Consider now a meta-analysis on the relationship between general cognitive ability and income. Suppose the study has no measure of ability, but has the same imperfect measure of amount of education as considered in the first example. The causal structure for these variables will differ from the causal structure in Figure 2.2. The assumed causal model for ability, education, and income is shown in Figure 2.3.

Figure 2.3 shows an arrow from general cognitive ability to income. This corresponds to the fact that once people are working at the same job, differences in cognitive ability are a prime determinant of job performance and, hence, of how high the person rises in the job and of income level. However, Figure 2.3 also shows an arrow from amount of education to income. The amount of education determines what job the person starts in and, hence, sets limits on how high the person will rise. This arrow from education to income distinguishes the structure of the causal models in Figures 2.2 and 2.3. The path coefficients for the arrows to the dependent variable are no longer simple correlations but are beta weights, the multiple regression weights for cognitive ability, b_{AY}, and education, b_{EY}, in

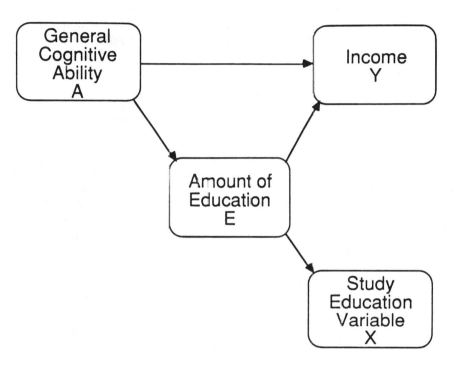

Figure 2.3 The Path Model Showing the Assumed Causal Structure of Ability, Income, and Education

jointly predicting income. The study effect size correlation r_{XY} is given by path analysis to be

$$r_{XY} = r_{EX} (b_{EY} + r_{AE} b_{AY})$$
$$= r_{AE} r_{EX} b_{AY} + r_{EX} b_{EY}.$$

By contrast, the simple education formula would have been

$$r_{XY} = r_{AE} r_{EX} r_{AY}.$$

In both models, the effect of random error of measurement is the same. In both models, it is true that

$$r_{XY} = r_{EX} r_{EY}.$$

The difference between the models lies in the structure of the correlation between education and income. If education has a causal impact on income, as in Figure 2.3, then the correlation between education and income is

$$r_{EY} = r_{AE} \, b_{AY} + b_{EY} ,$$

whereas in the simpler model the correlation would have been

$$r_{EY} = r_{AE} \, r_{AY} .$$

The larger the causal impact of education on income, the greater the difference between the models. The most extreme case would be one in which the assumption (known to be false) is made that there is no direct causal impact of ability at all. That is, assume that the beta weight for ability is 0, i.e., $b_{AY} = 0$. Then for the complex model

$$r_{EY} = r_{AY}/r_{AE}$$

instead of

$$r_{EY} = r_{AY} \, r_{AE} .$$

That is, in this extreme case the effect of substitution would be to divide the effect size correlation by the construct validity rather than to multiply the effect size correlation by the construct validity!

The key to the product rule in the previous examples is the assumption that the only causal connection between the dependent variable and the proxy variable is the intended independent variable. In the first example, the intended independent variable (ability) is causally prior to the proxy variable, and the proxy variable has no link to the dependent variable. It is also possible to have the proxy variable be causally prior to the intended variable. However, the product rule will fail if there is any path from the proxy variable to the dependent variable that does not go through the intended variable.

Consider a third example. Suppose that we hypothesize that teachers with a strong knowledge of their subject matter will do a better job of teaching due in part to having more time saved by eliminating look-up tasks, and in part to having more cognitive options for presentation, and so on. A large metropolitan high school system has national test scores for students that can be averaged for each class. Thus, we have a dependent variable for student performance. However, it is impractical to construct knowledge tests for all the teaching areas. Assume that the amount learned in a specialty is primarily a function of how well the teacher learns and how much the teacher studies in general. Learning in general would be measured by the college grade-point average. So instead of a specialized knowledge test, we use the teacher's college grade-point average as a proxy variable for knowledge of area. The total grade point is not available, but a code for grades in key education courses is stored in the computer. The design for this construct validity problem is shown as a path diagram in Figure 2.4.

Figure 2.4 shows an arrow from Teacher's GPA to Teacher's knowledge of area. Thus, the proxy variable is causally prior to the intended independent variable. There is no other path from GPA to the dependent variable. The path coefficient from GPA to knowledge is the construct validity of GPA as a measure of specialized knowledge. This path coefficient measures the extent of systematic error in the GPA measure. There is an arrow from overall GPA to GPA in the key education courses. The size of this path coefficient measures the extent of random error in the study variable. The correlation between the study grade-point variable X and the performance measure Y is the product

$$r_{XY} = r_{KG} \, r_{GX} \, r_{KY} \,.$$

Thus, the desired population correlation r_{KY} is multiplied by two other population correlations: the construct validity of GPA as a measure of knowledge (r_{KG}) and the square root of the reliability of the study GPA measure (r_{GX}). Denote the product of these two correlations by a. That is, define a by

$$a = r_{KG} \, r_{GX} \,.$$

Then a is the operational quality of the study independent variable as a measure of specialized knowledge. The desired population correlation r_{KY} is related to the study population r_{XY} by the equation

$$r_{XY} = a \, r_{KY} \,.$$

Since a is a fraction, this is an attenuation formula. The observed correlation is attenuated by the factor a. That is, the lower the operational quality of the study independent variable, the greater the attenuation of the study correlation between independent and dependent variable.

We can now summarize the two most common cases in which construct validity of the independent variable can be quantified and where system-

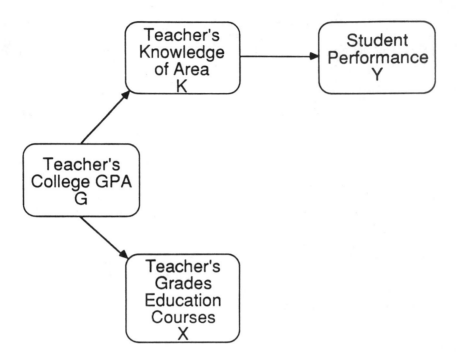

Figure 2.4 The Path Model Showing the Assumed Causal Structure of Teacher's Specialized Knowledge, Teacher's Overall GPA, Teacher's Grade Point in Selected Education Courses, and Student Performance

atic error of measurement is easily corrected. The imperfect construct validity will be correctable if the imperfect measure or proxy variable stands in one of two causal relations to the intended independent variable and the dependent variable. Consider the path diagrams in Figure 2.5. Figure 2.5a shows the imperfect variable as causally dependent on the intended independent variable and as having no other connection to the dependent variable. Figure 2.5b shows the imperfect variable as causally antecedent to the intended independent variable and as having no other connection to the dependent variable. The key to both path diagrams is the assumption that there is no extraneous causal path from the imperfect variable to the dependent variable that does not go through the intended independent variable.

Figure 2.5a shows the case in which the intended independent variable is antecedent to the study independent variable. This case can be described by saying that the study variable is influenced by "extraneous factors."

Figure 2.5 Path Models for Cases in Which the Effect of Imperfect Construct Validity Is To Attenuate the Desired Effect Size Correlation by Multiplying the Effect Size by the Construct Validity of the Proxy Variable (r_{xx}, in both cases)

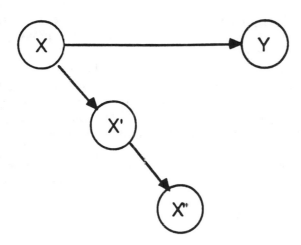

Figure 2.5a Extraneous Factors in the Study Independent Variable

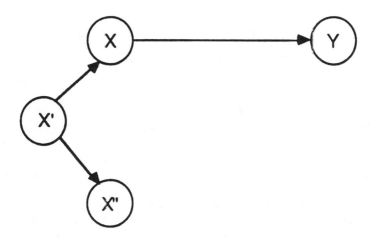

Figure 2.5b The Study as a Causal Antecedent of the Intended Independent Variable

This is the most common case for a proxy variable. For example, many employers use educational credentials as a proxy variable for general cognitive ability (Gottfredson, 1985). While cognitive ability is an important determinant of amount of education, education is influenced by many other variables (such as family wealth) as well. The path diagram in Figure 2.5a assumes that these other influences are not correlated with the dependent variable (say job performance) and, hence, are "extraneous factors" from the point of view of using the study variable as a proxy variable.

Figure 2.5b shows the case in which the study variable is causally antecedent to the intended variable. For example, the intended variable in a study of political values might be "political sophistication." The study variable might be general cognitive ability. While cognitive ability is an important determinant of sophistication, it does not measure other causal determinants of political sophistication such as political socialization by politically active parents.

In either Figure 2.5a or 2.5b, the correlation between the observed study independent variable X'' and the dependent variable Y can be written as a triple product:

$$r_{X''Y} = r_{X''X'} r_{X'X} r_{XY}.$$

In the notation of this paper, this triple product would be

$$r_o = abr$$

where

$a = r_{X''X'}$ = square root of the reliability of X'' and
$b = r_{X'X}$ = the construct of validity of X'.

If X' were a perfect measure of X, then the value of b would be 1.00 and the triple product would reduce to the equation for random error of measurement. If the measure is imperfect, then b will be less than 1.00 and the triple product will represent a reduction beyond that caused by error of measurement. That is, ab will be less than a to the extent that X' is not perfectly construct valid.

Note that in this path diagram, X is assumed to be perfectly measured. Thus, path coefficient b is the correlation between X' and X corrected for attenuation due to random error of measurement. Note that parameter a is the usual square root of the reliability of X'' that would be used to correct $r_{X''Y}$ for attenuation due to error in X''. The presence of the third factor b

represents the difference between a model of imperfect construct validity and a model of random error of measurement.

As an example, suppose that education were used as a proxy for general cognitive ability and assume that the "extraneous" factors in education are unrelated to the dependent variable. Assume that the correlation between ability and education is .50 and that the reliability of the study education measure is .90. The multipliers would be given by $a = \sqrt{.90} = .95$ and $b = .50$. The study correlation would be related to the actual correlation by

$$r_o = ab\,r = (.95)\,(.50)\,r = .48\,r\,.$$

In this example, there would be little error if random error were ignored (a 5% error) but a large error if imperfect construct validity were ignored.

Imperfect Construct Validity in the Dependent Variable

There can also be deviations from perfect construct validity in the dependent variable. Some deviations can be corrected, but some cannot.

Figure 2.6 shows one case in which the effect of imperfect validity can be quantified. Figure 2.6a shows the abstract case in which the study variable is causally dependent on the intended variable. Figure 2.6b shows a concrete example taken from personnel selection research.

Consider the example in Figure 2.6b: the use of supervisor ratings to measure job performance in a personnel selection validation study. The ideal measure would be an objective measure of job performance such as a construct valid, perfectly reliable, work sample test. Instead the study uses supervisor perception (ratings) as the measure. The ideal rating would be a consensus judgment across a population of supervisors. Instead, the observed study variable is the rating of the immediate supervisor. Thus, the idiosyncrasy of that supervisor's perceptions is a part of the error of measurement in the observed ratings. Extraneous factors that may influence human judgment include friendship, physical appearance, moral and/or life-style conventionality, and more.

The triple product rule for this quantifiable form of imperfect construct validity is given by path analysis:

$$\rho_{xy''} = \rho_{xy'}\ \rho_{yy'}\ \rho_{y'y''}\ .$$

That is,

$$\rho_0 = ab\rho\,.$$

Figure 2.6 Correctable Imperfect Construct Validity in the Dependent Variable

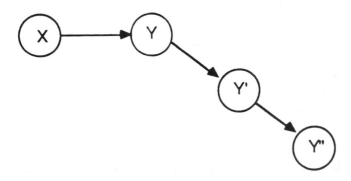

Figure 2.6a Extraneous Factors in the Study Measure of the Intended Dependent Variables

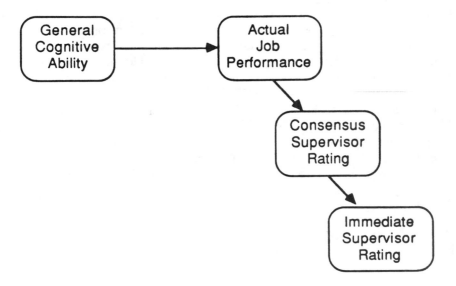

Figure 2.6b Using Supervisor Ratings as a Measure of Job Performance

where

$a = r_{y'y''}$ = square root of reliability of y'' and
$b = r_{yy'}$ = the construct validity of y'.

In the case of the example in Figure 2.6b, cumulative empirical data from a meta-analysis indicates that the correlation between actual job performance and consensus ratings is only .52 (Hunter, 1986). The reliability of the immediate supervisor rating depends on the quality of the rating instrument. For a summating rating, the reliability would average .47; for a single global rating the reliability would average .36 (Hunter & Hirsh, 1987; King, Hunter, & Schmidt, 1980). The reduction in validity from using a global rating measure would be given from $a = \sqrt{.36} = .60$ and $b = .52$, i.e.,

$$\rho_0 = ab\rho = (.60)(.52) \rho = .31\rho,$$

a reduction of 69%.

In this example, the new factors in the dependent variable were not only extraneous to the intended dependent variable, but were also uncorrelated with the independent variable. However, in some cases the extraneous variable is related to both the dependent *and* the independent variables. Such cases are more complex, and it is not always possible to correct for the effect of the extraneous variable on the construct validity of the dependent variable. These cases are beyond the scope of this book.

Errors in the Data

The most difficult artifact in meta-analysis is data errors. Bad data can arise from any step in the scientific process. The raw data may be incorrectly recorded or incorrectly entered into the computer. The computer may correlate the wrong variable because the format was incorrectly specified or because a transformation formula was incorrectly written. The sign of the correlation may be wrong because the analyst reverse scored the variable, but the person who read the output did not know that, or because the reader thought the variable had been reverse scored when it had not. When computer output is put into tables, the correlation can be incorrectly copied; the sign may be lost or digits may be reversed, or, when the table is published, the typesetter may miscopy the correlation.

Errors of these kinds are much more frequent than we would like to believe (Tukey, 1960; Wolins, 1962). Tukey maintains that all real data sets contain errors. Gulliksen (1986) made the following statement:

I believe that it is essential to check the data for errors before running my computations. I always wrote an error-checking program and ran the data through it before computing. I find it very interesting that in every set of data I have run, either for myself or someone else, there have always been errors, necessitating going back to the questionnaires and repunching some cards, or perhaps discarding some subjects [p. 4].

Further, some errors are likely to result in outliers, and outliers have a dramatic inflationary effect on the variance. In a normal distribution, for example, the SD is 65%, determined by the highest and lowest 5% of data values (Tukey, 1960). Data errors of various kinds probably account for a substantial portion of the observed variance in correlations and d values in many research literatures.

The upshot of this is that virtually every meta-analysis with a large number of correlations and some meta-analyses with a small number of studies will contain some bad data. If the bad data could be located, it could be thrown out. But the only bad data that can be identified are correlations that are so far out of the distribution that they are clearly outliers. Outlier analysis is discussed in Chapter 5. Outlier analysis works best where study sample sizes are at least moderate in size. If sample sizes are small, it is difficult to distinguish true outliers from extremely large sampling errors.

Thus, even if the present list of artifacts were complete (probably false) and even if all known artifacts were controlled (rarely possible), there would still be variation in study outcomes due to bad data. In actual meta-analyses there is always attenuation and false variation due to unknown and uncontrolled artifacts in addition to bad data. These considerations led Schmidt and Hunter (1977) to propose their "75% rule," which asserted as a rule of thumb that in any data set in which known and correctable artifacts account for 75% of the variance in study correlations, it is likely that the remaining 25% is due to uncontrolled artifacts. It is very unwise to assume that all unexplained variance is due to real moderator variables.

Extraneous Factors Introduced by Study Procedure

The measurement process or observation procedure of the study might cause variation on the dependent variable due to a variable that would not have existed (or that would have been constant) had the study been done perfectly. As an example, consider the effect of job experience in a concurrent validation study of job performance. In personnel selection, applicants can be considered as a cohort. When applicants are compared,

they are implicitly being compared as if they were to start work simultaneously. In a concurrent validation study, performance is measured on all
current workers, workers with different amounts of experience on the job.
This means that workers will differ in performance because they differ in
job experience (Schmidt, Hunter, & Outerbridge, 1986). This would not
be true of applicants hired at the same time. Thus, the differences in
experience constitute an extraneous variable created by the study observation procedure.

The abstract path diagram for this process is shown in Figure 2.7a, while
Figure 2.7b shows the case for job experience. If there had been no
extraneous variable introduced into the situation, this would be equivalent
to computing the partial correlation between the independent variable and
the dependent variable with the extraneous variable held constant. Since
the extraneous variable is not correlated with the independent variable, the
formula for the partial correlation is

$$\rho_{xy.z} = \rho_{xy} \, / \, \sqrt{1 - \rho_{zy}^2} \,.$$

This can be regarded as a correction for attenuation due to experience. If
we reverse the equation, we obtain the attenuation formula. Let a be the
reciprocal of the denominator of the equation for the partial correlation,
i.e.,

$$a = 1 \, / \, \sqrt{1 - \rho_{zy}^2} \,.$$

Then,

$$\rho_o = a\rho.$$

The reader may ask why we don't just compute the partial correlation
in the study itself. The fact is that that would solve the problem. That is,
if experience were recorded and the partial correlation were used as the
study correlation, then there would be no need for further statistical
correction. This would also eliminate the increase in sampling error
produced by statistical correction. This correction is like that for dichotomization. If the right correlation were given in the original research report
(or if the additional correlations necessary to compute it were given), then
there would be no need to use after-the-fact statistical correction.

Bias in the Sample Correlation

From time to time, quantitatively sophisticated investigations have
noted that the sample correlation is not an "unbiased" estimate of the

Figure 2.7 Path Diagrams for an Extraneous Variable Produced by the
Study Procedure

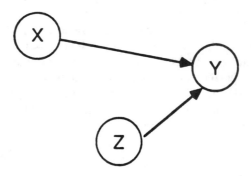

Figure 2.7a The Path Diagram for an Extraneous Variable *Z* Introduced by
Study Procedure

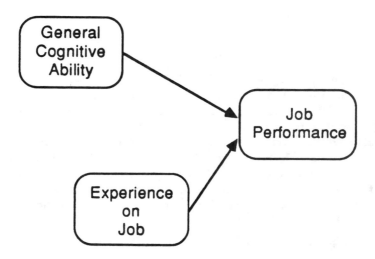

Figure 2.7b Experience Differences as an Extraneous Variable Produced
by Concurrent Validation Procedure

population correlation, where the word "unbiased" is used in the strict sense of mathematical statistics. From this, they have often then leaped to two conclusions: (1) that the bias is large enough to be visible and (2) that use of the Fisher z transformation will eliminate the bias (see for example, James, Demaree, & Mulaik, 1986). However, Hunter, Schmidt, and Coggin (1988) have shown that for sample sizes greater than 20, the bias in the correlation coefficient is less than rounding error. Even in meta-analysis, the bias for smaller sample size domains (i.e., $N < 20$) would be trivial in comparison to sampling error. They also showed that the positive bias in the Fisher z transformation is always larger than the negative bias in r (and especially so if the population correlations vary across studies). Thus, it is always less accurate to use the Fisher z transformation (though usually only to a very small degree). Further, it would be a very rare case in which it would be worthwhile to correct for bias at all. However, so the reader can make his or her own decision, we include the attenuation formula and correction here.

The average sample correlation is slightly lower than the population correlation. Assume that the population correlation has already been attenuated by all other artifacts. Then the bias in the sample correlation is given to a close approximation (Hotelling, 1953) by

$$E(r) = \rho - \rho(1 - \rho^2) / (2N - 2).$$

In our present multiplier notation, we would write

$$\rho_0 = a\rho$$

where the attenuation multiplier is

$$a = 1 - (1 - \rho^2) / (2N - 2),$$

though the ρ_0 is not the usual population correlation, but rather the expected sample correlation.

The bias is greatest and, therefore, the bias multiplier is smallest if $\rho = .50$, so that

$$a = 1 - .375 / (N - 1).$$

In personnel selection research, the average sample size is 68 and the multiplier is therefore $1 - .006 = .994$, which differs only trivially from 1.00. Since the typical attenuated correlation is less than .25 in value, the bias in personnel selection research would be less than the difference between the average sample correlation of .2486 and the population correlation of .25, a difference less than rounding error.

Only in meta-analysis with an average sample size of 10 or less would the bias be visible at the second digit. If correction is desired, then the attenuation formula above can be used with the average study correlation as the estimate of ρ. For population correlations less than .50, the attenuation factor is closely approximated by the linear multiplier $(2N - 2)/(2N - 1)$, and the correction for bias is effected by multiplying the observed correlation by $(2N - 1)/(2N - 2)$.

Sampling Error, Statistical Power, and the Interpretation of Research Literatures

An Illustration of Statistical Power

Traditional methods of interpreting research literatures lead to disastrous errors (Schmidt, Ocasio, Hillery, & Hunter, 1985). For example, consider research on the validity of nontest procedures for predicting job performance as measured by supervisory ratings. Hunter and Hunter (1984) found that the average observed correlation for reference checks was .20. For college grade point average (GPA), $\bar{r}$ was .09, and for interests, it was .08. Consider a predictor of job performance that has a mean observed validity of .10. Suppose this is the population correlation and it is constant across all settings. If 19 studies were then conducted and arranged by order of observed validity, the results would be as shown in Table 2.2. Table 2.2 presents findings for studies based on three sample sizes: (1) the classic recommended minimum of $N = 30$; (2) the median N of 68 found for Lent, Auerbach, and Levin (1971a) for studies published in the Validity Information Exchange in *Personnel Psychology*; and (3) $N = 400$, a sample size considered by many psychologists to be "large."

Clearly, the correlations in Table 2.2 vary over a wide range. Bearing in mind that the actual value of the correlation is always .10, we will now examine two traditional interpretations of these "findings": (1) that of the naive reviewer who takes observed correlations at face value and does not use significance tests, and (2) that of the "more sophisticated" reviewer who applies significance tests.

If the studies are each based on 30 people, the naive reviewer reaches the following conclusions:

1. Six of 19 studies (or 32%) found negative validities. That is, 32% of the studies show that job performance is predicted in reverse rank order of actual job performance.

Table 2.2 Nineteen Studies

	N=30	*N=68*	*N=400*
Study 1	.40**	.30**	.18**
Study 2	.34*	.25**	.16**
Study 3	.29	.23*	.15**
Study 4	.25	.20*	.14**
Study 5	.22	.18	.13**
Study 6	.20	.16	.13**
Study 7	.17	.15	.12**
Study 8	.15	.13	.11**
Study 9	.12	.12	.11**
Study 10	.10	.10	.10**
Study 11	.08	.08	.08*
Study 12	.05	.07	.09*
Study 13	.03	.05	.08*
Study 14	−.00	.04	.08
Study 15	−.02	.02	.07
Study 16	−.05	−.00	.06
Study 17	−.09	−.03	.05
Study 18	−.14	−.05	.04
Study 19	−.20	−.10	.02

**Significant by two-tailed test
*Significant by one-tailed test

2. Using a liberal standard of .20 for "moderate" correlations, in only 32% of the settings did the validity reach even a moderate level.
3. Overall conclusion: In most cases, the procedure cannot predict job performance.

If the naive reviewer is faced with 19 studies, each based on $N = 68$, he or she concludes as follows:

1. Four of 19 studies (or 21%) find negative validity.
2. In only 21% of settings (4 of 19) did the validity reach the moderate level of .20.
3. Overall conclusion: In most cases, the procedure cannot predict job performance.

If each study is based on $N = 400$, the naive reviewer concludes that

1. no studies find negative validity;
2. no studies report validity even as high as the "moderate" .20 level;
3. overall conclusion: The selection method predicts performance poorly in all settings and almost not at all in many settings.

Naive reviewers do not even begin to reach correct judgments unless the typical study has a sample size of 400 or more. Even at $N = 400$, there is enough sampling error to produce validity coefficients that differ in magnitude by a factor of $.18/.03 = 6$ to 1.

It has been a traditional belief that the use of significance tests enhances the accuracy of study interpretations. So let us examine the interpretations of a reviewer who applies significance tests to the studies in Table 2.2. If the studies are each based on $N = 30$, that reviewer reaches following conclusions.

1. Only 2 of the 19 studies (11%) found significant validity.
2. The procedure is not valid almost 90% of the time; that is, it is "generally invalid."

When each study is based on $N = 68$, the reviewer concludes as follows:

1. Only 4 of 19 studies (21%) found significant validity.
2. Thus, in the overwhelming majority of cases, the procedure is invalid.

The reviewer's conclusions from the $N = 400$ studies are

1. only 13 of 19 studies (68%) found significant validity;
2. thus, in 32% of settings, the procedure does not work;
3. conclusion: The method predict's job performance in some settings, but not in others. Further research is needed to determine why it works in some settings, but not in others.

These conclusions are *not* more accurate that those of the naive reviewer. With small sample sizes ($N < 400$), conclusions are no more accurate using the significance test, and, even with a sample size of 400, reviewers relying on traditional interpretations of significance tests do not reach correct conclusions from cumulative research. The reason the significance tests lead to errors of interpretation is that it has a very high error rate. An error is the failure to detect the true correlation of .10 in a study. The percentage of time that the statistical test will make this error in our example is

	$N=30$	$N=68$	$N=400$
Two-tailed test	92%	88%	48%
One-tailed test	86%	80%	36%

These error rates are very high. The percentage of the studies in which the significance test does *not* make this error is called its statistical power. Statistical power is 100% minus the error rate. For example, when one tailed tests are used in our 19 studies, and $N = 68$ in each study, the error rate is 80%. The statistical power is 100% − 80% = 20%. That is, the significance test is correct only 20% of the time. The next section examines statistical power in more detail.

A Detailed Examination of Statistical Power

The problems created by low statistical power in individual studies are central to the need for meta-analysis. This section explores the question of statistical power in more detail.

Suppose the population correlation between supervisory consideration and job satisfaction is .25 in all settings. This is the correlation prior to corrections for unreliability (measurement error). Now, suppose studies are conducted in a large number of settings, each with $N=83$. For simplicity, assume that the same instruments are used in all studies to measure these two variables, so reliabilities are constant across studies. Assume also that the subjects in each study are a random sample from the population of all possible employees, and range variation and the other artifacts discussed above do not vary across studies. Then the average observed correlation across all these studies will be .25, the true value. However, there will be substantial variability due to sampling error; the SD of the correlations will be

$$SD_r = \sqrt{\frac{(1 - .25^2)^2}{83 - 1}} = .103 \, .$$

This distribution of correlations is shown on the right in Figure 2.8a. The other distribution in Figure 2.8a is the one that would have resulted if the true population correlation were $\rho=0$, instead of $\rho=.25$. This null distribution is the basis of the statistical significance test. Its mean is zero. The SD of the null distribution is not the same as the SD of the real distribution, because the true value of ρ is zero,

$$SD_{NULL} = \sqrt{\frac{(1 - 0^2)^2}{83 - 1}} = .110 \, .$$

The .05 significance value for a one-tailed test is the point in the null distribution where only 5% of the correlations would be larger than that value. The 5% significance level is thus 1.645 SDs above the mean of the

Figure 2.8 Statistical Power: Two Examples

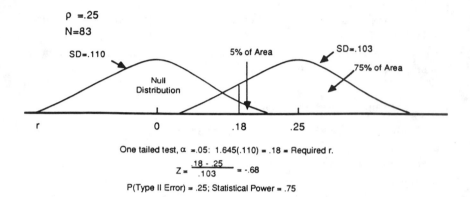

ρ =.25
N=83

One tailed test, α =.05: 1.645(.110) = .18 = Required r.

$$Z = \frac{.18 - .25}{.103} = -.68$$

P(Type II Error) = .25; Statistical Power = .75

Figure 2.8a Statistical Power Greater Than .50

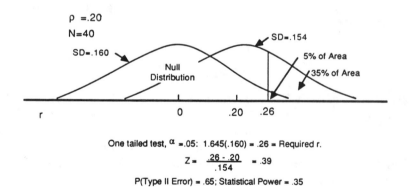

ρ =.20
N=40

One tailed test, α =.05: 1.645(.160) = .26 = Required r.

$$Z = \frac{.26 - .20}{.154} = .39$$

P(Type II Error) = .65; Statistical Power = .35

Figure 2.8b Statistical Power Less Than .50

NOTE: 1. 65% of all studies will reach a false conclusion.
2. The more studies conducted, the greater the certainty of a false conclusion.

null distribution, i.e., above zero. Therefore, to be significant, a study r must be at least as large as 1.645 (.110) = .18. If the true ρ really were zero, only 5% of study correlations would be as large as .18 or larger. That is, the Type I error rate would be 5%. But since ρ = .25, and not zero, there can be no Type I errors, only Type II errors. What percent of the study rs will be .18 or larger? If we convert .18 to a z score in the r distribution, we get

$$z = \frac{.18 - .25}{.103} = -.68.$$

The percent of values in a normal distribution that is above -.68 standard deviations below the mean is .75, as can be determined from any normal curve table. Therefore, statistical power is .75; 75% of all these studies will obtain a statistically significant correlation. In Figure 2.8a, this represents the area to the right of .18 in the observed r distribution. That area contains 75% of the observed rs. For the remaining 25% of the studies, the traditional conclusion would be that the correlation, being nonsignificant, is zero. This represents the area to the left of .18 in the observed r distribution. That area contains 25% of the observed rs. This conclusion is false; the correlation is always .25, and it has only that one value. Thus the probability of Type II error (concluding there is no relation where there is) is .25.

The studies in this example have higher statistical power than many real studies. This is because the true correlation (.25) is larger than is often the case for real world population correlations. Also, the sample size ($N = 83$) is larger here than is often the case in real studies, further increasing statistical power. For example, the mean validity coefficient for a typical employment test measuring a single aptitude is about .20 before correction for range restriction and criterion unreliability, and sample sizes are often smaller than 83.

Figure 2.8b illustrates a case that is more representative of many real studies. In Figure 2.8b the true value of the correlation (the population correlation) is .20, and each study is based on a sample size of $N = 40$. The standard deviation of the observed correlations across many such studies is

$$SD_r = \sqrt{\frac{(1 - .20^2)^2}{40 - 1}} = .154.$$

The SD in the null distribution is

$$SD_{NULL} = \sqrt{\frac{(1-0^2)^2}{40-1}} = .160 \, .$$

In order to be significant at the .05 level (again, using a one-tailed test), a correlation must be above the zero mean of the null distribution by 1.645 (.160) = .26. All correlations that are .26 or larger will be significant; the rest will be nonsignificant. Thus, to be significant, the correlation must be larger than its true value! The actual value of the correlation is always .20; observed values are larger (or smaller) than the true value of .20 only because of random sampling error. In order to get a significant correlation, we must be lucky enough to have a positive random sampling error. Any study in which r is equal to its real value of .20 — that is, any study that is perfectly accurate in estimating r — will lead to the false conclusion that the correlation is zero! What percent of the correlations will be significant? When we convert .26 to a z score in the observed r distribution, we get

$$z = \frac{.26 - .20}{.154} = .39 \, .$$

The percent of values in a normal distribution that is above a z score of .39 is 35%. In Figure 2.8b, this 35% is the area above the value of .26 in the observed r distribution. So only 35% of all these studies will get a significant r, even though the true value of r is always .20; it is never zero. Statistical power is only .35. The majority of studies — 65% — will falsely indicate that $\rho=0$; 65% of all studies will reach a false conclusion.

A vote-counting procedure has often been used in the past (see Chapter 11) in which the majority outcome is used to decide whether a relationship exists. If a majority of the studies show a nonsignificant finding, as here, the conclusion is that no relationship exists. This conclusion is clearly false here, showing that the vote-counting method is defective. But even more surprising is the fact that the larger the number of studies that are conducted, the greater is the certainty of reaching the false conclusion that there is no relationship (i.e., that $\rho=0$)! If only a few studies are conducted, then just by chance a majority might get significant correlations, and the vote-counting method might not result in an erroneous conclusion. For example, if only five studies are done, then by chance three might get significant correlations. But if a large number of studies are conducted, we are certain to zero in on approximately 35% significant and 65% nonsignificant. This creates the paradox of the vote-counting method: If statistical power is less than .50, and if the population correlation is not zero, then the more research studies there are, the more likely the reviewer is to reach the false conclusion that $\rho = 0$ (Hedges & Olkin, 1980).

These examples illustrate statistical power for correlational studies, but they are equally realistic for experimental studies. In experimental studies, the basic statistic is not the correlation coefficient, but the standardized difference between the means of two groups, the experimental and control groups. This is the difference between the two means in standard deviation units and is called the d-value statistic (see Chapters 6 and 7). The d statistic is roughly twice as large as the correlation. Thus, the example in Figure 2.8a corresponds to an experimental study in which $d = .51$; this is a difference of one-half a standard deviation, a fairly substantial difference. It corresponds to the difference between the 50th and 69th percentiles in a normal distribution. The corresponding sample sizes for Figure 2.8a would be $N = 42$ in the experimental group and $N = 41$ in the control group (or vice versa). These numbers are also relatively large; many studies have far less in each group.

The example in Figure 2.8b translates into a more realistic analogue for many experimental studies. Figure 2.8b corresponds to experimental studies in which there are 20 subjects each in the experimental and control groups. We have seen many studies, especially laboratory studies in organizational behavior and decision making, in which there were 20 or less (sometimes 5 or 10) in each group. The ρ of .20 corresponds to a d value of .40, a value as large or larger than many observed in real studies.

Thus, these two examples illustrating the low statistical power of small sample studies and the errors in conclusions that result from traditional use of significance tests in such studies generalize also to experimental studies. Since the properties of the d statistic are somewhat different, the exact figures given here for statistical power will not hold; statistical power is actually somewhat lower in the experimental studies. However, the figures are close enough to illustrate the point.

How would meta-analysis handle the studies shown in Figure 2.8a and 2.8b? First, meta-analysis calls for computing the mean r in each set of studies. For the studies in Figure 2.8a, the mean r would be found to be .25, the correct value. For Figure 2.8b, the computed mean would be .20, again the correct value. These $\bar{r}$s would then be used to compute the amount of variance expected from sampling error. For the studies in Figure 2.8a, this would be

$$S_e = \frac{(1 - \bar{r}^2)^2}{N - 1} \text{ and}$$

$$S_e^2 = \frac{(1 - .25^2)^2}{83 - 1} = .0107.$$

This value would then be subtracted from the amount of variance in the observed correlations to see whether any variance over and above sampling variance was left. The observed variance is $(.10344)^2 = .0107$. Thus the amount of real variance in the correlations across these studies is $S_\rho^2 = .0107 - .0107 = 0$. The meta-analytic conclusion is that there is only one value of $\rho - .25$ — and all of the apparent variability in rs across studies is sampling errors. Thus, meta-analysis leads to the correct conclusion, while the traditional approach led to the conclusion that $\rho=0$ in 25% of the studies and varied all the way from .18 to approximately .46 in the other 75% of the studies.

Likewise, for the studies in Figure 2.8b, the expected sampling error is

$$S_e^2 = \frac{(1 - .20^2)^2}{40 - 1} = .0236.$$

The variance actually observed is $(.1537)^2 = .0236 = S_r^2$. Again, $S_r^2 - S_e^2 = 0$, and the meta-analytic conclusion is that there is only one value of ρ in all the studies — $\rho=.20$ — and all the variability in rs across different studies is just sampling error. Again, meta-analysis leads to the correct conclusion, while the traditional use of statistical significance tests leads to false conclusions. The principle here is identical for the d statistics. Only the specific formulas are different (see Chapter 7).

The examples in Figure 2.8a and 2.8b are hypothetical, but they are not unrealistic. In fact, the point here is that real data often behave in the same way. For example, consider the real data in Table 2.3. These data are validity coefficients obtained in a study of nine different job families in Sears, Roebuck and Company (Hill, 1980). For any of these seven tests, validity coefficients are significant for some job families but not for others. For example, the Arithmetic test has significant validity coefficients for job families 1, 2, 5, 8, and 9; the validity is not significant for job families 3, 4, 6, and 7. One interpretation of these findings — the traditional one — is that the Arithmetic test should be used to hire people only in job families 1, 2, 5, 8, and 9, because it is valid for these job families but not for the others. This conclusion is erroneous. Application of the meta-analysis methods that we present in this book shows that for the tests in Table 2.3 all the variation in validities across job families is due to sampling error. The nonsignificant validities are due only to low statistical power. Another example in which sampling error accounts for all of the variation in study outcomes in real data is given in Schmidt, Ocasio, Hillery, and Hunter (1985). In that extensive study, observed correlation coefficients varied across different studies all the way from −.16 to .61, a range of .78 correlation points. Yet the true value of ρ was

Table 2.3 Validity Coefficients from the Sears Study

Job Family	N	Sears Test of Mental Alertness			Sears Clerical Battery			
		Linguistic	Quantitative	Total Score	Filing	Checking	Arithmetic	Grammar
1. Office Support Material Handlers	86	.33*	.20*	.32*	.30*	.27*	.32*	.25*
2. Data Processing Clerical	80	.43*	.53*	.51*	.30*	.39*	.42*	.47*
3. Clerical – Secretarial (Lower Level)	65	.24*	.03	.20	.20	.22	.13	.26*
4. Clerical – Secretarial (Higher Level)	186	.12*	.18*	.17*	.07	.21*	.20	.31*
5. Secretarial (Top Level)	146	.19*	.21*	.22*	.16*	.15*	.22*	.09
6. Clerical with Supervisory Duties	30	.24	.14	.23	.24	.24	.31	.17
7. Word Processing	63	.03	.26*	.13	.39*	.33*	.14	.22*
8. Supervisors	185	.28*	.10	.25*	.25*	.11	.19*	.20*
9. Technical, Operative, Professional	54	.24*	.35*	.33*	.30*	.22*	.31*	.42*

*$P < .05$

constant in every study at .22. (In fact, each study was a random sample from a single large study.) Sampling error in small sample studies creates tremendous variability in study outcomes. Researchers have underestimated this variability for years.

Of course, sampling error does not explain all variation in all sets of studies. In most cases, other artifacts also operate to cause variance in study outcomes, as discussed earlier in this chapter. And in some cases even the combination of sampling error and other artifacts (such as measurement error and range restriction differences between studies) cannot explain all the variance. However, these artifacts virtually always account for important amounts of variance in study outcomes.

When and How to Cumulate

In broad outline, a meta-analytic cumulation of results across studies is conceptually a simple process.

1. Calculate the desired descriptive statistic for each study available, and average that statistic across studies.
2. Calculate the variance of the statistic across studies.
3. Correct the variance by subtracting the amount due to sampling error.
4. Correct the mean and variance for study artifacts other than sampling error.
5. Compare the corrected standard deviation to the mean to assess the size of the potential variation in results across studies in qualitative terms. If the mean is more than two standard deviations larger than zero, then it is reasonable to conclude that the relationship considered is always positive.

In practice, cumulation usually involves a variety of technical complexities that we will take up in later chapters.

Cumulation of results can be used whenever there are at least two studies with data bearing on the same relation. For example, if your study at Crooked Corn Flakes contains a correlation between job status and job satisfaction, then you might want to compare that correlation with the correlation found in your earlier study at Tuffy Bolts. However, to correct for sampling error with two correlations, it is possible to use a strategy different from the corrected variance procedures presented in Chapters 3 and 4. It is possible to simply test the correlations to see if they are significantly different. If they are not significantly different, then the difference between them may be due solely to sampling error. The fact that one study was done in the food industry while the other study was done in manufacturing is probably irrelevant.

Cumulation of results should ideally be based on a large number of studies located by exhaustive search procedures (see Chapter 12). However, cumulation is also valid for "convenience" samples of studies that just happen to lie at hand, as long as they are a random sample of existing studies. This is particularly true if the corrected standard deviation suggests that all the variation across studies is due to sampling error. If all the variation is due to sampling error, then the accuracy of the mean value in relation to the one true population value is determined by the total number of subjects across studies. Even a relatively small number of studies may have a large cumulative sample size.

If a convenience sample of studies has a small corrected standard deviation, then one concludes that there is little or no variation in the results across the population of studies that is implicitly sampled. However, the investigator may have *systematically* excluded studies that others would have put in the same population of studies. In this case, the basis for the exclusion might be a real moderator variable and the population of excluded results might cluster around a different population correlation value. Reliance on a convenience sample always involves some risk.

It has long been alleged that published studies have larger correlations and effect sizes than unpublished ones, partly because the published studies are better designed, but partly because editorial reviewers have a substantial preference for studies with statistically significant results. There may be some research areas in which the true effect size is zero. In such an area, if some studies with Type I errors get published, and most studies without Type I errors do not get published, an assessment limited to published studies would be biased. Even if the true effect size is not zero, there may still be bias in the estimation of its *size* (although by definition there could be no Type I errors).

Two studies provide some evidence that unpublished studies do have smaller effect sizes. Smith and Glass (1977) analyzed the standardized effect sizes of 375 studies on psychotherapy. They found that studies published in books had an average effect size of .8σ, those published in journals had an average effect size of .7σ, dissertations averaged .6σ, and unpublished studies averaged .5σ. Rosenthal and Rubin (1978a, 1978b) found that, in a sample of interpersonal expectancy effect studies, the average effect size of 32 dissertations was .35σ and the average effect size of 313 nondissertations was .65σ. Neither set of authors reported an assessment of the relative methodological quality of the published and unpublished studies. Most of the difference between the average effect size of the published and unpublished studies may be due to differences in the methodological quality. If attenuation effects were properly corrected for, differences might disappear (see Schmidt & Hunter, 1977, pp. 536-537). This question is discussed in more detail in Chapter 13.

Undercorrection for Artifacts in the Corrected Standard Deviation

The corrected standard deviation of results across studies should always be regarded as an overestimate of the true standard deviation. Procedures developed to date correct for only some of the artifacts that produce spurious variation across studies. There are other artifacts that have similar effects. The largest of these is computational or reporting errors. If you have 30 correlations ranging from .00 to .60, and one correlation of −.45 (a case we encountered in our own studies), then it is virtually certain that the outlier resulted from some faulty computational or reporting procedure; for example, failing to reverse the sign of a variable that is reverse scored, or using the wrong format in a computer run, or a typographical error, and so on. Other artifacts that create spurious variation across studies include differences in the reliability of measurement, differences in the construct validity of measurement (such as criterion contamination or criterion deficiency in personnel selection studies), differences in the variances of measured variables in different studies (such as differences in restriction in range in personnel selection studies), and differences in the amount of the treatment (in experimental studies). Indeed, the relevant question in many settings is: Is all of the variation across studies artifactual? In the personnel selection area, this has been the conclusion in a number of areas, such as single group validity, differential validity by race or ethnic group, specificity of test validity across setting or time, and amount of halo in ratings made using different methods (cf., Schmidt & Hunter, 1981; Schmidt, Hunter, Pearlman, & Hirsh, 1985).

Some artifacts can be quantified and corrected for. Corrections for differences in reliability and restriction in range were first made by Schmidt and Hunter (1977) and Schmidt, Hunter, Pearlman and Shane (1979); these are described in Chapter 3. Differences in the construct validity of measures can be corrected using similar techniques if there is an integrated study available that provides a path analysis relating the alternate measures to each other (see discussion earlier in this chapter). Quantitative differences in treatment effects (such as magnitude of incentive) can be coded and corrected after the initial cumulation establishes the relation (if any) between that aspect of the treatment and study outcome (see Chapters 6 and 7).

However, these corrections depend on additional information that is frequently not available. For example, reliabilities and standard deviations are often not included in correlational studies. They are not even considered in most experimental studies. And, alas, computational and reporting errors will never be fully quantified and eliminated.

If there is large, real variation in results across studies, then any conclusion based solely on the summary result entails a certain amount of error. This is the familiar problem of ignoring interactions or moderator effects. However, errors of even greater magnitude can be made if variation caused by artifacts is attributed to nonexistent methodological and substantive moderators. For example, one well-known psychologist recently became so discouraged by the variation in results in several research areas that he concluded it was unlikely that any finding in psychology would ever hold from one generation to the next, since each cohort would always differ on some social dimension that would alter research outcomes (Cronbach, 1975). In our judgment, such a position is likely to reflect the reification of sampling error variance and other artifactual variance. Such reification leads not only to epistomological disillusionment, but also to immense wasted effort in endlessly replicating studies when enough data already exist to answer the question.

If there is a large corrected standard deviation, it may be possible to explain the variation across studies by breaking the studies into groups on the basis of the relevant difference between them. This breakdown can be an explicit subdivision of studies into categories, or it can be an implicit breakdown using regression methods to correlate study outcomes with study characteristics. Both of these will be considered in detail in Chapters 3, 4, and 7. However, we will show in the next section that such a breakdown should by attempted only if there is a substantial corrected variance. Otherwise, the breakdown can introduce error into the interpretation of the studies by virtue of capitalization on chance.

Coding Study Characteristics and Capitalization on Chance

The process of meta-analysis is defined by Glass and his associates (Glass, McGaw, & Smith, 1981) as a composite process: (1) cumulation of descriptive statistics across studies; (2) the coding of perhaps 50 to 100 study characteristics, such as date of study, number of threats to internal validity, and so forth; and (3) regression of study outcome onto the coded study characteristics. Such coding can be 90 to 95% of the work in the research integration process. Yet this coding work may be entirely wasted. In our own research, in which we have made corrections for sampling error and other artifacts, we have usually found no significant variation across studies remaining after these corrections. That is, it is our experience that there is usually no important variation in study results after sampling error and other artifacts are removed. Thus, all observed correlations with study characteristics would be the result of sampling error and capitalization on chance due to the small number of studies.

If there is little variation other than sampling error, then the dependent variable (study outcome: the r or d statistics) has low reliability. For example, if 90% of between-study variance in correlations is due to artifacts, then the reliability of the study outcome variable is only .10. Therefore, large observed correlations between study characteristics and study outcomes could occur only because of sampling error. Correlating study characteristics with study outcome leads to massive capitalization on chance when the correlations that are large enough to be statistically significant are identified ex post facto. Sampling error is very large because the *sample size* for looking at study characteristics is not the number of persons in the studies but the *number of studies*. For example, the multiple regression of study outcome onto 40 study characteristics (typical of current meta-analyses) with only 50 studies as observations (typical of current meta-analyses) would lead by chance to a multiple correlation near one. Indeed, some studies have more study characteristics than studies, a situation in which the multiple correlation is always 1.00 by fiat.

Many meta-analyses are conducted in the following manner. The researchers first look through their 40 study characteristics to find the 5 that are most highly correlated with study outcomes. Then they use multiple regression with those 5, using a shrinkage formula (if one is used at all) for 5 predictors. But to pick the best 5 out of 40 is approximately the same as doing a step-up regression from 40 predictors, and hence one should use 40 in the shrinkage formula rather than 5 (Cattin, 1980). In many cases, the proper shrinkage correction would show the actual multiple correlation to be near zero.

Table 2.4 illustrates how severe the problem of capitalization on chance is when only those study characteristics that correlate highest with study outcomes are retained and entered into the regression analysis. Table 2.4 depicts a situation in which every study characteristic correlates zero with study outcomes and all study characteristics correlate zero with each other. Thus, the true value of all multiple correlations in Table 2.4 is zero, and all the multiple correlations in the table are produced solely by capitalization on chance. Consider a typical example. Suppose the number of study characteristics coded is 20 and the 4 that correlate highest with study characteristics are retained and used in the regression analysis. Then if the number of studies is 100, the expected multiple R is .36, a value that is highly "statistically significant" ($p=.0002$). If there are 60 studies, then the spurious multiple R will on average be .47. If there are only 40 studies, it will be .58, even though in every case the true multiple R is zero. The

Table 2.4 Expected Values of the Multiple *R* of Study Characteristics
with Study Outcomes When All Study Characteristics
Correlate Zero with Study Outcomes and with Each Other

Number of Study Characteristics in Regression Equation	Total Number of Study Characteristics	Number of Studies							
		20	40	60	80	100	200	400	800
2		.49	.34	.28	.24	.21	.15	.11	.07
3	6	.51	.36	.29	.25	.22	.16	.11	.08
4		.53	.37	.30	.26	.23	.16	.12	.08
2		.53	.37	.30	.26	.23	.17	.12	.08
3	8	.57	.40	.33	.28	.25	.18	.13	.09
4		.61	.42	.35	.30	.27	.19	.13	.09
2		.57	.40	.32	.28	.25	.18	.12	.09
3	10	.62	.43	.35	.31	.27	.19	.13	.10
4		.66	.46	.38	.33	.29	.21	.14	.10
2		.61	.43	.35	.30	.27	.19	.13	.09
3	13	.67	.47	.38	.33	.29	.21	.14	.10
4		.72	.50	.41	.36	.32	.22	.16	.11
2		.64	.45	.36	.32	.28	.20	.14	.10
3	16	.71	.49	.40	.35	.31	.22	.16	.11
4		.77	.54	.44	.38	.34	.24	.17	.12
2		.68	.48	.37	.34	.30	.21	.15	.11
3	20	.76	.53	.43	.37	.33	.23	.16	.12
4		.83	.58	.47	.41	.36	.26	.18	.13
2		.70	.49	.40	.35	.31	.22	.15	.11
3	25	.79	.55	.45	.39	.34	.24	.17	.12
4		.86	.60	.49	.43	.38	.27	.19	.13
2		.73	.51	.41	.36	.32	.22	.16	.11
3	30	.82	.57	.46	.40	.36	.25	.18	.13
4		.90	.63	.51	.44	.39	.28	.20	.14
2		.75	.52	.42	.37	.33	.23	.16	.11
3	35	.84	.59	.48	.42	.37	.26	.18	.13
4		.93	.65	.53	.46	.41	.29	.20	.14
2		.76	.53	.43	.38	.33	.24	.17	.12
3	40	.87	.61	.50	.43	.38	.27	.19	.13
4		.97	.68	.55	.48	.42	.30	.21	.15
2		.80	.55	.45	.39	.35	.24	.17	.12
3	50	.90	.63	.51	.44	.39	.28	.20	.14
4		1.00	.70	.57	.49	.44	.31	.22	.15

values in Table 2.4 are *mean* values; they are not the largest values. Approximately half the time the observed multiple Rs will be *larger* than the values in the table. The situation in which 4 study characteristics out of 20 are retained is representative of some actual meta-analyses. However, often large numbers of study characteristics are coded; for example, it is not unusual for 40 to 50 characteristics to be coded. If 40 are coded and 4 are retained, the spurious multiple R can be expected to be .68 with 40 studies, .55 with 60 studies, and .48 with 80 studies. The reason the multiple R is spuriously large is that the retained study characteristic correlations are biased upward from their true value of zero by capitalization on (chance) sampling errors. For example, if there are 60 studies and 40 study characteristics are coded but only the top 4 are retained, then the correlation for the retained 4 will average .23. These retained characteristics then yield a multiple R of .55. Thus, it is apparent that the problem of capitalization on chance in conventional meta-analysis moderator analysis is extremely severe. Many moderators identified in published meta-analyses using regression and correlation methods are probably not real. Those that were identified purely empirically, and were not predicted a priori by a theory or hypothesis, are particularly likely to be illusions created by capitalization on sampling error.

On the other hand, those moderators that *are* real are unlikely to be detected because of low statistical power. The discussions of statistical power earlier in this chapter apply to correlations between study characteristics and study outcomes just as well as to other correlations. The sample size — the number of studies — is usually small (e.g., 40 to 100), and the study characteristics correlations are likely to be small because much of the variance of observed study outcomes is sampling error variance and other artifactual variance. Thus, statistical power to detect real moderators will typically be quite low. Hence, the real moderators are unlikely to be detected, and, at the same time, there is a high probability that capitalization on chance will lead to the "detection" of nonexistent moderators. This is indeed an unhappy situation.

To take all variation across studies at face value is to ignore sampling error. Since most studies are done with small samples (e.g., less than 500 subjects), the sampling error is actually quite large in comparison to observed outcome values. Thus, to ignore sampling error is to guarantee major statistical errors at some point in the analysis. The classical reviewer's error is to report the range of outcome values; the range is determined by the two most extreme sampling errors in the set of studies. The error in current meta-analyses is capitalization on chance and low statistical power in relating variation across studies in r or d values to coded study characteristics.

We do not claim that we have the answer to the problems of capitalization on chance and low statistical power in moderator analysis. In our judgment, there is no solution to this problem within statistics. It is well known within statistics that the statistical test does not solve the problem; the Type I versus Type II error trade-off is unavoidable. Thus, if issues are to be resolved solely on statistical grounds, then the answer to subtle questions can only be to gather more data, often vast amounts of data. The other alternative is to develop theories that allow new data to be drawn indirectly into the argument. This new data may then permit an objective resolution of the issue on theoretical grounds (see Chapter 11).

A Look Ahead in the Book

The two most common research designs for empirical studies are the correlational study and the two-group intervention study (i.e., an experimental study with independent treatment and control groups). Strength of relationship in correlational designs is usually measured by the correlation coefficient. We present methods for cumulating the correlation coefficient in Chapters 3 and 4. Some have argued that the slope or covariance should be cumulated, rather than the correlation. However, slopes and covariances are comparable across studies only if exactly the same instruments are used to measure the independent and dependent variables in each study. It is a rare set of studies in which this is true. Thus, only in rare cases can the slope or covariance be cumulated because it is in the same metric in all studies. Furthermore, the strength of relationship represented by a slope or covariance can only be known when these numbers are compared to the standard deviations, i.e., only when the correlation coefficient is computed. We examine the cumulation of slopes and intercepts in detail in Chapter 5.

The statistic most commonly reported in intervention studies is the t-test statistic. However, t is not a good measure of strength of effect since it is multiplied by the square root of sample size and, hence, does not have the same metric across studies. When sample size is removed from the t statistic, the resulting formula is the effect size statistic d. We will consider the effect size statistic d in Chapters 6, 7, and 8. We will also consider its correlational analogue, the point-biserial correlation. Often it is better to convert d values to point-biserial correlations, conduct the meta-analysis on these correlations, and then transform the final result back to the d-value statistic. Some would argue for use of proportion of variance instead of r or d, but proportion of variance accounted for (or explained) has many defects. For example, it does not preserve the sign or direction of the treatment effect. Also, as a consequence of the loss of sign, the squared effect measure mean is biased. Proportion of variance indices are discussed and critiqued further in Chapter 5.

Chapters 3, 4, and 5 on the correlation coefficient and 6, 7, and 8 on d values assume that each entry is based on a statistically independent sample. However, it is frequently possible to obtain more than one relevant estimate of a correlation or effect size from the same study. How then should multiple estimates of a relation from within the same study contribute to a cumulation across studies? This issue is taken up in Chapter 10.

PART II

Meta-Analysis of Correlations

3 Meta-Analysis of Correlations Corrected Individually for Artifacts

Introduction and Overview

In Chapter 2, we examined 11 study design artifacts that can affect the size of the correlation coefficient. At the level of meta-analysis, it is possible to correct for all but one of those artifacts: reporting or transcriptional error. Except for outlier analysis, we know of no way to correct for bad data. Outlier analysis (discussed in Chapter 5) will detect some but not all bad data. Sampling error can be corrected for, but the accuracy of the correction depends on the total sample size that the meta-analysis is based on. The correction for sampling error becomes perfect as total sample size approaches infinity. Our discussion of meta-analysis in this chapter and in Chapter 4 will implicitly assume that the meta-analysis is based on a very large number of studies. If the number of studies is small, then the formulas presented here still apply, but there will be sampling error in the final meta-analysis results. This is the problem of "second order" sampling error, which will be discussed in Chapter 9.

The 10 potentially correctable study design artifacts are listed in Table 3.1. To correct for the effect of an artifact, we must have information about the size and nature of the artifact. Ideally, this information would be given for each study (i.e., each correlation) individually for each artifact. In that case, each correlation could be corrected individually, and the meta-analysis would be done on corrected correlations. This type of meta-analysis is the subject of this chapter.

Artifact information is often available only on a sporadic basis and is sometimes not available at all. However, the nature of artifacts is such that in most research domains, the artifact values will be independent across studies. For example, there is no reason to suppose that reliability of measurement will be either higher or lower if the sample size is large or small. If the artifacts are independent of each other and independent of the size of the true population correlation, then it is possible to base meta-analysis on artifact distributions. That is, given the independence assump-

Table 3.1 Study Artifacts That Alter the Value of Outcome
Measures—With Examples From Personnel Research

1. Sampling error:
   Study validity will vary randomly from the population value because of sampling error.
2. Error of measurement in the dependent variable:
   Study validity will be systematically lower than true validity to the extent that job performance is measured with random error.
3. Error of measurement in the independent variable:
   Study validity for a test will systematically understate the validity of the ability measured since the test is not perfectly reliable.
4. Dichotomization of a continuous dependent variable:
   Turnover—the length of time that a worker stays with the organization is often dichotomized into "more than . . ." or "less than . . ." where . . . is some arbitrarily chosen interval such as one year or six months.
5. Dichotomization of a continuous independent variable:
   Interviewers are often told to dichotomize their perceptions into "acceptable" versus "reject."
6. Range variation in the independent variable:
   Study validity will be systematically lower than true validity to the extent that hiring policy causes incumbents to have a lower variation in the predictor than is true of applicants.
7. Attrition artifacts: Range variations in the dependent variable:
   Study validity will be systematically lower than true validity to the extent that there is systematic attrition in workers on performance, as when good workers are promoted out of the population or when poor workers are fired for poor performance.
8. Deviation from perfect construct validity in the independent variable:
   Study validity will vary if the factor structure of the test differs from the usual structure of tests for the same trait.
9. Deviation from perfect construct validity in the dependent variable:
   Study validity will differ from true validity if the criterion is deficient or contaminated.
10. Reporting or transcriptional error:
    Reported study validities differ from actual study validities due to a variety of reporting problems: inaccuracy in coding data, computational errors, errors in reading computer output, typographical errors by secretaries or by printers.
    Note: These errors can be very large in magnitude.
11. Variance due to extraneous factors:
    Study validity will be systematically lower than true validity if incumbents differ in experience at the time they are assessed for performance.

tion, it is possible to correct for artifacts at the level of meta-analysis even though we cannot correct individual correlations. This type of meta-analysis is the subject of the next chapter, Chapter 4. Finally, if no information is available on an artifact, then the meta-analysis cannot correct for that artifact. Note that this doesn't mean that the artifact does not exist or that it has no impact. It merely means that the meta-analysis does not correct for that artifact. If no correction is made for an artifact, then the estimated mean and standard deviation of true effect size correlations are not corrected for the effect of that artifact. The estimates will be inaccurate to the extent that uncorrected artifacts have large, rather than small, impact in that research domain.

Although there are 10 potentially correctable artifacts, they will not all be discussed at the same level of detail. First, sampling error is both nonsystematic and of devastating effect in contemporary narrative reviews of the literature. Thus, sampling error will be discussed first and in considerable detail. The other systematic artifacts will then be considered one by one. Here, too, there will be differences in the length of the presentation. This does not mean that some are less important than others. Rather, it is a matter of mathematical redundancy. Most of the artifacts have the effect of attenuating the true correlation by a multiplicative fraction, and hence, these artifacts all have a very similar mathematical structure. Once we look at error of measurement and range variation in detail, the others are mathematically similar and, hence, can be treated more briefly. However, it is important to remember that an artifact which may have little or no effect in one research domain may have a huge effect in another. For example, there are research domains where the dependent variable has never been dichotomized and hence there need be no correction for that artifact at all. However, in research on turnover almost every study dichotomizes the dependent variable, and the dichotomization is based on administrative conventions that often lead to very extreme splits. Thus, none of the artifacts in Table 3.1 can be routinely ignored, no matter how short our treatment of that artifact may be and regardless of whether it can be corrected or not.

Consider the effect of sampling error on the study correlation. At the level of the single study, sampling error is a random event. If the observed correlation is .30, then, unknown to us, the population correlation could be higher than .30 or lower than .30, and there is no way that we can know the sampling error or correct for it. However, at the level of meta-analysis, sampling error can be estimated and corrected for. Consider first the operation of averaging correlations across studies. When we average correlations, we also average the sampling errors. Thus the sampling error in the average correlation is the average of the sampling errors in the individual correlations. For example, if we average across 30 studies with a total sample size of 2,000, then sampling error in the average correlation is about the same as if we had computed a correlation on a sample of 2,000. That is, if the total sample size is large, then there is very little sampling error in the average correlation. The variance of correlations across studies is another story. The variance of correlations is the average *squared* deviation of the study correlation from its mean. Squaring the deviation eliminates the sign of the sampling error and, hence, eliminates the tendency for errors to cancel themselves out in summation. Instead, sampling error causes the variance across studies to be systematically larger than the variance of population correlations that we would like to know. However, the effect of sampling error on the variance is to add a known constant, which we will call the sampling error variance. This constant can be subtracted from the observed variance. The difference is then an estimate of the desired variance of population correlations.

To eliminate the effect of sampling error from a meta-analysis, we must derive the distribution of population correlations from the distribution of observed correlations. That is, we would like to replace the mean and standard deviation of the observed sample correlations by the mean and standard deviation of population correlations. Since sampling error cancels out in the average correlation across studies, our best estimate of the mean population correlation is simply the mean of the sample correlations. However, sampling error adds to the variance of correlations across studies. Thus, we must correct the observed variance by subtracting the sampling error variance. The difference is then the variance of population correlations across studies.

Once we have corrected the variance across studies for the effect of sampling error, it is possible to see if there is any real variance in results across studies. If there is a large amount of variance across studies, then it is possible to look for moderator variables to explain this variance. To test our hypothesized moderator variable, we break the set of studies into subsets using the moderator variable. For example, we might split the studies into those done on large corporations and those done on small businesses. We then do separate meta-analyses within each subset of studies. If we find large differences between subsets, then the hypothesized variable is indeed a moderator variable. The meta-analysis within subsets also tells us how much of the residual variance within subsets is due to sampling error and how much is real. That is, the meta-analysis tells us whether or not we need look for a second moderator variable.

Although it is pedagogically convenient for us to present the search for moderator variables immediately after presenting the method for eliminating the effects of sampling error, that search is actually premature. Sampling error is only one source of artifactual variation across studies. We should eliminate other sources of variance before we look for moderator variables. Another important source of correctable variation across studies in most domains is variation in error of measurement across studies. That is, a variable such as job satisfaction can be measured in many ways. Thus, different studies will often use different measures of the independent variable or different measures of the dependent variable. Alternate measures will differ in the extent to which they are affected by random error of measurement. Differences in amount of error produce differences in the size of the correlation. Differences in correlations across studies due to differences in error of measurement would look like differences due to a moderator variable. Thus, we obtain a true picture of the stability of results across studies only if we eliminate the effects of measurement error. The same is true of other study design artifacts.

Correctable artifacts other than sampling error are systematic rather than unsystematic in their impact on study correlations. Let us discuss error of measurement as one example of a correctable systematic artifact. At the level of the individual person, error of measurement is a random event. If Bill's observed score is 75, then his true score could be either greater than 75 or less than 75, and there is no way of knowing which. However, when we correlate scores across persons, the random effects of error of measurement produce a systematic effect on the correlation coefficient. Error of measurement in either variable causes the correlation to be lower than it would have been with perfect measurement. We will present a formula for "attenuation" that expresses the exact extent to which the correlation is lowered by any given amount of error of measurement. This same formula can be algebraically reversed to provide a formula for "correction for attenuation." That is, if we know the amount of error of measurement in each variable, then we can "correct" the observed correlation to provide an estimate of what the correlation would have been had the variables been perfectly measured.

The amount of error of measurement in a variable is measured by a number called the "reliability" of the variable. The reliability is a number between 0 and 1 that measures the percentage of the observed variance that is due to the true score. That is, if the reliability of the independent variable is .80, then 80% of the variance is due to the true score, and, by subtraction, 20% of the variance is due to error of measurement. To correct for the effect of error of measurement on the correlation, we need to know the amount of error of measurement in both variables. That is, to correct the correlation for attenuation, we need to know the reliability of both variables.

Error of measurement can be eliminated from a meta-analysis in either of two ways: at the level of single studies or at the level of averages across studies. If the reliability of each variable is known in each study, then the correlation for each study can be separately corrected for attenuation. We can then do a meta-analysis on the corrected correlations. This type of meta-analysis is the subject of this chapter. However, many studies do not report the reliability of their instruments. Thus reliability information is only sporadically available. Under such conditions we can still estimate the distribution of the reliability of both the independent and the dependent variables. Given the distribution of observed correlations, the distribution of the reliability of the independent variables, and the distribution of the reliability of the dependent variable, it is possible to use special formulas to correct the meta-analysis to eliminate the effects of error of measurement. Meta-analysis based on such artifact distributions is the subject of the next chapter.

If each individual correlation is corrected for attenuation, then the meta-analysis formulas will differ slightly from the formulas for meta-analysis on uncorrected correlations. The average corrected correlation is a good estimate of the average population correlation between true scores. But the variance is again too large because of the additive nature of sampling error on variance. The observed variance can be corrected for sampling error simply by subtracting a constant—the sampling error variance. However, the sampling error in a corrected correlation is larger than the sampling error in an uncorrected correlation. Therefore, a different formula must be used to compute the sampling error variance for corrected correlations.

The other correctable artifact most studied in psychometric theory (and in personnel selection research) is range restriction (though our formulas handle the case of range enhancement or range variation, too). In many contexts, the distribution of the independent variable is approximately the same across studies. In such cases, the meta-analysis need not correct for range variation. However, if the standard deviation of the independent variable differs radically from study to study, then there will be corresponding differences in the correlation from study to study. These differences across studies will look like differences produced by a moderator variable. Thus, if there are big differences in the range of the independent variable across studies, then a true picture of the stability of results will appear only if the effects of range variation are eliminated. To do this, we compute the value that the correlation would have had had the study been done on a population with some reference level of variance on the independent variable.

Range deviation can be corrected at the level of the single study. If we know the standard deviation of the independent variable in the study, and if we know the standard deviation in the reference population, then there is a range correction formula that will produce an estimate of what the correlation would have been had the standard deviation of the study population been equal to the standard deviation of the reference population. If we correct a correlation for range departure, then the corrected correlation will have a different amount of sampling error than an uncorrected correlation. Therefore, a meta-analysis on corrected correlations would use a different formula for the sampling error variance.

In an ideal research review, we would have complete information about artifacts on each study. For each study, we would know the extent of range departure and the reliabilities of both variables. We could then correct each correlation for both range departure and error of measurement. We would then do a meta-analysis of the fully corrected correlations.

Alas, information on range departure is usually only sporadically available. However, we may be able to compile information about the distribution of range departure across studies. If we can, then there is a formula for correcting the meta-analysis to eliminate the effects of range variation. These formulas are given in Chapter 4.

Discussion of other correctable artifacts will be taken up when the needed mathematical tools have been presented. Skipping these artifacts at this time is by no means intended to imply that they are less important. For example, in turnover studies dichotomization has an even larger attenuating effect on study correlaions than does error of measurement.

The remainder of this chapter will be presented in four main sections. First, there will be a complete treatment of meta-analysis with correction for sampling error only. Second, there will be a detailed treatment of error of measurement and range departure, both in terms of the corrections for single studies and in terms of the effect of the correction on sampling error. Third, there will be a more abreviated treatment of each of the other correctable artifacts. Fourth, there will be the presentation of meta-analysis for the case of individually corrected correlations, i.e., meta-analysis as it is done when full information is available on the artifact values in each study.

At present, we know of no research domain where the information has been available to correct for every one of the correctable artifacts listed in Table 3.1. Some meta-analyses methods (e.g., Glass, McGaw, & Smith, 1981) do not even correct for samplirg error; they take each study outcome at face value. In personnel selection research, correction is typically made only for error of measurement and range restriction. Most current meta-analyses have made no correction for dichotomization or imperfect construct validity. Furthermore, there will probably be more correctable artifacts defined and quantified over the coming years. And even if all correctable artifacts were corrected, there is still reporting error and bad data.

It is important to keep in mind that even a fully corrected meta-analysis will not correct for all artifacts. Even after correction, variation across studies should be taken with a grain of salt (see Chapters 2 and 5). Small residual variance is probably due to uncorrected artifacts rather than to a real moderator variable.

Bare Bones Meta-Analysis: Correcting for Sampling Error Only

We will now present a detailed discussion of sampling error. To keep the presentation simple, we will ignore other artifacts. The resulting presentation is thus written as if the study population correlations were free of other artifacts. In later sections, we will discuss the relationship between sampling error and other artifacts. This section also presents the mathematics of a meta-analysis in which sampling error is the only artifact corrected. Alas, there are those who do not believe that other artifacts exist. There are also whose who believe that if there are artifacts in the original studies, then those same artifacts *should be* reflected in the meta-analysis. They believe that meta-analysis should describe only observed results and should not correct for known problems in current research design (see Chapter 11). However, most scientists believe that the goal of cumulative research is to produce better answers than can be obtained in isolated studies. From that point of view, a meta-analysis that does not correct for as many artifacts as possible is an unfinished meta-analysis. We hold that view. If a meta-analysis corrects only for sampling error, then it is the mathematical equivalent of the ostrich with its head in the sand: it is a pretense that if we ignore an artifact then its effects on study outcomes will go away.

Estimation of Sampling Error

If the population correlation is assumed to be constant over studies, then the best estimate of that correlation is not the simple mean across studies but a weighted average in which each correlation is weighted by the number of persons in that study. Thus, the best estimate of the population correlation is

$$\bar{r} = \frac{\Sigma\,[\,N_i\,r_i\,]}{\Sigma N_i}$$

where r_i is the correlation in study i and N_i is the number of persons in study i. The corresponding variance across studies is not the usual sample variance, but the frequency weighted average squared error

$$s_r^2 = \frac{\Sigma\,[\,N_i\,(r_i - \bar{r})^2\,]}{\Sigma N_i}\;.$$

Two questions are often asked about the procedure above. First, is the weighted average always better than the simple average? Hunter and Schmidt (1987a) present a detailed discussion of this. Their analysis shows that it would be a very rare case in which an unweighted analysis would be better. Second, why do we not transform the correlations to Fisher z form for the cumulative analysis? The answer is that the Fisher z transformation produces an estimate of the mean correlation that is upwardly biased and less accurate than an analysis using untransformed correlations (see Chapter 5 and Hunter, Schmidt, & Coggin, 1988).

The frequency weighted average gives greater weight to large studies than to small studies. If there is no variance in population correlations across studies, then the weighting always improves accuracy. If the variance of population correlations is small, then the weighted average is also always better. If the variance across studies is large, then as long as sample size is not correlated with the size of the population correlation, the weighted average will again be superior. That leaves one case in which the weighted average could prove troublesome. For example, in one meta-analysis, we found thirteen studies on the validity of bio-data in predicting job success. One of these studies was done by an insurance consortium with a sample size of 15,000. The other 12 studies were done with sample sizes of 500 or less. The weighted average will give the single insurance study over 30 times the weight given to any other study. Suppose that the insurance study were deviant in some way. The meta-analysis might then be almost entirely defined by one deviant study. In a situation such as this, we recommend two analyses: a first analysis with the large sample study included and a second analysis with the large sample study left out. We have not yet had to figure out what to do should the two analyses show a major discrepancy. (In our case, they did not.)

What about the Fisher z transformation? In our original work, we carried out calculations both ways. For preliminary calculations done by hand, we averaged the correlations themselves, but on the computer we used what we thought to be a superior Fisher z transformation. For several years we noticed no difference in the results for these two analyses, but in our validity generalization study for computer programmers (Schmidt, Gast-Rosenberg, & Hunter, 1980), the difference was notable. The average validity using the Fisher z transformation was larger (by about .03) than the average validity when correlations were averaged without this transformation. Careful checking of the mathematics then showed that it is the Fisher transformation that is biased. The Fisher z transformation gives larger weights to large correlations than to small ones, hence the positive bias. This problem is discussed in more detail in Chapter 5.

Although the Fisher z transformation produces an upward bias when it is used in averaging correlations, the transformation does serve its original purpose quite well. The original purpose was not to create a method for averaging correlations. Fisher's purpose was to create a transformation of the correlation for which the standard error (and, therefore, confidence intervals) would depend solely on sample size and would not depend on the size of the statistic. The standard error of the Fisher's z statistic is $1 / (N - 3)^{1/2}$, and so this goal was achieved. This means that, unlike the case for the correlation, it is unnecessary to have an estimate of the population value to compute the standard error and confidence intervals.

There has been considerable confusion in the literature produced by the fact that there is a slight bias in the correlation coeffcient (a bias that can be corrected, as noted in Chapter 2 and below). There is a wide-spread false belief that the Fisher z eliminates that bias. The fact is that the Fisher z replaces a small underestimation or negative bias by a typically small overestimation, or positive bias, a bias that is always greater in absolute value than the bias in the untransformed correlation. This bias is especially large if there is variation in the population correlations across studies (Hunter, Schmidt, & Coggin, 1988). Thus, meta-analysis is never made more accurate by using the Fisher z transformation (though in practice it usually doesn't make much difference in the final outcome of the meta-analysis).

Correcting the Variance for Sampling Error and an Example

Consider the variation in correlations across similar studies on a research question. The observed variance s_r^2 is a confounding of two things: variation in population correlations (if there is any) and variation in sample correlations produced by sampling error. Thus an estimate of the variance in population correlations can be obtained only by correcting the observed variance s_r^2 for sampling error. The following mathematics shows that sampling error across studies behaves like error of measurement across persons, and that the resulting formulas are comparable to standard formulas in classical measurement theory (reliability theory).

We begin with a treatment of sampling error in an isolated study. In an isolated study, the correlation is based on a sample: a specific sample of the population of people who might have been in that place at that time, a sample of the random processes in each person's head that generate error of measurment in test responses or supervisor ratings, and so on, and a sample of time variation in person and situational parameters. This is represented in statistics by noting that the observed correlation is a sample from a population distribution of correlation values that might have been observed if the study were replicated except for the random factors. These replications are hypothetical in the sense that a real study usually obtains only one such sample. However, the replications are not hypothetical in the sense that they represent variation that does not exist. There have been thousands of actual experiments testing the theory of statistical sampling error, and all have verified that theory. Sampling error in an isolated study is unseen but present nonetheless.

For any study then, there is a real population correlation ρ (which is usually unknown) that can be compared to the study correlation r. The difference between them is the sampling error, which we will denote by e. That is, we define sampling error e by the formula

$$e = r - \rho$$

or

$$r = \rho + e .$$

The distribution of observed correlations for the (usually hypothetical) replications of the study is always centered about the population correlation ρ, although the sampling error varies randomly. If we ignore the small bias in the correlation coefficient (or if we correct for it as discussed below), then the average sampling error will be zero and the standard deviation of the sampling error will depend on the sample size. The sampling error in a particular correlation can never be changed (and in particular is not changed when a statistical significance test is run). On the other hand, if replications of the study could be done, then sampling error could thus be reduced. Since the average error is zero, the replicated correlations could be averaged, and the average correlation would be closer to the population correlation than the individual correlations. The sampling error in the average correlation would be the average of the individual sampling errors and would thus be much closer to zero than the typical single sampling error. The average correlation has smaller sampling error in much the same way as a correlation based on a larger sample size. Indeed, the formula for sampling error in the average correlation is very similar to the formula for sampling error in an isolated correlation with the same total sample size. Thus, replicating studies could potentially solve the problem of sampling error.

Whereas replication is not possible in most individual studies, replication does take place across different studies. Consider the ideal special case: a meta-analysis for a research domain in which there is no variation in the population correlations across studies and in which all studies are done with the same sample size. This case is mathematically identical to the hypothetical replications that form the basis of the statistics of isolated correlations. In particular, the average correlation across studies would have greatly reduced sampling error. In the case where the population correlation varies from one study to another, the replication is more complicated, but the principle is the same. Replication of sampling error across studies enables us to use averaging to reduce the impact of sampling error. If the number of studies is large, the impact of sampling error can be virtually eliminated.

How big is the typical sampling error? Since sampling error has a mean of zero, the mean sampling error does not measure the size of sampling error. That is, since a negative error of $-.10$ is just as bad as a positive error of $+.10$, it is the absolute value of the error that counts. To assess the size of errors without the algebraic sign, the common statistical practice is to square the errors. The average squared error is the variance, and the square root of that is the standard deviation of the errors. It is the standard deviation of sampling error that is the best representation of the size of errors. Consider then the isolated study. In the common case where the underlying distribution is the bivariate normal distribution, the standard deviation of the sampling error is given by

$$\sigma_e = (1 - \rho^2) / \sqrt{(N - 1)}$$

where N is the sample size. Technically, our use of this formula throughout is tantamount to the assumption that all studies are done in contexts where the independent and dependent variables have a bivariate normal distribution, but the statistics literature has found this formula to be fairly robust in the face of departures from normality. However, under conditions of range restriction, the above formula underestimates sampling error variance to some extent. That is, actual sampling variance is greater than the value predicted by the formula, leading to undercorrections for sampling error variance (Milsap, 1989). This could create the appearance of a moderator where none exists.

The effect of averaging across replications is dramatic in terms of sampling error variance. If the sample size in each replication is N and the number of studies is K, then the sampling error variance in the average of K correlations is the variance of the average error e, i.e.,

$$\text{Var}(\bar{e}) = \text{Var}(e) / K$$

That is, the effect of averaging across K studies is to divide the sampling error variance by K. Since the total sample size in K studies is K times the sample size in a single study, this means that to increase the sample size by a factor of K is to reduce the sampling error variance by a factor of K. This is exactly the same rule as that for increasing the sample size of a single study. Thus, replication can reduce sampling error in the same way as using larger samples.

In practice, the effect of increasing sample size is not quite as impressive as the previous formula would suggest. Unfortunately, it is not the variance but the standard deviation that counts. The standard deviation of the average error is divided only by the square root of the number of studies. Thus, to cut error in half, we must average 4 studies rather than 2. This is important in judging the number of missing studies in a meta-analysis when that number is small. For example, if an investigator randomly misses 10 out of 100 potential studies, the sampling error variance is increased by 10%, but the sampling error standard deviation is increased by only 5%. Thus, missing a few studies randomly usually does not reduce the accuracy of a meta-analysis by nearly as much as might be supposed.

We come now to the meta-analysis of correlations; the study of correlations computed across different studies. The power of meta-analysis to reduce the problem of sampling error lies in the fact that sampling errors are replicated across studies. The ultimate statistical error in meta-analysis will depend on two factors: the size of the average sample size for the individual studies and the number of studies in the meta-analysis. For the mean correlation, it is the total sample size that determines the error in the meta-analysis. For the estimate of the variance of correlations, the computations are more complicated but the principle is similar.

Let us use the subscript i to denote study number. Then the error variable e_i represents the sampling error in the sample correlation in study i, i.e., we define e_i by

$$r_i = \rho_i + e_i .$$

Then the mean of the error within hypothetical replications is 0. The average error across studies is the same

$$E(e_i) = 0 .$$

The variance across hypothetical replications is denoted

$$\sigma_{e_i}^2 = \frac{(1 - \rho_i^2)^2}{N_i - 1} .$$

In going across studies, this hypothetical and unobserved variation becomes real and potentially observable variation. This is similar to the case of observing a sample of people or scores from a distribution of people or scores. It differs from the usual case in statistics, because the error variance differs from one study to the next. Nonetheless, the critical fact is that the variance of sampling error becomes visible across studies. The formula

$$r_i = \rho_i + e_i$$

is analogous to the true score, error score formula

$$X_p = T_p + e_p$$

where X_p and T_p are the observed and true scores for person p. In particular, sampling error (signed sampling error, not sampling error variance) is unrelated to population values across studies. Thus, if we calculate a variance across studies, then the variance of sample correlations is the sum of the variance in population correlations and the variance due to sampling error, i.e.,

$$\sigma_r^2 = \sigma_\rho^2 + \sigma_e^2 .$$

The implication of this formula is that the variance of observed correlations is larger than the variance of population correlations, often much larger. The reason it is larger is because squared errors are always positive and do not cancel out when averaged. Thus, the average squared deviation of observed correlations is systematically larger than the average squared deviation of population correlations, because sampling error makes a systematically positive contribution to the squared deviation.

The formula $\sigma_r^2 = \sigma_\rho^2 + \sigma_e^2$ has three variances. If any two of the variances were known, the third could be computed by subtraction. In particular, if the sampling error variance σ_e^2 were known, then the desired variance of population correlations would be

$$\sigma_\rho^2 = \sigma_r^2 - \sigma_e^2 .$$

Of these three variances, only the variance of observed correlations is estimated using a conventional variance, i.e., average squared deviation of given numbers. If we knew the value of the sampling error variance, then it would not matter that we could not compute it as a conventional variance. The fact is that the sampling error variance need not be given as an empirical number; it is given by statistical formula. The error variance across studies is just the average of the error variance within studies. If study correlations are weighted by sample size N_i, then the error variance across studies is

$$\sigma_e^2 = \text{Ave } \sigma_{e_i}^2 = \frac{\Sigma \left[N_i \sigma_{e_i}^2 \right]}{\Sigma N_i} = \frac{\Sigma \left[N_i \left[\frac{(1 - \rho_i^2)^2}{N_i - 1} \right] \right]}{\Sigma N_i}.$$

The fraction $N_i / (N_i - 1)$ is close to unity. If we take this fraction as unity, and we use the approximation that average $(\rho^2) \cong (\text{average } \rho)^2$, then we have the almost perfect approximation

$$\sigma_e^2 = \frac{(1 - \bar{r}^2)^2 K}{T}$$

where K is the number of studies and $T = \Sigma N_i$ is the total sample size. The corresponding estimate of the variance of population correlations is thus

$$\text{est } \sigma_\rho^2 = \sigma_r^2 - \sigma_e^2 = \sigma_r^2 - \frac{(1 - \bar{r}^2)^2 K}{T}.$$

There is an even better estimate of the sampling error variance. Consider the special case in which all studies are run with the same sample size N. The ratio $N_i / (N_i - 1)$ is then simply the constant $N/(N-1)$, which factors out of the summation. We then have

$$\sigma_e^2 = \text{Ave} (1 - \rho_i^2)^2 / (N - 1).$$

If we estimate ρ_i by the average correlation across studies, we have the approximation

$$\sigma_e^2 = (1 - \bar{r}^2)^2 / (N - 1).$$

This formula is exactly analagous to the formula for sampling error in the single study

$$\sigma_e^2 = (1 - \rho^2)^2 / (N - 1).$$

The relationship between the first approximation and the second approximation stems from the fact that

$$K / T = 1 \ / \ (T / K) = 1 / N .$$

That is, the approximation above with K in the numerator and T in the denominator is equivalent to having average sample size in the denominator. Thus, the improvement is to use $N-1$ instead of N — a small change for typical sample sizes of 100, but a noticeable improvement in those unusual meta-analyses done in research areas with very small sample sizes. For example, psychotherapy studies have a typical sample size of about 20.

Consider again the typical case where sample size varies from one study to the next. Let the average sample size be denoted $\overline{N}$, i.e.,

$$\overline{N} = T / K .$$

Our first approximation could be written

$$\sigma_e^2 = (1 - \overline{r}^2)^2 / \overline{N}$$

while the second improved approximation is

$$\sigma_e^2 = (1 - \overline{r}^2)^2 \ / \ (\overline{N} - 1) .$$

Mathematical work not presented here (Hunter & Schmidt, 1987a) shows that the second approximation is accurate not only when the population correlations are all the same — when it is optimal — but also when there is variation in population correlations (when complicated weighting schemes based on knowledge of the distribution of sample size — not usually known in a meta-analysis — would improve the estimate slightly). The corresponding estimate of the variance of population correlations is

$$\sigma_\rho^2 = \sigma_r^2 - \sigma_e^2 = \sigma_r^2 - (1 - \overline{r}^2)^2 \ / \ (\overline{N} - 1) .$$

An Example: Socioeconomic Status and Police Performance

Bouchard (1776, 1860, 1914, 1941) postulated that differences in upbringing would produce differences in response to power over other people. His theory was that since lower-class parents obtain obedience by beating their children to a pulp while middle-class parents threaten them with loss of love, lower-class children would grow into adults who are more likely themselves to use physical force to gain compliance. He tested his theory by looking at the relationship between socioeconomic status and brutality in police departments. His independent measure was socioeconomic status measured in terms of six classes, ranging from 1 = upper, upper class to 6 = lower, lower class. His brutality measure was the number of complaints divided by the number of years employed. Only patrol officers were considered in the correlations, which are shown in Table 3.2. The meta-analysis of these data is as follows.

$$\bar{r} = \frac{100\,(.34) + 100\,(.16) + 50\,(.12) + 50\,(.38)}{100 + 100 + 50 + 50} = \frac{75.00}{300} = .25$$

$$\sigma_r^2 = \frac{100\,(.34-.25)^2 + 100\,(.16-.25)^2 + 50\,(.12-.25)^2 + 50\,(.38-.25)^2}{100 + 100 + 50 + 50}$$

$$= \frac{3.31}{300} = .011033$$

The average sample size is

$$\bar{N} = T/K = 300/4 = 75.$$

Thus, the sampling error variance is estimated to be

$$\sigma_e^2 = (1 - \bar{r}^2)^2 / (\bar{N} - 1) = (1 - .25^2)^2 / 74 = .011877.$$

The estimate of the variance of population correlations is thus

$$\sigma_\rho^2 = \sigma_r^2 - \sigma_e^2 = \sigma_r^2 - (1 - \bar{r}^2)^2 / (\bar{N} - 1)$$

$$= .011033 - .011877 = -.000844.$$

Since the estimated variance is negative, the estimated standard deviation is 0, i.e.,

$$\sigma_\rho = 0.$$

Some readers have been bothered by this example. They ask, "How can a variance be negative, even if only −.0008?" The answer is that the estimated variance of population correlations is not computed as a conventional variance, i.e., the average squared deviation of given numbers. Rather it is computed as the difference between the given variance of observed correlations and the statistically given sampling error variance. While there is little error in the statistically given sampling error variance,

Table 3.2 Correlations Between Socioeconomic Status and Police Brutality (U.S.)

Location	Date	Sample Size	Correlation
Philadelphia	1776	100	.34*
Richmond, VA	1861	100	.16
Washington, DC	1914	50	.12
Pearl Harbor	1941	50	.38*

*Significant at the .05 level.

the variance of observed correlations is a sample estimate. Unless the number of studies is infinite, there will be some error in that empirical estimate. If the population difference is 0, then error will cause the estimated difference to be positive or negative with probability one-half. Thus, in our case, sampling error caused the variance of observed correlations to differ slightly from the expected value, and that error caused the estimating difference to be negative. There is no logical contradiction here. For those who know analysis of variance, estimation of components of variance using expected mean square formulas also produces negative observed estimates for similar reasons. This question is discussed further in Chapter 9.

Consider the empirical meaning of our results. Bouchard claimed that his results varied dramatically from city to city. His explanation was that Washington and Richmond are southern cities, and southern hospitality is so strong that it reduces the incidence of brutality in the lower classes and, hence, reduces the correlation in those cities. However, our analysis shows that the variation in his results is just sampling error.

A Significance Test for Variation Across Studies

If the corrected variance across studies is positive, it may still be trivial in size. Indeed, it may even be due to sampling error. This section presents a statistical significance test for whether the observed variation is greater than that expected by chance. However, we do not endorse this significance test because it asks the wrong question. Significant variation may be trivial in magnitude, and even nontrivial variation may still be due to research artifacts.

If a sample correlation is drawn from a population in which the variables are approximately bivariate normal (or are dichotomous), then the sample correlation has mean

$$E(r) = \rho$$

where ρ is the population correlation, and a variance of

$$\sigma_r^2 = \frac{(1 - \rho^2)^2}{N - 1}$$

where N is the sample size for that study. For a single study, the following modified squared deviation has a chi-square distribution with 1 degree of freedom

$$\chi_1^2 = \frac{(N - 1)}{(1 - \rho^2)^2} (r - \rho)^2$$

If these squared deviations are summed across studies, then the sum has a chi-square distribution with K degrees of freedom, where K is the number of studies

$$\chi_K^2 = \sum_i \frac{N_i - 1}{(1 - \rho_i^2)^2} (r_i - \rho)^2 .$$

Under the null hypothesis that all population correlations are equal, i.e., under the assumption that $\rho_i = \rho$ for all i, the best estimate of ρ for them is $\bar{r}$, the weighted average sample correlation, i.e.,

$$E(\bar{r}) = \rho$$

and the modified deviation statistic using $\bar{r}$ for ρ has a chi-square distribution with $K - 1$ degrees of freedom.

$$\chi_{K-1}^2 = \sum_i \frac{(N_i - 1)(r_i - \bar{r})^2}{(1 - \bar{r}^2)^2}$$

To a close approximation, this is equal to:

$$\chi_{K-1}^2 = \frac{1}{(1 - \bar{r}^2)^2} \sum_i N_i (r_i - \bar{r})^2 .$$

If we now multiply through by unity in the form of T/T, where $T = \Sigma N_i$ is the total number of persons across studies, we get

$$\chi^2_{K-1} = \frac{T}{(1 - \bar{r}^2)^2}\, s_r^2 .$$

This statistic can be used for a formal test of no variation, although if the meta-analysis has very many studies, it has very high statistical power and will therefore reject the null hypothesis, given even a trivial amount of variation across studies. Thus, if the chi square is not significant, this is strong evidence that there is no true variation across studies, but if it is significant, the variation may still be negligible in magnitude. If variation due to artifacts in addition to sampling error is present (almost always the case), this test will have a Type I bias: It will be significant more than 5% of the time when all observed variance is artifactual. Also, the s_r^2 used in this test must be the *observed* variance, not the variance remaining after correction for sampling error. Finally, see the discussion of statistical significance tests in Chapters 2 and 10; there are good reasons for avoiding the use of significance tests.

Moderator Variables Analyzed by Grouping the Data and an Example

A moderator variable is a variable that causes differences in the correlation between two other variables. For example, in the police study above, Bouchard postulated that geographic region (North versus South) would be a moderator variable for the relationship between socioeconomic status and brutality. If there is true variation in results across studies, then there must be such a moderator variable (or possibly more than one) to account for such variance. On the other hand, if the analysis shows that the variation in results is due to sampling error, then any apparent moderating effect is due to capitalization on chance. This was the case in Bouchard's work.

If the corrected standard deviation suggests substantial variation in population correlations across studies, then a moderator variable derived from a theory or hypothesis can be used to group the observed correlations into subsets. Within each subset, we can calculate a mean, a variance, and a variance corrected for sampling error. A moderator variable will show itself in two ways: (1) the average correlation will vary from subset to subset, and (2) the corrected variance will *average* lower in the subsets than for the data as a whole. These two facts are not mathematically independent. By a theorem in analysis of variance, we know that the total variance is the mean of the subset variances plus the variance of the subset means. Thus, the mean uncorrected within subset variance must decrease to exactly the extent that the subset means differ from one another.

An Example: Police Brutality in Transylvania

In order to justify a European sabbatical, Hackman (1978) argued that Bouchard's work on police brutality needed a cross-cultural replication. So he gathered data in four cities in Transylvania, carefully replicating Bouchard's measurement on socioeconomic status and brutality. His data are given along with Bouchard's in Table 3.3.

Analysis of the Whole Set:

$$\bar{r} = \frac{100(.34) + \dots + 100(.19) + \dots + 50(.23)}{100 + \dots + 100 + \dots + 50} = \frac{105.00}{600} = .175$$

$$\sigma_r^2 = \frac{100(.34 - .175)^2 + \dots + 50(.23 - .175)^2}{100 + \dots + 50} = \frac{9.995}{600} = .016658$$

$$N = T / K = 600 / 8 = 75$$

$$\sigma_e^2 = \frac{(1 - .175^2)^2}{74} = .012698$$

$$\sigma_\rho^2 = .016658 - .012698 = .00396$$

$$\sigma_\rho = .063$$

The corrected standard deviation of .063 can be compared to the mean of .175: $.175/.063 = 2.78$. That is, the mean correlation is nearly 2.8 standard deviations above 0. Thus, if the study population correlations were normally distributed, the probability of a 0 or below 0 correlation is virtually nil. So the qualitative nature of the relationship is clear: the population correlation is positive in all studies.

However, the variation is not trivial in amount relative to the mean. This suggests a search for moderator variables. The moderator analysis is as follows:

America	*Transylvania*
$\bar{r} = .25$	$\bar{r} = .10$
$\sigma_r^2 = .011033$	$\sigma_r^2 = .011033$
$\sigma_e^2 = .011877$	$\sigma_e^2 = .013245$
$\sigma_\rho^2 = -.000244$	$\sigma_\rho^2 = -.002212$
$\sigma_\rho = 0$	$\sigma_\rho = 0$

Table 3.3 Correlations Between Socioeconomic Status and Police
Brutality (U.S. and Transylvania)

Investigator	Location	Sample Size	Correlation
Bouchard	Philadelphia	100	.34*
Bouchard	Richmond, VA	100	.16
Bouchard	Washington, DC	50	.12
Bouchard	Pearl Harbor	50	.38*
Hackman	Brasov	100	.19
Hackman	Targul-ocna	100	.01
Hackman	Hunedoara	50	−.03
Hackman	Lupeni	50	.23

*Significant at the .05 level.

Analysis of the subsets shows a substantial difference in mean correlations, $\bar{r} = .25$ in America and $\bar{r} = .10$ in Transylvania. The corrected standard deviations reveal that there is no variation in results within countries.

Hackman explained the difference between the two countries by noting that vampires in America live quiet, contented lives working for the Red Cross, while vampires in Transylvania must still get their blood by tracking down and killing live victims. Vampires in Transylvania resent their low station in life and focus their efforts on people of high status, whom they envy. Middle-class policemen who work at night are particularly vulnerable. Thus, there is less variance in social class among the policemen in Transylvania, and this restriction in range reduces the correlation. Later in this chapter, we will examine range corrections that can be used to test this hypothesis.

After a heated exchange at the Academy of Management convention, Bouchard bared his fangs and showed Hackman that American vampires can still be a pain in the neck. Bouchard then noted that the difference in the results reflected the fact that his studies were done at times when the country was going to war. This increase in aggressive excitement increased the general level and the variance of brutality and, thus, increased its reliability of measurement and, hence, the level of coordination. This hypothesis can be tested using the corrections for measurement error discussed later in this chapter.

Correcting Feature Correlations for Sampling Error and an Example

Suppose that some study feature is coded as a quantitative variable y. Then that feature can be correlated with the outcome statistic across studies. For example, if correlations between dependency and school achievement varied as a function of the age of the child, then we might code average age in study i as y_i. We could then correlate age of children with size of correlation across studies. An example of this method is given by Schwab, Olian-Gottlieb, and Heneman (1979). However, such a correlation across studies is a confounding of the correlation for population values with y and the noncorrelation of the sampling error with y. This is directly analogous to the role of error of measurement in attenuating correlations based on imperfectly measured variables. Thus, the observed correlation across studies will be smaller than would be the case had there been no sampling error in the correlations.

To avoid confusion between the basic statistic r, which is the correlation over persons within a study, and correlations between r and study features over studies, the correlations over studies will be denoted by the symbol "Cor." For example, the correlation between the correlation r and the study feature y across studies will be denoted Cor (r, y). This is the observed correlation across studies, but the desired correlation across studies is that for population correlations, ρ_i, the desired correlation across studies is Cor(ρ, y). Starting from the formula $r_i = \rho_i + e_i$, we calculate a covariance over studies and use additivity of covariances to produce

$$\sigma_{ry} = \sigma_{\rho y} + \sigma_{ey} = \sigma_{\rho y} + 0 = \sigma_{\rho y}.$$

If this covariance across studies is divided by standard deviations across studies, then we have

$$\text{Cor}(r, y) = \frac{\sigma_{ry}}{\sigma_r \sigma_y} = \frac{\sigma_{\rho y}}{\sigma_r \sigma_y}$$

$$= \frac{\sigma_{\rho y}}{\sigma_\rho \sigma_y} \frac{\sigma_\rho}{\sigma_r}$$

$$= \text{Cor}(\rho, y) \frac{\sigma_\rho}{\sigma_r}.$$

But the covariance of r_i with ρ_i is

$$\sigma_{r\rho} = \sigma_{\rho\,\rho} = \sigma_{e\,\rho} = \sigma_{\rho\,\rho} + 0 = \sigma_{\rho}^2$$

and hence the correlation across studies is

$$\mathrm{Cor}\,(r, \rho) \;=\; \frac{\sigma_{r\,\rho}}{\sigma_r\,\sigma_\rho} \;=\; \frac{\sigma_\rho^2}{\sigma_r\,\sigma_\rho} \;=\; \frac{\sigma_\rho}{\sigma_r} .$$

Thus, the observed correlation across studies is the product of two other correlations, the desired correlation and reliability-like correlation.

$$\mathrm{Cor}\,(r, y) = \mathrm{Cor}\,(\rho, y)\,\mathrm{Cor}\,(r, \rho)$$

The desired correlation is then the ratio

$$\mathrm{Cor}\,(\rho, y) = \frac{\mathrm{Cor}\,(r, y)}{\mathrm{Cor}\,(r, \rho)} ,$$

which is precisely the formula for correction for attenuation due to error of measurement if there is error in one variable only. What is the correlation between r and ρ over studies? We have the variance of r as estimated by s_r^2. We need only the variance of ρ, which was estimated in the previous section of this chapter. Thus the "reliability" needed for use in the attenuation formula is given by

$$\text{Reliability of } r = \left\{\, \mathrm{Cor}\,(r, \rho) \,\right\}^2$$

$$= \frac{\sigma_\rho^2}{\sigma_r^2} = \frac{\sigma_r^2 - (1 - \overline{r}^2)^2 \,/\, (\overline{N} - 1)}{\sigma_r^2} .$$

An Example: The Tibetan Employment Service

Officials in the Tibetan Employment Service have been using a cognitive ability test for some years to steer people into various jobs. Although they have relied on content validity for such assignments, they have also been gathering criterion-related validity data to test their content validity system. In their content validity system, test development analysts rate each occupation for the extent to which it requires high cognitive ability, with rating from 1 = low to 3 = high. They have concurrent validity studies on six occupations chosen to stratify the full range of the content validity continuum. These data are shown in Table 3.4. The analysis is as follows:

$$\bar{r} = .30$$

$$\sigma_r^2 = .048333$$

$$\bar{N} = T / K = 600 / 6 = 100$$

$$\sigma_e^2 = .008365$$

$$\sigma_\rho^2 = .048333 - .008365 = .039968$$

$$\sigma_\rho = .20$$

$$Rel(r) = \frac{\sigma_\rho^2}{\sigma_r^2} = \frac{.0400}{.0483} = .83 .$$

Let y_i be the cognitive rating of the ith occupation. Then

$$Cor(r, y) = .72$$

$$Cor(\rho, y) = \frac{.72}{\sqrt{.83}} = .79 .$$

The study found very large variation in validity even after correction for sampling error. The correlation was .72 between rating and observed correlation, and rose to .79 after correction for sampling error. In this case only 17 percent of the variance of the correlations was due to artifacts, so the reliability was .83 (i.e., $1 - .17$). Ordinarily, reliability would be much lower and, hence, the correction would be much larger. For example, if 70 percent of the variance were due to artifacts, then the reliability would be only $1 - .70 = .30$. The correction factor would be $1 / (.30)^{1/2} = 1.83$.

Artifacts Other than Sampling Error

Error of Measurement and Correction for Attenuation

Variables in science are never perfectly measured. Indeed, sometimes the measurement is very crude. Since the late 1890s, we have known that the error of measurement attenuates the correlation coefficient. That is, error of measurement systematically lowers the correlation between *measures* in comparison to the correlation between the variables themselves. This systematic error is then exaggerated by the unsystematic distortions of sampling error. In this section we will review the theory of error of measurement and derive the classic formula for correction for attenuation.

Table 3.4 Tibetan Employment Service Test Validities

Occupation	Rating	Validity (Correlation)	Sample Size
Monastery Abbot	3	.45*	100
Magistrate	3	.55*	100
Holy Man	2	.05	100
Farmer	2	.55*	100
Bandit	1	.10	100
Yak Chip Collector	1	.10	100

*Significant at the .05 level.

We will then look at the impact of error of measurement on sampling error and confidence intervals. In particular, we will derive the confidence interval for corrected correlations. From this base we will later consider the impact of error of measurement as it varies in amount from one study to another.

Let us denote by T the true score that would have been observed on the independent variable had we been able to measure it perfectly. We then have

$$x = T + E_1$$

where E_1 is the error of measurement in the independent variable. Let us denote by U the true score that would have been observed on the dependent variable had we been able to measure it perfectly. We then have

$$y = U + E_2$$

where E_2 is the error of measurement in the dependent variable. Let us use the traditional notation by denoting the reliabilities by r_{xx} and r_{yy}, respectively. We then have

$$r_{xx} = \rho_{xT}^2$$

$$r_{yy} = \rho_{yU}^2 .$$

The desired correlation is the population correlation between perfectly measured variables, i.e., ρ_{TU}, but the observed correlation is the sample correlation between observed scores r_{xy}. There are two steps in relating the one to the other: the systematic attenuation of the population correlation by error of measurement and the unsystematic variation produced by sampling error.

The systematic attenuation can be computed by considering the causal pathways from x to T to U to y.

$$\rho_{xy} = \rho_{xT} \; \rho_{TU} \; \rho_{Uy} = \rho_{xT} \; \rho_{yU} \; \rho_{TU}$$

$$= \sqrt{r_{xx}} \; \sqrt{r_{yy}} \; \rho_{TU}$$

At the level of population correlations, this leads to the classic formula for correction for attenuation.

$$\rho_{TU} = \frac{\rho_{xy}}{\sqrt{r_{xx}} \; \sqrt{r_{yy}}}$$

At the level of observed correlations, we have

$$r_{xy} = \rho_{xy} + e$$

where e is the sampling error in r_{xy} as before. Thus,

$$\sigma_r^2 = \sigma_\rho^2 + \sigma_e^2$$

where the error variance is given by the formulas of earlier sections.

If we correct the observed correlation using the population correlation formula, then we have the following equation.

$$r_c = \frac{r_{xy}}{\sqrt{r_{xx}} \; \sqrt{r_{yy}}} = \frac{\sqrt{r_{xx}} \; \sqrt{r_{yy}} \; \rho_{TU} + e}{\sqrt{r_{xx}} \; \sqrt{r_{yy}}}$$

$$= \rho_{TU} + \frac{e}{\sqrt{r_{xx}} \; \sqrt{r_{yy}}}$$

We can write a new equation for the corrected correlation

$$r_c = \rho_c + e_c$$

where e_c is the sampling error in the corrected correlation r_c, and where the population value $\rho_c = \rho_{TU}$. The error variance for the corrected correlation can then be computed from the error variance for uncorrected correlations and the reliabilities of the two variables.

$$e_c = \frac{e}{\sqrt{r_{xx}} \ \sqrt{r_{yy}}}$$

$$\sigma_{e_c}^2 = \frac{\sigma_e^2}{r_{xx} \ r_{yy}}$$

Thus, if we correct the observed correlation for attenuation, we increase the sampling error correspondingly. In particular, to form the confidence interval for a corrected correlation, we apply the correction formula to the two endpoints of the confidence interval for the uncorrected correlation. That is, in the case of correction for attenuation, just as we divide the point estimate of the correlation by the product of the square roots of the reliabilities, so, too, we divide each endpoint of the confidence interval by the same product.

An Example of Correction for Attenuation

Suppose that if organizational commitment and job satisfaction were perfectly measured, then the correlation between true scores would be $\rho_{TU} = .60$. Suppose instead that we measure organizational commitment with reliability $r_{xx} = .45$ and that we measure job satisfaction with reliability $r_{yy} = .55$. Then the population correlation between observed scores would be

$$\rho_{xy} = \sqrt{r_{xx}} \ \sqrt{r_{yy}} \ \rho_{TU} = \sqrt{.45} \ \sqrt{.55} \ \rho_{TU}$$

$$= .50 \, (.60) = .30 \, .$$

That is, the effect of error of measurement in this example is to reduce the correlation between true scores by 50%; from a true score population correlation of .60 to a study population correlation of .30 between observed scores. If we apply the correction formula we have

$$\rho_{TU} = \frac{\rho_{xy}}{\sqrt{r_{xx}} \ \sqrt{r_{yy}}} = \frac{.30}{\sqrt{.45} \ \sqrt{.55}} = \frac{.30}{.50} = .60 \, .$$

That is, correction for attenuation works perfectly for population correlations, i.e., it is perfectly accurate when sample size is infinite.

Consider the impact of sampling error. If the sample size for the study is $N = 100$, then the standard deviation of the observed correlation (from $\rho_{xy} = .30$) is $(1 - .30^2) / \sqrt{99} = .091$. Thus, it would not be uncommon to observe a correlation of .20 in the actual study. If we compare the observed correlation of .20 to the desired correlation of .60, then we see that there is a massive error. However, this error can be broken into two components; the systematic error of attenuation and the unsystematic error due to sampling error. The systematic error reduced the correlation from .60 to .30. The unsystematic error is shown in the comparison of .20 to the population attenuated correlation .30.

Let us correct for attenuation and look at the error in the corrected correlation.

$$r_c = \frac{r_{xy}}{\sqrt{r_{xx}}\ \sqrt{r_{yy}}} = \frac{.20}{\sqrt{45}\ \sqrt{.55}} = \frac{.20}{.50} = .40$$

The sampling error in the corrected correlation is the difference between the estimated .40 and the actual .60. Thus, we have

$$r = \rho_{xy} + e = \rho_{xy} - .1$$

$$r_c = \rho_c + e_c = \rho_c - .2\ .$$

So, as we doubled the observed attenuated correlation to estimate the unattenuated correlation, we doubled the sampling error as well. On the other hand, we reduced the systematic error from .30 to 0. The standard error for the observed correlation would be calculated as

$$\frac{1 - .20^2}{\sqrt{99}} = .096\ .$$

The 95% confidence interval for the observed correlation is given by $r \pm 1.96\,\sigma_e = .20 \pm 1.96\ (.096)$ or $.01 \le \rho \le .39$, which does include the actual value of $\rho_{xy} = .30$. We then correct each endpoint of the confidence interval to obtain

Lower Endpoint	Upper Endpoint
$r_1 = .01$	$r_2 = .39$
$r_{1c} = \dfrac{.01}{\sqrt{.45}\ \sqrt{.55}}$	$r_{2c} = \dfrac{.39}{\sqrt{.45}\ \sqrt{.55}}$
$= \dfrac{.01}{.50} = .02$	$= \dfrac{.39}{.50} = .78$

Let us compare the confidence intervals of corrected and uncorrected correlations.

$$.01 \le \rho_{xy} \le .39$$

$$.02 \le \rho_{TU} \le .78$$

We see that the center of the confidence interval changes from the uncorrected correlation .20 to the corrected correlation .40. At the same time, the width of the confidence interval doubles, reflecting the increased sampling error in the corrected correlation.

This point can be made dramatically with confidence intervals. If measurement of both variables were perfectly reliable, then the population correlation would be .60, and the sampling error would be $(1 - .60^2)$ / $\sqrt{99} = .064$. This is much smaller than the sampling error for a correlation of .30, which is .091. Thus, if we can eliminate error of measurement substantively, then we can obtain larger observed correlations *and smaller confidence intervals*. Substantive elimination of error of measurement is vastly superior to elimination by statistical formula after the fact.

We could have obtained the same confidence interval in a different way. Suppose that we erected the confidence interval around the corrected correlation using the sampling error formula for e_c. The center of the confidence interval is then $r_c = .40$. The sampling error variance is then given by

$$\sigma_{e_c}^2 = \frac{\sigma_e^2}{r_{xx} r_{yy}} = \frac{\sigma_e^2}{(.45)\,(.55)} = \frac{(1 - .2^2)^2 / 99}{.2475} = .0376$$

That is, the sampling error standard deviation for the corrected correlation is $\sigma_{e_c} = (.0376)^{1/2} = .19$. The confidence interval is then given by $.40 \pm 1.96 \, \sigma_{e_c}$ or $.02 \le \rho_{TU} \le .78$. This is the same confidence interval obtained earlier.

Statistical Versus Substantive Correction

If we use statistical formulas to correct for attenuation, we obtain larger corrected correlations with a wider confidence interval. There are two conclusions that might be drawn from this fact. (1) *False conclusion:* Since correcting for attenuation increases the amount of sampling error, maybe we should not correct for attenuation. *Key fact:* If we do not correct for attenuation, then we do not eliminate the *systematic* error. In our example, the error in the uncorrected correlation was .60 − .20 = .40. Thus the error in the corrected correlation was only half as large as the error in the uncorrected correlation. (2) *True conclusion:* We could greatly im-

prove our statistical accuracy if we could eliminate the error of measurement substantively, i.e., by using better measurement procedures in the
first place.

Using the Appropriate Reliability Coefficient

Computation of a reliability coefficient requires the specification of the
nature of the error of measurement in the research domain and requires the
gathering of some sort of data that make the error visible. In most current
meta-analyses, the unit of analysis is the person (or rat or pigeon or . . .)
and the variable measured is some behavior of the person. For this case,
there is an extensive theory of reliability developed primarily by psychometricians and there has been extensive testing of that theory. This is
the case that will be discussed in this book. However, meta-analyses are
being conducted in other areas. For example, Rodgers and Hunter (1986)
did a meta-analysis is which the unit of analysis was the organization and
the data was whole unit productivity measures. They were convinced that
there is error of measurement in the productivity measures, but there is as
yet no theory and no data to estimate the reliability. Suppose that the unit
of analysis in the study is persons. The measure is usually obtained in one
of three ways: direct recording of behavior (as in test scores or closed
ended questionnaire answers (here called "response data"), assessment by
an observer (here called a "judgment or rating"), or the behavior is
observed and recorded by an observer (here called "coded response data").
The reliability considerations differ by case.

Response Data. Response data behavior is used for measurement of a
given variable under the assumption that the variable to be measured is
the primary causal agent that determines that behavior. Error of measurement is present to the extent that the behavior is determined by other causal
agents. At least three kinds of error have been identified by psychometric
theory: random response error, specific error, and transient error. The
ubiquitous error agent is randomness in behavior. Except for highly prac-
ticed responses, such as giving one's name, most human acts have a
sizeable random element. This is called "random response error." Sometimes the behavior is influenced by something peculiar about the measurement situation, for example, an idiosyncratic response to one of the
specific words used in an opinion item. The influence of such situation or
stimulus specific agents is called "specific error." Sometimes the behavior
is influenced by an agent which varies randomly over time, such as mood
or illness. The influence of a time varying factor is called "transient error."
Each of these three forms of error of measurement enter differently into
the designs traditionally used to measure reliability. One design makes

error visible by obtaining multiple responses in a given measurement session — eliciting behaviors to various situations or stimuli that are equivalent in the extent of causal influence from the variable to be measured. The independent responses allow for new sampling of the random response error and allow for new sampling of the specific error. Thus, reliability computed from this design detects and measures the extent of random response error and specific error. However, if there is transient error, this design will not detect it and, thus, the reliability coefficient will be too large by the relative amount of transient error. This form of reliability is properly called "parallel forms reliability" and is improperly called "internal consistency reliability," although better language would substitute the phrase "reliability estimate" for the word "reliability." Another common design is the test-retest design. A behavior is measured at two points in time that are far enough apart so that the transient error factor is not repeated, but close enough in time so that there is not significant change in the variable to be measured. The two behaviors will allow for new sampling in the random response error and new sampling in the transient error. However, if there is specific error, then this design will not detect it and thus the reliability coefficient will be too large by the relative amount of specific error. This form of reliability is called "test-retest reliability," although better language would substitute the phrase "reliability estimate" for the word "reliability." If all three kinds of error are present, then the correct reliability will be obtained only by a design in which both the situational determinants of specific error and the temporal determinants of transient error are resampled. This design is called the "delayed parallel forms" design. Given two situational forms and two times, it is possible to separately estimate the extent of each of the three kinds of error. If all three kinds of error are present, then the delayed parallel forms reliability will be smaller than either the parallel forms reliability estimate or the test-retest reliability estimate. The effect of using the wrong reliability estimate is to underestimate the impact of error of measurement. Thus, correction using the wrong reliability means that some source of error is not corrected and the correlation is thus not corrected for attenuation due to that error source. That is, correction using the wrong reliability means that the corrected correlation will correspondingly underestimate the actual correlation between constructs.

Judgments by Raters. If a construct such as job performance is assessed by an observer such as the person's immediate supervisor, then there are two sources of error in the measurement: error in the judgment and idiosyncracy in rater perception. First, the judgment is itself a response by the rater and is thus subject to random response error and potentially subject to specific error and/or transient error. These are the sources of error studied by data methods that consider only data from one rater. Second, in no area has human perception of other people proved to be without idiosyncracy. In fact, in most areas, there are large differences in the perceptions of different raters. Thus, the proper reliability estimate must take differences in perception into account as well as randomness in the judgment made by each judge. The easy estimate of reliability for judgment is to have judgments made independently by different raters. The correlation between judges will be low to the extent that there is either randomness in the judgment or differences in perception. If two judgments (say, "quality of work" and "quantity of work") are each made by two raters, then it is possible to separately estimate the effect of random response error, specific error, and idiosyncracy error (also called "halo"). If there is transient error, and if the cause of transient error is independent in the two judges, then this correlation will be appropriately lowered by transient error also, although it will not be distinguished from idiosyncracy error. In this case, the reliability is called "interrater reliability," although it too would be better called a reliability estimate.

Coded Response Data. Some behaviors are too complicated to be directly recorded. Thus, the data used is a coding of the behavior by an observer. For example, we might code the extent of need for achievement expressed in a story inspired by a picture shown to the subject. Differences between the codings by different observers are called "coding error." The key error often made in this context is to consider as error only the discrepancy between coders. While coding error is one important source of error in the measurement, there are also random response error, specific error, and transient error in the behavior coded. For example, suppose that coders were so well trained that they agreed to a correlation of .95 in their assessments of stories. However, suppose that from one week to the next, there is only a correlation of .10 between the achievement imagery in successive stories told by the same person. The "reliability" of .95 would not be affected by the random response error in inventing stories and would thus greatly overestimate the actual reliability in question.

A complete treatment of measurement models and error of measurement can be found in Hunter (1987). Cronbach (1947) is another good source.

Restriction or Enhancement of Range

If studies differ greatly in the range of values present on the independent variable, then the correlation will differ correspondingly. Thus, correlations are directly comparable across studies only if they are computed on samples from populations with the same standard deviation on the independent variable. There is a range correction formula that will take a correlation computed on a population with a given standard deviation and produce an estimate of what the correlation would have been had the standard deviation been different. That is, the range correction formula estimates the effect of changing the study population standard deviation from one value to another. To eliminate range variation from a meta-analysis, we can use the range correction formula to project all correlations to the same reference standard deviation. For each study we need to know the standard deviation of the independent variable s_i. Range departure is then measured by relating that standard deviation to the reference standard deviation S. The comparison used is the ratio of the standard deviation in the study group to the reference standard deviation, i.e., $u = s / S$. The ratio u is less than 1 if the study has restriction in range and greater than 1 if the study has enhancement of range. The correlation in the study will be greater than or less than the reference correlation depending on whether the ratio u is greater than or less than 1, respectively. These corrections depend on two assumptions. First, the relation in question must be linear (or at least approximately so). Second, the variance of the independent variable must be equal (or at least approximately so) at each level of the dependent variable. This latter condition is known as homoscedacity (Gross & McGanney, 1987).

In this section, we will consider range departure in the context of a single study in which population correlations are known. In the following section we will consider the effect of correcting a sample correlation for range departure. We will find that the sampling error of the corrected correlation differs from that of the uncorrected correlation, and we will show how to adjust the confidence interval correspondingly. We will then briefly note the relation between the ratio u and the "selection ratio" in personnel selection research. After this treatment of range correction in single studies, we will consider the effect of range correction in meta-analysis.

We cannot always study the population that we wish to use as a reference point. Sometimes we study a population in which our independent variable varies less than in the reference population (restriction in range) and sometimes we study a population in which it varies more widely than in the reference population (enhancement of range). In either case, the same relationship between the variables produces a different correlation coefficient. In the case of enhancement of range, the study population correlation is systematically larger than the reference population correlation. This problem is compounded by sampling error and by error of measurement.

Consider personnel selection research. The reference population is the applicant population, but the study is done with people who have already been hired (since we cannot get job performance scores except for those who get to work). If the people hired were a random sample of the applicants, then the only problems would be sampling error and measurement error. But suppose that the test we are studying has been used to select those who are hired. For example, suppose that those hired are those who are above the mean on the test. Then the range of test scores among the job incumbents is greatly reduced in comparison to the applicant population. We would thus expect a considerable reduction in the size of the population correlation that we wish to estimate. If test scores are normally distributed in the applicant population, then the standard deviation for people in the top half of the distribution is only 60% as large as the standard deviation for the entire population. Thus, if the standard deviation were 20 in the applicant population, it would be only .60(20) = 12 in the incumbent population of those hired. The degree of restriction in range would thus be $u = 12/20 = .60$.

The formula for the correlation produced by a change in distribution in the independent variable is called the <u>formula for restriction in range</u>, although it <u>works for enhancement,</u> too, as we shall see. Let ρ_1 be the reference population correlation and let ρ_2 be the study population correlation. Then

$$\rho_2 = \frac{u\rho_1}{\sqrt{(u^2 - 1)\, \rho_1^2 + 1}}$$

where

$$u = \frac{\sigma_{x_2}}{\sigma_{x_1}}$$

is the ratio of standard deviations in the two populations. In the case of restriction in range, we have $u < 1$ and, hence, $\rho_2 < \rho_1$. In the case of range enhancement, we have $u > 1$ and, hence, $\rho_2 > \rho_1$.

In the case of our personnel selection example, we have $u = .60$ and, hence,

$$\rho_2 = \frac{.60\, \rho_1}{\sqrt{(.60^2 - 1)\, \rho_1^2 + 1}} = \frac{.60\, \rho_1}{\sqrt{1 - .64\, \rho_1^2}} \ .$$

For example, if the correlation between test and job performance in the applicant population were .50, then the correlation in the study population would be

$$\rho_2 = \frac{.60\,(.50)}{\sqrt{(1 - .64\,(.50)^2}} = \frac{.60\,(.50)}{.92} = .33\,.$$

That is, if the study is done on only the top half of the distribution on the independent variable, then the population correlation would be reduced from .50 to .33. If undetected, this difference between .50 and .33 would have profound implications for the interpretation of empirical studies.

But suppose we have the data, i.e., $\rho_2 = .33$ and $u = .60$, and we wish to correct for restriction in range. We could reverse the roles of the two populations. That is, we could regard the applicant population as an enhancement of the incumbent population. We could then use the same formula above with the ρs reversed, i.e.,

$$\rho_1 = \frac{U\,\rho_2}{\sqrt{(U^2 - 1)\,\rho_2^2 + 1}}$$

where

$$U = \frac{\sigma_{x_1}}{\sigma_{x_2}} = \frac{1}{u}$$

is the ratio of standard deviations in the opposite order. This formula is called the correction for restriction in range, although it also works for correction for enhancement. In the personnel example, we plug in $\rho_2 = .33$ and $U = 1/u = 1/.60 = 1.67$ to obtain

$$\rho_1 = \frac{1.67\,(.33)}{\sqrt{(1.67^2 - 1)\,(.33)^2 + 1}} = \frac{1.67\,(.33)}{1.09} = .50\,.$$

Thus, at the level of population correlations (i.e., when N is infinite), we can use the formula for restriction in range to move back and forth between populations of different variance with perfect accuracy.

The situation is more complicated if there is sampling error. If we apply the formula for correction for restriction in range to a sample correlation, then we get only an approximation to the reference group population correlation. Moreover, the corrected correlation will have a different amount of sampling error. This situation is analogous to that in correction for attenuation due to measurement error. There is a tradeoff. In order to eliminate the systematic error associated with restriction in range, we must accept the increase in sampling error that goes with the statistical correction formula. If we could correct substantively, i.e., if the study could be done on the reference population, then there would be no increase in sampling error. In fact, in the case of restriction in range, the study done on the applicant population (if it could be done) would have the larger correlation and, hence, the smaller confidence interval.

The confidence interval for the corrected correlation is easy to obtain. The correction formula can be regarded as a mathematical transformation. This transformation is monotone (but not linear) and hence it transforms confidence intervals. Thus, the confidence interval is obtained by correcting the endpoints of the confidence interval using the same formula that is used to correct the correlation. That is, the same range correction formula is applied to the endpoints of the confidence interval as is applied to the correlation itself.

Consider the personnel example in which the population correlations are .50 for the applicant population and .33 for the study population. If the sample size is 100, then the sampling error for a correlation of $\rho = .33$ is $\sigma_c = (1 - .33^2) / \sqrt{99} = .09$. If the sample correlation came out low, it might be something such as .28, which is low by .05. Corrected for restriction in range of $U = 1.67$ we have

$$r_c = \frac{1.67(.28)}{\sqrt{(1.67^2 - 1)(.28^2) + 1}} = \frac{.47}{1.07} = .44$$

The 95% confidence interval on the observed r of .28 is:

Lower Endpoint	Upper Endpoint
$r_1 = .10$	$r_2 = .46$
$r_{c_1} = \dfrac{1.67(.10)}{\sqrt{(1.67^2 - 1).10^2 + 1}}$	$r_{c_2} = \dfrac{1.67(.46)}{\sqrt{(1.67^2 - 1).46^2 + 1}}$
$= .16$	$= .65$

Thus, the confidence interval for the corrected correlation is $.16 \leq \rho_c \leq .65$, which includes the actual value of $\rho_c = .50$. This confidence interval is much wider than the confidence interval for the uncorrected correlation and wider yet than the confidence interval that would have been found had the study been done in the reference population itself.

Range Correction and Sampling Error

There is no difficulty in obtaining a confidence interval for a corrected correlation using the range correction formula; we simply correct the two

endpoints of the confidence interval for the uncorrected correlation. However, it is not so easy to compute the standard deviation of the sampling
error. Correction for attenuation due to measurement error is a linear
operation; the uncorrected correlation is just multiplied by a constant.
Thus, the sampling error and the error standard deviation are multiplied
by the same constant. However, the range correction formula is not linear,
and there is no exact formula for the resulting standard deviation. The
extent of nonlinearity depends on the size of the numbers involved, i.e.,
the extent to which U is different from 1 and the extent to which the
uncorrected correlation has a square much greater than 0. If the nonlinearity is not too great, then we can approximate the sampling error by
pretending that we have just multiplied the uncorrected correlation by the
constant

$$\alpha = \frac{r_c}{r} .$$

The sampling error would then be approximately

$$\sigma_{e_c}^2 = \alpha^2 \sigma_e^2 .$$

To see the extent of this approximation, let us consider our personnel
research example. We center our confidence interval for the corrected
correlation about the corrected correlation itself, i.e., around $r_c = .44$. The
error standard deviation for the uncorrected correlation is $(1 - .28^2)$ /
$\sqrt{99} = .093$, and the ratio of corrected to uncorrected correlations is .44 /
.28 = 1.57. Hence, the estimated error standard deviation for the corrected
correlation is $(1.57) (.093) = .146$. The corresponding confidence interval
is $.15 \leq \rho_c \leq .73$. This implied confidence interval differs only slightly
from the confidence interval obtained by correcting the endpoints, i.e.,
$.16 \leq \rho_c \leq .65$.

There is a more accurate estimate of the standard deviation that can be
obtained using Taylor's series as suggested by Raju, Burke, and Normand
(1983). For large sample size, the sampling error in the corrected correlation induced by the sampling error in the uncorrected correlation is
proportional to the derivative of the correction function. Whereas the
correlation is multiplied by the constant α, the standard deviation is
multiplied by the number $a\alpha$ where

$$a = 1 / [(U^2 - 1) r^2 + 1] .$$

The variance would be multiplied by $a^2 \alpha^2$. In the personnel example, we have $\alpha = 1.57$ and

$$a = 1 / [\ 1.67^2 - 1\ (.28)^2 + 1\ ] = 1 / 1.0352 = .966.$$

Thus, the standard deviation is multiplied by $.966(1.57) = 1.52$ instead of 1.57. The confidence interval found using the improved estimate of the confidence interval is

$$.16 < \rho < .72$$

in comparison to the correct interval obtained by correcting endpoints, which was

$$.16 < \rho < .65.$$

This improved estimate of the standard deviation is hardly worth the trouble for hand calculations, although it is easy to introduce into computer programs, and we have done so. The meta-analysis program VG6 in the Appendix contains this refinement.

An Example: Confidence Intervals. Consider a personnel selection validation study based on job performance ratings by a single supervisor. Given an observed correlation of .30 with a sample size of 100, the confidence interval for the uncorrected validity coefficient is $P\ [.12 \le \rho \le .48] = .95$. From King, Hunter, and Schmidt (1980), we know that the reliability of the supervisor ratings on the applicant pool is at most .60. If the selection ratio is 50%, then the formulas in Schmidt, Hunter, and Urry (1976) show that the ratio of the standard deviation of the application group to that of the incumbent population is 1.67. The point correction of the observed validity coefficient is therefore

$$r_1 = \frac{1.67\ r}{\sqrt{(1.67^2 - 1)\ r^2 + 1}} = .46$$

$$r_2 = \frac{r_1}{\sqrt{.60}} = .60$$

The confidence interval for the corrected validity is obtained by applying the same corrections to the endpoints of the confidence interval for the uncorrected validity.

Lower Endpoint	Upper Endpoint
$r_1 = \dfrac{1.67(.12)}{\sqrt{1.67^2 - 1).12^2 + 1}}$	$r_1 = \dfrac{1.67(.48)}{\sqrt{(1.67^2 - 1).48^2 + 1}}$
$= .20$	$= .67$
$r_2 = \dfrac{.20}{\sqrt{.60}} = .26$	$r_2 = \dfrac{.67}{\sqrt{.60}} = .86$

Hence, the confidence interval for the corrected validity is

$$P\left\{ .26 \leq \rho \leq .86 \right\} = .95 .$$

Range Restriction and the Selection Ratio

In personnel research, the restriction in range often comes about in a very particular way. People are hired from the top down using the test that is to be validated. Only those hired appear in the validation study. Thus, those who appear in the study are chosen from the top portion of the reference population distribution of test scores. Since test score distribution in applicant populations is typically normal or nearly normal distribution, the range restriction parameter u can be computed indirectly from the selection ratio.

The selection ratio is defined as the proportion of applicants selected by the test. For example, if all applicants in the top tenth of the distribution are offered employment, then the selection ratio is 10%. The test selection ratio will be equal to the percentage of applicants offered jobs if hiring is based solely on test scores from the top down (Schmidt, Hunter, McKenzie, & Muldrow, 1979). If hiring is also based on other requirements, then the overall selection ratio will differ from the test selection ratio. For example, police departments often require applicants to pass a medical exam, a psychiatric exam, and a background investigation in addition to the selection test. Typically, about two-thirds of the applicants fail one or the other of these additional screens. Thus if the proportion of persons offered jobs is 13%, then the test selection ratio is 39% (i.e., $3(13) = 39$). The effect of range restriction on the correlation is determined by the test selection ratio rather than the overall ratio.

Let p be the selection ratio as a proportion (i.e., as a fraction such as .10, rather than a percentage). If we are hiring from the top of a normal distribution, then, corresponding to any selection ratio p, there is a cutoff score C such that

$$P[x \geq C] = p.$$

If that cutoff score is given in standard score form, then it can be looked up using the normal distribution table backward. Once the cutoff score is known, then we can compute the mean and variance in test scores among those selected in standard score form using the following formulas.

$$\mu_x = \frac{\varphi(C)}{p}$$

where $\varphi(C)$ is the value of the normal density function at the cutoff (also called the "normal ordinate") and

$$\sigma_x^2 = 1 - \mu_x(\mu_x - C) = 1 - \mu_x^2 + C\mu_x.$$

Since the applicant population has a variance of 1 in standard scores, the number σ_x is equal to the parameter u in the range restriction formula.

For example, if the selection ratio is 10%, then the normal distribution table shows that a cutoff score of 1.28 is required to select the top tenth. The mean standard score among those selected will be

$$\mu_x = \frac{1}{p} \frac{1}{\sqrt{2\pi}} e^{-C^2/2} = 10 \frac{1}{2.507} e^{-.82} = 1.76.$$

The variance among those selected is

$$\sigma_x^2 = 1 - 1.76^2 + 1.28(1.76) = .1552.$$

The standard deviation and, hence, the parameter u is then the square root of .1552, which is .39. That is, with a selection ratio of 10%, the standard deviation in the study population will be only 39% as large as the standard deviation in the applicant population.

Dichotomization of Independent and Dependent Variables

The mathematics of dichotomization is very similar to that of correction for attenuation and will thus be developed succinctly. Some aspects of dichotomization were discussed in Chapter 2; a more detailed treatment is presented in Hunter and Schmidt (in press). The key fact is that the impact of dichotomizing a continuous variable is to multiply the population correlation by an attenuating factor. This systematic attenuation can be corrected by dividing the attenuated correlation by the same factor. That is, if we know the factor by which the study correlation was attenuated, then we can restore the study correlation to its original value by dividing by that same attenuation factor. If we divide a variable by a constant, then the mean and the standard deviation are divided by that same constant. Thus, the corrected correlation coefficient has a mean that is divided by the attenuation factor — that is, the original unattenuated population correlation — and a sampling error that is divided by the attenuation factor. Thus, the sampling error in the corrected correlation is larger than the sampling error in the uncorrected correlation. However, there is no other way to eliminate the systematic error introduced by the dichotomization.

Consider an example. Suppose the independent variable is split at the median. Then the attenuation factor is .80 and, thus, the population correlation is reduced by 20%. If ρ is the true population correlation and ρ_o is the attenuated population correlation, then

$$\rho_o = .80\,\rho\;.$$

This equation is algebraically reversible. To undo multiplication by .80, we divide by .80.

$$\rho_o\,/\,.80 = (.80\,\rho)\,/\,.80 = \rho$$

That is,

$$\rho = \rho_o\,/\,.80$$

is the formula for correction for dichotomization. The formula works perfectly for population correlations and works to eliminate the systematic error in the sample correlation.

The study sample correlation r_o is related to the study population correlation in the usual manner.

$$r_o = \rho_o + e_o$$

where e_o is the usual sampling error. If we correct the point biserial correlation to eliminate the attenuation due to dichotomization, then the corrected correlation r is given by

$$r = r_o\,/\,.80 = (\rho_o + e_o)\,/\,.80 = \rho_o\,/\,.80 + e_o\,/\,.80$$
$$= (.80\,\rho)\,/\,.80 + e_o\,/\,.80$$

$$= \rho + e_o \, / \, .80$$

Let us denote by e the sampling error in the corrected correlation. We then have

$$r = \rho + e$$

Thus, the population correlation corresponding to the corrected sample correlation is the desired true correlation; i.e., the systematic part of the sample correlation is restored to its pre-dichotomization value ρ. However, the sampling error e is not the usual sampling error associated with a population correlation of ρ. Rather e is the sampling error associated with a corrected correlation centered about the attenuated correlation ρ_o. Had there been no dichotomization, the standard deviation of the sampling error would have been

$$\sigma_e = (1 - \rho^2) \, / \, \sqrt{(N-1)} \, .$$

Instead, the standard deviation of the sampling error in the corrected correlation σ_e must be computed from the sampling error of the uncorrected correlation σ_{eo}. The sampling error standard deviation of the uncorrected correlation is

$$\sigma_{eo} = (1 - \rho_o^2) \, / \, \sqrt{(N-1)}$$
$$= [\, 1 - (.80\rho)^2 \,] \, / \, \sqrt{(N-1)}$$
$$= [\, 1 - .64\rho^2 \,] \, / \, \sqrt{(N-1)} \, .$$

The sampling error standard deviation of the corrected correlation is

$$\sigma_e = \sigma_{eo} \, / \, .80 = 1.25 \, \sigma_{eo} \, .$$

Consider an example. Suppose that the population correlation for the original continous variables is $\rho = .50$. The population correlation with the independent variable split at the median is

$$\rho_o = .80\rho = .80(.50) = .40 \, .$$

If the sample size were $N=100$, then the sampling error standard deviation for non-dichotomized variables would have been

$$\sigma_e = (1 - .50^2) / \sqrt{99} = .0754.$$

The sampling error standard deviation of the uncorrected correlation is

$$\sigma_{eo} = (1 - .40^2) / \sqrt{99} = .0844.$$

The sampling error standard deviation of the corrected correlation is

$$\sigma_e = \sigma_{eo} / .80 = .0844 / .80 = .1055.$$

Whereas 95% of sample correlations for non-dichotomized variables would have spread over

$$.35 < r < .65,$$

the corrected correlations spread over the range

$$.29 < r < .71.$$

For a more extreme split, the cost of correction would have been higher. For a 90-10 split, the attenuation factor is .59, and the contrasting probability intervals are much more different.

$$.35 < r < .65 \text{ if no dichotomization}$$

$$.20 < r < .80 \text{ if one variable is split } 90\text{-}10$$

The situation is even more extreme if both variables are dichotomized. Consider a case from personnel selection. Hunter and Hunter (1984) found an average correlation of .26 between (continuous) reference recommendations and job performance ratings. Suppose there were no error of measurement in the study. However, suppose that for purposes of communicating to the employer, the company psychologist decided to dichotomize the two variables. He dichotomizes the reference variable into "generally positive" versus "generally negative." He finds that 90% of past employers give positive ratings while 10% give negative ratings. He splits the supervisor performance ratings at the median to produce "above average" versus "below average." The effect of the double dichotomization (Hunter & Schmidt, in press) is to attenuate the correlation of .26 to

$$\rho_o = (.59)(.80)\rho = .472\rho = (.472)(.26) = .12.$$

The corrected correlation is thus

$$r = r_o \, / \, .472 = 2.12 \, r_o \,.$$

That is, the observed correlation must be more than doubled to overcome the attenuation produced by the dichotomization. The sampling error is correspondingly increased. For a sample size of $N=100$, the 95% confidence intervals in sample correlations are

$.08 < r < .44$ if the variables are not dichotomized and

$-.15 < r < .67$ for a 10-90 and a 50-50 split.

Furthermore, it is not likely that the reference evaluations in a local validation study will have reliability as high as that in the Hunter and Hunter (1984) data. The reference check studies reviewed by Hunter and Hunter checked across three or more past employers and used professionally developed scales to assess employer ratings. The correlation of .26 is corrected for the attenuation due to error of measurement in the performance ratings only. Suppose the validation study asks for references from just one past employer and uses performance ratings by the immediate supervisor. If good rating scales are used in both cases, the reliability of each variable would be expected to be about .60. Since both reliabilities are equal, the square roots are also equal at .77 . The attenuation factor for error of measurement is thus

$$\rho_o = a_1 a_2 \; \rho = (.77)(.77) \; \rho = .60 \; \rho = (.60)(.26) = .156 \,.$$

This correlation is then attenuated by double dishotomization

$$\rho_{oo} = a_3 a_4 \; \rho_o = (.59)(.80) \; \rho_o = .472 \; \rho_o = .472(.156) = .074 \,.$$

The net attenuation for both error of measurement and dichotomization is

$$\rho_{oo} = (.60)(.472) \; \rho = .2832 \; \rho \,.$$

This value of .2832 is thus the attenuation factor for the correction of the sample correlation. That is, the corrected correlation r will be

$$r = r_{oo} \, / \, .2832 = 3.53 \, r_{oo} \,.$$

That is, one must more than triple the observed sample correlation to correct for the attenuation produced by both error of measurement and double dichotomization. The sampling error is similarly increased. For a sample size of $N = 100$, the 95% probability intervals are

$.08 < r < .44$ if perfect measurement and no dichotomization and

$-.43 < r < .95$ if the correlation is corrected for measurement error and dichotomization in both variables.

Imperfect Construct Validity in Independent and Dependent Variables

We define the construct validity of a measure as its true score correlation with the actual construct or trait it is supposed to measure. The case of construct validity is similar to the case of error of measurement if the path analysis permits a simple multiplicative attenuation (see Chapter 2 for the required conditions). If error of measurement is treated separately, then the impact of imperfect construct validity is to multiply the true population correlation by an attenuation factor equal to the construct validity of the variable. If there is imperfect construct validity in both variables, and if both proxy variables satisfy the path analysis requirements, then the effect is a double attenuation, i.e., multiplication by the product of the two construct validities. Since the attenuation effect is systematic, it can be algebraically reversed. To reverse the effect of multiplying the correlation by a constant, we divide the correlation by the same constant. Thus, to restore the correlation to what it would have been had the variables been measured with perfect construct validity, we divide the study correlation by the product of the two construct validities. Note that for perfect construct validity, we divide by 1.00, which leaves the correlation unchanged. So perfect construct validity is a special case of imperfect construct validity.

For example, let the construct validity of the independent variable be a_1 and let the construct validity of the dependent variable be a_2. The impact of imperfect construct validity is to multiply the true correlation by the product $a_1 a_2$. That is,

$$\rho_o = a_1 a_2\, \rho\,.$$

The correction formula is to divide by the same attenuation factors

$$\rho_o \,/\, a_1 a_2 = (a_1 a_2\, \rho)\,/\,a_1 a_2 = \rho\,.$$

The corrected sample correlation is thus

$$r = r_o / a_1 a_2 = (1 / a_1 a_2) r_o,$$

which multiplies the sampling error by the same factor $(1 / a_1 a_2)$.

The attenuating effect of imperfect construct validity combines with the attenuating effect of other artifacts. Consider another example.

$a_1 = .90 =$ the square root of the reliability of X; $r_{XX} = .81$

$a_2 = .90 =$ the square root of the reliability of Y; $r_{YY} = .81$

$a_3 = .90 =$ the construct validity of X

$a_4 = .90 =$ the construct validity of Y

$a_5 = .80 =$ the attenuation factor for splitting X at the median

$a_6 = .80 =$ the attenuation factor for splitting Y at the median

The total impact of the six study imperfections is

$$\rho_o = (.9)(.9)(.9)(.9)(.8)(.8)\rho = .42\ \rho.$$

Thus, even minor imperfections add up. Had the true correlation been .50, the study population correlation would be

$$\rho_o = .42\ \rho = .42(.50) = .21.$$

a reduction of over one-half. The formula for the corrected correlation is

$$r = r_o / .42 = 2.38\ r_o.$$

Thus, to restore the systematic value of the study correlation, we must more than double the correlation.

Attrition Artifacts

As noted in Chapter 2, attrition artifacts can usually be treated as range variation on the dependent variable. If there is range variation on the dependent variable, but NOT on the independent variable, then the mathematical treatment is identical to the treatment of range variation on the independent variable; we merely interchange the role of variables X and

Y. As we complete this book, there are no meta-analysis methods that correct for range restriction on both the independent and the dependent variables. However, as noted in Chapter 2, we are currently developing such methods. We expect such methods to be important in the area of validity generalization and perhaps in certain other research areas.

Extraneous Factors

As noted in Chapter 2, easily correctable extraneous factors in the research setting usually enter into the causal model for the research design in much the same form as the extraneous factors in the measurement of a proxy variable for the dependent variable. At the level of the study, it would be possible to correct the study effect correlation by partialling out the extraneous factor. If the extraneous factor was not controlled in the original analysis, then the attenuation factor is

$$a = \sqrt{(1 - \rho_{EY}^2)}$$

where ρ_{EY} is the correlation between the extraneous factor and the dependent variable. The impact on the study effect correlation is to attenuate the population correlation by the multiplicative factor

$$\rho_o = a \ \rho \ .$$

This formula can be algebraically reversed

$$\rho = \rho_o \ / \ a$$

to yield the correction formula for the sample correlation

$$r = r_o \ / \ a \ .$$

The sampling error is divided by the same factor and increases correspondingly.

The mathematics is otherwise identical to that for attenuation due to error of measurement. The impact of extraneous factors can combine with the impact of other artifacts. The compound impact is to multiply the attenuation factors for the other factors by the attenuation factor for the extraneous factor.

Bias in the Correlation

As noted in Chapter 2, the purely statistical bias in the sample correlation as an estimate of the population correlation is normally trivial in magnitude, and it is rarely worthwhile to correct for it. This is why this bias is not listed in Table 3.1 (or in Table 2.1 in Chapter 2). However, we provide the computations to check the size of the bias in any given application. The impact of bias is systematic and can be captured to a close approximation by an attenuation multiplier. If the population correlations are less than .70 (usually the case), then the best attenuation multiplier for meta-analysis is the linear attenuation factor (Hunter, Schmidt, & Coggin, 1988).

$$a = 1 - 1 / (2N - 1) = (2N - 2) / (2N - 1).$$

This attenuation factor is most useful in meta-analysis because it is independent of the population correlation ρ. For applications with population correlations larger than .70 (a rare condition), the more accurate attenuation factor is

$$a = 1 - (1 - \rho^2) / (2N - 1).$$

Note that, if the above nonlinear attenuator is used, then correction for bias should always be the last artifact considered. In the case of multiple artifacts, the "ρ" in the attenuation formula will be the population correlation already attenuated for all other artifacts.

The impact of bias on the population correlation is a systematic reduction.

$$\rho_o = a\ \rho$$

The correction formula follows from the algebraic reversal of this equation

$$\rho = \rho_o / a$$

to yield

$$r = r_o / a.$$

The sampling error is divided by the same factor and increases correspondingly. The sampling error *variance* is divided by a^2.

Multiple Simultaneous Artifacts

Table 3.1 lists eleven artifacts; nine of these are potentially correctable by the use of multiplicative artifact attenuation factors. The other two artifacts are sampling error, which is corrected by a different strategy, and bad data, which can be corrected only if the bad data can be identified and thrown out (see Chapter 5). This section considers the compound of all the multiplicative artifacts. It is implicitly understood that range variation on both the independent and dependent variable are not simultaneously considered (Hunter & Schmidt, 1987b). Thus, the analysis would contain at most eight multiplicative artifacts. Note again that the artifact attenuation is caused by the real imperfections of the study design. The attenuation of the true correlation will thus occur whether we can correct for it or not.

Consider again the six artifact examples from the section on construct validity. The artifact attenuation factors are

a_1 = .90 = the square root of the reliability of X; r_{XX} = .81,
a_2 = .90 = the square root of the reliability of Y; r_{YY} = .81,
a_3 = .90 = the construct validity of X,
a_4 = .90 = the construct validity of Y,
a_5 = .80 = the attenuation factor for splitting X at the median,
a_6 = .80 = the attenuation factor for splitting Y at the median.

The total impact of the six study imperfections is determined by the total attenuation factor

$$A = (.9)\,(.9)\,(.9)\,(.9)\,(.8)\,(.8) = .42.$$

If the true correlation for the study is $\rho=.50$, the attenuated study correlation is only

$$\rho_o = .42\,\rho = .42\,(.50) = .21.$$

If the sample size is $N=26$, then the linear bias attenuation factor is

$$a_7 = 1 - 1/(2N - 1) = 1 - 1/25 = .96.$$

The total attenuation factor for all seven artifacts is thus

$$A = .42\,(.96) = .40$$

and the attenuated study population correlation is

$$\rho_o = .40 \ \rho = .40(.50) = .20.$$

The sampling error variance of the uncorrected correlation is

$$Var(e_o) = [1 - .20^2]^2 / (26 - 1) = .0368.$$

The sampling error variance of the corrected correlation is

$$Var(e) = Var(e_o) / A^2 = .0368 / .40^2 = .2304.$$

Thus, the sampling error standard deviation is $\sqrt{.2304} = .48$. The 95% probability interval for the observed *corrected* correlation is

$$-.44 < r < 1.44.$$

If the sample size were increased to $N = 101$, the probability interval for the corrected correlation would shrink to

$$.03 < r < .97.$$

The preceding example is an extreme case, but not unrealistic. All artifact values were derived from the empirical literature. This example shows that there is only limited information in the best of small sample studies. When that information is watered down with large methodological artifacts, then there may be almost no information in the study. Ideally, studies with approximately perfect methodology would eliminate these artifacts substantively and, hence, eliminate the need for statistical correction. However, most methodological artifact values are determined by the feasibility limitations of field research. Thus, researchers frequently have little leeway for improvement. This means that there will nearly always be a need for statistical correction and, hence, there will nearly always be a need to greatly reduce sampling error.

Meta-Analysis of Individually Corrected Correlations

The examples of the preceding sections show that individual studies contain only very limited information. The random effects of sampling error are unavoidable. Furthermore, the other artifacts in study designs are often caused by factors outside the control of the investigator. Thus, the information in most studies is diluted by statistical artifacts such as those listed in Table 3.1, and perhaps still further by artifacts yet to be delineated and quantified in future research. Solid conclusions can thus only be built on cumulative research combining the information across studies. The traditional narrative review is clearly inadequate to this complex task (see Chapter 11). Thus, there is no alternative to meta-analysis. If one pretends that the only study artifact is sampling error, then the meta-analysis techniques given earlier in this chapter are used. But if other artifacts are acknowledged and if information about the artifacts is available, then the values estimated by meta-analysis will be much more accurate if the study artifacts are corrected.

There are three kinds of artifacts in Table 3.1. First, there is bad data: recording, computing, reporting, and transcriptional errors. If the error is so large that the resulting correlation is an outlier in the meta-analysis, then the deviant result can be detected and eliminated (see Chapter 5). Otherwise, bad data goes undetected and, hence, uncorrected. Second, there is the nonsystematic and random effect of sampling error. These effects can be eliminated in meta-analysis. Third, the table contains nine artifacts that are systematic in nature. These we call the "correctable artifacts." For each correctable artifact, there is a quantitative parameter which must be known to correct the study correlation for that artifact. Given the necessary artifact values for the research domain in question, meta-analysis can correct for that artifact.

There are three cases in meta-analysis : (1) artifact values are given in each individual study for all artifacts, (2) artifact values are only sporadically given for any artifact in the various studies, and (3) artifact values are given for each study on some artifacts but are only available sporadically on other artifacts. The case of individually available artifact information is treated in this chapter. The case of sporadically available information is covered in Chapter 4, as is the case of mixed artifact information.

We now consider the case where artifact information is available on nearly all individual studies. The missing artifact values can be estimated by inserting the mean or modal value across the studies where information is given. At that point, each artifact value is available for each study. There are then three phases to the meta-analysis: (1) computations for each of the individual studies, (2) combining the results across studies, and (3) computing the estimated mean and variance of true effect size correlations in the designated research domain.

Individual Study Computations

The computations for each study are the computations used in correcting the correlation for artifacts. We begin with the observed study correlation and the sample size for that study. We next collect each piece of artifact information for that study. These values are placed in a table and may be read into a computer file.

We next do the computations to correct for artifacts. Under most conditions, the effect of each correctable artifact is to reduce the correlation by an amount that can be quantified as a multiplicative factor less than 1.00, which we call the "attenuation factor." Under these conditions, the net impact of all the correctable artifacts can be computed by simply multiplying the separate artifact attenuation factors. This results in a compound artifact attenuation factor. Dividing the observed study correlation by the compound attenuation factor corrects the study correlation for the systematic reduction caused by those artifacts.

For each study, we first compute the artifact attenuation factor for each artifact. Denote the separate attenuation factors by $a_1, a_2, a_3, \ldots$ The compound attenuation factor for the several artifacts is the product

$$A = a_1 \, a_2 \, a_3 \ldots$$

We can now compute the corrected study correlation r. We denote the observed study correlation by r_o, and the corrected correlation by r. The corrected correlation is then

$$r = r_o \, / \, A \, .$$

For purposes of estimating sampling error, it is necessary to estimate the mean uncorrected correlation. However, there is an important difference in the present context. If the corrected study correlations are to be weighted according to artifact values as recommended below, then those same weights should be used in computing the mean uncorrected correlation.

The sampling error variance in the corrected correlation is computed in two steps. First, the sampling error variance in the uncorrected correlation is computed. Then the sampling error variance in the corrected correlation is computed from that. The sampling error variance in the uncorrected correlation, $\text{Var}(e_o)$, is:

$$\text{Var}(e_o) = \left[\, 1 - \bar{r}_o^2 \, \right]^2 / \, (N_i - 1)$$

where $\bar{r}_o$ is the mean uncorrected correlation across studies and N is the sample size for the study in question. The sampling error variance in the corrected correlation is then given by

$$\text{Var}(e) = \text{Var}(e_o) \, / \, A^2$$

where A is the compound artifact attenuation factor for that study. For simplicity, denote the sampling error variance by ve. That is, define ve by

$$ve = \text{Var}(e).$$

The preceding computation of sampling error variance is corrected for all artifacts. However, we can refine our estimate of the contribution of the range correction to sampling error. Since the attenuation factor for range variation contains the correlation itself, the corresponding sampling error increase is only in proportion to the derivative of the attenuation instead of the attenuation factor itself. This difference is small in most cases so there is little error in ignoring this departure from linearity. However, a more accurate estimate can be computed using a more complicated formula for sampling error variance. Compute a first estimate of ve using the formula above. Label the first estimate ve'. The improved estimate is then

$$ve = \alpha^2 \, ve'$$

where α is computed as

$$\alpha = 1 \, / \, [\, (U^2 - 1) \, r_o{}^2 + 1 \,] .$$

Consider an extreme example: Suppose only the top half of the ability distribution had been selected in a personnel selection study. The study population standard deviation is smaller than the reference population standard deviation by the factor $u = .60$. The reciprocal of u would be $U = 1/.60 = 1.67$. If the study correlation were .20, then the refining factor would be $\alpha^2 = .96$. That is, the sampling error variance for that study would be 4% smaller than estimated using the simple attenuation factor.

Thus, for each study i we generate four numbers: the corrected correlation r_i, the sample N_i, the compound attenuation factor A_i and the sampling error variance ve_i. These are the numbers used in the meta-analysis proper.

Combining Across Studies

Meta-analysis reduces sampling error by averaging errors. Thus, an important step in meta-analysis is the computation of certain critical averages: the average correlation, the variance of correlations (the average squared deviation from the mean), and the average sampling error variance. To do this, we must decide how much weight to give to each study.

What weights should be used? The first step in the meta-analysis is to average certain numbers across studies. This averaging can be done in several ways. In averaging corrected correlations, a simple or "unweighted" average gives as much weight to a study with a sample size of 12 as to a study with a sample size of 1,200. Yet the sampling error variance in the small sample study is 100 times greater than in the large sample study. Schmidt and Hunter (1977) noted this problem and recommended that each study be weighted by its sample size. Hunter, Schmidt, and Jackson (1982, pp. 41-42) noted that this is an optimal strategy when there is little or no variation in population correlations across studies — the "homogeneous" case. They noted that there can be a problem if correlations differ a great deal across studies. The problem is potentially acute if the meta-analysis contains one study with very large sample size while all the other studies have much smaller sample size. If the large sample size study is deviant in some way, then, because it dominates the meta-analysis, the meta-analysis will be deviant. This case arises rarely in practice.

The homogeneous case was considered in technical detail in Hedges and Olkin (1985, Chapter 6). They noted the key mathematical theorem for that case. If the population correlations do not differ from one study to the next, then the optimal weights are obtained by weighting each study inversely to its sampling error variance. In the case of correlations that are not corrected for any artifact, the sampling error variance is

$$\text{Var}(e_i) = (1 - \rho_i^2)^2 / (N_i - 1).$$

The optimal weight for this homogeneous case would thus be

$$w_i = (N_i - 1) / (1 - \rho_i^2)^2.$$

Since the population correlation ρ_i is not known, this optimal weight cannot be used. Although Hedges and Olkin (1985) do not note it, even in the nonhomogeneous case, the substitution of the observed study correlation r_{oi} for the study population correlation ρ_i does not lead to the most accuate alternative weights. A more accurate alternative is to substitute the mean observed correlation $\bar{r}_o$ for each study population ρ_i (see Chapter 5). Since the resulting multiplicative term

$$1 / (1 - \bar{r}_o^2)^2$$

is the same for all studies, it can be dropped. That is, the corresponding weighting can be more easily accomplished by using the weight

$$w_i = N_i - 1 .$$

As Hedges and Olkin noted, this differs only trivially from the Schmidt and Hunter recommendation to weigh each study by sample size.

$$w_i = N_i$$

When studies differ greatly on one or more of the artifacts corrected, then more complicated weighting will make better use of the information in the studies. Studies with more information should receive more weight than studies with less information. For example, studies in which one or both of the variables is dichotomized with extreme splits should receive much less weight than a study with a near even split. The same is true if one study has very low reliability while a second study has high reliability.

Consider the optimality theorem presented by Hedges and Olkin (1985). The sampling error variance of the corrected correlation is

$$\text{Var}(e_i) = [(1 - \rho_i^2)^2 / (N_i - 1)] / A_i^2 .$$

Thus, if there were no variation in population correlations across studies, the optimal weight for each study would be

$$w_i = A_i^2 [(N_i - 1) / (1 - \rho_i^2)^2]$$
$$= [(N_i - 1) A_i^2] / (1 - \rho_i^2)^2 .$$

Since the study population correlation ρ_i is not known, some substitution must be made. In the homogeneous case, the most accurate substitution is to substitute the mean observed correlation $\bar{r}_o$ for each study population correlation ρ_i. This has the effect of eliminating the term with ρ_i and thus yields the weights

$$w_i = (N_i - 1) A_i^2 .$$

This, in turn, differs only trivially from the more simple weights

$$w_i = N_i A_i^2 .$$

That is, the weight for each study is the product of two factors: the sample size N_i and the square of the artifact attenuation factor A_i. The attenuation factor is squared because to multiply a correlation by the factor A_i is to multiply the sampling error variance by the square of that factor; i.e, by A_i^2. This weighting scheme has the desired effect: The more extreme the artifact attenuation in a given study, the less the weight assigned to that study. That is, the more information contained in the study, the greater its weight.

Consider two studies with sample size 100. Assume that (1) both variables are measured with perfect reliability and without range restriction, (2) the population correlation ρ is the same in both studies, and (3) in both studies, the dependent variable is dichotomized. In study 1, there is a 50-50 split so that the true population correlation ρ_1 is reduced to a study population correlation of .80 ρ_1. In study 2, there is a 90-10 split so that the true population correlation ρ_2 is reduced to a study population correlation of .59 ρ_2. To correct for the attenuation due to artificial dichotomization, the study 1 observed correlation r_{o1} must be multiplied by the reciprocal of .80, i.e., $1/.80 = 1.25$.

$$r_1 = 1.25\, r_{o1}$$

Thus, the sampling error variance is multiplied by the square of 1.25, i.e., $1.25^2 = 1.5625$. To correct for the attenuation due to artificial dichotomization, the study 2 observed correlation r_{o2} must be multiplied by the reciprocal of .59, i.e., $1 / .59 = 1.695$.

$$r_2 = 1.695\, r_{o2}$$

Thus, the sampling error variance is multiplied by the square of 1.695, i.e., $1.695^2 = 2.8730$. Before the correction, the sampling error in both correlations was the same: the sampling error implied by equal sample sizes of 100 and equal population correlations of ρ_i. However, after the correction for dichotomiztion, the second study has sampling error variance that is $2.8730/1.5625 = 1.839$ times larger than the sampling error variance in the first study. Thus, the second study deserves only $1/1.839 = .544$ times as much weight in the meta-analysis. The weights assigned to the studies by the formula

$$w_i = N_i\, A_i^2$$

do just that.

$$w_1 = 100 \ (.802)^2 = 100 \ (.64) = 64$$

$$w_2 = 100 \ (.592)^2 = 100 \ (.35) = 35$$

where $64/35 = 1.83$. Thus, to use round numbers, the study with twice the information is given twice the weight (1.00 versus .544).

In summary, there are three typical types of weights that might be used in averaging. First, one could ignore the differences in quality (information content) between studies and give as much weight to high error studies as to low error studies. The case of equal weights is represented by $w_i = 1$. Second, one might consider the effect on quality of unequal sample size but ignore the effects of other artifacts. This leads to the sample size weights recommended by Schmidt and Hunter (1977): $w_i = N_i$. Third, one might consider the optimal weights for the homogeneous or near homogeneous case: $w_i = N_i \ A_i^{\ 2}$.

We recommend the use of these last weights, because they give less weight to those studies that require greater correction and, hence, have greater sampling error.

Final Meta-Analysis Estimation

Once the researcher has corrected each study correlation for artifacts and has decided on the weights, there are three meta-analysis averages to be computed using the corrected rs:

$$\bar{r} = \Sigma \ w_i \ r_i \ / \ \Sigma \ w_i$$

$$\text{Var} \ (r) \ = \Sigma \ w_i \ [\ r_i - \bar{r} \ ]^2 \ / \ \Sigma \ w_i$$

$$\text{Ave} \ (ve_i) \ = \Sigma \ w_i \ ve_i \ / \ \Sigma \ w_i$$

The mean actual correlation is then estimated by the mean corrected correlation.

$$\bar{\rho} = \bar{r}$$

The variance of actual correlations is given by the corrected variance of corrected correlations.

$$\text{Var} \ (\rho) = \text{Var} \ (r) - \text{Ave} \ (ve)$$

The standard deviation is estimated by the square root of the variance estimate if it is positive. If the standard deviation is actually zero, then the variance estimate will be negative half the time by chance. A negative variance estimate suggests that the actual variance is zero (see Chapter 9).

It is possible to develop a chi-square test for homogeneity of the true effect size correlations across studies. The significance test statistic Q is only approximately chi square in distribution if the test is based on unit weighted or simple sample size weighted averages. The approximation is much closer if the artifact weights are used (Hunter & Schmidt, 1987b). Define the test statistic Q by

$$Q = K \operatorname{Var}(r) / \operatorname{Ave}(ve)$$

where K is the number of studies in the meta-analysis. Under the null hypothesis that all actual correlations are equal, Q has approximately a chi-square distribution with $K-1$ degrees of freedom. Note that this is a chi-square test for *corrected* correlations, unlike the chi-square test presented in Hunter et al. (1982, pp. 46-47). If the correlations are fully corrected for artifacts, the chi-square test presented here does not suffer from a Type I bias caused by variance due to artifacts that have not been corrected for. A chi-square test computed on uncorrected correlations does have such a bias. Nevertheless, it is usually undesirable to rely on statistical tests of homogeneity; the dangers of doing so are discussed in Chapter 11.

An Example: Validity Generalization

Validation studies are usually done on incumbent worker populations that have been selected using either the same or a similar test to that being validated. Thus, they are subject to sometimes extreme restriction of range. Criterion measures may have high reliability (job knowledge tests or training school scores) or low reliability (supervisor ratings). Thus, observed validity coefficients are subject to both restriction in range and to error of measurement. Table 3.5 presents the summary of findings for a hypothetical meta-analysis of validation studies. Table 3.5a presents the validity coefficients generated by assuming that all population correlations are the same ($\rho = .50$), and then reducing the correlation according to the degree of unreliability and restriction of range shown and adding sampling error. The observed correlations are then corrected using the usual formulas. The criterion reliabilities are values for the applicant pool; therefore, range restriction corrections are made first, then reliability corrections. We weight each study as follows:

$$w_i = N_i \, A_i^2$$

The work sheet for these calculations is shown in Table 3.5b. The attenuation factor for each study is most easily computed as the ratio of the uncorrected correlation to the corrected correlation. For study 1,

$$A_1 = .35/.70 = .50 \,.$$

Thus the study weight shown in the next to last column is

$$w_1 = 68\,(.50)^2 = 68\,(.25) = 17.0 \,.$$

The average uncorrected sample correlation is .28. The sampling error variance of the uncorrected correlation in study 1 is thus:

$$\text{Var}\,(e) = (1 - .28^2)^2 \,/\, 67 = .012677 \,.$$

Since all studies in this hypothetical example have the same sample size, this is the estimate of sampling error variance in the uncorrected correlations for every study (not shown in Table 3.5b).

The sampling error variance in the *corrected* correlations can be estimated in two ways. We could use the simple estimate that ignores the nonlinearity of the range restriction correction. That is the formula

$$\text{Var}\,(ve) = \text{VAR}\,(e) \,/\, A^2 \,.$$

For study 1, this value is

$$\text{Var}\,(ve) = .012677/\,(.50)^2 = .050708 \,.$$

This estimate is recorded in the column "Simple Error Variance" in Table 3.5b. However, a more accurate estimate is obtained by using the correction factor computed using the derivative of the correction transformation:

$$\alpha = 1 \,/\, [\,(U^2 - 1)\,r_o^2 + 1\,]$$

For study 1, the standard deviation ratio is

$$U = 1 \,/\, u = 1 \,/\, .468 = 2.1368$$

So the correction factor is

Table 3.5 A Meta-analysis on Hypothetical Personnel Selection Studies

Table 3.5a Hypothetical Validity and Artifact Information

Study	Selection Ratio	s/S (u)	Criterion Reliability	Sample Size	Observed Correlation	Corrected Correlation
1.	.20	.468	.80	68	.35**	.70
2.	.20	.468	.60	68	.07	.19
3.	.20	.468	.80	68	.11	.26
4.	.20	.468	.60	68	.31*	.74
5.	.50	.603	.80	68	.18	.32
6.	.50	.603	.60	68	.36**	.71
7.	.50	.603	.80	68	.40**	.66
8.	.50	.603	.60	68	.13	.27
9.	.90	.844	.80	68	.49**	.62
10.	.90	.844	.60	68	.23	.35
11.	.90	.844	.80	68	.29*	.38
12.	.90	.844	.60	68	.44**	.65

*p < .05 (two-tailed).
**p < .01 (two-tailed).

Table 3.5b The Meta-analysis Worksheet

Study	Sample Size	Attenuation Factor	Simple Error Variance*	Refined Error Variance*	Study Weight	Corrected Correlation
1.	68	.50	.0507	.0246	17.0	.70
2.	68	.37	.0926	.0894	9.3	.19
3.	68	.42	.0719	.0661	12.0	.26
4.	68	.42	.0719	.0399	12.0	.74
5.	68	.56	.0404	.0362	21.3	.32
6.	68	.51	.0489	.0324	17.7	.71
7.	68	.61	.0340	.0208	25.3	.66
8.	68	.48	.0550	.0519	15.7	.27
9.	68	.79	.0203	.0169	42.4	.62
10.	68	.66	.0291	.0279	29.6	.35
11.	68	.76	.0220	.0205	39.3	.38
12.	68	.68	.0274	.0236	31.4	.65

NOTE: Applies to the *corrected* correlations.

$$\alpha = 1 \ / \ [\ (2.1368^2 - 1)\,(.35)^2 + 1\ ] = 1 \ / \ 1.4368 = .6960.$$

Thus the refined estimate of sampling error variance in study 1 is

$$\text{Var}\ (ve) = \alpha^2\ (.050708) = .024564$$

as shown in the column "Refined Error Variance" in Table 3.5b.

Again, we note that the corrected correlations are denoted as r. The three weighted averages are

$$\bar{r} = .505$$

$$\text{Var}\,(r)\ = .030938$$

$$\text{Var}\,(e)\ = .037637\quad\text{(Simple method)}$$

$$\text{Var}\,(e)\ = .030390\quad\text{(Refined method)}.$$

Since all population correlations were assumed to be the same, the variance of population correlations is actually zero. Thus, the sampling error variance should equal the observed variance. For the simple estimation method, we have

$$\text{Var}\ (\rho) = \text{Var}\ (r) - \text{Var}\ (e)\ = .030938 - .037637 = -.006699,$$

which correctly suggests a standard deviation of zero but which is a poorer estimate than we would like. For the refined estimation method, we have

$$\text{Var}\ (\rho) = \text{Var}\ (r) - \text{Var}\ (e)\ = .030938 - .030390 = -.000548.$$

Although the value .000548 is much closer to the true value of 0, there is still a small error. This small error results from approximations used in the meta-analysis. For example, even the refined approximation for the effect of correction for range restriction is not exact.

The small error in estimating the variance of correlations leads to a corresponding error in estimating the standard deviation; though the error is larger in size. The estimated standard deviation is the square root of the estimated variance; i.e., .02. The square root of a small fraction is much larger than the original fraction in relative terms. Thus while the error in estimating the variance was .0005, the error in stimating the standard deviation is .02.

For comparison purposes, sampling error corrections are made for the observed correlations as well as for the corrected correlations. The results are as follows.

Uncorrected Correlations	Corrected Correlations
$\bar{r}_o = .28$	$\bar{r} = .50$
$\sigma^2_{r_o} = .017033$	$\sigma^2_r = .030938$
$\sigma^2_e = .012677$	$\sigma^2_e = .030390$
$\sigma^2_\rho = .004356$	$\sigma^2_\rho = .000548$
$SD_\rho = .07$	$SD_\rho = .02$

The results for uncorrected correlations show an incorrect mean of .28 (versus the true value of .50) and a standard deviation of .07 (versus an actual standard deviation of 0). The meta-analysis of uncorrected correlations is very inaccurate in comparison to the actual effect size correlation used to generate these hypothetical data. However, the error in the uncorrected correlation meta-analysis is exactly consistent with the known artifacts. The average attenuation factor is .563 (using the weights that would be used for the meta-analysis of uncorrected correlations, i.e. weighting by sample size). The mean correlation would then be expected to be reduced from .50 to .563 (.50) = .282, which matches the mean uncorrected correlation. A check of Table 3.5b shows considerable variation in the attenuation factors due to variation in the artifact values across studies. In uncorrected correlations, this variation across studies is all artifactual; that is, the uncorrected correlations vary due to differential range restriction and criterion unreliability.

If the variance in uncorrected correlations is interpreted to mean that there is a real moderator variable present, then there is a major substantive error of interpretation. However, if it is correctly noted that no correction for artifacts other than sampling error was made and that the remaining variation might be due to such artifacts, then the substantive error could be avoided. The moral of this story is this: Even meta-analysis will not save a review from critical errors if there is no correction for study artifact in addition to sampling error. Such artifacts are present in virtually every research domain.

This method of meta-analysis, in which each study correlation is individually corrected for attenuating artifacts, can only occasionally be used. The reason is obvious. Few sets of studies provide all the needed artifact information. For an example of a large-scale meta-analysis in which this method could be and was applied, see Rothstein, Schmidt, Erwin, Owens, and Sparks (in press). This study was a consortium validation effort in which numerous employers participated. Quite a number of such consortia studies have been conducted over the last 15 to 20 years (e.g., Dunnette et al., 1982; Peterson, 1982; Dye, 1982). The meta-analysis methods described in this chapter could be applied to the data from these studies.

Summary of Meta-Analysis Correcting
Each Correlation Individually

Correlations are subject to many artifactual sources of variation that we can control in a meta-analysis: the random effect of sampling error and the systematic attenuation produced by correctable artifacts such as error of measurement, dichotomization, imperfect construct validity, or range variation. Sampling error and error of measurement are found in every study and, hence, a full meta-analysis should always correct for both (unless there is no published data on the reliability of the measures used). Some domains are not subject to significant amounts of range variation across studies, but in areas with high degrees of subject selection, such as personnel selection research, the effects of range restriction can be as large as the effects of error of measurement. The attenuation produced by dichotomization is even larger than than the effects produced by error of measurement in most domains. Failure to correct for these artifacts results in massive underestimation of the mean correlation. Failure to control for variation in these artifacts may mean a large overstatement of the residual variance and, thus, a potential false assertion of moderator variables where there are none.

All meta-analyses can be corrected for sampling error. We need only know the sample size N_i for each sample correlation r_i. This has come to be called "bare bones" meta-analysis. However, in this analysis the correlations analyzed are the correlations between imperfectly measured variables (which are therefore systematically lowered by error of measurement); the correlations are computed on observed rather than reference populations (so that these correlations are not corrected for range variation); the correlations may be greatly attenuated by dichotomization; and the correlations may be much smaller than they would have been had the construct validity in each study been perfect. Thus, the mean correlation of a "bare bones" meta-analysis is a biased estimate of the desired mean correlation, i.e., the correlation from a study conducted without the imperfections that stem from limited scientific resources. Furthermore, although the variance in a "bare bones" meta-analysis is corrected for sampling error, it is still biased upward because it contains variance due to differences in reliability, differences in range (if any), differences in extremity of split in dichotomization (if any), and differences in construct validity. Moreover, there may be further artifacts that have not yet been studied, and there may be bad data. Thus, the "bare bones" variance is a potentially very poor estimate of the real variance.

If, for any artifact, the needed artifact information is available on each study, then each correlation can be separately corrected for that artifact. The corrected correlations can then be analyzed by meta-analysis to eliminate sampling error. This chapter presented detailed procedures for this form of meta-analysis: meta-analysis of correlations corrected individually for the effects of artifacts. In most sets of studies to be subjected to meta-analysis, such complete artifact information will not be available. But such study sets do occur. In two cases to date where this information has been available (Dye, 1982; Rothstein, Schmidt, Erwin, Owens, & Sparks, in press), this form of meta-analysis has found virtually all between-study variance in correlations to be due to artifacts. But, if the fully corrected variance of correlations across studies is far enough above zero to suggest that there is a moderator variable, then appropriate candidate variables can be checked by analyzing subsets of studies. That is, a separate meta-analysis is conducted within each subset of studies. Alternatively, study characteristics that are potential moderators can be coded and correlated with study correlations. This chapter described methods for both these approaches to moderator analysis.

In many sets of studies, information on particular artifacts is available in some studies, but not in others. Because some (often much) artifact information is missing, it is not possible to fully correct each study correlation for the attenuating effects of every artifact. Nevertheless, it is possible to conduct accurate meta-analyses that correct the final meta-analytic results for all artifacts. This is accomplished using distributions of artifact effects compiled from studies that do provide information on that artifact. These methods of meta-analysis are the subject of the next chapter.

4   Meta-Analysis of Correlations Using Artifact Distributions

The preceding chapter assumed that the correlation in each individual study could be corrected for artifacts. However, it is rare that every study in meta-analysis provides all the information required to correct for attenuation on all the study artifacts that impact on that study. In any given meta-analysis there may be several artifacts for which artifact information is only sporadically available. Indeed, this may be the case for all artifacts. For example, suppose measurement error and range restriction are the only relevant artifacts beyond sampling error. In such a case, the typical meta-analysis is conducted in three stages. First, the studies are used to compile information on four distributions: the distribution of the observed correlations, the distribution of the reliability of the independent variable, the distribution of the reliability of the dependent variable, and the distribution of range departure. That is, there are then four means and four variances compiled from the set of studies, using each study to provide whatever information it has. Second, the distribution of correlations is corrected for sampling error. Third, the distribution corrected for sampling error is then corrected for error of measurement and range variation. This fully corrected distribution is the final result of the meta-analysis (unless the data are analyzed by subsets to test for moderator variables). Thus, the broad conceptual outline of meta-analysis based on artifact distributions is very simple. However, there are numerous statistical considerations involved in the third step here. These are examined in this chapter.

In the first section of this chapter, we consider the case in which information on all artifacts (except sampling error) is only sporadically available in the studies. That is, except for sample size, there is no artifact on which information is given in every study. Thus, for every artifact except sampling error, correction is accomplished by use of a distribution of artifact values that is compiled across the studies that do provide information on that artifact. In fact, information on some artifacts may be drawn from studies that do not present any study correlations. For example, the reliabilities of scales measuring the independent and dependent

158

variables (e.g., widely used scales for job satisfaction or work commitment) may be obtained from such studies.

In the second section of this chapter, we consider the mixed case. In the mixed case, every study presents information on one or more artifacts, while information on other artifacts is missing from many but not all of the studies. For example, all studies may present information on reliability of the independent variable and on dichotomization of the dependent variable, but only sporadic information on other artifacts. In this case, correlations are first corrected individually for the artifacts for which there is complete information. Next, meta-analysis is performed on these partially corrected correlations. Finally, the results of that interim meta-analysis are corrected using artifact distributions. This step yields the final meta-analysis results (unless there is subsequent search for moderators).

Full Artifact Distribution Meta-Analysis

In full artifact distribution meta-analysis, there is no artifact other than sampling error for which information is given in all studies. In this form of meta-analysis, the initial or interim meta-analysis is a meta-analysis of the uncorrected (observed) study correlations. The questions are these: How can the mean and standard deviation of uncorrected correlations be corrected for the impact of artifacts? How do we restore the mean observed correlation to the value that it would have had had the studies been conducted without design imperfections? How do we subtract the variance in study correlations produced by variation in artifact values across studies? The answer lies in the algebra of the correctable artifacts. Since most correctable artifacts can be quantified in the form of a multiplicative factor, certain average products can be computed as the product of averages. This enables us to correct the means and variances of the interim meta-analysis even though we cannot correct the individual values that go into that analysis.

The algebraic formulas used in this meta-analysis make certain assumptions, namely that artifact parameters are (1) independent of the actual correlation and (2) independent of each other. Examination of the substantive nature of artifacts suggests that the independence assumptions are reasonable; most artifact values are less a matter of scientific choice and more a function of situational and resource constraints. The constraints for different artifacts usually have little to do with each other. (See Pearlman et al., 1980, and Schmidt, et al., 1980, for a discussion of the reasons why artifacts will usually be independently distributed.) However, it should be noted that this reasoning justifies the assumptions of independence for the study universe and not necessarily for the studies in hand. For the studies in hand, independence would only be satisfied to within second-order sampling error. That is, the independence assumptions will become more valid as the number of studies increases. By chance, there could be meta-analyses with a small number of studies for which the independence assumptions are violated to a sizable degree. However, in meta-analyses on a small number of studies, the problem of sampling error is usually more serious (see Chapter 9).

Suppose there is sporadic information on some artifact, say the reliability of the independent variable. Some studies report the reliability while other studies do not. Indeed, as we noted above, we may obtain reliability estimates for some scales by looking at studies that never used the dependent variable studied in the meta-analysis, i.e., studies outside the original research domain for the meta-analysis. Data on the construct validity of the independent variable is likely to come predominantly from studies outside the research domain for the meta-analysis. For the studies available, we can use the artifact information (e.g., the reliability of our independent variable as reported in that study) to compute the attenuation factor for that artifact (the square root of the reported reliability). These attenuation factor values can then be compiled across studies to generate a distribution for that artifact.

Consider then the nature of the meta-analysis to be done. We have the study values to do a meta-analysis of uncorrected correlations. For each of several correctable artifacts, we have a mean and standard deviation of the artifact attenuation factor. These artifact distribution values are then used to correct the initial meta-analysis for the effects of those artifacts. The fact that we can combine analyses of the artifacts done separately into an analysis of how they operate jointly stems from the independence assumption and the fact that compound attenuation factor is simply the product of the separate attenuation factors.

The Mean Correlation

For a meta-analysis of uncorrected correlations, we write the fundamental equation for sampling error as

$$r_{oi} = \rho_{oi} + e_i$$

where r_o and ρ_o are the uncorrected study sample correlation and study population correlation, respectively. The average of the uncorrected study correlations across studies is related to average population correlations and to average sampling error by

$$\text{Ave} \; (r_{oi}) = \text{Ave} \; (\rho_{oi}) + \text{Ave} \; (e_i)$$

for whatever set of weights is used to combine study values. Across a large enough set of studies, the average sampling error will be zero. Thus, for a large meta-analysis, the mean sample correlation is equal to the mean population correlation

$$\text{Ave} \; (r_{oi}) = \text{Ave} \; (\rho_{oi}) .$$

We know that the mean uncorrected correlation will be smaller than the mean of actual effect size correlations because the study correlations have been attenuated by artifacts such as error of measurement. The question is: Just how much has the mean correlation been attenuated? Since the effect of the correctable artifacts is systematic it is reasonable to hope that the answer to this question will be an algebraic equation such that the artifact impact can be reversed algebraically. We will now derive that equation.

While the compound artifact multiplier A_i is not known for most studies, it is a definite number and can thus be entered into our equations as if it were known. The equation for the study population correlation is

$$\rho_{oi} = A_i \rho_i$$

where ρ_i is the actual effect size correlation for that study. When we average study correlations, we have

$$\text{Ave} \; (\rho_{oi}) = \text{Ave} \; (A_i \, \rho_i).$$

That is, the average study correlation is the average of the products of the actual study correlation and the artifact attenuation factor for that study. If the two variables in a product are independent, then the average product is the product of the averages. That is, suppose that two variables X and Y are independent. Then

$$\text{Ave} \; (X_i Y_i) = \text{Ave} \; (X_i) \, \text{Ave} \; (Y_i).$$

If the extent of the artifact impact in a study is independent of the size of the study effect size correlation, then

$$\text{Ave} \; (\rho_{oi}) = \text{Ave} \; (A_i \, \rho_i) = \text{Ave} \; (A_i) \; \text{Ave} \; (\rho_i) .$$

If the average artifact attenuation factor Ave (A_i) were known, then this equation could be algebraically reversed to produce

$$\text{Ave } (\rho_i) = \text{Ave } (\rho_{oi}) / \text{Ave } (A_i) .$$

Note that this equation is exactly analogous to the formula for the correction of an individual correlation

$$\rho_i = \rho_{oi} / A_i .$$

That is, given the independence assumption, we can use the average attenuation factor to correct the average correlation for artifacts.

Thus, we have the answer to the question: How much is the average uncorrected correlation attenuated by artifacts? If the number of studies is large enough to eliminate sampling error, then

$$\text{Ave } (r_{oi}) = \text{Ave } (A_i) \text{ Ave } (\rho_i)$$

and, hence,

$$\text{Ave } (\rho_i) = \text{Ave } (r_{oi}) / \text{Ave } (A_i) .$$

Where the number of studies is not large enough to completely eliminate sampling error, we use the same equation to estimate the mean actual correlation. However, that equation will now be wrong by sampling error. The sampling error in the estimation equation will be exactly determined by the average sampling error. The sampling error in our estimation formula is

$$\text{Error} = \text{Ave } (e_i) / \text{Ave } (A_i).$$

Estimation of the size of that sampling error is beyond the scope of this book (see Hunter & Schmidt, 1987a).

The Average Attenuation Factor

If artifact information is sporadic, it is possible that the compound attenuation factor would not be known for any study. How then do we estimate the average across studies? The key lies in the independence of the artifacts. The causes of extreme values in one artifact are different from the causes of extreme values in another. Thus, any one attenuation factor is independent of any other. It is this fact that enables us to compute the average compound attenuation factor from the average of the component attenuation factors considered separately.

When each study correlation is corrected individually, the compound artifact attenuation factor is the product of the component artifact attenuation factors. That is, if we write the separate single artifact attenuation factors as a, b, c, $\ldots$; then the compound attenuation factor A is given by the product

$$A = a\,b\,c\,\ldots$$

Since the artifacts are independent, the average compound attenuation factor is the product of the averages of the component attenuation factors

$$E(A) = E(a)\,E(b)\,E(c)\ldots$$

Artifact information is given for one artifact at a time. Thus, we usually collect information on artifact values a and b and c and so on separately. The mean of each artifact is denoted $E(a)$ or $E(b)$ or $E(c)$, and so on, where the average is computed across the studies where the information is present. The mean of the compound attenuation factor is the product of the averages for the separate attenuation factors

$$E(A) = E(a)\,E(b)\,E(c)\ldots$$

The Final Correction

This is the last step needed to compute the mean effect size correlation. We compute the mean compound attenuation factor as the product of the separate mean attenuation factors for the individual artifacts. Then we divide the mean uncorrected correlation by that mean compound attenuation factor. That is, our estimate of the average unattenuated study effect correlation is

$$\text{Ave}(\rho) = \text{Ave}(r) / E(A).$$

The Standard Deviation of Correlations

The meta-analysis of uncorrected correlations provides an estimate of the variance of study population correlations. However, these study population correlations are themselves uncorrected. They have been attenuated by the study artifacts and are thus systematically reduced in magnitude. Furthermore, the variation in artifact extremity across studies causes the study correlations to be attenuated by different amounts in different studies. This produces variation in the size of the study correlations that could be mistaken for variation due to a real moderator variable. Thus, the variance of population study correlations computed from a meta-analysis of uncorrected correlations is erroneous for two different reasons. It is smaller than it should be because of the systematic reduction in the magnitude of the study correlations, and it is larger than it should be because of variation in artifact extremity across studies. Both problems must be solved to estimate the standard deviation of true correlations across studies.

Let us begin with notation. An actual study correlation free of study artifacts is denoted ρ_i and the compound artifact attenuation factor for that study is denoted A_i. The attenuated study correlation ρ_{oi} is computed from the actual study correlation by

$$\rho_{oi} = A_i \, \rho_i \, .$$

The study sample correlation r_{oi} departs from the study population correlation ρ_{oi} by sampling error e_i defined by

$$r_{oi} = \rho_{oi} + e_i = A_i \, \rho_i + e_i \, .$$

Consider now a meta-analysis on the uncorrected correlations from all the studies in the meta-analysis. We know that the variance of sample correlations is the variance of population correlations added to the sampling error variance. That is,

$$\text{Var} \, (r_o) = \text{Var} \, (\rho_o) + \text{Var} \, (e).$$

Since the sampling error variance can be computed by statistical formula, we can subtract it to yield

$$\text{Var} \, (\rho_o) = \text{Var} \, (r_o) - \text{Var} \, (e).$$

That is, the meta-analysis of uncorrected correlations produces an estimate of the variance of attenuated study population correlations — the actual study correlations after they have been reduced in magnitude by the study imperfections.

At the end of a meta-analysis of uncorrected correlations, we have the variance of attenuated study population correlations $\text{Var} \, (\rho_o)$, but we want the variance of actual unattenuated correlations Var (ρ). The relationship between these is

$$\text{Var}(\rho_o) = \text{Var}(A_i \rho_i).$$

That is, Var (ρ_o) is the variance of a variable that is the product of two other variables. We know that the A_i and ρ_i variables are independent. We can use this fact to compute the variance of the product. We will derive the formula for the variance of a product later, but for the moment let us use the final result. Let us denote the average actual study correlation by $\bar{\rho}$ and denote the average compound attenuation factor by $\bar{A}$. Then, to a close approximation

$$\text{Var}(A_i \rho_i) = \bar{A}^2 \text{Var}(\rho_i) + \bar{\rho}^2 \text{Var}(A_i).$$

We can then rearrange this equation algebraically to obtain the desired equation for the variance of actual study correlations free of artifact.

$$\text{Var}(\rho_i) = [\text{Var}(A_i \rho_i) - \bar{\rho}^2 \text{Var}(A_i)] / \bar{A}^2.$$

That is, starting from the meta-analysis of uncorrected correlations, we have

$$\text{Var}(\rho) = [\text{Var}(\rho_o) - \bar{\rho}^2 \text{Var}(A_i)] / \bar{A}^2.$$

The right-hand side of this equation has four numbers:

1. Var (ρ_o): the population correlation variance from the meta-analysis of uncorrected correlations
2. $\bar{\rho}$: the mean of unattenuated or actual study population correlations whose estimate was derived in the preceding section
3. $\bar{A}$: the mean compound attenuation factor that was estimated as part of the process of estimating the mean unattenuated correlation ρ
4. Var (A_i): the variance of the compound attenuation factor; this has not yet been estimated.

How do we compute the variance of the compound attenuation factor A? We are given the distribution of each component attenuation factor. These must be combined to produce the variance of the compound attenuation factor. The key to this computation lies in two facts: (1) the compound attenuation factor is the product of the component attenuation factors and (2) the attenuation factors are independent. That is, since the compound attenuation factor A_i for any single study is

$$A_i = a_i \, b_i \, c_i \ldots$$

the variance of the A_i across studies is the variance of a product variable across studies

$$\text{Var} \, (A_i) = \text{Var} \, (a_i \, b_i \, c_i \ldots).$$

We can also express this without the subscripts

$$\text{Var} \, (A) = \text{Var} \, (a \ b \ c \ldots).$$

The variance of the compound attenuation factor is the variance of the product of independent component attenuation factors. We will derive the formula for the variance of the product later. Here let us simply use the result.

   For each separate artifact we have a mean and a standard deviation for that component attenuation factor. From the mean and the standard deviation, we can compute the "coefficient of variation," which is the standard deviation divided by the mean

$$\text{CV} = \text{SD} \, / \, \text{Mean}.$$

   For each artifact, we now compute the *squared* coefficient of variation. For the first artifact attenuation factor a, we compute

$$v_1 = \text{Var} \, (a) \, / \, [\, \text{Ave} \, (a) \,]^2.$$

For the second artifact attenuation factor b, we compute

$$v_2 = \text{Var} \, (b) \, / \, [\, \text{Ave} \, (b) \,]^2.$$

For the third artifact attenuation factor c, we compute

$$v_3 = \text{Var} \, (c) \, / \, [\, \text{Ave} \, (c) \,]^2$$

and so on. Thus, we compute a squared coefficient of variation for each artifact. These are then summed to form a total

$$V = v_1 + v_2 + v_3 + \dots$$

Recalling that $\overline{A}$ denotes the mean compound attenuation factor, we write the formula for the variance of the compound attenuation factor (to a close approximation) as the product

$$\text{Var}(A) = \overline{A}^2 V.$$

We now have all the elements to compute the variance in actual study correlations $\text{Var}(\rho)$. The final formula is

$$\text{Var}(\rho) = [\text{Var}(\rho_o) - \overline{\rho}^2 \text{Var}(A_i)] / \overline{A}^2$$

$$\text{Var}(\rho) = [\text{Var}(\rho_o) - \overline{\rho}^2 \overline{A}^2 V] / \overline{A}^2.$$

Decomposition of Variance

Buried in the derivation above is a decomposition of the variance of uncorrected correlations. Let us pull that decomposition together here.

$$\text{Var}(r) = \text{Var}(\rho_o) + \text{Var}(e)$$

$$\text{Var}(\rho_o) = \text{Var}(A \rho) = \overline{A}^2 \text{Var}(\rho) + \overline{\rho}^2 \text{Var}(A)$$

$$\text{Var}(A) = \overline{A}^2 V$$

That is,

$$\text{Var}(r) = \overline{A}^2 \text{Var}(\rho) + \overline{\rho}^2 \overline{A}^2 V + \text{Var}(e)$$

$$\text{Var}(r) = S_1^2 + S_2^2 + S_3^2$$

where (1) S_1^2 is the variance in uncorrected correlations produced by the variation in actual unattenuated effect size correlations, (2) S_2^2 is the variance in uncorrected correlations produced by the variation in artifacts and (3) S_3^2 is the variance in uncorrected correlations produced by sampling error.

In this decomposition, the term S_1^2 contains the estimated variance of effect size correlations. This estimated variance has corrected for those artifacts that were corrected in the meta-analysis. This is usually not all the artifacts that affect the study value. Thus, S_1^2 is an upper bound estimate of the component of variance in uncorrected correlations due to real variation in the strength of the relationship and not due to artifacts of the study design. To the extent that there are uncorrected artifacts, S_1^2 will overestimate the real variation, possibly greatly overestimating that variation.

Schmidt and Hunter (1977) noted this overestimation and recommended that if the term S_1^2 is less than 25% of the total variance, then it is probably true that the remaining variance is also artifactual and is due to uncorrected artifacts. This is the often cited "75% rule." In that article, we were arguing that in any given meta-analysis it is probably the case that the unknown and uncorrected artifacts account for 25% of the variance. Thus, if the real variance estimate is not at least this high, it suggests that there may be no real variance.

The 75% rule has been widely misinterpreted. Some authors have taken this to be a rule for judging whether or not the variance is explained by second order sampling error (see Chapter 9). Consider a meta-analysis in a research domain where the number of studies is small. If the number of studies in the meta-analysis is small, there is sampling error in the observed variance of sample correlations, i.e., second-order sampling error. Thus, by chance the observed value of Var (r) may be larger than would be predicted by the sampling error variance formula. Some authors have falsely assumed that the 75% rule is intended to be a statistical test for such chance fluctuation.

Consider the null hypothesis that there is no real variance in unattenuated correlations; that all of the observed variance is due to variation in artifacts and to sampling error. A chi-square test can be used to test that hypothesis. If there were no real variance in unattenuated correlations, then the observed variance of uncorrected study correlations would equal that due to artifacts and sampling error alone, i.e., terms S_2^2 and S_3^2 in the decomposition above. Denote the predicted variance by $\hat{s}^2$ where

$$\hat{s}^2 = S_2^2 + S_3^2 = \bar{\rho}^2 \bar{A}^2 V + \text{Var}(e).$$

Define the test statistic Q by

$$Q = K \text{ Var}(r) / \hat{s}^2$$

where K is the number of studies. Then under the null hypothesis, Q will have an approximately chi-square distribution with $K-1$ degrees of freedom.

Note, however, that the Schmidt and Hunter (1977) argument still applies. If there are uncorrected artifacts, then the null hypothesis for the meta-analysis will be wrong even if the null hypothesis is true in fact. As long as there are uncorrected artifacts, there will be artifactual variation in study correlations produced by variation in those uncorrected artifacts.

Because there usually will be such uncorrected artifacts, this chi-square test will usually have a Type I bias, i.e., it will tend to be significant even when Var $(\rho) = 0$.

Variance of a Product: Two Variables

This section and the following two sections are mathematical in nature. They demonstrate the derivation of the formulas that were used in the prceeding two sections. Readers uninterested in these derivations may want to skip ahead to the section "An Example: Error of Measurement," page 173. Formulas for the variance of a product were invoked at several points in the preceding development. We now proceed to derive those formulas. First we note an identity for the variance that will be heavily used in these computations. Consider any variable X. The identity for the variance of X is

$$\text{Var } (X) = E \ (X^2) - [E \ (X) \ ]^2.$$

That is, the variance equals the mean of the squares minus the square of the mean. This identity can also be used in the reverse direction

$$E \ (X^2) = [E \ (X) \ ]^2 + \text{Var } (X).$$

Consider first the product of two independent variables a and b. We first compute the mean of the square, after which we subtract the square of the mean. The expected square is

$$E \ [\ (ab)^2 \ ] = E \ [\ a^2 \ b^2 \ ].$$

Since a and b are independent, the squares a^2 and b^2 are independent. Thus, the mean of the product equals the product of the means

$$E \ [\ a^2 \ b^2 \ ] = E \ (a^2) \ E \ (b^2).$$

The reverse identity for variables a and b separately is

$$E \ (a^2) = [E \ (c) \ ]^2 + \text{Var } (a)$$
$$E \ (b^2) = [E \ (b) \ ]^2 + \text{Var } (b).$$

These are then substituted into the expected square of the product

$$E \ [\ a^2 \ b^2 \ ] = \{ \ [E \ (a) \ ]^2 + \text{Var } (a) \} \ \{ \ [E \ (b) \ ]^2 + \text{Var } (b) \} = E \ (a)^2 \ E \ (b)^2 +$$
$$E \ (a)^2 \ \text{Var } (b) + E \ (b)^2 \ \text{Var } (a) + \text{Var } (a) \ \text{Var } (b).$$

The mean of the product is the product of the means

$$E\,(ab) = E\,(a)\,E\,(b)\,.$$

Thus, the square of the mean is

$$[\,E\,(ab)\,]^2 = [\,E\,(a)\,E\,(b)\,]^2 = E\,(a)^2\,E\,(b)^2\,.$$

This is subtracted from the mean square to produce the variance. The variance of the product of two independent variables is thus

$$\text{Var}\,(ab) = E\,(a)^2\,\text{Var}\,(b) + E\,(b)^2\,\text{Var}\,(a) + \text{Var}\,(a)\,\text{Var}\,(b).$$

For our purposes, we will argue that the last term, Var (a) Var (b), is so small that it can be dropped with no visible error. This would leave the formula used to compute Var $(A\,\rho)$.

All the variables considered in this part of the book are fractions. The mean of a fraction variable is a fraction and its variance is a smaller fraction. Thus, we will argue that the product Var (a) Var (b) is so small that it makes no visible contribution to the variance of the product.

As an illustration of this fact, consider the attenuation factor for the reliability of the independent variable. Suppose that the 95% interval for that reliability is

$$.64 < r_{XX} < .81.$$

Then the 95% interval for the square root of the reliability is

$$.80 < \sqrt{r_{XX}} < .90\,.$$

Thus, the mean would be about .85 and the standard deviation about .025, a coefficient of variation of

$$CV = SD\,/\,\text{Mean} = .025\,/\,.85 = .0294.$$

That is, for this attenuation factor, the mean is 34 times larger than the standard deviation. The comparison is even more striking when we square the mean and standard deviation. The squared coefficient of variation is

$$CV^2 = \text{Var}\,/\,\text{Mean}^2 = .025^2\,/\,.85^2 = .000625\,/.7225 = .000865.$$

That is, the squared mean is 1156 times larger than the variance.

Suppose now that a is the attenuation factor for error of measurement in the independent variable and that b is the attenuation factor for error of measurement in the dependent variable. If both have the distribution given in the previous paragraph, then the variance of the product is

$$\text{Var}(ab) = E(a)^2\,\text{Var}(b) \quad + E(b)^2\,\text{Var}(a) \quad + \text{Var}(a)\,\text{Var}(b)$$

$$= (.64)(.0025) \quad + (64)(.0025) \quad + (.0025)(.0025)$$

$$= .0016 \quad\quad + .0016 \quad\quad + .00000625.$$

The last term is less than one two-hundredth of either of the first two terms and would make little difference if dropped. If we drop the product of the variances, the estimated variance of the product is .0032. If the last term is tacked on, the figure for the variance of the product is .00320625. This tiny difference is invisible unless calculations are carried out to 5 digits. This illustrates our argument that virtually no error is incurred in dropping the product of the variances from the formula for the variance of the product.

Variance of the Product: Three Variables

Consider the product of three variables, a, b, and c. If these variables are independent, then the mean of the product is the product of the means, i.e.,

$$E[abc] = E[a]\,E[b]\,E[c].$$

If three variables are independent, then so are their squares. Hence,

$$E[a^2b^2c^2] = E[a^2]\,E[b^2]\,E[c^2].$$

We can now derive a formula for the variance of a triple product if all three variables are independent.

$$\sigma^2_{abc} = E[(abc)^2] - (E[abc])^2$$
$$= E[a^2b^2c^2] - (E[a]\,E[b]\,E[c])^2$$
$$= E[a^2]\,E[b^2]\,E[c^2] - \bar{a}^2\bar{b}^2\bar{c}^2$$
$$= (\bar{a}^2 + \sigma^2_a)(\bar{b}^2 + \sigma^2_b)(\bar{c}^2 + \sigma^2_c) - \bar{a}^2\bar{b}^2\bar{c}^2$$

$$= \bar{a}^2\,\bar{b}^2\,\sigma_c^2 + \bar{a}^2\,\bar{c}^2\,\sigma_b^2 + \bar{b}^2\,\bar{c}^2\,\sigma_a^2$$
$$+ \bar{a}^2\,\sigma_b^2\,\sigma_c^2 + \bar{b}^2\,\sigma_a^2\,\sigma_c^2 + \bar{c}^2\,\sigma_a^2\,\sigma_b^2$$
$$+ \sigma_a^2\,\sigma_b^2\,\sigma_c^2$$

The terms in this variance have been listed in a special order. The first three terms have two means and one variance, the next three terms have one mean and two variances, and the last term is the product of the three variances. The order is important because in our context, the variables a, b, and c are all fractions and have means much larger than variance. Thus the last four terms in our formula are negligible in size and can be dropped.

The resulting formula for the variance of the product is

$$\text{Var}\,(abc) = \bar{a}^2\,\bar{b}^2\,\text{Var}\,(c) + \bar{a}^2\,\bar{c}^2\,\text{Var}\,(b) + \bar{b}^2\,\bar{c}^2\,\text{Var}\,(a).$$

This can be written in a form which shows a pattern of substitution. Consider the product of the squares

$$E\,(abc)^2 = \bar{a}^2\,\bar{b}^2\,\bar{c}^2.$$

If one substitutes a variance for a squared mean for each of the variables in turn, one gets the terms in the variance of the product:

$$\text{Var}\,(abc) = \text{Var}\,(a)\,\bar{b}^2\,\bar{c}^2 + \bar{a}^2\,\text{Var}\,(b)\,\bar{c}^2 + \bar{a}^2\,\bar{b}^2\,\text{Var}\,(c).$$

For example, the term for the b variable substitution can be written

$$\bar{a}^2\,\text{Var}\,(b)\,\bar{c}^2 = [\,\bar{a}^2\,\bar{b}^2\,\bar{c}^2\,]\,[\text{Var}\,(b)\,/\,\bar{b}^2\,]$$
$$= [\,\overline{abc}\,]^2\,[\,\text{Var}\,(b)\,/\,\bar{b}^2\,].$$

The second term $[\text{Var}\,(b)\,/\,\bar{b}^2]$ is the square of the coefficient of variation of factor b. Denote the squared coefficient for b by v_2, and denote the squared coefficients for a and c by v_1 and v_3, respectively. Let A be the triple product, $A = \overline{abc}$. Then we have shown that the variance of the product is given by

$$\text{Var}\,(abc) = A^2\,(v_1 + v_2 + v_3).$$

This is the formula used to derive the variance of the compound attenuation factor.

Variance of a Product: General Case

The preceding derivation extends immediately to any number of factors. For example, the variance of the product of four variables is

$$\text{Var } (abcd) = \text{Var } (a) \, \overline{b}^{\,2} \overline{c}^{\,2} \overline{d}^{\,2} + \overline{a}^{\,2} \text{ Var } (b) \overline{c}^{\,2} \overline{d}^{\,2} + \overline{a}^{\,2} \overline{b}^{\,2}$$

$$\text{Var } (c) \, \overline{d}^{\,2} + \overline{a}^{\,2} \overline{b}^{\,2} \overline{c}^{\,2} \text{ Var } (d).$$

That is, in each term there is the substitution of a variance for a squared mean. If the squared quadruple product $A^2 = [\,\overline{abcd}\,]^2$ is factored out, then each such substitution is represented by the square of the coefficient of variation. Thus,

$$\text{Var } (abcd) = A^2 \, (v_1 + v_2 + v_3 + v_4) = A^2 \, V$$

using the notation

$$V = v_1 + v_2 + v_3 + v_4 \, .$$

Formulas for full artifact distribution meta-analysis were first developed in the specialized area of personnel selection research under the rubric "validity generalization" (Schmidt & Hunter, 1977). However, there is a certain quirk in research in personnel selection; specifically, there are reasons for not correcting for error of measurement in the predictor (independent) variable, as explained later in this chapter. As a result, the formulas from validity generalization must be modified to be useful in the broader general context of research integration in the social and behavior sciences generally. We will develop three sets of formulas here. First, we will consider the most common case: error of measurement in both variables x and y, but no restriction in range. We will then develop a set of formulas for the case in which all three of these artifacts are to be corrected for. Finally, we will present the validity generalization formulas as they are currently used in personnel selection research. Thus, for purposes of clarity of presentation, we exactly reverse the historical order in which the formulas were developed.

An Example: Error of Measurement

Variables in the social sciences are often only poorly measured. Thus, results must be corrected to eliminate error of measurement. Suppose that error of measurement is the only artifact that attenuates the studies in a given area. Or, alas, more realistically, assume that it is the only artifact on which information is available. The attenuation model for this study is

$$\rho_o = ab\,\rho$$

where

$$a = \sqrt{r_{XX}}$$
$$b = \sqrt{r_{YY}}\,.$$

Table 4.1 presents the basic computations for the meta-analysis of a hypothetical set of studies of the correlation between organizational commitment and job satisfaction. Table 4.1a presents the basic findings and the artifact information for eight studies. The studies are listed in three groups. The first pair of studies presents no correlational data pertaining to organizational commitment or job satisfaction, but these studies do contain reliability data on organizational commitment. The first is the classic study in which Ermine presented his measure of organizational commitment. The second study is one in which Ferret used "the key items from Ermine" and then correlated commitment with other variables (not including job satisfaction). The second pair of studies contains only reliability information on job satisfaction scales. Finally, the last four studies contain only correlational information (although each study had the item data and hence could have computed reliability coefficients for that study). In Table 4.1a we see that two of the correlations were significant while two were not.

Table 4.1b presents the meta-analysis worksheet. The column for a presents the attenuation factor for the first correctable artifact, i.e., the square root of the reliability of the independent variable. The column for b presents the attenuation factor for the second correctable artifact, i.e., the square root of the reliability of the dependent variable. At the bottom of the table, the mean and standard deviation of each entry is given.

Consider first the meta-analysis of the uncorrected correlations.

$$\bar{\rho}_{xy} = \bar{r} = .18$$
$$\sigma_r^2 = .014650$$
$$\sigma_e^2 = \frac{4\,(1-.18^2)^2}{4\,(67)} = .013974$$
$$\sigma_{\rho_{xy}}^2 = \sigma_r^2 - \sigma_e^2 = .014650 - .013974 = .000676$$
$$\sigma_{\rho_{xy}} = .026\,.$$

Table 4.1 Organizational Commitment and Job Satisfaction

Table 4.1a The Basic Artifact Information— Hypothetical Results

	Organizational Commitment Reliability (r_{xx})	Job Satisfaction Reliability (r_{yy})	Sample Size (N_i)	Sample Correlation (r_{xy})
Ermine (1976)	.70			
Ferret (1977)	.50			
Mink (1976)		.70		
Otter (1977)		.50		
Polecat (1978)			68	.01
Stoat (1979)			68	.14
Weasel (1980)			68	.23*
Wolverine (1978)			68	.34**

*Significant at the .05 level.
**Significant at the .01 level.

Table 4.1b The Meta-Analysis Worksheet

Study	a	b	N	r_0
1	.84			
2	.71			
3		.84		
4		.71		
5			68	.01
6			68	.14
7			68	.23
8			68	.34
Ave	.775	.775	68	.18C
SD	.065	.065	0	.121

This analysis of sampling error shows that there is little variation in the correlations across studies. The 95% credibility interval is $.13 \leq \rho_{xy} \leq .23$. Thus, the two studies that fail to find statistical significance make Type II errors.

To correct for the artifacts, we first compute the mean compound artifact attenuation factor

$$\overline{A} = \text{Ave}\,(a)\,\text{Ave}\,(b) = (.775)\,(.775) = .600625.$$

From this we compute the mean actual study correlation, i.e., the study correlation restored to its preattenuated value.

$$\rho = \text{Ave}\,(\rho_i) = \text{Ave}\,(r)\,/\,\overline{A} = .18\,/\,.600625 = .2997$$

Next we compute the sum of squared coefficients of variation.

$$V = .065^2\,/\,.775^2 + .065^2\,/\,.775^2 = .014069$$

The variance due to artifact variation is thus

$$S_2^2 = \overline{\rho}^{\,2}\,\overline{A}^{\,2}\,V = (.2997^2)\,(.600625^2)\,(.014069) = .000456.$$

The variance in true correlations is thus

$$\text{Var}\,(\rho) = [\,\text{Var}\,(\rho_o) - \overline{\rho}^{\,2}\,\overline{A}^{\,2}\,V\,]\,/\,\overline{A}^{\,2}$$

$$= [\,.000676 - .000456\,]\,/\,(.600625^2)$$

$$= .000610.$$

The standard deviation of effect size correlations is thus estimated to be the square root of .000610, or SD = .0247. In round numbers, the actual study correlations are estimated to have a mean of .30 and a standard deviation of .025. If the effect size correlations have a normal distribution, then the 95% credibility interval is

$$.25 < \rho < .35.$$

It is important to remember that only two study artifacts were corrected: the error of measurement in the independent and the dependent variable. Thus, the residual variation attributed to the actual correlations contains variation due to uncorrected artifacts such as imperfect construct validity or bad data, and so on. Therefore, the true standard deviation may be less than the .025 nominal estimate.

Let us consider the impact of artifacts in this example. The impact of sampling error on the mean correlation was assumed to be negligible (although that would not really be true with a total sample size of only 272). However, the impact of sampling error on the variance across studies is massive. The variance of the sample correlation is .01465, of which sampling error is .013974, variance due to variation of reliability is .000456, and "else" is .000220. That is, 95% of the variance in correlations across studies is due to sampling error, 3% is due variation in reliability, and 1.5% is due to unspecified other determinants.

On the other hand, the impact of error of measurement is largely on the mean correlation. The error of measurement caused the mean correlation to be depressed from .30 to .18.

An Example: Unreliability and Range Restriction

Suppose we have artifact information on three artifacts: error of measurement in the independent variable, error of measurement in the dependent variable, and range restriction on the independent variable. The three attenuation artifacts are

$$a = \sqrt{r_{XX}}$$
$$b = \sqrt{r_{YY}}$$
$$c = [\,(1 - u^2)\,\bar{r}^{\,2} + u^2\,]^{\frac{1}{2}} \ (\text{Callender \& Osburn}, 1980)$$

where $\bar{r}$ is the average observed correlation. The attenuation formula is

$$\rho_o = a\,b\,c\,\rho.$$

Table 4.2 presents both the artifact information in raw form and the computed attenuation factors for each artifact for 16 hypothetical studies. The example in Table 4.2 was created by assuming that the population correlation between true scores on the two variables in the reference population is always $\rho = .60$. The first five columns of Table 4.2 are the data extracted from the 16 hypothetical studies. The last three columns are the values of a, b, and c, computed from the values of r_{xx}, r_{yy}, and u, respectively.

The four means and variances needed are

$$\bar{r} = .175 \qquad \bar{a} = .75 \qquad \bar{b} = .75 \qquad \bar{c} = .525$$
$$\sigma_r^2 = .015100 \quad \sigma_a^2 = .0025 \quad \sigma_b^2 = .0025 \quad \sigma_c^2 = .009025.$$

Table 4.2 Sixteen Hypothetical Studies

	N	r_{xx}	r_{yy}	u	r_{xy}	a	b	c
(1)	68	.49	—	.40	.02	.70	—	.43
(2)	68	—	.64	—	.26*	—	.80	—
(3)	68	.49	.64	—	.33*	.70	.80	—
(4)	68	—	—	.60	.09	—	—	.62
(5)	68	.49	—	—	.02	.70	—	—
(6)	68	—	.49	.40	.24*	—	.70	.43
(7)	68	.49	.49	—	.30*	.70	.70	—
(8)	68	—	—	.60	.06	—	—	.62
(9)	68	.64	—	.40	.28*	.80	—	.43
(10)	68	—	.64	—	.04	—	.80	—
(11)	68	.64	.64	—	.12	.80	.80	—
(12)	68	—	—	.60	.34*	—	—	.62
(13)	68	.64	—	—	.26*	.80	—	—
(14)	68	—	.49	.40	.02	—	.70	.43
(15)	68	.64	.49	—	.09	.80	.70	—
(16)	68	—	—	.60	.33*	—	—	.62

*Significant at the .05 level (two-tailed test).

We first use the mean and variance of the observed correlations to correct for sampling error.

$$\bar{\rho}_{xy} = \bar{r} = .175$$

$$\sigma^2_{\rho_{xy}} = \sigma^2_r - \sigma^2_e = .015100 - .013819 = .001281$$

These values can then be corrected to eliminate the effects of error of measurement and range variation. First, we compute the mean compound attenuation factor A.

$$\bar{A} = (.75)\,(.75)\,(.525) = .2953$$

This can be used to correct the mean uncorrected correlation.

$$\text{Ave}\,(\rho_i) = .175 / .2953 = .5926$$

We then compute the sum of the squared coefficients of variation.

$$V = [.05 / .75]^2 + [.05 / .75]^2 + [.095 / .525]^2 = .041633$$

The variance due to variation in artifacts is

$$S_2^2 = \bar{\rho}^2 \bar{A}^2 \, V = (.5926^2)\,(.2953^2)\,(.041633) = .001275.$$

The residual variance in the uncorrected population correlations is thus

$$S_{res}^2 = \text{Var}\,(\rho_o) - S_2^2 = .001281 - .001275 = .000006.$$

The estimated variance of true correlations is thus

$$\text{Var}\,(\rho = S_{res}^2 \,/A^2 = .000006 \,/ .2953^2 = .000069.$$

The estimated standard deviation is thus .008. Since this example was constructed assuming no real variation, the standard deviation should be near zero, and it is. Thus, the final meta-analysis results are $\bar{\rho} = .59$ and $SD_\rho = .008$. These results are almost identical to the true values (the values used to generate the data): $\bar{\rho} = .60$ and $SD_\rho = 0$. The slight difference indicates the extent to which artifact distribution meta-analysis is an approximation rather than an exact calculation.

An Example: Personnel Selection with Fixed Test

Personnel selection is a special case because in the practical application, the predictor test is used in imperfect form. Thus, the relevant population correlation for purposes of assessing the practical impact of the test is corrected for error of measurement in the dependent variable but not in the independent variable. The validity of the test is given by the applicant population correlation between uncorrected test scores and job performance true scores. This means we should correct for measurement error in the job performance measure and correct for restriction in range, but not correct for error of measurement in the test. (Of course in the *theory* of personnel selection, we would want fully corrected correlations.)

Personnel selection research is vexed by all the artifacts shown in Table 3.1 in the previous chapter In particular, restriction in range on the independent variable is created by selective hiring. Suppose all studies in a meta-analysis use exactly the same test so there is no variation across studies in the reliability of the independent variable.

Suppose that error of measurement in the dependent variable (job performance) and range restriction are the only other artifacts for which artifact information is available. The attenuation factors would then be

$$a = \sqrt{r_{YY}}$$

$$b = [\,(1 - u^2)\,\bar{r}^{\,2} + u^2\,]^{\frac{1}{2}}$$

where $\bar{r}$ is the average uncorrected correlation across studies. The attenuation formula is

$$\rho_o = a\,b\,\rho\,.$$

Table 4.3 presents hypothetical data for 12 personnel selection studies of this type. These are the same data presented in Table 3.5 in the previous chapter. In that chapter, we meta-analyzed these data, correcting each correlation individually. Here we will analyze the same data, treating the artifact information as distributions since complete artifact information is given in Table 4.3 for each observed correlation, the artifact distribution method ordinarily wouldn't be used; instead each correlation would be corrected individually, as was done in Chapter 3. But we present the artifact distribution analysis here because the results can be directly compared to those obtained in Chapter 3 with the same data. The last two columns of Table 4.3 show the attenuation factors. The necessary means and variances are shown below.

$$\bar{a} = .8345 \qquad \bar{b} = .6763 \qquad \bar{r} = .28$$

$$\sigma_a^2 = .00354 \qquad \sigma_b^2 = .01849 \qquad \sigma_r^2 = .01703$$

$$\sigma_e^2 = .01249$$

$$\sigma_{\rho_o}^2 = .00454$$

The compound attenuation factor is

$$\bar{A} = (.8345)\,(.6763) = .5644.$$

Thus, the mean actual correlation is

$$\text{Ave}\,(\rho_i) = .28\,/\,.5644 = .496.$$

The sum of squared coefficients of variation is

$$V = [.00354\,/\,.8345^2] + [.01849\,/\,.6763^2] = .045509.$$

Table 4.3 Cumulative Analysis of Personnel Selection Validities

Study	Selection Ratio	u	Criterion Reliability	Sample Size	Observed Correlation	a	b
(1)	.20	.468	.80	68	.35**	.894	.529
(2)	.20	.468	.60	68	.07	.775	.529
(3)	.20	.468	.80	68	.11	.894	.529
(4)	.20	.468	.60	68	.31*	.775	.529
(5)	.50	.603	.80	68	.18	.894	.643
(6)	.50	.603	.60	68	.36**	.775	.643
(7)	.50	.603	.80	68	.40**	.894	.643
(8)	.50	.603	.60	68	.13	.775	.643
(9)	.90	.844	.80	68	.49**	.894	.857
(10)	.90	.844	.60	68	.23	.775	.857
(11)	.90	.844	.80	68	.29*	.894	.857
(12)	.90	.844	.60	68	.44*	.775	.857

*p < .05 (two-tailed)
**p < .01 (two-tailed)

The variance in the uncorrected correlations caused by variation in artifacts is

$$S_2^2 = .496^2 \, .5644^2 \, (.045509) = .003566.$$

The residual variance in uncorrected correlations is

$$S_{res}^2 = .00454 - .003566 = .000974.$$

The variance of actual study correlations is thus

$$\text{Var}(\rho) = S_{res}^2 / \overline{A}^2 = .000974 / .5644^2 = .003056.$$

Hence, the standard deviation is estimated to be .055.

The final estimates are thus $\overline{\rho} = .50$ and $SD_\rho = .05$. The mean value of .50 is exactly correct and the SD_ρ estimate is not much different from the correct value of zero. These estimates can be compared with those obtained in Table 3.5 in the last chapter, when for the same data each correlation was corrected individually. Those values were $\overline{\rho} = .50$ and $SD_\rho = .02$. Thus both methods yield the correct value for the mean (.50). Both methods overestimate SD_ρ, with the individual correction being the more accurate. However, the SD_ρ estimates of .02 and .05 relative to a mean of .50 both represent a small variation and would not lead to any difference in practice within personnel selection.

An Example: Personnel Selection with Varying Tests

The test used for prediction is usually only specified in terms of the construct to be measured; for example, arithmetic reasoning. There are many arithmetic reasoning tests available that are equivalent in general content but different in reliability. This variation in reliability contributes to the variation in correlations across studies if the review covers all studies using a given predictor rather than a fixed test.

There have been two responses to this in the literature. In our earliest work, we ignored the variation in the reliability of the predictor (as did Callender and Osburn, 1980). Later, we used a hybrid solution. We corrected the variance across studies for all artifacts, but we corrected the mean only for restriction in range and for error of measurement in job performance. That is, we did not correct the mean for the attenuating effect of error of measurement in the predictor variable. This gives the parameters for a distribution of validities in which the reliability of the predictor is always fixed at the average value for the study population. If the results are to be applied in a context in which the actual test used has a reliability equal to the average reliability, then our results could be used as such. However, if the results are to be used in a context in which the reliability is different from the average, then the user would modify our numbers. The mean validity and the standard deviation must first be corrected for attenuation using the square root of the mean test reliability. Then the resulting true score validity and true score standard deviation must be attenuated using the square root of the reliability of the actual test to be used (Schmidt, Gast-Rosenberg & Hunter, 1980).

There is a more straightforward procedure. Simply compute the fully corrected mean and standard deviation in the first place (including correction for error of measurement in the independent variable and including any other artifacts that information is available for). The procedures presented in this chapter do that as a matter of course. Then report two means and two standard deviations: (1) the fully corrected mean and the standard deviation and (2) a mean and standard deviation attenuated to the level of the mean reliability of the predictor variable.

Personnel Selection: Findings and Formulas in the Literature

The major application of artifact distribution meta-analysis to date has been the examination of the validity of tests and other methods used in personnel selection. Meta-analysis has been used to test the hypothesis of "situation specific validity." In personnel selection it had long been believed that validity was specific to situations; that is, it was believed that the validity of the same test for what appeared to be the same job varied from employer to employer, region to region, across time periods, and so forth. In fact, it was believed that the same test could have high validity (i.e., a high correlation with job performance) in one location or organization and be completely invalid (i.e., have zero validity) in another. This belief was based on the observation that obtained validity coefficients for similar tests and jobs varied substantially across different studies. This variability was explained by postulating that jobs that appeared to be the same actually differed in important ways in what was required to perform them. This belief led to a requirement for local or situational validity studies. It was held that validity had to be estimated separately for each situation by a study conducted in the setting; that is, validity findings could not be generalized across settings, situations, employers, and the like. (Schmidt & Hunter, 1981). In the late seventies, meta-analysis of validity coefficients began to be conducted to test whether validity might not in fact be generalizable (Schmidt & Hunter, 1977; Schmidt, Hunter, Pearlman, & Shane, 1979), and, thus, these meta-analyses were called "validity generalization" studies. If all or most of the study to study variability in observed validities was due to artifacts of the kind discussed in this book, then the traditional belief in situational specificity of validity would be seen to be erroneous, and the conclusion would be that validity findings did generalize.

To date, artifact distribution meta-analysis has been applied to over 500 research literatures in employment selection, each one representing a predictor-job performance combination. These predictors have included nontest procedures, such as evaluations of education and experience and interviews, as well as ability and aptitude tests. In many cases, artifacts accounted for all variance across studies; the average amount of variance accounted for by artifacts has been 80% to 90%. As an example, consider the relation between quantitative ability and overall job performance in clerical jobs (Pearlman et al., 1980). This substudy was based on 453 correlations computed on a total of 39,584 people. Seventy-seven percent of the variance of the observed validities was traceable to artifacts, leaving a negligible variance of .019. The mean validity was .47. Thus, integration of this massive amount of data leads to the general and generalizable principle that the correlation between quantitative ability and clerical performance is .47, with very little (if any) true variation around this value. Like other similar findings, this finding shows that the old belief that validities are situationally specific is false (Schmidt & Hunter, 1981).

Today many organizations — including the federal government, the U.S. Employment Service, and some large corporations — use validity generalization findings as the basis of their selection-testing programs. Validity generalization has been included in standard texts (e.g., Anastasi, 1986) and in the *Standards for Educational and Psychological Tests* (AERA-APA-NCME, 1985). Proposals have been made to include validity generalization in the federal government's Uniform Guidelines on Employee Procedures when this document is next revised. In recent litigation in Canada, the use of validity generalization findings as the basis for the use of a group intelligence test in selecting tax collectors was upheld (Maloley et al. v. Department of National Revenue, 1986). A recent report by the National Academy of Sciences (Hartigan & Wigdor, 1989) devotes an entire chapter (Chapter 6) to validity generalization and endorses its methods and assumptions.

In some validity generalization studies (e.g., Hirsh, Northrop & Schmidt, 1986; Schmidt, Hunter, & Caplan, 1981a, 1981b), the artifact values used in the artifact distributions were taken directly from the studies that contributed validities to the meta-analysis; that is, the procedure described earlier in this chapter was used. In other studies, however, the information on artifacts from the studies analyzed was too sparse. In those studies, artifact distributions were used that were estimated based on familiarity with the personnel selection literature in general. For example, a distribution of u values ($u = s/S$) was constructed that was believed to be typical of this research literature as a whole. Later, when it was possible to compare some of these artifact distributions to empirically cumulated distributions from bodies of research studies, the constructed artifact distributions were found to fairly closely match the empirical distributions (Schmidt, Hunter, Pearlman, & Hirsh, 1985, Q&A No. 26; Alexander, Carson, Alliger, & Cronshaw, 1989).

The artifact distribution methods presented in this book go beyond those used in validity generalization studies in adding new correctable artifacts. The artifacts corrected for in validity generalization meta-analysis have typically been limited to measurement error in both variables and range restriction (although some studies have used outlier analysis to partially correct for bad data). The formulas used in the validity generalization literature to compute $\bar{\rho}$ are basically the same as those presented earlier in this chapter. (The one difference that exists was discussed in the preceding section.) However, the formulas used to estimate the variance of the corrected validities contain somewhat different terms, resulting from the fact that each was derived using a slightly different set of assumptions. This is not to imply that any of the formulas are more (or less) "correct" than any of the others. The different formulas for the estimation of the same parameter (S_ρ^2) are all correct relative to their derivational assumptions (Schmidt, Hunter, & Pearlman, 1981). (This is the same situation that holds in the case of the various formulas derived to estimate the shrinkage of multiple correlations; each is correctly derived, given the assumptions of the derivation [Cattin, 1980].) Nor does it necessarily imply that any one formula is more accurate than another; as it turns out, computer simulation studies have shown that all are quite accurate (Callender & Osburn, 1980; Raju & Burke, 1983).

The first formula in the literature was our noninteractive formula (Pearlman et al., 1980; Schmidt, Hunter, Pearlman, & Shane, 1979; Schmidt, Gast-Rosenberg & Hunter, 1980)

$$\sigma_{\rho_{xU}}^2 = \frac{(\sigma_r^2 - \sigma_e^2) - \bar{\rho}_{TU}^2 (\sigma_a^2 + \bar{a}^2 \sigma_b^2 + \bar{a}^2 \bar{b}^2 \sigma_c^2)}{\bar{a}^2 \bar{c}^2}$$

where

ρ_{TU} = the fully corrected (true score) correlation between the two variables;

a = $(r_{yy})^{\frac{1}{2}}$;

b = $(r_{xx})^{\frac{1}{2}}$;

c = $[(1 - u^2)\bar{r}^2 + u^2]^{\frac{1}{2}}$; and

$\sigma_{\rho_{xU}}^2$ = the variance of validities corrected for range restriction, and for measurement error in job performance measure (y), but not in the predictor (x).

Other terms are as defined in previous sections. This procedure corrects for variance in validities due to variability in r_{xx}, but not the attenuating effect of mean r_{xx}. The reasons for this were given in the previous section. Further details on this formula and its assumptions are given in Schmidt, Gast-Rosenberg and Hunter (1980). The computer program given in the Appendix for artifact distribution meta-analysis of correlations uses the noninteractive equation for σ_ρ^2. The next formula developed for σ_ρ^2 was our interactive formula. The estimation procedure associated with this formula theoretically has the advantage of taking into account the slight interaction between the effects of measurement error and range restriction, which the noninteractive equation does not. This interaction occurs because the effect of measurement error is greater in studies where there is less range restriction (cf., Schmidt, Gast-Rosenberg & Hunter, 1980; Schmidt, Hunter, & Pearlman, 1981). The formula is

$$\sigma^2_{\rho_{xU}} = \frac{(\sigma^2_r - \sigma^2_e) - \bar{\rho}^2_{TU} \sigma^2_{abc}}{\bar{a}^2 \bar{c}^2}.$$

All terms except σ^2_{abc} are as defined earlier; however, the term σ^2_{abc} is not self-explanatory. The interactive procedure differs from the noninteractive procedure in that variances due to between-study differences in criterion reliability, test reliability, and range restriction are computed simultaneously rather than sequentially. This composite step can be summarized as follows.

1. Compute the sample-size weighted mean of the observed coefficients $(\bar{r})$ and correct this value for range restriction, criterion unreliability, and test unreliability, using mean values of these artifacts. The result is $\bar{\rho}_{TU}$.

2. Create a three-dimensional matrix, the cells of which are all possible combinations of range restriction u values, criterion unreliability, and test unreliability.

3. For each cell, compute the expected value of the observed coefficient for that combination of artifacts, using the fully corrected correlation from Step 1. The fully corrected correlation (ρ_{TU}) will be attenuated to a different value in each cell.

4. Compute the variance of the resulting coefficients across cells, weighting each by its cell frequency. Cell frequency is determined by artifact level frequencies; since range restriction frequencies are assumed to be uncorrelated with (applicant pool) reliabilities, the joint (cell) frequency is the product of the three marginal frequencies. This computed variance is the variance in observed coefficients that would be expected due to criterion and test reliability differences and range restriction differences if the true validity were constant. This variance can be symbolized as the variance of a four-way product: $\sigma^2_{abc\rho_{TU}}$. But since ρ_{TU} is a constant, this becomes $\rho^2_{TU} \sigma^2_{abc}$, which is the term in the equation above.

Callender and Osburn (1980) have also derived an equation for $\sigma^2_{\rho_{xU}}$.

$$\sigma^2_{\rho_{xU}} = \frac{(\sigma^2_r - \sigma^2_e) - \bar{\rho}^2_{xU}(\bar{c}^2 \sigma^2_b + \bar{b}^2 \sigma^2_c + \sigma^2_b \sigma^2_c)}{(\bar{b}^2 + \sigma^2_b)(\bar{c}^2 + \sigma^2_c)}$$

All terms are as defined earlier, except that in this equation $b = (r_{yy})^{1/2}$, instead of $(r_{xx})^{1/2}$. This equation has been used in published validity generalization studies. Finally, Raju and Burke (1983) have derived two equations for $\sigma^2_{\rho_{xt'}}$, both based on Taylor series approximations but starting with slightly different assumptions. The complexity of these equations precludes their reproduction here. To our knowledge, these equations have not been used in empirical meta-analysis.

Computer simulation studies by Callender and Osburn (1980) showed that the noninteractive, interactive, and Callender-Osburn equations are all about equally accurate, and all are more than accurate enough for operational use. Raju and Burke (1983) conducted similar computer simulation studies on these three equations, plus their two new equations. All five equations were quite accurate and all were about equally accurate. In both computer simulation studies, some of the simulated conditions were much more realistic than others. The most realistic conditions were those in which range restriction levels and independent and dependent variable reliabilities all varied simultaneously. All equations, and in particular the noninteractive, were very accurate under these conditions.

Mixed Meta-Analysis: Partial Artifact Information in Individual Studies

Artifacts differ in terms of the information given in studies. The sample size is almost always given so we can correct for sampling error variance. The same is true for dichotomization whenever it occurs. The degree of split for dichotomization is usually given in the research report. For example, a study may state that 70% were in the successful group and 30% were in the unsuccessful group; or that 20% quit their jobs and 80% did not. Thus, it is usually possible to correct individual study correlations for the attenuating effects of dichotomization. Reliability is reported more frequently since meta-analysis has become known, but it is uncommon in older studies and frequently not given even in recent studies. Thus, error of measurement is usually corrected using artifact distributions. The problems are even more serious with the other artifacts, such as range variation, construct validity, attrition artifacts, and extraneous factors. Information is often extremely sporadic. Thus, there are research domains where some correctable artifacts can be corrected for in each individual study while others can be corrected only using artifact distributions. This is the "partial information" case to be treated in this section.

There are three ways to conduct meta-analysis in such an area. First, the easiest way is to ignore the fact that one or more of the artifacts is given for each individual study. One would then use only the distribution of the artifact multipliers and compute the meta-analysis using the methods of the preceding section. Averages across studies would use simple sample size weights $w_i = N_i$. As we saw earlier in the analysis of the data in Table 4.3, this procedure yields approximate results that are quite accurate.

Second, one could improve accuracy by weighing each study in accordance with the known amount of sampling error produced by attenuation due to dichotomization (or any other individually correctable artifact). That is, one could give low weight to the low quality studies and high weight to the high quality studies. For each study, one would compute the attenuation multiplier A_i as if it were to be corrected. Then one would weight each study by

$$w_i = N_i A_i^2 .$$

These weights are used in computing both the mean and variance of study correlations and in computing the artifact mean and variance for the artifacts that contribute to the artifact multiplier A_i. In the case where dichotomization is the only artifact with information given on individual studies, this can be approximated by using a study weight that depends on the split in that study. Let the proportions for the split in study i be given by P_i and $Q_i = 1 - P_i$. Then the approximation weights would be

$$w_i = N_i P_i Q_i .$$

For two studies with sample size 100, a study with a 50-50 split would receive weight

$$w = 100 \ (.50) \ (.50) = 25$$

while a study with a 90-10 split would receive weight

$$w = 100 \ (.90) \ (.10) = \ 9.$$

The ratio $25/9 = 2.78$ differs somewhat from the ratio 1.84 for optimal weights.

Third, the optimal strategy is to do a two-step meta-analysis. In the first step, the individually known artifacts are corrected. In the second step, the sporadically given artifacts are corrected. This method will now be presented.

First, the individually known artifacts are used to do a meta-analysis using individual study correction. This meta-analysis produces a mean correlation corrected for the individually known artifacts and a variance corrected for those artifacts and for sampling error. Denote the partially corrected mean and variance by PR and PV respectively. The methods of artifact distributions can then be used to finish the corrections.

The first step is to correct the mean correlation. This is done by computing the average attenuation factor for the remaining artifacts and using that factor to correct the partially corrected mean correlation from the first meta-analysis. Consider each sporadically available artifact separately. For each artifact, compute the mean and standard deviation of the corresponding attenuation factor. Combine the effects of the separate sporadic artifacts by multiplication; the mean compound attenuation factor is the product of the means of the separate artifacts. If the sporadic artifacts are designated a, b, c . . . ; then the mean of the compound attenuation factor A is given by

$$\text{Ave } (A_i) = \text{Ave } (a_i)\,\text{Ave } (b)\,\text{Ave } (c_i) \ldots$$

Denote the average by $\overline{A}$. The fully corrected mean correlation is then the partially corrected mean correlation PR divided by the compound sporadic artifact attenuation factor A, i.e.

$$\text{Ave } (\rho) = \text{PR} / \overline{A} \quad .$$

Denote the fully corrected mean correlation by $\overline{R}$, i.e., define $\overline{R}$ by

$$\overline{R} = \text{Ave}(\rho = \text{PR} / \overline{A}) \quad .$$

The next step is to correct the partially corrected variance PV for the effects of the sporadic artifacts. First, estimate the variance in the partially corrected correlations due to sporadic artifact variance. Compute the sum of the squared coefficients of variation across the separate sporadic attenuation factors.

$$V = [\text{Var } (a) / \text{Ave } (a)^2] + [\text{Var } (b) / \text{Ave } (b)^2] + \ldots$$

The variance in partially corrected study correlations accounted for by variation in sporadic artifacts is the product

$$S_4^2 = \overline{R}^2 \overline{A}^2 V.$$

The unexplained variance in partially corrected study correlations explained by variation in the sporadic artifacts is

$$S_5^2 = \text{PV} - S_4^2 .$$

Note that some if not all of this residual variance is due to uncontrolled artifacts, such as recording, computational, transcriptional errors and other bad data.

The upper-bound estimate of the variance of actual correlations can then be computed from the residual variance. Since some of the residual variance is due to uncontrolled artifacts, the residual variance is an upper-bound for the unexplained variance in study correlations. This number is the numerator of the estimate of the variance of actual correlations. Since this number is an upper-bound estimate, the ratio is also an upper-bound estimate. The variance of actual correlations should be less than the ratio

$$\text{Var} (\rho) = S_5^2 / \overline{A}^2 .$$

An Example: Dichotomization of Both Variables

Tenure is the length of time that a person stays with an employer. Termination from the firm can be voluntary or involuntary. We will consider only voluntary termination — people who leave the job of their own accord. There are many factors that determine tenure, but one of the main factors is performance. People with low performance are frequently under pressure from supervisors and/or peers for a variety of problems that they cause others. This pressure often leads to quitting. So we consider a hypothetical meta-analysis of the correlation between performance and tenure.

If working conditions are poor, workers may quit for that reason, thus reducing the correlation between tenure and performance. Thus, we postulate that the correlation between performance and tenure will be higher in jobs with good working conditions than in jobs with poor working conditions, and we code the studies for working conditions as a potential moderator variable.

Table 4.4a presents the basic information for 24 hypothetical studies. Information is available on all studies for both the independent and dependent variable as to whether or not the variable was dichotomized. If it was dichotomized, the resulting split is given. On the other hand, reliability information is sporadic for both variables. No information was available on other potential artifacts, such as imperfect construct validity or extraneous factors.

Table 4.4b presents the artifact information recorded as attenuation factors. Note that if a variable is not dichotomized, then the dichotomiza-

Table 4.4 Hypothetical Meta-Analysis of Performance and Turnover

Table 4.4a Basic Study Information

Study Number	Sample Size	Ratings Split	Tenure Split	Ratings Reliability	Tenure Reliability	Sample Correlation
Jobs with good working conditions						
1	50	50-50	90-10	.47	—	.46*
2	50	50-50	90-10	—	.81	.08
3	50	not	90-10	.64	—	.46*
4	50	not	90-10	—	.81	.18
5	50	50-50	50-50	.47	—	.44*
6	50	50-50	50-50	—	.81	.16
7	50	not	50-50	.64	—	.52*
8	50	not	50-50	—	.81	.24
9	50	50-50	rot	.47	—	.51*
10	50	50-50	rot	—	.81	.24
11	50	not	rot	.64	—	.68*
12	50	not	rot	—	.81	.40*
Jobs with poor working conditions						
13	50	50-50	90-10	.47	—	.23
14	50	50-50	90-10	—	.64	−.05
15	50	not	90-10	.64	—	.27
16	50	not	90-10	—	.64	−.01
17	50	50-50	50-50	.47	—	.26
18	50	50-50	50-50	—	.64	−.02
19	50	not	50-50	.64	—	.32*
20	50	not	50-50	—	.64	.04
21	50	50-50	not	.47	—	.29*
22	50	50-50	not	—	.64	.01
23	50	not	not	.64	—	.36*
24	50	not	not	—	.64	.08

tion attenuation factor is 1.00. To multiply by 1 is to leave the correlation unattenuated by that factor.

Table 4.4c presents the worksheet for the first meta-analysis of the studies, a meta-analysis that uses individual study correction for the dichotomization artifact on both independent and dependent variables. The corrected correlations are corrected for dichotomization but not for error of measurement. Thus, they are partially corrected correlations. The mean and variance of the partially corrected correlations are

$$PR = .364$$

$$PV = \text{Var}\,(r) - \text{Ave}\,(ve) = .251823^2 - .031494 = .031921.$$

Table 4.4b Attenuation Factors

Study Number	Sample Size	Ratings Split	Tenure Split	Ratings Reliability	Tenure Reliability	Sample Correlation
Jobs with good working conditions						
1	50	.80	.59	.69	—	.46*
2	50	.80	.59	—	.90	.08
3	50	1.00	.59	.80	—	.46*
4	50	1.00	.59	—	.90	.18
5	50	.80	.80	.69	—	.44*
6	50	.80	.80	—	.90	.16
7	50	1.00	.80	.80	—	.57*
8	50	1.00	.80	—	.90	.29*
9	50	.80	1.00	.69	—	.51*
10	50	.80	1.00	—	.90	.24
11	50	1.00	1.00	.80	—	.68*
12	50	1.00	1.00	—	.90	.40*
Jobs with poor working conditions						
13	50	.80	.59	.69	—	.23
14	50	.80	.59	—	.80	−.05
15	50	1.00	.59	.80	—	.27
16	50	1.00	.59	—	.80	−.01
17	50	.80	.80	.69	—	.26
18	50	.80	.80	—	.80	−.02
19	50	1.00	.80	.80	—	.32*
20	50	1.00	.80	—	.80	.04
21	50	.80	1.00	.69	—	.29*
22	50	.80	1.00	—	.80	.01
23	50	1.00	1.00	.80	—	.36*
24	50	1.00	1.00	—	.80	.08

From Table 4.4b, we compute the mean and variance of each sporadic attenuation factor, i.e., the mean and variance of the attenuation factors for error of measurement of the two variables:

$$\text{Ave } (a) = .745 \qquad \text{Var } (a) = .003025$$
$$\text{Ave } (b) = .850 \qquad \text{Var } (b) = .002500.$$

The mean compound attenuation factor for the sporadic factors is

$$\overline{A} = \text{Ave } (a) \text{ Ave } (b) = (.745) (.850) = .63325.$$

Thus, the fully corrected mean correlation is

$$\overline{R} = \text{Ave } (\rho_i) = \text{PR} / \overline{A} = .364 / .63325 = .5748.$$

Table 4.4c Worksheet for the Interim Meta-Analysis

Study Number	Sample Size	Ratings Split	Tenure Split	Compound Atten.	Uncorr. Correl.	Cor'ted Correl.	Error Variance	Study Weight
		Jobs with good working conditions						
1	50	.80	.59	.472	.46*	.97	.076846	11.1
2	50	.80	.59	.472	.08	.17	.076846	11.1
3	50	1.00	.59	.59	.46*	.78	.049181	17.4
4	50	1.00	.59	.59	.18	.31	.049181	17.4
5	50	.80	.80	.64	.44*	.69	.041797	20.5
6	50	.80	.80	.64	.16	.25	.041797	20.5
7	50	1.00	.80	.80	.57*	.71	.026750	32.0
8	50	1.00	.80	.80	.29*	.36	.026750	32.0
9	50	.80	1.00	.80	.51*	.64	.026750	32.0
10	50	.80	1.00	.80	.24	.30	.026750	32.0
11	50	1.00	1.00	1.00	.68*	.68	.017120	50.0
12	50	1.00	1.00	1.00	.40*	.40	.017120	50.0
Ave					.414	.519	.031494	
SD					.172227	.204412		
		Jobs with poor working conditions						
13	50	.80	.59	.472	.23	.49	.076846	11.1
14	50	.80	.59	.472	−.05	−.11	.076846	11.1
15	50	1.00	.59	.59	.27	.46	.049181	17.4
16	50	1.00	.59	.59	−.01	−.02	.049181	17.4
17	50	.80	.80	.54	.26	.41	.041797	20.5
18	50	.80	.80	.54	−.02	−.03	.041797	20.5
19	50	1.00	.80	.30	.32*	.40	.026750	32.0
20	50	1.00	.80	.30	.04	.05	.026750	32.0
21	50	.80	1.00	.30	.29*	.36	.026750	32.0
22	50	.80	1.00	.80	.01	.01	.026750	32.0
23	50	1.00	1.00	1.00	.36*	.36	.017120	50.0
24	50	1.00	1.00	1.00	.08	.08	.017120	50.0
Ave					.167	.208	.031494	
SD					.146216	.191532		
Overall					.290	.364		
SD					.201923	.251823		

The sum of the squared coefficients of variation for the sporadic artifacts is

$$V = [.003025 / .745^2] + [.002500 / .850^2] = .008910.$$

The residual variance is

$$S_5^2 = PV - \overline{R}^2 \overline{A}^2 V = .031921 - .5748^2 .63325^2 .008910 = .030741.$$

The standard deviation of actual correlations is thus .175. This is a fairly large standard deviation, even in comparison to a mean correlation of .575. This is consistent with the hypothesis of a major moderator variable. Working conditions were hypothesized a priori to be a moderator of the correlation between performance and tenure. To test this hypothesis, we can perform a meta-analysis within each set of studies separately.

Jobs With Good Working Conditions

The meta-analysis of partially corrected correlations is obtained from the averages and standard deviations in the top part of Table 4.4c.

$$PR = \text{Ave } (r) = .519$$

$$PV = \text{Var } (r) - \text{Var } (e) = .204412^2 - .031494 = .010290$$

The mean and standard deviation of each sporadic artifact can be computed from the top part of Table 4.4b.

Ave $(a) = .745$	Var $(a) = .003025$
Ave $(b) = .900$	Var $(b) = 0$

The mean compound attenuation factor for the sporadic artifacts is

$$\overline{A} = \text{Ave } (a) \text{ Ave } (b) = (.745)(.900) = .6705.$$

The fully corrected mean correlation is thus

$$\overline{R} = \text{Ave } (\rho) = PR \ / \ \overline{A} = .519 \ / \ .6705 = .774.$$

The sum of squared coefficients of variation for the sporadic artifacts is

$$V = [.003025 \ / \ .745^2] + [\ 0 \ / \ .900^2] = .005487.$$

The residual variance is

$$S_5^2 = PV - \overline{R}^2 \, \overline{A}^2 \, V = .010290 - .774^2 \, .6705^2 \, .005487 = .008812.$$

The fully corrected variance is thus

$$\text{Var } (\rho_i) = S_5^2 \ / \ \overline{A}^2 = .008812 \ / \ .6705^2 = .019601.$$

The standard deviation is thus estimated to be .14.

Within the studies conducted on jobs with good working conditions, the mean correlation is, therefore, .77 and the standard deviation is .14.

Jobs With Poor Working Conditions

The meta-analysis of partially corrected correlations is obtained from the averages and standard deviations in the bottom part of Table 4.4c.

$$\text{PR} = \text{Ave} (r) = .208$$

$$\text{PV} = \text{Var} (r) - \text{Var} (e) = .191532^2 - .031494 = .005191$$

The mean and standard deviation of each sporadic artifact can be computed from the top part of Table 4.4b.

$$\text{Ave} (a) = .745 \qquad \text{Var} (a) = .003025$$

$$\text{Ave} (b) = .800 \qquad \text{Var} (b) = 0$$

The mean compound attenuation factor for the sporadic artifacts is

$$\overline{A} = \text{Ave} (a) \, \text{Ave} (b) = (.745) \, (.800) = .5960.$$

The fully corrected mean correlation is thus

$$\overline{R} = \text{Ave} (\rho_i) = \text{PR} \, / \, \overline{A} = .208 \, / \, .5960 = .349.$$

The sum of squared coefficients of variation for the sporadic artifacts is

$$V = [.003025 \, / \, .745^2] + [\, 0 \, / \, .800^2] = .005487.$$

The residual variance is

$$S_5^2 = \text{PV} - \overline{R}^2 \, \overline{A}^2 \, V = .005191 - .349^2 \, .5960^2 \, .005487 = .004954.$$

The fully corrected variance is thus

$$\text{Var} (\rho_i) = S_5^2 \, / \, \overline{A}^2 = .004954 \, / \, .5960^2 = .013945.$$

The standard deviation is thus estimated to be .118.

Thus, within the studies conducted on jobs with poor working conditions, the mean correlation is .35 and the standard deviation is .12.

The Moderator Variable Evaluated

For jobs with good working conditions, the mean correlation is .77 with a standard deviation of .14. If the distribution of correlations within this condition is normal, then the 95% credibility interval would be

$$.49 < \rho < 1.00 \qquad \text{(good working conditions).}$$

For jobs with poor working conditions, the mean correlation is .35 with a standard deviation of .12. If the distribution of correlations within this condition is normal, then the 95% credibility interval would be

$$.21 < \rho < .59 \qquad \text{(poor working conditions).}$$

The mean correlations are quite different, .77 versus .35. This finding suggests that working conditions are a moderator variable. There is residual variation within each set of studies, although we cannot know how much of this remaining variance is due to unknown and uncorrected artifacts. As is indicated by the credibility intervals, the two distributions overlap, but this could be explained by the fact that the moderator variable (working conditions) is actually a continuum that was split at the median. Thus, the upper end of one set is the bottom end of the other. It may be that much of the residual variation could be explained by fine-grained variation in working conditions.

Finally, in computing these meta-analyses, the overall mean uncorrected r of .290 was in the sampling error calculations variance for the subset meta-analyses. The results could be computed using the separate mean rs shown in Table 4.4c (.414 and .167 for good and poor working conditions). We leave this as an exercise for the reader.

Summary of Artifact Distribution Meta-Analysis of Correlations

Ideally there would be artifact information on every artifact for every study. However, publication practice has not yet reached this level of completeness in reporting research. Typically, artifact information comes at three levels. For some artifacts, information is available for all or nearly all studies. This information can be used to correct studies individually. For some artifacts, information is available on a random subset of studies, enough to estimate the distribution of artifact values across studies. Although individual studies cannot be corrected, the meta-analysis results can be corrected for those artifacts. For some artifacts, no information is available and no correction can be made. We recommend that meta-analysis be conducted in two stages, corresponding to the artifact information available.

The first-stage meta-analysis corrects for those artifacts for which information is available for all or nearly all studies. In some research domains, that will be a bare bones meta-analysis. The methods for the first stage meta-analysis were presented in Chapter 3. The main product of the first stage meta-analysis is the estimate of the mean and standard deviation of population correlations corrected for those artifacts controlled in the first-stage meta-analysis. If a moderator variable was identified, then there will be a meta-analysis for each corresponding subset of studies.

The purpose of the second-stage meta-analysis is to correct the first-stage meta-analysis for those artifacts where information is available on a sporadic basis. The phrase, "the artifacts," means the sporadic artifacts in this context. There are two phases to the second-stage meta-analysis: analysis of each artifact separately followed by an analysis for the compound effect of the artifacts.

Phase 1

For each sporadic artifact, the artifact information is used to generate the artifact multiplier for those studies where it can be computed. These values are then cumulated across studies. That is, we compute a mean and a standard deviation for each artifact multiplier. For each artifact distribution, we also compute the coefficient of variation, the standard deviation divided by the mean, and the square of the coefficient of variation, here denoted v.

Phase 2a: Correcting the Mean Correlation

The compound impact of the artifacts on the mean correlation is computed by the compound multiplier. That is, the mean attenuated correlation is the product of the mean true correlation and the mean compound artifact multiplier. The mean compound multiplier is the product of the means of the separate artifact multipliers. To correct for the compound effect of the sporadic artifacts, we take the mean correlation from the first-stage meta-analysis and divide by the mean compound multiplier.

Phase 2b: Correcting the Standard Deviation of Correlations

The compound effect of the artifacts on the variance of correlations is more complicated. On the one hand, the attenuating effect of artifacts tends to reduce the variation of population correlations. On the other hand, the variation in artifacts across studies causes an artifactual increase in the variance of correlations across studies. Computationally, we first correct for artifact variation. From the variance found in the first-stage meta-analysis, we subtract a term computed from the sum of the squared coefficients of variation of the separate artifacts. We then correct for the attenuation effect by dividing the reduced variance by the square of the mean compound multiplier. That number is the desired variance of correlations corrected for all artifacts with available artifact information.

The main product of the second-stage meta-analysis is the mean and standard deviation of population correlations corrected for those artifacts for which sporadically available artifact information has been gathered. To the extent that important artifacts have not been corrected, the mean will be an underestimate and the standard deviation will be an overestimate. If the artifacts not corrected have only a small impact, and if we are lucky enough to have little bad data in the research domain, then the mean and the standard deviation will be accurate estimates of the true correlation distribution. In any case, the estimates will be far more accurate than the single-study uncorrected correlations that form the basis of most current scientific inferences.

5 | Technical Questions in Meta-Analysis of Correlations

This chapter discusses technical questions that arise in the meta-analysis of correlations. These include the question of whether r or r^2 should be used in meta-analysis, and the question of whether meta-analysis of regression slopes and intercepts is preferable to meta-analysis of correlations. In earlier chapters, we have stated that estimates of SD_ρ must always be considered to be upper bound values. This chapter discusses five technical factors and shows how they contribute to inflation in SD_ρ estimates. Finally, six criticisms that have been leveled at meta-analysis of correlations using the methods presented in Chapters 3 and 4 are examined. These criticisms are taken up here rather than in Chapter 13 because the criticisms do not apply to meta-analysis methods in general, but only to the methods of Chapters 3 and 4.

r versus r^2: Which Should Be Used?

Chapter 3 focuses on the correlation coefficient as the statistic to be cumulated across studies. But some have argued that it is the squared correlation — r^2 — that is of interest, not r itself. They argue that r^2 is the proportion of variance in one variable that is accounted for by the other variable, and this is the figure that provides the true description of the size of the relationship. Further, the advocates of r^2 typically hold that relationships found in the behavioral and social sciences are very small. For example, they maintain that $r = .30$ is small because $r^2 = .09$, indicating that only 9% of the variance in the dependent variable is accounted for. Even $r = .50$ is considered small: only 25% of the variance is explained.

The "percent variance account for" is statistically correct but substantively erroneous. It leads to severe underestimates of the practical and theoretical significance of relationships between variables. This is because r^2 (and all other indices of percent variance accounted for) are related only in a very nonlinear way to the magnitudes of effect sizes that determine their impact in the real world.

The correlation is the standardized slope of the regression of the dependent variable on the independent variable. If x and y are in standard score form, then $\hat{y} = rx$. Thus, r is slope of the line relating y to x. As such, it indexes the predictability of y from x. For example, if $r = .50$, then for each increase of one SD in x, there is an increase of $\frac{1}{2}$ SD in y. The statistic r^2 plays no role in the regression equation. The same principle applies in raw score regression; here the slope again is based on r, not r^2. The slope is $B = \dfrac{r\,SD_y}{SD_x}$. The raw score regression equation is

$$\hat{Y} = \left\{ r\frac{SD_y}{SD_x} \right\} X + C,$$

where C is the raw score intercept.

The problem with all percent variance accounted for indices of effect size is that variables that account for small percentages of the variance often have very important effects on the dependent variable. Variance-based indices of effect size make these important effects appear much less important than they actually are, misleading both researchers and consumers of research. Consider an example. According to Jensen (1980) and others, the heritability of IQ true scores is about .80. This means that 80% of the (true) variance is due to heredity and only 20% is due to environmental differences, yielding a ratio of "importance" of .80 / .20 or 4 to 1. That is, based on percent variance accounted for indices, heredity is 4 times more important than environment in determining intelligence. But this picture is very deceptive. (For purposes of this example, we assume heredity and environment are uncorrelated; that is close to true, and in any event the principle illustrated here is not dependent on this assumption.) The functional relationships between these two variables and intelligence are expressed by their respective standard score regressions, not by the figures of .80 and .20. The correlation between IQ and heredity is $\sqrt{.80} = .894$, and the correlation between environment and intelligence is $\sqrt{.20} = .447$. Thus, the functional equation for predicting IQ from each (when all variables are in standard score form) is

$$\hat{Y}_{IQ} = .894\,(H) + .447\,(E).$$

Thus, for each one SD increase in heredity (H), there is a .894 SD increase in IQ, and for each one SD increase in environment (E), there is a .447 SD increase in IQ. This is the accurate statement of the power of H and E to produce changes in IQ; that is, it is the true statement of their effects on IQ. The relative size of these effects is .894 / .447 = 2. That is, the true

impact of heredity on IQ is only twice as great as that of environment, not
4 times as great, as implied by the percent variance accounted for indices.
The variance-based indices underestimate the causal impact of environment relative to heredity by a factor of two. Further, the absolute causal
importance of environment is underestimated. The correct interpretation
shows that if environment could be improved by two SDs, the expected
increase in IQ (where $SD_{IQ} = 15$) would be .447 (2.00) (15) = 13.4. This
would correspond to an increase from 86.6 to 100, which would have very
important social implications. This correct analysis shows the true potential impact of environment, while the variance-based statement that environment accounts for only 20% of IQ variance leaves the false impression
that environment is not of much importance. (Note: The fact that no one
seems to know *how* to increase environment by 2 SDs is beside the point
here.)

This is not an unusual case. For example, the Coleman Report (1966)
concluded that when other variables were controlled for, money spent per
student by school districts accounted for only a small percent of the
variance of student achievement. The report concluded that financial
resources and facilities, such as libraries and labs, were not very important
because they provide little "leverage" over student achievement. But later
analyses showed that this small percent of variance corresponded to a
standardized regression coefficient for this variable that was much larger,
and demonstrated that improvements in facilities could yield increases
in student achievement that were significant socially and practically
(Mosteller & Moynihan, 1972).

Variance-based interpretations have led to the same sort of errors in
personnel selection. There it was said that validity coefficients of, for
example, .40 were not of much value since only 16% of the variance of
job performance was accounted for. But a validity coefficient of .40 means
that for every 1 SD increase in mean score on the selection procedure, we
can expect a .40 SD increase in job performance — a substantial increase
with considerable economic value. In fact, a validity coefficient of .40 has
40% of the practical value to an employer of a validity coefficient of
1.00 — perfect validity (Schmidt, Hunter, McKenzie, & Muldrow, 1979).

Variance-based indices of effect size are virtually always deceptive and
misleading and should be avoided, whether in meta-analysis or in primary
research. In meta-analysis, such indices have an additional disadvantage:
They obscure the *direction* of the effect. Being nondirectional, they do not
discriminate between an r of .50 and an r of −.50; both would enter the
meta-analysis as $r^2 = .25$.

To illustrate that r, and not r^2, is the appropriate index of effect size
and to show that "small" rs (e.g., .20-.30) indicate substantial relation-

ships, Rosenthal and Rubin (1979b; 1982c) have introduced the Binomial Effect Size Display (BESD). Although this technique requires that both variables be dichotomous (e.g., treatment versus control or "survived" versus "died") and requires 50% on each side of each dichotomy, it does forcefully illustrate the practical importance of "small" correlations. For example, a correlation of .32 (r^2 = .10) between treatment with a particular drug and patient survival corresponds to a reduction in the death rate from 66% to 34% (Rosenthal, 1984, p. 130). Thus, a relationship that accounts for only 10% of the variance means a reduction in the death rate of almost 50%. Small correlations can have large impacts. The Rosenthal and Rubin (1979b) BESD uses a special case — that of truly dichotomous variables — to illustrate the same principle we have presented using the more general regression analysis method.

r versus Regression Slopes and Intercepts in Meta-Analysis

On the surface, it often appears that some hypotheses or theories could be tested as effectively or more effectively by cumulating raw score slopes and intercepts rather than correlations. For example, a theory advanced by Hackman and Oldham (1975) states simply that the relationship between the "motivating potential" of a job and the job satisfaction of incumbents will be stronger for those incumbents with high "growth need strength" (GNS) than for those low in GNS. Since the theory is not explicit, it seems plausible a priori that it could be tested by cumulation of either regression slopes or correlations. Although some hypotheses or theories specify correlation- or regression-based relationships, most are like the Hackman-Oldham Theory. Some have advocated that all such theories should be tested using (raw score) regression analyses. What is the relative feasibility and usefulness of meta-analysis based on slopes and intercepts versus correlations? The disadvantages of using raw score regression slopes and intercepts rather than correlations outweigh the advantages.

Range Restriction

Correlations are affected by range restriction and, therefore, need to be corrected to a common SD for the independent variable to remove the resulting differences and the overall attenuation. When range restriction on the independent variable is direct, it has no effect on estimates of slopes and intercepts, and, therefore, there is no need for range corrections. This appears to be an important advantage, but unfortunately, range restriction is often indirect, and thus slopes and intercepts can be affected.

Measurement Error

Correlations are attenuated by unreliability in the measures of both independent and dependent variables, and they have to be corrected for both. These corrections were described in Chapter 3. Raw score regression slopes and intercepts are also attenuated by measurement error, but only measurement error in the independent variable. They are not affected by unreliability in the dependent variable, and, thus, one need neither know that reliability nor make that correction. The correction for unreliability in the independent variable is (Hunter & Schmidt, 1977)

$$\hat{B}_T = B \ / \ r_{XX}, \text{ and}$$

$$\hat{C}_T = \overline{Y} - (B \ / \ r_{XX}) \, \overline{X},$$

where $\hat{B}_T$ is the estimated true score slope, $\hat{C}_T$ is the estimated true score intercept, and r_{XX} is the reliability of the independent variable. From these equations, it is apparent that measurement error reduces the observed slope and increases the observed intercept; these corrections reverse those effects. Thus, uncorrected slopes and intercepts can be just as deceptive as uncorrected correlations, underestimating true relations. And the corrections, with their corresponding increase in sampling error, are often about the same in magnitude. Although B is corrected only for measurement error in the independent variable, division is by r_{XX}, not $\sqrt{r_{XX}}$, and, thus, the correction is larger. Both range restriction and reliability corrections increase sampling error; for this reason, it would be better if such corrections were unnecessary. But this statement is far more important for single studies than for meta-analyses; a major strength of meta-analysis is that, unlike single studies, it corrects for the effects of sampling error. Thus, even if fewer or smaller corrections sometimes have to be made to the slope and intercept, meta-analysis cancels out this advantage.

Comparability of Units Across Studies

A major disadvantage of regression slopes and intercepts is that they are usually not comparable across studies, and, thus, cannot be meaningfully cumulated in a meta-analysis. The formulas for the bivariate regression slope (B) and intercept (C) are

$$B = r \, \frac{SD_y}{SD_x}$$

$$C = \overline{Y} - B\overline{X}.$$

The values for B are comparable across studies only when all studies have used exactly the same scales to measure X and Y. For example, if X is job satisfaction, then every study must have used a single job satisfaction scale, say the JDI. If Y is life satisfaction, again the same scales must have been used in all studies. If different scales are used, slopes are not comparable even if those scales correlate 1.00 corrected for unreliability. For example, suppose one study uses a shortened form of the same job satisfaction scale used by another study. Even though the two scales measure the same construct, the short form will have a smaller SD, and that scale difference alone will greatly increase the observed slope. In personnel selection, suppose two studies both use rating scales to measure job performance and use the same test (X). If one study uses a rating scale with 20 subscales and the other a scale with only 7, the SD_y in the first study might be twice as large, causing the slope to be twice as large. This problem makes it impossible to meaningfully compare slopes across the two primary studies. In meta-analysis, it is usually impossible to use slopes and intercepts as the statistic to be cumulated for this reason. The correlation coefficient, on the other hand, is in the same units in all studies and can be cumulated across studies; it is scale-independent.

This problem of noncomparable scales is unique to the behavioral and social sciences. In the physical sciences, even if different studies use different scales, all studies can be put on a common scale and the slopes and intercepts can then be cumulated. Pounds can be converted to kilograms, inches to centimeters, quarts to liters, and vice versa. These scales are fully translatable to each other because each has a rational zero point; each is some constant times the other. We can define zero weight, but it is difficult to define zero verbal ability; thus, our studies cannot be converted to the same units of measurement. Instead, we must convert all to the same scale-free unit, the correlation (or the d value; see Chapters 5 and 6). This important distinction between the physical and social sciences has been overlooked by those who have criticized the correlation coefficient and advocated the use of slopes instead (e.g., the Society to Abolish the Correlation Coefficient).

It is sometimes maintained that this comparability problem can be solved by simply standardizing the independent and dependent variables within each study, creating equal standard deviations across studies; but the resulting standardized regression weights are then equal to the correlation. There is then no point in not starting with r.

Comparability of Findings across Meta-Analyses

If all available studies have been conducted using the same measurement scales (a very rare event), then one can apply meta-analysis to slopes and intercepts. Methods for doing this have been developed in detail by Raju, Fralicx, and Steinhaus (1986) and have been discussed by Callender (1983). For example, virtually all of the studies testing the Hackman-Oldham theory have used the same scales — the original scales developed by Hackman and Oldham. Also, where a consortium study is carried out in many organizations, the same scales are usually used in all organizations. The problem now is that the results of such a meta-analysis cannot be compared to other meta-analyses. For example, we cannot ask whether the strength of the relation between job satisfaction and job performance is the same in the consortium study as in other meta-analyses in the literature. These latter meta-analyses will be in correlation units (or more rarely, some *different* raw score unit). As we noted in Chapter 1, the development of theories requires that the results of different meta-analyses can be brought together and integrated into a coherent explanation. Thus, noncomparability of meta-analyses is a serious drawback to cumulation of slopes and intercepts. What it means is that, even in those rare cases in which meta-analysis of slopes and intercepts is statistically possible, one must still do a meta-analysis in correlations to have a set of findings that can be linked to the wider developing nomological net (Callender, 1983).

Intrinsic Interpretability

In addition to the above problems, slopes and intercepts are very difficult to interpret. It is easy to grasp the meaning of the correlation: it is the standardized regression coefficient of y or x.

$$\hat{y} = rx$$

For every increase of 1 unit (1 SD) on x, there is an increase of r SDs on y. If $r = .50$, increasing x by 1.00 SD increases y by .50 SD. But suppose the raw score regression equation is

$$\hat{Y} = 3.8X + 13.2 .$$

It is very hard to see whether this is a strong relation or a weak one. For every one unit increase in X, we get a 3.8 unit increase in Y. But is this a large or small increase? Perhaps SD_y is just very large. After all, the scaling is arbitrary. To make sense of this equation, one must somehow translate it into standard score units — and then one is back to the correlation!

In summary, the disadvantage of conducting meta-analysis using slopes and intercepts rather than correlations is substantial. Ordinarily, meta-analysts will have few occasions to prefer slopes and intercepts over correlations.

Technical Factors That Cause Overestimation of SD_ρ

Throughout this book, we have stressed that much of the variation in correlations across studies is caused by the operation of statistical and measurement artifacts. These artifacts were defined in Chapter 2, and methods for correcting for many of them were presented in Chapters 3 and 4. This section discusses five additional factors that contribute to overestimation of SD_ρ, the standard deviation of population correlations. Thus, these factors lead to an overestimation of the amount of variability in actual correlations. These factors are (1) presence of non-Pearson correlations in the meta-analysis, (2) presence of outliers (extremely large or small correlations) in the meta-analysis, (3) the use of study observed correlations in the formula for sampling error variance, (4) undercorrection for sampling error variance when there is direct range restriction, and (5) failure to allow for the nonlinearity in range corrections in meta-analyses based on artifact distributions. The first three of these factors apply in all meta-analyses; the fourth applies only when some or all of the correlations have been affected by range restriction; the fifth applies only to meta-analyses that use artifact distributions. However, most meta-analyses to date have used artifact distributions.

Presence of Non-Pearson *r*s

It is well known that commonly used non-Pearson correlation coefficients, such as the biserial and tetrachoric, have larger standard errors than do Pearson *r*s. Thus, the formula for the sampling error variance of the Pearson correlation underestimates the amount of sampling error variance in these correlations. When such correlations are included in a meta-analysis, they are treated as if their standard errors were those of Pearson *r*s. This deflates the estimated variance accounted for by artifacts and inflates the estimate of SD_ρ in any distribution of correlations in which biserial and tetrachoric correlations are present. More accurate results can be obtained if non-Pearson *r*s are deleted prior to the meta-analysis. Of course, such deletion is more feasible when the total number of correlations is large to begin with. In large sets of validity studies, we have found that deleting non-Pearson *r*s increased the average percent of variance accounted for by sampling error by almost five percentage points (Hirsh, Schmidt, Pearlman, & Hunter, 1985; Schmidt, Law, Hunter, Rothstein, & Pearlman, 1989). It should be noted that Spearman's Rho is the Pearson *r* between ranks and has the same sampling error variance as the Pearson *r*. Hence, it should not be deleted.

Presence of Outliers

The use of least squares statistical methods to estimate the mean and variance of the distribution of correlations is based on the assumption that the data contain no aberrant values (i.e., outliers). When this assumption does not hold, the statistically optimal properties (efficiency and unbiasedness) of least squares estimates disappear. Under these circumstances, least squares estimates become very inaccurate because of their extreme sensitivity to outliers (Huber, 1980; Tukey, 1960; see also Barnett & Lewis, 1978; Grubbs, 1969). The presence of even a single outlier can produce a radical increase in the observed standard deviation, and a somewhat smaller distortion of the mean. Data sets in any research area are likely to contain data points that are erroneous due to computational, transcriptional, and other errors (Guilliksen, 1986; Wolins, 1962). Based on his extensive experience with data sets of all kinds, Tukey (1960) judges that virtually all data sets contain outliers and other errors. One of our best-known psychometricians recently expressed the following statement (Guilliksen, 1986):

> I believe that it is essential to check the data for errors before running my computations. I always wrote an error-checking program and ran the data through it before computing. I find it very interesting that in every set of data I have run, either for myself or someone else, there have always been errors, necessitating going back to the questionnaires and repunching some cards, or perhaps discarding some subjects. (p. 4)

Unfortunately, the failure to conduct such checks is very widespread. In the physical sciences (e.g., physics and chemistry) extreme values have been routinely eliminated for centuries (Hedges, 1987). The psychological and social sciences have recently begun to recognize the need for such "trimming" prior to data analysis. Tukey (1960) and Huber (1980) recommend deletion of the most extreme 10% of data points — the largest 5% and the smallest 5% of values. In our study (Hirsh et al., 1985; Schmidt, Law et al., 1989), we found that deletion of only the top and bottom 2% resulted in a five-percentage-point increase in the average percent of variance accounted for by artifacts.

Use of r instead of $\bar{r}$ in the Sampling Error Formula

The formula for the sampling error variance in a correlation coefficient is

$$S_e^2 = \frac{(1 - \rho_{xy}^2)^2}{N - 1},$$

where N is the sample size and ρ_{xy} is the population (uncorrected) correlation. ρ_{xy} is, of course, unknown, and to use this formula, some method must be found to estimate it. In single studies, the estimate of ρ_{xy} typically used — because it is the only one available — is the observed correlation in the study at hand. In our early meta-analyses of employment test validities, we followed this tradition: The value used to estimate the sampling error variance in every study was the observed correlation in that study. Subsequent simulation studies and studies with real data have shown that this procedure is not optimal. The mean observed r ($\bar{r}_{obs}$) — a good estimate of ρ_{xy} — is typically about .20 in this literature. Sample sizes are usually small, so there are substantial departures in both directions from ρ_{xy}. When the sampling error is large and positive (e.g., + .20, so that $r = .40$), the estimated S_e^2 is substantially reduced (by 23% in this example). But this effect is not symmetrical. When sampling error is large and negative (e.g., -.20, so that r = .00), estimated S_e^2 is increased by only a small amount (by 9% in this example). Thus, on balance, the sampling error in a set of correlations is substantially underestimated. The smaller the sample size in the studies analyzed, the greater this underestimation will be. Also, the smaller the (attenuated) population correlation, the greater the underestimation will be (because smaller ρ_i have larger sampling error variances, sample sizes equal). The result is underestimation of the amount of variance accounted for by sampling error and overestimation of SD_ρ. This distortion can be eliminated by using the $\bar{r}$ for the set of studies rather than individual rs in the formula for sampling error. The $\bar{r}$ contains little sampling error, and extreme values are very unlikely. The result is more accurate estimates of SD_ρ (Hirsh et al., 1985; Schmidt, Law et al., 1989).

Milsap (1988), in a Monte Carlo study, used r rather than $\bar{r}$ in the formula for sampling error variance. In his study, all ρ were equal so S_ρ^2 was zero, and the variance of the observed rs was solely sampling error variance, i.e., $S_r^2 = S_e^2$. However, he found that his formula-derived estimates of S_e^2 were slightly smaller than S_r^2 figures, and this difference was larger for smaller sample sizes. He attributed this finding to inaccuracy in the formula (the formula is an approximation), but the phenomenon described in this section is in large part the explanation for his findings. He also found that the negative bias in his formula-derived estimates of sampling error variance was larger for smaller levels of reliability of measures. This finding is explained by the fact that lower reliability leads to lower values of ρ_i, the operative population correlation (see Chapter 3). Lower ρ_i values have larger sampling error variances for any fixed sample size, thus intensifying the process described above. Thus, contrary to Milsap's (1988) conclusion, it was not unreliability (measurement error) per se that caused the increase in the underestimation, but rather the reduced value of the population correlation.

Undercorrection for Sampling Error Variance in the Presence of Range Restriction

The formula for sampling error variance assumes that the independent and dependent variables are at least approximately normally distributed. Where there is direct range restriction (truncation) on one or both variables, this assumption is violated. For example, in personnel selection, there may be direct restriction on the test (the independent variable). For example, job offers may be made only to those applicants above the mean test score. Milsap (1989), using computer simulation studies, found that under such conditions the sample (or study) correlations have larger sampling error variances than indicated by the sampling error variance formula. That is, the formula underestimates the true amount of sampling error, leading to undercorrections for sampling variance and, therefore, overestimation of the residual variance and SD_ρ. The undercorrection is largest when sample sizes are 60 or less. As an example, if $N = 60$ and $\rho = .40$ in all studies, and all variance is in fact due only to sampling error, then estimated residual SD (SD_{res}) will on average be .046. The estimated SD_ρ value will typically be about .09. The correct value in both cases is, of course, zero. Thus, many nonzero estimates of SD_ρ in the published literature could be due, in whole or in large part, to this effect because many are in the .08 to .12 range. In many studies, range restriction is indirect rather than direct. For example, people may be selected based on a different test that might correlate .60 to .70 with the independent variable test. Studies are needed to determine what the effect of such indirect range restriction is on the accuracy of the formula for sampling error variance.

Nonlinearity in the Range Correction

In artifact distribution based methods of meta-analysis, the mean (ρ) and standard deviation (SD_ρ) of true correlations are estimated from the mean ($\bar{r}_{res}$) and standard deviation (SD_{res}) of the residual distribution. The residual distribution is the distribution of observed correlations expected across studies if N were always infinite (i.e., no sampling error) and reliability, range restriction, and other artifacts were always constant at their respective mean values. To correct the residual distribution for unreliability, we could divide every value in that distribution by the mean of the square roots of reliabilities. But since that value is a constant, we can instead just divide both $\bar{r}_{res}$ and SD_{res} by that constant and get the same result. This is what artifact distribution-based procedures do. But these procedures do exactly the same thing in correcting the residual distribution for the effects of mean range restriction — and here things do not work out quite so neatly. Using the mean level of range restriction (in the form of the ratio of the restricted to the unrestricted predictor standard deviations), current procedures correct $\bar{r}_{res}$. This increases $\bar{r}_{res}$ by some factor, say 1.50. Then SD_{res} is multiplied by this same factor to estimate the SD of a distribution in which each r has been corrected for the mean level of range restriction. But, unlike the reliability correction, the range restriction correction is not linear in r. The correction is not the same for every value of r in the residual distribution. It is larger for smaller rs and smaller for larger rs. Thus, the approximation based on the assumption of linearity in artifact distribution-based meta-analysis procedures leads to overestimates of SD_ρ. Simulation studies (Callender & Osburn, 1980; Raju & Burke, 1983) have demonstrated that the interactive procedure — theoretically, our most sophisticated method; see Chapter 4 and Schmidt, Gast-Rosenberg, & Hunter (1980) — yields estimates of SD_ρ that are too large by about .02. This overestimation occurs in simulated data in which sample sizes are infinite and sources of artifactual variance such as computational errors, outliers, and non-Pearson rs, do not exist. This overestimation stems from failure to take into account the nonlinearity of range restriction corrections. This nonlinearity can be taken into account by correcting each value in the residual distribution separately for the mean level of range restriction. To take this nonlinearity into account, the following method can be used. After determining the mean and SD of the residual distribution, identify 60 additional values in that distribution by moving out from the mean in .1 SD units to 3 SD above and below the mean. Then correct each of these values individually for range restriction, using the mean of the s / S ratio. The formula used to correct each value is

$$R = \frac{r(S/s)}{\{([S/s]^2 - 1)r^2 + 1\}^{1/2}}$$

where

r = the value of the correlation in the residual distribution;
R = the corrected value;
S = the unrestricted standard deviation;
s = the restricted standard deviation.

Each range corrected r is then corrected for the mean effect of un-reliability. The relative frequency of each value of r is indexed by the normal curve ordinate associated with its z score in the residual distribution. These frequencies are applied to the corresponding corrected correlations (ρ_i). The frequency weighted mean of the distribution of the corrected correlations $(\bar{\rho})$ is then determined, and the following (relative) frequency weighted variance formula is used to find S_{ρ}^2:

$$S_{\rho}^2 = \frac{\Sigma f_i (\hat{\rho}_i - \bar{\rho})^2}{\Sigma f}$$

where f_i is the relative frequency associated with $\hat{\rho}_i$.

In our studies (Hirsh et al. 1985; Schmidt, Law et al., 1989), the estimated true standard deviations resulting from this improved procedure were found to be smaller than the analogous values derived from the original procedure. Our current computer programs based on the interactive model for artifact distribution-based meta-analysis of correlations incorporate this refinement.

Other Factors Causing Overestimation of SD_ρ

Every research area can be expected to have additional factors that cause overestimation of SD_ρ in that particular research literature. The meta-analyst should be alert to this fact and should describe these factors even if no correction can be made for them. This section presents some examples from the meta-analysis of employment test validities. In that literature, some studies used ratings of job performance that had earlier been made for administrative purposes (e.g., pay raises, promotions, and so on), while other studies were based on special ratings that were used solely for the research study. Administrative ratings are known to be strongly influenced by nonperformance considerations (Whetzel, McDaniel, & Schmidt, 1985) and to yield smaller observed correlations with selection procedures than research ratings. This difference is a source of artifactual variance in the observed correlations that could not be corrected for; it thus caused SD_ρ to be an overestimate. Another artifactual source of variance stemmed from the fact that some studies assessed job performance using content valid work sample measures, while other studies use supervisory ratings of job performance. Work samples are by far the better measure of job performance. We now know that employment tests correlate more highly with work sample measures than with ratings of job performance (Hunter, 1983f; Nathan & Alexander, 1988). This difference between studies inflates estimates of SD_ρ. Another factor causing SD_ρ to be overestimated is inclusion of two or more correlations from the same studies whenever the study contained two different tests measuring the same ability in the same sample (e.g., two different tests measuring spatial ability). These correlations are not independent, and the result is inflation of both the observed SD (SD_r) and SD_ρ (see Chapter 10). Finally, we now know that differences between employees in amount of job experience reduce the observed validities of employment tests (Schmidt, Hunter, Outerbridge, & Trattner, 1986; McDaniel, Schmidt, & Hunter, 1988). Thus, studies in which employees vary widely in job experience can be expected to report smaller correlations on average than studies in which employees vary little in time on the job. The result is additional variation in correlations across studies that is not corrected for. Again, the effect is inflate the estimate of SD_ρ.

The specific nature of the factors that cause SD_ρ to be overestimated will vary from one research literature to another. But they will virtually always be present. Even if no method can be found to correct for their effects, these factors should be described clearly in the meta-analysis report. As we emphasized in Chapter 2, it is important that every meta-analyst and every reader of meta-analyses constantly bear in mind the fact that all estimates of SD_ρ are likely to be overestimates. Even after the meta-analysis is completed, there is still less variation across studies than there appears to be.

Criticisms of Meta-Analysis Procedures for Correlations

This section examines criticisms that have focused specifically on meta-analysis procedures for correlations. Broader criticisms that apply to all forms of meta-analysis are discussed in Chapter 13. Meta-analysis procedures for correlations have been criticized by James, Demaree, and Mulaik (1986), Kemery, Mossholder and Roth (1987), Ladd and Cornwell (1986), Spector and Levine (1987), and Thomas (1988).

Does Meta-Analysis *Assume* $SD_\rho = 0$?

James et al. (1986) have contended that meta-analysis rests on the built in *assumption* that $SD_\rho = 0$. For example, they state, "The key 'what if' *assumption* for the validity generalization procedure is: what is the population is *assumed* to be the same over studies (Callender & Osburn, 1980; Hunter, Schmidt, & Jackson, 1982)" (p. 441; emphasis added). The James et al. article fails to distinguish between hypothesis testing (that is, use of the 75% rule, the chi-square test, or computer sampling simulation to choose between the hypotheses of constant versus variable true correlations) and parameter estimation (that is, estimation of the mean and standard deviation of true validity). In hypothesis testing, one compares parameter estimation results (in particular, the estimate of SD_ρ) with the value expected given the hypothesis — not the assumption — that ρ is constant across studies, that is, the hypothesis that ρ is constant tested. In *parameter estimation*, and in particular in estimating SD_ρ, there is no hypothesis that ρ is constant across studies; nor is there any hypothesis or assumption that ρ is variable across studies. In parameter estimation, all meta-analysis equations used in validity generalization (Callender & Osburn, 1980; Raju & Burke, 1983; Schmidt, Hunter, Pearlman, & Shane, 1979) treat ρ as a random variable that is free to take on any distribution of values. Callender and Osburn (1980) provide an explicit explanation (p. 556) and mathematical demonstration (pp. 557-558) of these properties of the equations. James et al. treat validity generalization as if the hypothesis testing component were the only component, and then mistakenly imply that both the hypothesis testing and the estimation of ρ and SD_ρ are based on the *assumption* that true validity is constant. Neither hypothesis testing nor parameter estimation is based on an assumption that ρ is constant. Hypothesis testing tests the *hypothesis* that ρ is constant. In parameter estimation, there is not even the hypothesis that ρ is constant.

Bias in *r* and Use of Fisher's *z*

James et al. next turn to the long-known fact that there is a slight downward bias in *r* as an estimate of ρ, the population correlation. As a result of this tiny bias, *r* and *e* are slightly correlated, leading to a very slight underestimation of the sampling error variance in *r* and in sets of *r*s (a minuscule *conservative* bias). The bias in *r* decreases as sample size increases; for *N*s larger than 40, the bias is always less than .005; that is, it is less than rounding error and, therefore, disappears when *r* is rounded to the usual two places. When ρ varies across studies, there is a very tiny negative covariance (and, hence, correlation) between ρ and *e*. James et al.

are concerned that this could lead to underestimation of SD_ρ. This point was developed in detail by Hedges (1982), specifically in terms of its implications for validity generalization research. James et al. do not cite Hedges (1985), but they cite Linn and Dunbar (1982), who analyze Hedges's specific critique in some detail and conclude that "While Hedges' results are of theoretical interest, it is unlikely that the missing covariance term causes any serious difficulty in practice" (p. 15). They also state that the tiny departure from complete independence "is probably of no practical concern" (p. 15).

Callender and Osburn (1988) present evidence, based on extensive simulation studies, that the standard formula for the sampling error variance of the correlation is quite accurate, even when the ρ_i vary widely. James et al. point out that our early validity generalization research was conducted using Fisher's z, stating that we dropped Fisher's z in favor of using correlation "under the *assumption* that the formula for sampling error based on correlations was 'very accurate' (Schmidt, Gast-Rosenberg, & Hunter, 1980, p. 660)" (p. 448; emphasis added). On the same page they cite here, we state: "However, Callender, Osburn, and Greener (Note 7) have shown in simulation studies that the formula for the sampling error of the correlation coefficient that we now use in both procedures is very accurate." Thus, the change in procedures was not based on an *assumption* but on evidence.

Based on the slight bias in r, James et al. (1986) challenged the basic equation in the meta-analysis of correlations: $S_r^2 = S_\rho^2 + S_e^2$. This equation states that the sampling error variance and the variance of ρ across studies combine additively to produce the observed variance of correlations. They present three arguments: (1) that classical measurement theory assumes homogeneous errors while the sampling error of r varies with the population correlation; (2) that sampling errors are not independent of the correlation; and (3) that Fisher's z transformation yields homogeneous errors and is additive. First, the fact that classical error theory assumes homogeneous errors is irrelevant. Meta-analysis does not assume homogeneous errors. For example, Hunter et al. (1982, p. 43) and Chapter 3 of this book show the dependence of sampling error variance on the population correlation, and this formula is used in the derivation of subsequent estimation formulas. Meta-analysis does not require the assumption of homogeneous errors.

Second, it is true that sampling error variance is not independent of the population correlation. If there is variation in the population correlation, then there is a negative correlation across studies between the population correlations and squared sampling errors (sampling error variance). Thus, population correlations and sampling error variance are not independent.

However, the additivity of the variance of ρ and the variance of e does not assume independence of ρ and e; it requires only that ρ and e be *uncorrelated*. That is, it is the across-study correlation between population correlation and *signed* sampling error ($r_{\rho_i e_i}$) that is relevant; the across-study correlation between population correlation and *squared* sampling error (sampling error variance) ($r_{\rho_i S_{ei}^2}$) is irrelevant. Consider an example.

Suppose that the study domain consisted of two sets of studies: one set with population correlation $\rho = .00$ and the other set with population correlation $\rho = .50$. Assume all studies are done with sample size 101. The sampling error variance for the studies with $\rho = .00$ will be .01, a standard deviation of .10. The sampling error variance for the studies with $\rho = .50$ will be .005625, a standard deviation of .075. Thus, typical errors from each set would be +.10 and −.10 or +.075 and −.075. If we form population correlation-error pairs, we have (.00, −.10), (.00, +.10), (.50, −.075), (.50, +.075). Across these pairs, ρ and e are uncorrelated, and the variance of the sum is the sum of the variances. However, if we consider squared errors, the pairs are (.00, .01), (.00, .01), (.50, .0056), (.50, .0056). Across these pairs there is a negative correlation between the population correlation and the squared error. James et al. lost track of the sign of sampling error in their argument. This is a critical error in quantitative terms and leads to their error in conclusions.

However, it is true that the population correlation and signed sampling errors are not *perfectly* uncorrelated. But *that* correlation is extremely small under all realistic conditions. Hedges (1982) noted that, since the correlation is not perfectly unbiased, a negative correlation can be expected between population correlations and sampling errors. However, this bias is so small that it becomes visible only under extreme conditions. One extreme example that Hedges used assumed a study domain with two sets of studies: one set where the population correlation is +.90 and a second set with population correlation −.90, each with equal frequency. All studies were assumed to have a sample size of 70. The positive correlations will not have an average of exactly .90; rather the average will be .8975, a bias of −.0025. Similarly, the average correlation in the negative set will be only -.8975 instead of -.90; a bias of +.0025. Thus, across the whole domain, there will be a negative correlation between population correlations and sampling errors. However, the expected correlation is only −.11 in this most extreme example. In real data sets, the correlation will typically be much smaller. Moreover, even in this most extreme example, the validity generalization formulas are very accurate. Using the individual study estimation formula (Chapter 3), the estimated standard deviation of ρ is .8975 instead of .9000, an error of −.0025, or one-third of one percent. Even in this most extreme example, the error would be invisible if the estimate were rounded to two digits, as is customarily done. In real data sets, the corresponding estimation error is much smaller.

Third, James et al. erroneously assert that use of the Fisher z transformation produces additivity. They start by asserting that the error variance is homogeneous for z across population z values. This would be irrelevant even if it were true, because it relates to the across-study correlation between population correlated and *squared* error instead of the across study correlation between population and *signed* error. The formula for the sampling error of Fisher's z is $\sigma_e^2 = 1 / (N-3)$. This formula is an approximation; it assumes that $\rho = .00$ and it assumes very large sample size. If we require accuracy to four digits (the criteria James et al. implicitly use for the correlation coefficient), then the formula breaks down for sample sizes less than 100 or population correlations different from zero. Thus, by the extreme standards of James et al., the Fisher z does not have homogeneous error variance. Furthermore, if we duplicate Hedge's analysis for the Fisher z transformation, we find that population z and signed sampling error are positively correlated. The bias in z is larger than the bias in r, and, hence, the mathematically expected across-study correlation between population z and signed sampling error is larger than the across study correlations for the correlation coefficient. The Fisher z transformation actually yields estimates of variance that are less accurate than the estimate based on the correlation coefficient.

The challenge to the equation $\sigma_r^2 = \sigma_\rho^2 + \sigma_e^2$ issued by James et al. was based on indirect arguments. These arguments are shown here to be erroneous. Their belief in the accuracy of the Fisher z transformation is based not on evidence but on assumption. The Fisher z transformation — like the untransformed correlation — is only approximately unbiased. It is only approximately uniform in variance. These approximations are not accurate to four digits. Ironically, by four-digit accuracy standards, the validity generalization estimates for the correlation coefficient are actually more accurate than the formulas for z (although often only trivially so).

There are two additional problems in using Fisher's z. First, there is no good method available for transforming standard deviation estimates in Fisher's z (SD_{Fz}) back into the corresponding correlation value, that is, into SD_ρ. *Mean* Fisher's z can easily be transformed into an estimated *mean* correlation using tables for Fz to r transformation (or using the Fz to r equation), but this is *not* true for SD_{Fz}. And it should be remembered that for interpretation and for applied use, results must be presented in correlational form. Second, use of Fisher's z produces an upward bias in the estimation of the mean correlations, while use of r produces a much smaller downward bias (Hunter, Schmidt, & Coggin, 1988). It was because of this tendency of Fisher's z to inflate true correlations in real data (sometimes by as much as .03) that we replaced Fisher's z with r in our validity generalization computer programs (Schmidt, Gast-Rosenberg, & Hunter, 1980; Schmidt, Hunter, & Pearlman, 1982). This bias is illustrated by the hypothetical data in Table 1 of James et al. The mean validity in that table is .50. The mean of Fisher's z is .56. When this value is transformed back into a correlation to estimate the mean validity, one obtains .51. Thus, mean validity has been inflated by .01 — in this case — a 2% increase. This inflationary factor may seem small, but it is from three to thirty times larger than the minuscule biases in variance estimates dwelt on at length by James et al. Furthermore, there is no need to tolerate the bias; it can be eliminated simply by using r instead of z.

We have recently examined the question of bias in estimated validities for r and Fisher's z in some detail (Hunter, Schmidt, & Coggin, 1988). This investigation found that when there is no variation in the population correlations (ρ_i), r has a small negative bias that is less than rounding error (that is, less than .005) unless N is smaller than 40. With sample sizes less than 40, the downward bias can be reduced to below rounding error by multiplying each r by the linear correction factor $(2N - 1) / (2N - 2)$. For Fisher's z, when the ρ_i do not vary, the bias is in the opposition direction — a positive bias — and is always larger in magnitude than the bias in r. When there is variation in the ρ_i, this variation introduces an additional bias component into both r and Fisher's z. This bias component is positive. In r, this positive bias acts in a direction opposite to the initial negative bias, reducing the overall bias. Further, both bias components and total bias decrease for r as N increases. For Fisher's z the story is different. The additional positive bias resulting from variation in the ρ_i (the transformation bias) is added to the previously existing positive bias, producing a larger positive bias. Furthermore, the transformational bias is independent of sample size; it does not decrease as sample size increases. For further details, formulas, derivations, and tables of bias values, see Hunter, et al. (1988). The discovery of a transformational bias in Fisher's z that is independent of sampling error is an additional new reason for not employing that statistic in validity generalization methods. Further, the Fisher's z transformation is frequently employed in the averaging of correlations outside of meta-analyses. These findings indicate that Fisher's z should not be used for that purpose either. Its use can lead to inflation of obtained averages by substantial amounts — up to .06 or more under extreme circumstances (Hunter, Schmidt, & Coggin, 1988).

Erroneous Use of Confidence Intervals

James et al. propose that whenever a researcher hypothesizes that ρ varies across studies, meta-analysis should not be used. Instead, they argue that it is better to use a confidence interval procedure that they describe. They propose placing confidence intervals around the largest and smallest observed correlations; the endpoints of their combined confidence interval for all values of ρ_i are then the lower bound of the confidence interval around the smallest observed correlation and the upper bound of the confidence interval around the largest observed correlation.

In estimating the variation of population correlations, it is clear that it would be a naive error to take the variation in observed correlations at face value, that is, to use the standard deviation of observed correlations as the estimate of the standard deviation of population correlations. Every method of meta-analysis — including the Fisher z method that we originally used and that James et al. propose to return to — recognizes that the standard deviation of observed correlations is generally larger than the standard deviation of population correlations. Yet the James et al. misuse of confidence intervals is even more inaccurate than naive use of the face value standard deviation. In the hypothetical data they present in their article, meta-analysis indicates that the 95% range for the ρ_i is .39 to .61, a width of .22. The naive 95% range estimate based on the observed standard deviation of .105 would on average be .29–.71, a width of .42, which is almost twice as wide as the meta-analysis range. The misuse of confidence intervals recommended by James et al. produces on average a range of .04 to .84, a width of .80, which is more than three times the meta-analysis range and almost twice the range yielded by the naive face value method. The large error in their hypothetical example is no accident. The error will always be large unless sample sizes are so large that sampling error is trivial. The James et al. method makes no correction for sampling error; rather it multiplies the effect of sampling error.

Homogeneous Studies: An Example

The nature of the error made by James et al. can be most easily seen in the case where all population correlations are actually equal (homogeneous studies). Consider 30 studies conducted in different settings where, unknown to the researcher, the population correlation is constant at .50. Since all population correlations are the same, the actual 95% range in population correlations is .50 to .50, with a width of zero. Assume that all studies have a sample size of 70; there will thus be considerable variation in the observed correlations. If 30 numbers are drawn randomly from a normal distribution, then on average (i.e., in the median sample) the largest value will be 2.00 standard deviations abcve the mean and the smallest value will be 2.00 standard deviations below the mean. In this example, the range of correlations would on average be .32 to .68, with a band width of .36. Thus, a naive meta-analyst would be led to believe that the range of population correlations is .32 to .68 instead of .50 to .50, a massive error. On average the largest correlation :n our example is .68, which would have a 95% confidence interval of .55 to .81. Thus, .81 will be the largest of the upper bounds. The smallest correlation will on average be .32, which would have a confidence interval of .11 to .53. Thus, .11 will be the smallest of the lower bounds. The James et al. estimate of the 95% range of population correlations is thus .11 to .81 with a width of .70. In summary, the actual range of population correlations in this example is .50 to .50, a band width of 0. The observed sample correlations will on the average have a 95% range of .32 to .68; a band of width .36. If this range is naively accepted as the estimate of the range of population correlations, the result is a very large error in estimation. The James et al. approach to confidence intervals produces an estimated range of .11 to .81, a band width of .70. Thus, the James et al. "sophisticated" approach is even more inaccurate than the naive estimate, almost twice as inaccurate.

Heterogeneous Case: An Example

In the James et al. hypothetical example, the meta-analysis estimate of the standard deviation of population correlations is .054. If population correlations have a standard deviation of .054 (rather than zero), then there will be two components to the variation in *sample* correlations: sampling error and real variation. The result is an addition of variance in population correlations plus the sampling error variance. In the James et al. hypothetical example, the observed variance would on average be .008152 + .002874 = .011026, resulting in a standard deviation of .105. Across a set of 30 studies, the high and low sample correlations would on average vary by two standard deviations from the mean. Thus, the range of observed sample correlations would be on average .29 to .71, a band of width .42. This band is much wider than the 95% range of .22: .42 / .22 = 1.91, or almost twice as wide. Thus, the naive estimation of variation produces a value in this example that is two times too wide. Now consider the result produced by the James et al. method. On average, the largest sample correlation would be .71, which has a confidence interval of .59 to .83. Thus, the largest upper bound is .83. On average, the smallest sample correlation would be .29, which has a confidence interval of .07 to .51. Thus, the smallest lower bound is .07. The James et al. misuse of confidence intervals produces an estimate of .07 to .83, a band of width .76. The meta-analysis estimate of the range of population correlations in their example is only .39 to .61. The James et al. estimated range width is off by a factor of .76 / .22 = 3.45. That is, their estimate is more than three times larger than the best estimate of the range. To summarize, the 95% range of population correlations in the James et al. hypothetical example is best estimated as .39 to .61, a width of .22. The range of observed correlations is .29 to .71, a band of .42, which is almost twice as wide as the actual band. The range of combined confidence intervals is .07 to .83, a band of width .76, which is more than three times as wide as the actual band. Thus, the James et al. misuse of confidence intervals leads to an error even larger than the error made by a naive observer who ignores sampling error and relies on the standard deviation of the observed correlations. The James et al. error is larger by a factor of (.78–.22) / (.44–.22) = 2.54. That is, the James et al. error is over 2.5 times larger than the naive error. Further analysis of the James et al. (1986) article can be found in Schmidt, Hunter and Raju (1988).

Is Sampling Error Variance Inaccurately Estimated?

Spector and Levine (1987) conducted a computer simulation study aimed at evaluating the accuracy of the formula for the sampling error variance of r. In their study, the value of ρ was always zero, so the formula for the sampling error variance of observed rs was $S_e^2 = 1 / (N-1)$. They conducted simulation studies for various values of N, ranging from 30 to 500. The number of observed rs per meta-analysis was varied from 6 to 100. For each combination of N and number of rs, they replicated the meta-analysis 1,000 times and then evaluated the average value of S_e^2 / S_r^2 across 1,000 meta-analyses. That is, they focused their attention on the average ratio of variance predicted from the sampling error formula to the average observed variance of the rs across studies. They did not look at $S_r^2 - S_e^2$, the difference between predicted and observed variances. They found that for all numbers of r's less than 100, the ratio S_e^2 / S_r^2 averaged greater than 1.00. For example, when there were 10 rs per meta-analysis and $N = 75$ in each study, the average ratio was 1.25. Kemery, Mossholder, and Roth (1987) obtained similar results in their simulation study. The smaller the number of rs per meta-analysis, the more the ratio exceeded 1.00. They interpreted these figures as demonstrating that the formula for S_e^2 overestimates sampling variance when the number of correlations in a meta-analysis is less than 100. Their assumption was that if the S_e^2 formula were accurate, the ratio S_e^2 / S_r^2 would average 1.00.

This conclusion was startling. Could it really be that one of the most basic formulas in all of statistics — a formula that had been accepted by all statisticians for over 80 years — was really grossly erroneous? That did not seem likely, and indeed it was not true. The Spector and Levine (1987) study was critiqued by Callender and Osburn (1988), who showed that if one assessed accuracy by the difference $S_r^2 - S_e^2$, the sampling error variance formula was shown to be extremely accurate, as had also been demonstrated in their numerous previous simulation studies. There was no bias. They also demonstrated why the average ratio S_e^2 / S_r^2 is greater than 1.00 despite the fact that S_e^2 is an unbiased estimated of sampling variance. When the number of correlations in a meta-analysis is small, then by chance, the S_r^2 will sometimes be very small; that is, by chance all observed rs will be very similar to each other. Since S_r^2 is the denominator of the ratio, these tiny S_r^2 values lead to very large values for S_e^2 / S_r^2, sometimes as large as 30 or more, and if S_r^2 should by chance be zero, the ratio is *infinitely large*. These extreme values pull the mean ratio up above 1.00; the *median* ratio is very close to 1.00. The analysis by Callender and Osburn (1988) fully explains the bizarre conclusions of Spector and Levine (1987) and demonstrates that the fundamental sampling variance formula for the correlation is unbiased.

It should be noted that Spector and Levine would not have reached this same conclusion had they used the reciprocal of their ratio; that is, if they had used S_r^2 / S_e^2 instead of S_e^2 / S_r^2, they would have found that the mean ratio was 1.00. With this reversed ratio, the most extreme possible value is zero (rather than infinity), and the distribution of ratios is much less skewed. This point has important implications for second-order meta-analyses, that is, meta-analyses of meta-analyses (see Chapter 9). Second-order meta-analyses may be conducted by averaging the percentage of variance accounted for by artifacts over similar meta-analyses. In any given meta-analysis, this percentage is the ratio of artifact-predicted variance (sampling variance plus that due to other artifacts) to the observed variance. One over this ratio is the reversed ratio, S_r^2 / S_e^2. In second-order meta-analysis, this reversed ratio should be averaged across studies, and then the reciprocal of that average should be taken. This procedure prevents the upward bias that appeared in the Spector and Levine study and results in an unbiased estimate of the average percent of variance in the meta-analyses that is due to artifacts. For an example application, see Rothstein, Schmidt, Erwin, Owens, and Sparks (in press).

Errors in the Kemery, Mossholder and Roth (1987) Study

Kemery et al. (1987) conducted a computer simulation study to examine the accuracy of meta-analysis results under highly artificial and unrealistic conditions: situations in which ρ assumes only two different values, zero and .60. For example, in one condition that they simulated, half of all studies were from populations where $\rho = 0$ and the other half were from populations where $\rho = .60$. It is difficult to imagine such a situation in real data. Even if it did occur, the moderator variable would almost certainly be recognized by the meta-analyst, and separate meta-analyses would be conducted on the two groups of studies, obviating the problem focused on by Kemery et al. Writing in the context of meta-analysis applied to employment test validities, Kemery et al. stated, "Because there is no substantive theoretical reason for the assumption of a unimodel distribution (of ρ), it is perhaps just as reasonable to postulate a multimodel continuum of validities" (p. 31). Actually, there is strong evidence to indicate unimodel distributions for ρ in validity generalization research. The larger the average sample size for the rs, the closer the distribution of r comes to resemble the distribution of ρ. Large-sample validity studies are available from military research, and these distributions are almost invariably unimodel, indicating that the distribution of ρ is also unimodel. And the meta-analysis results indicate that SD_ρ is typically a very small value, or zero, which argues against a multimodel or bimodel distribution of ρ.

Kemery et al. evaluated the accuracy of meta-analysis estimates of $\bar{\rho}$, SD_ρ and the 90% confidence value when ρ was bimodelly distributed, with some $\rho = 0$ and some $\rho = .60$. Since "actual" values of ρ were known, the actual values of $\bar{\rho}$ and SD_ρ could be computed directly. The meta-analysis estimates of $\bar{\rho}$ were very close to the actual values, and this is indicated in the article. But instead of comparing the meta-analysis estimates of SD_ρ with the actual value of SD_ρ, Kemery et al. mistakenly computed and reported the SD of the correlations corrected for artifactual variance, but not for attenuation due to measurement error and range restriction. The SD they reported was the residual SD (SD_{res}), which is much smaller than SD_ρ (see Chapter 4). Kemery et al. mistakenly concluded that since the square of the residual SD — the residual variance, S^2_{res} — was smaller than the actual S^2_ρ, meta-analysis overestimated the amount of variance due to artifacts. Enough information was given in the article to allow us to compute the meta-analysis estimates of SD_ρ to a close degree of approximation. These values averaged very close to the actual SD_ρ values; the difference did not exceed those expected from sampling error.

The case of the 90% confidence values was somewhat different. Again, the meta-analysis estimates closely approximated the values that were computed using the known values of ρ. However, in this case these "known values" were erroneous because they were computed by finding the value in ρ distribution that was 1.28 SDs below the mean. This method assumes a normal distribution, and will be inaccurate if the distribution is markedly non-normal, as in the case of the bizarre bimodel distribution imposed by Kemery et al. in their simulation study. Thus, even though the meta-analysis produced estimates very similar to those yielded when the computations were done on the ρs themselves, Kemery et al. (1987) argued that the meta-analysis estimates were inaccurate. However, it is clear that this "inaccuracy" stems completely from the imposition of the unrealistic bimodel distribution of ρ, a distribution that they themselves described as "admittedly contrived." Kemery, Mossholder, and Dunlap published a second, very similar article in 1989. Most of the comments presented here apply to that article also. Neither study appears to have important implications for meta-analyses of real data.

Are Estimates of SD_ρ "Unreliable"?

Ladd and Cornwell (1986) stated that "the accuracy of the estimate of the true variance (S_ρ^2) of the effect size has not been addressed in previous research on the meta-analytic procedure" (p. 1). This seems a strange statement in light of the extensive computer simulation studies of Callender and Osburn (1980) and Raju and Burke (1983) showing that the mean accuracy of the estimates of S_ρ^2 and SD_ρ produced by the artifact distribution formulas given in Chapter 4 is quite high. In discussing the results of their computer simulation study Ladd and Cornwell (1986) state, "The first and foremost point of this study is that the reliability of a meta-analysis in estimating true variance (S_ρ^2) is unacceptable" (p. 5). Thus, Ladd and Cornwell concluded that estimates of S_ρ^2 are unreliable and inaccurate, while Callender and Osburn (1980) and Raju and Burke (1983) concluded just the opposite.

What accounts for this apparent contradiction? The earlier simulation studies defined accuracy as the difference between estimated S_ρ^2 and actual S_ρ^2, and found that these differences were very small. This is the index of accuracy that is the most useful and appropriate. Ladd and Cornwell defined accuracy in a different manner. They started with a number of hypothetical sets of studies, each having a slightly different actual value of S_ρ^2 for each study set using simulated meta-analysis. Instead of computing the difference $S_\rho^2 - \hat{S}_\rho^2$, as done in the earlier studies, they correlated

$\hat{S}_\rho^2$ with S_ρ^2. For meta-analyses based on 60 or more studies, these rs ranged from about .60 to .80. They then squared these correlations and labeled them reliability coefficients. Thus, the range from .60 to .80 became .36 to .64. They then concluded that these "reliabilities" were "unacceptably low," showing that meta-analysis yields estimates of S_ρ^2 that are inaccurate. This is an inappropriate index of accuracy. The Ladd and Cornwell co-efficient indexes the reliability of *differences* between their different meta-analysis in S_ρ^2 estimates. This index is not useful for two reasons. First, it depends entirely on how large the researcher arbitrarily makes the differences in S_ρ^2 between study sets (meta-analyses). If these differences are made very large, this "reliability" can arbitrarily be made as large as desired, and vice versa. Second, their reliability index does not provide the information one needs to assess the accuracy of $\hat{S}_\rho^2$ in one's meta-analysis. The meta-analyst would like to know how different the S_ρ^2 esti-mate in his or her study is from the true value, i.e., how large is $S_\rho^2 - \hat{S}_\rho^2$ on average. Whether or not the estimate of S_ρ^2 in his or her meta-analysis is reliably different from the estimate of S_ρ^2 in another meta-analysis on a different research literature and examining a different relation is rarely of any interest. The Ladd and Cornwell study thus examines an irrelevant index of accuracy.

Overestimation of Variance Due to Artifacts

This section discusses a computational error in Paese and Switzer (1988) and critiques their interpretation of the corrected figures in Paese and Switzer (1989). Paese and Switzer (1988) concluded that the results of their computer simulation study showed that meta-analysis based on artifact distributions overestimates the amount of variance in study corre-lations that is due to study differences in reliability of the independent and dependent variables. Their study focused specifically on estimates of residual variance produced by the interactive and noninteractive proce-dures (discussed in Chapter 4) that have been used in validity generaliza-tion research. They concluded that even when the distribution of indepen-dent and dependent variable reliabilities used in the meta-analysis were exactly the same as those used to create their simulated data, the inter-active and noninteractive methods overestimated the amount of variance due to measurement error differences. However, they later discovered an error in their computer program that rendered their figures inaccurate. In the corrected study (Paese and Switzer, 1989), they concluded that the interactive method is accurate when the appropriate reliability distribu-tions are used. However, they concluded that the noninteractive method overestimated the variance due to reliability differences. They reported that the amount of variance accounted for could range up to 17% more than the actual amount due to reliability differences. However, when these results are expressed in terms of the actual amounts by which the interactive method overestimated the variance, the discrepancies are seen to be very small. For example, for the two reliability distributions most commonly used in past studies, the average amount of overestimation was .00063. For the second set of reliability distributions they examined, this figure was even smaller (.00033). And for the final two sets of reliability distributions they examined, the noninteractive method slightly *underestimated* the variance due to reliability differences (again, by very small amounts). Thus, their findings actually indicate that the noninteractive (as well as the interactive) procedure is quite accurate. Further, the effect of these small discrepancies on the estimate of the residual standard deviation (SD_{res}) is quite limited (see below).

Paese and Switzer (1989) also examined the effects of a mismatch between the reliability distributions used in a meta-analysis and the actual distributions that apply to that set of studies. As would be expected, they found that if the reliability distributions used were more (less) variable than the correct ones, then the meta-analysis attributed more (less) variance in observed correlation to between-study differences in reliability than was the actual case. This finding could have been predicted a priori on logical grounds. Again, they presented these discrepancies in percentage terms (for example, stating that the estimated artifactual variance was 20% larger than the actual values). But in terms of actual deviations from correct variance values, the distortions produced by use of incorrect reliability distributions were very small and would be unlikely to affect conclusions in meta-analyses of real data. For example, for the reliability distribution set with means of .60 and .80, overestimation of variance due to artifacts averaged .00217 and .00119 for the noninteractive and interactive methods, respectively, when the distributions used in the meta-analyses were too variable. These differences would not have much impact. For example, using the .00217 figure for the noninteractive procedure, if the actual SD_{res} were .12, then the estimated residual variance would be $(.12)^2 - .00217 = .01223$, yielding a SD_{res} estimate of .11 (versus the correct value of .12). The .01 difference in the SD_{res} estimate would be unlikely to affect conclusions from the meta-analysis. When the distributions used were not variable enough, artifact variance was *underestimated* by an average of .00137 and .00173, respectively. In cases where all variance was due to artifacts, these latter two values would lead to estimates of the residual standard deviation (SD_{res}) of .037 and .042, respectively, instead of the correct value of zero. If the actual SD_{res} were

.12, the estimated residual variance for the noninteractive procedure would be $(.12)^2 + .00137 = .01577$, yielding a SD_{res} estimate of .1256 (versus the correct value of .12). Errors of such small magnitude would not be likely to affect overall conclusions from a meta-analysis. This is especially true in the case of validity generalization meta-analysis. In those studies (e.g., Pearlman et al., 1980; Schmidt, Gast-Rosenberg, & Hunter, 1980), meta-analyses that made *no correction* for variance due to reliability (or range restriction) differences between studies reached the same conclusions as the full artifact distribution meta-analyses (see also Schmidt, Hunter, Pearlman, & Hirsh, 1985). Both concluded that the presence of substantial validities could be generalized across settings, employers, and so on. The major concern of Paese and Switzer (1988, 1989) appears to have been the possibility that "overcorrection" of variance due to study reliability differences might result in erroneous conclusions about validity generalizability. There appears to be no such danger.

Alleged Problems with the Sampling Error Variance Model

Thomas (1988) claimed to have found fundamental problems in the basic model $\hat{S}^2_{\rho_{xy}} = S^2_r - S^2_e$ used to correct the observed variance of correlations (S^2_r) for sampling error variance (S^2_e). His conclusions were evaluated by Osburn and Callender (1989). First, Thomas (1988) called the model into question on grounds that the expected value of the estimate $\hat{S}^2_\rho$ [i.e., $E(\hat{S}^2_\rho)$] can be a (very small) negative number when the true value (i.e., S^2_ρ) is zero. However, Osburn and Callender (1989) showed that negative expected values do not occur unless ρ is at least .80 or larger, which is very rare in real data. Furthermore, negative expected values do not occur even in the presence of such large ρ values unless study sample sizes are less than about 45, which again is rare in real data. Finally, the negative expected values are very close to zero when they do occur. They typically show up only in the fifth decimal place and would have no effect on conclusions. The correct conclusion that $S^2_\rho = 0$ would always be reached.

Second, Thomas contended that $E(\hat{S}^2_\rho)$ can sometimes be larger when $S^2_\rho = 0$ than when $S^2_\rho > 0$. If true, this would indeed be an anomaly. But Osburn and Callender showed that this conclusion holds only if one assumes very different values for $\bar{\rho}$ when $S^2_\rho = 0$ and $S^2_\rho > 0$. For example, if the true value of ρ is always .325 (i.e., $S^2_\rho = 0$), then given study Ns of 10, 40, 50, and 180, $E(\hat{S}^2_\rho)$ is larger than when the ρ values vary and are .9, .85, .9, and .85 (.00183 vs. .00042). But this comparison is very unrealistic. Thomas overlooked the fact that in real studies, the estimate of the variance is made in conjunction with an estimate of the mean. In the above example, if ρ is allowed to vary but $\bar{\rho}$ is set at .325, this seeming anomaly never occurs. That is, $E(\hat{S}_\rho^2)$ is always smaller when $S_\rho^2 = 0$ than when $S_\rho^2 > 0$. Osburn and Callender (1989) showed that this is always the case when $\bar{\rho}$ is the same across the two elements of the comparison. Thus, Thomas's point appears to be irrelevant to any evaluation of the model for correcting for sampling error.

Finally, Thomas (1988) contended the model was defective because, under certain circumstances (when $S_\rho^2 = 0$ is very small), $\hat{S}_\rho^2$ has a substantial probability of being negative. The question of negative values for S_ρ^2 is discussed in some detail in Chapter 9 and in Hunter, Schmidt and Raju (1986). Such estimates create no problem. Osburn and Callender (1989) noted this same point and presented a simulation study showing that where Hedges's (1988) procedure is used to correct the small bias in r, the number of negative $\hat{S}_\rho^2$ values *increases*. Osburn and Callender conclude that Thomas has offered no valid reasons for questioning the basic model for correcting for sampling error.

PART III

Meta-Analysis of Experimental Effects and Other Dichotomous Comparisons

6   Treatment Effects: Experimental Artifacts and Their Impact

This chapter presents a substantive discussion of the evaluation of experiments and interventions. The next chapter (Chapter 7) will present the quantitative methods and formulas for meta-analysis and other more technical material. For purposes of simplicity, we will consider only a two group experiment. The principles developed here apply equally to more complicated designs.

This presentation will be parallel to that for correlational studies in Chapter 2. For typical studies, sampling error causes error in treatment effects and causes studies to appear to be inconsistent with each other. If the usual analysis were based on confidence intervals, the large effects of sampling error would be recognized, and spurious differences between studies would be properly attributed to sampling error. Instead most investigators rely on the statistical significance test, which aggravates rather than reduces the problem. Meta-analysis can disentangle differences due to sampling error from differences due to real moderator variables. Treatment effects are also distorted by other artifacts: error of measurement in the dependent variable, error of measurement in the treatment variable (i.e., differences between the nominal treatment and the actual treatment), dichotomization of a continuous dependent variable, range variation on the dependent variable, lack of perfect construct validity in the dependent variable, lack of perfect construct validity in the treatment variable (e.g. confounding of the intended treatment impact with other unintended impacts), bias in the estimation of the treatment effect, as well as bad data due to reporting errors, computation errors, transcription errors, and so on.

The distortions in treatment effects produced by artifacts were camouflaged by the traditional dichotomous description of treatment effects as either "had an effect" or "had no effect." Most artifacts reduce the size of the treatment effect. Had there been no effect to reduce, the artifact would cause no distortion. Thus, under the null hypothesis of "no effect," artifacts other than sampling error become irrelevant and were traditionally ignored. However, meta-analysis has shown that the nihilistic null hypothesis is rarely true. In most research domains, the null hypothesis is not true and the reduction of an effect by artifacts has a real and important effect. Among other things, reduction of the size of the study effect by an artifact increases the error rate of the conventional statistical significance test (which is high in the best of conditions for most studies). Differences in the extent of artifacts between studies cause apparent differences in effects across studies; i.e., produce the appearance of situation (or setting) by treatment interactions where there are none.

This chapter will begin with a discussion of the quantification of the treatment effect. We will then present hypothetical across-study data showing the effects of sampling error and the failure of the conventional statistical significance test in the context of the review study. We will then present a substantive discussion of artifacts other than sampling error. These other artifacts can be just as large in size even though they are usually systematic rather than random in nature.

Quantification of the Treatment Effect:
The *d* Statistic and the Point-Biserial Correlation

A key issue is the description of treatment effects as quantitative or dichotomous. The traditional description is dichotomous: to say that the treatment either had an effect or had no effect. Methodologists have long argued that we should instead describe the treatment in quantitative form, i.e., estimate the actual size of the treatment. A dichotomous description is poor for several reasons. First, there is a great loss of information, information that can be used (1) to assess the practical importance of a treatment, (2) to compare the effectiveness of treatments, (3) to determine whether a theory has been confirmed or disconfirmed, and (4) to test quantitative theories such as path models. Second, the implicit assumption in dichotomizing the treatment effect is that most treatments have no effect. If this were true, then there would be important information in the statement that the treatment effect is not zero. But meta-analyses have now shown that treatments rarely have no effect at all. The conclusion, "The treatment had no effect," is usually erroneous. Thus, the question for a treatment is really not whether it had an effect, but whether the effect is as large as a theory predicts, whether the effect is large enough to be of practical importance, or whether the effect is larger or smaller than some other treatment or some variation of the treatment. These questions can only be answered by quantifying the size of the treatment effect.

The dichotomization of treatment effects is also related to the statistical analysis of treatments. If it were true that most treatments have no effect, then good statistical analysis would focus on "Type I" error: falsely concluding that there is an effect when there is no such effect. The conventional significance test guarantees that Type I errors will occur no more than 5% of the time. However, meta-analysis has now shown that this nihilistic null hypothesis is rarely true. If the null hypothesis is false, then all statistical errors will be "Type II" errors: falsely concluding that there is no effect when there is in fact an effect. As we shall see, for typical sample sizes, the Type II error rate is quite high. For sample sizes of 100, the Type II error rate for textbook experiments is around 50% and the Type II error rate for more subtle follow-up research is higher yet. There are many important research domains where the significance test error rate is as high as 85%.

Since the null hypothesis is false in most research domains, the conventional significance test has a very high error rate. This high error rate means that the conventional significance test is actually counterproductive at the level of review studies. The high error rate for the conventional significance test means that results interpreted using the significance test must necessarily look inconsistent across studies. For example, if the significance test is wrong 50% of the time, then half the studies will have a significant treatment effect, but the other half will falsely appear to show no treatment effect.

This is quite evident in comparing the results of meta-analyses to the conclusions of narrative reviews. For most questions studied, meta-analysis shows that the treatment effect was not zero — although treatment effects are sometimes quite small. Narrative reviews on the other hand have been inconsistent. Some reviewers are selective; they throw out studies on "methodological" grounds — frequently of an entirely hypothetical nature. They throw out studies until those that remain have consistent results. They then base their conclusions on the remaining studies. Unfortunately, different reviewers will throw out different studies and, hence, come to different — sometimes opposite — conclusions. Comprehensive reviewers make a different error: they usually conclude that treatment effects are sporadic. They conclude that the treatment effect is present in some studies but absent in others.

The natural quantitative description of the treatment effect is just the difference between the means on the dependent variable. Let Y be the dependent variable. Denote the means for the control and experimental groups as follows.

$$Y_E = \text{the mean for the experimental group}$$

$$Y_C = \text{the mean for the control group}$$

To say, "The treatment increased performance by 3.2 feet," is to say that the difference $Y_E - Y_C$ is 3.2 feet; i.e.,

$$Y_E - Y_C = 3.2.$$

If the dependent variable were identically measured in all studies, then the raw score difference between means would be the conventional measure of the treatment effect. But this is rarely true. Consider the measurement of the job performance of sewing machine operators. One would think that a measure such as "number of garments sewn per week" would be the same variable across studies. But workers at different places are sewing different kinds of garments. To sew three dresses might be very different from sewing three coats. Thus, typically the units of the dependent variable vary from one study to the next.

If the dependent variable is the same in two different studies except for units, then it would in principle be possible to calibrate the two measures by finding the constant of proportionality between the two units. But consider the problem of matching the units for sewing machine operators in two different studies. In one study the workers sew dresses while the workers in the other study sew coats. To transform scores from one metric to the other, the workers at one place would have to sew the other kind of garment. Furthermore, they would have to be given exactly the same training in sewing that other kind of garment to be exactly comparable. This would be prohibitively expensive even if it were possible. Thus, exact calibration of independent variables is also impossible in most research domains.

There is an alternative method of matching across studies, although it depends on a substantive assumption. We can eliminate units within a study by using standard scores instead of raw scores. The treatment effect in standard scores would then be given by

$$d = (Y_E - Y_C) / \sigma$$

where σ is the standard deviation of the raw scores in that study. The only question is, "Which standard deviation?" This question will be considered in detail in the next chapter. For population data, the natural definition would be to use the population standard deviation of the control group. However, for sample data the standard deviation is much better estimated by using the "within group variance", i.e., by averaging the experimental and control group standard deviations. This sample statistic is Cohen's (1977) "d statistic," which is the most widely used statistic in the meta-analysis of experimental or intervention studies. For the population value, we will use the Greek letter for d, i.e., δ.

Suppose that the distribution of garment sewing performance per month has a mean of 100 and a standard deviation of 25. If a training program increases performance by 10 garments per month, then the treatment effect in standard scores would be

$$\delta = 10 / 25 = .40.$$

That is, the treatment effect would be .40 standard deviations.

There is a closely related measure of treatment effect that will be discussed in detail in the next chapter: the "point biserial" correlation. The point biserial correlation is actually an ordinary Pearson correlation; the special name comes from the nature of the data on which it is computed. We create a single data set by pooling the data across the control group and the experimental group. We define a treatment variable (sometimes called a "dummy variable" or "contrast variable") by assigning different scores to the people in the two different groups. For example, we might define the variable T by assigning the score zero to those in the control group and assigning the score one to those in the experimental group. The correlation computed on the pooled data between that treatment variable and the dependent variable is the point biserial correlation. The point biserial correlation has the advantage that it can be treated like any other correlation coefficient. In particular, the meta-analysis could be done using the methods of Chapters 3 and 4 on the correlation coefficient. The mathematics is then much easier than that for the d statistic. The correlation is much easier to fit into advanced statistical analyses such as reliability analysis, path analysis, and so on. The point biserial correlation is the second most often used quantification of the treatment effect in meta-analysis. As noted in the next chapter, the two statistics, r and d, can be algebraically transformed back and forth from each other. Thus, it is conceptually arbitrary which statistic is used. However, in this chapter we will primarily use d. For the usual empirical range of d of $-.41 < d < +.41$, the conversion formulas between r and d are trivial.

$$d = 2r \quad \text{for } -.21 < r < +.21$$

$$r = .5d \quad \text{for } -.41 < d < +.41$$

How close is this approximation? Consider the worst case, $d = .40$. The approximation $.5d$ yields $r = .20$, while the actual correlation is .196.

The δ statistic is comparable across studies if the standard deviation of the dependent variable (measured in any one set of units) is the same across studies. This is a typical finding for standardized variables in psychology. While means often differ considerably from one setting to the next, standard deviations often differ little. In a research domain where this is not true, then variation in results due to differing units could only be corrected by making a "correction for range variation."

Sampling Error in *d* Values: Illustrations

Is an argument more effective if it is expressed in intense language or if it is cast in "wishy-washy" language? A meta-analysis by Hamilton and Hunter (1987) has shown the difference in attitude change to be about .20 standard deviations (i.e., $d = .20$ or $r = .10$). Assume that this is the population value of the d statistic for all studies in a hypothetical meta-analysis. What would the review data look like? That depends on the sample sizes used in the studies collected. For simplicity, suppose that all studies had used exactly the same sample size. The study results would be approximately distributed as in Table 6.1. (Note: The distributions in Table 6.1 are 19-study distributions that exactly match the sampling distribution for replicated studies. An actual 19-study meta-analysis would find values that departed from this distribution somewhat because the 19 observed sampling errors would not match the exact population distribution of sampling errors.)

Case 1: $N = 30$

Suppose that 19 studies were done with a total sample size of 30 (15 subjects in each group) in each study. The study treatment effects would distribute themselves as the first column of Table 6.1. Six of the studies would have had negative observed treatment effects. The authors of these studies would believe that intense language is counterproductive and reduces the persuasive effect. On the other hand, six studies would have found treatment effects of $d = .40$ or more, effects as large as textbook examples. These authors would believe that intense language is one of the most powerful persuasive agents known. Both sets of authors would be wrong. Only study 10 — the median study — has an effect size of $d = .20$, the actual population value for all studies.

One classic but crude method of reviewing research is to count the number of studies in the predicted direction. This count is 13 out of 19. This is greater than the 9.5 out of 19 expected by chance, though not significantly so (using a binomial test). However, had there been 190

Table 6.1 Hypothetical Meta-Analysis Data for the Effect of Language Intensity on Persuasion.

Study	N=30	N=68	N=400
1	.80**	.60**	.36**
2	.68*	.50**	.32**
3	.58	.46*	.30**
4	.50	.40*	.28**
5	.44	.36	.26**
6	.40	.32	.26**
7	.34	.30	.24**
8	.30	.26	.22**
9	.24	.24	.22**
10	.20	.20	.20**
11	.16	.16	.18*
12	.10	.14	.18*
13	.06	.10	.16
14	−.00	.08	.16
15	−.04	.04	.14
16	−.10	−.00	.12
17	−.18	−.06	.10
18	−.28	−.10	.08
19	−.40	−.20	.04

**Significant by two-tailed test.
*Significant by one-tailed test.

NOTE: In each case the population treatment effect is given by $\varepsilon=.20$ in all studies and all deviation from that value is entirely due to sampling error. The sample size is the total sample size across control (low intensity) and experimental (high intensity) groups. Thus, "$N=30$" means "15 in each group."

studies instead of 19, the expected count of studies in the predicted direction would be 130/190, which is significantly greater than the 95 expected by chance. Thus, a count of the studies in the predicted direction would show that intensity increased persuasion more often than chance. However, it would falsely suggest that intensity acted in the *opposite* direction 32% of the time.

The statistical significance test was designed to reduce the impact of sampling error. Under certain conditions, it should reduce errors of inference to 5%. How does the conventional significance test fare in this example? There are two ways to do this significance test. Had each study been analyzed using analysis of variance, it would have been analyzed using a two-tailed significance test, and only the study with $d = .80$ would have been significant. That is, analysis of variance yields the correct inference for only one study, an error rate of 18/19 or 95%. That is, the error rate for the two-tailed significance test is not 5% but 95% in this example.

Had the data been analyzed using the t test, the authors would have had the option of doing a one-tailed test. For a one-tailed test, both studies 1 and 2 have significant treatment effects. Thus, this significance test yields a correct inference for only 2 of the 19 studies, an error rate of 17/19 or 89%. Thus, for a one-tailed t test, the error rate is not 5% but 89% in this example.

In this example, the two-tailed test (conventional analysis of variance) is correct in only 1 of 19 studies. The one-tailed test is correct in 2 of 19 studies which doubles the power of the two-tailed test. However, in either case the error rate is far higher than the 5% error rate that most people believe to be the error rate for the statistical significance test.

Why is the error rate higher than 5%? The conventional statistical significance test assumes a nihilistic null hypothesis of $\delta = 0$. If the null hypothesis were true, then the error rate would be only 5%. But the null hypothesis is false for this research domain and, thus, the error rate is not constrained to be 5%, but will be higher. In this example, the error rate rose to 89% (one-tailed test) or 95% (two-tailed test), which is close to the theoretical maximum error rate.

Consider the position of a reviewer faced with study results such as those in Table 6.1. If the reviewer counts results in the expected direction, then there is a weak indication of results in the expected direction. It is true that nearly a third of the studies go in the wrong direction, but that is counterbalanced by the third of the studies with effects as large as classic textbook effects in social psychology. That reviewer would probably conclude that intense language is more persuasive most of the time but would warn that there are some settings, where for unknown reasons, intense language is counterproductive. This would be a false interpretation of the data.

Suppose the reviewer ignored the size of the treatment effects and considered only a count of the number of significant findings using a two-tailed test. This reviewer would almost certainly conclude that language intensity has no effect on persuasiveness. That, too, would be a false conclusion. Ironically, the reviewer who uses the significance test — the more "sophisticated" method – is even farther off base than the reviewer who naively looks at raw results!

Note that the inferences of reviewers would not materially improve with more data. If the number of studies rose from 19 to 190, the number of studies with results significant by a one-tailed test would rise from 2 to 20. However, the proportion of significant findings would still be the same,

20/190 = 2/19. Thus, a reviewer who depended on the significance test would still draw the same false conclusions even though there were 10 times as much data.

As we will see, the method of meta-analysis presented in this book will deal with this data correctly. This method would estimate the average treatment effect to be $\delta = .20$ to within the sampling error left by using a total sample size of $N = 19 (30) = 570$. If there were 190 studies, the error in estimating the mean effect size would drop to that left by a total sample size of $N = 190 (30) = 5,700$. As more and more studies become available, this method of meta-analysis has less and less error. This method would also have correctly concluded that all or nearly all the variance in observed study effects was due to sampling error.

Is this example far-fetched? The size of the treatment effect for language intensity is that found in actual studies. On the other hand, the sample size of $N = 30$ is lower than the actual studies ($N = 56$). However, there are important research domains with sample sizes this low. For example, Allen, Hunter, and Donahue (1988) did a meta-analysis on studies of the effect of psychotherapy on problems of shyness and fear of public speaking. For the studies using systematic desensitization, the average sample size was 23. For the studies using rational-emotive therapy, the average sample size was only 19.

Case 2: $N = 68$

The median sample size of studies in personnel selection is 68 (Lent, Auerbach, & Levin, 1971a, 1971b). This seems not far from sample sizes in other psychological study domains although there are exceptions both larger and smaller. The average sample size for the language intensity meta-analysis done by Hamilton and Hunter (1987) was $N = 56$, which is about the same as the 68 used in Table 6.1. If all 19 studies were done with a sample size of $N = 68$, then the study values would have an expected distribution like that of the second column of Table 6.1.

A reviewer who looked at the results at face value would now see 15 of 19 values in the expected direction and only 4 of 19 negative values. This split is significantly different from a 50-50 split using a binomial comparison. At the same time, the four large values are not quite as large as textbook examples. This reviewer would probably conclude that the studies in the wrong direction were just sampling errors from a zero effect. Thus, the reviewer would probably conclude that language intensity usually increases persuasion, although there are a minority of cases where it does not. This conclusion is false since the effect is actually $\delta=.20$ in all cases.

The conventional two-tailed statistical significance test of analysis of variance registers only the two largest values as significant. Thus, the conventional two-tailed test is correct in only 2 of 19 cases, an error rate of 17/19 or 89%. A reviewer who counted significant findings would probably conclude that language intensity is irrelevant to persuasion. This conclusion would be a grave error in this example.

The one-tailed significance test registers the top four values as significant. Thus, the one-tailed test is correct four times, which means that the one-tailed test has twice the power of the two-tailed test in this example. However, the one-tailed test is still wrong in 15/19 studies, an error rate of 79%. A reviewer who counts one-tailed significant findings would probably conclude that 4 times in 19 is noticeably greater than the 1 in 20 expected by chance. If not, then if the number of studies were raised to 190, the reviewer would certainly notice that 40 out of 190 is much greater than the 190/20 = 9.5 expected by chance. The reviewer would probably conclude that language intensity does have an impact in about (40–10)/190 or 16% of settings, but has no effect otherwise. This is an improvement over the error made by the reviewer who looks at two-tailed tests, but is worse than the conclusion drawn by the reviewer who ignores the significance test altogether.

The method of meta-analysis presented here would estimate the treatment effect to within the sampling error left by a total sample size of $N =$ 19 (68) = 1292. If there were 190 studies, the error in the mean effect size would be down to that left by a total sample size of $N = 190 (68) = 12,920$. The method would also correctly conclude that all or nearly all of the variance across studies is due to sampling error.

Case 3: $N = 400$

Most psychologists think of a sample size of 400 as if it were infinity. However, pollsters know differently from experience. The typical study results for 19 studies with a sample size of $N = 400$ are shown in the third column of Table 6.1.

A reviewer who looks at the results at face value would now note that all results are in the expected direction, although the smallest results are small indeed. The largest results are still moderate in size. Thus, the reviewer would probably conclude that language intensity always increases persuasion (a correct conclusion) although in some settings the impact is negligible in magnitude (an incorrect conclusion).

A reviewer who counts two-tailed significance tests would find that 10 of 19 study values are significant. This reviewer would probably conclude that language intensity increases persuasion in about half of the settings but does not work in the other half. This conclusion is quite far from the truth.

A reviewer who counts one-tailed significance tests would find that 13 of 19 study values are significant. Thus, in this example, the one-tailed test is 13/10 times more powerful than the two-tailed test, i.e, about 30% more powerful. This reviewer would probably conclude that language intensity increases persuasion in about two-thirds of the settings, but does not work in the other third. This conclusion is also quite far from the truth.

Even with a sample size of 400, the reviewer who naively looks at face value results is closer to the truth than a reviewer who counts statistical significance findings. Thus, even with a sample size of 400, the significance test still works so poorly that it is counterproductive in comparison to doing no analysis for sampling error at all.

With an average sample size of 400, our method of meta-analysis would estimate the mean effect size to within the sampling error left by a total sample size of $N = 19 (400) = 7,600$. The analysis would also correctly conclude that all or nearly all of the variance across studies is due to sampling error.

From the viewpoint of review studies, the statistical significance test does not correctly deal with sampling error. The statistical significance test works only in a research context in which we know the null hypothesis to be true. But if we know the null hypothesis to be true, then we need not do the test at all. Thus, we should abandon the use of the statistical significance test in doing review studies. There are now many sets of mathematically equivalent meta-analysis formulas that take sampling error into account correctly for mean effect sizes, including the method presented here. In an example where there is no variance in population effect sizes, there are now many equivalent chi-square tests for homogeneity that would correctly (to within sampling error) conclude that the variance across studies is entirely due to sampling error. Our method will also work when there is real variance in effect sizes across studies. We will estimate the size of the standard deviation of population effect sizes. Some authors stop with a test for homogeneity and present no method for estimating the standard deviation if it is not zero.

Error of Measurement in the Dependent Variable

Ordinary English interprets the phrase "error of measurement" as having two meanings: systematic and unsystematic error. Systematic error is a departure from measuring exactly what was intended. In psychometric theory, this is called "imperfect construct validity." In psychometric theory, the phrase "error of measurement" is used for unsystematic error, also called "random error" or "unreliability." We will follow psychometric terminology here. This section will present the effects of unsystematic or random error of measurement and a later section will cover imperfect construct validity.

In psychology, most of the unsystematic error of measurement is caused by randomness in subject response. This kind of error usually has a mean of zero, i.e., is equally likely to be positive or negative, and is uncorrelated with the true value. If we write the observed score on the dependent variable as Y, write the true score as U, and write the error of measurement as e, then

$$Y = U + e$$

where the population mean of e is 0 and the population correlation between e and U is 0.

Since the average error is 0, the mean of errors does not describe the typical size of an error. Rather the typical size of errors is described by either the error variance — the average squared error — or by the error standard deviation. The number σ_e is called the "standard error of measurement" in psychometric theory. The practical impact of error of measurement is relative to the size of differences between people. If two people differ on the dependent variable by 10 points, then errors of size -1 or $+1$ would have little effect on the comparison of those people. On the other hand, if the difference between two subjects were .5, then errors of -1 or $+1$ would completely obscure the comparison. One measure of the relative error of measurement is the "noise to signal" ratio σ_e / σ_U although this is not commonly used. Instead, the more useful measure of relative error is the correlation between true and observed score, i.e., r_{UY}. By historical convention, the square of this correlation is called the "reliability" of the dependent variable and is denoted r_{YY}. That is, we define the reliability of the dependent variable r_{YY} by

$$r_{YY} = r_{YU}^{2}.$$

The error standard deviation and the reliability of the dependent variable are related by

$$\sigma_e = \sigma_Y \sqrt{(1 - r_{YY})}.$$

The size of the reliability depends on the extent of random error in the process measured — usually a response in psychology — and on the number

of primary measurements used to generate the final response — frequently
the number of items on a scale. High quality measurement often provides
reliability in the region of $r_{YY} = .81$. Moderate quality usually falls around
$r_{YY} = .64$. Measurement based on a single response frequently has reliability no higher than $r_{YY} = .25$. It should be noted that the reliability of a single
response is not determined by the cost of obtaining that response. For
example, in equity studies in social psychology, subjects may spend as
much as an hour before the criterion act. But the only measurement of the
dependent variable is a single response: the amount of money given to the
partner. The reliability of that single response is the correlation between
that response and the response that would have been made on some other
randomly chosen day. The reliability of single responses is rarely higher
than $r_{YY} = .25$.

The size of the reliability depends both on the extent of error in the
measurement process and on the extent of individual differences on the
dependent variable. For instance, Nicol and Hunter (1973) found that the
same semantic differential scale that had a reliability of .90 measuring
attitudes toward the polarized issue "law and order" had only a reliability
of .20 measuring attitudes toward the issue "pollution."

The observed score for a given person p is related to the true score for
that person by

$$Y_p = T_p + e_p .$$

If we average scores across persons, the mean score is related to the mean
true score by

$$\overline{Y} = \overline{T} + \overline{e} .$$

That is, errors of measurement are averaged across persons. The population mean of scores across persons averages the errors of measurement
across an infinity of errors and is thus zero. That is, at the population level,
error of measurement has no impact of the mean.

The raw score treatment effect is defined as the difference between
population means.

$$\text{Raw Score } \delta_Y = Y_E - Y_C$$

Since population mean error of measurement is zero, each mean observed
score is equal to the mean true score. Thus,

$$\text{Raw Score } \delta_U = U_E - U_C = Y_E - Y_C = \text{Raw Score } \delta_Y.$$

That is, random error does not alter the raw score treatment effect. This is the reason that traditional statistics has ignored error of measurement in the treatment of experimental design.

However, it is not the raw score treatment effect but rather the standard score treatment effect that is of primary interest in statistics. For purposes of meta-analysis it is normally necessary to use standard score treatment effects to achieve comparability across studies. However, the standard score treatment effect is also central to traditional statistics because it is the standard score treatment effect that is assessed by the statistical test for significance. In particular, the power of the conventional significance test depends on the standard score treatment effect.

Error of measurement does not affect the mean of the dependent variable but it *does* affect the variance. The variance of observed scores is related to the variance of true scores by

$$\sigma_Y^2 = \sigma_U^2 + \sigma_e^2.$$

That is, error of measurement increases the variance and, hence, the standard deviation of the dependent variable. Consider then the experimental versus control group comparison. Adding error does not change the means, but it increases the spread of scores about the mean. This effect is shown in Figure 6.1.

The extent of separation between two groups depends on the extent of overlap between the two distributions. The extent of overlap between the distributions depends on the difference between the means in relation to the extent of spread about the means. The greater the spread about the means, the greater the overlap between the two distributions. Figure 6.1 shows that the extent of overlap is greatly increased by the presence of error of measurement. The lower the reliability, the larger the spread about the means and, hence, the greater the overlap. That is, as the amount of error of measurement increases, the difference is more and more obscure. In terms of statistical power, the more obscure the difference between the means, the more difficult that difference is to detect.

Consider then the standardized effect size for true scores and observed scores.

$$\delta_U = (U_E - U_C) / \sigma_U$$

$$\delta_Y = (Y_E - Y_C) / \sigma_Y$$

Figure 6.1 The Effect of Error of Measurement on the Separation Between the Control and Experimental Groups for a Case in Which the True Score Treatment Effect is $\delta = 1.00$

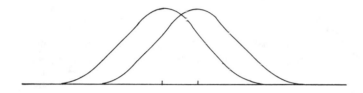

Figure 6.1a Perfect Measurement, $r_{yy} = 1.00$

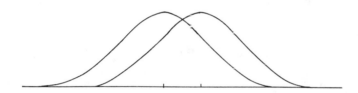

Figure 6.1b Typical Good Measurement, $r_{yy} = .81$

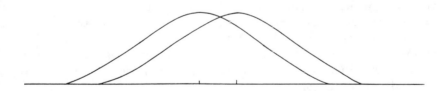

Figure 6.1c Typical Moderate Measurement, $r_{yy} = .50$

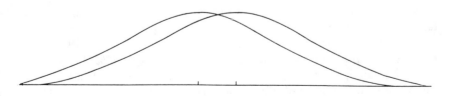

Figure 6.1d Typical Poor Measurement, $r_{yy} = .25$

Because population means are not affected by error of measurement, the numerators are equal. However, error of measurement increases the standard deviation and, hence, the denominators are different. The increase in standard deviation is given by

$$\sigma_Y = \sigma_U / \sqrt{r_{YY}}$$

where we note that to divide by a number less than 1 is to increase the ratio. If this identity is substituted into the equation for δ_Y we have

$$\delta_Y = \delta_U \sqrt{r_{YY}} .$$

That is, the standardized effect size for the observed score is the standardized effect size for the true score multiplied by the square root of the reliability. For example, if the reliability were $r_{YY} = .81$, the effect size would be reduced to

$$\delta_Y = .90\ \delta_U,$$

i.e., reduced by 10%.

If the effect size is reduced by error of measurement, the effect is more difficult to detect by the conventional significance test. This is illustrated in Table 6.2. Table 6.2 computes the power of the conventional significance test for studies of sample size $N = 100$; a value roughly typical for empirical studies. An effect size of $\delta = .40$ is about the size of large introductory textbook examples from the social psychology experimental literature. The effect size of $\delta = .20$ is about the size of effects in the more sophisticated research that follows up textbook examples, i.e., research that studies variation in textbook manipulations rather than the crude manipulation itself.

Table 6.2 first shows the reduction in the treatment effect produced by different levels of error of measurement. As the reliability decreases from $r_{YY} = 1.00$ to $r_{YY} = .25$, the treatment effect is reduced by half; e.g. from $\delta = .40$ to $\delta = .20$ or from $\delta = .20$ to $\delta = .10$. The probability of detecting the effect using a conventional significance test drops correspondingly. For textbook size effects with $\delta = .40$, the power drops from an already low 51% to 17%; a power level only one-third the size. Stated the other way, the error rate for the significance test rises from 49% to 83%. For sophisticated research, the initial power level is smaller to begin with and, hence, there is less distance to fall. If with perfect measurement the effect size is $\delta = .20$, then, if the dependent variable is based on a single response, the

Table 6.2 The Power of the Conventional Significance Test for Studies with Sample Size *N*=100

I. *The reduction in the effect size: the value of δy for various values of the reliability of the dependent variable*

Reliability	$\delta_U=.10$	$\delta_U=.20$	$\delta_U=.30$	$\delta_U=.40$
1.00	.10	.20	.30	.40
.81	.09	.18	.27	.36
.64	.08	.16	.24	.32
.25	.05	.10	.15	.20

II. *The reduction in power: the power of the conventional .05 level statistical significance test for various values of the reliability of the dependent variable; expressed as a percent*

Reliability	$\delta_U=.10$	$\delta_U=.20$	$\delta_U=.30$	$\delta_U=.40$
1.00	7.2	16.6	31.8	51.2
.81	6.5	14.3	26.7	43.2
.64	5.9	12.1	22.0	37.3
.25	4.3	7.2	11.2	16.6

observed effect size would be about $\delta = .10$ and the power would drop from 17% to 7%; a reduction of slightly more than half. The error rate for the significance test rises from 83% to 93%.

The next chapter will show that for population effect sizes the reduction of the treatment effect can be corrected if the reliability of the dependent variable is known. While the application of that same correction formula to sample values eliminates the systematic effect of error of measurement, the increased sampling error and reduced statistical power cannot be corrected. This shows in the fact that the significance test on the corrected effect size is algebraically equivalent to the significance test on the uncorrected effect size.

Error of Measurement in the Treatment Variable

The treatment variable is defined by group assignment. Since the investigator usually knows exactly which group each subject belongs to, this variable is usually regarded as perfectly measured. However, this definition ignores the interpretation of the results. In interpreting the results, it is not group assignment but the treatment process that is assumed to be the independent variable. From that point of view, the nominal treatment variable may be quite different from the actual treatment variable.

Consider an attitude change experiment directed to the topic of acid rain. The investigator seeks to manipulate the credibility of the source of the change-inducing message. At one point in the instructions the sentence "The author of the message is . . ." is completed with either the phrase, "a famous scientist in the area," or with, "a marine drill instructor." Assume that the instructions are correctly read to each subject so that we do know correctly and exactly the group assignment of each subject. However, suppose that 30% of the subjects are not paying careful attention to the instructions. They do not hear the sentence stating the author of the message. They do not think about the author of the message until they read it. Assume that the subjects who did not hear the author's identity then *assume* one. Suppose that half the subjects assume the author to be an expert while half the subjects assume the author to be some know-nothing graduate assistant. Then, in this study, 15% of the control group subjects will assume an expert source and will act as if they had been exposed to the experimental group instructions, while 15% of the experimental group subjects will assume a know-nothing source and will act as if they had been exposed to the control group instruction. In this example, the nominal treatment group variable is the reverse of the actual treatment variable 15% of the time. The observed effect size will be correspondingly reduced.

How much will the treatment effect be reduced? The idea is simple, but the computations are complicated. In our example, where 15% of the subjects were misidentified in each group, we could compute the effect of the treatment variable error by assuming each treatment group to be the pooling of 85% from the corresponding true treatment group and 15% from the other true treatment group. The outcome is easily stated in correlational terms. Denote the nominal treatment variable by X and denote the true treatment variable by T, i.e.

X = the observed group assignment of the subject;

T = the actual treatment value for that subject.

If the correlation between X and T is r_{XT} then the observed treatment effect correlation r_{XY} is related to the true treatment effect correlation r_{TY} by the equation

$$r_{XY} = r_{XT} r_{TY}.$$

The formula for the reduction in the δ statistic can be obtained by substituting the above product into the formula for r to d conversion.

The product rule for the treatment effect correlation is a special case of the attenuation formula from psychometric theory. Let us denote the "reliability of the treatment" by r_{XX} and define it to be the square of the correlation between true and observed treatment identifications, i.e., we define r_{XX} by

$$r_{XX} = r_{XT}^2 .$$

Then our product formula is a special case of the psychometric formula

$$r_{XY} = \sqrt{r_{XX}} \ r_{TY} .$$

In our attitude change example, we assumed 15% misidentification in each group. The correlation between the observed and true treatment is thus $r_{XT} = .70$ and, hence, the observed treatment effect correlation is

$$r_{XY} = .70 \ r_{TY} .$$

That is, the observed treatment effect correlation is reduced by 30%.

If the treatment effect correlation is reduced, then statistical power will be reduced correspondingly. Suppose in our example that the true treatment effect was $\delta_T = .40$ with a sample size of $N = 100$. The true treatment effect correlation would then be $r_{TY} = .20$. The observed treatment effect correlation would then be $r_{XY} = (.70)(.20) = .14$ and the observed treatment effect would be $\delta_X = .28$. Had there been no error in the treatment identification, the statistical power would have been 51%. Instead, it is 28%, reduced by nearly half.

If the reliability of the treatment variable is known, then the attenuation effect can be corrected. The formula is the usual psychometric formula for correction for attenuation due to error in the independent variable.

$$r_{TY} = r_{XY} / \sqrt{r_{YY}}$$

This correction works perfectly at the population correlation level. However, the correction at the sample data level corrects for only the systematic attenuation. It does not correct for the increased sampling error introduced by the measurement error. The significance test on the corrected correlation is algebraically equivalent to the significance test on the uncorrected correlation.

In the above example of attitude change experiment, errors of measurement in the independent variable had two effects: (1) Within both the experimental and control groups, the within group variance on the dependent variable was increased; and (2) the raw score mean difference on the dependent variable was reduced, that is, $\overline{Y}_E - \overline{Y}_C$ was reduced. In such a case, the observed d value will be reduced for two reasons: because the numerator is reduced and because the denominator is increased. There are other cases of measurement error in the independent variable in which the numerator, $\overline{Y}_E - \overline{Y}_C$, is unaffected but the denominator, the pooled within group SD, is inflated, leading to artifactually lowered estimates of d.

For example, suppose an experiment is conducted to determine the effect of personal attention and sympathetic listening by work counselors on the job-related attitudes of problem employees. Each member of the experimental group is supposed to get 12 hours of personal interaction (6 two-hour sessions) with a counselor. However, because of interruptions of scheduled sessions, lateness, and other problems, some people in each study get less than that: some 10 and some 11 hours. Because some counselors run past the stopping time without realizing it, other members of the experimental group get more than 12 hours: some 13 and some 14 hours. The average amount of time might be approximately correct: 12 hours. If the impact of treatment strength differences is approximately linear over the range of variation in the study (true in most cases), then the average effect will be determined by the average treatment strength. The individual variations will cancel out, and the mean of the treatment group will be the same as if there had been no variation in treatment. Thus, the numerator of the effect size formula for d (i.e., $\overline{Y}_E - \overline{Y}_C$) will not be affected. But the individual variations in treatment strength will cause variations in outcome that will contribute to variation in the dependent variable. Thus, the denominator of the effect size will be larger than would be true if there were no variation in treatment strength. If the denominator of the effect size is increased, then the effect size would be reduced. Thus, within study variation in treatment strength that has no effect on $\overline{Y}_E - \overline{Y}_C$ nevertheless reduces the effect size.

Furthermore, since the extent of within study variation is likely to differ from one study to the next, failure to correct for attenuation due to treatment variation will lead to artificial variation in effect size across studies. This uncorrected variation could be falsely interpreted as showing the existence of a nonexistent moderator variable.

Variation in the treatment effect increases the experimental group standard deviation, but does not change the control group standard deviation. The increase in the experimental group standard deviation increases the within group standard deviation and, hence, reduces the observed effect size value. However, this artificial increase in the experimental standard deviation could also cause another error. If there were no true treatment by subject interaction and if there were no variation in the treatment effect, then the control and experimental group standard deviations would be equal. The artificial increase in the experimental group standard deviation might be falsely interpreted as an indication of a treatment by subject interaction.

If there is no true treatment by subject interaction, then the increase in the experimental group standard deviation can be used to quantify the impact of treatment variation. If there is no interaction, then the desired effect size is

$$\delta = (Y_E - Y_C) / SD_c .$$

The observed population effect size is

$$\delta_o = (Y_E - Y_C) / SD_w .$$

The two effect sizes differ by

$$\delta_o = a \, \delta$$

where the attenuation factor a is given by

$$a = SD_c / SD_w .$$

For equal sample sizes, the attenuation factor can be computed from the ratio comparing the experimental and control group standard deviations. Denote the standard deviation comparison ratio by v. That is, define v by

$$v = SD_e / SD_c .$$

Then, the within group standard deviation is related to v by

$$SD_w = \sqrt{[\,(SD_c^2 + SD_e^2\,) / 2\,]} = SD_c \sqrt{[\,(1 + v^2) / 2\,]} .$$

Thus,

$$a = SD_c / SD_w = 1 / \sqrt{[\,(1 + v^2) / 2\,]} .$$

If v is not much larger than 1, then we have the approximation

$$a = 1 - (v^2 - 1) / 2 .$$

In summary, within study variation in treatment strength causes an inflation in the experimental dependent variable standard deviation. If there is no real treatment by subject interaction, then variation in treatment strength causes the experimental group standard deviation to be artificially larger than the control group standard deviation. If treatment variation is not suspected, then this increase could be falsely interpreted as indicating a treatment by subject interaction. If it is known that there is no interaction, then the attenuation in the effect size can be computed from comparison ratio of the experimental to control group standard deviation.

Variation Across Studies in Treatment Strength

In the example above, the mean raw score treatment effect, $\overline{Y}_E - \overline{Y}_C$, is the same in all studies. In other cases, however, this value may vary across the studies in a meta-analysis — because the amount of treatment given to the experimental group might differ, causing $\overline{Y}_E$ to vary across studies. If these differences are known (that is, if they are given in each study), they can be coded and treated as a potential moderator variable. But if the strength of treatment values is not known, then variation in treatment strength will produce variation in effect sizes that cannot be accounted for. This variation could cause an actually homogeneous treatment effect to appear to be heterogeneous and, thus, suggest a nonexistent moderator variable. (Alternately, the effects of variation in treatment strength will be confounded with the real moderator variable.)

Consider an example: Suppose in a *series* of studies evaluating a new training method, the experimental group was supposed to get 10 hours of training in each study. But, due to administrative and communications problems, the experimental people in some studies get 8, 9, 11 ,or 12 hours of training; although *within* each study, each subject received exactly the same number of hours of training, only some of the studies hit exactly the desired 10 hours. If the mean across studies is 10 hours, then the mean effect size for the meta-analysis will not be affected. However, the variation in training time across studies will create additional variance in effect sizes beyond that created by sampling error. The formulas presented in this book do not correct for this. If the number of training hours is given in each study, this variable can be coded and analyzed as a moderator. However, this information would rarely be given since the deviations from 10 hours all represent errors in carrying out the study plan — errors that the experimenters themselves may not even be aware of.

In the example here, average treatment strength across studies was equal to the target value of 10 hours. This is what would be expected if the measurement error were random. If the mean were discrepant from the goal — say 9 hours instead of 10 — then the mean effect size would be affected, as well as the variance. However, in this example we assume a mean (expected value) of zero for the measurement errors.

This form of measurement error is analogous to unintended differences between studies in range restriction in correlational studies, that is, differences in range restriction (or enhancement) that might appear despite the fact that researchers took special steps to obtain the same variation in all studies, just as the experimenters attempted here to have exactly the same treatment across studies. In many meta-analyses, the strength of treatment conditions will vary across studies, not because of measurement error, but because the different experimenters did not have a common goal for treatment strength to begin with. This condition is closely analogous to the naturally occurring range variation that occurs across correlational studies. As noted and illustrated earlier, this problem can be addressed by a moderator analysis when the needed information on treatment strength is given in individual studies. But this information will often not be given.

Range Variation on the Dependent Variable

The raw score treatment effect is determined by the nature of the treatment process. Thus, if the same process is used in different settings, it should stay about the same. However, the standard deviation of the study group is not determined by the treatment process but by the nature of the selection of the group in question. Thus, the study population might be more homogeneous in some settings than others. The standardized treatment effect would vary correspondingly.

Consider an attitude change study done on a polarized political topic. Initial attitudes would be much more homogeneous in a group of Republicans than in a politically unselected population. Assume that the standard deviation among Republicans is only half the size of the standard deviation in a mixed population, say $\sigma = 50$ in the mixed population and $\sigma = 25$ for Republicans. If the change produced by the message is 10 points in raw score form, then a study done on a mixed population would produce a standardized effect size of $10/50 = .20$, while the same study done on a Republican population would produce a standardized effect size of $10/25 = .40$, a standardized effect size twice as large.

From the viewpoint of statistical power, there is a considerable advantage to doing a study using a more homogeneous population. Consider the political attitude example again. The investigator doing the study on a general population would have an effect size of $\delta = .20$, while the same study done on a Republican population would have an effect size of $\delta = .40$. Given a study sample size of $N = 100$, the statistical power for the study on a general population would be 17%, while the power on the homogeneous population would be 51%, three times higher.

The investigator studying the general population could have obtained a similar gain in power by breaking his data down into Republicans and Democrats and then properly merging the results from the two within group comparisons. This is the gain in power that results from analysis of covariance, or use of the "treatment by levels" design.

For purposes of meta-analysis, let us choose some population as a reference population. We want all effect sizes expressed in terms of that reference population. To do so, we must know the ratio of the standard deviation of the study population to the standard deviation of the reference population. Denote the standard deviations of the two populations by

$$\sigma_P = \text{standard deviation of reference population;}$$

$$\sigma_S = \text{standard deviation of the study population.}$$

The ratio of study to reference standard deviation is denoted u, i.e.,

$$u = \sigma_S / \sigma_P .$$

If the raw score treatment effect is the same in both populations, then the standardized treatment effect in the study population is given by

$$\delta_S = \delta_P / u .$$

That is, the more homogeneous the study population in comparison to the reference population, the larger the study effect size.

To correct for range variation, we need merely use the above equation in reverse order, i.e.,

$$\delta_P = u\delta_S .$$

In meta-analysis, this formula could be used to correct each of the study effect sizes to the same reference population value and, thus, eliminate differences in effect size due to differences in homogeneity. However, this correction requires that the same scale of measurement for the dependent variable be used in all studies. This is rarely the case, so this correction can usually not be made.

Dichotomization of the Dependent Variable

In some studies, a continuous dependent variable is dichotomized. For example, in research on the effect of a realistic job preview on subsequent turnover, most investigators do not use the natural dependent variable of tenure, the length of time the worker stays with the firm. Instead, they dichotomize tenure to create a binary "turnover" variable; e.g., they might see if a worker stays more than six months or not. The loss of information inherent in dichotomization causes a reduction in the effect size and a corresponding loss in statistical power. Within a wide range of values, this artificial reduction in effect size can be corrected. However, within a single study, the statistical correction formula does NOT restore the higher level of statistical power.

Denote the treatment variable by T and denote the continuous dependent variable by Y. Denote the dichotomized dependent variable by Y'. The effect of the dichotomization is to replace the correlation r_{TY} by the correlation $r_{TY'}$, which is lower in magnitude. The statistical significance test is then done on the smaller $r_{TY'}$ with correspondingly lower power. What we seek is a correction formula that restores the value $r_{TY'}$ to the value r_{TY}. There is an approximate formula that works at the population level. Application of that formula at the sample level eliminates the systematic error in the correlation, but does not eliminate the larger sampling error that arises from the loss in information due to dichotomization. The formula works well in meta-analysis where the impact of sampling error is greatly reduced.

For a cross-sectional correlation, dichotomization of the dependent variable reduces the correlation by a product rule formula similar to that for attenuation due to error of measurement. The correction formula is known as that which creates a "biserial correlation" from a "point biserial correlation." This formula does not work for treatment correlations because the dependent variable does not have a normal distribution. The treatment effect causes the distribution of the experimental group to be displaced from that of the control group. When the two groups are pooled, the combination distribution is not normal. To see this, consider the extreme case in which the treatment effect is three standard deviations in magnitude. The two distributions hardly overlap and the combined distribution is distinctly bimodal — one mode at each of the subgroup means.

However, we will show that the biserial correlation formula works quite well as an approximation over the usual range of effect sizes and distribution splits. This corresponds to the fact that the combined distribution is

Table 6.3 The Comparison Ratio of Corrected/Actual Correlations—
Expressed as Percents—Where the Corrected Correlation is
the Estimated Correlation for the Continuous Dependent
Variable Computed by Correcting the Dichotomous Variable
Correlation Using the Biserial Correction Formula.

d	.10	.20	.30	.40	.50	.60	.70	.80	.90
	Combined proportion "high" on the dependent variable								
.10	100	100	100	100	100	100	100	100	100
.20	100	100	100	100	100	100	100	100	100
.30	100	100	101	101	101	101	101	100	100
.40	99	100	101	101	101	101	101	100	99
.50	99	101	101	102	102	102	101	101	99
.60	98	101	102	103	103	103	102	101	98
.70	97	101	103	104	104	104	103	101	97
.80	96	101	103	105	105	105	103	101	96
.90	95	101	104	106	106	106	104	101	95
1.00	94	101	105	107	107	107	105	101	94
1.10	93	101	105	108	109	108	105	101	93

NOTE: The statistic d is the population effect size for the continuous variable; i.e., approximately twice the value of the population continuous variable treatment correlation.

approximately normal unless the treatment effect is very large. Suppose that in the combined groups the proportion of people in the "high" split is p while the proportion in the "low" split is $q = 1 - p$. For a normal distribution, there would be a z value corresponding to such a split (although the combined distribution is not exactly normal). Call this value the "cutoff" value and denote it by c. The value of the normal density function or "normal ordinate" at c is denoted $\varphi(c)$. The attenuation in the treatment correlation is approximately given by the biserial attenuation formula

$$r_{TY'} = a \, r_{TY}$$

where

$$a = \varphi(c) / \sqrt{pq} \, .$$

The corresponding correction formula is the biserial formula

$$r_{TY} = r_{TY'} / a \, .$$

The range over which the formula is accurate is shown in Table 6.3. Table 6.3 presents the comparison ratio for the actual continuous variable correlation and the attenuated dichotomous variable correlation corrected using the biserial correction formula. The ratio is in the order corrected/actual and is expressed as a percent. For example, for a population continuous $d = .40$ and a median split on the combined population $p = .50$, the ratio is 101. That is, whereas the actual continuous treatment correlation is $r_{TY} = .20$, the corrected dichotomized correlation is $1.01(.20)=.202$, an error less than rounding error. The error is always less than rounding error for the range of values, $-.51 < d < +.51$ and $.09 < p < .91$, the range of values in most current meta-analyses. For the most extreme case in Table 6.3, $d = 1.10$ and $p = .90$, the actual correlation is .48 and the corrected correlation is $.93(.48) = .45$, an error that is visible but still not large in practical terms.

Imperfect Construct Validity in the Dependent Variable

Suppose that there is some systematic error in the measurement of the dependent variable; i.e., we measure a dependent variable that is different to some extent from the intended dependent variable. What effect will this have on the effect size and can it be corrected? A full treatment of this problem requires considerable knowledge of path analysis and knowledge of the nature of the dependent variable and its relations with other variables. However, there are certain common cases that are relatively straightforward.

The most common case is the use of a dependent variable that is an indirect measure of the desired dependent variable. For example, a good assessment of a juvenile delinquency treatment program would require an objective assessment of the subsequent behavior of the clients. Instead, investigators must often rely on indirect measures such as the subsequent arrest record. Figure 6.2 shows the assumed path model of the relations between the two measures of behavior and the treatment variable.

Let Y be the measure of the client's actual delinquent behavior, and let Y' be the arrest record. The desired treatment effect correlation r_{TY} is related to the observed treatment correlation by the product rule

$$r_{TY'} = r_{TY}\, r_{YY'}.$$

If the correlation between behavior and arrest were only $r_{YY'} = .30$, then the treatment correlation would be attenuated to

$$r_{TY'} = .30\, r_{TY},$$

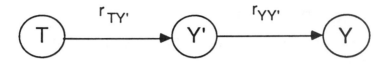

Legend:
     T = Deliquency Treatment Variable
     Y' = Posttreatment Behavior
     Y = Posttreatment Arrest Record

Figure 6.2 The Path Model for the Relationship Between the Delinquency Treatment Program, the Desired Measure of Actual Posttreatment Behavior, and the Observed Posttreatment Arrest Record

i.e., attenuated by 70%. In this case, the observed correlation could be corrected by reversing the algebraic equation

$$r_{TY} = r_{TY'} / r_{YY'} .$$

The corrected d statistic would then be obtained by transforming this corrected correlation. In the delinquency example the correction would be

$$r_{TY} = r_{TY'} / .30 .$$

The observed correlation must be more than tripled in this case to correct for the imperfect construct validity. If the observed d statistic were $d_{Y'} = .12$, then $r_{TY'} = .06$, which corrects to $r_{TY} = .06/.30 = .20$ and, hence, to $d_Y = .40$.

While the treatment correlation, or d statistic, can be corrected to eliminate the systematic reduction in the correlation produced by imperfect construct validity, the effect of increased sampling error cannot be corrected. The proper significance test for the corrected effect size is

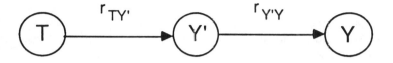

Legend:
  T = Training Treatment Variable
  Y' = Training Learning Measure
  Y = Posttreatment Social Behavior

Figure 6.3 The Path Model for the Assumed Relationship Between the Social Skills Training of Supervisors, Program Mastery, and Subsequent Behavior on the Job

algebraically equivalent to the significance test for the uncorrected effect size.

Imperfect construct validity does not always reduce the size of the effect size. Consider social skills training for supervisors. Assessment of the training program would ideally require measuring the interactive skills of the trainee after the program. Instead, the only available measure might be a measure of how well the person mastered the training program. But mastery of the material is only antecedent to behavior change; it may take time or special experience for the trainee to put that learning into operation. The path model for this hypothesis is shown in Figure 6.3.

The desired treatment correlation r_{TY} and the observed treatment correlation $r_{TY'}$ are related by the product rule

$$r_{TY} = r_{TY'} \, r_{Y'Y} \, .$$

If the correlation between the cognitive learning measure and subsequent social behavior was only $r_{YY'} = .30$, then the desired correlation r_{TY} would be lower then the observed correlation $r_{TY'}$.

$$r_{TY} = .30 \, r_{TY'}$$

This product rule is itself the correction formula for the treatment correlation. The correction for the d statistic is obtained by transforming the corrected treatment correlation to a d value.

On the other hand, if this path model is known to be correct, and if the value $r_{YY'} = .30$ is known a priori, then the proper significance test for r_{TY} is the test on $r_{TY'}$ which has higher power than would the test for the lower correlation r_{TY}.

Imperfect Construct Validity in the Treatment Variable

Imperfect construct validity in the treatment variable is a confounding of the intended treatment effect with an effect due to some other causal agent. This problem can be attacked using path analysis (Hunter, 1986, 1987), and, under certain conditions, it can be corrected in a manner that could be used in meta-analysis. Correction of confounding requires the use of a multiple dependent variable design where an intervening variable is observed that measures the process induced by the confounding causal agent. The desired correlation is then the partial correlation between the treatment variable and the dependent variable with the intervening variable held constant. This approach is a rigorous, quantitative replacement for doing an analysis of covariance with the intervening variable used as a concomitant variable (Hunter, 1988). Detailed treatment of this method is beyond the scope of the present book.

Bias in the Effect Size

The effect size statistic is subject to a statistical phenomenon known by the forbidding title "bias." For sample sizes greater than 20, bias is trivial in magnitude. However, there have been papers arguing that a major problem with meta-analysis is the use of "biased methods." This section will present a correction for bias, although the primary intent of the section is to show that the bias is of trivial magnitude.

Consider a set of perfectly replicated studies, all with the same sample size and the same population effect size. The average sample effect size will differ slightly from the population effect size. This discrepancy is called "bias" in the statistical estimation literature. The size of the bias depends on the sample size. The bias is in different directions for the effect size statistic d and the treatment correlation r. The average d is slightly larger than δ while the average correlation is slightly smaller than ρ.

A complete treatment of bias in the treatment correlation is given by Hunter, Schmidt, and Coggin (1988), who show that the bias is trivial in all but very small sample studies and small for small sample studies. Some authors have suggested using the Fisher z transformation to reduce the bias, but the bias using Fisher's z turns out to be even larger, although in the opposite direction. The bias in the treatment correlation is given by

$$E(r) = a\rho$$

where

$$a = 1 - (1 - \rho^2) / (2N - 2).$$

How small is this bias? Consider perfectly replicated studies with a population correlation of $\rho = .20$ and a sample size of $N = 100$. The multiplier for the average observed correlation would be $a = 1 - .00485 = .995$. The average correlation would be .199 instead of .200. The trivial size of the bias in the correlation is the reason that bias has traditionally been ignored. However, for very small sample size meta-analyses (average sample size less than 10), or for very fastidious analysts, it is possible to correct the observed treatment correlation for bias. The nonlinear correction corresponding to the equation above would be

$$r' = r / a$$

where

$$a = 1 - (1 - r^2) / (2N - 2).$$

If the meta-analysis is studying treatment correlations below .70 in magnitude, then the correction is very closely approximated by the linear correction

$$r' = r / a$$

where

$$a = (2N - 3) / (2N - 2).$$

The linear correction has the advantage that it can be applied *after* the meta-analysis. Just divide both the estimated mean and the estimated standard deviation of population correlations by the multiplier computed with N set at the average sample size. Note that the corrected correlation will be trivially larger than the uncorrected correlation.

A complete treatment of bias in the d statistic is given in Hedges and Olkin (1985). Although the bias is trivial for all but very small sample studies, they recommend routine correction for that bias. Indeed, they use the symbol "d" only for the corrected statistic. The bias in d is approximately given by

$$E(d) = a \delta$$

where

$$a = 1 + 3 / (4N - 12).$$

How large is this bias? Consider a study with a textbook-sized effect $d = .40$ based on a sample size of $N = 100$. The multiplier is $a = 1 + .0077 = 1.0077$. The average study effect size would be .403 instead of .400. On the other hand, consider a study done with extremely small sample size, say, $N = 10$ (5 subjects in each group). The multiplier would be $a = 1 + .107 = 1.107$ and the average effect size would be .443 rather than .400. The correction is straightforward; just divide by a.

$$d' = d / a$$

Note that this is a linear correction. Thus, it could be applied *after* the meta-analysis. Just divide both the estimated mean and the estimated standard deviation of corrected d values by the multiplier a. The corrected effect sizes will be slightly smaller than the uncorrected effect sizes.

Recording, Computational, and Transcriptional Errors

Meta-analysis will inevitably include some studies with bad data. There might be a recording error in gathering the primary data or in entering it into the computer. The study effect size could be erroneous because of computational error or an error in algebraic sign in the effect size. Finally, error can arise in transcription: from computer output to analyst table, from analyst table to manuscript table, from manuscript table to published table. Some have even suggested than a meta-analyst might miscopy a figure, but it is well known that meta-analysts do not make errors.

Study results should always be examined for outliers. This will eliminate the extreme cases of bad data. However, smaller erroneous effect sizes may not be detectable. Thus, any meta-analysis with a very large number of effect sizes will usually have at least a few bad data points.

Since bad data cannot be completely avoided, it is important to consider variation in study results with some caution. A certain percentage of the original observed variation will be due to bad data. A larger proportion of the residual variation — that left after all other study artifacts have been corrected — may be due to bad data.

Multiple Artifacts and Corrections

Alas, there is no rule that says that a study can be hurt by only one artifact. Sampling error will be present in all studies. Error of measurement in the dependent variable will be present in all studies, although it may occasionally be trivial in magnitude. Imperfect control of the nominal treatment variable will be unavoidable in most studies. Thus, a meta-analysis free of artifact will usually require that effect sizes be corrected for a number of sources of error.

Other than the removal of outliers, there is no correction for bad data. Sampling error acts differently from other artifacts in that it is (1) additive and (2) unsystematic. While a confidence interval for the effect size provides an unbiased estimate of potential sampling error for the single study, there is no correction for sampling error at the level of the single study. We will consider correcting the problem of sampling error in meta-analysis in the next chapter.

The artifacts other than sampling error and bad data are systematic in nature and, thus, potentially correctable. The key is to have the necessary information about the size of the artifact process (e.g., knowledge of the extent of unreliability or the extent of range restriction or the extent of imperfect construct validity). You can correct each artifact where there is adequate artifact information, be this one artifact or seven. Every artifact left uncorrected results in a corresponding underestimate of the true effect size. Furthermore, variation in uncorrected artifacts across studies looks like true variance in treatment effect. This may create the appearance of across setting variation where there is none. If there is true variation in treatment effect, then uncorrected artifacts mask the true differences. That is, variation in apparent effect size due to uncorrected artifacts may override the differences due to true moderator variables and, thus, make it difficult to identify the true moderator variable by examining the studies after the fact.

Correction for artifacts is not difficult if the information on each artifact is given. Consider an example: A study of social skill training for first-line

supervisors is conducted in a factory setting. The measure of job performance is performance ratings by the immediate manager of each supervisor on a single 100-point graphic rating scale. Because the investigator
doubted that performance ratings are measured on a ratio scale (a fact),
the investigator decided that parametric statistics could not be used (a
statistical error on his part). So the investigator decided to do a sign test
on the data. The combined group data were split at the median and a
chi-square test was run comparing the proportion of above average performance among the supervisors with and without the skills training. Assume
the treatment effect for training on consensus performance ratings is $d_{TY}=$
.40. The true population treatment correlation is thus r_{TY} = .20. The
interrater reliability of performance ratings by a single superior on a single
rating scale averages .28 (Hunter & Hirsh, 1987; King, Hunter, & Schmidt,
1980). Thus, the effect size is reduced from d_{TY} = .40 to

$$d_{TY'} = d_{TY} \sqrt{.28} = .53\, d_{TY} = .53\,(.40) = .21\,.$$

For a study with total sample size 100, this would reduce statistical power
from an already low 51% to a very low 18%. The effect of a dichotomization using a median split for a d value less than .50 is simply to decrease
the value by 20%, that is,

$$d_{TY''} = .80\, d_{TY'} = .80\,(.21) = .17\,.$$

This reduces the statistical power from a very low 18% to an even lower
13%. That is, the two artifacts together reduce the effect size from .40 to
.17, i.e., to less than half its proper value. The statistical power is reduced
from an already undesirable 51% to only 13%; an increase in the error rate
for the significance test from 49% to 87%.

   The systematic effect of the artifacts can be eliminated from the study
by correction formulas. We have

$$d_{TY} = d_{TY'} / .53 = (d_{TY''} / .80) / .53 = d_{TY''} / .424$$

$$= 2.36\, d_{TY''}\,.$$

That is, if the artifacts reduce the size of the effect by 58%, we can restore
the value by dividing by the corresponding factor .42. However, while this
correction eliminates the systematic error in the effect size, it does not
eliminate the increased sampling error. The proper statistical test on the
corrected effect size is algebraically equivalent to the test on the uncor-

rected effect size. Thus, statistical correction formulas do not restore the lost statistical power.

Consider the preceding example in abstract form. The effect of the first artifact was to multiply the effect size by a multiplicative factor a_1 as in

$$d' = a_1 d.$$

The effect of the second artifact was to multiply by a second factor a_2 as in

$$d'' = a_2 d'.$$

The impact of the two factors is

$$d'' = a_2 d' = a_2 (a_1) d = a_1 a_2 d,$$

i.e., to multiply the effect size by a multiplicative factor a, which is the product of the two separate artifact multipliers. That is,

$$d'' = a d$$

where

$$a = a_1 a_2.$$

The effect size is then restored to its original value by the correction formula

$$d = d'' / a.$$

The preceding example was typical of correction for multiple artifacts in effect sizes of moderate size. Each artifact reduces the effect size by a multiplicative factor. The net effect is to reduce the effect size by a multiplicative factor that is the product of the separate multipliers. That is, the attenuating effect of several artifacts is to reduce the effect size by the product of the separate attenuating factors. The corresponding correction restores the effect size to its original size by dividing by the attenuation multiplier.

There is one caveat to the preceding discussion: It is exactly true for the treatment correlation but only an approximation for the effect size d. If a treatment effect is so large that the approximation $d = 2r$ breaks down, then the multiplicative formula should be applied only to the treatment correlation. The treatment effect d can then be computed by the usual conversion formula.

For example, consider the social skill training example for a very large treatment effect, say $d = 1.50$. The observed treatment correlation satisfies the attenuation equation

$$r_{TY''} = .42\, r_{TY}.$$

The effect size $d = 1.50$ corresponds to a treatment correlation of .60. The artifacts reduce this correlation from .60 to

$$r_{TY''} = .42\,(.60) = .25.$$

This attenuated treatment correlation corresponds to an attenuated effect size of $d = .52$. The attenuation in the d statistic is from 1.50 to .52, which is by a factor of .35 rather than the factor .42 for the treatment correlation.

The treatment of multiple artifacts is very straightforward for the treatment correlation. The reduction in the size of the treatment correlation by a series of artifacts is to attenuate the correlation by a total multiplier that is the product of the separate artifact attenuation multipliers. The treatment correlation can be restored to its proper size by correcting for those artifacts by dividing by the attenuation multiplier.

For the d statistic, correction for artifacts is only slightly more difficult. If the unattenuated population d value falls in the moderate range $-.50 < d < +.50$, then the formulas for the treatment correlation apply directly to the d statistic. If the population effect size falls outside the moderate range, then the d value can be converted to a correlation, the correlation can be corrected, and the corrected correlation can be converted to a corrected d value.

7 Meta-Analysis Methods for *d* Values

This chapter presents the meta-analysis formulas for effect sizes from experimental studies. In this chapter, we consider only the posttest—only independent groups experimental designs. In such designs, different people are assigned to different treatment groups, hence, the label "independent groups" designs. The next chapter will consider "within subjects" or "repeated measures" designs. Studies with more than two levels for a treatment variable could be handled within the present framework using contrasts, but this is beyond the scope of the present manuscript.

Independent groups studies could be analyzed using correlations. The size of the treatment effect could be measured by the (point-biserial) correlation between treatment and effect. This use of correlation to measure the treatment effect has the advantage of lending itself to multivariate techniques such as partial correlation, multiple regression, and path analysis. However, most meta-analysts have chosen to use a measure of effect size called "*d*," the difference between the group means divided by the standard deviation. It matters little since either statistic can be algebraically transformed into the other.

The *d* statistic is affected by all the same artifacts as the correlation, including sampling error, error of measurement, and range variation, but the terminology is the same only for sampling error. Many experimenters believe that error of measurement in the dependent variable is irrelevant in experiments since it averages out in the group means. However, error of measurement enters the variance of the dependent variable and, hence, enters the denominator of *d*. Thus the value of *d* is systematically lowered by error of measurement, and differences across studies in the reliability of the dependent variable produce spurious differences in the value of *d*.

Error of measurement in the independent variable is also not acknowledged by most experimenters. In their mind, persons are unequivocally assigned to one treatment group or the other. But those who have used manipulation checks have found that what is nominally the same treatment for all may be a very different thing to different persons. Some hear the instructions while some do not. Some give one meaning to ambiguous instructions while others give another. Error of measurement in the independent and dependent variables is discussed in more detail later in this chapter (see also Chapter 6).

Range variation goes under another name in experimental work, namely, "strength of treatment." In dichotomous experiments, the independent variable is scored 0-1, regardless of how strong the treatment is. However, if differences in treatments across studies can be coded, then treatment effects can be projected to a common reference strength and the results of different studies become comparable. However, studies often do not give the information needed to code for treatment strength. The resulting problems are discussed later (see also Chapter 6).

Effect Size Indices: d and r

Consider an intervention such as training managers in interpersonal skills. The effect of such an intervention might be assessed by comparing the performance of managers who have had such training (the experimental group) with performance of comparable managers who have not (the control group). The usual comparison statistic is t (or F, which in this context is just the square of t, i.e., $F = t^2$). However, this is a very poor statistic since its size depends on the amount of sampling error in the data. The optimal statistic (which measures size of effect in a metric suitable for path analysis or analysis of covariance or other effects) is the point-biserial correlation r. The great advantage of the point-biserial correlation is that it can be inserted into a correlation matrix in which the intervention is then treated like any other variable. For example, the partial correlation between the intervention and the dependent variable with some prior individual difference variable held constant is equivalent to the corresponding analysis of covariance (Hunter, 1988).

Path analysis can be used to trace out the difference between direct and indirect effects of the intervention (Hunter, 1986, 1987). For example, training might enhance the interpersonal skills of supervisors. This in turn might increase their subordinates' satisfaction with the supervisor, which in turn might cause a decrease in subordinate absenteeism. If this is the case, then path analysis would show the training to have a direct effect only on the supervisors' interpersonal skills, even though the intervention was also having second-order and third-order indirect effects on subordinate satisfaction and absenteeism, respectively.

The theory of sampling error for the point-biserial correlation is identical to the theory for the Pearson correlation given in the previous section, except that the point-biserial correlation may need to be corrected for unequal sample sizes before cumulation (as discussed below).

When one variable is dichotomous, the usual formula for the Pearson product-moment correlation will yield the point-biserial correlation r_{bp}. Thus, popular statistical packages, such as SPSS and SAS can be used to compute the point-biserial. There are also other formulas for r_{pb}.

$$r_{pb} = (\sqrt{pq}) \; (\overline{Y}_E - \overline{Y}_C) / SD_y$$

where Y_E is the mean of the experimental group on the continuous (usually the dependent) variable, Y_C is the mean for the control group, and p and q are the proportion in the experimental and control groups, respectively. It is important to note that SD_y is *not* the within group SD used in computing d; SD_y is the pooled standard deviation of *all* scores on the dependent variable. The two groups need not be experimental and control groups; they can be any two groups, for example, males and females or high school graduates and nongraduates. Another formula for r_{pb} is

$$r_{pb} = (\overline{Y}_E - \overline{Y}_T) \sqrt{p/q} \; / SD_y$$

where $\overline{Y}_T$ is the total group mean for the continuous variable, and all other terms are as defined above.

Maximum Value of Point-Biserial *r*

Many texts (e.g., Nunnally, 1978) state that the maximum value of r_{pb} is not 1.00 as it is for the Pearson correlation, but rather .79. They further state that this is the maximum value only when $p = q = .50$; otherwise, the maximum value is lower than .79. However, this theorem is false for experiments. The implicit assumption in this theorem is that the two groups were formed by dichotomizing a normally distributed variable, such as mental ability. This is the case treated in Chapter 2 under the rubric "dichotomization." Assume that two variables X and Y have a bivariate normal distribution. If a dichotomous variable X' is formed by splitting the distribution of X, then the correlation between the dichotomous variable X' and Y is equal to the original correlation between X and Y multiplied by a constant, which is at most .79. Hence, the statement that the point-biserial correlation is at most .79.

Suppose the two groups in the study are defined as those who are above the median on anxiety versus those below the median on anxiety. The question is: Which group will perform better in an assessment center group exercise? Then, if the continuous anxiety variable had a bivariate normal relationship to the dependent variable, the theorem in Chapters 2 and 3 would apply. If the correlation between the anxiety test and performance on the group task is .30, then the point biserial correlation for the two group mean comparisons will be (.79)(.30) = .24.

However, in a typical experiment, the dichotomous variable is defined by treatment groups rather than by splitting some continuous variable. The treatment group is defined by some experimental process. For example, at the end of World War II, some Jews migrated to Israel while other Jews remained in Europe. The two groups were then subjected to the impact of radically different environments. Where the groups are defined by process or treatment differences, the theorem given in Chapter 3 does not apply. Instead the size of the correlation is determined by the size of the treatment effect. The larger the treatment effect, the higher the correlation. As the treatment effect becomes larger and larger, then the implied correlation gets closer and closer to 1.00.

In a purely statistical sense, the difference between the two cases lies in the assumption that the continuous independent variable has a bivariate normal relation to the continuous dependent variable. That constraint places distinct limits on how far apart the two group means on the dependent variable can be. The largest difference occurs if the continuous variables are perfectly correlated. In this case, the two groups are the top and bottom halves of a normal distribution. The largest difference for such groups occurs if the split is at the mean, a difference of 1.58 standard deviations.

If the groups are defined by a treatment process, then there is no mathematical limit on the size of the difference between the two groups. Consider the impact of education on knowledge of history. Consider first two groups of first graders. One group goes to school for the usual nine months while the other group goes to school for ten months. The two distributions are likely to overlap substantially, and the point biserial correlation would be low. On the other hand, consider two groups from a third-world country such as India. One group is raised in a mountain village where children rarely go to school at all, while the other group is educated in Bombay where they go all the way through college. There is likely to be no overlap between the two knowledge distributions. The difference could be 100 or 1,000 standard deviations, and the point-biserial correlation could be arbitrarily close to 1.00. (Note: In such cases the formulas given by Kemery, Dunlap and Griffeth [1988] cannot be used. These formulas assume that the underlying distribution of the dependent variable is normal and will give erroneous results when this is not the case, as here.)

The Effect Size

Glass (1977) and his associates and Cohen (1977) have popularized a transform of the point-biserial correlation called the effect size statistic "*d*." The effect size *d* is the difference between the means in standard score form, i.e., the ratio of the difference between the means to the standard deviation. The two variants of the effect size statistic are determined by considering two different standard deviations that might be used for the denominator. The standard deviation that will be used here is the pooled within-group standard deviation used in analysis of variance. The alternative is the control-group standard deviation as used by Smith and Glass (1977). However, since there is rarely a large difference between the control and experimental group (a comparison that can be separately cumulated), it seems reasonable to use the statistic with the least sampling error. The within-group standard deviation has only about half the sampling error of the control-group standard deviation.

If the variance for the experimental group is V_E, the variance for the control group is V_C, and the sample sizes are equal, then the within-group variance V_W is defined by

$$V_W = (V_E + V_C) / 2 .$$

That is, it is the average of the two within-group variances. If the sample sizes are not equal, then a sample size weighted average could be used.

$$V_W = (N_E V_E + N_C V_C) / (N_E + N_C)$$

where N_E and N_C are the sample sizes for the experimental group and control group respectively. This is the maximum liklihood estimate of the population within-group variance. As it happens, the most common current analysis of variance formula is the modified formula popularized by Fisher. Fisher chose to use slightly different formulas for his analysis of variance. He weighted each variance by its degrees of freedom, i.e., by $N - 1$ instead of N.

$$V_W = [(N_E - 1) V_E + (N_C - 1) V_C] / [(N_E - 1) + (N_C - 1)]$$

In view of the convention, we will use the Fisher formula, although it actually makes little difference.

The effect-size statistic *d* is then defined by

$$d = (Y_E - Y_C) / S_W$$

where S_W is the within-group standard deviation, i.e., the square root of the within-group variance. That is, d is the difference between the means divided by the within-group standard deviation.

Most researchers are used to comparing group means using the t statistic. However, the t statistic depends on the sample size and, thus, is not a proper measure of the size of the treatment effect. That is, for purposes of testing a difference for statistical significance, it is true that the larger the sample size the more "significant" a given observed difference would be. But the treatment effect we want to estimate is the population treatment effect, which is defined without reference to sample size. The statistic d can be thought of as a version of t that is made independent of sample size.

The three statistics, d, t, and r, are all algebraically transformable from one to the other. These transformations will be shown below for the special case of equal sample sizes in the two groups, i.e., for $N_E = N_C = N / 2$ where N is the total sample size for that study. The most common statistic reported is t. Thus, in meta-analysis, we often want to convert t to either d or r. The transformation formulas are

$$d = 2t / \sqrt{N}$$

$$r = t / \sqrt{t^2 + N - 2} \ .$$

For example, if the total sample size is $N=100$ and the study value of t is 2.52, then

$$d = (2 / \sqrt{100}) \ (2.52) = .2\,(2.52) = .504$$

$$r = 2.52 / \sqrt{2.52^2 + 98} = 2.52 / \sqrt{104.3504} = .247 \ .$$

If the d statistic is given, then it can be transformed to either r or t.

$$r = (d/2) / [\,(N - 2) / N + (d/2)^2\,]^{\frac{1}{2}}$$

$$t = (\sqrt{N} / 2)\,d$$

For example, reverse the previous case for $N = 100$ and $d = .504$.

$$r = (.504/2) / [\,98/100 + (.504/2)^2\,]^{\frac{1}{2}} = .247$$

$$t = (\sqrt{100} / 2)\,d = (10/2)\,(.504) = 2.52 \ .$$

If the point biserial correlation *r* is given, then

$$d = \sqrt{[(N-2)/N]} \; 2r / \sqrt{(1-r^2)}$$

$$t = \sqrt{(N-2)} \; [r/\sqrt{(1-r^2)}] \; .$$

For example, given $N = 100$ and $r = .247$, we have

$$d = \sqrt{(98/100)} \; 2(.247) / \sqrt{(1-.247^2)} = .505$$

$$t = \sqrt{98} \; (.247) / \sqrt{(1-.247^2)} = 2.52 \; .$$

The value for *d* is off from .504 by rounding error.

The preceding formulas are complicated by the fact that the Fisher estimate of the within-group variance is used. If the maximum liklihood estimate were used, then the formulas relating *r* and *d* would be

$$d = 2r / \sqrt{(1-r^2)}$$

$$r = (d/2) / \sqrt{[1+(d/2)^2]} = d/\sqrt{(4+d^2)} \; .$$

These formulas are also quite accurate approximations for the Fisher estimate, except for very small sample sizes.

The *d* to *r* and *r* to *d* conversions are especially simple for the usual small treatment effect sizes. If $-.4 < d < +.4$ or $-.2 < r < +.2$, then to a close approximation we have

$$d = 2r$$

$$r = d / 2 \; .$$

The formulas above are for the equal sample size case. If the control group and experimental group have different sizes, then the number "2" is replaced by

$$\text{“2”} = 1 / \sqrt{(pq)}$$

where *p* and *q* are the proportion of persons in the two groups.

Some studies characterize the outcome in statistics other than *t*, *d*, or *r*. Glass, McGaw, and Smith (1981) provide transformation formulas for many such cases. However, the transformed value in such cases will not have the sampling error given by our formulas. In particular, probit transformations yield effect sizes with much larger sampling errors than do our formulas for d and r. This will lead to undercorrections for error variance for such estimates of d and r.

Correction of the Point Biserial for Unequal Sample Sizes

Conceptually, the effect size is normally thought of as independent of the sample sizes of the control and experimental groups. However, in a natural environment, the importance of a difference depends on how often it occurs. Since the point biserial correlation was originally derived for natural settings, it is defined so as to depend on the group sample sizes. As it happens, for a given-sized treatment effect, the correlation is smaller for unequal sample sizes. For sample size differences as large as 90-10 or 10-90, the correlation is smaller by a factor of .60, i.e., 40% smaller. Thus, extremely uneven sampling can cause substantial understatement of the correlation.

In a typical experiment, any large difference between the sample sizes is usually caused by resource limitations rather than fundamental frequencies in nature. Thus, the point-biserial correlation that we want is the point biserial correlation that we would have gotten had we been able to do the study with equal sample sizes. That is, we would like to "correct" the observed correlation for the attenuation effect of unequal sampling. The formula for this correction is

$$r_c = a\,r\,/\,\sqrt{[\,(a^2-1)\,r^2+1\,]}$$

where

$$a = \sqrt{[\,.25/pq\,]}\,.$$

For example, if our study were cut short before we had finished the control group, we might have finished with 90 subjects in the experimental group but only 10 in the control group. We thus have $p = .90$, $q = .10$, and

$$a = \sqrt{.25/[\,(.90)\,(.10)\,]} = \sqrt{2.7777} = 1.6667.$$

If the correlation for the unequal groups were .15, then the equal group correlation would have been

$$r_c = 1.67\,(.15)\,/\,\sqrt{[\,(1.67^2-1)\,(.15^2)+1\,]} = .246\,.$$

The effect-size *d* is already expressed independently of the two sample sizes, although that poses certain problems for natural groups of quite uneven sizes (such as persons with and without migraine headache).

Kemery, Dunlop et al. (1988) have critized this correction formula and have offered an alternative that first converts the point-biserial correlation to a biserial correlation and then converts the biserial correlation to a point-biserial with a 50-50 split. The Kemery et al. formulas yield accurate results only if the underlying distribution of the dichotomized variable is normal. Where this does not hold, the results are very inaccurate. The normal distribution assumption is usually not appropriate in experiments.

Examples of the Convertibility of *r* and *d*

The *d* statistic is often used to express the difference between treatment and control groups in experimental studies. Indeed, that is our major focus in this chapter. However, *d* can also be used to express the difference between any two groups. Differences between naturally occurring groups expressed in *d* form are often very informative, and the same relations can be expressed using the point-biserial *r*. For example, females average higher than males on measures of perceptual speed; *d* is approximately .70. What is the correlation in the population between sex and perceptual speed?

$$r = (d/2) / \sqrt{\{1 + (d/2)^2\}} = .35 / 1.05948 = .33$$

Thus, the population correlation is .33. Since men and women are about equal in numbers in the population (i.e., $p \cong q \cong .50$), the value of *r* computed from *d* is the same as would be computed from representative samples from the population.

As another example, the sex difference on height in the population is approximately *d* = 1.50. This translates into a population correlation between sex and height of *r* = .60.

Consider another example: In the United States, the difference in academic achievement between black and white students is approximately one standard deviation, that is, *d* = 1.00. What is the correlation between race and academic achievement? Consider first the formula assuming equal numbers of blacks and whites.

$$r = .50 / \sqrt{(1 + .50^2)} = .45$$

This correlation of .45 is the value that would apply if there were equal numbers of black and white students (i.e., $N_W = N_B$). But this is not the case; black students are only about 13% of the total. Thus, this value must be adjusted to reflect that fact. The correlation reflecting these unequal frequencies is $r = .32$. Thus, for natural populations, if the two groups have greatly different sizes, the natural correlation is substantially smaller.

Problems of Artificial Dichotomization

Throughout this chapter, we focus on true binary variables such as the control group versus experimental group distinction. If the binary variable is created by dichotomizing a continuous variable — as when people are classified as "high anxious" or "low anxious" using a median split on a continuous anxiety measure — then it is important to remember that the word "correlation" becomes ambiguous. There is the correlation between the continuous variable and the dependent variable — ingenuously called the "biserial" correlation — and the correlation between the binary variable and the dependent variable — called the "point-biserial" correlation. The conversion formulas given in this chapter apply to the point biseral correlation. To convert from d to the continuous correlation, one would first convert from d to the point-biserial correlation using the formula in this chapter. Then, one would convert the point-biserial correlation to the biserial correlation using the formula to correct for dichotomization given in Chapter 3.

In experimental studies, it is common for authors to define a binary variable such as "anxiety" by a median split on a continuous measure. If the split is the same across studies, there is no problem in simply igoring the dichotomiztion for purposes of the initial meta-analysis. The final values for d can be converted to the biserial correlation if desired. However, if the binary variable is created using different splits across studies, then the point-biserial correlation and the corresponding d values will vary across studies artifactually because of the variation in split. In the case of "turnover" studies, the variation can be extreme, for example, 50-50 for one author versus 95-5 for another. In such cases, it would be wise to do the meta-analysis on correlations and use the correction formulas from Chapter 3 and Chapter 4.

An Alternative to d: GLASS' d

Glass has often used a variation on the d statistic. He uses the control group standard deviation instead of the within-group standard deviation. His reason for this is that the treatment may have an effect on the experimental group standard deviation as well as on the experimental group mean. That point is well taken; where there is a treatment effect, there may well be a treatment by subject interaction. However, if we wish to check for this, there is a much more effective procedure than altering the definition of d. We can do a meta-analysis that compares the values of the standard deviations directly.

Let v be the ratio of the experimental group standard deviation to the control group standard deviation, i.e.,

$$v = s_E / s_C .$$

The value of v will be 1.00 (to within sampling error) if the usual assumptions of the t test are met, i.e., if there is no treatment by subject interaction. If the meta-analysis produces a mean value other than 1, then this is evidence of a treatment by subject interaction. The direction of the departure from 1.00 will provide an inkling as to its nature.

Let us use the symbol d_G to denote the Glass variation on the effect size d. That is, let us define the symbol d_G by

$$d_G = (Y_E - Y_C) / s_C .$$

If the meta-analysis shows the value of v to be 1, then the population values of d and d_G are the same. If the meta-analysis shows the value of v to be other than 1, then the meta-analysis value for d can be transformed into the meta-analysis value of d_G by the following identity:

$$d_G = (s_W / s_C) d = d \sqrt{[(1 + v^2)/2]} .$$

For example, suppose our meta-analysis found the average d to be .20 and the average value of v to be 1.50. Then, the Glass d_G would be given by

$$d_G = [.20] \sqrt{[(1 + 1.5^2)/2]} = .255 .$$

There are two principle advantages to using the within group standard deviation rather than the control group standard deviation, i.e., using d rather than d_G. First, the control group standard deviation (and hence d_G) has much more sampling error than does the within group standard deviation (and hence d). Second, most reports have a value for t or F and, hence, permit the computation of d. Many reports do not present standard deviations, and so d_G cannot be computed. Therefore, we have chosen to develop and present meta-analysis formulas only for d.

Meta-Analysis Formulas for S_E and S_C

This section is technical and many readers may wish to skip over it; it is devoted to the sampling error variance formulas required for the meta-analysis of v. Let the population value of v be denoted $\varnothing$ and the sampling error by e. Then

$$v = \varnothing + e.$$

Denote the total sample size by N, i.e.,

$$N = N_E + N_C .$$

If the two sample sizes are about equal and the total sample size is greater than 50 (25 in each group), then, to a close approximation

$$E(e) = 0$$

$$\text{Var } (e) = \varnothing^2 / (N-6).$$

The standard deviation ratio is not perfectly unbiased and the bias shows in research domains such as psychotherapy where the average sample size is about $N = 20$ (10 in each group). The actual bias is approximately

$$E(e) = \varnothing / (N-2).$$

The bias can be eliminated by a multiplicative correction formula. Since

$$E(v) = a \varnothing$$

where

$$a = 1 + 1/(N-2) = N / (N-2)$$

we can form an unbiased estimator v^* by dividing by the bias multiplier, i.e.

$$v^* = v / a.$$

The sampling error is similarly divided.

$$v^* = \varnothing + e^* \quad \text{where } e^* = e / a$$

We then have approximately

$$E(e^*) = 0$$

$$\text{Var}(e^*) = \text{Var}(e) / a^2 = [\varnothing^2 / (N{-}6)] / a^2.$$

For a total sample size of 20 or more, the sampling error variance is approximately

$$\text{Var}(e^*) = \varnothing^2 / (N{-}4).$$

If the sample sizes in the two groups are quite different, then it is necessary to use more complicated formulas. For the simple estimator, the bias is

$$E(v) = a \varnothing$$

where the bias multiplier is

$$a = 1 + b$$

where

$$b = [.75 / (N_C - 3) - .25 / (N_E - 1)].$$

The sampling error variance is approximately

$$\text{Var}(e) = [\varnothing^2 / 2] [1/(N_C - 3) + 1/(N_E - 1) + 1.5/\{(N_C - 3)(N_E - 1)\}].$$

An unbiased estimator can be formed by dividing by the multiplier. That is, we define v^* by

$$v^* = v / a.$$

The sampling error mean and variance are approximately

$$E(e^*) = 0$$

$$\text{Var}(e^*) = \text{Var}(e) / a^2.$$

The exact formulas for the expected value and the sampling error variance can be computed using the gamma function $\Gamma(x)$. Write the expected value of v using the bias multiplier a as

$$E(v) = a\ \varnothing$$

where a is the product

$$a = b\ c$$

where

$$b = \Gamma(N_E/2) / [\ \Gamma(\{N_E - 1\}/2)\ \sqrt{(N_E/2)}\ ]$$

$$c = [\ \Gamma(\{N_C - 2\}/2)\ (\{N_C - 2\}/2)\ ] / \Gamma\ (\{N_C - 1\}/2).$$

The bias is given by

$$E(e) = (a - 1)\ \varnothing$$

and the sampling error variance is given by

$$\text{Var}\ (e) = \varnothing^2\ [\ b^2\ (\{N_C - 1\}/\{N_C - 3\} - c^2)]$$

$$+\ c^2\ (1 - b^2)$$

$$+\ (\{N_c - 1\}/\{N_C - 3\} - c^2)\ (1 - b^2)\ ].$$

The unbiased estimator is defined by

$$v^* = v\ /\ a$$

for which

$$E(v^*) = 0$$

$$\text{Var}\ (e^*) = \text{Var}\ (e)\ /\ a^2.$$

Sampling Error in the *d* Statistic

The Standard Error for *d*

Let us denote the population value of the effect-size statistic by δ. The observed value *d* will then deviate from δ by sampling error. As with correlations, we can write the sampling error formula as

$$d = \delta + e$$

where *e* is the sampling error. For large samples,

$$E(e) = 0$$

and

$$\text{Var } (e) = (4/N) (1 + \delta^2 / 8)$$

where *N* is the total sample size. These formulas work well for sample sizes of $N = 50$ (25 in each group) or more. However, more accurate approximations are noted in the next few paragraphs.

The important alteration is a more accurate formula for the sampling error variance. The more accurate estimate is

$$\text{Var } (e) = [(N-1)/(N-3)] \left[(4/N) (1 + \delta^2 / 8) \right].$$

This formula differs from the large sample formula only by the multiplier $[(N-1)/(N-3)]$. This multiplier differs only slightly from 1 for $N > 50$. But it makes a bigger difference for sample sizes of 20 or less.

An excellent discussion of sampling error in very small sample-size values of *d* is presented in Hedges and Olkin (1985). However, the reader is warned that the statistic that is traditionally denoted "*d*" is called "*g*" by Hedges and Olkin. They reserve the symbol "*d*" for their approximately unbiased estimator. We will denote the approximately unbiased estimator by "*d**." The mean value of *d* across sample replications is

$$E(d) = a \ \delta$$

where to a close approximation

$$a = 1 + .75 / (N-3).$$

For a sample of size $N = 100$, the bias multiplier is

$$a = 1 + .75/97 = 1 + .0077 = 1.01,$$

which differs only trivially from 1.00. However for very small samples — as in therapy research — the bias may warrant correction. For a sample size of $N = 20$, the muliplier a is

$$a = 1 + .75/17 = 1 + .044 = 1.044.$$

To correct for the bias, we divide by the bias multiplier. If we denote the (approximately) unbiased estimator by d^*, then

$$d^* = d / a.$$

This correction mechanically decreases the value of d and, hence, the sampling error is similarly decreased. If we define sampling error by

$$d^* = \delta + e^*$$

then we have approximately

$$E(e^*) = 0$$

$$\text{Var }(e^*) = \text{Var }(e) / a^2.$$

There is a small error in Hedges and Olkin (1982) in this regard. They offer the approximation

$$\text{Var }(e^*) = (4/N)(1 + \delta^2 / 8).$$

This approximation assumes the further approximation

$$[(N-1)/(N-3)] / a^2 = 1.$$

This approximation breaks down for sample sizes of 20 or less, where the more accurate approximation

$$[(N-1)/(N-3)] / a^2 = 1 + .25 / (N-3)$$

yields the formula that we have given.

For a bare bones meta-analysis, bias can be corrected either study by study or after the meta-analysis has been done. If the meta-analysis is done on the usual *d* statistic, then the correction for bias would be

$$\text{Ave } (\delta) = \text{Ave } (d^*) = \text{Ave } (d) \, / \, a$$

where

$$a = 1 + .75 \, / \, (N{-}3)$$

where N is the average sample size across studies.

The corresponding estimate of the standard deviation of population effect sizes would be

$$\text{Unbiased SD}_\delta = \text{SD}_\delta \, / \, a.$$

Thus, to correct for bias after the fact, we merely divide both the mean and the standard deviation by the bias multiplier computed using the average sample size.

The Confidence Interval for δ

The *d* statistic has mean δ and variance

$$\text{Var } (e) = [(N{-}1)/(N{-}3)] \, [\, (4/N) \, (1 + \delta^2 / 8) \,].$$

The square root of the sampling error variance Var (e) is the standard error of *d*. Denote the standard error by S. Except for very small sample sizes, the *d* statistic is approximately normally distributed. Thus the 95% confidence interval for δ is given to a close approximation by

$$d - 1.96 \, S < \delta < d + 1.96 \, S$$

The exact value of the standard error requires knowledge of δ. Since δ is unknown, we estimate the sampling error variance by substituting *d* for δ. That is, we estimate S^2 by

$$\text{Var } (e) = [(N{-}1)/(N{-}3)] \, [\, (4/N) \, (1 + d^2 / 8) \,].$$

The estimated standard error S is then the square root of Var (e).

Cumulation and Correction of
the Variance for Sampling Error

At this point, we begin the discussion of the meta-analysis of d. We start with a "bare bones" meta-analysis, which makes no correction to the mean or variance for artifacts such as error of measurement. This form of meta-analysis corrects only for sampling error variance. We consider a meta-analysis that estimates the distribution of uncorrected population effect sizes δ_i from information about the study sample effect sizes d_i. We will return to the consideration of other artifacts in later sections. However, the reader should note that our final coverage of artifacts for the d statistic will be far less extensive than our coverage for correlations. This reflects the greater complexity of correction formulas for d than for r. The simplest way to do a meta-analysis correcting for artifacts such as dichotomization and imperfect construct validity is to do the meta-analysis using r. This is done in four steps.

1. Convert all the ds to rs using the formula above. The maximum likelihood formula is

$$r = d \, / \, \sqrt{(4 + d^2)} \, .$$

2. Use the methods described in Chapters 3 and 4 to conduct the meta-analysis on r correcting for all possible artifacts.

3. Convert the final results for the mean correlation to a mean effect size using the conversion formula for r to d. The maximum liklihood formula is

$$d = 2r \, / \, \sqrt{(1 - r^2)} \, .$$

4. Convert the standard deviation of correlations to the standard deviation for effect sizes using the formula

$$SD\,(\delta) = a \, SD\,(\rho)$$

where

$$a = 2 \, / \, (1 - r^2)^{1.5} \, .$$

For example, suppose the meta-analysis on r yielded a mean treatment correlation of Ave $(\rho) = .50$ and a standard deviation of SD $(\rho) = .10$. The conversion to mean effect size would be

$$\text{Ave } (\delta) = 2\,(.50) \, / \, \sqrt{[\,1 - (.50)^2\,]} = 1.1547$$

$$\text{SD } (\delta) = a\,(.10)$$

where $a = 2\,/\,(1 - .25)^{1.5} = 2\,/\,.6495 = 3.0792$. That is, Ave $(\delta) = 1.15$ and SD $(\delta) = .31$.

The reader who starts this book with this chapter is warned that many important issues regarding the *d* statistic are discussed in Chapter 6. Chapter 6 should be read before this chapter. The reader is also cautioned that this chapter is less detailed than Chapters 3 and 4 because many explanations are identical to the corresponding explanation for the meta-analysis of *r* and are not repeated here for want of space. That is, to avoid repetition, many conceptual issues are discussed in Chapters 4 and 5 that are not repeated in this chapter.

Bare Bones Meta-Analysis

The basic cumulation process is the same for effect sizes as for correlations: One computes the frequency weighted mean and variance of the effect size over studies, and then corrects the variance for sampling error.

Consider any set of weights w_i. There are three averages to be computed: (1) the weighted average of *d*, (2) the correspondingly weighted variance of *d*, and (3) the average sampling error variance. If we denote the average value of *d* by *D*, then the averages are

$$\text{Ave } (d) = \Sigma\, w_i\, d_i \, / \, \Sigma\, w_i = D$$

$$\text{Var } (d) = \Sigma\, w_i\, [\, d_i - D\,]^2 \, / \, \Sigma\, w_i$$

$$\text{Var } (e) = \Sigma\, w_i\, \text{Var } (e_i) \, / \, \Sigma\, w_i\, .$$

The tricky computation is the average sampling error variance, Var (*e*). The problem is that the sampling error variance within each study requires knowledge of the effect size for that study. That is,

$$\text{Var } (e_i) = (4/N_i)\,(1 + \delta_i^{\,2} / 8)$$

depends on the population effect size δ_i, which is unknown. A good approximation in most cases is to substitute the mean value of *d* for δ_i in each study. In the case of the frequency weighted average, this leads to the equation

$$\text{Var } (e) = (4/N) \, (1 + D^2 / 8)$$

where N is the average sample size. That is, if we denote the total sample size by T and the number of studies by K, then

$$T = \Sigma \, N_i$$

$$N = T / K.$$

The more accurate formula for the sampling error variance is

$$\text{Var } (e) = [(N{-}1)/(N{-}3)] \, [(4/N) \, (1 + D^2 / 8)]$$

where N is the average sample size and D is the frequency weighted value of d_i.

The variance of population effect sizes Var (δ) is the observed variance of effect sizes corrected for sampling error. The variance of population effect sizes is found by subtracting the sampling error variance from the observed variance. That is,

$$\text{Var } (\delta) = \text{Var } (d) - \text{Var } (e).$$

This difference can be interpreted as subtracting the variance in d due to sampling error. In that sense, subtracting the average sampling error variance can be regarded as correcting the variance for the effect of sampling error. The standard deviation of study population effect sizes is the square root of the variance

$$SD_\delta = \sqrt{\text{Var } (\delta)} \, .$$

Thus, for bare bones meta-analysis, if the observed distribution of effect sizes is characterized by the values Ave (d) and Var (d), then the study population effect size is characterized by

$$\text{Ave } (\delta) = \text{Ave } (d)$$

$$\text{Var } (\delta) = \text{Var } (d) - \text{Var } (e)$$

$$SD_\delta = \sqrt{\text{Var } (\delta)} \, .$$

If the effect size is really the same across studies, then the variance of population effect sizes is zero. That is, if there is no real variation in population effect sizes, then the observed variance will exactly equal the variance due to sampling error. Even if there is some variation across studies, the variance may still be small enough to ignore for practical or theoretical reasons. If the variation is large, especially if it is large relative to the mean value, then there should be a search for moderator variables.

A Numerical Example

The reader is cautioned that the discussions of examples in this chapter take certain liberties. To present an example and illustrate computations, we must present examples with a small number of studies. This means that the total sample size in the example is not nearly large enough to eliminate the effect of sampling error. That is, the estimates from the meta-analysis will still have sampling error in them. However, in this chapter we want to discuss the results as if the sampling error had been removed. Thus, for each example in this chapter, our discussion will be phrased as if the number of studies were much larger than shown in the example. The estimation of sampling error in the estimates from a meta-analysis will be considered in its own right in Chapter 9. That chapter contains sampling error estimates for many of the examples shown here.

Consider an example for bare bones meta-analysis.

N	d
100	−.01
90	.41*
50	.50*
40	−.10

(*Significant at the .05 level)

Two of the effect sizes are significant while two are not. By the usual logic, a reviewer would assume from this that there is some moderator variable that causes the treatment to have an effect in some settings but have no effect in others. Could this be sampling error?

The bare bones meta-analysis is

$$T = 100 + 90 + 50 + 40 = 280$$

$$N = T / K = 280 / 4 = 70$$

$$\text{Ave }(d) = [\ 100\,(-.01) + 90\,(.41) + 50\,(.50) + 40\,(-.10)\ ]\ /\ 280$$

$$= 56.9\ /\ 280 = .20$$

$$\text{Var }(d) = [\ 100\,(-.01 - .20)^2 + 90\,(.41 - .20)^2$$

$$+ 50\,(.50 - .20)^2 + 40\,(-.10 - .20)^2\ ]\ /\ 280$$

$$= 16.479\ /\ 280 = .058854.$$

Using D for the average value of d, the large sample estimate of the sampling error variance is

$$\text{Var }(e) = (4/N)\,(1 + D^2\ /8) = (4/70)\,(1 + .20^2\ /8) = .057429.$$

Thus, we estimate the distribution of study population effect sizes by

$$\text{Ave }(\delta) = \text{Ave }(d) = .20$$

$$\text{Var }(\delta) = \text{Var }(d) - \text{Var }(e) = .058854 - .057429 = .001425$$

$$\text{SD }(\delta) = \sqrt{.001425} = .038.$$

We now consider an interpretation of this meta-analysis written as if the number of studies were much larger than 4. This meta-analysis has only 4 studies and a total sample size of 280. Thus, there is actually room for considerable sampling error in the meta-analysis estimates. This will be considered in Chapter 9.

Suppose these meta-analysis estimates were very accurate; e.g., assume the number of studies to be 400 rather than 4. If population effect sizes were normally distributed, then the middle 95% of population effect sizes would lie in the interval

$$.20 - 1.96\,\text{SD}_\delta < \delta < .20 + 1.96\,\text{SD}_\delta$$

$$.13 < \delta < .27.$$

In order for a population effect size to be 0, it would represent a standard score of

$$[\ 0 - .20\ ]\ /\ .038 = -5.26.$$

This is an extremely unlikely possibility. Thus, in this example, meta-analysis shows the usual review logic to be quite wrong. It is not the case that the treatment has no effect in 50% of settings. There are no settings where the treatment effect is 0. Thus, in the two studies with nonsignificant effect sizes, there was a Type II error. That is, in this example, the error rate for the significance test was 50%.

Consider the use of the more accurate formula for the sampling error variance.

$$\text{Var}(e) = [(N-1)/(N-3)][4/N][1 + D^2/8]$$

$$= [69/67][.057429] = .059143$$

There is little difference in the estimate of the sampling error variance. However there is a larger difference in the estimate of the study population effect size variance.

$$\text{Var}(\delta) = \text{Var}(d) - \text{Var}(e) = .058854 - .059143 = -.000289$$

Using the less accurate large-sample formula, the difference between observed variance and variance due to sampling error was .001425; i.e., the observed variance was larger than expected on the basis of sampling error. However, the more accurate formula shows that the variance was almost exactly equal to the level expected from sampling error. The fact that the difference is negative shows that with only four studies, there is some second-order sampling error (see Chapter 9) in Var (d). The corresponding estimate of the standard deviation is $SD_\delta = 0$. Thus, using the more accurate sampling error formula generates a description of the study population correlations, which is

$$\text{Ave}(\delta) = .20$$

$$SD_\delta = 0.$$

This estimate shows that there was no variation in the study population effect sizes. That this is true is known from the fact that the authors generated the data using the same population effect size for all studies. In a real meta-analysis based on only four studies, the same finding would be only provisional.

To correct for bias, we first compute the bias multiplier

$$a = 1 + .75/(N-3) = 1 + .75/67 = 1.007.$$

The corrected mean and standard deviation are thus

$$\text{Ave }(\delta) = .20 \,/\, 1.007 = .1985 = .20$$

$$SD_\delta = 0 \,/\, 1.007 = 0 \,.$$

Thus, for an average sample size of 70, the effect of correction for bias is smaller than rounding error.

Another Example: Leadership Training by Experts

Organizational psychologists have long suspected that training in interpersonal or leadership skills improves the performance of managers. Professor Fruitloop decided that he wanted to know the amount of improvement and, therefore, laid out the design of a meta-analysis. He decided that studies should meet two criteria. First, each training program must contain at least three key skills: active listening, negative feedback, and positive feedback. Second, the study should be run under controlled training conditions. To assure this he used only studies in which the training was done by outside experts (see Table 7.1).

Of the five studies, only one shows a significant effect. Two of the studies show effects in the opposite direction. Thus, using normal review standards, Fruitloop would be led to conclude that training in interpersonal skills had no impact (or uncertain impact) on performance of supervisors in a majority of settings. But, fortunately, Fruitloop had heard of meta-analysis. The meta-analysis of the five studies in Table 7.1 is

$$T = 200$$

$$N = 40$$

$$\text{Ave }(d) = .20$$

$$\text{Var }(d) = .106000.$$

Using the more accurate formula

$$\text{Var }(e) = [\,39/37\,]\,[\,4/40\,]\,[\,1 + .20^2 \,/\, 8\,] = .105932$$

$$\text{Var }(\delta) = \text{Var }(d) - \text{Var }(e) = .106000 - .105932 = .000068$$

$$SD_\delta = .01 \,.$$

Table 7.1 Leadership Training (Studies with Training by Outside Experts)

Author	Sample Size	Effect Size
Apple	40	−.24
Banana	40	−.04
Cherry	40	.20
Orange	40	.44
Melon	40	.64*

*Significant at the .05 level.

For a meta-analysis of five studies with an average sample size of 40, the total sample size is only $T = 200$. Thus, the potential sampling error in the meta-analysis estimates would be as large as the sampling error in a single study with $N = 200$, and that is very large (though these figures were set up so that such large errors did not occur). Computation of confidence intervals about the estimates from this meta-analysis will be presented in Chapter 9.

It is not our purpose here to focus on the sampling error in meta-analysis with a small number of studies. Rather, we used only a small number of studies so that it would be easy for the reader to replicate the computations to check understanding of formulas. For purposes of argument, assume that the residual variance of .000068 is not due to sampling error; i.e., accept the standard deviation of .01 as real. A real standard deviation of .01 would mean that there is real variation in the study population effect sizes. But would that mean that there was real variation in actual effect sizes? Certainly not. In a bare-bones meta-analysis, we control for only one artifact: sampling error. No control was made for variation in error of measurement, or variation in the degree of imperfection of construct validity, or variation in the degree of imperfection of construct validity, or variation in the strength of the treatment, and so on. Thus, there are many other artifacts that might have caused variance in the study effect size.

It is even more important to remember that this is a bare-bones analysis in interpreting the size of the treatment effect. Most of the artifacts not controlled have the effect of lowering the observed effect size. Thus, the observed mean of .20 is almost surely an underestimate, and possibly a massive underestimate.

Consider the difference between a narrative review and a meta-analysis, assuming these same results from a meta-analysis of 500 studies. Only 100 of the 500 studies would produce significant results. As many as 200 of the 500 studies would produce results in the wrong direction. Thus, the contemporary narrative review would probably conclude that training has an effect in only a minority of settings; on the other hand, 20% of the studies with significant results would find large effect sizes, *d* values of .60 or more. Thus, a narrative review might well conclude that in those settings where training works, it works quite well.

Using meta-analysis, Fruitloop discovered a very different pattern to population effect sizes. He found that virtually all the variation in oberved results was actually due to sampling error. Thus, the available studies actually showed perfect consistency in the effect of training, a uniform effect size of $\delta = .20$. Thus, the effect size is never 0, and it is also never as large as .40, much less .60, the levels found in isolated studies.

Analysis of Moderator Variables

The impact of an intervention might vary from setting to setting. For example, training programs might vary in quality, quantity, or in the average learning ability of the trainees. If this were so, then the cumulation formulas would yield nonzero variance for the population effect sizes, i.e., a nonzero value for SD_δ. The search for and detection of the moderator variables that account for such variation is identical to the procedure followed in looking for moderator variables in correlational studies. Indeed, the general mathematics is identical for both. In particular, if the number of studies is small and the number of coded study characteristics is large, then blind search is highly prone to capitalization on chance (see Chapter 2).

There are two ways to see if a study characteristic is a moderator variable or not: Use the characteristic to break the data into subsets or correlate the study characteristic with effect size. There have now been enough meta-analyses done with both methods to generate an opinion as to which method works better. It is our impression that the correlation method — which is usually touted as "more sophisticated" — is much more often used incorrectly. Thus, for most purposes we would recommend the subset method be used.

Finally, we note that meta-analysis can examine moderators only at the study level. For example, if some studies have been conducted on males and some on females, then meta-analysis can examine sex as a potential moderator. However, if every study is based on a combination of males and females and reports only the total group results, sex cannot be tested as a moderator. Guzzo et al. (1986) criticized meta-analysis for this "limitation," a criticism we consider inappropriate and ingenuous. No other method of integrating study findings can test for moderators under these circumstances either (see Chapter 13).

Using Study Domain Subsets

If the studies are broken down into subsets, then there is no new computational tool to be learned. The researcher merely performs a separate meta-analysis within each subset. For a bare-bones meta-analysis there is nothing more to say. However, if artifacts other than sampling error are to be corrected — a critical feature in many research areas — then we do have one additional word of advice. Often, artifact information for other artifacts is only sporadically available. In most cases, the artifact distributions are better computed for the entire set of studies rather than recomputed within subsets. The whole domain artifact distribution values are then used in the computation of the within-subsets meta-analyses.

If the data are broken into subsets, then there are two ways that a moderator variable would show itself. First, there should be large differences in the mean effect size between subsets. Second, there should be a reduction in variance within subsets. These are not independent events. We know from analysis of variance that the total variance in effect size is the sum of the variance in mean effect sizes between subsets plus the average within-subset variance. Thus, if there is a large difference between the subset mean effect sizes, then the within-subset variance must be smaller than the overall variance.

This theorem applies equally well to either observed effect sizes or to population effect sizes. If the usual formula for components of variance is applied to the corrected variances rather than to uncorrected variances, then the result is the same: a large difference between subset means implies a lower value for average within-subset variance than for overall variance.

Using Study Characteristic Correlations

Consider instead the correlation approach to the search for moderator variables. In this approach, we compute a correlation over studies between the coded study characteristic and the observed effect size. The effect of sampling error on this correlation is directly analogous to the effect of error of measurement on a correlation between variables over subjects: The correlation is systematically reduced. Thus, to correct a correlation between effect size and study characteristic for the effect of sampling error is to increase that correlation in proportion to the relative size of the real variation in effect size to the artificial variation caused by sampling error. This is directly analogous to correction for attenuation. This correction of Var (*d*) for sampling error is comparable to correcting the usual within-experiment variance for error of measurement

If the observed sample effect size is correlated with a study characteristic, then the correlation will be attenuated by the sampling error in the observed effect size in the same manner that the ordinary correlations across persons are attenuated by error of measurement. Consider the sampling error formula

$$d_i = \delta_i + e_i$$

and consider a study characteristic denoted y_i. Denote the correlation across studies between d and y as "Cor (d,y)." The covariance is

$$\text{Cov } (d,y) = \text{Cov } (\delta,y) + \text{Cov } (e,y).$$

For a large set of studies, the covariance between sampling error and study characteristics will be zero. Thus, in the research domain as a whole, sampling error does not contribute to the covariance of study characteristic and effect size. However, since

$$\text{Var } (d) = \text{Var } (\delta) + \text{Var } (e)$$

sampling error does contribute to the variance of the effect sizes. Thus, the effect of sampling error is to increase the variance in the denominator of the study characteristic correlation while making no corresponding increase in the numerator. Thus the effect of sampling error is to decrease the size of the correlation.

The study characteristic correlation can be corrected for sampling error using a formula that is exactly analagous to the formula for correction of a correlation for error of measurement. To do this we use the error of measurement to define a "reliability" denoted "Rel (d)" and then use it to correct the observed correlation "Cor (d,y)" in the usual manner. In measurement theory, the reliability of a variable affected by random error e_p is the relative variance of true scores T_p to observed scores X_p.

$$r_{XX} = \text{Var } (T) \, / \, \text{Var } (X)$$

where

$$\text{Var } (X) = \text{Var } (T) + \text{Var } (e).$$

The analagous formula for meta-analysis is

$$\text{Rel }(d) = \text{Var }(\delta) / \text{Var }(d).$$

To correct the over subjects correlation between variables X and Y for error of measurement in X is to divide by the square root of the reliability, i.e.

$$r_{TY} = r_{XY} / \sqrt{r_{XX}}.$$

The corresponding theorem for meta-analysis is

$$\text{Cor }(\delta, y) = \text{Cor }(d,y) / \sqrt{\text{Rel}(d)}.$$

This formula generates an estimate of the study characteristic correlation, had all the studies been done with very large samples.

It is important to note that the formula above is derived using the assumption that sampling error will be uncorrelated with any study characteristic. This theorem is true for the research domain and is approximately true for any meta-analysis done with a large number of studies. However, for a meta-analysis done with a small number of studies, the sampling errors in those particular studies may by chance be correlated with some of the study characteristic values for that sample of studies. This is the problem of capitalization on chance (see Chapter 2). As one sorts through potential moderator variables, some study charateristics may have a high-chance correlation with the sampling errors. This variable would then look like a strong moderator variable.

For a meta-analysis with a small number of studies, there is no statistical solution to the problem of capitalization on chance. In a research domain with good theories, there is a possible solution. Test first only that moderator variable predicted by a good theory that is well supported by other research. If that variable does not moderate the effect size, then treat all the remaining potential moderators with a very large grain of salt. If there is a theory to go with the discovered moderator variable, then check the literature to see if there is any independent corroboration of that theory.

An Example: Training by Experts Versus by Managers

In his dissertation, Jim Russell tested the hypothesis that training of supervisors in interpersonal skills should be conducted by their own managers rather than by outside experts. That idea derived from the proposition that since managers act as role models for supervisors, the supervisors are much more likely to identify with procedures recommended by managers than with those recommended by outside experts.

Table 7.2 Training in Interpersonal Skills by Managers Versus by Experts

Author	Trainer	Sample Size	Effect Size
Apple	Expert	40	−.25
Banana	Expert	40	−.05
Cherry	Expert	40	.20
Orange	Expert	40	.45
Melon	Expert	40	.65*
Cucumber	Manager	40	−.05
Tomato	Manager	40	.15
Squash	Manager	40	.40
Carrot	Manager	40	.65*
Pepper	Manager	40	.85*

*Significant at the .05 level (two-tailed test).

Although his results were negative, we will present a hypothetical example showing positive results here.

Consider again the hypothetical cumulative study done by Fruitloop. Fruitloop discarded all studies done by managers as "lacking in experimental control." Thus Fruitloop analyzed only studies where the training was done by experts. Suppose instead that all studies were analyzed. The results might look like those in Table 7.2. In this collection of studies, only four of ten have significant effects, and three of ten go in the opposite direction. Thus, normal review practice would probably conclude that the effect of training in interpersonal skills is problematic.

The overall meta-analysis for the studies in Table 7.2 is

$$T = 40 + 40 + \ldots = 400$$

$$N = T / 10 = 40$$

$$\text{Ave } (d) = .30$$

$$\text{Var } (d) = .116000$$

$$\text{Var } (e) = [\, 39/37 \,][\, 4/40 \,][\, 1 + .30^2 / 8 \,] = .106591$$

$$\text{Var } (\delta) = .116000 - .106591 = .009409$$

$$SD_\delta = .097 .$$

For purposes of computational convenience, we have again presented a meta-analysis with only a small number of studies. A set of 10 studies with an average sample size of 40 represents only a total sample size of 400. Thus, there would still be a large potential sampling error in the estimates from the meta-analysis. The formulas for confidence intervals are presented in Chapter 9.

Since we are not interested in such sampling error in this example, let us assume that we obtained similar results not with 10 studies but with 100 studies. The standard deviation of study effect size is .097, which is noticably greater than 0. The standard deviation of .097 is also large relative to a mean effect size of .30. However, it is not large enough to suggest that there are any settings where the effect size is 0. If variation in effect size were normally distributed (it actually turns out to be dichotomous in this example), the middle 95% of effect sizes would be

$$.30 - 1.96\,(.097) < \delta < .30 + 1.96\,(.097)$$

$$.11 < \delta < .49.$$

However, this is a large range of possible effect, and a search for moderator variables is justified.

Consider again the performance of the statistical significance test on this dataset. Only 3 of the 10 effect sizes were significant. Yet the meta-analysis shows that all of the population effect sizes were positive. Thus the (Type II) error rate for the significance test in this example is 70%. Furthermore, the variation in observed effect sizes covered a massive range: from −.25 to +.85. In fact, the meta-analysis shows that most of this variation is due to sampling error. Few values would actually be found outside the interval $.11 < \delta < .49$. On the other hand, there is still quite a bit of variability in results and, thus, a search for moderator variables is well advised.

In this example, the moderator was hypothesized before the meta-analysis. Thus, we break the studies down into those where the training was by outside experts versus those where the training was done by managers. The within subset meta-analyses are:

Training by experts

$$T = 40 + 40 + \ldots = 200$$

$$N = T / 10 = 40$$

$$\text{Ave}\,(d) = .20$$

$$\text{Var}\,(d) = .106000$$

$$\text{Var }(e) = [39/37] [4/40] [1 + .20^2 / 8] = .105932$$

$$\text{Var }(\delta) = .106000 - .105932 = .000068$$

$$\text{SD}_\delta = .008$$

Training by managers

$$T = 40 + 40 + \ldots = 200$$

$$N = T / 10 = 40$$

$$\text{Ave }(d) = .40$$

$$\text{Var }(d) = .106000$$

$$\text{Var }(e) = [39/37] [4/40] [1 + .40^2 / 8] = .107514$$

$$\text{Var }(\delta) = .106000 - .107514 = -.001514$$

$$\text{SD}_\delta = .0$$

Again, we note that the small number of studies was meant only for computational convenience. Assume that there were not 10, but 1,000 studies, 500 studies of each kind. That is, let us interpret the results of the meta-analysis as if there were no sampling error in the estimates.

In this example, breaking studies down by type of trainer shows the moderator effect in two ways. First, there is the wide difference between mean effect sizes: Ave $(d) = .20$ for training by experts but Ave $(d) = .40$ for training by managers. Furthermore, the breakdown by trainer eliminates virtually all variation in effect size (beyond that due to sampling error). Thus, training by outside experts always has an effect of .20 standard deviations, while training by managers always has an effect of twice that size, .40 standard deviations.

Note that assuming a normal distribution for effect sizes produced a 95% interval from .11 to .49, suggesting that 2.5% of studies would produce values lower than $\delta = .11$ and that 2.5% of studies would produce values higher than $\delta = .49$. In fact the distribution was not normal. Instead, half the studies had a population effect size of $\delta = .20$ (those with outside expert trainers) and half had a population effect size of $\delta = .40$ (those with manager trainers). Thus, the assumption of normality overestimated the actual spread of effect sizes.

Another Example: Amount of Training

We now present an example in which the impact of training on inter-personal skills varies as a function of the number of hours of training. The data are shown in Table 7.3. The measure of number of hours is the amount of time that the trainee is in actual interaction with the trainer (as opposed to watching the trainer work with someone else).

In this example, the effect size was significant only 1 in 12 times and the results were positive in only 7 of the 12 studies. That is, nearly half the studies found effects in the opposite direction. Normal review practice would probably conclude that training in interpersonal skills has no effect. The meta-analysis results are:

All studies

$$T = 40 + 40 + \ldots = 480$$

$$N = 480 / 12 = 40$$

$$\text{Ave } (d) = .15$$

$$\text{Var } (d) = .109717$$

$$\text{Var } (e) = .105702$$

$$\text{Var } (\delta) = .004015$$

$$\text{SD}_\delta = .063$$

Again, we duck the issue of the small total sample size of 480 in this example (to which we return in Chapter 9). Suppose there had been not 12, but 1,200 studies. That is, assume that there is essentially no sampling error in the meta-analysis estimates. We describe the distribution of pop-ulation effect sizes as having a mean of .15 and a standard deviation of .063. How much would study effect sizes vary from one setting to the next? Consider the assumption of a normal distribution of effect sizes. If the variation in effect sizes were normally distributed (it is not), the middle 95% of effect sizes would be

$$.15 - 1.96\,(.063) < \delta < .15 + 1.96\,(.063)$$

$$.03 < \delta < .27 .$$

Table 7.3 Training in Interpersonal Skills by Hours

Number Hours	Sample Size	Effect Size
2	40	−.39
2	40	.54
2	40	.25
2	40	−.05
3	40	−.29
3	40	.00
3	40	.30
3	40	.59
4	40	−.24
4	40	.64*
4	40	.35
4	40	.05

*Significant at the .05 level (two-tailed test).

This would suggest that there are probably no settings in which the training has no effect.

Compare the results of the meta-analysis with the conclusions of a narrative review. Only 100 of the 1,200 studies would have statistically significant effects. This could be interpreted to mean that training only has an effect in about 1 setting in 12. The cumulative analysis shows this to be wrong. At the level of observed study effects, results ranged from −.25 to +.85. The cumultive analysis shows that most of this variation is due to sampling error.

Thus, the meta-analysis reveals a very different story. The average effect size is a weak .15, but most of the variation is due to sampling error. If variation in effect size were normally distributed, then 95% of settings would have effect sizes in the range $.03 < \delta < .27$.

On the other hand, a range in effect of .03 to .27 would be a whopping difference in impact. Thus, it would be very important to know which studies had the large and which studies had the small effects. Thus, we begin the search for a moderator variable. Consider hours of training as a moderator. Since 3 levels of amount of training are represented in the domain of studies, we break the total set of studies into 3 subsets, those with 2 hours, 3 hours, or 4 hours of training. The separate bare-bones meta-analyses follow.

2 Hours Training

$$T = 40 + 40 + \ldots = 160$$

$$N = 160 / 4 = 40$$

Ave (d) = .10

Var (d) = .108050

Var (e) = .105537

Var (δ) = .002513

SD_{δ} = .050

3 Hours Training

$T = 40 + 40 + \ldots = 160$

$N = 160 / 4 = 40$

Ave (d) = .15

Var (d) = .108050

Var (e) = .105702

Var (δ) = .002348

SD_{δ} = .048

4 Hours Training

$T = 40 + 40 + \ldots = 160$

$N = 160 / 4 = 40$

Ave (d) = .20

Var (d) = .108050

Var (e) = .105932

Var (δ) = .002118

SD_{δ} = .046

The moderator analysis shows that the amount of training is an important determinant of the effect of training. As the amount grows from 2 to 3 to 4 hours, the mean treatment effect grows from .10 to .15 to .20. That is, the mean treatment effect is proportional to the amount of training time within the range of training times studied. Thus, even greater impact would be projected if still more time were devoted to the training. On the other hand, the nonlinear learning curves in the literature on learning suggest that we could not just project out linearly; rather, diminishing returns would set in at some point.

In this example, the one moderator variable does not explain all the variation in results. The overall standard deviation of .063 droppd to .050, .048, and .046 for the three within subset analyses. This is a decrease in variation, but it is not 0. Consider the 4 hour training studies. The mean effect size is .20, but the standard deviation is .046. If effect sizes varied normally, the middle 95% of the distribution of effect sizes would be

$$.20 - 1.96(.046) < \delta < .20 + 1.96(.046)$$

$$.11 < \delta < .29.$$

Thus, if another moderator variable — perhaps job complexity — could be found, it would add substantially to our understanding of interpersonal training.

However, it should be noted that there may not be another moderator variable. A bare-bones meta-analysis corrects only for the effects of sampling error. Other artifacts, such as error of measurement, have not been controlled. Thus, it is possible that the residual variation is due to uncontrolled artifacts rather than real differences in training contexts.

The Correlational Moderator Analysis

The corresponding correlational moderator analysis defines hours of training as a quantitative variable H. This can then be correlated with the observed effect size. The correlation between H and d in Table 7.3 is

$$\mathrm{Cor}(d, H) = .125.$$

The "reliability" is

$$\mathrm{Rel}(d) = \mathrm{Var}(\delta) / \mathrm{Var}(d) = .004015 / .109717 = .0366.$$

Thus, the correlation for population effect sizes would be

$$\mathrm{Cor}(\delta, H) = \mathrm{Cor}(d, H) / \sqrt{\mathrm{Rel}(d)} = .125 / \sqrt{.0366} = .65.$$

That is, the effect of sampling error was to reduce the correlation of .65 between population effect sizes and hours of training to a correlation of only .125.

Correcting *d* Value Statistics
for Measurement Error in the Dependent Variable

In Chapter 6 we showed that error of measurement in the dependent variable reduces the effect size estimate. If the reliability of measurement is low, the reduction can be quite sizeble. Failure to correct for the attenuation due to error of measurement yields an erroneous effect size estimate. Furthermore, since the error is systematic, a bare bones meta-analysis on uncorrected effect sizes will produce an incorrect estimate of the true effect size. The extent of reduction in the mean effect size is determined by the mean level of reliability across the studies. Variation in reliability across studies causes variation in the observed effect sizes above and beyond that produced by sampling error. If the true effect size is actually homogeneous across studies, the variation in reliability would produce a false impression of heterogeneity in a bare bones meta-analysis. A bare bones meta-analysis will not correct for either the systematic reduction in the mean effect size or the systematic increase in the variance of effect sizes. Thus, even meta-analysis will produce correct values for the distribution of effect sizes only if there is a correction for the attenuation due to error of measurement.

In meta-analysis, there are two ways to eliminate the effect of error of measurement. Ideally, one could compile information on reliability for all or nearly all the individual studies. In this case, each effect size could be individually corrected and the meta-analysis could be done on the corrected effect sizes. However, if information on reliability is only available sporadically, then it may only be possible to generate an estimate of the distribution of reliability across studies. If the level of reliability in studies is independent of the level of effect sizes, then it is possible to correct a bare bones meta-analysis for the effect of error of measurment. That is, if reliability information is only available in the form of a distribution, then we first do a bare bones meta-analysis and we then correct the bare bones meta-analysis estimates for attenuation (the mean effect size) and inflation (the variance of effect sizes) after the fact.

Some authors would rather incur the error of attenuation than correct for it. They defend this choice by saying that underestimation of effect sizes is acceptable; only overestimation is bad. That is, some believe that only positive errors count and negative errors don't matter. But theoretical work often requires the comparison of effect sizes. If some of the effect sizes have been underestimated, the comparison may be wrong and, thus, lead to false inferences. It is our belief that the history of science shows that negative errors are just as damaging as positive errors. Thus, we believe that correction is always desirable.

The problem in meta-analysis is that some studies do not report the reliability of the measures used. Sometimes this problem can be eliminated by going to studies outside the research domain that use the same measure and report its reliability. If none of the studies that use a given measure ever report a reliability (often the case in behavioristic work), then even in meta-analysis no correction can be made. However, even if correction for attenuation is to be ignored, it is important to have some idea of how large the corresponding error in estimation will be. One way to do this would be to look at the reliability of similar measures.

The key to computing the effect of error of measurement on effect sizes is to measure the extent of random measurement error in the dependent variable. This is done in psychometric theory using the reliability coefficient. If the reliability of the dependent measure is known, then the extent of attenuation can be exactly computed. It is then possible to algebraically reverse the attenuation; the process called "correction for attenuation."

If the true population effect size is δ, then the study population effect size would be as high as δ only if the dependent variable is perfectly measured. If the reliability of the dependent variable is less than 1.00, then there will be a corresponding reduction in the study population effect size. If the reliability of the dependent variable measure is r_{YY}, then the attenuated population effect size δ_o is given by

$$\delta_o = a\,\delta$$

where $a = \sqrt{r_{YY}}$. For example, if the reliability of the dependent variable is $r_{YY} = .64$, then the study population effect size is

$$\delta_o = .80\,\delta$$

i.e., reduced by 20%. If we know that a number has been reduced by 20%, then we can find the original number by division. That is, if we know that $\delta_o = .80\delta$, then we can divide by .80 to obtain δ, i.e. $\delta = \delta_o \,/\, .80$. Thus, the population effect size δ_o could be algebraically corrected for attenuation by dividing both sides of the equation by a. That is,

$$\delta_o \,/\, a = (a\,\delta)\,/\,a = \delta.$$

The formula for correction for attenuation works perfectly with population effect sizes. The sample effect size can also be corrected for attenuation using the same formula. That correction eliminates the systematic attenuation of the sample effect. Thus, in principle, we can use a statistical correction formula to eliminate the effects of random error of measurement. However, there is still sampling error in the corrected effect size. The crucial fact for meta-analysis is that the formula for sampling error in a corrected effect size is different from the formula for the sampling error in an uncorrected effect size. Thus, meta-analysis on corrected effect sizes uses a slightly different formula to correct the variance for sampling error.

If correction for attenuation can eliminate the attenuation produced by error of measurement, one might ask why we should bother to try to use good measurement in the first place. The answer lies in the sampling error of corrected effect sizes. A careful analysis of the correction process shows that we pay a price for statistical correction: The sampling error in a statistically corrected effect size is larger than the sampling error in a study done with perfect measurement. The higher the reliability, the less the increase in sampling error. Thus, the better the original measurement, the less the sampling error in the corrected effect size. That is, we can obtain the results for perfect measurement without being able to achieve perfect measurement in our studies, but the price for statistical correction is increased sampling error. The higher the reliability, the lower the price. The price for low reliability in an individual study is very high. However, the larger sample sizes in meta-analysis make it possible to get good estimates of effect sizes even if all the studies done in a domain have low reliability.

We will show that correcting the effect size for attenuation increases sampling error. Consider the sample effect size d_o.

$$d_o = \delta_o + \epsilon = a\,\delta + e$$

The attenuated sample effect size can be corrected for the effect of error of measurement. Denote the corrected effect size by d.

$$d = d_o\,/\,a = (\delta_o + e)\,/\,a$$

$$= \delta_o\,/\,a + e\,/\,a$$

$$= \quad \delta \quad + \quad e'$$

where e' is the sampling error in the corrected effect size. The sampling error in e' is given by

$$\text{Var}(e') = \text{Var}(e) / a^2 = \text{Var}(e) / r_{YY}.$$

To divide by a fraction is to increase the ratio. Thus, the increase in sampling error variance is exactly proportional to the reliability. The standard error of the corrected effect size is the square root of the variance. For the standard error, we have

$$\text{SD}_{e'} = \text{SD}_e / a.$$

That is, to divide the effect size by the attenuation factor is to divide the standard error by the same factor. The lower the reliability, the greater the increase in sampling error.

For example, if the reliability of the dependent variable is .64, then the sampling error variance of the corrected effect size is

$$\text{Var}(e') = \text{Var}(e) / .64 = (1/.64)\,\text{Var}(e) = 1.56\,\text{Var}(e).$$

The corresponding standard error is

$$\text{SD}_{e'} = \sqrt{1.56}\,\text{SD}_e = 1.25\,\text{SD}_e.$$

That is, if the study reliability is as low as .64, then the corrected effect size has 25% more sampling error than the uncorrected effect size. Thus, to eliminate the 20% systematic error in the uncorrected effect size, we must incur a 25% increase in the unsystematic error.

In meta-analysis, we must not only worry about the extent of reliability in single studies, but about variation in reliability across studies. If there is variation across studies in the reliability of measures of dependent variables, then different effect sizes are attenuated by different factors. This fact will cause variation in observed d values beyond the variation due to sampling error. Thus, in a bare bones meta-analysis, there will be artifactual variance in the effect sizes that is not subtracted when the variance is corrected for the effect of sampling error. This variation is eliminated if each effect size is individually corrected for unreliability.

Meta-Analysis of *d* Values Corrected Individually and an Example

If the reliability of the dependent variable is known for all individual studies, then each effect size can be individually corrected for attenuation.

If the reliability is known for almost all studies, then there is little error in using the average reliability for the missing cases. The meta-analysis is then computed on the corrected effect sizes. The steps in the meta-analysis are the same as those for a bare bones meta-analysis: (1) Compute the mean and variance of the effect sizes; (2) Compute the variance in effect sizes due to sampling error; and (3) subtract that from the variance of the sample effect sizes. However, there is one complication: The weights that are optimal for uncorrected effect sizes are not optimal for corrected effect sizes. Optimal weights are inversely related to the sampling error in the effect size. In an uncorrected effect size, sampling error is primarily determined by the sample size. But in a corrected effect size, the sampling error also depends on the extent of the correction for attenuation. Studies that require a large correction should get less weight than studies that require only a small correction. For uncorrected effect sizes, the optimal weight for each study is its sample size N_i. For corrected effect sizes, the optimal weight for each study is

$$w_i = N_i \, a_i^2 = N_i \, r_{YY_i} \, .$$

That is, the mean effect size is better estimated if we weight each study proportional to its reliability. The lower the reliability in the study, the lower the optimal weight for that study.

For each study, we compute three numbers: (1) the corrected effect size, (2) the weight to be given to the study, and (3) the sampling error variance for that study. The formula for the sampling error variance presents one small problem: It depends on the population effect size. A good approximation is to use the mean effect size in the sampling error formula. Thus, the sampling error in the corrected effect size is approximately

$$\text{Var}(e_i') = \text{Var}(e_i) / a_i^2 = \text{Var}(e_i) / r_{YY_i}$$

where

$$\text{Var}(e_i) = [\,(N_i - 1)/(N_i - 3)\,]\,[\,4/N_i\,]\,[\,1 + D_o^2 / 8\,]$$

where D_o is the mean uncorrected effect size. Thus, estimation of the sampling error for the corrected effect sizes requires the computation of the average uncorrected effect size.

Let us denote the observed sample effect size by d_o and the corrected effect size by d. Denote the population uncorrected effect size by δ_o and the population corrected effect size by δ. Denote the sampling error variance estimate of study i by ve_i and denote the mean corrected effect size by D. Then the three averages required for the meta-analysis are the three weighted averages

$$\text{Ave}\,(d) = \Sigma\, w_i\, d_i\, /\, \Sigma\, w_i$$

$$\text{Var}\,(d) = \Sigma\, w_i\, (d_i - D)^2\, /\, \Sigma\, w_i$$

$$\text{Var}\,(e) = \Sigma\, w_i\, ve_i\, /\, \Sigma\, w_i\,.$$

The variance of population effect sizes is then estimated by subtraction.

$$\text{Var}\,(\delta) = \text{Var}\,(d) - \text{Var}\,(e)$$

Now let us consider an example. Alex Lernmor, a psychologist at New York University, developed a new method of training dopplegangers in the facts they need to operate the machinery on their jobs. His training program has been adopted by many firms in the Northeast that employ dopplegangers. So far, four studies have been done in these firms to evaluate the effectiveness of the program, and the same 100-item measure of job knowledge was used in all four studies. In all cases, there were twenty people in the trained group and twenty in the control group (see Table 7.4). Alphonso Kopikat of the University of Texas learned about this program and, in connection with his consulting work, introduced it into many Texas businesses employing dopplegangers. Four studies evaluating the method have now been completed in Texas. These studies are much the same as the earlier ones, although, to save time, a short 12-item measure of job knowledge was used instead of the lengthy 100-item scale used by Lernmor. The results for this set of studies are also shown in Table 7.4.

Kopikat felt that his studies did not replicate Lernmor's findings. Whereas all of Lernmor's findings were positive, one of Kopikat's studies went in the wrong direction — a finding that greatly bothered the company at which the study was done. Furthermore, where two of Lernmor's findings were significant — half the studies done — this was true for only one of Kopikat's four studies. He interpreted the difference in results in terms of a theory that suggested that Texans were slower learners.

However, a colleague warned Kopikat about sampling error and urged him to do a meta-analysis. Kopikat then did the bare bones meta-analysis shown in Table 7.4. For the overall analysis, he found a mean of Ave $(\delta) = .42$ with a standard deviation of SD $= .09$, which, using a normal

Table 7.4 Bare Bones Meta-Analyses on Hypothetical Studies on Training Dopplegangers

Research findings

Author	Location	Sample Size	Effect Size
Lernmor	NE	40	.07
Lernmor	NE	40	.36
Lernmor	NE	40	.66*
Lernmor	NE	40	.95*
Kopikat	Texas	40	−.11
Kopikat	Texas	40	.18
Kopikat	Texas	40	.48
Kopikat	Texas	40	.77*

*Significant at .05 level.

Bare bones meta-analysis	*Within subset bare bones meta-analyses*	
	Texas studies	*Northeastern studies*
$T = 40 + 40 + \ldots = 320$	$T = 40 + 40 + \ldots = 160$	$T = 40 + 40 + \ldots = 160$
$N = 320 / 8 = 40$	$N = 160 / 4 = 40$	$N = 160 / 4 = 40$
Ave $(d) = .42$	Ave $(d) = .33$	Ave $(d) = .51$
Var $(d) = .116150$	Var $(d) = .108050$	Var $(d) = .108050$
Var $(e) = .107730$	Var $(e) = .106840$	Var $(e) = .108832$
Var $(\delta) = .008420$	Var $(\delta) = .001210$	Var $(\delta) = -.000782$
SD $\delta = .092$	SD $\delta = .034$	SD $\delta = 0$

approximation, implies a middle range of $.24 < \delta < .60$. He also did the meta-analysis corresponding to his belief that the studies in Texas had different results. Those meta-analyses are also reported in Table 7.4. The mean effect was still positive in Texas as in the northeastern states, but the effect size was only a little bigger than half as large, i.e. .33 versus .51. Furthermore, the within subsets standard deviations were .03 and 0, considerably smaller than the overall standard deviation of .09. Thus, Kopikat admitted that the Texas results replicated the northeastern results in sign, but he claimed that the moderator effect confirmed his theory of regional work force differences. Kopikat's study was widely acclaimed as yet

Table 7.5 Worksheet for Meta-Analysis of Studies in Table 7.4

Location	N	d_o	r_{YY}	d	ve	w_i
NE	40	.07	.81	.08	.132999	32.4
NE	40	.36	.81	.40	.132999	32.4
NE	40	.66	.81	.73	.132999	32.4
NE	40	.95	.81	1.06	.132999	32.4
Texas	40	−.11	.34	−.19	.316852	13.6
Texas	40	.18	.34	.31	.316852	13.6
Texas	40	.48	.34	.83	.316852	13.6
Texas	40	.77	.34	1.33	.316852	13.6

Overall meta-analysis	*Within subsets meta-analyses*	
T = 160		
N = 40	*Northeastern states*	Texas studies
Ave (d) = .568	Ave (d) = .568	Ave (d) = .570
Var (d) = .189528	Var (d) = .133669	Var (d) = .322600
Var (e) = .187356	Var (e) = .132999	Var (e) = .316852
Var (δ) = .000217	Var (δ) = .000670	Var (δ) = .005748
SD δ = .047	SD δ = .026	SD d = .076

another convincing demonstration of the importance of moderator variables when it was published in the *Statistical Artifact Review* (1990, 66: 398-447).

Lernmor did not believe that Texans were slower learners. He was also bothered by the fact that Kopikat used only 12 items in his job knowledge test. Lernmor had found a reliability of .81 with his 100-item test. He used the Spearman-Brown formula to compute the reliability of a 12-item test and found the reliability to be only .34. So Lernmor redid Kopikat's meta-analysis, correcting for attenuation. Those meta-analyses are shown in Table 7.5.

Lernmor's overall meta-analysis found a mean effect size of .57 with a standard deviation of .05, an implied middle range of .47 < δ < .57 . Lernmor also did the meta-analyses on the two areas. He found a mean effect size of .57 in the northeastern studies and a mean effect size of .57

in the Texas studies. He concluded that region is not a moderator variable. Instead, he concluded that Kopikat's low values had resulted from the use of a lower reliability measure of the dependent variable.

Artifact Distribution Meta-Analysis and an Example

Reliability is sometimes available only on a sporadic basis. In that case, we cannot correct each individual effect size. However, if we can estimate the distribution of reliabilities in the research domain, then we can correct the values obtained in a bare bones meta-analysis for the effects of error of measurement. The methods for this are developed fully in Chapter 5 (for correlations) and will be only sketched here.

The mean true effect size. The key to the analysis is to look at the effect of error of measurement on the statistics computed in a bare bones meta-analysis: the mean and variance of uncorrected effect sizes. The formula relating the actual effect size and the sample effect size is

$$d_o = \delta_o + e = a\,\delta + e$$

where δ is the actual effect size, a is the attenuation factor (the square root of the reliability), and e is the sampling error. Across a research domain, the mean observed effect size is

$$E\,(d_o) = E\,(a\,\delta + e) = E\,(a\,\delta) + E\,(e)\,.$$

If we ignore the slight bias in d, then the mean sampling error is 0.

$$E\,(d_o) = E\,(a\,\delta)$$

If the level of reliability of measurement is independent of the true effect size, then the mean of the product is the product of the means.

$$E\,(d_o) = E\,(a)\,E\,(\delta)$$

The desired mean true effect size is thus attenuated by the average of the attenuation factors for individual studies. If the mean attenuation factor is known, then we can correct the observed mean effect size using the same formula we would use to correct an individual effect size.

$$E\,(\delta) = E\,(d_o)\,/\,E\,(a)$$

Thus, to compute the mean effect size, we do not need to know the attenuation factor for each individual study, we need only know the mean attenuation factor across studies.

Note that the factor a is not the reliability but its square root. Thus, from the distribution of reliabilities, we must extract the distribution of attenuation factors. If the reliabilities are given individually, we merely transform to square roots before computing the mean and standard deviation. If the reliability distribution is given as a histogram, then we change the histogram labels to square roots.

The Variance of True Effect Sizes

The variance of observed effect sizes is given by

$$\text{Var}(d_o) = \text{Var}(\delta_o + e) = \text{Var}(\delta_o) + \text{Var}(e).$$

The bare bones meta-analysis uses this to compute the variance of study population effect sizes $\text{Var}(\delta_o)$ by subtracting the sampling error variance $\text{Var}(e)$ from the variance of observed effect sizes $\text{Var}(d_o)$. That residual variance has been corrected for sampling error, but not for error of measurement. The corrected variance from the bare bones meta-analysis is connected to the desired variance of true effect sizes $\text{Var}(\delta)$ by

$$\text{Var}(\delta_o) = \text{Var}(a\,\delta).$$

If the level of reliability is independent of the true effect size across studies, then to a close approximation

$$\text{Var}(\delta_o) = [E(a)]^2 \text{Var}(\delta) + [E(\delta)]^2 \text{Var}(a).$$

This equation can be solved for the desired variance $\text{Var}(\delta)$.

$$\text{Var}(\delta) = \left\{ \text{Var}(\delta_o) - [E(\delta)]^2 \text{Var}(a) \right\} / [E(a)]^2$$

The right-hand side of this equation has 4 entries. The entry $\text{Var}(\delta_o)$ is the corrected variance from the bare bones meta-analysis. The entry $E(a)$ is the average attenuation factor across studies. The entry $\text{Var}(a)$ is the variance of the attenuation factor across studies. The entry $E(\delta)$ is the average true effect size as computed in the previous section. The numerator

$$\text{Var}(\delta_o) - [E(\delta)]^2 \text{Var}(a)$$

can be regarded as subtracting the variance in observed effect sizes due to variation in reliability. That is, the variance in study effect sizes can be partitioned

$$\text{Var}(\delta_o) = [E(a)]^2 \text{Var}(\delta) + [E(\delta)]^2 \text{Var}(a) + \text{Var}(e)$$

$$= \quad A \quad + \quad B \quad + \quad C$$

where *A* is the variance due to variation in true effect size,
  B is the variance due to variation in reliability, and
  C is the variance due to sampling error.

Reliability Distribution: An Example

One of the oldest hypotheses in psychology is that a failure experience produces anxiety. For example, this is the hypothesis that links job stress to health problems, such as high blood pressure or stomach ulcers. Stress produces fear of failure, which produces anxiety, which produces autonomic arousal, which causes high levels of blood pressure and high levels of stomach acid. This has been studied in the laboratory by putting subjects in a situation where it is predetermined that they will fail, and then measuring the resulting level of state anxiety. Table 7.6 presents the data base for a meta-analysis of eight hypothetical experimental studies.

Jones (1987) located the eight studies but did only a bare bones meta-analysis of the data. Thus, Jones saw only the columns for sample size and effect size in Table 7.6. His results are given as the first meta-analysis in Table 7.7. He found a mean effect size of .31 and a standard deviation of .075. Using the normal distribution as a guide, he estimated the 95% range to be $.16 < \delta < .46$. He concluded that the effect is always positive, but that the size of the effect varied across studies by as much as 3 to 1. Jones looked for a moderator variable but found none.

Smith (1988) had read Hunter et al. (1982) and he worried about the reliability of the measurement of anxiety in these studies. He went back to the eight studies to see which studies reported the reliability of the dependent variable. Two studies reported reliability, the two studies with values listed in Table 7.6. He then did a meta-analysis correcting for reliability using the values found in the studies. This is the second meta-analysis shown in Table 7.7.

For the two studies that reported reliability, the attenuation factors are .77 and .81, which have a mean of .79 and a standard deviation of .02. The corrected meta-analysis yielded a mean effect size of .39 with a standard deviation of .09. The normal distribution middle 95% range would be $.21 < \delta < .57$. Smith then noted that Jones was right in asserting that the effect

Table 7.6 A Meta-Analysis of Hypothetical Studies Looking at the Effect
of a Failure Experience on State Anxiety

Effect size studies

Author	Sample Size	Effect Size	Number Items	Reliability	Attenuation Factor
Callous (1949)	40	.82	5	—	—
Mean (1950)	40	.23	5	.60	.77
Cruel (1951)	40	−.06	5	—	—
Sadistic (1952)	40	.53	5	.65	.81
Villainous (1983)	40	.38	1	—	—
Vicious (1984)	40	−.20	1	—	—
Fiendish (1985)	40	.68	1	—	—
Diabolical (1986)	40	.10	1	—	—

Reliability studies

Author	Number Items	Reliability	Reliability Of One Item
Uneasy (1964)	2	.45	.29
Nervous (1968)	2	.35	.21
Concerned (1972)	4	.60	.27
Anxious (1976)	4	.54	.23
Distressed (1980)	6	.68	.26
Paralyzed (1984)	6	.66	.24

Average reliability of one item = .25 or a = .50
Implied reliability of five items = .625 or a = .79

is always positive, but Jones had underestimated the strength of the mean
effect by 21%. On the other hand, Smith, too, found that the size of the
effect varied by as much as 3 to 1.

Black (1989) thought that Smith was right to worry about reliability,
but he worried that the two studies that reported reliability might not have
been representative of the domain as a whole. Black looked at each report
to see what was said about the nature of the measurement. What he found
was that the four older studies were done before behavioristic methodology had had much impact on personality research. Those studies all
worried about the quality of measurement and constructed scales to assess

Table 7.7 Meta-Analyses Performed on the Studies of Failure and Anxiety in Table 7.6

Bare bones meta-analysis (Jones, 1987)

$T = 320$

$N = T / 8 = 40$

Ave $(d) = .310$

Var $(d) = .112225$

Var $(e) = .106672$

Var $(\delta_o) = .005553$

$SD_{\delta_o} = .075$

Bare bones analysis corrected for error of measurement using the reliability information given in the experimental studies (Smith, 1988)

Ave $(a) = [.77 + .81] / 2 = .79$

Var $(a) = [(.77 - .79)^2 + (.81 - .79)^2] / 2 = .000400$

Ave $(\delta) = $ Ave $(d) / $ Ave $(a) = .31 / .79 = .392$

Var $(\delta) = \{ $ Var $(\delta_o) - [$Ave $(\delta)]^2$ Var $(a) \} / \{$Ave $(a)\}^2$

$\qquad = \{ .005553 - (.392)^2 (.00040) \} / (.79)^2 = .008799$

$SD_\delta \qquad = .094$

Bare bones meta-analysis corrected for error of measurement using the information from the reliability studies (Black, 1989)

Ave $(a) = [.79 + .50] / 2 = .645$

Var $(a) = [(.79 - .645)^2 + (.50 - .645)^2] / 2 = .021025$

Ave $(\delta) = $ Ave $(\delta_o) / $ Ave $(a) = .310 / .645 = .481$

Var $(\delta) = \{ $ Var $(\delta_o) - [$Ave $(\delta)]^2$ Var $(a) \} / \{$Ave $(a)\}^2$

$\qquad = \{ .005553 - (.481)^2 (.021025) \} / (.645)^2 = .001655$

$SD_\delta \qquad = .041$

---

state anxiety. Each older study used a five-item scale to measure anxiety. The four newer studies were done after behavioristic methodology became dominant in personality research. These studies were unconcerned with the quality of measurement and assessed state anxiety by a single response, i.e., a one item scale. Black then looked up six studies that reported the reliabilities of various scales measuring state anxiety. The reported reliabilities are shown in Table 7.6. The reliabilities are not comparable because the scales vary in the number of items. So Black used the Spearman-

Brown formula to compute the reliability of one item, a common reference point for all studies. This formula is

$$r_1 = [\, r_n \,/\, n \,] \,/\, [\, 1 - (1 - 1/n)\, r_n \,]$$

where n is the number of items on the scale with reliability r_n. The one-item reliabilities are reported in Table 7.6. All one-item reliabilities are close to .25, and the variation in reliabilities is no more than would be expected from sampling error. From this, Black knew that the reliability in the newer one item studies was only .25, while he used the Spearman-Brown formula to compute a reliability of .625 for the older five-item studies, a value that agrees with the two reliabilites reported. He then used that information to do the third meta-analysis shown in Table 7.7. Black found a mean effect size of .48 with a standard deviation of .04. The normal distribution middle range would be $.40 < \delta < .56$. Black noted that Jones had underestimated the mean effect of failure by 65% while Smith had underestimated it by 19%. He also noted that both authors had very greatly overestimated the extent of variation across studies. Variation in reliability produced a variance of

$$[\, E\,(\delta)\,]^2 \, \text{Var}\,(a) = (.481)^2\, (.021025) = .004864$$

in study population correlations whose variance was .005553. That is, variation in reliability accounts for .004864/.005553 or 88% of the variance in effect sizes. Black noted that it would be quite possible that variation in other artifacts might account for the remaining 12% of the variance. That is, it is not unreasonable to suspect that the actual treatment effect is actually approximately constant across studies.

Measurement Error in the Independent Variable in Experiments

The preceding section shows that error of measurement in the dependent variable can have a considerable impact on the effect size, both in terms of reducing the apparent size of the mean effect and in terms of producing artificial variation in effect sizes across studies. The analysis in Chapter 6 showed that error of measurement in the independent variable can have just as large an effect. The important point is to remember that group membership is a *nominal* designation. It represents what the experimenter intended to happen to the subject and may or may not represent the actual process designation. If the subject is not listening closely to the instructions, then an experimental difference in instructions may not apply to many of the nominally experimental group subjects. In naturalistic dichotomies, such as "schizophrenic" versus "normal," some of the nominal schizophrenics may not be psychotic and some of the nominal normals may be schizophrenic. The practical problem for meta-analysis is that in most curent studies there is no information on the extent of misidentification on the independent variable. Without such information, there can be no analysis of its impact. This is very unfortunate, because the fact that experimenters ignore such error does not make the error go away. Thus, in the typical meta-analysis, there will be no correction for error of measurement in the independent variable. It is important to remember this in the interpretation of the meta-analysis. If this artifact is ignored, then the mean treatment effect is correspondingly underestimated and the variance of treatment effects is correspondingly overstated.

If the correlation between nominal and actual identification is denoted a, then the population study effect size correlation is

$$\rho_o = a\,\rho$$

where ρ is the actual treatment correlation (attenuated for the other artifacts in the study). Thus, if the meta-analysis were done measuring the treatment effect as a correlation, the analysis would be directly symmetric to the analysis of the impact of error of measurement in the dependent variable. The analysis of the d statistic is complicated by the nonlinearity of the transformation from r to d:

$$d = 2r / \sqrt{(1 - r^2)}$$

In the present case, we have

$$\delta_o = 2\,\rho_o / \sqrt{(1 - \rho_o^{\,2})} = 2\,(a\,\rho) / \sqrt{(1 - a^2\rho^2)}$$

where

$$\rho = \delta / \sqrt{(4 + \delta^2)}\;.$$

In most contemporary meta-analyses, the population treatment effects are not large. Those of textbook social psychology experiments are rarely larger than $\delta = .40$. Those for more sophisticated research domains are smaller yet. We will show that, for domains where the population treatment effects are no larger than .40, we have the close approximation

$$\delta_o = c\,\delta\;.$$

This approximation is perfectly symmetric to the equation for the impact of error of measurement in the dependent variable. Thus, the mathematics of the meta-analysis is the same except for the change in the meaning of the attenuation factor "a." For the present case, "a" is the correlation between nominal and actual group membership. For the case of error in the dependent variable, "a" was the square root of the reliability of the dependent variable. This difference is less than it might seem. The square root of the reliability of the dependent variable is the correlation between observed dependent variable score and the true dependent variable score. Thus, the meaning of "a" is actually symmetric between the case of the independent variable and the case of the dependent variable.

It is important to note that the approximation is used here for population effect sizes and not for sample effect sizes. Sample effect sizes will often be larger than .40 because of sampling error. If the population effect size was δ = .20 and the sample size was N = 40, it would not be unlikely to see a sample effect size as large as d = .64. However, sampling error is not a part of the approximation process. Rather, sampling error is added *after* the attenuation effect. That is, the sampling error equation is additive.

$$d_o = \delta_o + e$$

Thus, the sampling error equation uses the approximation

$$d_o = \delta_o + e = a\,\delta + e$$

which does not alter the value of e.

In most real meta-analyses, the study population effect size is attenuated by other artifacts, such as error of measurement in the dependent variable. In this case, the extraneous attenuation has the effect of extending the range of the linear approximation. Suppose that the true treatment effect is δ = .60, but it is attenuated to δ_1 = .40 by error of measurement in the dependent variable. The linear approximation applies to the attenuated effect size .40 rather than the unattenuated effect size .60. Thus, we have the approximation

$$\delta_o = a\,\delta_1$$

which becomes

$$\delta_o = a\,b\,\delta$$

with the substitution $\delta_1 = b\,\delta$ where b is the attenuation factor for error of measurement in the dependent variable. Thus, in this case, the linear approximation is still quite close even though the true effect size is as large as .60.

Finally, we show that for effect sizes no larger than .40, the impact of nonlinearity is slight. Suppose that $\delta = .40$. Then,

$$\rho = \delta / \sqrt{(4 + \delta^2)} = .40 / \sqrt{(4 + .16)} = (.40/2) / \sqrt{1.04}$$

which, to a close approximation, is

$$\rho = (\delta/2)(1.02) = \delta / 2 .$$

That is, for population treatment effects in the usual range, the transformation from d to ρ is approximately linear. Using this approximation, we have the approximation

$$\delta_o = [\, 2\, a\, (\delta/2)\,] / \sqrt{[\, 1 - a^2\, (\delta/2)^2\,]}$$

$$= [\, a\, \delta\,] / \sqrt{[\, 1 - .25\, \delta^2\, a^2\,]} .$$

For population treatment effects no larger than $\delta = .40$, the denominator satisfies the following inequality.

$$\sqrt{[\, 1 - .25\, \delta^2\, a^2\,]} > \sqrt{[\, 1 - .04\, a^2\,]}$$

$$> 1 - .02\, a^2 > 1 - .02$$

Thus, if the population treatment effect is no larger than .40, there is little error in the approximation

$$\delta_o = [\, a\, \delta\,] / 1 = a\, \delta .$$

For population treatment effects no larger than .40, we have the close approximation

$$\delta_o = a\, \delta .$$

Other Artifacts and Their Effects

In this chapter, we have considered the following artifacts: sampling error, random measurement error in the dependent variable, and random measurement error (causal misidentification) in the independent or treatment variable. Other artifacts were discussed in Chapter 6: imperfect construct validity of the dependent variable, imperfect construct validity (confounding) in the independent or treatment variable, dichotomization of a continuous dependent variable, variation in the strength of the treatment, and attrition artifacts. Given certain information about the extent and nature of the artifact, it is possible to correct the meta-analysis for the effects of that artifact. We have shown how to do this for a meta-analysis of correlations, but we have not presented the corresponding computations for the d statistic. The computations can be done, although the correction formulas for the d statistic are usually nonlinear and more cumbersome than the formulas for r. The simplest method is to convert the ds to rs and do the meta-analysis on r, as we noted earlier in this chapter.

We would like to emphasize that the reason that we did not present the formulas is not because the artifact effects are small. Where such artifacts have been tracked, they have sometimes proven to be large. Of special concern is the effect of imperfect construct validity in experimental studies. Experimental studies are often metaphorical in nature. The investigator sees helping someone pick up their computer cards as altruism and, thus, treats that dependent variable measure as if it were equivalent to signing up for the Peace Corps. Or the investigator believes that a failure experience is an attack on self-esteem and, thus, treats failure at a laboratory problem solving task as if it were the same as the effect of flunking out of college. In the organizational literature, there is often a considerable gap in the construct validity of lab and field studies. This has shown up in many meta-analyses conducted on organizational interventions.

It is important to correct for as many artifacts as possible, even if the formulas to do so are not given in this chapter. Finally, it is important to remember that there is an artifact that is difficult to detect and, thus, is rarely corrected: bad data. There can be error in coding raw data, error in computing statistics or recording the numbers computed, error in typing manuscripts, error in printing numbers, and, according to certain cynics, error in meta-analytic recording (especially in converting from some strange statistic to d or r). At a minimum, one should be on the lookout for outliers, i.e., effect sizes that are extremely different from other studies. Unfortunately, in many research domains the average sample size is so small that it is difficult to distinguish between an outlier and a large sampling error. At least, it is always wise to consider residual variance with a large grain of salt. The residual variance virtually always contains the effects of uncorrected artifacts, even if the meta-analyst convinces himself or herself that the artifact does not exist.

Correcting for Multiple Artifacts

The previous sections of this chapter treated error of measurement in the independent variable as if one or the other occured, but not both. The fact is that both errors can occur in a given study. Furthermore, any given study may also be affected by the many artifacts listed in Chapter 6 that have not been considered in this chapter to this point. Thus, a proper meta-analysis will have to correct for multiple artifacts.

In Chapter 6, we noted that the effect of most artifacts on the effect size statistic *d* often requires a very complicated formula. These complicated formulas make it cumbersome to correct for the artifact individually and make it very difficult to correct for several artifacts jointly. The complicated artifact formulas also create problems for meta-analysis. In this section, we will derive an approximation formula for the correction of *d* for multiple artifacts. This approximation formula permits the development of very straightforward formulas for meta-analysis.

Attenuation Effect of Multiple Artifacts and Correction for the Same

The artifacts other than sampling error are systematic. At the level of population statistics, the attenuation produced by the study artifacts can be algebraically computed. That algebra can be reversed. Thus it is possible to start with the attenuated effect size and compute the true effect size. In the form of an equation, this process would be called "correction for attenuation." The classic formulas were developed for random error of measurement, but similar correction formulas could be generated for any systematic artifact.

Observed study effect sizes are influenced not only by the systematic artifacts but by sampling error as well. The algebraic formulas that work exactly for population statistics do not work exactly for sample statistics. Instead, there is a more complicated interaction between sampling error and the systematic effect of the other artifacts. This section will describe the attenuating effect of systematic errors on population statistics. The effects of sampling error will be considered in the following section.

The complication of artifact formulas for *d* is in sharp contrast to the simple formulas for artifact effects on the correlation. For the artifacts currently identified, the effect on the correlation is to multiply the correlation by a constant that measures the impact of the artifact. In many of the cases in Chapter 6, we capitalized on this fact to indirectly compute the effect of an artifact on *d*. There are three steps to this method. First, transform the actual treatment effect δ into the corresponding treatment effect correlation ρ. Second, compute the effect of the artifact on the treatment correlation, that is, compute the attenuated treatment correlation ρ_o. Third, transform the attenuated treatment correlation ρ_o back into the d statistic form as δ_o. We will now use this same strategy to compute the attenuating effect of multiple artifacts.

For correlations, it is as easy to handle multiple artifacts as to handle one. Each of the artifacts currently listed can be quantified in the form of a product in which the unaffected correlation is multiplied by a constant. Denote the actual population correlation by ρ and the artifactually attenuated population correlation by ρ_o. Then the effect of any one artifact is quantified as

$$\rho_o = a\,\rho$$

where a is an artifact multiplier (such as the square root of the reliability) that measures the effect of that artifact on the correlation. If the correlation is affected by several artifacts, then the study correlation is simply multiplied by the several corresponding artifact multipliers. For example, if three artifacts were measured by a, b, and c, then

$$\rho_o = a\,b\,c\,\rho \,.$$

The net impact of the several artifacts can be combined into one artifact multiplier as in

$$\rho_o = A\,\rho$$

where the combined artifact multiplier A is given by the product

$$A = a\,b\,c \,.$$

That is, the combined artifact multiplier A is the product of the individual artifact multipliers. Except for the change of notation from a to A, the math of the compound effect of several artifacts is not different from the math of a single artifact.

We will now derive a procedure to compute the attenuated study effect size δ_o from the actual treatment effect δ. This is done in three steps. First, we transform δ to ρ. Second, we use the simple multiple artifact formulas for correlation to compute the attenuated study treatment correlation ρ_o. Third, we transform the attenuated study correlation ρ_o into the attenuated study effect size δ_o. The complexity of formulas for the d statistic stems from the nonlinearity of the relationship between d and r. Consider the true treatment effect size δ and the corresponding true treatment correlation ρ. The relationship between them is given by the conversion formulas

$$\delta = 2\rho / \sqrt{(1 - \rho^2)}$$
$$\rho = \delta / \sqrt{(4 + \delta^2)}.$$

Note that sample size does not appear in these conversion formulas because they are formulas for population parameters.

Attenuation

To compute the attenuating effect of several artifacts, we first transform the unattenuated effect size δ to obtain the unattenuated treatment correlation ρ.

$$\rho = \delta / \sqrt{(4 + \delta^2)}$$

We then compute the attenuated treatment correlation ρ_o. The combined impact of several artifacts is computed for the treatment correlation by the product

$$\rho_o = A\rho$$

where A is the combined artifact multiplier (the product of the individual artifact multipliers). We now compute the attenuated treatment effect size δ_o. The study population effect size δ_o is given by

$$\delta_o = 2\rho_o / \sqrt{(1 - \rho_o^2)}.$$

Correction for Attenuation

For the systematic artifacts, the attenuation effect can be computed algebraically. This algebra can be reversed to produce a formula that corrects the observed treatment effect for attenuation. That is, we can produce an algebraic procedure that takes the study effect size δ_o, which has been reduced in size by the study artifacts, and algebraically restores it to the size of the actual treatment effect δ. This is most easily done for the treatment effect statistic by transforming to treatment correlations. The steps are: (1) transform the attenuated study effect size δ_o to the attenuated study treatment correlation ρ_o; (2) correct the study treatment correlation for attenuation, that is, algebraically restore the attenuated value ρ_o to the correct treatment correlation ρ; and (3) transform the disattenuated correlation ρ into the disattenuated treatment effect δ.

Suppose we are given the attenuated study treatment effect δ_o. The attenuated study treatment correlation is computed by the conversion formula to be

$$\rho_o = \delta_o / \sqrt{(4 + \delta_o^2)} \; .$$

From the fact that the study artifacts reduced the treatment correlation ρ to

$$\rho_o = A \, \rho$$

we algebraically deduce the fact that

$$\rho = \rho_o / A \; .$$

This is the formula for the correction of the treatment correlation for attenuation due to the artifacts measured by the compound artifact multiplier A. The true treatment effect δ is then computed by transforming the true treatment correlation ρ.

$$\delta = 2 \, \rho / \sqrt{(1 - \rho^2)}$$

Disattenuation and Sampling Error: The Confidence Interval

The causal structure of study errors has a definite order. The substantive nature of the systematic artifacts causes a reduction in the size of the study population effect size. Randomness in the sampling of people and response processes then produces sampling error in the observed study effect size. Disentangling the errors is most easily done by considering the errors in a corresponding order. To go backward from the observed effect size to the true effect size, we first "correct" for the effect of sampling error and then correct for the effect of the systematic artifacts.

In an isolated study, we cannot correct for the effect of sampling error. Instead we use a confidence interval to generate a band of potential population values that would be reasonable given the observed value. Given the observed study value d_o, we generate the upper and lower ends of the confidence interval. Call them d_- and d_+ respectively. Thus, we deal with sampling error by generating three estimates for the study effect size δ_o. The most likely value for δ_o is the observed value d_o. The lowest reasonable estimate of δ_o is d_-. The highest reasonable value for δ_o is d_+.

If the population study effect size δ_o were known, then we would compute the actual effect size by disattenuating the effects of the systematic artifact algebraically. The sampling error analysis produces three estimates of the population study effect size. Each of these estimates can be disattenuated using the same method. This then produces a corresponding sampling error analysis of the true treatment effect. That is, since d_o is the most likely value of δ_o, the corrected value generated using d_o is the most likely value for δ. Since the lowest reasonable value for δ_o is d_-, the lowest reasonable value for δ is obtained by correcting d_- for attenuation. Since the highest reasonable value for δ_o is d_+, the highest reasonable value for δ is obtained by correcting d_+ for attenuation. The three corrected effect sizes thus provide the best estimate and the confidence interval for the true effect size δ.

A Formula for Meta-Analysis with Multiple Artifacts

The preceding procedure for computing the attenuating impact of systematic artifacts on study effect sizes works fine for isolated study effects. However, it is not sufficient for meta-analysis. For meta-analysis, we need a formula that enables us to compute sampling error variance and relate it to the variation in effect sizes across studies. That is, we need a formula relating the sample study d statistic to the true effect size δ. To get this formula, we need a formula for the attenuated study effect size as a function of the attenuation multiplier A and the true treatment effect δ. The exact formula is untractable for meta-analysis because of the nonlinearity of the relationship of d to r. However, we will show that there are close approximations that yield formulas that can be used for meta-analysis.

The formula relating the sample study effect size d_o to the population effect size δ_o is

$$d_o = \delta_o + e .$$

We then need a formula that relates the study effect size δ_o to the actual effect size δ. The exact formula will be shown to be

$$\delta_o = c A \delta$$

where δ is the true treatment effect, A is the compound attenuation multiplier, and

$$c = 1 / \sqrt{(1 + b)}$$

where

$$b = (1 - A^2) \, \delta^2 / 4 \; .$$

The problem with this formula is that the number c varies from study to study in a nonlinear way. We will show that for the typical meta-analysis, there is little error incurred by ignoring the variation in the value of c across studies. That is, there is little error in the meta-analysis if the individual study values of c are replaced by the average value of c. To show this, we will first show that c differs little from 1. In fact, there is not much error in a meta-analysis that uses the approximation

$$\delta_o = A \, \delta \; .$$

In meta-analyses in which this approximation is suitable, the formulas for the meta-analysis of d would be exactly parallel to those for the correlation.

Derivation of c

The exact formula for the attenuated treatment effect δ_o is obtained by tracing the transformation method symbolically. We are given the true treatment effect δ. This is converted to the true treatment correlation ρ by

$$\rho = \delta / \sqrt{(4 + \delta^2)} \; .$$

The effect of the systematic artifacts on the treatment correlation can be measured by the compound artifact multiplier A, which is the product of the individual artifact multipliers. That is, the attenuated study treatment correlation ρ_o is

$$\rho_o = A \, \rho \; .$$

The attenuated study treatment effect δ_o is then given by

$$\delta_o = 2 \, \rho_o / \sqrt{(1 - \rho_o{}^2)} \; .$$

This formula states δ_o in terms of the study correlation ρ_o. What we need is a formula for the attenuated effect size that relates it directly to the true effect size. This can be done by making algebraic substitutions that trace our steps backward. The attenuated effect size can be computed from the true treatment correlation ρ. This formula is obtained by substituting $A\rho$ for ρ_o in the equation for δ_o.

$$\delta_o = 2 [A \rho] / \sqrt{(1 - [A \rho]^2)}$$

$$= 2 A \rho / \sqrt{(1 - A^2 \rho^2)}$$

The attenuated effect size can then be computed from the true treatment effect size δ. This formula is obtained by substituting

$$\rho = \delta / \sqrt{(4 + \delta^2)}$$

for ρ in the equation for δ_o.

$$\delta_o = 2 A [\delta/\sqrt{(4 + \delta^2)}] / \sqrt{(1 - A^2 [\delta^2/(4 + \delta^2)]}$$

$$= 2 A \delta / \sqrt{(4 + [1 - A^2] \delta^2)}$$

$$= A \delta / \sqrt{(1 + b)}$$

where

$$b = (1 - A^2) \delta^2 / 4 .$$

The numerator $A\delta$ is the same simple product that applies to compound artifacts for the correlation. However the denominator is a highly non-linear function of A and δ. Thus, the denominator is a potential problem.

The impact of the denominator is better seen if we convert it to a multiplier. Let c be defined by

$$c = 1 / \sqrt{(1 + b)} .$$

Then

$$\delta_o = c A \delta .$$

The potential impact of the denominator depends on how much the multiplier c differs from 1. We will show that in contemporary meta-analyses c is close to 1.00.

There are many meta-analyses in which the denominator of the effect size can simply be dropped. The key questions are: (1) How large is the true effect size? (2) How large are the artifact impacts? If the true effect size is small or if the artifacts are small, then to a close approximation, we can write

$$\delta_o = A \, \delta \, .$$

and develop meta-analysis formulas for d that are exactly parallel to those for the correlation.

The analysis of the denominator starts with the approximation

$$\sqrt{(1 + x)} = 1 + x/2 \, .$$

This approximation is close if x is close to 0. For example,

$$\sqrt{(1 + .01)} = 1.00499 \text{ versus } 1 + .01/2 = 1.00500$$

$$\sqrt{(1 + .10)} = 1.04881 \text{ versus } 1 + .10/2 = 1.05000$$

$$\sqrt{(1 + .50)} = 1.22474 \text{ versus } 1 + .50/2 = 1.25000.$$

The approximation is not too inaccurate even for values of x as large as 1. For example,

$$\sqrt{(1 + 1)} = 1.414 \text{ versus } 1 + 1/2 = 1.500 \, .$$

Consider then the denominator

$$\sqrt{(1 + b)}$$

where

$$b = (1 - A^2) \, \delta^2 \, / \, 4 \, .$$

If the number b is small, then to a close approximation

$$\sqrt{(1 + b)} = 1 + b/2$$

and, hence,

$$c = 1 \, / \, \sqrt{(1 + b)} = 1 - b/2 \, .$$

The effect of the denominator on the attenuated effect size would then be closely approximated by

$$\delta_o = c\, A\, \delta$$

where $c = (1 - b/2)$. That is, the numerator $A\delta$ is multiplied by the number $c = (1 - b/2)$. If b differs little from 0, then $(1-b/2)$ would differ little from 1. If the multiplier c differs little from 1, then there would be little error incurred by dropping it.

How close is b to 0? The artifact A is a fraction. Thus,

$$1 - A^2 < 1$$

and, hence,

$$b < \delta^2 / 4\,.$$

Even textbook effect sizes are rarely larger than $\delta = .50$. Thus, for a meta-analysis with $\delta = .50$,

$$b < (.50)^2 / 4 = .0625\,.$$

For such cases, the reciprocal of the denominator is closer to 1 than

$$1/\sqrt{(1 + b)} = 1 - .03\,.$$

If the attenuated effect size is about $\delta_o = .30$, then a 3% error would mean overestimating the effect size to be .31 instead of .30. In the end, this would lead to a similar sized error in the estimated mean effect size, although the error would be in the opposite direction. For example, if the true mean effect size was actually Ave $(\delta) = .50$, we would be off by 3% to generate the estimate Ave $(\delta) = .50\,(1+.03) = .515$. Unless the number of studies is large, this error is smaller than sampling error. So for small effect sizes and moderate artifact impacts, the approximation

$$\delta_o = A\, \delta$$

is sufficiently accurate.

The principal problem caused by the multiplier c in developing formulas for meta-analysis is the fact that it varies from one study to the next. However, since the multiplier c does not vary much from the number 1, it cannot vary much from one study to the next. This suggests that we replace the individual multipliers by the average multiplier across studies. We compute the average attenuation multiplier A across studies. We compute the average treatment effect across studies. From these we compute an estimate of the average value of b across studies.

$$\text{Ave}\,(b) = [\,1 - \text{Ave}\,(A)^2\,][\,\text{Ave}\,(\delta)\,]^2 / 4$$

The average value of c is then estimated by

$$\text{Ave}\,(c) = 1 / \sqrt{[\,1 - \text{Ave}\,(b)\,]}\,.$$

Estimation of c

The preceding discussion of the constant c was circular. We said that to estimate c you compute the average value of A and the average value of δ across studies. However, in order to compute the average actual treatment effect, you must correct the attenuated study treatment effects for attenuation. To correct the study treatment effects for attenuation, you need the value of c. This sounds like an infinite regress, but there is an easy numerical solution.

From the previous section, we know that

$$\text{Ave}\,(c) = 1 / \sqrt{[\,1 - \text{Ave}\,(b)\,]}$$

where

$$\text{Ave}\,(b) = [\,1 - \text{Ave}\,(A)^2\,][\,\text{Ave}\,(\delta)\,]^2 / 4\,.$$

Thus, to compute Ave (c), we need to compute Ave (A) and Ave (δ). Since the artifact information is assumed to be given as part of the meta-analysis, the computation of Ave (A) presents no conceptual problem. However, Ave (δ) is the average actual effect while the original data provide only the attenuated study effects. Thus, computation of Ave (δ) is a by-product of the meta-analysis and we must estimate Ave (c) in order to compute the meta-analysis. The solution is to do a small meta-analysis before doing the main meta-analysis.

For each study in the meta-analysis, the exact equation for the study effect size is

$$\delta_o = c\,A\,\delta + e\,.$$

Average the study effect sizes.

$$\text{Ave} (\delta_o) = \text{Ave} (c A \delta) + \text{Ave} (e)$$

For a large number of studies, the average sampling error is zero. Thus,

$$\text{Ave} (\delta_o) = \text{Ave} (c A \delta).$$

Since there is little error in ignoring the variation in c, assume that it is constant. Then, it factors out of the average.

$$\text{Ave} (\delta_o) = (c) \text{Ave} (A \delta)$$

That is, to a close approximation, we have

$$\text{Ave} (\delta_o) = \text{Ave} (c) \text{Ave} (A \delta).$$

Since the substantive processes that determine the size of the artifacts are independent of the substantive processes that determine the actual treatment effect, the numbers A and δ will be independent across studies. Thus, for a large number of studies,

$$\text{Ave} (A \delta) = \text{Ave} (A) \text{Ave} (\delta).$$

Thus, we have to a close approximation

$$\text{Ave} (\delta_o) = \text{Ave} (c) \text{Ave} (A) \text{Ave} (\delta).$$

If c were known, then we could compute Ave (δ) by

$$\text{Ave} (\delta) = \text{Ave} (\delta_o) / [\text{Ave} (c) \text{Ave} (A)].$$

We now have two equations: one that computes Ave (c) from Ave (δ) and one that computes Ave (δ) from Ave (c). These are two equations in two unknowns. We could solve these by ordinary algebra if they weren't so nonlinear. However there is an easy iterative solution.

Start with approximation Ave $(c) = 1$. Then use the equation for Ave (δ) to compute the corresponding approximation for Ave (δ). Use that value of Ave (δ) in the equation for Ave (c) to generate a new approximation for Ave (c). This new estimate of Ave (c) will be more accurate than the original approximation Ave $(c) = 1$. The new estimate of Ave (c) can then be used to generate a new estimate of Ave (δ) that can be used to generate a new estimate of Ave (c), and so on. This process converges rapidly to the desired estimate. A computer program to do the iteration is available from the authors.

Consider an example. Suppose that the average study effect is Ave (δ_o) = .30 and the average artifact multiplier is Ave (A) = .50. From the estimate Ave (c) = 1, we obtain the estimate

$$\text{Ave } (\delta) = \text{Ave } (\delta_o) / [\text{ Ave } (c) \text{ Ave } (A)] = .30 / [(1)(.50)] = .60.$$

From the estimate Ave (δ) = .60, we generate a new estimate of Ave (c).

$$\text{Ave } (b) = [1 - \text{Ave } (A)^2] \text{ Ave } (\delta)^2 / 4$$

$$= [1 - .50^2][.60]^2 / 4 = .0675$$

$$\text{Ave } (c) = 1 / \sqrt{[1 + \text{Ave } (b)]} = 1 / \sqrt{1.0675} = .968$$

From this new estimate of Ave (c), we obtain the new estimate.

$$\text{Ave } (\delta) = \text{Ave } (\delta_o) / [\text{ Ave } (c) \text{ Ave } (A)]$$

$$= .30 / [(.968)(.50)] = .620$$

From that we have a new estimate of Ave (c),

$$\text{Ave } (c) = 1 / \sqrt{(1 + .0721)} = .966,$$

which differs little from the previous estimate of .968. The new estimate of Ave (δ) is

$$\text{Ave } (\delta) = .30 / [(.966)(.50)] = .621,$$

which differs only trivially from the previous estimate of .620. The next approximations for Ave (c) is

$$\text{Ave } (c) = .966,$$

which is identical to the previous estimate to three digits. Thus, the process has converged to three places.

Meta-Analysis of Individually Corrected Studies

Suppose the artifact information is known for each individual study. Then, the observed study values can be individually corrected and the meta-analysis can be performed on the corrected *d* statistics. For study *i*, we have

$$d_{oi} = \delta_{oi} + e_i$$

$$= c\, A_i\, \delta_i + e_i \,.$$

Before the correction can be carried out for each study, a preliminary meta-analysis must be done to furnish the information needed to estimate *c*. The two numbers to be computed are Ave (d_{oi}) and Ave (A_i). The best weights for these averages would be

$$w_i = N_i\, A_i{}^2$$

where N_i is the sample size for study *i*.

Once the value of *c* has been estimated, the corrected effect sizes can be computed by

$$d_i = d_{oi} / [\, c A_i\,] = \delta_i + e_i / [\, c A_i\,] \,.$$

Denote the average uncorrected effect size by D_o. Then, the error variance for study *i* is

$$ve_i = \mathrm{Var}\,(e_i) / [\, c A_i\,]^2$$

where

$$\mathrm{Var}\,(e_i) = [\,(N_i - 1)/(N_i - 3)\,]\,[\, 4/N_i\,]\,[\, 1 + D_o^2 / 8\,]\,.$$

Denote the mean corrected effect size by *D*. Then the three averages required for the meta-analysis are the three weighted averages

$$\mathrm{Ave}\,(d) = \Sigma\, w_i\, d_i / \Sigma\, w_i = D$$

$$\mathrm{Var}\,(d) = \Sigma\, w_i\,(d_i - D)^2 / \Sigma\, w_i$$

$$\mathrm{Var}\,(e) = \Sigma\, w_i\, ve_i / \Sigma\, w_i \,.$$

The variance of population effect sizes is then estimated by subtraction.

$$\text{Var}\,(\delta) = \text{Var}\,(d) - \text{Var}\,(e)$$

The chi-square test for homogeneity is

$$Q = K\,\text{Var}\,(d) \,/\, \text{Var}\,(e)$$

with $K-1$ degrees of freedom.

Meta-Analysis with Artifact Distributions

If the artifact information is given sporadically, then the main meta-analysis is the bare bones meta-analysis that eliminates the effect of sampling error (if the number of studies is large). It is then necessary to correct the bare bones meta-analysis for the effect of the systematic artifacts.

Bare bones meta-analysis. The bare bones meta-analysis is carried out using the methods given above. Denote the average uncorrected effect size by D_o and denote the estimated variance of population study effect sizes by V_o. Denote the error variance by V_e.

Artifact distributions. If artifact information is sporadic, then the information is usually given one artifact at a time. Thus, the distribution of the compound artifact multiplier must be constructed from distributional information on the individual artifacts. This process was discussed in detail in Chapter 4 and will be presented here in very abbreviated form.

For each individual artifact a, compute three numbers: Ave (a), Var (a), and the squared coefficient of variation.

$$\text{CV}\,(a) = \text{Var}\,(a) \,/\, [\,\text{Ave}\,(a)\,]^2$$

To combine the artifact information, let us number the individual artifact multipliers $a_1, a_2, \ldots$ The compound artifact multiplier is the product of the individual multipliers

$$A = a_1\,a_2\,a_3\,\ldots\,.$$

Because the artifacts are independent, the mean of the product is the product of the means. That is,

$$\text{Ave}\,(A) = \text{Ave}\,(a_1)\,\text{Ave}\,(a_2)\,\text{Ave}\,(a_3)\,\ldots\,.$$

The variance of the product is computed from the squared coefficients of variation.

$$\text{Var}(A) = [\text{Ave}(A)]^2 [\text{CV}(a_1) + \text{CV}(a_2) + \text{CV}(a_3) + \ldots]$$

The corrected meta-analysis. Because $\delta_o = cA\delta$ the mean uncorrected population effect size is

$$\text{Ave}(\delta_o) = c\text{ Ave}(A\delta) = c\text{ Ave}(A)\text{ Ave}(\delta).$$

Rearranging this equation, we get the formula for correcting the mean study effect size for attenuation.

$$\text{Ave}(\delta) = \text{Ave}(\delta_o) / [c\text{ Ave}(A)] = D_o / [c\text{ Ave}(A)]$$

Denote the average true effect size by D.
The variance of uncorrected effect sizes is

$$\text{Var}(\delta_o) = c^2 \text{Var}(A\delta)$$
$$= c^2 \{[\text{Ave}(A)]^2 \text{Var}(\delta) + [\text{Ave}(\delta)]^2 \text{Var}(A)\}.$$

Rearranging this equation, we get the formula for correcting the variance of population study effect sizes for the effect of variation in artifacts across studies.

$$\text{Var}(\delta) = \{\text{Var}(\delta_o) - c^2 [\text{Ave}(\delta)]^2 \text{Var}(A)\} / \{c^2 [\text{Ave}(A)]^2\}$$
$$= \{V_o - c^2 D^2 \text{Var}(A)\} / \{c^2 [\text{Ave}(A)]^2\}$$

Denote by V_a the amount of variance in observed effect sizes caused by variation in artifacts. That value is given by

$$V_a = c^2 D^2 \text{Var}(A).$$

The variance of observed effect sizes can thus be partitioned into

$$V_o = \text{Var}(\delta_o) + V_a + V_e.$$

If these numbers are divided by V_o, then they can be called the percentage of variance in observed effect sizes due to real variation in treatment effects, due to variation in artifacts, and due to variation in sampling error, respectively.

Summary of Meta-Analysis of *d* Values

Although statisticians have consistently warned against it, the conventional evaluation of experiments and programs has been the statistical significance test. In a two-group design, this means that the number most likely to be published is the *t* statistic. The value of *t* does not answer the most relevant question: "How large was the treatment effect?" Instead, the value of *t* answers the question: "How far out is the observed treatment effect under the assumption that the population treatment effect is zero?" This chapter began by presenting alternative measures of the size of the treatment effect: the raw score mean difference, the standard score mean difference (d or δ), and the point-biserial correlation (r or ρ). Because different authors use different measures of the dependent variable, the raw score difference is not usually reasonable for meta-analysis. Thus, the usual statistics used to characterize the size of the treatment effect are d and r. If the point-biserial correlation is used (and it is the easier of the two in terms of formulas), then the relevant chapters are Chapters 2 through 4. This chapter presented formulas for meta-analysis using the d statistic. The d statistic is influenced by a number of error factors or artifacts as listed in Chapter 6: sampling error, error of measurement in either variable, imperfect construct validity in either variable, artifactual dichotomization of the dependent variable, and so on. For each such artifact, there is artifact information that would make it possible to control for that artifact in meta-analysis. However, primary researchers are only just beginning to orient publication practices to include the collection and presentation of the information needed to control artifacts. Thus, it is often the case that the only piece of artifact information available is the sample size N, the number needed to control for the effect of sampling error.

If sample size is the only piece of artifact information available in a given research area, then the only meta-analysis that can be done is a bare bones meta-analysis that controls for no artifact other than sampling error. Because other artifacts are not controlled, the bare bones meta-analysis will greatly underestimate the mean treatment effect and will greatly overestimate the standard deviation of treatment effects across studies, especially in relation to the mean (i.e., the coefficient of variation of treatment effects will be greatly overestimated). The key formula for the bare bones meta-analysis of the d statistic is the sampling error variance formula for d. The exact formula uses the gamma function and is mathematically intractable. However, approximation formulas are available, formulas that become progressively more complicated as sample size becomes smaller. Once the approximation formula is chosen, the bare bones meta-analysis is very straightforward. The mean population δ is estimated by the mean *d* statistic across studies, where the mean is computed weighing each study by its sample size.

The variance of population effect sizes is estimated by subtracting the sampling error variance from the observed variance of *d* statistics across studies. The subtraction of the sampling error variance is the statistical control for sampling error that completely eliminates the effects of sampling error once the number of studies in the meta-analysis becomes large enough. For a meta-analysis with a small number of studies, there is still sampling error in the meta-analysis values (a topic considered in Chapter 9). Thus, bare bones meta-analysis uses the mean of sample effect size, the standard deviation of sample effect sizes, and the sample size for each study to produce an estimate of the mean and standard deviation of population effect sizes. For most purposes, the key question is this: Is the standard deviation of effect sizes small in comparison to the effect size? If the answer is yes, then most inferences about the treatment effect will be correctly made if the mean effect size is used as "the" effect size. However, it is important to remember that the mean effect size from a bare bones meta-analysis underestimates the actual effect size because there is no correction for attenuation due to study artifacts other than sampling error. It is also important to remember that the standard deviation of population effect sizes in a bare bones meta-analysis is NOT corrected for variation in the other artifacts and, thus, overestimates the extent of real variation in effect sizes across studies. If some theory predicts that effect sizes will vary between certain kinds of studies, or if the standard deviation of population effect sizes is large in proportion to the mean effect size, then the meta-analysis should be extended to analyze potential moderator variables. If the theory predicts that studies of Type A will yield effect sizes larger than those of Type B, that distinction is the moderator variable. Otherwise, the moderator variable must be sought by trial and error, usually starting with some set of study characteristics that are coded for each study for descriptive purposes.

The use of bare bones meta-analysis to study a potential moderator variable requires no new math. The potential moderator variable is used to break the studies into subsets. A bare bones meta-analysis is then run on each subset separately. The impact of the potential moderator is registered in two ways: the difference in the mean effect size across subsets and a reduction in the standard deviation of effect sizes within subsets. Because the number of studies within subsets is smaller, the theory of second-order sampling error in Chapter 9 will show that the difference in means is better estimated than is the reduction of variance within subsets. In the case of the theoretically predicted moderator variable, the subset strategy works well. In the case of trial and error, there is a further problem of capitalization on chance. As discussed in Chapters 1 and 2, if you analyze a large number of potential moderator variables, then at least one will appear to be significant by chance. There will always be a combination of potential moderator variables that appears to account for variation in effect size, but it could just be the equivalent of a large multiple correlation produced by capitalization on the specific sampling errors in specific studies. If there is information on artifacts other than sampling error (and experience has shown that where the data are available these artifacts prove to be large and important), then the meta-analysis can be considerably more accurate than a bare bones meta-analysis. Consider any single artifact. There are two cases: (1) The artifact information is known for all or almost all studies, and (2) the artifact information is known only for a random subset of studies. In the first case, individual d values can be corrected for the artifact. In the second case, knowledge of the distribution of the artifact can be used to correct a meta-analysis conducted on the studies not corrected for that artifact. Meta-analysis controlling for artifacts beyond sampling error is thus done in two stages: (1) a meta-analysis of corrected effect sizes followed by (2) correction of those meta-analysis results for the effects of sporadically studied artifacts. Stage 1: First, the study effect sizes are corrected for each artifact that is known for all or most studies (the mean value is used for studies with missing data). A meta-analysis is then done on the corrected effect sizes. Stage 2: First, a study is made of each of the artifacts for which only sporadic information is available. Those artifact values known are coded in the attenuation factor form. The mean and standard deviation of the attenuation factor is computed. The means and standard deviations for each attenuation factor are then combined across artifacts to generate an estimate of the mean and variance of the compound artifact multiplier. These numbers are used to correct the meta-analysis done in the first stage.

8

Technical Questions in Meta-Analysis of *d* Values

This chapter discusses technical questions that arise in the meta-analysis of experimental effect sizes. By far the most important of these questions is the effect of different experimental designs on the properties of the resulting *d* values. In particular, *d* values for meta-analysis, and the sampling error variances of the *d* values, are computed differently for within-subjects designs as compared to between-subjects designs. Other technical questions are the slight positive bias in (correctly) computed *d* values, the Hedges and Olkin (1985) concept of fixed vs. random effects models in *d* value meta-analysis, and the Hedges and Olkin (1985) critique of Glass's use of regression in moderator analysis of *d* values. We discuss each of these topics in turn in this chapter.

Within-Subjects Experimental Designs

The preceding chapter on the meta-analysis of *d* values assumed that the study was run with a particular design: random assignment of subjects to experimental and control groups. Different subjects are assigned to different groups, and the design is called an "independent subjects," "between subjects," or "independent groups" design. This design is so often used in research that our 1982 book on meta-analysis made no mention of alternative designs. However, alternative designs are used occasionally and the data from such studies must be analyzed in different ways using different formulas for sampling error. In particular, there is a very different relation between *d* and *t* for the within-subjects design (see Kulik & Kulik, 1986). This section will consider the "within-subjects" or "repeated measures" design. In order to explain why different formulas are used, we must also discuss the derivation of the within-subjects design. That also gives us the opportunity to demonstrate that under most conditions, the within-subjects design is far superior to the between-subjects design. In particular, if the dependent variable is measured with high reliability, then the within-subjects design has much higher statistical power than does the between-subjects design. This chapter presents a much more complete statistical treatment of the within-subject design than exists in the current literature. In particular, we present formulas that are either new or hard to find in the statistical literature: (1) confidence intervals for both the raw score and standardized treatment effect, (2) a significance test for the treatment by subject interaction, and (3) confidence intervals for both the raw score and standardized interaction variance. Finally, we describe how to incorporate the results of within-subjects studies into meta-analysis.

Many myths have grown up about the within-subjects design. These myths lead many to reject any study using a within-subjects design without consideration for the concrete details about the substantive nature of the design. For example, many researchers believe that studies that use a pre-post design should be discarded when conducting a meta-analysis. The explanation is usually something like this: "The within subject design is fundamentally flawed by threats to internal and external validity," citing Campbell and Stanley (1963). This chapter will show (1) that is *not* what Campbell and Stanley said, and (2) it isn't true in fact. Campbell and Stanley listed things to *think about* when evaluating a within-subjects design. They repeatedly say that one is not to *assume* that a threat is realized, but to see if there is actual evidence that the threat was realized. Thus, they were only listing *potential* problems of internal or external validity, problems to be considered concretely in each study. They explicitly and deliberately refused to assume the existence of such problems in advance. We will show by example that it is possible to have a pre-post study in which not a single threat to internal validity is realized. This demonstration is proof that the discard position is erroneous. On the other hand, we can offer only a statement of our own experience as to the likelihood of a violation. We have found violations of the Campbell and Stanley list to be rare. We have found few cases in which a within-subjects design could not be used.

In addition to misunderstanding Campbell and Stanley (1963), this chapter will address other widespread misconceptions and problems concerning the within-subjects research design: (1) misunderstanding the statistical power problem for the independent groups design, (2) misunderstanding the problem of treatment by subjects interactions and the implications for the independent groups design, and (3) inaccessible formulas for the evaluation of the basic statistics, especially the measurement of the treatment by subject interaction. This chapter urges experimenters to use the more powerful within-subjects design whenever possible. In particular, if the dependent variable is measured with high reliability, then the within-subjects design has much higher statistical power than does the independent groups subjects design.

The reason the independent groups design is so commonly used is not because it is a good design. As we noted in the previous chapter, the independent groups design has very low power. There are better designs. One way to create a better design is to lay out the theory of the intervention in a process model. The processes can then be mapped by various dependent variables. The full multiple-dependent variable model can then be tested using path analysis. This approach, however, is beyond the scope of this book (but, see Hunter, 1986, 1987).

Another way to increase power is by using a "within-subjects" or "repeated measures" design such as the pre-post design. Consider a department that produces widgets, and suppose that quality circles are to be introduced into the department. We could measure productivity before the intervention and then at several stages after the intervention. For simplicity, assume that we have just one post-measure of productivity. For each worker in the study, we have a pre-intervention measure called the "pretest score" and a post-intervention measure called the "posttest score." We can then check for gain in performance by subtracting the pretest score from the posttest score. That is, we can analyze gain at the level of the individual worker. The main problem in this regard is error of measurement. If the measure of productivity were perfect, then the gain score would be an exact measurement of the treatment effect for that worker. However, if there is error of measurement, then the observed difference score would differ from the true difference score by some random amount. If the error of measurement is large enough, and if the treatment effect is small enough, then the error in the gain score may overshadow the true gain for individual subjects. In that case, the treatment effect may be reliably observed only at the level of the mean gain score across subjects. In that case, the power of the within-subjects design will be no higher than the power of the between-subjects design.

The Potentially Perfect Power of the Pre-Post Design

The rule in analysis of variance is that a main effect must never be separately interpreted if there is a higher order interaction. In the case of the independent groups design, the difference between the group means is the treatment main effect. To be certain that the interpretation of that main effect is correct, there must be no higher order interaction. In particular, this means that the conventional interpretation of the between-subjects design assumes that there is no treatment by subject interaction. That is, the conventional independent groups design assumes that the treatment effect is the same for every subject. We will now consider the implications of this assumption for the within-subjects design. If the treatment effect is the same for each subject, and if the dependent variable is measured perfectly, then we will see that the power of the corresponding t test on gain scores would be perfect even for very small sample sizes. That is, if there were no treatment by subject interaction, then the use of the within-subjects design would potentially free us from the tyranny of sampling error. The reason why it does not in practice is the presence of error of measurement. We will see that error of measurement reintroduces the problem of sampling error in a different form.

Suppose that the introduction of quality circles increases the daily production of widgets by 5.2. Consider the production of three workers perfectly measured.

	Pretest Score	Posttest Score	Gain Score
Ernesto ("Ernie")	31.3	36.5	5.2
Horacio ("Buddy")	41.4	46.6	5.2
Antonio ("Tony")	51.5	56.7	5.2

In this data, the treatment effect is reflected in the gain of any one single subject. There is no need to observe a population of subjects. In this data, the fact that there is no treatment by subject interaction shows in the fact that the gain score is exactly the same for all subjects. Thus, both the key facts about this study are shown without sampling error in a sample of subjects as small as $N = 3$!

The statistical analysis for the within-subjects design is a t test on the gain scores. The mean and standard deviation of the gain scores are

Mean gain: 5.2
SD of gain: 0

The t test value is

$$t = \text{Mean} / (\text{SD} / \sqrt{N}) = 5.2 / (0 / \sqrt{3}) = 5.2 / 0 = \infty.$$

The t value of ∞ is significant at any level whatsoever. Thus, even for a sample of three subjects, the t test has perfect power.

Unfortunately, we will see that perfect power is lost if there is any measurement error at all, and there is always some measurement error.

The Deficiencies of the Between-Subjects Design

If there is no treatment by subject interaction, the within-subjects design has potentially perfect power. Why does the between-subjects design have such low power? The answer lies in missing data. There is a sense in which the independent groups design has *half* the data missing, one of two scores for each subject. In fact, there is a sense in which *all* the data is missing: there is no observed *gain* score for any subject.

Consider the widget producing department again. Suppose that we organize it into two (geographically separated) subdepartments for purposes of using an independent groups design to assess the effect of quality circles. Each worker is randomly assigned to either the quality circle group or to the control group. We assume for purposes of this example that there is no measurement error in the dependent variable. Corresponding to the three-person data considered for the within-subject design, we have six workers, three in each group.

	Productivity Score
Control Group	
Ernesto ("Ernie")	31.3
Horacio ("Buddy")	41.4
Antonio ("Tony")	51.5
Experimental group	
Samuel ("Sam")	38.3
Gilberto ("Gill")	48.4
Alberto ("Speedie")	58.5

The statistical analysis consists of comparing the two group means in relation to the within-groups variance.

	Control	Experimental
Mean	41.4	48.4
SD	10.1	10.1

Mean difference = 48.4 − 41.4 = 7.0

Within-groups variance = 102 01

Within-groups SD = 10.1

The value of the d statistic is

$$d = 7.0 / 10.1 = .69.$$

Since the within-groups variances were computed using $N_i - 1$ instead of N_i, the formula for the t test statistic is

$$t = \frac{\overline{Y}_E - \overline{Y}_C}{\left[\left[\frac{(N_1 - 1) S_1^2 + (N - 1) S_2^2}{N_1 - N_2 - 2}\right]\left[\frac{N_1 - N_2}{N_1 N_2}\right]\right]^{\frac{1}{2}}}$$

$$t = .85$$

which is not significant at the .05 level.

There are several problems with this new data. First, the treatment effect is wrong. The difference between the means is 7.0 instead of 5.2. Second, the difference is not significant and, hence, the significance test has registered a Type II error.

Where did the errors in the independent groups design come from? Suppose that we had done a pre-post study. Under the assumptions of our example, the data would have been

	Pretest Score	Posttest Score	Gain Score
Control Group			
Ernesto ("Ernie")	31.3	36.5	5.2
Horacio ("Buddy")	41.4	46.6	5.2
Antonio ("Tony")	51.5	56.7	5.2
Experimental group			
Samuel ("Sam")	33.1	38.3	5.2
Gilberto ("Gill")	43.2	48.4	5.2
Alberto ("Speedie")	53.3	58.5	5.2

Had we done a pre-post study, the gain score would have been 5.2 for every subject. Instead, for the subjects in the control group, there was no intervention and, hence, the "posttest" score was actually the pretest score. For the subjects in the experimental group, the pretest score was not observed. Thus, the data in the independent groups design is actually represented by the following table.

	Pretest Score	Posttest Score	Gain Score
Control Group			
Ernesto ("Ernie")	31.3	—	—
Horacio ("Buddy")	41.4	—	—
Antonio ("Tony")	51.5	—	—
Experimental group			
Samuel ("Sam")	—	38.3	—
Gilberto ("Gill")	—	48.4	—
Alberto ("Speedie")	—	58.5	—

In this table, we see that for each worker only one of his two scores is observed. In that sense, the independent groups design is a design in which *half the data is missing*. But there is an even more severe problem. The gain score is not observed for any subject. In that sense, for an independent groups design, *all the data on individual treatment effects is missing*.

In the independent groups design, we estimate the treatment difference by comparing the two group means. The experimental group mean is the experimental group posttest mean, while the control group mean is the control group pretest mean. Given within-subjects data, we could instead compare the posttest and pretest mean for each group separately. We would have

	Pretest Mean	Posttest Mean	Mean Difference
Control Group	41.4	46.6	5.2
Experimental group	43.2	48.4	5.2

For the within-subjects data, the difference between pretest and posttest means is, in fact, 5.2 for each group. That is, for the pre-post design, the mean difference between posttest and pretest is the treatment effect for either group.

What happened to sampling error? Note that in the within-subjects design, the two subgroups do have different means. That is, by chance the pretest mean is 41.4 for the control group and 43.2 for the experimental group. This is sampling error. However, in the within-subjects design, the comparison of means is done within each group. That is, we compute the treatment effect mean difference for the control subgroup as the difference between their posttest mean and their pretest mean. For the experimental subgroup, we compute the mean difference using the two experimental subgroup means. Since comparisons are made within groups, the between-groups difference on the pretest does not enter the estimation of the treatment effect.

For the independent groups design, we estimate the treatment effect by subtracting the pretest mean for one group from the posttest mean for the other group. The sampling error difference in pretest means is $43.2 - 41.4 = 1.8$. Because the means compared come from the two different groups, this sampling error difference enters the estimated treatment effect. That is, note that

$$5.2 + 1.8 = 7.0.$$

Suppose we define

DA = Actual treatment effect

e = Sampling error difference between pretest means

DO = Observed treatment effect estimate

then

$DO = DA + e.$

Thus, the sampling error in the conventional independent groups design stems from a conceptual defect. Because we do not observe the treatment effect for any individual subject, we are forced to estimate the effect for individuals from data on groups. Since the groups are different, the sampling error difference between the groups is confounded with the true treatment effect. This sampling error difference can be considerable unless the number in each group is large, which is rarely the case.

The Independent Groups Design and the Treatment by Subjects Interaction

Another key problem for the independent groups design is the potential treatment by subject interaction. If the treatment has different effects on different people, then there is an interaction between treatment and subjects. If so, then it is possible that the between-groups design may be rendered quite misleading. The between-groups design considers the main effect of treatment under the assumption that there is no interaction between the treatment and subjects. Suppose that the treatment increases the dependent variable by +5 units for half the subjects, but decreases the dependent variable by −5 units for the other half of the subjects. The average treatment effect is zero, and so the mean for the experimental group will then equal the mean for the control group and the usual interpretation of between-groups data would be that the treatment had no effect. This interpretation is completely false. Thus, if there is a treatment by subject interaction, then it is possible for the between-groups design to be completely invalid.

A key question for the independent groups design is this: Is it possible to run any test of the independent groups data to see if there is a treatment by subjects interaction? The answer is, "There is no sure test." Some treatment by subjects interactions show up because the differences in treatment effects causes a difference between the standard deviation of the control and experimental groups. However, (1) this is not always true, and (2) the statistical power for detecting the difference in standard deviations may not be very high. So the between-groups design must ASSUME that there is no interaction; this design does not gather the data necessary to test that assumption.

We will show that the within-subjects design does gather the data necessary to detect a treatment by subjects interaction if it occurs. Furthermore, the size of the interaction can be measured in this design. Given information on the size of the interaction, it is possible to see if the treatment effect is always in the same direction or not. That is, the within-subjects design provides a test for whether the usual treatment effect is a reasonable interpretation of the data or not.

The within-subjects design allows a treatment by subject interaction to be detected and measured. However, to say that change scores vary across subjects is not to say why those change scores vary. Thus, the interaction may be detected and measured without being identified. It is not possible to identify the interaction without data on the relevant individual difference variable that determines the subject's response to the treatment. So, if the within-subjects design detects the interaction, it may be necessary to gather additional data to identify that interaction. New data would not be necessary if the individual difference variable had been measured in the first place. In the design of any study, it is important to ask whether there might be differences in the treatment effect and what variable might predict such differences. That variable can then be measured and used as a "control" variable in the final analysis. In a pre-post design, the treatment by subject interaction can be identified as a correlation between the individual difference variable and the change scores.

The independent groups design must ASSUME that there is no treatment by subject interaction; it does not provide the data needed to test for the interaction. Suppose that the independent groups designs were chosen after a careful theoretical consideration of the question of treatment by subjects showed that there could be no interaction. There would then be an interaction in the study only if that theory were wrong. If the theory is empirically very well grounded, then it fits a great many findings. Thus, inferences drawn about the new study design based on the theory are likely to be correct, and theoretically justified choice of the independent groups design is probably well warranted.

However, informal interviewing shows that experimenters rarely consider the possibility of a treatment by subject interaction. In fact, when asked if all subjects will respond to the treatment in exactly the same way, most investigators say, "No." Often they will state specific hypotheses as to individual differences in treatment response. Thus, most investigators actually expect a treatment by subject interaction, but do not realize the significance of that expectation. Thus, use of the independent groups design is a matter of faith, faith that is usually NOT grounded in a deliberate theoretical consideration of potential interaction and that is often contrary to the beliefs of the investigator. Most experimenters are just not aware that the independent groups design may be invalidated by the presence of such an interaction.

Error of Measurement and the Within-Subjects Design

The effect of error of measurement on the within-subjects design is quite direct: It blurs the observation of the individual treatment effect. Consider the case for Ernie.

True pretest score	= 31.3
True posttest score	= 36.5
True gain score	= 5.2

Suppose instead that there is error of measurement. Then,

Observed pretest score	= 31.3 + first error
Observed posttest score	= 36.5 + second error
Observed gain score	= 5.2 + difference between errors

If we denote the observed gain score by OG and the errors of measurement by e_1 and e_2 respectively, then

$$OG = 5.2 + (e_2 - e_1).$$

When errors are subtracted, they do not necessarily cancel out. For example, suppose the first error is +2.3 and the second error is −2.3. We then have

Observed pretest score	= 31.3 +	2.3 =	33.6
Observed posttest score	= 36.5 +	(−2.3) =	34.2
Observed gain score	= 34.2 −	33.6 =	.6
	= 5.2 −	4.6	
	= 5.2 + ([+2.3] − [−2.3])		

Half the time, the errors of measurement will have the same sign and will approximately cancel out. But half the time, the errors of measurement will have opposite signs and will thus add to each other in absolute value. Thus, error of measurement blurs the observation of the treatment effect for individual subjects. The larger the error of measurement relative to the treatment effect, the more difficult t is to detect the treatment effect in single scores.

Error of measurement does cancel out in averages across subjects. Thus, the treatment effect could potentially be perfectly observed since it equals the average gain score. The word "potentially" reflects the fact that it is only the population average error that is zero; the sample mean will differ from zero by sampling error. Thus, the introduction of error of measurement into individual data causes our summary statistics to suffer from sampling error, namely, sampling error in the statistics computed on the errors of measurement. This section spells out the sampling error effects quantitatively.

Let us denote the compound error by f. That is, the error of measurement in the gain score is given by

$$f = e_2 - e_1 .$$

If the gain true score is denoted TG, then the observed score gain score is related to the true gain score by

$$OG = TG + f.$$

If we replace the notation "OG" by "X" and replace "TG" by "T" and replace "f" by "E," this equation would be

$$X = T + E,$$

the traditional equation for error of measurement. This equation would be fully justified if (1) the mean error $E(f)$ is 0, and (2) the error f is uncorrelated with the true score TG. The population mean error is

$$E (f) = E (e_2 - e_1) = E (e_2) - E (e_1) = 0 - 0 = 0.$$

To see that the error in the gain score is uncorrelated with the true gain score, consider the composition of each. Denote the true score of the pretest by T_1 and the true score of the posttest by T_2. Then,

$$TG = T_2 - T_1$$

$$f = e_2 - e_1 .$$

Since each of the component errors in f is uncorrelated with each of the component true scores in TG, f is uncorrelated with TG. Thus, the f acts as the error of measurement in the gain score OG in exactly the manner of classical reliability theory.

How large is the error in the gain score? Since the component errors are not correlated with each other, the population variance of the gain score error is

$$\text{Var} (f) = \text{Var} (e_1 - e_2) = \text{Var} (e_1) + \text{Var} (e_2) - 2 \text{Cov} (e_1, e_2)$$

$$= \text{Var} (e_1) + \text{Var} (e_2) - 0$$

$$= \text{Var} (e) + \text{Var} (e)$$

$$= 2 \text{Var} (e)$$

That is, the error variance of the gain scores is exactly twice the error variance of the pretest and posttest scores. If the pretest and posttest scores are denoted Y_1 and Y_2, respectively, then the error variance of the dependent variable scores is

$$\text{Var} (e) = [1 - r_{YY}] \text{Var} (Y)$$

where r_{YY} is the reliability of the dependent variable. The gain score error variance is thus

$$\text{Var} (f) = 2 \text{Var} (e) = 2 [1 - r_{YY}] \text{Var} (Y).$$

Note that if the reliability were perfect $r_{YY} = 1.00$, then the error variance would be 0, as in the perfect measurement example above.

What is the effect of error of measurement on sampling error? Consider mean gain. The sample mean is given by

$$\text{Ave }(OG) = \text{Ave }(TG + f) = \text{Ave }(TG) + \text{Ave }(f).$$

If there is no treatment by subject interaction, then each true gain score is identical and, hence,

$$\text{Ave }(TG) = TG = \text{Raw score gain.}$$

That is, if there is no treatment by subject interaction, then there is no sampling error in the average true gain score because there is no variance. (The case of the treatment by subject interaction will be considered in the next section.) The average error of measurement is given by

$$\text{Ave }(f) = E(f) + \text{sampling error} = 0 + \text{sampling error}$$

$$= \text{sampling error}$$

The sample average error is not 0, but differs from 0 by sampling error. Thus, the sample average error of measurement will not be 0 unless sample size is extremely large. The size of the potential sampling error is given by its variance

$$\text{Var }[\text{ Ave }(f)] = \text{Var }(f) / N$$

where N is the sample size.

Thus, the effect of error of measurement on the observed raw score treatment effect is: If there is no treatment by subject interaction, then the sample mean gain score will differ from the raw score treatment effect by the sampling error in the mean gain score error of measurement.

Consider now the sample variance of the observed gain scores. If there is no treatment by subject interaction, then the true gain score is constant across subjects. The population variance of observed gain scores is thus

$$\text{Var }(OG) = \text{Var }(TG + f) = \text{Var }(f).$$

That is, if there is no interaction, then the variance of observed gain scores is variance of errors of measurement. The sample variance differs from the observed variance in the usual manner. Denote the sample variance of the observed gain scores by SVO. Let Q be ratio of the sample variance to the population variance multiplied by the factor, sample size minus 1. That is, Q is defined by

$$Q = (N - 1) \, \text{SVO} / \text{Var} \, (OG).$$

Then Q has a chi-square distribution with $N - 1$ degrees of freedom.

Thus, error of measurement introduces sampling error into both the sample mean gain score and the sample gain score variance. This causes the corresponding t test to have less than perfect power, and it introduces error of measurement into the estimate of the treatment effect from the data.

The Treatment Effect in Standard Scores

Up to now, the focus has been on the treatment effect for raw scores. For meta-analysis, results must be in a form that is the same across all studies. If all studies were done with identically the same variable, then the raw score treatment effect could be cumulated across studies. However, in most research domains the same construct is used across studies, but it is measured in different units from one study to the next. Thus, the usual measure of the treatment effect is measured in standard score units, which tend to be the same across studies. In the case of the treatment effect, the main treatment effect δ is defined in standard score units.

$$\delta = E \, (TG) \, / \, \sigma$$

where σ is the within-groups standard deviation for true scores. If the posttest standard deviation is the same as the pretest standard deviation (i.e., "homogeneity of variance"), then

$$\text{Var} \, (T_2) = \text{Var} \, (T_1) = \sigma^2$$

and the within-groups standard deviation is unambiguously defined.

If the posttest standard deviation is different from the pretest standard deviation, then there are three choices for the "within-groups" standard deviation: (1) the pretest standard deviation, (2) the posttest standard deviation, and (3) an average standard deviation. In theory, the best choice is probably the pretest standard deviation. That is, the baseline level of individual differences is the level before the treatment. In practice, the best choice of standard deviation is the standard deviation that will be used in meta-analysis. If a large portion of the studies in the domain will be independent groups studies, then the meta-analysis will have probably used the square root of the within-groups variance as its within-groups standard deviation. Thus, the best choice of within-groups standard deviation for the within-subjects would be the corresponding average standard deviation.

Note that the desired standard deviation is the standard deviation of true scores, not the standard deviation of observed scores. However, if the reliability of the dependent variable is known, then it is easy to obtain an estimate of the true score standard deviation from the corresponding observed score standard deviation,

$$\text{Var}\,(T) = r_{YY}\,\text{Var}\,(Y)$$

for the pretest, for the posttest, or for the average.

Digression

Before going on to the discussion of interactions, we will pause to set up helpful language.

"Level" scores. There are two kinds of scores: (1) the change score and (2) the pretest and posttest scores. To be able to refer to pretest and posttest by one name, we will call both "level" scores. The language is derived by thinking of the pretest and posttest as the "level" that the subject is at, while the change score measures the treatment impact.

The pretest-posttest correlation. A key statistic not mentioned thus far is the correlation between pretest and posttest. This is sometimes called the "test-retest correlation," and in some contexts it can be used as an estimate of the reliability. However, in some contexts, the test-retest correlation might be a poor estimate of the reliability. The distinction is primarily determined by whether or not there is a treatment by subject interaction.

Let us first define notation. The correlation between pretest and posttest will be denoted r_{12} while the reliability is denoted r_{YY}. The treatment of error of measurement here assumes that the nature of the error is "random response error" and/or "transient error." There is another kind of error called "specific error." If the dependent variable has specific error, then the exact treatment of the within-subjects design is slightly more complicated.

If there is no specific error, then the relationship between the test-retest correlation r_{12} and the reliability r_{YY} is straightforward. If there is no treatment by subject interaction, then the population test-retest correlation equals the reliability. However, if there is a treatment by subject interaction, then the test-retest correlation will be smaller than the reliability by an amount that is related to the size of the interaction. That is, the test-retest correlation will be lower than the reliability to the extent that the change score standard deviation σ_{TG} is large in comparison to the level score standard deviation σ_T.

Confidence intervals. Most statistics are averages and, therefore, have approximately normal distributions except for very small sample sizes. Thus, to generate a confidence interval, we need only know the sampling error standard deviation or "standard error." Suppose the sample statistic value is denoted V and the population PV. If S is the standard error of V, then the 95% confidence interval is

$$V - 1.96\,S < PV < V + 1.96\,S.$$

In this formula, it is assumed that S is the population value of the standard error. If a sample variance is used to estimate S, then the width of the confidence interval is wider because of the sampling error in S. In most cases, we merely substitute a value from the t distribution for the value 1.96 from the normal distribution. The 95% t value is

$$t = 1.96[\,1 + 1.2104/(N-1)\,]$$

unless there are fewer than 16 subjects, in which case one should use

$$t = 1.96[\,1 + 1.2104/(N-1) + 1.4402/(N-1)^2\,].$$

The corresponding confidence interval is

$$V - t\,S < PV < V + t\,S.$$

Throughout the text, we will typically present only the confidence interval for the known standard error and will make the reference "use of t," or the like, to refer to the substitution above.

The Treatment by Subject Interaction

If there is a treatment by subject interaction, then the treatment effect is different for different subjects. For example, suppose that some subjects learn better techniques from quality circle discussions while other subjects are too rigid to change their work habits and, thus, gain no advantage from the new ideas expressed there. The treatment effect then varies across the population of subjects. The simplest statistical description of the raw score treatment effect would be given by the population mean and the population standard deviation of individual treatment effects. These statistics are the population mean and standard deviation of the true gain scores, i.e., the gain scores free of error of measurement. On the other hand, the observed statistics will be computed on observed scores and will have components due to error of measurement. Thus observed statistics will not only have sampling error, but error of measurement as well. It is possible to correct for the systematic effect of error of measurement in a single study, but it is possible to correct for sampling error only by conducting a meta-analysis across studies.

The significance test of the treatment main effect computed on corrected statistics is equivalent to the corresponding significance test computed on uncorrected statistics. Thus, the tradition in analysis of variance has been to present only the test for uncorrected scores. If the null hypothesis were true — the guiding principle for traditional statistical usage — both the corrected and uncorrected treatment main effect would be zero. Thus, if there were no treatment main effect, there would be no need to compute corrected effect sizes anyway. The failure of classic texts to mention correction formulas indirectly reflects the implicit assumption that the null hypothesis is always true. That is, the bias in classic statistics texts shows in the fact that there is no discussion of practical computations that assume that the null hypothesis might be false.

Our treatment will be evenhanded. We will first define the treatment main effect without error of measurement. We will then relate the corresponding observed main effects to the actual main effects. Psychometrically, this is equivalent to correction for the attenuation produced by error of measurement.

There is an even greater bias in the classic statistics tests. We have said that if there is a treatment by subjects interaction, then we must estimate two statistics: the mean and the standard deviation of treatment effects across subjects. Yet, in the conventional treatment of the within-subjects *t* test, there is no mention of the standard deviation at all. This corresponds to the tacit assumption of the global null hypothesis that the null hypothesis is true *for each individual subject*. If there is no treatment effect at all, then both the mean treatment effect and the standard deviation would be zero, and there would be no need to either report the standard deviation or to quantify its size. It could just be ignored. Thus, again the odd omissions of classic statistics texts can be explained by the fact that the authors implicitly assume that the null hypothesis is always true.

Perfect Measurement

Suppose that there is a treatment by subject interaction. There is variation in the treatment effect across subjects. The raw score treatment main effect is defined as the average treatment effect across subjects. If we use the notation "raw score δ" for the raw score treatment main effect, then

$$\text{Raw score } \delta = E\,(TG)\,.$$

If the standard deviation of pretest true score gain scores is denoted σ_T, then the true standard score treatment effect is

$$\delta = \text{Raw score}\,\delta \,/\, \sigma_T = E\,(TG) \,/\, \sigma_T\,.$$

Note that the standard deviation in this formula is the standard deviation of the pretest true scores and NOT the standard deviation of gain scores. This is an important distinction not always made clearly in conventional statistics texts.

If there is a treatment by subject interaction, then the extent of variation in the treatment effect can be measured in raw score form as the standard deviation of gain scores. This definition differs slightly from the definition in analysis of variance texts in that we measure the interaction by the standard deviation instead of the variance. However, this is necessary if the main effect and the interaction are to be compared since they must be computed in the same units. Analysis of variance texts usually confuse this issue by using an ambiguous definition of the treatment main effect. In their substantive discussions and concrete examples, they talk about the treatment effect as the mean difference. However, in their formal analysis of variance formulas, the "treatment main effect" is defined as the *square* of the treatment difference. By squaring the treatment main effect, they put it into the same (alas, meaningless) units as the treatment variance.

Let us denote the standard deviation of true gain scores by σ_{TG}. The quantitative measure of the interaction in raw score form is thus

$$\text{Raw score interaction} = \sigma_{TG}.$$

This standard deviation can be compared to the treatment main effect directly. Suppose the raw score treatment main effect or mean gain score is 5.2 and the raw score interaction (gain score standard deviation) is 1.1. If the treatment effect were normally distributed across subjects, then the middle 95% of subjects would be described by

$$E(TG) - 1.96\,\sigma_{TG} < TG < E(TG) + 1.96\,\sigma_{TG}$$

$$5.2 - 1.96\,(1.1) < TG < 5.2 + 1.96\,(1.1)$$

$$3.04 < TG < 7.36$$

From the fact that 0 is $5.2 / 1.1 = 4.73$ standard deviations below the mean, we would conclude that it is very unlikely that the treatment effect is negative for any subject. That is, it is unlikely that any subject was affected in the opposite direction from that suggested by the mean gain. This is called a "homogeneous interaction."

By contrast, suppose the mean is 5.2 but the standard deviation is also 5.2. According to the normal distribution, the middle 95% of the raw score effect size would be

$$5.2 - 1.96\,(5.2) < TG < \quad 5.2 + 1.96\,(5.2)$$

$$-4.99 < TG < 15.39$$

While this interval would suggest that some people increased by three times as much as average, it would also suggest that some people decreased. When different subjects respond in different directions, the interaction is said to be "heterogeneous."

The normal distribution is not always a natural assumption for treatment effect differences. In our quality circle example, we assumed that some subjects learn from the thoughts of others, while other subjects are too rigid to change their work habits. Suppose that half the subjects are flexible and they gain 10.4 units in productivity, while the other half of the subjects are rigid and gain 0. The mean gain would 5.2 and the standard deviation would also be 5.2. The flexible half of the subjects are exactly one standard deviation above mean gain at $5.2 + 5.2 = 10.4$. The rigid half of the subjects are exactly one standard deviation below mean gain at $5.2 - 5.2 = 0$. Note that in this dichotomous case, the spread in effect is not 4 standard deviations, but only 2.

There are two problems with raw score treatment main effects and interactions: (1) There is no indication of whether the change is large or small in comparison to ordinary individual differences in performance, and (2) it is given in arbitrary units. Both problems are solved by using standard score units. The treatment main effect in standard score units is

$$\delta = E(TG) / \sigma_T .$$

The subject by treatment interaction in standard score units is

$$s = \sigma_{TG} / \sigma_T .$$

Note the distinction between the two different standard deviations in this formula: σ_{TG} the standard deviation of *change* scores versus σ_T the standard deviation of *level* scores. If the treatment effect were the same for everyone, the standard deviation of change scores would be 0 as would the interaction. That is, the interaction can be 0 no matter how large the level score standard deviation of the dependent variable.

The raw score standard deviation of gain scores σ_{TG} measures the raw score treatment by subject interaction. This interaction can be compared to either of the two corresponding main effects. In raw score form, the subject main effect is measured by the level score standard deviation (the "within-groups" standard deviation) σ_T. Thus, the comparison of the raw score interaction to the raw score subject main effect is the ratio σ_{TG} / σ_T, which is the standardized interaction. That is, the standardized interaction is the ratio of the treatment by subject interaction effect to the subject main effect.

The interaction can also be compared to the treatment main effect. For raw scores, this is the ratio $E(TG) / \sigma_{TG}$, which was used earlier in discussing the identification of homogeneous versus heterogeneous interactions. Note also that the standardized mean and standard deviation have the same ratio as do the raw score mean and standard deviation. That is,

$$\delta / s = [E(TG) / \sigma_T] / [\sigma_{TG} / \sigma_T] = E(TG) / \sigma_{TG} .$$

Thus, the ratio of the treatment main effect to the treatment by subject interaction is the same for standard scores as for raw scores.

Homogeneity of variance. It is important to compare the pretest and posttest standard deviations. If they are equal, then we have "homogeneity of variance"; otherwise, "heterogeneity of variance." If the treatment effect is the same for everyone, then the posttest score is related to the pretest score by

$$T_2 = T_1 + TG = T_1 + \text{Raw score}\,\delta .$$

Since the variance is not effected by an additive constant, this means

$$\text{Var}(T_2) = \text{Var}(T_1) .$$

That is, if there is no treatment by subject interaction, then homogeneity of variance is guaranteed. In particular, if there were no treatment effect, then since $T_2 = T_1$ for all subjects, the variances too must be equal.

Suppose an independent groups design is used. Then the investigator is betting that there is no interaction. If the investigator is right, then the data will satisfy homogeneity of variance. If the investigator finds heterogeneity of variance, then there must be a treatment by subject interaction. Thus, a finding of heterogeneity of variance is a very important finding for substantive reasons. In particular, if there is heterogeneity of variance, then the mean difference is only the MEAN treatment effect, and the treatment effects for different individuals might be quite different. This will be further discussed in the section on interactions later.

If the independent groups design is used, then a statistical test for heterogeneity of variance is a preliminary test for a treatment by subject interaction. If the pretest and posttest variances are different, then there is definitely an interaction. If there is homogeneity of variance, then it would be nice if we could conclude that there is not interaction. However, it is easy to create hypothetical data in which there is a massive interaction but no difference between variances. Consider

	Pretest	Posttest	Gain
Henry	10	6	– 4
Sam	5	5	0
Peter	6	10	+ 4
average	7	7	0
SD	2.6	2.6	4

The mean difference is $7 - 7 = 0$, which suggests that there is no treatment effect. The posttest standard deviation and pretest standard deviation are both 2.6, which is homogeneity of variance. Thus, there is nothing in the independent groups data to suggest that there is an interaction and that the mean difference is misleading. However, if we consider the individual gain scores, a different pattern becomes clear. The mean treatment effect is 0, which suggests that there is no treatment effect. But the finding of "no treatment effect" is true only for Sam. Peter went up by 4 units (more than a standard deviation) and Henry went down by 4 units (more than a standard deviation). Thus, the treatment had large effects for 2 out of 3 subjects; the effects were just in opposite directions.

The first step in the analysis of independent groups data should be a test for homogeneity of variance. If the variances are different, then there is a treatment by subjects interaction, and the mean treatment effect may be a very misleading picture of the typical treatment effect for individual subjects. If the variances are not different, then there may or may not be an interaction.

Error of Measurement

Traditional analysis of variance has ignored error of measurement. The observed score statistics are treated as if they were unaffected by error of measurement. Why is this true?

Some of the confusion stems from considering only the raw score main effect. Since the population mean error of measurement is zero, the population mean observed score is the same as population mean true score. Thus, the raw score treatment main effect for observed scores equals (in expectation) the raw score treatment main effect for true scores. That is, error of measurement does not alter the population raw score treatment main effect.

However, the treatment effect parameter that is crucial for power calculations and that is crucial to meta-analysis is not the raw score treatment effect but the standard score treatment effect. The standardized treatment effect (also called the "power parameter" in advanced texts) is the mean gain divided by a standard deviation. While error of measurement does not alter the population mean, it increases the population variance. Thus, to divide by the enlarged standard deviation is to reduce the ratio. That is, error of measurement reduces the size of the power parameter and, hence, reduces power. It also reduces the size of the observed standardized effect size (the effect size needed for meta-analysis).

Ideally, error of measurement would be reduced, if not eliminated, by better experimental measurement techniques. But some imperfection will nearly always remain. Thus, we need a method of correcting the observed treatment statistics for error of measurement. In this section, we will derive correction formulas using population statistics.

There are four key statistics in a within-subjects design: the raw score treatment effect, the raw score interaction, the standardized treatment effect, and the standardized interaction. Each is impacted by error of measurement in a different way.

At the level of population statistics, the mean error of measurement across the population of subjects is zero. Thus, for population statistics, the mean observed gain score is the same as the mean true gain score, and the population raw score treatment effect is not changed by error of measurement.

The raw score interaction is measured by the standard deviation of gain scores. This standard deviation is increased by error of measurement, sometimes dramatically increased. In particular, the error variation in gain scores can cause the appearance of a treatment by subject interaction where there is none. The error variance is directly added to the true score variance. That is,

$$\text{Var}(OG) = \text{Var}(TG + f) = \text{Var}(TG) + \text{Var}(f).$$

Thus, we correct the raw score interaction variance by subtracting the error of measurement variance.

$$\text{Var}(TG) = \text{Var}(OG) - \text{Var}(f)$$

$$= \text{Var}(OG) - 2[1 - r_{YY}]\text{Var}(Y)$$

The square root of the corrected variance is the corrected standard deviation.

The standard score treatment effect is the ratio of the mean raw score effect size to the level standard deviation. The numerator of this ratio is the raw score treatment effect that is not changed by error of measurement. Thus, the numerator need not be corrected. However, the denominator is the level score standard deviation. Since the observed score standard deviation is inflated by error of measurement, it must be corrected before it can be used in the denominator of the standard score treatment effect. Error of measurement variance is directly added to true score variance. Thus, we have

$$\text{Var}(Y) = \text{Var}(T + e) = \text{Var}(T) + \text{Var}(e).$$

We correct the observed level score variance by subtracting the error variance.

$$\text{Var}(T) = \text{Var}(Y) - \text{Var}(e)$$

$$= \text{Var}(Y) - [1 - r_{YY}]\text{Var}(Y)$$

$$= r_{YY}\text{Var}(Y)$$

That is, by algebraic identity, to subtract the error variance from the observed level score variance is to multiply the level score variance by the level score reliability. The corrected standard deviation is then obtained by taking the square root of the corrected variance.

$$\sigma_T = \sqrt{r_{YY}} \; \sigma_Y$$

The corrected standardized treatment effect is

$$\delta = E\,(TG)\,/\,\sigma_T = E\,(OG)\,/\,[\,\sqrt{r_{YY}}\;\sigma_Y\,]$$

$$= [\,E\,(OG)\,/\,\sigma_Y\,]\,/\,\sqrt{r_{YY}}$$

$$= [\,\text{Raw score}\,\delta\,]\,/\,\sqrt{r_{YY}}$$

Thus, the standard score treatment effect is corrected by dividing the observed standard score treatment effect by the square root of the level score reliability.

The standard score interaction is the ratio of two standard deviations, each of which is inflated by error of measurement. Thus both the numerator and the denominator must be corrected before the correct ratio can be computed. Since variances are more easily corrected than standard deviations, we first square the interaction ratio. The squared interaction ratio is the ratio of the variance of true gain scores to the variance of true level scores, i.e.,

$$\text{Interaction}^2 = \text{Var}\,(TG)\,/\,\text{Var}\,(T)\,.$$

The correction of each variance has been given above.

$$\text{Var}\,(TG) = \text{Var}\,(OG) - \text{Var}\,(f)$$

$$= \text{Var}\,(OG) - 2\,[\,1 - r_{YY}\,]\,\text{Var}\,(Y)$$

$$\text{Var}\,(T) = \text{Var}\,(Y) - \text{Var}\,(e)$$

$$= \text{Var}\,(Y) - [\,1 - r_{YY}\,]\,\text{Var}\,(Y)$$

$$= r_{YY}\,\text{Var}\,(Y)$$

The square root of the corrected variances is the desired standard score interaction measure.

Consider an example. Assume population means and variances are known, and suppose the pretest mean observed level score is 20, the standard deviation of observed level scores is 7 for both pretest and posttest, the mean observed gain score is 5.2, the standard deviation of observed gain scores is 5.94, and the reliability of the observed level scores is .81. Since the population mean error of measurement is 0, the raw score treatment main effect is the same as the treatment effect for raw scores, i.e.,

$$\text{Raw score } \delta = E\,(TG) = E\,(OG) = 5.2\,.$$

The apparent interaction is the raw score interaction computed on observed scores.

$$\text{Apparent raw score interaction} = \sigma_{OG} = 5.94$$

This apparent interaction is not 0 and, thus, suggests that there might be a true interaction. If this apparent interaction is compared to the raw score treatment effect, we have

$$\text{Apparent relative interaction} = 5.94\,/\,5.2 = 1.14$$

which suggests a heterogeneous interaction. However, the standard deviation of observed scores is inflated by error of measurement. The corrected variance is

$$\text{Var}\,(TG) = \text{Var}\,(OG) - 2\,[\,1 - r_{YY}\,]\,\text{Var}\,(Y)$$

$$= 5.94^2 - 2\,[\,1 - .64\,]\,7^2$$

$$= 35.2836 - 35.28$$

$$= .0036$$

This number is so close to 0 as to potentially be rounding error (the actual fact in this example). However, let us take the value at face value. The square root is the raw score true gain standard deviation $\sigma_{TG} = .06$. If this is compared to the treatment main effect, we find

$$\text{True relative interaction} = .06\,/\,5.2 = .01\,.$$

Thus, while the observed score gain standard deviation suggested a heterogeneous interaction, the true score gain standard deviation reveals the fact that there was virtually no interaction.

To compute the standardized treatment main effect, we must compute the level true score standard deviation σ_T. This is computed from the level observed score standard deviation.

$$\text{Var}(T) = r_{YY}\,\text{Var}(Y) = (.81)7^2 = 39.69$$

The level true score standard deviation is $\sigma_T = \sqrt{39.69} = 6.3$. The standard score treatment main effect is thus

$$\delta = E\,(TG)\,/\,\sigma_T = 5.2\,/\,6.3 = .83\,.$$

The standard score interaction is

$$s = \sigma_{TG}\,/\,\sigma_T = .06\,/\,6.3 = .0095\,.$$

If the relative interaction is computed on standard score effect sizes, we have

$$\text{Relative interaction} = .0095\,/\,.83 = .01$$

as before.

Sampling Error

No Error of Measurement and No Interaction

If there is no error of measurement and no treatment by subject interaction, then there is no sampling error in the observed mean gain score. It is equal to the observed gain score for each individual subject, which is equal to the raw score treatment effect. There is also no sampling error in the standard deviation of gain scores since the sample standard deviation is always zero if the population standard deviation is zero. The null hypothesis is directly testable. If there is no treatment effect, then the gain score will be zero for every individual subject, and, hence, the mean gain score will also be zero without sampling error. Thus, if there is no error of measurement and no treatment by subject interaction, then the null hypothesis is perfectly tested by inspection. Either the mean gain is zero, or it is not.

If there is no treatment by subject interaction and there is no error of measurement, then the raw score treatment effect is measured without sampling error because it is observed and is the same for every subject.

However, the standard score effect size δ uses the population within-groups standard deviation in its definition.

$$\delta = E\,(TG)\,/\,\sigma$$

Since the within-groups standard deviation σ is not known, the standard-ized effect size will be estimated with sampling error. There are two difference estimates of the population within-groups variance that could be used: the sample variance of the pretest score $SV(Y_1)$ and the average variance

$$SV = [\,SV(Y_1) - SV(Y_2)\,]\,/\,2\,.$$

Note that because there is no error of measurement, the observed score Y is the true score T. Because there is no interaction, the posttest variance is equal to the pretest variance. Thus, in this case, the average variance is equal to the pretest variance, and there is no sampling error advantage in using the average variance. Using the chi-square distribution, we obtain a confidence interval for the population within-groups variance. To a close approximation for $N > 30$ and a good approximation for $N > 4$, the confidence interval can be written

$$b^2\,SV(T) < \sigma^2 < B^2\,SV(T)$$

where

$$b = \sqrt{(2N-2)}\,/\,[\,\sqrt{(2N-3)} + 1.96\sqrt{(1 - 1/4\{N-2\})}\,]$$

$$B = \sqrt{(2N-2)}\,/\,[\,\sqrt{(2N-3)} - 1.96\sqrt{(1 - 1/4\{N-2\})}\,]\,.$$

From this we obtain the confidence interval for the standardized effect size.

$$d\,/\,B < \delta < d\,/\,b$$

where $d = Ave\,(OG)\,/\,\sqrt{SV}$.

Error of Measurement But No Interaction

If there is no treatment by subject interaction, then the treatment effect is the same for all subjects. Thus, it makes sense to talk about "the treatment effect" without referring to some particular subject. In this case, "the treatment effect" is the treatment main effect and the interaction standard deviation is zero.

If there were no error of measurement, then the treatment effect and the zero treatment effect standard deviation would be directly observable without sampling error. But if there is error of measurement, then there is sampling error in both the mean observed change score and the standard deviation of observed change scores. In both cases, the sampling error is due to sampling error in the mean and standard deviation of the error scores. There will be a sampling error band around any treatment parameter that we estimate. Ideally, we would like confidence intervals about each of those parameter estimates. If zero were included in the confidence interval for the treatment effect, then the sample treatment effect would not be statistically significant. As in all cases, the use of the significance test without computing a confidence interval is a very biased way of looking at the data since only sampling error in one direction is considered, while sampling error in the other direction (probability, one-half) is ignored and, thus, implicitly (and falsely) assumed to be nonexistent.

The treatment effect. Consider the sample mean gain score

$$\text{Ave}(OG) = \text{Ave}(TG + f) = \text{Ave}(TG) + \text{Ave}(f).$$

If there is no interaction, the true gain score is the same for each individual subject and, hence,

$$\text{Ave}(TG) = TG = \text{Raw score } \delta$$

without sampling error. If we denote the raw score treatment effect by δ^*, then

$$\text{Ave}(OG) = \delta^* + \text{Ave}(f).$$

The average error of measurement will converge to zero only if many errors are averaged. Thus, on a finite sample, there will be sampling error in the average error. Denote the sampling error variance in Ave (f) by V_f. Then, the sampling error in the average error is given by

$$V_f = \text{Var}(f) / N$$

where N is the number of subjects and Var (f) is the population variance of the gain error scores. Denote the square root of Var (f) by S. If the population variance were known, then the confidence interval for the raw score treatment effect would be

$$\text{Ave}\,(OG) - 1.96\,S \;<\; \text{Raw score } \delta < \text{Ave}\,(OG) + 1.96\,S\,.$$

If the population variance of level scores Var (Y) were known, then the variance of errors could be computed using reliability theory

$$\text{Var}\,(f) = 2\,[\,1 - r_{YY}\,]\,\text{Var}\,(Y)\,.$$

However, the population variance of level scores is not usually known. If we use the notation "SV ( )" for sample variance, then one estimate of the error variance would be

$$\text{Est Var}\,(f) = 2\,[\,1 - r_{YY}\,]\,\text{SV}\,(Y)\,.$$

However, because there is no subject by treatment interaction, there is a better estimate that stems from the identity

$$SV\,(f) = SV\,(OG)\,.$$

That is, we estimate the sampling error standard deviation S by

$$\text{Est}\,S \; = \sqrt{[\,SV\,(OG)\,/\,N\,]}\,.$$

(This number will itself have sampling error whose extent could be estimated using the chi-square distribution.) The sampling error in the estimate of S renders the normal curve confidence interval slightly too narrow. A more precise interval requires use of the noncentral t distribution, which is beyond the scope of our work here. To a good first approximation, the implication of the sampling error in our estimate of S is captured by replacing 1.96 by the t value, as noted in the section on confidence intervals.

The standard score treatment effect is obtained by dividing the raw score treatment effect by the level true score standard deviation. Since true scores are not observed, there is also no direct estimate of the true score standard deviation. Instead, we estimate the true score standard deviation indirectly using reliability theory. From the fact that

$$\text{Var}\,(T) = r_{YY}\,\text{Var}\,(Y)$$

we obtain the sample estimate

$$\text{Est SV}\,(T) = r_{YY}\,\text{SV}\,(Y)\,.$$

Denote the square root of that estimate by $S(T)$. Then, the sample estimate of the standard score treatment effect is

$$\text{Est } \delta = \text{Ave } (OG) / S(T).$$

This estimate of the effect size is very similar to the d_t statistic of the independent groups design (see Chapter 7). It is so similar that we will abuse our notation by using the notation d_t for this estimate of the standard score treatment effect. That is, for the within-subject design, we define d_t by

$$d_t = \text{Est } \delta = \text{Ave } (OG) / S(T).$$

There is sampling error in both the numerator and the denominator.

Because of error of measurement, the posttest variance will differ from the pretest variance because errors are independently sampled. Thus, the best estimate of the within group variance is the average variance. If we define $SV(Y)$ by

$$SV(Y) = [SV(Y_1) + SV(Y_2)] / 2$$

then the confidence interval for d_t is

$$d_t - 1.96\,S < \delta < d_t + 1.96\,S$$

where

$$S^2 = [2(1-r)/N] + [\delta^2(1+r^2) / \{4(N-1)\}]$$

where for this case

$$r = r_{12} = r_{YY}.$$

In using d_t to denote the sample effect size, it is important to note that d_t is NOT related to the t statistic that tests the null hypothesis that the treatment is zero. If we divide the test statistic by the square root of sample size, then

$$t / \sqrt{N} = \text{Ave } (OG) / \sqrt{SV(OG)}$$

versus

$$d_t = \text{Ave}\,(OG)\,/\,\sqrt{[\,r_{YY}\,SV\,(Y)\,]}\;.$$

These numbers differ in two ways. First, the d_t value contains the reliability r_{YY} so as to correct for attenuation. But the two variances also differ. $SV\,(OG)$ is the sample variance of CHANGE scores, whereas $SV\,(Y)$ is the sample variance of LEVEL scores. Thus, in the within-groups design, there is no simple transformation from t to d as is true for the independent groups design.

The apparent treatment interaction. In this case, we have assumed that there is no actual treatment by subjects interaction. However, because of error of measurement, there will be a large apparent interaction. The formula for the inflation is

$$\text{Var}\,(TG) = 0$$

$$\text{Var}\,(OG) = \text{Var}\,(f) = 2\,\text{Var}\,(e) = 2\,[\,1 - r_{YY}\,]\,\text{Var}\,(Y)\,.$$

Even for moderately large reliability, this will be a very substantial inflation. This inflation must be corrected so that the true value of zero is observed.

The variance of gain scores will be inflated from zero to twice the error variance of level scores. If there were no sampling error, this algebraic effect could be simply subtracted, and there would be no room for doubt that the apparent interaction is actually nonexistent. But error of measurement not only introduces a systematic error into the estimate of the interaction, it introduces sampling error as well.

If there were an interaction, then

$$\text{Var}\,(OG) = \text{Var}\,(TG) + \text{Var}\,(f)\,.$$

The true raw score interaction variance would be

$$\text{Var}\,(TG) = \text{Var}\,(OG) - \text{Var}\,(f)\,.$$

To subtract, we need an estimate of the error variance, which is independent of the gain scores. That estimate is

$$\text{Var}\,(f) = 2\,[\,1 - r_{YY}\,]\,\text{Var}\,(Y_1)$$

where $\text{Var}\,(Y_1)$ is the pretest variance. (If there is an interaction, then the posttest variance may differ from the pretest variance.)

The sample estimate of the true raw score interaction variance is thus given by

$$\text{Est}\, SV\,(TG) = SV\,(OG) - \text{Est Var}\,(f)$$

where

$$\text{Est Var}\,(f) = 2\,[\,1 - r_{YY}\,]\,SV\,(Y_1)\,.$$

If there is no actual interaction, then this estimate of the interaction will differ from zero by sampling error. With probability one-half, sampling error will cause the estimate to be negative, and there will be little doubt that there is no true interaction. However, with probability one-half, sampling error will cause the estimate to be positive and will falsely suggest a true interaction. We need to distinguish this last case from a real interaction.

The question is this: Is the variance of gain scores larger than would be predicted by chance given error of measurement? To obtain a significance test, we compare the two variances by division instead of subtraction. That is, define the statistic F by

$$F = SV\,(OG)\,/\,\text{Est Var}\,(f)$$

$$= SV\,(OG)\,/\,[\,2\,(1 - r_{YY})\,SV\,(Y_1)\,]\,.$$

If there is no interaction, then the numerator and denominator of F are each estimates of the same population variance. Consider then the null hypothesis that there is no treatment by subjects interaction. If the numerator and denominator were independent, then the F ratio defined here would have an F distribution with $N-1$ and $N-1$ degrees of freedom. However, the numerator and denominator are not independent. We have

$$\text{Numerator} = SV\,(OG) = SV\,(e_1) + SV\,(e_2) - 2\,\text{Cov}\,(e_1, e_2)$$

$$\text{Denominator} = 2\,(1 - r)\,[\,SV\,(T) + SV\,(e_1) + 2\,\text{Cov}\,(T, e_1)\,]\,.$$

The two have $SV\,(e_1)$ in common. The correlation between the numerator and the denominator is

$$\text{Cor (num, den)} = (1 - r_{YY})\,/\,4\,.$$

For moderate to high reliability, this correlation is low. Even if the reliability is as low as .64, the correlation is .36/4 = .09. If the reliability is as high as .81, the correlation is .19/4 = .05. Thus, except for data with very low reliability, there is little error in assuming that this F has an F distribution if there is no interaction.

The null hypothesis. Consider the null hypothesis that there is no treatment effect. If there were no interaction, then every subject would have a gain score of zero. Because of error of measurement, the individual gain scores will depart randomly from zero. Since individual gain scores would be as likely to be negative as positive, we might also change terminology from "gain score" to "change score." For simplicity, we will continue to use the phrase "gain score" with the understanding that a negative gain score represents a decrease.

Since there is sampling error, the null hypothesis is not directly testable. Even if there were no treatment effect, the mean gain score would differ from zero by sampling error (the sampling error in the mean error score). There are then two ways to test the null hypothesis statistically. One way is to compute the confidence interval as noted above. The more dangerous way is to compute a significance test without generating the confidence interval. Suppose we first compute the confidence interval. The significance test is obtained by checking to see if the confidence interval contains zero or not. This test is unbiased in that the investigator can see how far the confidence interval extends in both directions and, thus, take the significance test with the required grain of salt.

On the other hand, it is common practice in the field to ignore confidence intervals. This leads to the test of the null hypothesis by a "dependent groups" t test or — what is equivalent — by the "treatment by subjects" or "repeated measures" analysis of variance. The statistical power is the same in either case. However, the person who looks at a wide confidence interval can tell when there is quite a stretch down to zero. The person who never sees a confidence interval has no concrete way of knowing how tenuous that null hypothesis may be.

Interaction but no Error of Measurement

If there is no error of measurement, the treatment effect is directly observed for each individual subject. However, if there is a treatment by subjects interaction, then that treatment effect will differ from one subject to the next. Thus, the phrase, "the treatment effect," has no meaning if separated from some individual subject. The conventional practice in this case is to create a single number to represent the treatment effects by averaging the treatment effect across a population of subjects. This average treatment effect is the *treatment main effect* of analysis of variance. Thus, if there is an interaction, we must be careful to always describe the average treatment effect as the "treatment main effect," and we must avoid the phrase "treatment effect."

If there is no error of measurement, then the treatment effect is exactly observed for each individual subject. However, the mean treatment effect is known only for the sample of subjects at hand. The sample average treatment effect will differ from the population average treatment effect by sampling error. In this case, the sampling error is traditional sampling error: One sample of subjects will differ randomly from another sample. Thus, we would like to have a confidence interval to estimate the potential error band around the sample mean treatment effect. We need two confidence intervals: one for the raw score treatment main effect and one for the standard score treatment main effect.

The treatment by subject interaction is the population standard deviation of gain scores. The sample standard deviation will differ from the population standard deviation by sampling error. Thus, we would like a confidence interval around our sample estimate of the interaction standard deviation. We would like two confidence intervals: one for the raw score interaction and one for the standard score interaction.

The treatment main effect. Since in this case we assume that there is no error of measurement, the gain scores observed in the study are the true gain scores. Thus, we can directly observe the sample mean true gain score and, hence, the sample raw score treatment effect. Denote the sample average by Ave (TG). The sample average is related to the population average E (TG) by

$$\text{Ave} \, (TG) = E \, (TG) + \text{sampling error}$$

$$= \text{Raw score} \, \delta + \text{sampling error}$$

The sampling error variance in the mean gain score is determined by the population variance of gain scores. If we denote the sampling error standard deviation by S, then

$$S^2 = \text{Var} \, (TG) \, / \, N$$

where N is the sample size. If the population variance of gain scores were known, then S would be known and the confidence interval would be

$$\text{Ave} \, (TG) - 1.96 \, S < E \, (TG) < \text{Ave} \, (TG) + 1.96 \, S \, .$$

Since the population variance is not known, we instead estimate S using the sample variance of gain scores. That is,

$$\text{Est } S^2 = SV(TG) / N.$$

The sampling error in this estimate of S further increases the width of the corresponding confidence interval. We replace the 1.96 by the corresponding value of t as noted in the section on confidence intervals.

To estimate the standard score treatment effect, we must estimate the level score standard deviation. Since there is an interaction, the pretest and posttest standard deviation may be different. Thus, we define the desired standard deviation to be the pretest standard deviation. That is, we would like to know the population variance Var (T_1). Since there is no error of measurement, the level scores observed in the study are level true scores. Thus, the sample standard deviation of level true scores is directly observable. The obvious estimate of the standard score treatment effect is obtained by dividing the sample treatment main effect by the pretest standard deviation.

$$\text{Est } \delta = \text{Ave } (TG) / S(T_1)$$

It is tempting to obtain the confidence interval the same way. We could just take the two endpoints of the confidence interval for the raw score treatment main effect and divide each by the level score pretest standard deviation. This is not entirely accurate because it does not take into account the sampling error in the pretest standard deviation, but it is a good first approximation.

The treatment by subject interaction. The raw score interaction is measured by the standard deviation of true gain scores. If there is no error of measurement, the gain scores observed are the true gain scores. The null hypothesis of no treatment by subject interaction would be directly testable. Either the standard deviation of gain scores is zero or it is not. If the standard deviation is greater than zero, then there is a treatment by subject interaction.

The sample standard deviation of gain scores is the sample standard deviation for the treatment by subject interaction. The population interaction differs from the sample standard deviation in the usual manner. The confidence interval can be computed using the chi-square distribution.

If the sample standard deviation is computed using N in the denominator, then define the statistic Q by

$$Q = N \, SV(TG) / \text{Var}(TG).$$

If the less accurate formula for the standard deviation using $N-1$ is used, then compute Q by

$$Q = (N - 1) SV(TG) / \text{Var}(TG).$$

If the gain scores have a normal distribution, then Q has a chi-square distribution with $N-1$ degrees of freedom, and the confidence interval can be figured from that distribution. Let L and U be the lower and upper 97.5% points of that distribution. The 95% confidence interval for the raw score interaction standard deviation is

$$S(TG) / \sqrt{U} < \sigma_{TG} < S(TG) / \sqrt{L}.$$

To a close approximation for $N > 30$ and a good approximation for $N > 4$, the confidence interval can also be written

$$b\,S(TG) < \sigma_{TG} < B\,S(TG)$$

where

$$b = \sqrt{(2N - 2)} / [\sqrt{(2N - 3)} + 1.96\sqrt{(1 - 1/4\{N - 2\})}]$$

$$B = \sqrt{(2N - 2)} / [\sqrt{(2N - 3)} - 1.96\sqrt{(1 - 1/4\{N - 2\})}].$$

The standard score interaction is defined as the ratio σ_{TG} / σ_T. To estimate this ratio, we must estimate the standard deviation of level scores. Since there is an interaction, the pretest and posttest standard deviation may be different. Thus, we define the desired standard deviation to be the pretest standard deviation. That is, we would like to know the population variance $\text{Var}(T_1)$. Since there is no error of measurement, the level scores observed in the study are level true scores. Thus, the sample standard deviation of level true scores is directly observable. The obvious estimate of the standard score interaction is obtained by dividing the sample raw score treatment by subject interaction by the pretest standard deviation.

$$\text{Est}\,s = S(TG) / S(T_1)$$

It is tempting to obtain the confidence interval the same way. We could just take the two endpoints of the confidence interval for the raw score treatment main effect and divide each by the level score pretest standard deviation. This is not entirely accurate because it does not take into account the sampling error in the pretest standard deviation, but it is a good first approximation.

The null hypothesis. Consider the null hypothesis that there is no treatment effect. This statement is ambiguous. If we mean that there is no treatment effect for any subject, then there is also no treatment by subject interaction. We treated this case earlier. However, it is also possible to define a null hypothesis by the possibility that the treatment *main* effect is zero even though the treatment by subject interaction is not zero. If the mean treatment effect is zero and the variance is not, then some subjects must have positive gain scores while other subjects have negative gain scores. Thus, the interaction is necessarily heterogeneous.

If there were no interaction, then every subject would have a gain score of zero. If there is an interaction, then the individual gain scores will depart from zero randomly. Since individual gain scores would be as likely to be negative as positive, we might also change terminology: from "gain score" to "change score." For simplicity, we will continue to use the phrase "gain score" with the understanding that a negative gain score represents a decrease.

Because subjects differ in their true gain scores, there is sampling error in the average gain score. Since there is sampling error, the null hypothesis is not directly testable. Even if there were no treatment main effect, the mean gain score would differ from zero by sampling error. There are then two ways to test the null hypothesis statistically. One way is to compute the confidence interval as noted above. The more dangerous way is to compute a significance test without generating the confidence interval. Suppose we first compute the confidence interval. The significance test is obtained by checking to see if the confidence interval contains zero or not. This test is unbiased in that the investigator can see how far the confidence interval extends in both directions and, thus, take the significance test with the required grain of salt.

If there is a treatment by subject interaction, then *the conventional t test does not work.* The conventional *t* test and the conventional repeated measures analysis of variance use the nominal interaction term as an error term to test the main effect. In doing this, they assume homogeneity of variance and independence between the interaction and the subject level scores. These assumptions are true if the apparent interaction is actually error of measurement. However, for real interactions, these assumptions are usually false. Thus, the conventional *F* test cannot be trusted. There have been experimental tests — the "quasi-*F*" — for such cases, but these too make independence assumptions that are quite implausible for most common interactions (such as a multiplicative treatment effect). These procedures are beyond the scope of the present text. Thus, if there is a treatment by subject interaction, then the confidence interval approach appears to be the only approach available.

Error of Measurement and an Interaction

If there is both error of measurement and an interaction, then there are two sources of sampling error: sampling of errors of measurement, and sampling of different levels of treatment effect. If there is error of measurement, then the treatment effect is only imperfectly observed at the level of individuals. Thus, we must rely heavily on indirect statistics, especially our estimate of the treatment main effect and our estimate of the treatment interaction standard deviation. In both cases, we must adjust observed score statistics for the effects of error of measurement, especially the apparent interaction standard deviation.

The treatment main effect. The treatment main effect is the population mean true gain score. Our estimate is the sample mean observed gain score. The sample mean observed gain score suffers from two sources of sampling error.

$$\text{Ave}(OG) = \text{Ave}(TG + f) = \text{Ave}(TG) + \text{Ave}(f)$$

where

$$\text{Ave}(TG) = E(TG) + \text{sampling error}$$

$$\text{Ave}(f) = 0 + \text{sampling error}.$$

The sampling error in the average true gain score stems from variation in the treatment effect across subjects. The sampling error in the average error of measurement stems from variation in errors of measurement across subjects. The error of measurement can be pooled, as in

$$\text{Ave}(OG) = E(TG) + \text{sampling error}.$$

If we denote the pooled sampling error standard deviation by S, then that variance is determined by the population variance of observed gain scores.

$$S^2 = \text{Var}(OG) / N$$

The corresponding confidence interval is

$$\text{Ave}(OG) - 1.96\,S < \text{Raw score } \delta < \text{Ave}(OG) + 1.96\,S.$$

If the population variance must be estimated by the sample variance SV (OG), then the underlying distribution for the confidence interval is no longer the normal distribution but the t distribution with $N-1$ degrees of freedom. Thus, the "1.96" must be replaced by the corresponding values from the 95% two-tail column of the t table. To a close approximation for $N > 14$, we replace 1.96 by

$$1.96\,[\,1 + 1.2104\,/\,(N-1)\,]$$

and for $14 > N > 5$ by

$$1.96\,[\,1 + 1.2104\,/\,(N-1) + 1.4402\,/\,(N-1)^2 + 1.3041\,/\,(N-1)^2\,].$$

The standard score treatment main effect is the ratio of the mean raw score effect size to the level standard deviation. Since there is an interaction, the standard deviation used is the pretest standard deviation. The numerator of the ratio is the raw score treatment main effect which is not changed by error of measurement. Thus, the numerator need not be corrected. However, the denominator is the level score standard deviation. Since the observed score standard deviation is inflated by error of measurement, it must be corrected before it can be used in the denominator of the standard score treatment main effect. Error of measurement variance is directly added to true score variance. Thus, we have

$$\text{Var}\,(Y_1) = \text{Var}\,(T_1 + e_1) = \text{Var}\,(T_1) + \text{Var}\,(e_1)\,.$$

We correct the observed level score variance by subtracting the error variance.

$$\begin{aligned}\text{Var}\,(T) &= \text{Var}\,(Y) - \text{Var}\,(e)\\ &= \text{Var}\,(Y) - [\,1 - r_{YY}\,]\,\text{Var}\,(Y)\\ &= r_{YY}\,\text{Var}\,(Y)\end{aligned}$$

That is, by algebraic identity, to subtract the error variance from the observed level score variance is to multiply the level score variance by the level score reliability. The corrected standard deviation is then obtained by taking the square root of the corrected variance.

$$\sigma_T = \sqrt{r_{YY}}\ \sigma_Y$$

The corrected standardized treatment main effect is thus

$$\delta = E\,(TG) \,/\, \sigma_T = E\,(OG) \,/\, [\,\sqrt{r_{YY}}\ \sigma_Y\,]\ .$$

It is also possible to compute an observed score treatment main effect "δ" defined by

$$\text{``}\delta\text{''} = E\,(OG) \,/\, \sigma_Y\ .$$

The true score or actual treatment main effect is related to the observed score treatment effect by

$$\delta = [\,E\,(OG) \,/\, \sigma_Y\,] \,/\, \sqrt{r_{YY}}$$

$$= [\,\text{Observed score ``}\delta\text{''}\,] \,/\, \sqrt{r_{YY}}\ .$$

This is the conventional formula for correcting a main effect for the error of measurement in the dependent variable. Thus, the actual standard score treatment main effect is corrected by dividing the observed standard score treatment main effect by the square root of the level score reliability.

The confidence interval for the standard score treatment main effect is most easily approximated by dividing the endpoints of the confidence interval for the raw score treatment main effect by the level score standard deviation. This would ignore the sampling error in the level score main effect. The exact formula for the standard error can be computed. Estimate the raw score treatment effect by

$$\text{Est}\,E\,(TG) = \text{Ave}\,(OG) = \text{Ave}\,(Y_2) - \text{Ave}\,(Y_1)$$

and estimate the pretest level true score standard deviation by

$$\text{Est}\,\sigma_T = \sqrt{r_{YY}\,SV\,(Y_1)}\ .$$

The standard score treatment main effect is then estimated by

$$d = \text{Est}\,\delta = \text{Est}\,E\,(TG) \,/\, \text{Est}\,\sigma_T\ .$$

The bias in this formula is given by

$$E\,(d) = \delta \,/\, J\,(N-1)$$

where

$$J(N) = \Gamma(N/2) / \sqrt{(N/2)\,\Gamma(\{N-1\}/2)}$$

which is closely approximated by

$$J(N-1) = 1 - .75 / (N-2).$$

That is,

$$E(d) = a\,\delta$$

where

$$a = 1 + .75 / (N-2).$$

This bias is very small even for sample sizes as low as 50 (although not so small for sample sizes of 20 or less). The bias can be corrected by dividing the estimate of *d* by the multiplier *a*.

The large sample sampling error variance of *d* is given by

$$\text{Var}(d) = [4/N][\mu + \delta^2 / 8]$$

where

$$\mu = [1 - r_{12}] / [4\,r_{YY}]$$

if there might be an interaction, and by

$$\mu = [1 - r_{YY}] / [4\,r_{YY}]$$

if there is no interaction. For small samples, the sampling variance is more closely computed by

$$\text{Var}(d) = [(N-1)/(N-3)][4/N][\mu + (\delta^2 / 8)(N/\{N-1\})].$$

Let the square root of this variance be denoted *S*. Then to a close approximation, the confidence interval for δ is

$$d - 1.96S < \delta < d + 1.96S.$$

The treatment by subjects interaction. The treatment by subjects interaction is measured by the population true gain score standard deviation.

The corresponding observed gain score standard deviation is greatly inflated by error of measurement. Thus, it must be corrected before it becomes a serious estimate of the actual interaction. Furthermore, it is very much worthwhile to test the interaction to see if it is really there.

Consider first the inflation of the interaction variance by error of measurement. The formula for the inflation is

$$\text{Var}(OG) = \text{Var}(TG) + \text{Var}(f)$$

where

$$\text{Var}(f) = 2\,\text{Var}(e) = 2[1 - r_{YY}]\,\text{Var}(Y_1).$$

Even for moderately large reliability, this will be a very substantial inflation, especially if there is actually no interaction.

The true raw score interaction variance can be computed by subtraction.

$$\text{Var}(TG) = \text{Var}(OG) - \text{Var}(f)$$

To subtract, we need an estimate of the error variance that is independent of the gain scores. That estimate is

$$\text{Var}(f) = 2[1 - r_{YY}]\,\text{Var}(Y_1)$$

where $\text{Var}(Y_1)$ is the pretest variance. If there is an interaction, then the posttest variance may differ from the pretest variance.

Using the notation "SV( )" for sample variance, the sample estimate of the true raw score interaction variance is given by

$$\text{Est Var}(TG) = SV(OG) - \text{Est Var}(f)$$

where

$$\text{Est Var}(f) = 2[1 - r_{YY}]\,SV(Y_1).$$

If there is no actual interaction, then this estimate of the interaction will differ from zero by sampling error. With probability one-half, sampling error will cause the estimate to be negative, and there will be little doubt that there is no true interaction. However, with probability one-half, sampling error will cause the estimate to be positive and will falsely suggest a true interaction. We need to distinguish this last case from a real interaction.

The question is this: Is the variance of gain scores larger than would be predicted by chance given error of measurement? To obtain a significance test, we compare the two variances by division instead of subtraction. That is, define the statistic F by

$$F = SV(OG) / \text{Est Var}(f)$$

$$= SV(OG) / [\, 2\,(1 - r_{YY})\,SV(Y_1)\,]\,.$$

Under the null hypothesis, there is no interaction. Thus, the previous discussion of the statistical properties of this F test in the earlier section for no interaction applies here. To a close approximation, this F ratio has an F distribution with $N-1$ and $N-1$ degrees of freedom.

The estimate of the standard score interaction is the raw score interaction divided by the level true score standard deviation. The corresponding variance is estimated by

$$\text{Est Var}(T_1) = r_{YY}\,SV(Y_1)\,.$$

That is,

$$\text{Est }s^2 = \text{Est Var}(TG) / \text{Est Var}(T_1)$$

$$= [\, SV(OG) - \text{Est Var}(f)\,] / \text{Est Var}(T_1)$$

where

$$\text{Est Var}(f) = 2\,[\, 1 - r_{YY}\,]\,SV(Y_1)\,.$$

To generate a confidence interval for s, we note first that

$$\text{Est }s^2 = [\, 1/r_{YY}\,]\,[\, SV(OG) / SV(Y_1)\,] - [\, 2\,(1 - r_{YY})/r_{YY}\,]\,.$$

That is, the estimated interaction square has the form

$$\text{Est }s^2 = \beta\,[\, SV(OG) / SV(Y_1)\,] - \alpha$$

where α and β are constants. The variance ratio $SV(OG) / SV(Y_1)$ would have an approximately F ratio if it were not for the fact that the numerator and denominator population variances are different. There is a modified ratio that does have an approximately F distribution,

$$F = [\text{Var}(Y_1) / Var(OG)] [SV(OG) / SV(Y_1)]$$

with degrees of freedom $(N - 1, N - 1)$. The corresponding endpoints for the confidence interval are obtained from the F endpoint tabled under $p =$ .025, although few tables have that value for the degrees of freedom characteristic of most studies. To a close approximation, the upper endpoint is given by

$$U = e^{2w}$$

where

$$w = 1.96 / \sqrt{(N - 2)}.$$

The lower endpoint is given by the reciprocal, i.e.,

$$L = 1 / U.$$

Define the constant β by

$$\beta = 2(1 - r_{YY}) / r_{YY}.$$

Then, the confidence interval for the squared interaction is

$$[\text{Est } s^2 + \beta] / U - \beta < s^2 < [\text{Est } s^2 + \beta] / L - \beta.$$

The confidence interval for the interaction s is obtained by taking the square root of each endpoint.

Meta-Analysis and the Within-Subjects Design

The d Statistic

Studies that report standard deviations are easy to code for meta-analysis. We estimate the true score level standard deviation σ_{T_1} by

$$S^2 = r_{YY} SV(Y_1).$$

We define d by

$$d = \text{Ave}(OG) / S = [\text{Ave}(Y_2) - \text{Ave}(Y_1)] / S.$$

We can relate this sample estimate to the population δ by the usual sampling error formula,

$$d = \delta + e.$$

The sampling error variance in *d* is given by

$$\text{Var}\,(e) = [\,(N - 1)/(N - 3)\,]\,[\,1/N\,]\,[\,\beta - \{\,\delta^2 / 2\,\}\{\,N / (N - 1)\,\}\,]$$

where

$$\beta = [\,\sigma_{OG} / \sigma_T\,]^2 = 2\,[\,1 - r_{12}\,] / r_{YY}$$

where r_{12} is the pretest-posttest correlation. If there is no treatment by subjects interaction, the test-retest correlation is equal to the reliability, i.e.,

$$r_{12} = r_{YY}.$$

For large samples,

$$\text{Var}\,(e) = [\,\beta + \delta^2 / 2\,] / N.$$

For small samples,

$$\text{Var}\,(e) = [\,(N - 1) / (N - 3)\,]\,[\,\beta + (\delta^2 / 2)\,(N/\{\,N - 1\,\})\,] / N.$$

Note that the sampling error in this *d* statistic is not the same as the sampling error of *d* for the independent groups design. Thus, if the meta-analysis is mixing within-subjects and between-subjects designs, then the sampling error must be computed separately for the two sets of studies.

The Treatment by Subjects Interaction

The independent groups design assumes no treatment by subject interaction. Furthermore, this is a stringent assumption because there is no way to test that assumption in an independent groups design. The within-groups design has a test for the interaction, namely

$$F = SV\,(OG) / \text{Est Var}\,(f)$$

$$= SV\,(OG) / [\,2\,(1 - r_{YY})\,SV\,(Y_1)\,]$$

with degrees of freedom $(N - 1, N - 1)$.

The standard score interaction is defined by

$$s = \sigma_{TG} / \sigma_T$$

which is estimated by

$$\text{Est } s^2 = \text{Est Var } (TG) / \text{Est Var } (T_1)$$

$$= [\, SV(OG) - \text{Est Var } (f) \,] / \text{Est Var } (T_1)$$

where

$$\text{Est Var } (f) = 2 \,[\, 1 - r_{YY} \,]\, SV(Y_1)$$

$$\text{Est Var } (T_1) = r_{YY} SV(Y_1) .$$

To generate a confidence interval for s, we note first that

$$\text{Est } s^2 = [\, 1/r_{YY} \,]\, [\, SV(OG) / SV(Y_1) \,] - [\, 2 \,(1 - r_{YY}) / r_{YY} \,] .$$

That is, the estimated interaction square has the form

$$\text{Est } s^2 = \beta \,[\, SV(OG) / SV(Y_1) \,] - \alpha$$

where α and β are constants. The variance ratio $SV(OG) / SV(Y_1)$ would have an approximately F ratio if it were not for the fact that the numerator and denominator population variances are different. There is a modified ratio that does have an approximately F distribution,

$$F = [\, \text{Var } (Y_1) / \text{Var } (OG) \,]\, [\, SV(OG) / SV(Y_1) \,]$$

with degrees of freedom $(N - 1, N - 1)$. The corresponding endpoints for the confidence interval are obtained from the F endpoint tabled under $p = .025$, although few tables have that value for the degrees of freedom characteristic of most studies. To a close approximation, the upper endpoint is given by

$$U = e^{2w}$$

where

$$w = 1.96 / \sqrt{(N - 2)} .$$

The lower endpoint is given by the reciprocal, i.e.,

$$L = 1 / U.$$

Define the constant β by

$$\beta = 2\,(1 - r_{12}) / r_{YY}.$$

Then, the confidence interval for the squared interaction is

$$[\,\text{Est}\,s^2 + \beta\,] / U - \beta < s^2 < [\,\text{Est}\,s^2 + \beta\,] / L - \beta.$$

The confidence interval for the interaction s is obtained by taking the square root of each endpoint.

   To estimate the standard error of this estimate of s, compute the width of the final confidence interval. The corresponding standard error is the width divided by $2(1.96) = 3.92$. The sampling error variance is the square of the standard error. That is, if we write the equation defining sampling error e as

$$\text{Est}\,s = s + e$$

then

$$\text{Var}\,(e) = \left\{ [\,\text{Est}\,s^2 + \beta\,] / L - [\,\text{Est}\,s^2 + \beta\,] / U \right\} / 1.96^2.$$

   The t statistic. The preceding discussion assumed that the study reported standard deviations. However, standard deviations are often left out of the report. Instead, authors report significance test statistics such as t. By analogy with the independent groups case, we might search for a way to transform the value of t to provide an estimate of δ. Without standard deviations, there is no way to estimate the interaction s.

   Consider now the t test for within-subjects designs.

$$t = \text{Ave}\,(OG) / \sqrt{[\,SV(OG) / N\,]}$$

If there were no treatment main effect, then this t statistic would have a central t distribution with $N-1$ degrees of freedom and its value could be compared to those in the conventional t table in the conventional manner. If there is a treatment main effect, then this t statistic will have a noncentral t distribution whose noncentrality parameter depends on the size of the treatment main effect relative to the standard deviation of observed gain scores.

Note that the relevant standard deviation for sampling is the standard deviation of gain scores rather than the standard deviation of level scores. This means that transforming this value of t to the conventional within-subjects power parameter creates a ratio with the wrong denominator (see also Kulik & Kulik, 1986). To see this, divide t by the square root of sample size and consider the value for very large samples.

$$\lim [\, t / \sqrt{N} \,] = E\,(OG) \,/\, \sigma_{OG}$$

Since $E\,(OG) = E\,(TG)$, we have

$$\delta = E\,(TG) \,/\, \sigma_T = E\,(OG) \,/\, \sigma_T\,.$$

Thus the t statistic has the wrong standard deviation (σ_{OG} instead of σ_T). We can relate the t statistic to δ by a ratio

$$\lim [\, t / \sqrt{N} \,] = \alpha\,\delta$$

where

$$\alpha = \sigma_T \,/\, \sigma_{OG}\,.$$

For the case of no interaction and no error of measurement, $\sigma_{OG} = 0$ and the ratio is infinite! If there is error of measurement but no interaction, then the ratio α can be computed from the reliability of the dependent variable. The square of α is given by

$$\alpha^2 = r_{YY} \,/\, [\, 2\,(1 - r_{YY})\,]\,.$$

Consider now the formula used to convert the independent groups t to d, i.e.,

$$\text{``}d\text{''} = 2\,t / \sqrt{N}\,.$$

The limit for large sample sizes is

$$\lim \text{``}d\text{''} = \alpha\,\delta$$

where

$$\alpha^2 = r_{YY} \,/\, (1 - r_{YY})\,.$$

This ratio would be 1 only for the special case $r_{YY} = .50$. For any other reliability, the formula would be wrong.

The desired formula transforming *t* to *d* is

$$d = a \, t / \sqrt{N}$$

where

$$a = \sqrt{[\, 2\,(1 - r_{12}) / r_{YY} \,]}$$

if there is an interaction and

$$a = \sqrt{[\, 2\,(1 - r_{YY}) / r_{YY} \,]}$$

if there is not. (The approximation $r_{12} = r_{YY}$ can be used if there is an interaction but the test-retest correlation is not reported.) If we define sampling error *e* for this *d* by

$$d = \delta + e$$

then the sampling error variance is

$$\text{Var}\,(e) = [\, 1/N \,] \; [\, (N - 1)/(N - 3) \,] \; [\, a^2 + \delta^2 / 2 \,].$$

The corresponding large sample formula is

$$\text{Var}\,(e) = [\, a^2 - \delta^2/2 \,] / N.$$

To put this in comparison with the formula for the independent groups *d* sampling error variance, consider the independent groups large sample formula

$$\text{"Var}\,(e)\text{"} = [\, 4/N \,] \; [\, 1 + \delta^2 / 8 \,].$$

The within-groups large sample formula can be written

$$\text{Var}\,(e) = [\, 4/N \,] \; [\, \beta^2 + \delta^2 / 8 \,]$$

where

$$\beta^2 = a^2 / 4 = [\, 1 - r_{YY} \,] / [\, 2\, r_{YY} \,].$$

The two formulas will agree only in the special case $\beta^2 = 1$, i.e., for the special case $r_{YY} = .33$. For higher reliabilities, the independent groups formula will overstate the sampling error in d.

Statistical Power in the Two Designs

We have given a substantive argument showing that the within-subjects design with high reliability of measurement has higher statistical power than the independent groups design. However, we have given neither formulas nor examples showing how much higher the power is. We will present such formulas in this section. For ease of presentation, we will assume that the independent groups design is justifiable; i.e., we will assume that if there is a treatment by subjects interaction, then that interaction is small enough to ignore. That is, like the conventional textbooks, we will assume that there is no treatment by subjects inter-action.

A key question in matching designs is to match the sample sizes. There are two different ways to do this: to match the number of subjects or to match the number of scores. In the independent groups design, the number of scores equals the number of people. That is, N_1 people in group 1 get N_1 scores on the dependent variable, while N_2 people in group 2 get N_2 scores. Thus there are $N_1 + N_2$ people and $N_1 + N_2$ scores. However, in the within-subjects design, there are N people and $2N$ scores since each person gets two scores, a score for the first condition and a score for the second condition (in our discussion a pretest and a posttest score). Thus, in matching designs, we can either match people or match scores.

The choice is not simple. In practice, the matching will be determined by a resource match. There are two extreme cases. In most field studies, the sample size is set by the number of people available for study. For example, if we want to study the introduction of quality circles into the machinist department of Acme Manufacture, then our sample will contain at most the 32 people who work there at this time. However, in most lab studies, the sample size is set by the number of hours the lab is available (or the number of assistant-hours available). If the lab is available for 40 hours and it takes 30 minutes to run a subject through a condition, then the study will have 80 scores.

Consider the typical field study. We have N subjects available. Our design choice is this: (1) Run all N subjects in a pre-post design, or (2) randomly split the N subjects into two half-samples of $N/2$ persons each and assign one-half of the sample to the control group and the other half-sample to the experimental group. Thus, we end up matching the designs by number of subjects, but we get twice as many scores in the pre-post design as in the independent groups design.

Consider the typical lab study. We have N units of observation time available. Our choice then is (1) to run $N/2$ subjects through each of the two conditions, or (2) to run one randomly chosen set of subjects in one condition and to run a second randomly chosen set of subjects in the other condition. Thus, we end up matching the designs on number of scores, but the independent groups design has twice as many people in it.

Designs Matched for Number of Subjects

Consider then the choice between the two designs with the same number of subjects. In the within-subjects design, all N subjects are observed in both conditions. In the independent groups design, the N subjects are randomly divided into two half-samples, with subjects in one sample observed in one condition and the subjects in the other sample observed in the other condition. Consider the power of the t test in each design.

First, we note that there will be a trivial difference in the degrees of freedom: $N-1$ for the within-subjects design and $N-2$ for the independent groups design. That difference doesn't matter and will be ignored here (assume $N > 19$).

If there were no treatment effect, then the only possible statistical error would be a Type I error. In both designs, the t statistic and t tables are designed so that the probability of a Type I error is .05. Thus, if the null hypothesis were true, then it would not matter which design is chosen.

Assume then that there is a treatment effect. Define the size by

$$\delta = E\,(TG)\,/\,\sigma_T = [\,E\,(T_2) - E\,(T_1)\,]\,/\,\sigma_T$$

where T stands for the actual dependent variable, i.e., the dependent variable scores that would have been observed had there been no error of measurement. For either design, the t test has a noncentral t distribution. Thus, it can be written

$$t = (\mu + z)\,/\,c$$

where z has a standard normal distribution, c is the square root of a chi-square divided by its degrees of freedom, z and c are independent, and μ is the systematic impact of the treatment effect. If the degrees of freedom are denoted v, then

$$E\,(t) = \mu\,/\,J\,(v)$$

$$\mathrm{Var}\,(t) = v/(v-2) + \mu^2\,[\,v/(v-2) - 1/J\,(v)\,].$$

To a close approximation

$$E\,(t) = (1 + .75/v)\,\mu$$

$$\mathrm{Var}\,(t) = [\,v/(v-2)\,]\,[\,1 + (\mu^2/2v)\,(1 + 3\,/\,\{v-1\})\,].$$

If the study designs are matched for the number of subjects, the designs differ only trivially in degrees of freedom. Thus, it is the parameter μ that differs between designs and that determines the relative power of the t test. In either design, we can write

$$\mu = \delta\,\sqrt{(N\,r_{YY}/b)}$$

where b — the divisor under the radical — differs between the designs. For within-subjects design, we have

$$b = 2\,(1 - r_{YY})$$

and, hence,

$$\mu_w = \delta\,\sqrt{[\,Nr_{YY}/(2\{1 - r_{YY}\})\,]}\,.$$

For the independent groups design, we have

$$b = 4$$

and, hence,

$$\mu_i = \delta\,\sqrt{[\,Nr_{YY}/4\,]}\,.$$

The relative size of the parameters is the ratio

$$\mu_w\,/\,\mu_i = \sqrt{[\,4/2\,(1 - r_{YY})\,]} = \sqrt{[\,2/(1 - r_{YY})\,]}\,.$$

The higher the reliability, the greater the relative advantage of the within-subjects design. As measurement nears perfection, the ratio nears infinity. This reflects the fact that if there is no interaction and no error of measurement, the within-subjects design always has perfect power (an infinite value of t), as shown earlier in this chapter. The lower the reliability, the lower the relative advantage. However, even as the reliability approaches 0, there is still a relative advantage of $\sqrt{2} = 1.41$, a 41% advantage. This reflects the fact that as the level scores approach perfect unreliability, the gain scores still represent twice as much data as the independent groups data because each subject has two measurements rather than one.

The mapping from power parameter to power is highly nonlinear. Thus, the power advantage is not proportional to the relative advantage in the power parameter. In part, this reflects the fact that as sample size increases, power tends to its upper bound of 1.00 in both designs. As both tests approach perfect power, there is no room for the power of the within-subjects design to be more than slightly higher than that for the independent groups design.

A power comparison is presented in Table 8.1. In Part I of the table, the effect size is always the same: $\delta = .40$. This is the typical effect size of major textbook examples (Cooper, 1984). Power is tabulated for varying values of sample size N and reliability r_{YY}. Since 5 levels of reliability are shown, there are 5 columns for each design. Counting sample size as column 1, there are 11 columns in Table 8.1. The 5 columns for the within-subjects design are columns 2-6, while the 5 columns for the independent groups design are columns 7-11. Corresponding columns represent the same level of measurement error.

Consider the row for a sample size of $N = 100$. As the reliability rises from .25 (the average reliability of an isolated response) to .81 (the reliability of professionally developed tests), the power of the independent groups design rises from 17% to 44%. That is, the error rate for the independent groups significance test drops from 83% to 56%. For the within-subjects design, the corresponding power values rise from 37% to 100%. That is, the error rate drops from 63% to 0. For a sample size of $N = 100$, the within-subjects design attains perfect power for reliabilities as low as .81, while the independent groups design never attains perfect power.

Consider the two columns for reliability $r_{YY} = .81$. The smaller the sample size, the greater the relative power advantage for the within-subjects design. At the extremely low sample size of $N = 10$, the relative power is 44/9 = 4.89; the within-subjects design is nearly 5 times more likely to detect the treatment effect than is the independent groups design. When the sample size reaches $N = 70$, the power of the within-subjects design reaches 100% — perfect power — and can grow no further. At $N = 70$, the relative power is 100/33 = 3.03 or 3 to 1. From that point on, the power of the within-subjects design remains fixed at 100% while the power of the independent groups design climbs to 44% at $N = 100$. At a

Table 8.1 The Power of the Within-Subjects and Independent Groups Designs for Two Effect Sizes When the Number of Subjects Is the Same in Both Designs

I. $\delta = .40$: Textbook Examples

N	Within-Subjects Reliability					Independent Groups Reliability				
	.25	.36	.49	.64	.81	.25	.36	.49	.64	.81
10	8	10	14	22	44	6	7	7	8	9
20	11	16	24	39	71	7	8	10	11	13
30	15	22	33	53	87	9	10	12	14	17
40	18	27	42	65	94	10	12	14	17	21
50	22	32	50	75	98	11	14	17	21	25
60	25	38	57	82	99	12	15	20	24	29
70	28	43	63	87	100	13	17	22	27	33
80	31	47	69	91	100	15	20	24	30	36
90	34	52	74	94	100	16	21	27	33	40
100	37	56	79	96	100	17	23	29	36	44

II. $\delta = .20$: Sophisticated Research

N	Within-Subjects Reliability					Independent Groups Reliability				
	.25	.36	.49	.64	.81	.25	.36	.49	.64	.81
10	6	6	7	9	15	5	5	6	6	6
20	7	8	10	13	26	6	6	6	6	7
30	7	9	12	18	36	6	6	7	7	8
40	8	10	14	23	45	6	7	7	8	9
50	9	12	17	27	54	6	7	8	9	10
60	10	13	20	31	61	7	8	8	10	11
70	10	14	22	35	68	7	8	9	10	12
80	11	16	24	39	74	7	8	10	11	13
90	12	17	26	43	78	8	9	10	12	14
100	13	19	29	47	82	8	9	11	13	15

NOTE: N is sample size, the effect size is δ, and the power is given as the percent of times the null hypothesis would be rejected.

sample size of 100, the relative power has dropped correspondingly to $100/44 = 2.27$, which is only a 2 to 1 advantage.

For more sophisticated research, the effect size is usually a contrast between versions of a treatment rather than the contrast of treatment versus control. Thus, effect sizes are much smaller. The bottom part of Table 8.1 illustrates sophisticated research; the effect size is $\delta = .20$. For $\delta = .20$, sample sizes up to $N = 100$, and reliability up to .81, the within-subjects design does not reach perfect power. Thus, in the table corresponding to the smaller effect size of sophisticated research, there is no ceiling effect for the within-subjects design, and it retains a massive relative advantage in all cells.

Designs Matched for Number of Measurements or Scores

Consider then the choice between two designs with the same number of scores. In the independent groups design, the N subjects are randomly divided into two half-samples, with subjects in one sample observed in one condition and subjects in the other sample observed in the other condition. There will be $N/2 + N/2 = N$ scores measured. In the within-subjects design, there will be only $N/2$ subjects, each of whom is observed in both conditions. There will be $2(N/2) = N$ scores measured. Thus, if measurement is expensive, then resource matching will match on number of scores rather than on number of subjects. Consider the power of the t test in each design.

First, we note that there will be a nontrivial difference in the degrees of freedom: $df = (N/2 - 1)$ for the within-subject design and $N - 2$ for the independent groups design. The ratio of degrees of freedom for independent groups design over the within-subjects design is

$$df_i \,/\, df_w = (N - 2) / (\{N/2\} - 1) = 2(N - 2) / (N - 2) = 2.$$

That is, the independent groups design has a 2 to 1 advantage in degrees of freedom. Note, however, that it is the square root of sample size that counts, and, hence, the relative advantage is the square root of 2, a 41% advantage in degrees of freedom. Furthermore, the number of degrees of freedom governs the extent of sampling error in the denominator of the t test. But we will see that the relative sampling error in the numerator is much greater.

If there were no treatment effect, then the only possible statistical error would be a Type I error. In both designs, the t statistic and t tables are designed so that the probability of a Type I error is .05. Thus, if the null hypothesis were true, then it would not matter which design is chosen.

Assume then that there is a treatment effect. Define the size by

$$\delta = E\,(TG)\,/\,\sigma_T = [\,E\,(T_2) - E\,(T_1)\,]\,/\,\sigma_T$$

where T stands for the actual dependent variable, i.e., the dependent variables scores that would have been observed had there been no error of measurement. For either design, the t test has a noncentral t distribution. Thus, it can be written

$$t = (\mu + z)\,/\,c$$

where z has a standard normal distribution, c is the square root of a chi-square divided by its degrees of freedom, z and c are independent, and μ is the systematic impact of the treatment effect.

The parameter μ differs between designs. In either design, we can write

$$\mu = \delta\,\sqrt{N\,r_{YY}\,/\,4\,b}$$

where b, the divisor under the radical, differs between the designs.

For the within-subjects design, we have

$$b = 1 - r_{YY}$$

and, hence,

$$\mu_w = \delta\,\sqrt{[\,Nr_{YY}/4\,\{1 - r_{YY}\}\,]}\,.$$

For the independent groups design, we have

$$b = 1$$

and, hence,

$$\mu_1 = \delta\,\sqrt{[\,Nr_{YY}/4\,]}\,.$$

The relative size of the parameters is the ratio

$$\mu_w\,/\,\mu_i = \sqrt{[\,1/(1 - r_{YY})\,]}\,.$$

The higher the reliability, the greater the relative advantage of the within-subjects design. As measurement nears perfection, the ratio nears infinity.

This reflects the fact that if there is no interaction and no error of measurement, the within-subjects design always has perfect power (an infinite value of t). The lower the reliability, the lower the relative advantage. As the reliability approaches zero, the relative advantage vanishes. This reflects the fact that as the level scores approach perfect unreliability, the gain scores still represent exactly the same amount of data as the independent groups scores because there are the same number of measurements in each design.

If the designs are matched for the number of scores, the advantage lies in opposite directions for the power parameter and for the degrees of freedom. The 2 to 1 advantage in degrees of freedom means that there is less sampling error in the denominator for the independent groups design than for the within-subjects design. The within-subjects advantage in the power parameter means that there will be less sampling error in the numerator of the within-subjects design than in the independent groups design. The question is: Which has the greater impact, sampling error in the numerator or in the denominator? The power tables in Table 8.2 show that the numerator is more important.

A power comparison is presented in Table 8.2. In Part I of the table, the effect size is always the same: $\delta = .40$. This is the typical effect size of major textbook examples (Cooper, 1984). Power is tabulated for varying values of number of measurements and reliability r_{YY}. Since 5 levels of reliability are shown, there are 5 columns for each design. Counting sample size as column 1, there are 11 columns in Table 8.2. The 5 columns for the within-subjects design are columns 2-6, while the 5 columns for the independent groups design are columns 7-11. Corresponding columns represent the same level of measurement error.

Consider the row for 100 measurements. As the reliability rises from .25 (the average reliability of an isolated response) to .81 (the reliability of professionally developed tests), the power of the independent groups design rises from 17% to 44%. That is, the error rate for the independent groups significance test drops from 83% to 56%. For the within-subjects design, the corresponding power values rise from 22% to 98%. That is, the error rate drops from 78% to 2%. Note that the power is always higher for the within-subjects design.

Consider the two columns for reliability $r_{YY} = .81$. The smaller the number of measurements, the greater the relative power advantage for the within-subjects design. At 10 measurements, the relative power is $25/9 = 2.78$; the within-subjects design is nearly 3 times more likely to detect the treatment effect than is the independent groups design. When the number of measurements reaches $N = 100$, the relative power is $98/44 = 2.28$ or still better than 2 to 1. Because the within-subjects design does not reach

Table 8.2 The Power of the Within-Subjects and Independent Groups Designs for Two Effect Sizes When the Number of Measurements Is the Same in Both Designs

I. $\delta = .40$: Textbook Examples

No. Msmts	Within-Subjects Reliability					Independent Groups Reliability				
	.25	.36	.49	.64	.81	.25	.36	.49	.64	.81
10	7	8	10	14	25	6	7	7	8	9
20	8	10	14	22	44	7	8	10	11	13
30	10	13	19	31	59	9	10	12	14	17
40	11	16	24	39	71	10	12	14	17	21
50	13	19	29	46	80	11	14	17	21	25
60	15	22	33	53	87	12	15	20	24	29
70	16	25	37	60	91	13	17	22	27	33
80	18	27	42	65	94	15	20	24	30	36
90	20	30	46	70	96	16	21	27	33	40
100	22	32	50	75	98	17	23	29	36	44

II. $\delta = .20$: Sophisticated Research

No. Msmts	Within-Subjects Reliability					Independent Groups Reliability				
	.25	.36	.49	.64	.81	.25	.36	.49	.64	.81
10	5	6	6	7	10	5	5	6	6	6
20	6	6	7	9	15	6	6	6	6	7
30	6	7	8	11	20	6	6	7	7	8
40	7	8	10	13	26	6	7	7	8	9
50	7	8	11	16	31	6	7	8	9	10
60	7	9	12	18	36	7	8	8	10	11
70	8	10	13	21	41	7	8	9	10	12
80	8	10	14	23	45	7	8	10	11	13
90	9	11	15	25	50	8	9	10	12	14
100	9	12	17	27	54	8	9	11	13	15

NOTE: The effect size is δ and the power is given as the percent of times the null hypothesis would be rejected.

the 100% ceiling in this table, the high relative advantage is largely maintained across the sample sizes displayed.

For more sophisticated research, the effect size is usually a contrast between different treatments rather than the contrast of treatment versus control. Thus, effect sizes are much smaller. The bottom part of Table 8.2 illustrates sophisticated research; the effect size is $\delta = .20$. For $\delta = .20$, sample sizes up to $N=100$, and reliability up to .81, the within subjects design does not reach perfect power. Thus in the table corresponding to the smaller effect size of sophisticated research, there is no ceiling effect for the within-subjects design, and it retains a relative power advantage in all cells.

For every cell in Table 8.2, the power is at least as large for the within-subjects design as for the independent-groups design. Thus, there is no case in this table where the advantage in degrees of freedom outweighs the advantage in power parameter.

Threats to Internal and External Validity

There are many who reject the within-subjects design before even considering issues such as the low power of the independent-groups design. This rejection is philosophical in nature and stems primarily from a misreading of the deservedly famous monograph by Campbell and Stanley (1963). In Table 1 of that monograph, they listed "sources of invalidity" for various designs, including seven sources for the within-subjects design. However, at the bottom of the table is the reminder that these are only POTENTIAL threats to validity and that they may not apply to any given study. Many have dropped the adjective "potential" in the phrase "potential threats to validity" and, thus, state that the within-subjects design has "threats to validity." Worse yet, some researchers have lost the word "threat" and interpret Campbell and Stanley as having said that the within-subjects design is "fundamentally flawed because it lacks internal and external validity." Nothing could be farther from what Campbell and Stanley wrote, and they themselves said so several times. Yet the topic of within-subjects designs can hardly come up in a group without someone citing Campbell and Stanley as stating that the within-subjects design is riddled with uncontrolled sources of internal and external invalidity.

Campbell and Stanley (1963) view potential threats to validity as source ideas of possible rival theories to explain an observed effect. But they stipulate that one must argue for the rival hypothesis—the claim that a threat was realized—with carefully documented concrete evidence of the same sort that is used for the original hypothesis. For example, on page 7 they say, "To become a *plausible* rival hypothesis, such an event should have occurred to most of the students in the group under study . . ." Note that they are interested only in *plausible* threats, not in vague hypothetical possibilities, and that they cast their argument in terms of a specific concrete event, not as an abstract argument such as "the within subject design is flawed by failure to control for history."

The purpose of this section is not to criticize Campbell and Stanley, but to remind researchers of what Campbell and Stanley actually said. Their intention was this: If you are planning to do a within-subjects design, check these potential problems to see if any apply to that study. If so, then change the study procedures to eliminate that problem (or abandon the study design). The frequent false conclusion is that their checklist is a statement of problems that apply to every within-subjects design. We will attempt to dispel these false beliefs by presenting a series of examples. On the one hand, we will take a typical example of a pre-post study in organizational psychology and show that not one of the Campbell and Stanley threats actually exists for that study. On the other hand, for each threat we will cite a study for which that threat would exist. Thus, we will be true to the actual content of Campbell and Stanley: a checklist of POSSIBLE problems, not a list of charges in an indictment of the design.

Some would argue that showing that a given example is free of the threats listed by Campbell and Stanley does not save the within-subjects design. They would say that only a rare study would be free of flaws and, thus, it is a waste of time to consider such a design in the first place. It is true that the logical conclusions that can be drawn from an example are limited. Not all within-subjects studies are ruled out by the Campbell and Stanley list. However, we believe that the probability implication in this argument is wrong. In our experience, the probability of each threat on the Campbell and Stanley list is actually very low. In fact we have rarely seen a study in which the within-subjects design could not be used. Our combined experience covers 45 years of scientific work in the field. So we do not believe that our opinion is based on limited experience.

Campbell and Stanley (1963, p. 8) list the following potential threats to the internal validity of the within-subjects design: history, maturation, testing, instrumentation, regression (they listed a question mark on this one), and interactions of these factors. They list the following potential threats to the external validity of the within-subjects design: interaction of testing and treatment, interaction of selection and treatment, and reactive arrangements (with a question mark). We will show by example that a within-subjects design could indeed suffer from a flaw of each kind. However, we will also show by example that there can be a study that suffers from none of these potential problems. The Campbell and Stanley list is intended to be a list of potential problems to consider, not a list of problems to assume.

The part of the psychological literature in which the within-subjects design is most commonly used is field studies of interventions, i.e., program evaluation. In most such studies, the subjects are adults who understand the program's objectives and who know that they are part of an intervention. However, it is also true that the dependent variable in most interventions is a behavior or event that is very difficult to change without intervention. These aspects of the study usually rule out all of the Campbell and Stanley potential threats to validity.

Consider a management training program. Supervisors are to be given a training experience that explains how to apply certain skills, such as active listening to supervisor problems. The dependent variable is the performance rating of the supervisor by the manager who is the supervisor's immediate superior. The pre-post design compares performance ratings before and after the training experience.

History

The experimenter interprets the change in the dependent variable as being caused by the intervention. But perhaps there was some concurrent event outside the scope of the study that actually caused the improvement. For example, suppose that we introduce goal setting to a group of small-car salesmen. During the test interval there is a massive oil price increase in the Middle East that drives buyers from the large cars they had bought before to smaller cars. An increase in sales could be due to the oil price increase rather than to the goal setting intervention. Thus, there could be a study in which history made the interpretation of the study result false.

But how often are there natural events that produce large change in important dependent variables? How often would such an event be overlooked by a seasoned scientific researcher working in an area that he knows well? Consider the skill training study. There is a long history of supervisor behavior study, which has found that even with intervention it is difficult to produce change in supervisor social behavior. What real event could change these supervisors that the experimenter would not know?

Maturation

Perhaps the change observed in the study could be due to some internal process in the subject that would have taken place whether the intervention was done or not. Consider a psychologist studying psychomotor skill training in children. He argues that the change he observed between ages five and six was due to the special training program that he administered. But psychomotor systems between the ages of five and six improve because of brain maturation. In this study, we would need some additional evidence to show that the increase in skill was not due to maturation rather than training.

But how often would a psychologist overlook the process of maturation? For most dependent variables, there is ample evidence showing that the variable changes little for adults unless there is some major event that causes a reorganization of that behavior domain. Consider the social skill training example. Most people change their basic social behavior little over the adult years. Thus, we know before doing the study that there is no maturation process for the behavior in question.

Testing

Perhaps the observed change could be due to the pretest rather than to the intervention. For example, suppose we believe that teaching mathematical reasoning will improve a person's problem-solving skills. We create a problem-solving test to assess skill. We see if the test score improves from before the reasoning module to after the reasoning module. The problem is memory. If people remember how they solved the problem the first time, they can use that same method of solution much more rapidly. So it is possible that the observed improvement was due to memory for the specific problems rather than due to the use of the skills taught. Thus, it is possible for the results of a study to be due to testing rather than to the intervention.

But how often does a psychologist have so little understanding of the dependent variable being used that he would overlook practice effects? In some social psychology experiments, subjects are deceived or misled as to the purpose of the study and it is critical to the study that they not figure out that purpose. In such cases, the testing is a clue to the purpose and, hence, produces undesired effects. But in field studies, the subject is usually told the purpose of the intervention and, hence, there is no secret to be revealed. Thus, testing rarely alerts the subject to anything not already known and provides no opportunity for practice.

Consider the social skill training example. The supervisors in the study have had performance ratings all of their working lives. Why should the performance rating before the training program change their fundamental social behavior? Testing is not a plausible rival theory for change in that study.

Instrumentation

Perhaps the change in a value is due to a change in the measuring instrument. If a spring is used to weigh a very heavy object, it will not spring all the way back to its original position. Consider studies in which the dependent variable is obtained from the subjective judgment of an observer. The observer may be tired or may have different standards after the study than he or she had before the study. For example, suppose that, unlike in our example, both the supervisor and his manager are put through the same training experience. Suppose the supervisor doesn't change, but the manger now has new standards for proper procedure. The manager evaluates the unchanged supervisor behavior negatively against the new standards and gives lower ratings after the training. So it is possible that a change in the instrument could produce a change in value, which is falsely attributed to the intervention.

In many studies, the instrument is not a subjective observer. In such studies, it is not likely that the instrument will change. If the dependent variable is a judgment, is it likely that a scientist familiar with the research area would overlook the possibility of change in the observer? In most studies with human observers, researchers go to a great deal of trouble to train the observers. One typical criterion for training is that the observer learn to give consistent responses to equivalent stimuli. Thus, even with subjective judgment, change in the instrument is rarely a plausible hypothesis.

Consider our social skill training study example. Managers usually have long experience in making performance ratings. They are not likely to change their standards because of a study in which they do not participate. In fact, studies have shown that it is difficult to change performance ratings even with extensive training on the rating process. Thus, in our example, change in the instrument is not a threat to validity.

Regression to the Mean

Suppose that people are preselected for the study. Perhaps the preselection biases the pretest scores and causes a false change effect when unbiased scores are obtained after the study. One such change is regression to the mean due to error of measurement. Consider an example from therapy to reduce anxiety about public-speaking. The study begins by giving a public speaking anxiety test to a large class of subjects. The top 20 of 100 students are put into a special lab that uses stimulus desensitization to reduce the anxiety. At the end of the class period, the same anxiety instrument is used to assess change. The problem is this: No instrument is without error of measurement. In particular, the anxiety test has less than perfect reliability. To pick out unusually high scores is to select people for positive errors of measurement. Thus, the selected group will not have an average error of zero on the pretest; the average error will be positive. Suppose there is no change in anxiety produced by the desensitization. After the study, each subject will have the same true score on anxiety. However, the new measurement will produce new errors of measurement. For each subject, the new error of measurement is as likely to be negative as positive. Thus for the group of subjects, the average posttest error of measurement is zero. The change in average error of measurement from positive to zero produces a negative change in mean score that could be falsely attributed to therapy. Thus, regression to the mean could cause a change to be falsely interpreted.

On the other hand, in most studies there is no preselection of subjects and, hence, no possibility of regression effects. If there is preselection, then there is an easy way to eliminate a possible regression effect: Use a double pretest. That is, use a first pretest for selection. Then use a second pretest to assess the preintervention level. The errors of measurement will be resampled on the second pretest, and, hence, the mean error will be zero on the second pretest, as on the posttest, thus eliminating the regression problem. Also, if the reliability of the dependent variable is known, and if the extent of selection is known, then it is possible to use a procedure similar to range restriction correction to correct the observed change for regression to the mean (Allen, Hunter, & Donohue, 1989), even without a double pretest.

Consider the social skills training study. All supervisors are to be given the training. There is no preselection and, hence, no possibility of a regression effect.

Reactive Arrangements

Reactive arrangements are interventions in which some seemingly trivial aspect of the treatment procedure causes a change that is not anticipated in the interpretation of the treatment as such. There are two possibilities: reactive measurement and reactive procedures.

Consider an example of potential reactive measurement. Suppose we believe that a certain dramatic movie (*Guess Who's Coming to Dinner?*) will produce altruistic thoughts on racial issues. We use a sentence completion test to assess racial imagery. A typical item is "Black people are. . . ." We see if the person expresses more racial altruism after the movie than before the movie. The problem is this: What will the person think when she (1) is given a test that taps attitudes towards blacks, and

(2) is then presented with a movie about prejudice? It may be that the person would then try to do a self-evaluation in the form of, "I'm not that prejudiced, am I?" The person would search memory for instances of nonprejudiced behavior. These biased memories might then form the substance of the apparently altruistic thoughts that register in the posttest. This would then lead the experimenter to a false conclusion.

Consider an example of reactive procedure. As part of a quality circles experiment, randomly selected workers are taken to a room off the factory floor. They might wonder what this is for and might form paranoid theories about assessment for labor union sympathies or dislike of their supervisor, or whatever. They might then be preset to have a negative reaction to the quality circles presentation. Thus, reactive procedure could produce a spurious change.

Consider the question of reactive measurement. Most field studies in political, organizational, or clinical psychology use measurements of important dependent variables, variables that are well known to the experimenters and are reasonably well understood by the participants. Thus, reactive measurement is rare in these fields.

Consider the question of reactive procedures. In laboratory experiments that depend critically on deception, this is a serious problem. But in most field studies the subjects are told the objectives of the study, and the nature of the measurements is obviously related to those objectives. Thus, the measurement cannot reveal secrets and cannot produce bizarre subject theories as to the experimenter's unknown objectives. That is, reactive procedures are rare in most areas of psychological research.

Consider the social skill training example. The subjects are told that they will be participating in a training exercise. They are told that the objective is to improve their skills as supervisors. The training exercise tells them what they are supposed to do, and successful exercises tell them why. Thus, both reactive measurement and reactive procedures are unlikely or impossible.

Interaction Between Testing and Treatment

What Campbell and Stanley call "interaction between testing and treatment" has been called "reactive measurement" here. This was covered in the preceding paragraphs on "reactive arrangements."

Interaction Between Selection and Treatment

The problem discussed by Campbell and Stanley (1963) under the rubric "interaction between selection and treatment" is not a problem of

404   METHODS OF META-ANALYSIS

false interpretation of the results of the study itself. That is, it is not a threat to "internal validity." Rather, they are worried about a generalization from the results of the study to some other context that might turn out to be wrong, i.e., a threat to "external validity." The interaction in question represents the assumption that the effect of a treatment might differ from one setting to the next. If there is such variation, then an experimenter who generalizes from one setting to another may make a false inference. However, if there is variation in results across settings, then the independent groups design will NOT work any better than the within-subjects design. If people in a given setting are randomly assigned to control and experimental groups, the mean difference will be the same as if a pre-post study had been done in that same setting. Thus, variation in treatment effects across settings creates the same logical problem for single setting studies — usually the only feasible study — for between-subjects designs as for within-subjects designs.

Meta-analysis is essential if there is variation in results across studies. That variation would not show in a single study. However the variation can be detected and identified in a meta-analysis (Hunter, Hamilton, & Allen, in press). However, detailed consideration of this issue shows that identification of the interaction is often critically dependent on the statistical power of single studies. For this reason, consideration of meta-analysis shows that within-subjects designs are to be preferred when feasible.

Bias in Observed d Values

Hedges (1981, 1982a) and Rosenthal and Rubin (1982a) have shown that there is a slight positive bias in the d value statistic presented in Chapters 6 and 7. That is, the computed d value is slightly too large. The size of this bias depends on δ (the population value) and N (the sample size). This bias is typically small enough to be ignored. For example, if $\delta = .70$ and $N = 80$, the bias is .007. Rounded to two places, this would be .01, a bias of no practical or theoretical significance. (Also, if the d value is converted to a correlation using the formulas given in Chapter 7, the bias in the correlation will be only about half as large.) The bias is large enough to be of concern only when the sample size is quite small. Green and Hall (1984) state that the bias can be ignored unless the sample size for a study is 10 or less. In the example above, if N were 20 instead of 80, computed d value would average approximately .03 too large, that is, about a 4% upward bias. Both Hedges (1981) and Rosenthal and Rubin (1982a) have presented formulas that provide approximate corrections for this bias. If study sample sizes are very small, these corrections should be used.

Otherwise, this tiny bias can safely be ignored. The articles presenting these corrections are an example of a phenomenon discussed in the Preface: highly detailed statistical elaborations on technical points that have limited relevance for real applications of meta-analysis. Finally, we note that this upward bias is small in comparison to the ever present downward bias created by measurement error in the dependent variable. For example, if the reliability of the measure of the dependent variable in our example were .75, then the average observed *d* value would be $(.75)^{1/2} (70) = .61$; that is, if no correction were made for measurement error (often the case in published meta-analyses), the negative bias would be .09. This is 9 times greater than the upward bias of .01 identified by Hedges (1981) and Rosenthal and Rubin (1982a) when $N = 80$, and 3 times larger than when $N = 20$. This places the upward bias in *d* values in its proper perspective.

Random Versus Fixed Effects Models

Hedges and Olkin (1985) devote separate chapters to what they term "random effects models" versus "fixed effects models" for meta-analysis. They state that Glass's methods of meta-analysis use fixed effects models while the Schmidt and Hunter methods use random effects models. This contention is actually erroneous on both counts. The Glass approach to effect size variance is too crude to allow application of either model, while applications of our methods have usually used the "fixed effects" model described in Hedges and Olkin (1985). The problem in Hedges and Olkin's (1985) reasoning stems from an error in their presentation of the "fixed effects model" in their Chapter 7: Their allegedly "fixed effects model" is actually a "mixed model" by analogy with analysis of variance. Their presentation of the random versus fixed effect distinction is confused by the fact that they associate the distinction with meta-analysis "models," whereas the distinction is actually meaningful only as a distinction between potential moderator variables.

Consider the fixed versus random effects distinction in analysis of variance. If all desired levels of a variable are present in the design, the variable is called a "fixed effect factor." However, if only a sample of the levels is present in the study, then the variable is called a "random effects factor." For example, consider an attitude change study that is designed to answer the question, "Will profanity make a message more persuasive?" An effective attitude change message is constructed without use of profanity. This message is given to the control group. Then a few profane words are added at appropriate points in the control message, and the profane message is given to the experimental group. The comparison of mean change in the control and experimental groups provides an estimation of the treatment effect of profanity. Suppose, in addition we hypothesize that men and women will react differently to the profanity. That is, we hypothesize that sex of subject will be a moderator variable for the profanity treatment effect. If we introduce sex as a variable into a primary research study, then both levels — men and women — will be present in the study. Sex would thus be a "fixed effect factor." The test for whether sex is a moderator variable would be the test of the profanity by sex interaction. On the other hand, suppose that we hypothesize that content will be a moderator variable. For example, we might believe that profanity would be acceptable in messages about topics such as sports or politics, while profanity would not be acceptable in messages about topics such as religion. Since there is an almost infinite variety of topics for attitude change messages, content as "topic" cannot be a "fixed effect factor." If two or more topics are used in the study, we might regard them as a sample of topics from the topic universe. In this case, content would be a "random effects factor." Note that this distinction in analysis of variance is well known to be problematic. For example, suppose we use two messages: one about sports and one about religion. Then, content has been transformed from a "random effects factor" with many levels into a "fixed effects factor" with two levels, i.e., "acceptable content" versus "unacceptable content."

The same distinction can be made between potential moderator variables in a meta-analysis. Suppose a set of primary studies had been done on the profanity issue and suppose that none of the primary studies had considered the question of sex or topic as potential interactive variables. Sex as a potential moderator variable could be considered in the meta-analysis by classifying studies as "All male subjects" versus "All females subjects" versus "Mixed set studies." Since studies of all three types would normally be present, the sex variable would be a "fixed effect potential moderator variable." On the other hand, consider content as a potential moderator variable. If topics can be classified into "Profanity acceptable" versus "Profanity unacceptable," then topic is also a fixed effect potential moderator variable. However, if topics are not classified, then the topics in the observed studies are only a sample of topics, and content would then be a random effects potential moderator variable.

The Hedges and Olkin (1985) presentation of this topic is confused by their implicit use of "study" as a random effects potential moderator variable. That is, in the chapter on "random effects models" (Chapter 9), they simply consider one set of "studies" with no further classification. Since the number of levels of "study" is essentially infinite, they regard the studies as a random sample from a study domain. Thus, "study" is a random effects potential moderator variable. The homogeneity test they recommend (the standard chi-square test — our test for the hypothesis that all variation is due solely to sampling error) has the null hypothesis that the effect size is the same in all studies. If this null hypothesis is true, then the potential moderator variable "study" is *not* a moderator variable is fact. Consider the null hypothesis for the homogeneity test for a fixed effect potential moderator. That null hypothesis also assumes that the potential moderator is in fact *not* an actual moderator variable. That is, the null hypothesis for the Hedges and Olkin homogeneity tests does not distinguish between random and fixed effect potential moderators. Thus, it is no surprise that the significance tests for the two "models" are identical. Since Hedges and Olkin do not go beyond homogeneity tests in their treatment of second-order sampling error, the distinction between fixed and random effects potential moderator variables is actually irrelevant to their book.

The treatment of the "fixed effect model" in Hedges and Olkin is confused. They do not consider one set of studies. Instead, they consider "classes" of studies. That is, they begin with the studies categorized into subsets using some potential moderator variable. They never introduce the question of whether all categories are present or not and, hence, do not correctly consider the question of whether the potential moderator variable "classes" is a random or fixed effect potential moderator variable. Instead they implicitly assume that all classes are present. That *implicit* assumption makes the potential moderator variable a fixed effect potential moderator variable.

Note, however, that they picture the set of studies as classes of studies. That is, they still have "study" as a potential moderator variable. However, studies are nested within classes. That is, the levels of "study" are nested within the levels of "classes." Thus, they are not considering a simple fixed model. Rather their "fixed effect model" is analogous to a *two*-factor model in which the random effect variable "study" is nested under the fixed effect variable "classes." That is, what they call a "fixed effect model" is actually analogous to a "mixed model" in analysis of variance in which a random factor is hierarchically nested within a fixed factor.

Hedges and Olkin (1985) implicitly assume that if the identified potential moderator variable is the only moderator variable, then each class of studies will be homogeneous in treatment effect. However, consider the present example. If sex is the only actual moderator variable, then the "All male" studies would be homogeneous and the "All female" studies would be homogeneous. However, the "mixed set" studies would NOT be homogeneous. Instead, the effect size in each study would depend on the proportion of men and women in each study. As this proportion varied between 100% and 0, the effect size would vary proportionately between the effect size for men and the effect size for women.

Use of Multiple Regression in Moderator Analysis

Glass (1977) was the first to advocate use of ordinary least squares multiple regression to identify moderator variables in meta-analysis. The procedure is conceptually very simple: The d values from a set of studies are regressed on the coded study characteristics, and those study characteristics with statistically significant regression weights are considered to be moderators of the effect size. This procedure has been used in meta-analyses of psychotherapy outcome studies (Smith & Glass, 1977) and the effects of class size (Smith & Glass, 1980), among other meta-analyses. Hedges and Olkin (1985, pp. 11-12, 167-169) have argued against this procedure on grounds that the assumption of homogeneity of observation sampling error variances is usually not met in meta-analysis data sets. The (error) variance of each "observation" (i.e., each d value) depends on the sample size on which it is based. If these sample sizes vary substantially, as they often do, then different effect size estimates will have very different error variances. Heterogeneity of variances can affect the validity of significance tests; actual alpha levels may be larger than nominal levels (e.g., .15 versus the nominal .05). Hedges and Olkin (1985, Chapter 8) present a weighted least squares regression procedure that circumvents this problem. However, when Hedges and Stock (1983) used this method to reanalyze the Glass and Smith (1979) studies on class size, they obtained results that were quite similar to the original results. Thus, the problem identified by Hedges and Olkin (1985) may not be serious. The general finding has been that most statistical tests are robust with respect to violations of the assumption of homogeneity of variance (e.g., see Glass, Peckham, & Sanders 1972). There is another consideration that is important here: As discussed in Chapters 2, 3, 7, and 11, statistical significance tests do not and should not play an important role in meta-analysis. Overreliance on significance tests has historically been the cause of many of the problems of inappropriate data interpretation that meta-analysis seeks to solve. But perhaps the most important fact here is this: The problem of potential distortion of alpha levels pointed out by Hedges and Olkin (1985, Chapter 8) pales in comparison to other, more serious problems that plague the use of multiple regression to identify moderators: capitalization on chance and low statistical power. As described graphically in Chapter 2, these latter problems can completely destroy the interpretability of the results of such moderator analyses. By comparison, the violation of the assumption of homogeneity of sampling error variances is almost academic. Finally, we note that, although this discussion appears in a chapter devoted to d values, it applies equally to meta-analyses based on correlations.

PART IV

General Issues in Meta-Analysis

9 Second-Order Sampling Error and Related Issues

This chapter is organized in a particular way. The first three sections are general conceptual overviews, while the remainder of the chapter is more technical and presents formulas and their derivations. The first two sections of the chapter present the general ideas related to second-order sampling error and statistical power in meta-analysis, respectively. The third section presents an overview of second-order meta-analysis. The following more technical section distinguishes between two types of second-order uncertainty in meta-analysis estimates of means and standard deviations, and presents formulas for confidence intervals for meta-analysis means. The next section explores the implications of second-order uncertainty in meta-analysis results for the detection of moderator variables. This section shows that statistical power is much higher in meta-analysis for detecting moderator variables that are predicted in advance from theory than for moderator variables that are not specified a priori. The latter must be tested using the chi-square test for homogeneity, which we show has low statistical power in commonly occurring situations.

Second-Order Sampling Error: General Principles

The outcome of any meta-analysis based on a small number of studies depends to some extent on which studies randomly happen to be available; that is, the outcome depends in part on study properties that vary randomly across studies. This is true even if the studies analyzed are all that exist at that moment. This phenomenon is called "second-order sampling error." It affects meta-analytic estimates of standard deviations more than it affects estimates of means. (This is also the case with ordinary, or first-order, sampling error and ordinary statistics: ordinary sampling error affects standard deviations more than means.)

Consider a hypothetical example. Suppose there were only ten studies available estimating the relation between trait A and job performance. Even if the mean sample size per study were only 68 (the median for

411

published validity studies reviewed by Lent, Auerbach, and Levin, 1971a, 1971b), the mean validity would be based on $N = 680$ and would be reasonably stable. The observed variance across studies would be based on only ten studies, however, and this variance, which we compare to the amount of variance expected from sampling error, would be based on only ten data points. Now suppose sampling error were in fact the only factor operating to produce between-study variance in observed correlations (validities). Then, if we randomly happened to have one or two studies with large positive sampling errors, the observed variance across studies would likely be larger than the predicted variance, and we might falsely wind up concluding, for example, that sampling error accounts for only 50% of the observed variance of validities across studies. On the other hand, if the observed validity coefficients of, say, five or six of the studies randomly happened to be very close to the expected value (population mean), then the observed variance across studies would likely be very small and would underestimate the amount of variance one would typically (or on the average) observe across ten such randomly drawn studies (from the population of such hypothetical studies that could be conducted). In fact, the observed variance might be smaller than the variance predicted from sampling error. The computed percent variance accounted for by sampling error would then be some figure greater than 100%, for example 150%. Of course, in this case, the correct conclusion would be reached: All of the observed variance could be accounted for by sampling error. But some people have been troubled by such outcomes. They are taken aback by results indicating that sampling error can account for more variance than is actually observed. Sometimes they are led to question the validity of the formula for sampling error variance (for example, see Thomas, 1988, and the reply by Osburn & Callender, 1989). This formula correctly predicts the amount of variance sampling error will produce on the average. However, sampling error randomly produces more than this sometimes and less at other times. The larger the number of studies (other things equal), the smaller the deviations of observed from expected variance. If the number of studies is small, however, these deviations can be quite large *on a percentage basis* (although *absolute* deviations are usually small, even in such cases).

Negative estimates of variances occur using other methods of statistical estimation. In one-way analysis of variance (ANOVA), for example, the variance of sample means is the sum of two components: the variance of population means and the sampling error variance. This is directly analogous to the meta-analytic breakdown of the observed variance of sample correlations across studies into the variance of population correlations (the real variance) and the sampling error variance (the false or spurious variance). In estimating the variance of population means in ANOVA, the first step is to subtract the within-group mean square from the between-group mean square. This difference can be, and sometimes is, negative, as a result of sampling error. Consider a case in which the null hypothesis is true; the population means are then all equal and the variance of population means is zero. The variance of observed means (i.e., sample means) is then determined entirely by sampling error. This observed between-group variance will vary randomly from one study to another. About half the time the within-group mean square will be larger than the between-group mean square, while half the time the within-group mean square will be smaller. That is, if the variance of population means is zero, then in half of the observed samples the estimated variance of population means will be negative. This is exactly the same as the situation in meta-analysis if all the population correlations are equal: The estimated variance will lie just above zero half the time and will lie just below zero half the time. The key here is to note that the variance of population correlations is estimated by subtraction: The known error variance is subtracted from the variance of sample correlations, which estimates the variance of sample correlations across a population of studies. Since the number of studies is never infinite, the observed variance of sample correlations will depart by sampling error from the expected value. Thus, when the variance of population correlations is zero, the difference will be negative half the time.

Another example is the estimation of variance components in generalizability theory. Cronbach and his colleagues (Cronbach, Gleser, Nanda, & Rajaratnam, 1972) proposed generalizability theory as a liberalization of classical reliability theory, and it is now widely used to assess the reliability of measuring instruments in situations where the techniques of classical reliability theory are considered inadequate. Generalizability theory is based on the well-known ANOVA model and requires estimated variance components for its application. One or more of the estimated variance components may be negative, as noted by Cronbach et al. (1972, pp. 57-58) and Brennan (1983, pp. 47-48) even though by definition population variance components are nonnegative. The same phenomenon was also noted by Leone and Nelson (1966). Cronbach et al. (1972) recommended substituting zero for the negative variance, and Brennan (1983) agreed with this recommendation.

Negative estimated variances are not uncommon in statistical estimation. The occurrence of negative estimates of variances in empirical research does not call into question a statistical theory such as the ANOVA or a psychometric theory such as meta-analysis or validity generalization. As described above, existing statistical sampling theory provides a sound rationale for observed negative estimates of variances in meta-analysis when the actual variance of true validities is zero or close to zero.

Statistical Power to Detect Moderators in Meta-Analysis: General Principles

The question of second-order sampling error is related to the question of statistical power in meta-analyses. The issue of statistical power arises both with respect to the mean and the variance in meta-analyses. With respect to the mean, the statistical power of a meta-analysis is the probability that the meta-analysis will detect the $\bar{r}$ (or $\bar{d}$) as significant when $\bar{\rho} > 0$ (or $\bar{\delta} > 0$), that is, when the mean population correlation or delta is in fact greater than zero. The statistical power of meta-analysis with respect to the mean is discussed later in this chapter. When the moderator variable is not specified in advance by theory, the statistical power of a meta-analysis with respect to the variance is the probability that it will detect variation in ρ or δ values across studies when such variation does in fact exist. One minus this probability is the probability of a Type II error: concluding that all the variance across studies is due to artifacts when in fact some of it is real. When all variance is indeed artifactually caused, there is no possibility of a Type II error, and there can be no statistical power question. Just as second-order sampling error becomes more of a problem as the number of studies becomes smaller, statistical power also becomes lower. A number of statistical tools have been used make the decision about whether any of the observed variance is real. In our meta-analytic research on test validities, we have used the 75% rule: If 75% or more of the variance is due to artifacts, we conclude that all of it is, on grounds that the remaining 25% is likely to be due to artifacts not corrected for. Another method is the chi-square test discussed in Chapters 3 and 7 and later in the present chapter. Callender and Osburn (1981) have presented another method, one based on simulation. Extensive computer simulation studies have been conducted to estimate the statistical power of meta-analyses to detect variation in ρ using these decision rules (Osburn, Callender, Greener, & Ashworth, 1983; Sackett, Harris, & Orr, 1986; Spector & Levine, 1987). These estimates have been obtained for different combinations of (1) numbers of studies, (2) sample size of studies, (3) amount of "true" variation in ρ, (4) mean ρ values, and (5) levels of measurement error. The findings of the Sackett et al. (1986) study are probably the most relevant to meta-analysis in general. Sackett et al. found that, under all conditions studied, the 75% rule had statistical power greater than (or equal to) the other methods (although it also showed a higher Type I error rate: concluding there was a moderator when there was not). This advantage in statistical pcwer was relatively the greatest when the number of studies was small (4, 8, 16, 32, or 64) and the sample size of each study was small (50 or 100). However, when the assumed population variance to be detected (s_ρ^2) was small, and both the number of studies and the sample size of the studies were small, all methods had relatively low statistical power. For example, if there were four studies ($N = 50$ each) with $\rho = .25$ and four ($N = 50$ each also) with $\rho = .35$ (corresponding to $s_\rho^2 = .01$), and if $r_{xx} = r_{yy} = .80$ in all studies, statistical power was .34 for the 75% rule (and only .08 for the other methods). However, a total sample size of 8(50) = 400 is very small, and eight is a small number of studies for a meta-analysis. Also, a difference of .10 is very small. If the difference in this example is raised to .30, power rises to .75. This difference between ρs is more representative of the moderators that it would be theoretically and practically important to study. Nevertheless, it is true that individual meta-analyses will have less than optimal statistical power in some cases.

The above discussion applies to "omnibus" tests for moderator variables — moderator variables that are not specified in advance by theories or hypotheses. In such cases, the existence of moderators must be detected by determining whether the variance of study effect sizes is larger than can be accounted for by the presence of variance-generating artifacts. The story is very different when the moderator hypotheses are specified in advance. In such cases, the studies in the meta-analysis can be subgrouped based on the moderator hypothesis (for example, studies done on blue versus white collar employees), and the means ($\bar{\delta}$ or $\bar{\rho}$) of the subgroup meta-analyses can be tested for statistically significant differences. As demonstrated later in this chapter, statistical power in meta-analysis is much higher for this approach to detecting moderators.

In most areas of research there should be sufficient development of theory to generate hypotheses about moderators. However, in one major meta-analytic research area — the generalizability of employment test validities — this has not been the case. It has not been possible to use the subgrouping approach to test the "situational specificity" hypothesis in personnel selection. To use this approach, the moderators must be specified. There must be a theory, or at least a hypothesis, that is specific enough to postulate that, for example, correlations will be larger for females than for males; or larger for "high-growth need" individuals than for "low-growth need" individuals; or larger in situations where supervisors are high in "consideration" than where supervisors are low. The situational specificity hypothesis does not meet this criterion; it postulates merely that there are unspecified subtle but important differences from job to job and setting to setting in what constitutes job performance, and that job analysts and other human observers are not proficient enough as information processors to detect these critical elusive differences (Albright, Glennon, & Smith, 1963, p. 18; Lawshe, 1948, p. 13). Since the operative moderators are actually unknown and unidentifiable, it is not possible to subgroup studies by hypothesized moderators. However, if one can show that all observed validity variance is due to artifacts, one has shown that no moderators can possibly be operating. This approach does not require that the postulated moderators be identified or even identifiable. Given that there is a broad and heterogenous range of situations represented in one's validity generalization meta-analysis, one can show that the postulated moderators do not exist, even without knowing what the moderators are. One would hope that situational specificity would be the first and only hypothesis of this nature to be tested using meta-analysis. We hope that theories and hypotheses tested in the future using meta-analysis will be far better specified and definite in the predictions they make. If so, they will allow use of the second approach to identifying moderators.

However, there is an unfortunate tradition in industrial-organizational psychology among some critics. Critics of particular theories or conclusions sometimes make statements like the following: "There are many factors that could affect outcomes. Supervisory style may have important effects; group membership, geographical location, type of industry, and many other variables would be expected to be moderators." Such "critiques" are usually not based on theoretical reasoning or empirical evidence. They are usually just vague speculations and, thus, are not scientifically useful. But they do occur, and since the number of hypothesized potential moderators is essentially unlimited, it will never be possible to test them all using the second procedure. However, the first procedure — the omnibus procedure we have used to test the situational specificity hypothesis — can be used to test all such moderators simultaneously, even those that have not (yet) been named by the critic. If the meta-analysis is based on a *large* group of studies that is heterogeneous across all potential moderators, then a finding that artifacts account for all between-study variance in correlations or effect sizes indicates that none of the postulated moderators are, in fact, moderators. Even where not all the variance is accounted for by artifacts, the remaining variance may often be small, demonstrating that even if some moderators might exist, their effect is far more limited in scope than implied by the critic. In fact, the results may often indicate that the moderators have at best only trivial effects. In this connection, it should always be remembered that the variance remaining after correction for artifacts indicates the *upper bound* of the effects of the moderators. This will almost always be true because there will almost always be some artifacts operating to create variance for which no corrections will be possible.

The facts of second-order sampling error and less than perfect statistical power in individual meta-analysis point up another reason for the importance of a principle we stated at the beginning of this book. The results of a meta-analysis should not be interpreted in isolation but rather in relation to a broader set of linked findings from other meta-analyses that form the foundation for theoretical explanations. Estimating a particular relationship is only the immediate objective of a meta-analysis; the ultimate objective is to contribute pieces of information that can be fitted into a wider developing mosaic of theory. But just as the results of a meta-analysis can contribute to this bigger picture, the bigger picture under development can contribute to the interpretation of the meta-analysis results. Results of "small" meta-analyses (those based on few and small N studies) that are inconsistent with the broader cumulative picture of knowledge thereby become suspect, and the credibility of those that are consistent is likewise enhanced. This is the universal pattern of reciprocal causation between data and theory in science.

Some have worried that inadequate statistical power in meta-analysis to detect moderators might be an almost insurmountable problem limiting scientific progress (even while admitting that better alternatives to meta-analysis do not appear to be available). Aside from the fact that this criticism applies only to the omnibus test for moderators (see above), the critical difficulty with this argument is that it focuses on single meta-analytic studies. Just as earlier researchers focused on the individual study, failing to realize that single studies cannot be interpreted in isolation, this position focuses on single meta-analyses — in particular, on the statistical power of single meta-analyses — not seeing that it is the overall pattern of findings from many meta-analyses that is important in revealing the underlying reality.

Consider an example. In personnel selection, the theory of situational specificity holds that the true (population) validity of any employment test varies substantially from one organization to another even for highly similar or identical jobs. This is the hypothesis that $S_\rho^2 > 0$. In meta-analysis (called validity generalization when used in personnel selection), this hypothesis is tested by determining whether artifacts such as sampling error account for the variation of observed validity coefficients across studies conducted in different organizations on similar jobs using measures of the same ability (e.g., arithmetic reasoning). In the initial validity generalization studies, the average percent of the observed validity variance accounted for by artifacts was less than 100%. But these meta-analyses were based on published and unpublished studies from a wide variety of sources and researchers, and we pointed out in all our studies that there were several sources of between-study variance that we could neither control for nor correct for (e.g., programmer errors, transcriptional errors). When all studies going into a validity generalization analysis are conducted by the same research team, strong efforts can be made to control these sources of errors. In two large-scale, nationwide consortium studies, such efforts were made (Dunnette et al., 1982; Peterson, 1982). In both cases, these studies found that, on the average, all variance across settings (i.e., companies) was accounted for by artifacts. We found the same to be true in data from studies conducted in 16 companies by Psychological Services, Inc. (Dye, 1982). Thus, our prediction that improved control of sources of error variance would show that all between-study variance is due to artifacts was borne out. These findings are strong evidence that there is no situational specificity.

This is not all the evidence against situational specificity, however. The situational specificity hypothesis predicts that if the situation is held constant and the tests, criteria, and job remain unchanged, validity findings should be constant across different studies conducted in that setting. That is, since the setting is constant, observed validities should be constant because it is differences between settings that are hypothesized to cause differences in observed validities. Meta-analytic principles predict that such observed validities will vary substantially, mostly because of sampling error. We tested these predictions in two studies (Schmidt & Hunter, 1984; Schmidt, Ocasio, Hillery, & Hunter, 1985) and found that observed validities within the same situation varied markedly, disconfirming the situational specificity hypothesis. In the second of these studies, the data from a large-sample validity study ($N = 1,455$) were divided into smaller, randomly identical studies (21 studies of $n = 68$ each). Since situational variables were controlled, the specificity hypothesis predicted that all the smaller studies would show the same observed validity. This was not the case, however. Instead, there was great variance among studies in both magnitude of validity and significance level, as predicted by the theory of artifacts, which is the basis of meta-analysis and validity generalization. The variation in validities was as great as that typically found across studies conducted in entirely different settings.

The final piece of evidence that fits into this network is this: Recent refinements in validity generalization methods have led to the conclusion that published validity generalization studies substantially underestimate the percentage of observed validity variance that is due to artifacts, further undercutting the situational specificity hypothesis. There are four such refinements. First, as recommended by Tukey (1960), outliers (see Chapter 5) are removed prior to analysis (using the methods recommended by Tukey). Second, non-Pearson validity coefficients are removed, because the sampling error formula for Pearson correlations substantially underestimates the sampling error in non-Pearson correlations such as the biserial and the tetrachoric (see Chapter 5). Third, within each meta-analysis, the population observed correlation used in the sampling error formula is estimated by the mean observed validity instead of the individual observed validity from the study at hand. This provides a more accurate estimate of sampling error (see Chapter 5). Fourth, the problem created by nonlinearity in the range restriction correction (cf., Chapter 5 and Schmidt, Gast-Rosenberg, & Hunter, 1980, Appendix) is solved by a new set of computational procedures. These refinements are discussed in Hirsh, et al. (1985) and Schmidt, Law et al. (1989). These improvements were applied to the massive validity data base in Pearlman et al. (1980), which consists of approximately 3,600 validity coefficients from published and unpublished studies from many organizations, researchers, and time periods. Each of these methodological refinements resulted in increases in the percentage of validity variance accounted for and/or smaller estimates of SD_ρ. Even in this heterogeneous group of studies, almost all validity variance was found to be due to artifacts.

All these pieces of interlocking evidence point in the same direction: toward the conclusion that for employment tests of cognitive abilities, the situational specificity hypothesis is false. The only conclusion consistent with the total pattern of evidence is that there is no situational specificity (or that situational effects are so tiny it is reasonable to consider them to be zero; some prefer this latter conclusion, which we regard as scientifically identical).

In some research areas, there may be no related meta-analyses with which one's meta-analytic results can be cross-referenced and checked for consistency. In such cases, one's results should be compared with the broader pattern of general research findings. Where even this is not possible, meta-analyses based on small numbers of studies should indeed be interpreted with caution, even though the meta-analysis provides the most accurate summary possible of existing research knowledge. We stress that, in cases such as this, the problem is created not by meta-analysis methods, but the limitations of the research literature. These limitations do not have to be permanent. Consider an example. McDaniel, Schmidt and Hunter (1988) found that only 15 criterion-related studies had ever been conducted on the validity of the behavioral consistency method of evaluating applicants' past job-related achievements and accomplishments. Based on these 15 studies, mean true validity is estimated at .45 (SD = .10; 90% credibility value = .33; percent variance accounted for = 82%). The appropriate interpretation of these findings is different from the interpretation that would be appropriate for exactly the same findings based on exactly the same number of studies in a meta-analysis of a cognitive ability. There are now literally hundreds of meta-analyses of cognitive abilities and job performance to which the latter findings could be cross-referenced to check for consistency. In the case of the behavioral consistency method, there are no other meta-analyses. Further, we have very little information as to precisely what the behavioral consistency procedure measures. For example, there are no reported correlations between cognitive abilities test scores and behavioral consistency scores. Behavioral consistency scores are not yet part of a rich, structured, complex, and elaborated network of established knowledge as cognitive abilities are. Therefore, this meta-analysis must stand alone to a much greater extent. We cannot be really certain that the results are not substantially influenced by outliers or by second-order sampling error. (For example, the actual amount of variance due to artifacts may be 100%, or it may be 50%). For these reasons, McDaniel, Schmidt and Hunter (1988) stated that these finding must be considered preliminary and recommended that additional validity studies be conducted, not to estimate "local validities" from local studies for local settings, but to have more studies to combine into the meta-analysis.

There are other areas of research in industrial-organizational psychology completely outside the area of personnel selection where (1) the number of studies now available is small, and (2) there is no elaborated structure of empirical and theoretical knowledge against which the meta-analytic results can be checked. In such cases, researchers should be on guard against the dangers of low statistical power to detect moderators and of Type I errors ("detecting" moderators where they don't exist) resulting from capitalization on chance in the search for moderators. Osburn et al. (1983) and Sackett et al. (1986) have discussed the problem of statistical power in meta-analyses to detect moderators and have conducted simulation studies to estimate power under various conditions. When meta-analytic results have less evidential value because the number of individual studies in the meta-analysis is small *and* there is no related structure of empirical and theoretical knowledge against which the meta-analytic results can be checked, the alternative is neither reversion to reliance on the single study nor a return to the narrative review method of integrating study findings; both are vastly inferior to meta-analysis in information yield. The appropriate reaction is to accept the meta-analysis provisionally while conducting (or awaiting) additional studies, which are then incorporated into a new and more informative meta-analysis. During this time, other forms of evidence bearing on the hypothesis in question may appear — forms of evidence analogous to the within-setting studies (Schmidt & Hunter, 1984; Schmidt, Ocasio, Hillery, & Hunter, 1985) in the area of situational specificity, in that they represent different approaches to the same question. Such evidence then allows the beginning of the construction of the kind of structured pattern of evidence described above.

Second-Order Meta-Analyses

In the research program described above, results in the form of percent variance accounted for were combined across different meta-analyses, in particular meta-analyses of different abilities used to predict job performance. In cases like this in which the same theoretical considerations apply to a number of meta-analyses, the problem of second-order sampling error can be addressed using a meta-analysis of meta-analyses, or a *second-order meta-analysis*. Validity generalization research on cognitive ability tests is an example. Under the situational specificity hypothesis, the hypothesized situational moderators would be essentially the same for different abilities, and under the alternate hypothesis, all variance would be hypothesized to be artifactual for all abilities. The second-order meta-analysis would involve computing the average percent of variance accounted for across the several meta-analyses. For example, in a large consortium study conducted by Psychological Services, Inc., in 16 companies, the percent of variance accounted for by sampling error ranged from about 60% to over 100% for the various abilities examined. The average percentage accounted for across abilities was 99%, indicating that once second-order sampling error was considered, all variance of validities across the 16 companies was accounted for by sampling error for all the abilities studied. It should be clear that in conducting a second-order meta-analysis, figures greater than 100% should not be rounded down to 100%. Doing so would obviously bias the mean for these figures, since those that are randomly lower than 100% are not rounded upward. Technical considerations in conducting second-order meta-analyses are discussed in Chapter 5. The key point is that it is the *reciprocal* of the percent variance accounted for that must be averaged across meta-analyses. For an example, see Rothstein et al. (in press). See also Callender and Osburn (1988).

Meta-analysis has made clear how little information there is in single studies because of the distorting effect of (first-order) sampling error. An examination of second-order sampling error shows that even several studies combined meta-analytically contain limited information about between-study variance (although they provide substantial information about means). Accurate analyses of between-study variance require either meta-analyses based on a substantial number of studies (we have had up to 882; cf., Pearlman et al., 1980), or meta-analyses of similar meta-analyses (second order meta-analyses.) These are the realities and inherent uncertainties of small-sample research in the behavioral and social sciences (or in any other area, e.g., medicine). There is no perfect solution to these problems, but meta-analysis is the best available solution. As the number of studies increases, successive meta-analyses will become increasingly more accurate.

Second-Order Sampling Error: Technical Treatment

The remainder of this chapter presents a more technical and analytical treatment of second-order sampling error and statistical power in meta-analysis. For the sake of simplifying the presentation, the results are presented for "bare-bones" meta-analyses, that is, meta-analyses for which sampling error is the only artifact that occurs and that is corrected for.

If a meta-analysis is based on a large number of studies, then there is little sampling error in the meta-analytic estimates. However, if the meta-analysis is based on only a small number of studies, then there will be sampling error in the meta-analytic estimates of means and standard deviations. This is called second-order sampling error. There are potentially two kinds of second-order sampling error: sampling error due to incompletely averaged sampling error in the primary studies, and sampling error produced by variation in effect sizes across studies. We will call unresolved sampling error from the primary studies "secondary second-order sampling error" or "secondary sampling error" for short. We will call sampling error due to variation in effect sizes "primary second-order sampling error." For simplicity, the following discussion will be written for analyses of the d statistic, but analyses based on other statistics are also subject to second-order sampling error when the number of studies is not large.

Consider secondary sampling error. Meta-analytic estimates are averages. Thus, the sampling error in individual studies is averaged across studies. If enough studies are averaged, then the averaged sampling error effects become exactly computable and, hence, exactly correctable. However, if the number of studies is small, then the average sampling error effects will still be partly random. For example, consider the mean effect size. Ignoring the small bias in the d statistic (see Chapter 8), the average d for the meta-analysis is

$$\text{Ave}\,(d) = \text{Ave}\,(\delta) + \text{Ave}\,(e).$$

If the number of studies is large, then the average sampling error across studies, $\text{Ave}\,(e)$, will equal its population value of 0. That is, if we average across a large number of particular sampling errors, then the sampling errors will cancel out exactly and yield an average of 0. If Ave (e) = 0, then

$$\text{Ave}\,(d) = \text{Ave}\,(\delta)\,.$$

That is, if the average sampling error in the meta-analysis is 0, then the average observed effect size in the meta-analysis is equal to the average population effect size in the meta-analysis. If Ave (e) differs from 0, then that is the effect of secondary sampling error.

If secondary sampling error were 0, then the average effect size in the meta-analysis would equal the average population effect size in the studies included in the meta-analysis. But the number that we want to know is the average population effect size across the entire research domain. The average effect size in the meta-analysis might differ from the average for the whole domain. If there were no variance in effect sizes across studies, then Ave $(\delta) = \delta$ for any meta-analysis, and there can be no difference between the mean for the meta-analysis and the mean for the research domain. But if there is variation across studies, then the mean in the meta-analysis could differ by chance from the mean in the domain as a whole. This is primary second-order sampling error.

If the number of studies is large and the studies are representative of the research domain, the average population effect size in the meta-analysis, Ave (δ), will differ little from the average effect size across the research domain. That is, if the number of studies is large, then the Ave (d) value in the meta-analysis will be almost exactly equal to the average across the entire potential research domain. Thus, for a large number of studies, there will be no primary second-order sampling error in the meta-analysis mean.

To summarize, if the number of studies is small, then there will be second-order sampling error in the mean effect size. Ave (d) will differ somewhat from the mean population effect size because the sampling errors in the individual studies will not have an average that is exactly zero (secondary sampling error) and possibly because of chance variation in the mean population effect size in the meta-analysis (potential primary second-order sampling error). In this section, we will derive a confidence interval to estimate the potential range of second-order sampling error in the meta-analysis mean.

Each of the other statistics considered in meta-analysis has second-order sampling error, although the exact relationship is more complicated in the case of variances than it is for means. If the number of studies is large, then the variance of the particular sampling errors in the meta-analysis, Var (e), will equal the value predicted from statistical theory. If the number of studies is small, then the observed sampling error variance may differ from the statistically expected value. Similarly, if the number of studies is large, then the variance in the particular effect sizes observed in the meta-analysis, Var(δ), will equal the variance for the research domain as a whole. But if the number of studies is small, then the variance of study population effect sizes in the meta-analysis may differ by chance from the variance of population effect sizes. If the number of studies is large, then the covariance between effect size and sampling error will be zero. If the number of studies is small, then the covariance in the meta-analysis may differ by chance from zero.

Let us consider primary second-order sampling error in more detail. One key question is whether there is any primary second-order sampling error. There are two possible cases. First, there is the "homogeneous case" in which the population effect sizes do not differ from one study to the next. Second, there is the "heterogeneous case" where there is variation in population effect sizes across studies. Consider first the primary case in which the population study effect, δ_i, does not vary across studies. That is, in the homogeneous case, we have

$$\delta_i = \delta \text{ for each study } i \text{ in the domain.}$$

In the homogeneous case it is possible to speak of "the" population effect size δ. Since δ_i is the same for each study,

$$\text{Ave}(\delta_i) = \delta \text{ for any set of studies from the domain}$$

$$\text{Var}(\delta_i) = 0 \text{ for any set of studies from the domain.}$$

The meta-analysis mean observed effect size is

$$\text{Ave}(d_i) = \text{Ave}(\delta_i) + \text{Ave}(e_i)$$

$$= \delta + \text{Ave}(e_i).$$

Thus, the meta-analytic average effect size differs from the effect size δ only to the extent that the average of the sampling errors in the meta-analysis differs from zero. That is, the only second-order sampling error in the mean effect size in the meta-analysis is the secondary sampling error, the sampling error resulting from primary sampling errors that by chance do not average to exactly zero.

In the homogeneous case, the population effect size is constant across studies. Thus,

$$\text{Var}(d_i) = \text{Var}(e_i).$$

If the number of studies were large, then the variance of the particular sampling errors in the meta-analysis would equal the variance predicted by the statistical theory for the research domain as a whole. However, if the particular sampling errors in the meta-analysis have a variance that is different by chance from the domain variance, then that unresolved primary sampling error will not have been eliminated from the meta-analysis. Thus, in the homogeneous case, the only second-order sampling error in the variance of observed effect sizes will be secondary sampling error, i.e., unresolved first-order study sampling error.

Now let us consider the heterogeneous case in which population effect sizes *do* differ from one study to the next. The average observed effect size in a meta-analysis is

$$\text{Ave}(d_i) = \text{Ave}(\delta_i) + \text{Ave}(e_i).$$

If the number of studies is small, then there can be error in each of the two terms: the average sampling error, $\text{Ave}(e_i)$, and the average population effect size, $\text{Ave}(\delta_i)$. Consider the average sampling error, $\text{Ave}(e_i)$. By chance the average sampling error for that meta-analysis, $\text{Ave}(e_i)$, is likely to depart from zero by at least some small amount. That is secondary sampling error. Secondary sampling error always converges to zero if the number of studies is large enough. However, it is possible for secondary sampling error to be small even if the number of studies is small. If the sample sizes in the primary studies were all very large — an unlikely event in psychological research — the average of the individual sampling errors would be near zero. The average sampling error would then be near zero even though the number of studies is small.

Now consider the other term in the average effect size, $\text{Ave}(\delta_i)$, the average population effect size for the meta-analysis. If the number of studies is large, then the average population effect size in the meta-analysis will differ little from the average population effect size for the whole research domain. However, if the number of studies is small, then the particular values of δ_i observed in the meta-analysis are only a sample of the effect sizes from the domain as a whole. Thus, by chance, the average effect size in the meta-analysis may differ by some amount from the average effect size for the entire research domain. This departure is primary second-order sampling error. Even if all primary studies were done with an infinite number of subjects (i.e., even if every primary study sampling error e_i were 0) then the particular effect sizes in the meta-analysis need not have an average that is exactly equal to the domain average.

Thus, in the heterogeneous case, both the mean and the standard deviation of population effect sizes in the meta-analysis will depart from the research domain values because the studies observed are only a sample of studies. This is "primary second-order sampling error."

The "Homogeneous" Case

In defining the word "homogeneity," it is important to distinguish between actual treatment effects and study population treatment effects. There are few studies that are methodologically perfect and, thus, few studies in which the study population treatment effect is equal to the actual treatment effect. In a research domain in which the actual treatment effect is the same for all studies, artifact variation across studies will produce artifactual differences in study effect sizes. In most current textbooks on meta-analysis, the definition of "homogeneous" is buried in implicit statistical assumptions. The usual definition of homogeneity requires that the study population effect sizes be exactly uniform across studies. In particular, most current chi-square tests thus not only assume that the actual treatment effect is constant across studies, but that there is no variation in artifact values either. This is very unlikely.

Nearly all contemporary meta-analyses of experimental treatments have been bare-bones meta-analyses; no correction has been made for error of measurement or variation in strength of treatment, or variation in construct validity, and more. For a bare-bones meta-analysis, it is very unlikely that the study population effect sizes would be exactly equal for all studies. To have uniformity in the study effect sizes, the studies would not only have to be uniform in actual effect size, but they would have to be uniform in artifact values as well. All studies would have to measure the dependent variable with exactly the same reliability and the same construct validity. All studies would have to have the same degree of misidentification — inadvertent treatment failure — in group identification, and so on (see Chapters 2 and 6). However, it may be useful in some cases to think of the homogeneous case as an approximation.

For purposes of this exposition of second-order sampling error, we assume homogeneity, and we denote the uniform study effect size by δ. Assume the average sample size to be 50 or more so that we can ignore bias in mean d values. Then, for each study individually, the treatment effect differs from δ only by sampling error. That is,

$$d_i = \delta + e_i \ .$$

We then have

$$\text{Ave}\,(d) = \delta + \text{Ave}\,(e_i)$$

$$\text{Var}\,(d) = \text{Var}\,(e_i)\ .$$

The average differs from δ only if the average sampling error is not the expected value of zero, i.e., only if the number of studies is too low for errors to average out to the expected value (to within rounding error). The variance of observed effect sizes differs from $\text{Var}\,(e)$ only if the variance of sampling errors $\text{Var}(e_i)$ differs from the expected variance $\text{Var}\,(e)$. This would not occur for a meta-analysis on a large number of studies. However, the sampling variation in the variance is larger than the sampling variation in the mean. Thus, in most meta-analyses, the sampling error in the variance of effect sizes is much more important than the sampling error in the average effect size.

In the homogeneous case, the sampling error in the mean effect size for a bare-bones meta-analysis is obtained from the sampling error equation

$$D = \delta + \varepsilon$$

where D is the mean effect size and ε is the average sampling error. The distribution of meta-analytic sampling error ε is described by

$$E\,(\varepsilon) = 0$$

$$\text{Var}\,(\varepsilon) = \text{Var}\,(e)\,/\,K$$

where K is the number of studies. Thus, under the assumption of homogeneity, the confidence interval for the mean effect size is

$$\text{Ave}\,(d) - 1.96\,\text{SD}_\varepsilon < \delta < \text{Ave}\,(d) + 1.96\,\text{SD}_\varepsilon \ .$$

The sampling error in the variance of effect sizes for a bare-bones meta-analysis is obtained by considering a variance ratio. For a large number of studies, the condition of homogeneity could be identified by computing the following ratio.

For a small number of studies, this ratio will depart from one by sampling error. The extent of such sampling error can be estimated using the chi-square distribution. Define the statistic Q by

$$Q = K \operatorname{Var}(d) / \operatorname{Var}(e).$$

Q is the comparison variance ratio multiplied by the number of studies. Under the assumption of homogeneity, Q has a chi-square distribution with $K - 1$ degrees of freedom. This is the most common "homogeneity test" of contemporary meta-analysis.

The homogeneity test has all the flaws of any significance test. If the number of studies is small, then a real moderator variable must be enormous to be detected by this test. On the other hand, if the number of studies is large, then any trivial departure from homogeneity, such as departures in artifact uniformity, will suggest the presence of a moderator variable where there may be none. However, research on human decision making has shown that when there is no good alternative available, people will grasp at straws. The homogeneity test is just such a straw.

The "Heterogeneous" Case

If the research domain is not homogeneous, then there can be primary second-order sampling error—error due to the fact that the number of studies is not infinite. In a real meta-analysis in the heterogeneous case, there will thus be two kinds of error: secondary sampling error and primary second-order sampling error. For purposes of discussion, we will focus first on just primary second-order sampling error. To do this, we will make a very unrealistic assumption: assume either (1) that all studies are done with essentially infinite size, or (2) (which is the same thing) that all study population effect sizes are known. After consideration of the special case, we will return to the realistic case of primary as well as second-order sampling error.

To make second-order sampling error clearly visible, let us eliminate primary sampling error. Suppose that population effect sizes do vary across studies. The individual study effect size is δ_i. Meta-analysis will compute the average and variance of the study effect sizes in the studies located.

$$\operatorname{Ave}(d) = \operatorname{Ave}(\delta_i)$$

$$\operatorname{Var}(d) = \operatorname{Var}(\delta_i)$$

However, if the number of studies is small, then the average population effect size in the studies observed is only a sample average of the population effect sizes across all possible studies in the research domain.

The simplest case of a moderator variable would be the binary case. For example, the foot-in-the-door persuasion technique works if the subsequent request is altruistic, but doesn't work for nonaltruistic requests. The statistical description of a binary variable has four pieces of information: the two values that are taken on by the binary variable and the probability of each value. Denote the two values by X_1 and X_2 and denote the respective probabilities by p and q. Since the sum of probabilities is 1, $p + q = 1$ and hence $q = 1 - p$. The mean value is

$$E(X) = p X_1 + q X_2.$$

Let D denote the difference between the values, i.e., define D by

$$D = X_1 - X_2.$$

The variance of the binary variable is

$$\text{Var}(X) = p q D^2.$$

Suppose that a research domain has a moderator variable such that for 50% of studies the effect size is $\delta = .20$, while for the other 50% of studies the effect size is $\delta = .30$. For the research domain as a whole, the mean effect size is

$$\text{Ave}(\delta) = .50(.20) + .50(.30) = .25.$$

The variance is given by

$$\text{Var}(\delta) = pq D^2 = (.50)(.50)(.30 - .20)^2 = .0025.$$

Thus, the standard deviation is $\text{SD}_\delta = .05$. Consider a meta-analysis with $K = 10$ studies. If the studies split 5 and 5, then for that meta-analysis the mean effect size would be .25 and the standard deviation would be .05. But suppose the studies by chance split 7 and 3. The mean would be

$$\text{Ave}(d) = (7/10)(.20) + (3/10)(.30) = .23$$

rather than .25. The variance would be

$$\text{Var}\,(d) = (7/10)\,(3/10)\,(.30 - .20)^2 = (.21)\,(.01) = .0021$$

instead of .0025. That is, the standard deviation would be .046 rather than .05. These deviations in the mean and standard deviation of effect sizes are primary second-order sampling error, variation due to the fact that the sample of studies has chance variations from the research domain, which is the study population.

How large is primary second-order sampling error? The answer is simple for the main effect size.

$$\text{Var}\,[\,\text{Ave}\,(\delta)\,] = \text{Var}\,(\delta)\,/\,K$$

The answer for the variance depends on the shape of the effect size distribution. That discussion is beyond the scope of the present book.

Consider now the case of a real meta-analysis with a small number of studies. There will be both primary and second-order sampling error. For the mean effect size in a bare-bones meta-analysis, each can be computed separately and easily.

$$\text{Var}\,[\,\text{Ave}\,(d)\,] = \text{Var}\,[\,\text{Ave}\,(\delta)\,] + \text{Var}\,[\,\text{Ave}\,(e)\,]$$

$$= \text{Var}\,(\delta)\,/\,K + \text{Var}\,(e)\,/\,K$$

$$= [\,\text{Var}\,(\delta) + \text{Var}\,(e)\,]\,/\,K$$

$$= \text{Var}\,(d)\,/\,K$$

Furthermore, this formula holds for whatever set of weights is used in the basic estimation equations.

The case for the standard deviation is much more complex and is beyond the scope of the present manuscipt.

A numerical example. Consider the first numerical example presented in Chapter 7.

N	d
100	−.01
90	.41*
50	.50*
40	−.10

(*Significant at the .05 level.)

The meta-analysis using the more accurate formula found

$$
\begin{aligned}
T &= 280 \\
K &= 4 \\
N &= 70 \\
\text{Ave}\,(d) &= .20 \\
\text{Var}\,(d) &= .058854 \\
\text{Var}\,(e) &= .059143
\end{aligned}
$$

The chi-square test for homogeneity is

$$ Q = K\,\text{Var}\,(d)\,/\,\text{Var}\,(e) = 4\,[\,.058854\,/\,.059143\,] = 3.98 $$

with 3 degrees of freedom. This is far below the value required for statistical significance. Thus, this test suggests the research domain to be homogeneous.

If the domain is considered to be homogeneous, then the standard deviation of effect sizes is zero and need not be estimated. Thus, the only second-order sampling error is the secondary sampling error in the mean effect size. For the homogeneous case, the sampling error in the mean is given by

$$ \text{Var}\,[\,\text{Ave}\,(d)\,] = \text{Var}\,(e)\,/\,K = .059143\,/\,4 = .014786 $$

and, thus, the standard error of the mean is .12. The confidence interval for the effect size δ is

$$ .20 - 1.96\,(.12) < \delta < .20 + 1.96\,(.12) $$

$$ -.04 < \delta < .44 . $$

Thus, the sampling error in this meta-analysis is substantial. We cannot be sure that the effect size is actually positive.

The problem in the previous meta-analysis is the total sample size. A total sample size of 280 would still be a small sample size for a single study. Thus, this meta-analysis can be expected to have considerable sampling error. To make this very explicit, suppose that the number of studies was $K = 40$ rather than 4. The total sample size would then be $T = 2,800$, which is far from infinite but still substantial. The sampling error variance would be

$$\text{Var}\,[\,\text{Ave}\,(d)\,]=\text{Var}\,(e)\,/\,k=.059143\,/\,40=.001479$$

and the standard error would be .04. The confidence interval would be

$$.20-1.96\,(.04)<\delta<.20+1.96\,(.04)$$

$$.12<\delta<.28\,.$$

Thus, given 40 studies with an average sample size of 70, the average value of δ is known to be positive (97.5% chance it is greater than .12) and the width of the 95% uncertainty interval shrinks from .48 to .16.

If the number of studies were 400, the total sample size would be 28,000 and the confidence interval would shrink to

$$.18<\delta<.22\,.$$

Thus, meta-analysis will eventually yield very accurate estimates of effect sizes in all research domains. But if the average sample size in the primary studies is very small, the number of studies required may be very large.

The leadership training by experts example. Consider the leadership effect size meta-analysis from Table 7.1 in Chapter 7. Let us illustrate the computation of confidence intervals about those estimates. The sampling error variance in the mean effect size is

$$\text{Var}\,[\,\text{Ave}\,(d)\,]=\text{Var}\,(d)\,/\,K=.106000\,/\,5=.021200$$

and the corresponding standard error is .146. The 95% confidence interval for the mean effect size is thus

$$.20-1.96\,(.146)<\text{Ave}\,(\delta)<.20+1.96\,(.146)$$

$$-.09<\text{Ave}\,(\delta)<.49\,.$$

Thus, with a total sample size of only 200, the confidence interval for the mean effect size is very wide.

But this would also be true for a single study with a sample size of only 200. For a single study with sample size 200 and an observed d of .20, the sampling error variance would be

$$\text{Var}\,(e)=[\,199/197\,]\,[\,4\,/200\,]\,[\,1+.20^2/8\,]=.020304\,.$$

The corresponding standard error is .142 and the 95% confidence interval would be

$$.20 - 1.96(.142) < \delta < .20 + 1.96(.142)$$

$$-.08 < \delta < .48.$$

The key to accuracy in the estimate of the mean effect size is to gather enough studies to generate a very large total sample size.

For this example with a total sample size of 200, the confidence interval for the mean effect size is $-.09 < \text{Ave}(\delta) < .49$. In particular, since the confidence interval goes down below zero, we cannot be sure that the mean effect size is positive. On the other hand, it is equally likely to be off in the other direction. Just as the mean effect size might be .00 rather than the observed mean of .20, so with equal liklihood it could be .40 rather than the observed value of .20.

The estimated variation in effect size is very small. The chi-square test for homogeneity yields

$$Q = 5 [.106000 / .105932] = 5.00$$

with 4 degrees of freedom. This value is far from significance. Thus, it is entirely possible that there is no variance in population effect sizes at all.

Assume now that we obtained similar results not for 5 studies but for 500 studies. For 500 studies with an average sample size of 40, the total sample size would be $500(40) = 20,000$. There would be little sampling error in the meta-analysis estimates. The sampling error in the mean effect size would be

$$\text{Var}[\text{Ave}(d)] = \text{Var}(d) / K = .106000 / 500 = .000212$$

and the standard error would be .015. The 95% confidence interval for the mean effect size would be

$$.20 - 1.96(.015) < \text{Ave}(\delta) < .20 + 1.96(.015)$$

$$.17 < \text{Ave}(\delta) < .23.$$

The chi-square test for homogeneity would yield

$$Q = 500 [.106000 / .105932] = 500.32$$

with 499 degrees of freedom, which is still far from significant.

Even with 500 studies, a standard deviation as small as .015 could well be a chance deviation from 0. Thus, this difference may well not really be there. Indeed the data were created as a homogeneous case.

The skills training moderator example. Consider the overall meta-analysis of the studies in Table 7.2 of Chapter 7. We have

$$T = 40 + 40 + \ldots = 400$$

$$K = 10$$

$$N = T / 10 = 40$$

$$\text{Ave}(d) = .30$$

$$\text{Var}(d) = .116000$$

$$\text{Var}(e) = [\,39/37\,]\,[\,4/40\,]\,[\,1 + .30^2 / 8\,] = .106591$$

$$\text{Var}(\delta) = .116000 - .106591 = .009409$$

$$SD_\delta = .097$$

The estimated standard deviation of effect sizes is .097, which is large. However the total sample size is only 400. The chi-square for homogeneity is

$$Q = 10\,[\,.116000 / .106591\,] = 10.88$$

with 9 degrees of freedom. This value is not significant. Thus, the chi-square test did not detect the moderator variable in this meta-analysis. However, remember that with 5 studies in each subset, the total sample sizes are only 200 in each subset meta-analysis.

Since the total sample size is only 400, we should worry about the sampling error in the mean effect size. Since the test for homogeneity is untrustworthy with such small total sample size, we ignore the results of the chi-square test and assume the heterogeneous case. The sampling error in the mean effect size is thus

$$\text{Var}[\,\text{Ave}(d)\,] = \text{Var}(d) / K = .116000 / 10 = .011600$$

and the standard error is .108. The confidence interval for the mean effect size is thus

$$.30 - 1.96(.108) < \text{Ave}(\delta) < .30 + 1.96(.108)$$

$$.09 < \text{Ave}(\delta) < .51.$$

That is, with a total sample size of 400, there is an very large potential sampling error in the mean effect size.

On the other hand, suppose that we obtained these results not with 10 studies but with 1,000 studies. The total sample size would be 1,000(40) = 40,000, and there would be very little sampling error in the mean effect size. The confidence interval for the mean effect size would be

$$.30 - 1.96(.0108) < \text{Ave}(\delta) < .30 + 1.96(.0108)$$

$$.28 < \text{Ave}(\delta) < .32.$$

The chi-square test for homogeneity would yield

$$Q = 1,000[.116000 / .106591] = 1,088.27$$

with 999 degrees of freedom. This value is statistically significant.

What is the minimum number of studies required for the chi-square test to be significant? In this example, the minimum number of studies is $K = 671$. This shows that the chi-square test has very low power in this example: 671 studies are required for a power of 50%.

The power of the chi-square test depends sharply on the average sample size in the primary studies. In this example, we considered a moderator with effect sizes $\delta = .20$ versus $\delta = .40$ and an average sample size of $N = 40$. The number of studies required for the power to be 50% is $K = 671$. Had the average sample size been $N = 68$, the minimum number of studies would have been only $K = 189$. Had the average sample size been $N = 100$, the minimum number of studies would have been only $K = 82$. Had the average sample size been $N = 200$, the minimum number of studies would have been only $K = 17$. Had the average sample size been $N = 236$, the minimum number of studies would have been only $K = 10$. That is, had the sample size in the primary studies been $N = 236$ rather than $N = 40$, the chi-square test would have been significant for the present example.

The low power of the chi-square test to detect a moderator variable stands in sharp contrast to the high power for the comparison of the means for the two moderator groups as discussed in the next section.

The Detection of Moderator Variables: Technical Treatment

The presence of second-order sampling error in meta-analysis means that under certain conditions it will be difficult to distinguish between sampling error and real variation in the population effect size. How then is a moderator variable to be detected? In this section, we will consider the detection of a moderator variable from a computational point of view. Since a complete treatment of this problem is beyond the scope of this book, we will present only the most common case: the binary moderator. For a binary moderator variable, the research domain can be split into two subdomains so that the mean effect size is different in each subdomain. We will contrast two statistical detection procedures: mean comparison and the chi-square homogeneity test.

In every statistical domain there is a trade-off between substantive knowledge and statistical power. That is, it is always possible for a clever statistician to use substantive knowledge about the statistic in question to reduce the effect of sampling error on inferences to be drawn. This is strikingly true of meta-analysis in the case of the binary moderator variable. Consider the substantively extreme cases: the theoretically predicted moderator variable versus the unsuspected moderator variable. We will show that the statistical power to detect the theoretically predicted moderator is far higher than the power to detect the unsuspected moderator variable.

Consider the theoretically predicted moderator variable. Since this moderator variable is predicted, it can be coded in the meta-analysis. The test for this moderator variable will be the comparison of subgroup meta-analyses on the two subgroups of studies in the original overall meta-analysis. We will present a statistical significance test for this comparison and show that under most circumstances it has high power.

Consider the unsuspected moderator variable. Since it is unsuspected, it will not be coded in the meta-analysis. Thus, it must be detected in the form of residual variation left after all identifiable artifacts have been controlled. In most current textbooks on meta-analysis, this detection takes on the form of a chi-square test for homogeneity. The leadership training example illustrates the fact that this chi-square test often has low power. An alternative to the chi-square test is to take the estimated residual standard deviation at face value (one implicit suggestion of our first book on meta-analysis). The statistical power of the face value approach is much higher, but it looks unsophisticated. It also runs a 50% error rate if there is actually no moderator variable, i.e., a 50% Type I error rate. (A third alternative is to use our 75% rule, discussed earlier in this chapter).

The Theoretically Predicted Moderator

Confidence Intervals

Consider the theoretically predicted binary moderator variable. Use this variable to split the overall meta-analysis with K studies into two subsets with K_1 and K_2 studies in each (where $K_1 + K_2 = K$). Perform a subgroup meta-analysis within each subset of studies using the set of weights judged optimal for the research domain in question. Denote by D_i the subgroup average effect size and denote by v_i the subgroup variance of observed effect sizes. If the two mean effect sizes, D_1 and D_2, differ in the predicted direction, this tends to confirm the predicted moderator variable. However, there is the possibility that the observed difference between means is due to second-order sampling error. The range of potential sampling error in each subset of studies can be estimated by computing a confidence interval for the mean effect size in each subset. For each subgroup, we can compute a confidence interval for the mean population effect size using the method derived earlier. To the extent that these confidence intervals do not overlap, we have sharp confirmation of the predicted moderator variable. One way to measure the extent of overlap of the confidence intervals is to compute a significance test on the difference between the two mean effect sizes.

We will first present the confidence interval method using a simpler notation to facilitate the development of the significance test and the computation of its power. We first write the second-order sampling error formula for the mean effect size as

$$D = \delta + \varepsilon$$

where D is the observed mean effect size, δ is the research domain mean effect size, and ε is the second-order sampling error. The sampling error variance is given by

$$\mathrm{Var}(\varepsilon) = \mathrm{Var}(d) / K$$

where $\mathrm{Var}(d)$ is the variance of observed effect sizes. The sampling error standard deviation for the confidence interval is the square root of $\mathrm{Var}(\varepsilon)$. Let us denote the second-order sampling error in D by S. We then have $S^2 = \mathrm{Var}(\varepsilon)$ and the confidence interval for the mean population effect size

$$D - 1.96S < \delta < D + 1.96S .$$

Consider now the confidence intervals for the two subsets of the overall meta-analysis.

$$D_1 - 1.96S_1 < \delta_1 < D_1 + 1.96S_1$$

$$D_2 - 1.96S_2 < \delta_2 < D_2 + 1.96S_2$$

To the extent that these confidence intervals do not overlap, we have sharp confirmation of the predicted moderator variable.

The Statistical Significance Test

Let us derive a significance test comparing the two mean effect sizes. The comparison difference C is defined by

$$C = D_1 - D_2$$

$$= (\delta_1 + \varepsilon_1) - (\delta_2 + \varepsilon_2)$$

$$= (\delta_1 - \delta_2) + (\varepsilon_1 - \varepsilon_2) .$$

Thus the sampling error variance of C is

$$\text{Var}(C) = \text{Var}(\varepsilon_1 - \varepsilon_2) = S_1^2 + S_2^2 .$$

Since the variances may not be equal, the best significance test in this case is the critical ratio. Define z by

$$z = C / \sqrt{\text{Var}(C)} .$$

Under the null hypothesis that the two mean effect sizes are equal, the statistic z has a standard normal distribution. Since the direction of the difference is predicted, the appropriate test is the one-tailed test. The 5% critical value for z is thus 1.64.

Statistical Power

There are two meanings to the phrase "statistical power." The conventional meaning assumes that the statistical parameters are given a priori. Power is then the probability that the significance test will reject the null hypothesis. In the second meaning, a "power" value is computed from observed statistics to suggest the power that applies to the study in question.

Consider first the conventional meaning of power. Assume that we want to compute the power for the significance test for the meta-analysis of a binary moderator variable. For each of the two subsets, we are given as a priori information the mean effect size δ, the variance of the effect sizes $\text{Var}(\delta)$, the average sample size N, and the number of studies K. For each subset, we then compute the sampling error variance $\text{Var}(e)$ and the observed effect size variance $\text{Var}(d)$; from the latter we compute the second-order sampling error variance for the mean effect size $\text{Var}(\varepsilon) = \text{Var}(d)/K$. The comparison statistic C has variance

$$\text{Var}(C) = \text{Var}(\varepsilon_1) + \text{Var}(\varepsilon_2).$$

Denote the standard deviation of C by S. That is, let S be defined by

$$S^2 = \text{Var}(\varepsilon_1) + \text{Var}(\varepsilon_2).$$

The power of the significance test is the probability that the null hypothesis will be rejected, i.e.,

$$\text{Power} = P\left\{z > 1.64\right\}$$

$$= P\left\{C/S > 1.64\right\}$$

$$= P\left\{C > 1.64\,S\right\}.$$

Since C has mean $(\delta_1 - \delta_2)$ and standard deviation S,

$$\text{Power} = P\left\{[C - (\delta_1 - \delta_2)]/S > [1.64\,S - (\delta_1 - \delta_2)]/S\right\}$$

$$= P\left\{x > c\right\}$$

where x is standard normal and the cutoff value c is

$$c = 1.64 - (\delta_1 - \delta_2)/S.$$

Power is then computed from the normal distribution using

$$\text{Power} = Q(c)$$

where Q is the function defined by the upper tail of the normal distribution function.

The "power statistic" for a given comparison is computed as follows. First, compute the variance of the comparison difference C by

$$S^2 = \text{Var}(d_1) / K_1 + \text{Var}(d_2) / K_2 .$$

Compute the normal curve cutoff value c by

$$c = 1.64 - C/S .$$

Compute the power using the upper tail of the normal distribution

$$\text{Power} = Q(c) .$$

The Unsuspected Moderator

If a moderator variable is not anticipated, then it can only be detected in the form of residual variation not explained by sampling error and variation in other artifacts. Our first book on meta-analysis implicitly recommended that the detection of the moderator be done by taking the estimated variance of population effect sizes at face value. That is, if the estimate of $\text{Var}(\delta)$ is positive, then one assumes there is some source of nonartifactual variation across studies. In our chapter on the correlation coefficient, we warned that few studies control for all artifacts and, therefore, the remaining variation in effect sizes may be artifactual. In personnel selection, we recommended ignoring the residual variance unless it was at least 25% of the observed variance. This is a good rule for small sample size research domains, although it works very differently for large sample research domains (McDaniel & Hirsh, 1986). Monte Carlo studies have consistently shown that our 75% rule has higher power for detecting moderator variables than does the chi-square homogeneity test (see earlier discussion in this chapter).

Most other current texts on meta-analysis recommend that moderator variables be detected using a chi-square test for homogeneity. We will show that this makes sense only for an unsuspected moderator variable. If the moderator is theoretically predicted, the t test for mean effect size has much higher power. In this section we will compute the power of the homogeneity test for the binary moderator. For simplicity, assume that no artifact other than sampling error is operating and assume that there is no other moderator variable. Consider an unsuspected binary moderator variable. What is the statistical power of the chi-square test?

We start with the specification of the population effect size distribution. Assume that studies with effect size δ_1 occur with probability p and that studies with effect size δ_2 occur with probability $q = 1 - p$. The mean effect size is

$$E(\delta) = p\,\delta_1 + q\,\delta_2$$

and the variance of effect sizes is

$$\mathrm{Var}(\delta) = pq\,(\delta_1 - \delta_2)^2 .$$

We then construct the parameters of the overall meta-analysis. Let the average sample size be N and let the number of studies be K. Denote the mean effect size by D, i.e., let

$$D = E(\delta).$$

The sampling error variance of observed effect sizes is

$$\mathrm{Var}(e) = [\,(N-1)/(N-3)\,]\,[\,4/N\,]\,[\,1 + D^2/8\,].$$

The variance of observed effect sizes is

$$\mathrm{Var}(d) = \mathrm{Var}(\delta) + \mathrm{Var}(e).$$

The extent of separation between the residual variance and the sampling error variance depends on the variance ratio

$$\Omega = \mathrm{Var}(d) / \mathrm{Var}(e).$$

This ratio is 1 if the mean effect sizes are equal, i.e., if the unsuspected moderator variable is in fact not a moderator variable. The more the ratio exceeds 1 in value, the greater the statistical separation between study subsets. The statistical power of the chi-square test depends directly on Ω and on the number of studies.

Denote the observed meta-analysis chi-square statistic by Q. That is, let

$$Q = K\,\mathrm{Var}(d) / \mathrm{Var}(e)$$

where $\mathrm{Var}(d)$ and $\mathrm{Var}(e)$ are the variances computed for that meta-analysis. If the population effect sizes do not vary, then Q has a chi-square distribution with $K - 1$ degrees of freedom. That is, if the unsuspected moderator were not an actual moderator, then Q would have a chi-square distribution.

If the two mean effect sizes differ, then Q will not have a chi-square distribution. However, Q can be scaled to produce a chi-square distribution. Consider the scaled value of Q defined by

$$x = Q \, / \, \Omega$$

where Ω is the comparison variance ratio. The scaled test value x has a chi-square distribution with $K - 1$ degrees of freedom. The null hypothesis is a special case. Under the null hypothesis, $\Omega = 1$ and hence $x = Q$. Let the 5% critical value for chi-square with $K - 1$ degrees of freedom be denoted $c*$. Under the null hypothesis,

$$P \{ Q > c* \} = .05 \, .$$

Power is the probability that Q exceeds the critical value when the null hypothesis is false. If the null hypothesis is false, then the rescaled value of Q has a chi-square distribution. That is,

$$P \{ Q/\Omega > c* \} = .05 \, .$$

Power is then given by

$$\text{Power} = P \{ Q > c* \} = P \{ Q/\Omega > c*/\Omega \}$$

$$= P \{ x > c*/\Omega \}$$

where x has a chi-square distribution with $K - 1$ degrees of freedom.

A computer program to compute the power of the chi-square test is available from the authors.

The Power of the Homogeneity Test

The two parameters that determine the power of the homogeneity test are K (the number of studies) and Ω (the variance comparison ratio). The number of studies in a meta-analysis typically ranges between 5 and 80 in current work. The variance comparison ratio is much less familiar. Two tables have been constructed to illustrate the value of Ω for various binary moderator conditions.

The "Failed Treatment" Moderator

Consider first the case of the failed treatment. Suppose that under some conditions the treatment has an effect while under other conditions the treatment has no effect. Assume there is one binary moderator variable that accounts for failure versus success. The treatment effect is $\delta = 0$ for studies done in the failure condition. Assume for simplicity that the treatment effect is homogeneous in the success condition. The treatment effect would then be a constant $\delta = \mu$ in the success condition. Thus, the binary moderator has treatment effects $\delta = 0$ in one level and $\delta = \mu$ in the other level. Table 9.1 presents the variance comparison ratio Ω for the failed treatment binary moderator under the assumption that the probablity of failure and success is 50% in the research domain. If the probability of failure is less than 50%, the variance comparison ratio is smaller than that shown in Table 9.1. If the failure rate is far less than 50%, the variance ratio is far less than that shown.

Table 9.1 presents the variance comparison ratio for successful treatment effect sizes varying from $\mu = .10$ to $\mu = 1.00$. Textbook-sized treatment effects are rarely larger than .40. Thus, the first four columns represent the typical large treatment effects in contemporary research. Table 9.1 presents the variance comparison ratio for study sample sizes running from $N = 10$ to $N = 1,600$. In psychological research, the average sample size is rarely larger than 100. So the most relevant rows of Table 9.1 are the first five rows. In certain areas of survey research, sample sizes of 1,000 or more are common, and the last four rows were added to represent such cases.

Most contemporary research domains are represented by the first five rows and first four columns of Table 9.1. For such meta-analyses, the variance comparison ratio Ω varies from 1.005 to 1.970. Thus, the comparison ratio runs from barely larger than 1 for small sample, small effect size domains to 1.97 for large sample, large effect size domains.

The "Doubled Treatment" Moderator

The difference between failed and successful treatments represents the largest possible moderator variable. The more realistic case is one in which the treatment effects differ quantitatively. Consider a binary moderator in which the treatment effect in the big effect studies is twice as large as the treatment effect in the small effect studies. For simplicity, assume that there is no variation in effect size within the two subdomains. Table 9.2 presents the variance comparison ratio for the "doubled effect" binary moderator variable under the assumption that the two moderator levels are equally likely. If the two levels have unequal probability in the

Table 9.1 The Variance Comparison Ratio for Meta-Analyses of a Treatment That Fails in 50% of Studies

				EFFEC	T SIZES					
δ_1	.00	.00	.00	.00	.00	.00	.00	.00	.00	.00
δ_2	.10	.20	.30	.40	.50	.60	.70	.80	.90	1.00
N										
10	1.005	1.019	1.044	1.077	1.120	1.171	1.231	1.299	1.375	1.458
20	1.011	1.045	1.100	1.177	1.275	1.394	1.532	1.688	1.862	2.053
30	1.017	1.070	1.156	1.277	1.430	1.615	1.830	2.1	2.3	2.6
50	1.030	1.120	1.268	1.475	1.738	2.1	2.4	2.8	3.3	3.8
100	1.061	1.244	1.548	1.970	2.5	3.2	3.9	4.8	5.7	6.8
200	1.124	1.494	2.1	3.0	4.0	5.4	6.9	8.6	10.5	12.6
400	1.249	1.993	3.2	4.9	7.1	9.8	12.8	16.3	20.2	24.4
800	1.498	3.0	5.5	8.9	13.3	18.6	24.7	31.7	39.5	47.9
1600	1.998	5.0	9.9	16.8	25.6	36.2	48.5	62.5	78.0	95.0

NOTE: The column headers are the two effect sizes, the row headers are the average sample size.

domain, then the variance comparison ratio will be smaller than that shown in Table 9.2.

Table 9.2 presents the variance comparison ratio for average treatment effect sizes varying from Ave (δ) = .075 to Ave (δ) = .75. Large textbook-sized treatment effects are rarely larger than .40. Thus, the first six columns represent the typical large treatment effects in contemporary research. Table 9.2 presents the variance comparison ratio for study sample sizes running from N = 10 to N = 1,600. In psychological research, the average sample size is rarely larger than 100. So the most relevant rows of Table 9.2 are the first five rows. In certain areas of survey research, sample sizes of 1,000 or more are common, and the last four rows were added to represent such cases.

Most contemporary research domains are represented by the first five rows and first six columns of Table 9.2. For such meta-analyses, the variance comparison ratio Ω varies from 1.001 to 1.536. Thus, the comparison ratio runs from barely larger than 1 for small sample, small effect size domains to 1.54 for large sample, large effect size domains.

A Power Table

For the failed treatment, the variance comparison ratio ranges from 1.005 to 1.97 as the treatment effect rises to textbook example size and as average sample size rises to N = 100. For the doubled treatment, the variance comparison ratio ranges from 1.001 to 1.57 as the treatment effect

Table 9.2 The Variance Comparison Ratio for Meta-Analyses in Which
the Effect Size in 50 Percent of Studies Is Twice the Effect
Size of the Other 50 Percent of Studies

					EFFECT SIZES					
δ_1	.05	.10	.15	.20	25	.30	.35	.40	.45	.50
δ_2	.10	.20	.30	.40	50	.60	.70	.80	.90	1.00
N										
10	1.001	1.005	1.011	1.019	1.030	1.043	1.057	1.074	1.093	1.113
20	1.003	1.011	1.025	1.044	1.069	1.098	1.132	1.170	1.213	1.259
30	1.004	1.017	1.039	1.069	1.107	1.153	1.206	1.266	1.332	1.405
50	1.007	1.030	1.067	1.118	1.184	1.262	1.354	1.457	1.571	1.695
100	1.015	1.061	1.137	1.242	1.375	1.536	1.722	1.933	2.2	2.4
200	1.031	1.123	1.276	1.489	1.759	2.1	2.5	2.9	3.4	3.9
400	1.062	1.248	1.556	1.983	2.5	3.2	3.9	4.8	5.7	6.8
800	1.125	1.497	2.1	3.0	4.1	5.4	6.9	8.6	10.5	12.6
1600	1.249	1.996	3.2	4.9	7.1	9.7	12.8	16.2	20.0	24.2

The column headers are the two effect sizes, the row headers are the average sample size.

rises to textbook example size and as average sample size rises to $N = 100$. This provides a background for looking at the parameters of the power of the test for homogeneity of a meta-analysis on the d statistic. Table 9.3 presents the power of the test for homogeneity for various levels of the variance comparison ratio and for various numbers of studies.

In current meta-analyses, the number of studies is typically in a range from 5 to 80. Thus, the first four columns of Table 9.3 are representative of most current meta-analyses. The average effect size in large textbook examples is rarely larger than Ave $(\delta) = .40$. Tables 9.1 and 9.2 suggest that the variance ratio for a moderator variable is not likely to be larger than 1.97 for the extreme case in which the treatment fails in 50% of studies and not larger than 1.54 for the case in which the large effects are twice as large as small effects. For the doubled effect examples, only the first twelve rows of Table 9.3 are relevant. For the failed treatment examples, the last row is just larger than the anticipated range.

Few meta-analyses have found evidence for failed treatments. So let us focus on the doubled effect research domain examples. In the best of cases, the variance ratio would attain values as large as 1.55. This row of Table 9.3 shows that the power of the test for homogeneity increases from 20% to 87% as the number of studies in the meta-analysis increases from 5 to 80. A power of 87% is acceptable. But note that the power reaches this level only for a case in which there are 80 studies with an average sample size of $N = 100$ (a total sample size of 8,000), and where the moderator is

Table 9.3 The Power of the Chi-Square Test for Homogeneity as a Function of the Variance Comparison Ratio and the Number of Studies in the Meta-Analysis (power expressed as a percent)

	NUMBER OF STUDIES									
	5	20	45	80	125	180	245	320	405	500
$\Omega*$										
1.00	5	5	5	5	5	5	5	5	5	5
1.05	6	7	8	9	11	12	14	16	18	20
1.10	7	10	12	16	20	24	29	34	40	46
1.15	8	13	18	24	31	39	48	56	64	72
1.20	10	16	24	33	44	55	66	75	83	89
1.25	11	19	30	43	57	69	80	88	94	97
1.30	13	23	37	53	68	81	90	95	98	99
1.35	14	27	44	62	78	89	95	98	99	100
1.40	16	31	51	70	85	94	98	99	100	100
1.45	17	35	57	77	90	97	99	100	100	100
1.50	19	39	63	83	94	98	100	100	100	100
1.55	20	43	69	87	96	99	100	100	100	100
1.60	22	47	74	91	98	100	100	100	100	100
1.65	23	51	78	93	99	100	100	100	100	100
1.70	25	55	82	95	99	100	100	100	100	100
1.75	26	58	85	97	100	100	100	100	100	100
1.80	28	61	87	98	100	100	100	100	100	100
1.85	29	64	90	98	100	100	100	100	100	100
1.90	30	67	92	99	100	100	100	100	100	100
1.95	32	70	93	99	100	100	100	100	100	100
2.00	33	72	94	100	100	100	100	100	100	100

*Ω is the variance comparison ratio

such that 50% of studies have a treatment effect of $\delta = .30$ while the other 50% have a treatment effect of $\delta = .60$ (see Table 9.2). Otherwise, the power is much lower.

There are many meta-analyses in which the average effect size is Ave$(\delta) = .20$ and where the average sample size is 50. For such meta-analyses, a doubled treatment effect moderator would generate a variance comparison ratio of only 1.067. If we round this figure up to 1.10, then the relevant row of Table 9.3 is the third row. For a variance ratio of 1.10, the statistical power of the homogeneity test increases from 7% for 5 studies to 16% for 80 studies. That is, the error rate for the chi-square test for homogeneity ranges from 93% for a meta-analysis of 5 studies down to 84% for a meta-analysis of 80 studies.

From this analysis, it is clear that in most meta-analyses, the chi-square test for homogeneity has rather low power to detect moderator variables. (Also, if artifacts in addition to sampling error are operating to produce spurious variance in effect sizes, the test will have spurious "power" to detect nonexistent "moderators"; that is, the Type I error rate will be higher than indicated by nominal alpha level.)

Comparison of Statistical Power

We have now developed the computational formulas for the power to detect theoretically predicted and unsuspected binary moderator variables. Therefore, we can compute the relative power of one over the other. The relative power depends on the difference between the mean effect sizes, the relative frequency of the two levels, the number of studies, and the average sample size in the primary studies. To show just how much the average sample size and number of studies matter, we have chosen to show these effects in our table. Therefore, we reduced the other dimensions to one illustrative case. Since power is maximized if the average effect size is large, we chose an example to match the large textbook effect sizes found in contemporary psychological research. The doubled treatment case with $\delta = .30$ versus $\delta = .60$ with a 50-50 split has an average effect size of Ave $(\delta) = .45$. That is the illustrative case for the power analysis shown in Table 9.4. The computer program written for this table can be run for any desired case.

If a moderator is theoretically predicted, then it will be coded for the meta-analysis and will be used to generate subset meta-analyses. Thus, the statistical test corresponding to the theoretically predicted moderator is the t test on the subset means. If the moderator is unsuspected, then it must be detected as residual variance in the overall meta-analysis. Since most researchers appear to feel that it is too unsophisticated to simply look at the residual variance, they use the chi-square test for homogeneity, which "looks good" but has lower power. Thus, the conventional test for the unsuspected moderator is the chi-square test for homogeneity.

Table 9.4 presents the power for each analysis for meta-analyses with the number of studies ranging from 6 to 160 and with the average sample size ranging from 10 to 800. For any entry in Table 9.4, the total sample size is the product of the these numbers, i.e., the product of the row and column headers. The average sample size in many psychological research domains is about 70. So the most representative values in Table 9.4 are the rows for $N = 70$. Consider first the separate power analyses.

Table 9.4 A Comparison of the Power to Detect a Theoretically Predicted Moderator versus the Power to Detect an Unsuspected Moderator Variable

	Power to detect a theoretically predicted moderator variable							Power to detect an unsuspected moderator variable					
	Number of studies							Number of studies					
	6	10	20	40	80	160		6	10	20	40	80	160
N^*							N^*						
10	13	16	24	37	58	83	10	6	6	7	8	9	11
20	19	26	40	63	88	99	20	7	8	10	12	15	22
30	25	34	54	80	97	100	30	9	10	13	17	24	37
50	35	49	74	95	100	100	50	12	15	20	30	45	68
70	44	61	86	99	100	100	70	16	20	29	44	66	88
100	56	75	95	100	100	100	100	21	28	42	63	86	98
200	82	95	99	100	100	100	200	40	53	76	94	100	100
400	98	99	100	100	100	100	400	65	82	97	100	100	100
800	100	100	100	100	100	100	800	86	96	100	100	100	100

	The relative power for the theoretically predicted moderator variable over the unsuspected moderator variable expressed as a percent					
	Number of studies					
	6	10	20	40	80	160
N^*						
10	214	258	350	491	671	793
20	258	318	426	539	566	451
30	277	337	427	470	398	270
50	286	332	365	318	220	146
70	279	307	298	225	152	113
100	261	266	225	158	116	102
200	207	178	130	106	100	100
400	151	122	103	100	100	100
800	117	104	100	100	100	100

$^*N$ is the average sample size

In both cases, the binary moderator has treatment effects of $\delta = .60$ in half of the studies and $\delta = .30$ in the other half of the studies. The theoretically predicted moderator is detected using a t test comparing the mean d for the two subsets of studies. The unsuspected moderator is detected using a chi-square test on the overall meta-analysis. Power is expressed as a percent. The rows represent variation in the average sample size.

Number of studies:	6	10	20	40	80	160
Power, theoretical:	44	61	86	99	100	100
Power, unsuspected:	16	20	29	44	66	88

The power to detect the theoretically predicted moderator is always greater than the power to detect an unsuspected moderator. If the number of studies is small, the power is low in either case, but is abysmally low for the homogeneity test. Consider the case of 5 studies, typically 3 of each kind. The total sample size is thus only 420 for the overall meta-analysis and 210 each for the subset meta-analyses. The power of 44% for the t test is the same as the power to detect the difference in the effect sizes between two studies with sample sizes of 210 each. This is greater than the power to detect the interaction in a single two-factor between-subjects analysis of variance study conducted with a sample size of 420. In the single study, the test for the interaction would be a two-tailed test while the test between studies is a one-tailed test because the direction is predicted. However, while the power of the t test may be a low 44%, the power of the homogeneity test is an abysmal 16%. Thus, the power for the t test is approximately $44/16 = 2.75$ times larger.

If the average sample size is $N = 70$, then in this example the power to detect the theoretically predicted moderator reaches 80% when the number of studies reaches $K = 18$. To detect an unsuspected moderator using the chi-square test, the power does not reach 80% until the number of studies reaches $K = 131$. Thus, the cost of ignorance is that $131/18 = 7.27$ times as many studies are needed to detect the moderator.

The relative power for the case of an average sample size of $N = 70$ is

Number of studies:	6	10	20	40	80	160
Relative power:	2.79	3.07	2.98	2.25	1.52	1.13

Thus for the typical number of studies in contemporary meta-analyses, the power to detect the theoretically predicted moderator is 2 to 3 times higher than the power to detect an unsuspected moderator using the chi-square homogeneity test.

Summary

In psychological research, the average sample size is usually 100 or less. Therefore, the largest component of second-order sampling error in meta-analysis is secondary sampling error, i.e., unresolved sampling error in the primary studies. In such meta-analyses, the main determinant of the size of confidence intervals and the main determinant of the statistical power to detect moderator variables is total sample size. Secondary sampling error is large enough to surprise most researchers even with a total sample size of $T = 1,500$. On the other hand, theoretical knowledge is also very important. If there is a moderator variable, then the power to detect it is much higher if it is theoretically predicted than if it is unsuspected.

10 Cumulation of Findings Within Studies

It is often possible to obtain more than one correlation or estimate of effect size from within the same study. Should these estimates be included in the meta-analysis as independent estimates? Or should they be combined somehow within the study so that only one value is contributed? There is no one answer to these questions since there are several different kinds of replications that can take place within studies. This chapter surveys the cases that are most frequent.

Many single studies have replication of observation of a relationship within the study. Thus, there can be cumulation of results within, as well as across, studies. However, the method of cumulation depends on the nature of the replication process used in the study. Three kinds of replication will be considered here: fully replicated designs, conceptual replication, and analysis of subgroups.

Fully Replicated Designs

A fully replicated design occurs in a study if that study can be broken into parts that are conceptually equivalent but statistically independent. For example, if data are gathered at several different organizations, then statistics calculated within organizations can be regarded as replicated across organizations. The outcome measures from each organization are statistically independent and can be treated as if they were values from different studies. That is, the cumulation process for these values is the same as that for cumulation across entirely different studies.

Conceptual Replication

Conceptual replication occurs within a study when more than one observation that is relevant to a given relationship is made on each subject. The most common example is replicated measurement, the use of multiple indicators to assess a given variable: for example, the use of several items to assess skill variety; the use of training grades, selection test scores, and job knowledge to assess cognitive ability for work performance; or the use of peer ratings, supervisor ratings, and production records to assess job performance. The second most common example is observation in multiple situations. For example, a participant in an assessment center may be asked to show problem-solving skills in Task A, Task B, and so on. The observation in the various situations can be regarded as replicated measurements of problem-solving skill.

The replication within the study can be used in either of two ways: (1) Each conceptual replication can be represented by a different outcome value, and these separate outcome values can either be cumulated within the study or contributed as a set to a larger cumulation, or (2) the measurements can be combined, and the resulting single-outcome measure can be used to assess the relationship in question.

Suppose that three variables are used as indicators of job performance: peer rating, supervisor rating, and a job sample test. Any potential test could then have three correlations that are conceptually all validity coefficients: the correlation between test and peer rating, the correlation between test and supervisor rating, and the correlation between test and job sample test. These values could contribute to a larger cumulative study in two ways: (1) The three correlations could be contributed as three separate values (the most common approach in contemporary studies), or (2) the three correlations could be averaged and the average could be contributed as the one value representing the study.

If the set of correlations is contributed to the larger study, then there is a problem for the cumulation formulas presented in Parts II and III of this book. These formulas assume that the values used are statistically independent of each other. This is guaranteed if the values come from different studies, but is only true in the present example if the correlations between peer rating, supervisor rating, and job sample test are all zero (as population values for that study), which is impossible if the measures are even approximately equivalent measures as they are believed to be. If the number of correlations or d values contributed by each study is small in comparison to the total number of correlations or d values, then there is little error in the resulting cumulation. However, if a very large number of values are contributed from one small study, then there can be considerable distortion if statistical significance tests are used (see, for example, Hunter, Schmidt, & Hunter, 1979; Schmidt, Pearlman, & Hunter, 1980).

To the extent that a meta-analysis contains groups of correlations or d values that come from the same study samples, the formulas for sampling error presented in Chapters 3 and 7 will underestimate the sampling error variance component in the observed variance of effect sizes (S_r^2 or S_d^2).

This means that there will be an undercorrection for sampling error and that the final estimate of S_ρ^2 or S_δ^2 will be too large. To this extent, the obtained meta-analysis results will be conservative; that is, they will underestimate the degree of agreement (or generalizability) across studies. In our own research on the validity of ability tests in personnel selection, whenever it was the ability (e.g., verbal ability) that had multiple measures, we included the individual correlations in the meta-analysis. Most studies contained only one measure of each ability and, thus, contributed only one correlation to the meta-analysis for that ability. A minority of studies had two measures (e.g., two measures of spatial ability). Therefore, this decision rule contributed only a slight conservative bias to our estimates of SD_ρ. Whenever a study contained multiple measures of job performance, these measures were combined into a composite as described below; if that was not possible, then the correlations were averaged and only the average correlation was entered into the meta-analysis. This decision rule ensured complete independence on the job performance side of the correlation.

It should be noted that while violations of the assumption of independence do affect (inflate) the observed variance of effect sizes across studies, such violations have no systematic effect on the mean d or mean r values in a meta-analysis. Thus, there need be no concern from this source about the accuracy of mean values in meta-analysis. However, unlike other approaches to meta-analysis, the methods described in this book focus strongly on estimating the true (population) variance (and SD) of study effects. The accuracy of estimates of SD_δ and SD_ρ is important because these estimates play a critical role in the interpretation of the results of the meta-analysis. This is in contrast to Glassian meta-analysis in particular, in which the focus is heavily on $\bar{d}$ and $\bar{r}$ and little emphasis is placed on the variance of study effects. Since violations of independence create an upward bias in estimates of SD_δ and SD_ρ, the question of statistical independence in the data deserves careful attention in applications of our meta-analysis methods.

If the average correlation is used to represent the study, then there is no violation of the independence assumption. However, what are we to use for the sample size of the average correlation? If we use the total number of observations that go into the average correlation (i.e., the product of sample size times the number of correlations averaged), then we greatly underestimate the sampling error since this assumes that we have averaged independent correlations. On the other hand, if we use the sample size of the study, then we overestimate the sampling error since the average correlation will have less sampling error than a single correlation. The exact sampling error in the average correlation will be made clear in the discussion of composite scores to follow. In most studies, there is much less error in assuming the simple sample size for the average correlation.

There is another potential problem with the average correlation. In those rare cases in which there is a strong moderator variable, i.e., cases in which there is a large, real, corrected standard deviation across studies, the moderator variable may vary within studies as well as across studies. In such a case, the average correlation would be conceptually ambiguous. For example, there is strong evidence that measures of ability have higher true-score correlations with job sample measures than with supervisory ratings (Hunter, 1983f; Nathan & Alexander, 1988). Identification of this difference in any meta-analysis would require that these two measures not be combined.

Conceptual Replication and Confirmatory Factor Analysis

Multiple measurements can be used to generate correlations with smaller measurement error or to estimate correlations without measurement error (Hunter & Gerbing, 1982). The crucial question is the extent to which measures believed to be equivalent are in fact measures of the same underlying trait. If the replicated measures are equivalent in the sense of reliability theory, then measurement error can be reduced by using a composite score formed by averaging the standard scores (or by just adding the raw scores if the standard deviations are all about the same). If the correlations for this composite score are corrected for attenuation, then measurement error is eliminated altogether. In the case of the items in a scale, the composite score is the test score, and the true score is the factor measured without error.

In confirmatory factor analysis, the same distinction is made in terms of the jargon of factor analysis. If the analysis is done "with ones in the diagonal," then the factor is the composite score. If the analysis is done "with communalities," then the factor is the underlying trait measured without error. If the alternate indicators are equivalent in the sense of reliability theory (i.e., they differ only by random response error), then the computations of confirmatory factor analysis are identical to those of reliability theory. However, confirmatory factor analysis is valid in certain situations in which reliability theory fails. Hunter and Gerbing (1982) note that if the indicator variables define a general factor, and if the specific factors are irrelevant to the other variables being considered, then, at the level of second-order factor analysis, the indicator variables satisfy the assumptions of reliability theory, and confirmatory factor analysis generates the correct correlation between the general factor that was intended to be measured and the other variable. For example, it is quite likely that peer rating, supervisor rating, and job sample test each measure specific factors in addition to the general factor of job performance. However, if these specific factors are uncorrelated with each other and with the selection test, then confirmatory factor analysis will generate a correct correlation between the test and job performance. However, in the case of second-order analysis, the correction for attenuation is not made with the reliability of the composite score, but with a slightly smaller number. The reliability of the composite would be Mosier's (1943) formula with indicator reliabilities in the numerator diagonal, whereas the equivalent correction formula for second-order analysis is Mosier's formula with communalities in the numerator diagonal. Thus, second-order factor analysis correctly treats the specific factors as error.

There is a strong algebraic relationship between the average correlation and the correlation for the composite score. Let the indicator variables be denoted $x_1, x_2, \ldots, x_n$; let the composite score be denoted X; and let the other variable be denoted y. Let $\bar{r}_{xy}$ be the average correlation between the individual indicators and y; i.e., let $\bar{r}_{xy}$ be the average of $r_{x_1 y}$, $r_{x_2 y}$, and so on. Let $\bar{r}_{xx}$ be the average correlation between the indicator variables; i.e., let $\bar{r}_{xx}$ be the average of $r_{x_1 x_2}$, $r_{x_1 x_3}$, $r_{x_2 x_3}$, and so on. Let $\bar{c}_{xx}$ be the average covariance between the indicators; i.e. let $\bar{c}_{xx}$ be defined by

$$\bar{c}_{xx} = \frac{1 + (n-1)\bar{r}_{xx}}{n}.$$

Then the relationship between the average correlation $\bar{r}_{xy}$ and the composite score correlation r_{Xy} is given by

$$r_{Xy} = \frac{\bar{r}_{xy}}{\sqrt{\bar{c}_{xx}}}.$$

The number $\bar{r}_{xx}$ is a fraction; $0 \le \bar{r}_{xx} \le 1$. The number $\bar{c}_{xx}$ is a weighted average of $\bar{r}_{xx}$ and 1 and hence is between them.

$$0 \le \bar{r}_{xx} \le \bar{c}_{xx} \le 1$$

Since $\bar{c}_{xx}$ is a fraction, its square root is also a fraction and it lies between $\bar{c}_{xx}$ and 1, i.e.,

$$0 \le \bar{r}_{xx} \le \bar{c}_{xx} \le \sqrt{\bar{c}_{xx}} \le 1.$$

To divide $\bar{r}_{xy}$ by a fraction is to increase its size. Thus, for positive correlations we have

$$r_{Xy} \geq r_{xy} .$$

That is, the composite score correlation is always larger in size than the average correlation. It is the composite correlation whose sampling error is given by the conventional formula with the study sample size. The standard error of the average correlation is smaller than that by exactly the multiplicative factor $\sqrt{\bar{c}_{xx}}$. Thus, the composite score correlation enters into a larger cumulation in exact accordance with the assumptions about sampling error made by the cumulation formulas in Chapter 3, while the average correlation is off. If the conceptual assumptions of the study are correct, then the composite score correlation is also more accurate numerically.

From a conceptual point of view, the number we really want is the correlation for the composite without measurement error, i.e., the correlation obtained from confirmatory factor analysis with communalities. This number will be larger than the composite score correlation (and hence larger than the average correlation), although often not by much. However, a corrected correlation does not have the same standard error as an uncorrected correlation; the standard error is larger by the same multiplicative factor of correction (as shown in Chapter 3). If the correlations are corrected for attenuation or generated using confirmatory factor analysis with communalities, then the cumulative variance should be corrected using the formulas given in Chapter 3.

For example, suppose that peer rating, supervisor rating, and a job sample test were each correlated .60 with each other. Then

$$\bar{r}_{xx} = .60, \ \bar{c}_{xx} = .73, \ \sqrt{\bar{c}_{xx}} = .86$$

and, hence,

$$r_{Xy} = 1.16 \ \bar{r}_{xy} .$$

That is, the composite score correlation would be about 16 percent larger than the average correlation. If T is job performance measured without error, then the trait correlation r_{Ty} is related to the others by

$$r_{Ty} = \frac{r_{Xy}}{\sqrt{r_{XX}}} = 1.10 \ r_{Xy} = 1.28 \ \bar{r}_{xy}$$

where r_{XX} is the "reliability" of the composite score calculated using Mosier's (1943) formula with communalities in the numerator diagonal (which is also equal to coefficient alpha [Cronbach, 1951] calculated using the correlations between the scales). Thus, the correlation for actual job performance is 10 percent larger than the composite score correlation, and 28 percent larger than the average correlation.

Conceptual Replication: An Alternative Approach

Since the methods of confirmatory factor analysis may not be familiar to all readers, it is worthwhile noting that the correlation of a variable with the sum of other variables can be computed using more familiar formulas for the correlation of variables with composites (Nunnally, 1978, Chapter 5). A basic formula for the Pearson correlation between any two variables a and b is

$$r_{ab} = \frac{\text{Cov}(a, b)}{\text{SD}_a \, \text{SD}_b} .$$

If one variable, say variable b, is a composite, then we need only replace SD_b with the expression for the variance of a composite and replace $\text{Cov}(a, b)$ with the expression for the covariance of a variable with a composite. Suppose we want to compute r_{xY}, where x is a single variable and Y is a composite that is the sum of the measures y_1, y_2, and y_3. Then if the y_i measures are all in z score form (i.e., if SD = 1 for all y_i), the value S_Y^2, the variance of the composite, is merely the sum of all the values in the intercorrelation matrix of the y_i measures. This sum is denoted $1'R_{yy}1$ in matrix algebra, where R_{yy} is the correlation matrix among the y_i measures (including the 1.00s in the diagonal). The 1s are vectors that indicate that values in R_{yy} are to be summed. The square root of this value is SD_Y, that is, $(1'R_{yy}1)^{1/2} = \text{SD}_Y$.

The covariance of a variable with a composite is the sum of the covariances of the variable with each of the component measures of the composite. In our example, this would be $\text{cov}(xy_1) + \text{cov}(xy_2) + \text{cov}(xy_3)$. But since all variables are standardized, this is $r_{xy_1} + r_{xy_2} + r_{xy_3}$. This is denoted in matrix algebra as $1'r_{xy_i}$. Thus, we have

$$r_{xY} = \frac{1' \, r_{xy_i}}{\text{SD}_x \sqrt{1' R_{yy} 1}} = \frac{\Sigma r_{xy_i}}{(1) \sqrt{n + n(n-1) \bar{r}_{y_i y_j}}}$$

where $\bar{r}_{y_i y_j}$ is the average off-diagonal correlation in the correlation matrix R_{yy}.

Suppose, for example, a measure of perceptual speed (x) were correlated in the same sample of people with three measures of job performance: supervisory ratings of job performance ($r = .20$), peer ratings of job performance ($r = .30$), and records of output ($r = .25$). Suppose the correlations among the job performance measures are reported and the average of these is .50, that is, $\bar{r}_{y_i y_j} = .50$. Then,

$$r_{xY} = \frac{(.20 + .30 + .25)}{\sqrt{3 + 3\,(2)\,(.50)}} = .31.$$

The obtained value of .31 is larger than the average r ($\bar{r}_{xy_i} = .25$), as expected. Also, the sampling error variance of r_{xY} is known; it is $(1-.31^2)^2 / (N - 1)$. If the meta-analysis is to be based on artifact distributions (see Chapter 4), this value of .31 should be entered directly into the meta-analysis. However, the reliability of the composite measure of job performance should be computed, using the methods discussed below, and entered into the artifact distribution for reliabilities. If the meta-analysis is to be based on correlations individually corrected for unreliability (see Chapter 3), then the correction for unreliability (and range restriction if appropriate) should be applied to the .31 value before it is entered into the meta-analysis.

The formula given above assumes that the y_i measures are to be weighted equally. All weights are unity and all variables are in standard score form; therefore, each y_i measure has the same effect on the final Y composite. If you make the calculations with the variance-covariance matrix instead of the correlation matrix, the y_i measures will be weighted by their standard deviations. If you make the calculations with the correlation matrix, you can still weight the y_i differentially, by assigning unequal weights instead of unity weights. For example, suppose that, based on construct validity considerations you decide to assign twice as much weight to production records as to supervisory ratings and three times as much weight to peer ratings as to supervisory ratings. This leads to the weight vector $w' = [1\ 3\ 2]$. The correlation between the independent variable x and the weighted composite Y is then

$$r_{xY_2} = \frac{w'\,r_{xyi}}{\sqrt{w'\,R_{yy}w}} = \frac{[1\,3\,2]\begin{bmatrix} .20 \\ .30 \\ .25 \end{bmatrix}}{\sqrt{[1\,3\,2]\begin{bmatrix} 1.00 & .50 & .50 \\ .50 & 1.00 & .50 \\ .50 & .50 & 1.00 \end{bmatrix}\begin{bmatrix} 1 \\ 3 \\ 2 \end{bmatrix}}}$$

$$= \frac{(1)(.20) + (3)(.30) + 2(.25)}{\sqrt{[3.5 \ 4.5 \ 4.0] \begin{bmatrix} 1 \\ 3 \\ 2 \end{bmatrix}}} = \frac{1.6}{5.0} = .32 .$$

Thus, the weighted correlation is .32, while the unweighted correlation was .31. This is a typical result; when measures in a composite are substantially positively correlated, weighting usually has little effect on the correlation of the composite with other variables. If some measures in a composite have higher construct validity, however, differential weighting should be considered. The weighted mean correlation is

$$\bar{r}_w = \frac{(1)(.20) + (3)(.30) + 2(.25)}{1 + 3 + 2} = .26 .$$

Again, the mean correlation is less than the composite correlation.

Sometimes a study sample will have multiple measures of both the independent and dependent variables. If the correlations among all measures are given, you can compute the correlation between the sum of the independent variable measures (composite X) and the sum of the dependent variable measure (composite Y). The measure within each composite can be weighted equally or differentially. If the k measures in the independent variable composite are $x_1, x_2 \ldots x_i \ldots x_k$ and the measures in the dependent variable composite are $y_1, y_2 \ldots y_i \ldots y_m$, then the correlation between the two composites when all variables are equally weighted is

$$r_{XY} = \frac{1 \ R_{xy} 1}{\sqrt{1' R_{xx} 1} \ \sqrt{1' R_{yy} 1}} .$$

Note that the first term in the denominator is SD_X and the second is SD_Y; these are the SDs of the two composites. R_{xy} is the matrix of cross-correlations between the x_i measures and the y_i measures. The sum of these correlations is the covariance of composite X with composite Y. Thus, this formula corresponds to the fundamental formula for the Pearson r, i.e.,

$$r_{XY} = \frac{\text{Cov}(X, Y)}{SD_X \ SD_Y} .$$

The measures contained in each composite can also be differentially weighted. If the vector of (unequal) weights to be applied to the y_i is w, as before, and the vector of weights for the x_i measures is v, then the correlation between the two weighted composites is

$$r_{XY} = \frac{v'R_{xy}w}{\sqrt{v'R_{xx}v}\ \sqrt{w'R_{yy}w}}.$$

If the measures in one composite are to be weighted unequally, but not the measures in the other composite, then the differential weights can be replaced by a vector of 1s for the composite whose measures are to be equally weighted. For example, if the x_i are to be equally weighted, then v should be replaced by 1.

The formulas for the correlation of variables with composites and composites with other composites can often be used to compute a better estimate of the correlation from a study with conceptual replications. Entering these correlations into the meta-analysis instead of the individual measure correlations, or the mean r, improves the precision of the meta-analysis. We have used these formulas repeatedly in our work; typically the composite correlations can be computed with a hand calculator when one is reading and coding data from the study. These formulas are also useful in data interpretation in general. For example, suppose you are reading a journal research report that employs three measures of job satisfaction that are all correlated with a measure of organizational commitment. It may be clear that the best measure of job satisfaction would be the sum of the three measures. If the study reports the correlations among measures, you can use the formulas in this section to quickly compute the correlation between the job satisfaction composite and the organizational commitment measure, thus, extracting an important piece of information not reported by the study's authors. You can also check reported research for errors. If the study reports correlations for composites, these rs should be as large or larger than rs for individual measures. If they are not, that indicates an error in the reported results.

If you compute composite correlations, then you should compute the reliability of the composite measure. If you are using the meta-analysis procedure that corrects each correlation individually (see Chapter 3), you should use this reliability to correct the correlation computed. If you are using artifact distribution meta-analysis (see Chapter 4), then you should enter this reliability into the distribution of reliabilities.

The Spearman-Brown formula can be used to compute the reliability of the composite, based on the $\bar{r}$ among the measures in the composite. In our example, this would be

$$r_{yy} = \frac{n\,\bar{r}_{yy}}{1+(n-1)\bar{r}_{yy}}$$

$$= \frac{3(.50)}{1+(3-1)(.50)} = .75 .$$

An identical estimate of reliability would be produced by Cronbach's alpha. The corrected correlation is then

$$r_{xY_T} = \frac{.31}{\sqrt{.75}} = .36 .$$

In most meta-analyses, one would correct for unreliability in the x measure also.

Use of Spearman-Brown or alpha reliabilities assumes that the specific factors measured by each component measure in the composite are unrelated to the construct measured by the other variable (in this case x, a measure of perceptual speed) and can be treated as random error. In our example, this would be the assumption that the specific factors in supervisory ratings, peer ratings, and production records are unrelated to perceptual speed (as well as unrelated to each other). It also assumes that these specific factors are not part of true job performance, i.e., are irrelevant to the construct of job performance. If either or both of the assumptions appears to be implausible, then each measure in the composite may be measuring some aspect of actual or true job performance that is not measured by the other y_i measures. If so, then a different measure of reliability must be used, one that treats specific factor variance as true variance. The appropriate formula is given by Mosier (1943).

$$r_{yy} = \frac{1\,(R_{yy} - D + D_{rel})\,1}{1'\,R_{yy}\,1}$$

The denominator of this formula is the total variance of the composite, as explained earlier. Since reliability is always the ratio of true to total variance, the numerator is true variance. The matrix D is a (k by k) diagonal matrix with ones in the diagonal (all other values are zero). Subtracting D from R_{yy} just takes all of the 1.00s out of the diagonal of R_{yy}. Then adding the matrix D_{rel} (also k by k) back in replaces all the diagonal values with the reliabilities of the y_i measures. D_{rel} is a diagonal matrix that contains only these reliabilities.

Suppose in our example the reliability of the y_i is as follows.

Supervisory ratings: $r_{y_1 y_1} = .70$

Peer ratings: $r_{y_2 y_2} = .80$

Production records: $r_{y_3 y_3} = .85$

Then the Mosier reliability is

$$r_{yy} = \frac{1' \begin{bmatrix} 1.00 & .50 & .50 \\ .50 & 1.00 & .50 \\ .50 & .50 & 1.00 \end{bmatrix} - \begin{bmatrix} 1 & 0 & 0 \\ 0 & 1 & 0 \\ 0 & 0 & 1 \end{bmatrix} + \begin{bmatrix} .70 & 0 & 0 \\ 0 & .80 & 0 \\ 0 & 0 & .85 \end{bmatrix} 1}{1' \begin{bmatrix} 1.00 & .50 & .50 \\ .50 & 1.00 & .50 \\ .50 & .50 & 1.00 \end{bmatrix} 1}$$

$$r_{yy} = \frac{.70 + .80 + .85 + 6\,(.50)}{3 + 6\,(.50)}$$

$$r_{yy} = \frac{5.35}{6.00} = .89 \,.$$

Because the Mosier reliability considers specific factor variance as true variance, the reliability estimate is larger than our Spearman-Brown estimate of .75. Therefore, the correlation corrected for unreliability is smaller.

$$r_{xY_T} = \frac{.31}{\sqrt{.89}} = .33$$

This value is 8% smaller than the previous value of .36. Thus, you should give careful consideration to the question of whether specific factors should be treated as random error variance or true construct variance. In general, the larger the number of measures contained in a composite, the less likely it will be that specific factor variance should be treated as true variance. However, the final answer depends on the definition and theory of the construct being measured, and so no general answer can be given. But in many cases, theory does provide fairly clear answers. For example, verbal ability may be *defined* as what different measures of verbal ability have in common, thus implying that specific factor variance is error variance. Other constructs, for example job satisfaction and role conflict, are often defined theoretically in the same way. In most cases that we have encountered, specific factor variance should be treated as random measurement error.

Alas, there is a practical side to this issue. Published studies typically do not currently present whole correlation matrices, but often show only selected correlations. Thus, the composite score correlation may not be computable and the confirmatory factor analysis may not be computable. The unifactor hypothesis cannot even be tested for many studies. For such studies, the choice defaults to the use of individual correlations versus the use of the average correlation.

Analysis of Subgroups

For many it has now become routine to compute correlations separately by race and sex, even though there is usually no reason to believe that either will act as a moderator. This practice stems in part from a common confusion between additive and moderator effects. For example, some have hypothesized that the technology of an organization sets limits on its managerial philosophy. For example, large-scale manufacturing requires rigid coordination of work and hence provides fewer opportunities for power sharing with subordinates. This leads to the prediction that the level of consideration will be lower in manufacturing organizations. Even if this is true, however, within such organizations it may still be true that those who bring workers into their decision-making structure will have higher production. Thus, the *correlation* need not be lower in such plants even though the mean is.

If demographic membership is a real and substantial moderator, then the subgroup correlations can be entered into the larger cumulation as independent outcome values. Statistically, outcome values for nonoverlapping groups have the same properties as values from different studies.

Subgroups and Loss of Power

But the analysis of subgroups exacts a terrible price. Consider an example in which 100 persons are evenly split by race and by sex. There will then be 4 subgroups: 25 black females, 25 black males, 25 white females, and 25 white males. An outcome value for a sample size of 25 has much more sampling error than an outcome based on 100 cases. In fact, the confidence interval for 25 cases is exactly twice as wide as that for 100 cases. For the full sample, an observed correlation of .20 would have a confidence interval of $.00 \leq p \leq .40$. For each subsample, the confidence interval would be $-.20 \leq p \leq .60$. There is actually very little information in an observed correlation based on as few as 25 cases (although it can be cumulated with other small-sample correlations and make a contribution in this way).

The immense statistical uncertainty and sampling error in subgroup analysis leads to massive capitalization on chance. For simplicity, suppose that there is no moderating effect. If the population correlation is zero, then there are four opportunities to make a Type I error instead of one, and the actual Type I error rate would not be .05 but .19. If the population correlation is not zero, then there are four opportunities to make a Type II error rather than just one. But the situation is worse than that. The probability of a Type I error is always .05 regardless of the sample size, but the probability of a Type II error increases drastically with a decrease in sample size. For example, if the population correlation is .20 and the sample size is 100, then the probability of statistical significance and a correct inference is only .50. But if the sample size is 25, then the probability of significance drops to .16; i.e., the investigator will be wrong 84 percent of the time. Furthermore, the probability of correctly concluding significance in all 4 subgroups is $(.16)^4 = .0007$, which is less than 1 in 1,000. That is, analysis by subgroups for a population correlation of .20 raises the Type II error rate from 50% to 99.9%.

Subgroups and Capitalization on Chance

The situation is even worse for the many investigators who select the data to present using significance tests. If there were 10 variables in the study, then the correlation matrix would have 45 entries. If all population correlations were 0, then the analysis of the whole sample would provide for a search through 45 entries to capitalize on chance. At least 2 such correlations would be expected to be significant and it would not be incredibly unlucky to get 5. For a sample size of 100, the largest correlation in a chance matrix would be expected to be .23. However, for a subgroup, the largest correlation among 45 would be expected to be .46. Furthermore, the analysis by subgroups provides a search list of $4(45) = 180$ elements on which to capitalize by chance, and hence a greater expected error and an expected 8 and possibly 20 false significant readings.

Even if the null hypothesis were false for every correlation (in which case every failure to find significance would be Type II error of about 84% frequency), the handful pulled out would be completely unrepresentative of the population correlations. The true value of each correlation is .20, but with a sample size of 25, only correlations of .40 or greater will be significant (two-tailed test, $p \leq .05$). Therefore, only those correlations that by chance are much larger than the population value will be statistically significant. The conclusion that these correlations are not zero will be correct; that is, in this 16% of cases there will be no Type II error. But these significant observed correlations will greatly overestimate actual population correlations. The significant observed correlations will in fact be about twice as large as the actual value.

Subgroups and Suppression of Data

There is a current practice in journals that acts to restrict publication of data. Under current pressures, it is likely that an author who analyzed four subgroups would be allowed to publish only one-fourth as much data on each group. From the point of view of future cumulation, this is a disaster. There are too many missing values as it is.

Subgroups and the Bias of Disaggregation

If the moderator effect is nonexistent or trivial in magnitude, then the desired correlation for cumulation is the total group correlation. But for all practical purposes, it is the average correlation that is entered into the larger cumulation. That is, if there is no moderator effect, then the larger cumulation will ultimately average all entries and hence implicitly average the entries for each study. As it happens, the average correlation in this case may be quite "biased" as an estimate of the total sample correlation. This bias is always in the direction of the average correlation being smaller in magnitude than the total sample correlation. This bias is produced by restriction in range in the subgroups.

Assume that the covariance structures are the same in each subgroup; i.e., assume that the regression line is the same in all groups. Then the correlation is smaller in a subgroup to the extent that the standard deviation in the subgroup is smaller than the total population standard deviation. Let u be the ratio of standard deviations; i.e., let u be defined by

$$u = \frac{\sigma_{subgroup}}{\sigma_{total}}.$$

Let r_t be the correlation in the total group and let r_s be the correlation in the subgroup. Then the conventional formula for restriction in range yields

$$r_s = \frac{ur_t}{\left(\left(u^2 - 1\right)r_t^2 + 1\right)^{1/2}}.$$

For small correlations, this formula differs little from $r_s = ur$; i.e., the subgroup correlation is lower by a factor of u. To show that u is less than 1, we note that

$$u^2 = \frac{\sigma^2_{\text{subgroup}}}{\sigma^2_{\text{total}}} = 1 - \eta^2$$

where η^2 is the correlation ratio between the grouping variable and the causally prior variable of the two being correlated.

Conclusion: Use Total Group Correlations

If the moderating effect of the demographic variable is to be studied, then of course subgroup correlations should be entered into the cumulation. However, once the demographic variable is known to have little or no moderator effect, then the major cumulative analysis should be done with total group correlations.

Summary

There are three common forms of replication within studies: fully replicated designs, conceptual replication, and analysis of subgroups. Each requires a different strategy for meta-analysis.

A fully replicated design is a study in which there are subparts that are independent replications of the study design. For example, the same study design might be carried out in three organizations. Results from each organization can then be entered into the meta-analysis as if the results were from three separate studies. If results are averaged rather than entered separately, then the average should be treated as if the sample size were the sum of the sample sizes across the three organizations.

Conceptual replication is multiple measurement. Either the independent or the dependent variable could be measured by several instruments or methods. Each such measure then produces its own correlation or effect size. Ideally, these alternate measures should be combined by using confirmatory factor analysis or formulas for the correlations of composites, to yield a single correlation or effect size. The study then contributes one value to the meta-analysis with a minimum error of measurement. If the study report does not contain the information to do a confirmatory factor analysis or to compute composite correlations then the best alternative is to average the conceptually equivalent correlations or effect sizes. Since the values are not independent, the sample size for the average is the same as the sample size for the study. The average value will be an underestimate of the value that would have been produced by confirmatory factor analysis.

Analysis of subgroups may be either important or frivolous. If the subgroups are defined by what is believed to be a large moderator variable, then there should be a corresponding meta-analysis of these subgroups across studies. However, if the analysis of subgroups simply stems from a ritual analysis by sex, race, or other subgrouping, then the total group correlation should be the only contribution to the meta-analysis. In any case, the total group correlation should be used for the main meta-analysis across studies. If the total group correlation is not given and cannot be computed from the information in the report, then the subgroup correlations can be used individually in the meta-analysis. Alternatively, the subgroup correlations can be averaged and the average correlation used in the meta-analysis with the total group sample size. This average correlation will usually be slightly smaller than the total group correlation.

Methods of Integrating Findings Across Studies

This chapter presents and critiques ten different methods for integrating study results across studies. These methods are presented and discussed in their approximate order of efficacy (from least to most efficacious) in extracting the information needed from the studies reviewed.

The Traditional Narrative Procedure

The oldest procedure, the narrative review, has also been described as "literary," "qualitative," "nonquantitative," and "verbal." In this procedure the reviewer takes the results reported in each study at face value and attempts to find an overarching theory that reconciles the findings. If few studies exist, this integration can be carried out even though there may be some conflict between reviewers who postulate different interactions. But if the number of studies is large (100 to 1,000), then the studies will almost never be precisely comparable in design, measures, and so forth, and findings will typically vary across studies in bizarre ways. As a result, the information-processing task becomes too taxing for the human mind. The result is usually one of three outcomes. First, the result may be "pedestrian reviewing where verbal synopses of studies are strung out in dizzying lists" (Glass, 1976, p. 4). That is, the reviewer may not even attempt to integrate findings across studies. Second, the reviewer may simplify the integration task by basing his or her conclusions on only a small subset of the studies. Reviewers often reject all but a few of the studies as deficient in design or analysis, and then "advance the one or two acceptable studies as the truth of the matter" (Glass, 1976, p. 4). This approach unjustifiably wastes much information, and, in addition, may base conclusions on unrepresentative studies. Third, the reviewer may actually attempt the task of mentally integrating findings across all studies—and fail to do an adequate job. Cooper and Rosenthal (1980) have shown that even when the number of studies reviewed is as small as seven, reviewers who use narrative-discursive methods and reviewers who use quantitative methods reach different conclusions.

The Traditional Voting Method

The traditional voting method was one of the first techniques developed to ease the information-processing burden on the reviewer. In its simplest form, it consists merely of a tabulation of significant and nonsignificant findings. Light and Smith (1971, p. 433) described this approach as follows:

> All studies which have data on a dependent variable and a specific independent variable of interest are examined. Three possible outcomes are defined. The relationship between the independent and dependent variable is either significantly positive, significantly negative, or there is no significant relationship in either direction. The number of studies falling into each of these three categories is then simply tallied. If a plurality of studies falls into any of these three categories, with fewer falling into the other two, the model category is declared the winner. This model categorization is then assumed to give the best estimates of the direction of the true relationship between the independent and dependent variable.

The voting method is sometimes used also in an attempt to identify correlates of study outcomes. For example, the proportion of studies in which training method A was superior to training method B might be compared for males and females.

An example of a review based on this method is Eagly's (1978). The voting method is biased in favor of large-sample studies that may show only small effect sizes. Even where variation in sample size does not cause problems in interpreting significance levels, and where the voting method correctly leads to the conclusion that an effect exists, the critical question of the size of the effect is still left unanswered. But the most important problem with the voting method is that it can and does lead to false conclusions. Consider an example. Based on a meta-analysis of 144 studies, Pearlman et al. (1980) found the correlation of general intelligence and proficiency in clerical work to be .51. That is, if a perfect validity study were done using the entire applicant population and a perfectly reliable measure of job proficiency, then the correlation between intelligence and performance would be .51. But proficiency measures cannot be obtained on applicants; performance can be measured only on those who are hired. Most organizations hire fewer than half of those who apply. Suppose that those hired are those in the top half of the distribution on intelligence. Then, because of restriction in range, the correlation between test and performance will only be .33, rather than .51. But it is also impossible to obtain perfect measures of job performance. Typically, the best feasible measure is the rating of the single supervisor who knows the person's work well enough to rate it. According to the review of King et al. (1980), the usual interrater reliability of a single rating by a single supervisor is only .31. If the rater were asked to make multiple judgments and those ratings were combined into a composite score, then the interrater reliability would rise to .62. In this "best" of cases, the reliability of the job performance measure would be .62 (actually less, although we will ignore here the reduction in reliability produced by restriction in range), and the potential correlation between test and performance would be dropped from .33 to .26.

So, because of problems inherent in doing field studies, the investigator begins work with an underlying population correlation of .26. What are the implications of doing such a study with a small sample? Suppose that Smith does a study with a sample size of 30. Then if the expected correlation of .26 were found, it would not be statistically significant, and Smith would label the test as "invalid." But suppose that Jones found the same correlation of .26 using the median sample size reported by Lent, Aurbach, and Levin (1971a), i.e., $N = 68$. Then the same correlation would be statistically significant, and Jones would label the test as "valid." Here we have a prime example of false "conflicting results in the literature"; the same correlation can be labeled "significant" in one study, but "non-significant" in another. Reviewers using the voting method treat all studies alike and completely ignore the fact that studies with different sample sizes have a completely different meaning for "significant."

But suppose that all studies were done with the same sample size. Would reviewers find the research literature consonant with the uniformity that we have defined our example to have? Certainly not. This example has thus far assumed that the observed correlations would equal the population correlations, but this is quite false. If all studies were done with fifty subjects, what would the effect of sampling error be? For fifty subjects, the correlation must be .28 to be significant at the .05 level using a two-tailed test. Given a population correlation of .26, the observed correlation will have a mean of .26 and a standard deviation of .13. The probability that the observed correlation will be larger than .28 and, hence, be labeled as "significant" is .44. Thus, across studies, the test would be correctly labeled "valid" 44% of the time and would be incorrectly labeled "invalid" 56% of the time, and the author list in the review on the negative side of the issue would be somewhat longer than the author list on the positive side of the issue. Note that all authors who claim the test is "invalid" are actually wrong. That is, the conclusion stated in the *majority* of studies is wrong. Thus, the "preponderance of data" using counts of statistical significance can be completely false.

Furthermore, Hedges and Olkin (1980) have pointed out (and proven) that if there is a true effect, then in any set of studies in which mean statistical power is less than about .50, the probability of a false conclusion using the voting method increases as the number of studies increases. That is, the more data examined, the greater the certainty of a false conclusion about the meaning of the data! Thus, the traditional voting method is fatally flawed statistically and logically. Although reviewers using the voting method often reach conclusions — false or otherwise — the typical conclusion is that the research literature is in deplorable shape. Some researchers get results; others do not. Sometimes a given researcher gets significant results, sometimes not. These reviewers almost invariably issue calls for better research designs, better experimental controls, better measures, and so on (Glass, 1976).

Cumulation of p-Values Across Studies

This procedure attempts to cumulate significance levels across studies to produce an overall p-value (significance level) for the set of studies as a whole. If this value is small enough, the reviewer concludes that existence of the effect has been established. Methods for combining p-values across studies go back at least three decades (Baker, 1952), but the most recent advocates of this approach have been Rosenthal and his associates (Cooper & Rosenthal, 1980; Rosenthal, 1978a).

The major problem with this method is that in most sets of studies the combined p-value will be significant, but the fact tells nothing about the magnitude of the effect. Obviously, the practical and theoretical implications of an effect depend at least as much on its size as on its existence. Rosenthal (1978a, p. 192) has recognized the necessity for analysis of effect sizes along with p-values, and in his later substantive reviews (e.g., Rosenthal & Rubin, 1978a) has used a combination of p-value and effect-size analysis.

This method — cumulation of p-values along with computation of the mean effect size (r or d) — has been labeled the Combined Probability Method by Bangert-Drowns (1986). Bangert-Drowns notes that the Combined Probability Method is best regarded as a "transitional" form of meta-analysis. The introduction of the mean effect size resulted from the recognition by Rosenthal and his colleagues (Rosenthal 1978a; Rosenthal & Rubin, 1982a, 1982b) of the need for an index of the magnitude of study outcomes; but at the same time the method provides no information about the variability of effect sizes across studies, and, therefore, lacks an important component available in some other forms of meta-analysis. With the introduction of the Combined Probability Method, the method of cumulating p-values alone was left with no major advocates. Rosenthal (1984) has provided an extensive discussion of methods for cumulating p-values across studies. Additional information can be found in Rosenthal (1983) and Rosenthal and Rubin (1979a, 1983). In Chapter 13, we present a discussion of the specific method of combining p-values favored by Rosenthal (the Stouffer method), but we do not emphasize these methods in this book because we consider them to be less informative than other available methods (cf., also Becker, 1987). For example, the Stouffer combined probability method has no greater statistical power than a test of the significance of the average effect size (power is the same), yet the latter provides an index of magnitude of effect size, while the former does not. Even more critical is the fact that use of effect sizes permits an assessment of the extent to which an effect varies across studies. Combined probability methods provide no assessment of variation in effect sizes.

In passing, we note a potentially useful technique developed by Rosenthal as a result of his work in cumulating p-values across studies. This technique was developed to address the so-called "file drawer problem." Suppose a researcher has demonstrated that the combined p-value across the studies reviewed is, say, .0001, and concludes that a real effect exists. A critic could then argue that this finding is due to nonrepresentativeness of the studies reviewed, on grounds that studies not showing an effect are much less likely to have been located by the reviewer. That is, the studies with negative findings are apt to have been tucked away in file drawers rather than circulated or published. Using Rosenthal's (1979) technique, the researcher can calculate the number of missing studies showing zero effect size that would have to exist in order to bring the combined p-value down to .05, .10, or any other level. This number typically turns out to be very large, e.g., 65,000 (Rosenthal & Rubin, 1978a). It is highly unlikely that there are 65,000 "lost" studies on any topic. The statistical formulas and the rationale for file drawer analysis are given in Chapter 13.

Statistically Correct Vote-Counting Methods

Although the traditional vote-counting method is statistically and logically deficient, there are methods of cumulating research findings across studies based on vote counting that are statistically correct. These methods fall into two categories: (1) those that yield only a statistical significance level for the body of studies, and (2) those that provide a quantitative estimate of the mean effect size.

Vote-Counting Methods Yielding Only Significance Levels

If the null hypothesis is true, then the population correlation or effect size is in fact zero. Thus, when study results are given in the form of p-values, half would be expected to be larger than .50 and half smaller than .50. The sign test can be used to test whether the observed frequencies of findings in the positive and negative directions depart significantly from the 50-50 split expected under the null hypothesis (Hedges & Olkin, 1980; Rosenthal, 1978a). Alternatively, the reviewer can use a count to determine the proportion of studies reporting statistically significant findings supporting the theory (positive significant results) and test this proportion against the proportion expected under the null hypothesis (typically, .05 or .01). The binomial test or the chi-square statistic can be used for this test (Brozek & Tiede, 1952; Hedges & Olkin, 1980; Rosenthal, 1978a). Hedges and Olkin (1980) note that some reviewers believe that most, if not the majority, of studies should show a positive significant result if the true effect size or true correlation is nonzero. In fact, this is typically not true. When the true effect size or true correlation is in the range of magnitude typically encountered, only a minority of studies will usually report significant positive findings because of low statistical power in the individual studies. They also point out that the proportion of positive significant findings required to reject the null hypothesis is much smaller than is commonly believed. For example, if ten studies are run using alpha = .05, the probability of three or more positive significant findings is less than .01. That is, three positive significant findings out of ten is sufficient to reject the null hypothesis.

These vote-counting methods, however, are most useful when the null hypothesis is true, not when it is false. For example, Bartlett, Bobko, Mosier, and Hannan (1978) and Hunter et al. (1979) showed that frequency of significant differences in employment test validities for blacks and whites did not differ from the chance frequencies expected under the null hypothesis and the alpha levels used. Bartlett et al., for example, examined over 1,100 such tests at the alpha = .05 level and found that 6.2% were significant. When the null hypothesis is not rejected in cumulative studies with high statistical power, this method does provide an estimate of population effect size or population correlation: zero. However, when the null hypothesis is false, the binomial or sign tests provide no estimate of effect size. This is a serious disadvantage.

Vote-Counting Methods Yielding Estimates of Effect Sizes

The probability of a positive result and the probability of a positive significant result are both functions of the population effect size and study sample size. If sample sizes are known for all studies, then the effect size can be estimated from either the proportion of positive results or from the proportion of positive significant results. Hedges and Olkin (1980) have derived formulas for both of these methods of estimating effect size. They also present formulas for determining the confidence intervals around the effect-size estimates. These confidence intervals will, in general, be wider than those resulting when effect sizes are determined individually for each study and then averaged, as advocated by Glass (1976). (In the latter case, confidence intervals are based on the standard error of the mean.) The confidence intervals are wider because estimation of effect sizes from counts of positive or positive significant results uses less information from the studies than the Glass procedure. Therefore, vote-counting-based estimates of effect sizes should typically only be used when the information needed to determine effect sizes in individual studies is not available or retrievable.

Most studies provide either r or d values or enough information to compute these values. If a few studies do not, ordinarily one would just omit these studies from the meta-analysis. If the entire set does not, one would have to use one of the methods presented by Hedges and Olkin; however, that would be unusual. It would be more likely that one would have a subset of studies (say ten studies) that do not provide enough information to compute r or d. You could then use the Hedges and Olkin method to derive an estimate of $\bar{d}$ for this subset of studies and thereby avoid losing these studies. Also, if you are reading a traditional review that gives only statistical significance and the direction of significance for each study (a common occurrence), you can use one of these methods to get an estimate of the $\bar{d}$ for the studies in the review; in effect, this would be an incomplete and less precise — but quick and convenient — meta-analysis of these studies.

Counting Positive Significant Findings

Suppose you have 10 studies in which $N_E = N_C = 12$ in each study, and suppose 6 of the 10 have significant positive results ($\hat{p} = 6/10 = .60$). Then, from Table A2 of Hedges and Olkin (1980), you can determine that the estimated $\hat{\delta} = .80$. You can also derive an estimate of the standard error of this $\hat{\delta}$ using the formula given by Hedges and Olkin for the confidence intervals for the p-value. The 90% confidence interval for $\hat{p}$ is

$$\frac{(2m\hat{p} + c_\alpha^2) \pm \sqrt{c_\alpha^4 + 4mc_\alpha^2 \, \hat{p}\,(1-\hat{p})}}{2(m + c_\alpha^2)},$$

where m = the number of studies (10 here) and c_α = 1.645. The 90% confidence interval in our example is then

$$\frac{\left\{2\,(10)\,(.6) + 1.645^2\right\} \pm \sqrt{1.645^4 + 4\,(10)\,(1.645)^2\,(.60)\,(1-.60)}}{2\,(10 + 1.645^2)}$$

$$= .35 < \hat{p} < .81 .$$

This confidence interval applies to $\hat{p}$. We must next transform the end points of this CI to δ values, again using Table A2 of Hedges and Olkin (1980). By linear interpolation, δ for $\hat{p} = .31$ is 1.10 and δ for $\hat{p} = .35$ is .53. The approximate standard error of δ is then

$$SE_{\hat{\delta}} = \frac{1.10 - .53}{2\,(1.645)} = .1733$$

and the sampling error variance of $\hat{\delta}$ is $(.1733)^2$ or .03003. Thus, for the 10 studies combined, there is only one entry into the meta analysis: $\hat{\delta} = .80$ and $S_e^2 = .03003$.

Note that the $SE_{\hat{\delta}}$ here is the SE of the $\bar{d}$, not the standard error of ds from each individual study. This SE is analogous to $SE_d / \sqrt{m}$ from an ordinary meta-analysis of observed (and uncorrected) ds. The analogous estimate of SE_d for individual d values would be $\sqrt{m}\,SE_{\bar{d}}$, which here is $\sqrt{10}\,(.1733) = .548$. This is the estimate of the observed SD of individual d values across the 10 studies, based only on the significance information. But here we have in effect combined the 10 studies into one "study" for entry into the meta-analysis. Hence, the variance value that should be used is S_d^2, which is .03003 here. This estimate, like the Hedges and Olkin vote-counting methods in general, assumes that δ does not vary across studies. If δ does vary, the estimate of S_d^2 is only approximate.

This procedure allows us to salvage some, but not all, of the information potentially in the 10 studies. We can compute how much information is lost by our inability to compute a d value for each study. The actual total N in the 10 studies is $10(12)(2) = 240$. We can solve the following equation for N to determine the effective N in this analysis.

$$S_e^2 = \frac{4}{N}\left(1 + \frac{\overline{d}^2}{8}\right)$$

$$.03003 = \frac{4}{N}\left(1 + \frac{.8^2}{8}\right)$$

$$N = 144$$

Thus, the effective N, when only significance is known, is reduced from 240 to 144; 40% of the information in the studies is lost because the researchers did not report enough information to allow computation of d values.

This example assumed that $N_E = N_C = $ some constant across all studies. This will virtually never be true. If sample sizes vary, some form of the average sample size should be used. Hedges and Olkin (1980) suggest the geometric mean, the square mean root, or the simple average sample size. The geometric means is

$$GM = {}^m\sqrt{N_1 N_2 \dots N_m}\,.$$

The square mean root is

$$SMR = \left[\sum_1^m \left[\frac{\sqrt{N_i}}{m}\right]\right]^2.$$

If sample sizes do not vary dramatically across studies, the simple average N will be reasonably accurate. The reader should note that in Hedges and Olkin's Table A2, n is the number in the control *or* experimental group. Total N is $2n$. Thus, when sample sizes are not equal, one should average both the N_E and N_C values together.

Hedges and Olkin do not provide a separate table for correlations. However, their Table A2 will yield approximately correct values for r if (1) you convert the δ values at the top of the table to r (actually ρ), using the formula in Chapter 7, and (2) you remember to use one-half of your N in entering the table.

Counting Positive Results

An estimate of $\overline{d}$ or $\overline{r}$ for a group of studies that does not provide enough information to compute d and r in individual studies can also be derived from the number of outcomes that favor the experimental group —

whether or not they are significant. If the null hypothesis is true, and there are no differences between experimental and control groups, then this expected frequency is 50%. This method uses departures from the expected 50% to estimate $\bar{d}$ or $\bar{r}$. Suppose you have 10 studies for which N_C = N_E = 14 in each study, and 9 of 10 results are in the positive direction (i.e., favor the experimental group whether they are significant or not). Entering this information into Table A1 of Hedges and Olkin (1980) yields $\hat{\delta}$ = .50. Confidence intervals and the SE and S_e^2 of $\hat{\delta}$ are computed in the same way as illustrated for counts of positive significant results above.

Counting Positive and Negative Significant Results

This method is more useful than the two above when you suspect that publication or other availability bias is distorting the sample of studies. That is, when you believe that significant results—both positive and negative—are being published or located and nonsignificant results are not being published or located. This means the available set of studies is unrepresentative of all studies that have been conducted. This method is based on the proportion of all significant findings that are *positive* significant results, i.e.,

$$\hat{p} = \frac{\text{No. positive significant results}}{\text{No. positive plus negative significant results}}.$$

If the null hypothesis is true, the expected value of $\hat{p}$ is .50. Departures from .50 are the basis for the estimate $\hat{\delta}$. For example, suppose you have 20 studies, each with N_E = N_C = 10. Ten studies report significant results, and of the 10, 8 are significant positive findings. Thus, $\hat{p}$ = .80. Table A3 of Hedges and Olkin (1980) shows that $\hat{\delta}$ is then .15. Confidence intervals and standard errors can be estimated in the same way as described above for counts of positive significant results. This method should be used only when (1) publication bias based on significance only (not direction) is suspected, and (2) the studies do not allow computation of d or r values. Thus, it is not a method that will be used frequently.

The Hedges and Olkin (1980) methods of estimating effect size based on vote counting assume that the population effect size (δ) does not vary across studies. If δ varies substantially across studies, these methods yield only approximate estimates of mean effect size and variance of observed effect sizes (S_d^2).

Meta-Analysis of Research Studies

In this book, we have limited the term meta-analysis to methods that focus on the cumulation of effect sizes, rather than significance levels, across studies. Much early systematic work on combining p-values across studies can be found in the literature (e.g., Fisher, 1932, 1938; Pearson, 1938). Although systematic methods for meta-analysis have been presented and advocated only recently, many of the basic concepts underlying meta-analysis have been employed by individual researchers and research teams over the decades. Thorndike (1933) cumulated test-retest reliability coefficients for the Binet intelligence test from 36 studies and even went so far as to correct the observed variance of these coefficients for the effects of sampling error. He found that not all of the observed variance could be explained by sampling error; some of the variation was due to the length of the interval between test and retest. Ghiselli (1949, 1955, 1966) cumulated validity coefficients from numerous studies for different types of tests and different jobs, presenting the results in the form of median values. Although he did not systematically analyze the variances of coefficients, he did cumulate a vast amount of information, which he presented in his 1966 book, followed by an update later (Ghiselli, 1973). Despite his consistent emphasis on the cumulation of significance levels across studies, Rosenthal was computing and publishing mean correlations as early as 1961 (Rosenthal, 1961, 1963). Bloom (1964) averaged correlation coefficients to summarize the large number of studies that had accumulated on the stability (and instability) of human traits and abilities. Erlenmeyer-Kimling and Jarvik (1963) used kinship correlations for intelligence test scores from many studies to piece together a picture of hereditary influences on mental ability. Fleishman and Levine and their associates cumulated effect sizes across experimental studies to determine the relation between alcohol intake and decrements in task performances dependent on different abilities (Levine, Kramer, & Levine, 1975) and to determine the effectiveness of an abilities classification system in the vigilance area of human performance (Levine, Romashko, & Fleishman, 1973). None of these authors, however, advanced a systematic body of meta-analysis methodology for use in solving the general problem of integrating findings across studies to produce cumulative knowledge. In recent years, systematic quantitative techniques for integrating research findings across studies have been introduced. Glass (1976) advanced the first such set of procedures and coined the term "meta-analysis" to refer to the analysis of analyses (studies). One reason he introduced this term was to distinguish such analyses from secondary analysis. In secondary analysis, the researcher obtains and reanalyzes the original data on which an earlier study was based (Light & Smith, 1971). Meta-analysis is the quantitative cumulation and analysis of effect sizes and other descriptive statistics across studies. It does not require access to original study data.

Glassian Meta-Analysis Methods

The primary properties of Glass's meta-analysis are:

1. A strong emphasis on effect sizes rather than significance levels. Glass believes the purpose of research integration is more descriptive than inferential, and he feels that the most important descriptive statistics are those that indicate most clearly the magnitude of effects. His meta-analysis typically employs estimates of the Pearson r or of d, where

$$d = (\overline{X}_E - \overline{X}_C) / \text{SD}$$

   and $\overline{X}_E$ and $\overline{X}_C$ are the means of the experimental and control groups, respectively. SD is the average SD or the SD of the control group. Glass (1977) has presented quite a number of useful formulas for converting statistics in studies to estimates of d or r. The initial product of a Glassian meta-analysis is the mean and standard deviation of effect sizes[1] across studies (e.g., see Smith & Glass, 1977).

2. Acceptance of the variance of effect sizes (S_{ES}^2) at face value. Glassian meta-analysis implicitly assumes that S_{ES}^2 is real and should have some substantive explanation. These explanations are sought in the varying characteristics of the studies, e.g., sex or mean age of subjects, length of treatment, and more. Study characteristics that correlate with study effect are examined for their explanatory power. The general finding has been that few study characteristics correlate significantly with study outcomes. Problems of capitalization on chance and low statistical power associated with this step in meta-analysis are discussed in Chapter 2 and later in this chapter.

3. A strongly empirical approach to determining which aspects of studies should be coded and tested for possible association with study outcomes. Glass (1976, 1977) feels that all such questions are "empirical questions," and he seems to de-emphasize the role of theory or logic in determining which variables should be tested as potential moderators of study outcome (see also Glass, 1972).

Glassian meta-analysis has been applied to research studies on the effects of psychotherapy (Smith & Glass, 1977), the effects of the Keller personalized instruction system (Kulik, Kulik, & Cohen, 1979), gender effects in sensitivity to nonverbal cues (Hall, 1978), effects of test anxiety on test performance (Hembree, 1988), and to many other sets of research studies. In each case, the results clarify what was previously a confusing set of results and allow fairly specific conclusions.

Criticisms of Glassian Meta-Analysis

In later sections of this chapter, we argue that Glassian meta-analysis is incomplete in important respects and that our methods as presented in this book extend and complete Glass's methods. However, others have also advanced criticisms of Glass's methods. As a result of these criticisms, new approaches to meta-analysis have been advanced, approaches that are essentially variations on the Glass methods. These new approaches are discussed below. The major criticisms are:

1. In Glassian meta-analysis, the study effect size estimate is the unit of analysis. Studies based on a single research sample often report several (sometimes numerous) estimates of effect sizes; in such cases Glass and his associates typically include all such estimates in the meta-analysis, resulting in violations of the assumption of statistical independence (see Chapter 10). The effect of this is to cast doubt on the validity of any inferential statistical tests that might be applied in the meta-analysis, for example, tests of the significance of the $\bar{d}$ value. This criticism is statistically correct, but it overlooks the important fact that for Glassian meta-analysis, the purpose of research integration is more descriptive than inferential. While statistical tests are usually used, they are secondary to the descriptive purpose. We agree with the de-emphasis of significance testing in Glassian meta-analysis. As we showed in Chapters 1 and 2, it is precisely the overreliance on statistical significance tests in psychology and the other social sciences that has led to our extreme difficulties in making sense out of our research literatures. Also, in most cases, such violations of independence have a conservative effect on meta-analysis outcomes; they lead to overestimates of what the observed variance of study outcomes would be if all study effects were independent. Another important consideration is that violations of independence can be expected to have no systematic effect on $\bar{d}$ or $\bar{r}$ values, and the focus of the Glass method is heavily on these two summary statistics. Nevertheless, when a very small percentage of studies contributes a large percentage of the effect sizes, the credibility of the meta-analysis is called into question. Technical issues related to this problem are discussed in Chapter 10.

2. The second criticism holds that Glass is mistaken in including all studies in the meta-analysis regardless of methodological quality (Bangert-Drowns, 1986; Slavin, 1986). Slavin (1986), for example, calls for replacement of Glass's method by what he calls "Best Evidence Synthesis," in which all but the studies judged to be methodologically strongest are excluded from the meta-analysis. We discuss this question in more detail in Chapter 12. Glass's position—one that we agree with—is that judgments of overall methodological quality are often very subjective, and inter-evaluator agreement is

often low. Therefore, the question should be decided empirically by meta-analyzing separately the studies judged methodologically strong and weak and comparing the results. If they differ, one should rely on the "strong" studies; if they do not, then all studies should be used.

3. The third criticism is that the Glass methods mix very different independent variables in the meta-analysis, thereby masking important differences in the mean outcomes for different independent variables. For example, the Smith and Glass (1977) meta-analysis of the effects of psychotherapy included ten different kinds of therapy (e.g., rational-emotive along with behavior modification therapies). The argument is that if some of these therapy methods are more effective than others, such a meta-analysis would never reveal that fact. This criticism ignores the fact that there is nothing in Glass's methods that precludes performing separate meta-analysis for each independent variable type as a second step; and in fact, this is typically done, allowing any such differences in treatment effects to emerge. However, Glass correctly argues that whether such finer grained meta-analyses are necessary depends on the purpose of the meta-analysis. If the research question is, "What is the relative effectiveness of different types of therapy?", clearly they are. But if the research question is whether therapy in general is effective (for example, to determine whether therapists should be reimbursed under government health insurance programs), then the overall analysis may be more appropriate (Wortman, 1983). Glass's critics are theoretically and analytically oriented and, therefore, find it hard to see why anyone would ever ask such a broad research question. In our research, we have typically asked narrower questions, and, therefore, our independent variables have been quite homogeneous.

4. The last major criticism is that Glassian methods mix measures of very different *dependent* variables. For example, in studies of educational interventions, *d* values for measures of attitudes, beliefs, disciplinary behavior, and academic achievement may all be included in the same meta-analysis. The critics are correct in contending that the results of such meta-analysis are difficult or impossible to interpret. It does not seem likely that the impact of, say the open classroom, would be the same on such conceptually diverse dependent variables. Again, however, there is nothing inherent in Glass's methods that precludes conducting separate meta-analyses for each dependent variable construct. The problem is that this has often not been done. In our research, we have confined the dependent variable measures within a single meta-analysis to measures of a single construct. In our validity generalization research, for example, the dependent variable has always been a measure of overall job performance.

Most of these criticisms do not stem from the nature of the Glassian statistical methods for meta-analysis per se. Instead they are criticisms of the applications of these methods made by Glass, his associates, and some others. The criticisms stem from the fact Glass and his critics have very different concepts of what the purpose of meta-analysis is. For Glass, the purpose of meta-analysis is to paint a very general, broad, and inclusive picture of a particular research literature. The questions to be answered are very general; for example, does psychotherapy — regardless of type — have an impact in general on the kinds of things that therapist-researchers consider important enough to measure, regardless of the nature of the construct (e.g., self-reported anxiety and counts of emotional outbursts and . . .). His critics believe meta-analysis must answer much narrower, more specific questions if it is to contribute to cumulative knowledge, understanding, and theory development. Actually, meta-analysis can be used for both purposes. A more general quantitative summary may be useful as a first step; for those who believed that there was no cumulativeness — and indeed no order whatsoever other than randomness — in social science research literatures, the results of such meta-analysis could be (and probably have been) a heartening step back from epistimological despair. However, they can only be a first step; further advances in scientific understanding do require that meta-analysis answer more specific questions. For example, we must look separately at the impact of a given organizational intervention on job satisfaction and job knowledge.

Study Effects Meta-Analysis

One variation on Glass's methods has been labeled Study Effect Meta-Analysis by Bangert-Drowns (1986). It differs from Glass's procedures in several ways. First, only one effect size from each study is included in the meta-analysis, thus assuring statistical independence within the meta-analysis. If a study has multiple dependent measures, those that assess the same construct are combined (usually averaged), and those that assess different constructs are assigned to different meta-analyses. These steps are similar to those we have followed in our research. Second, this procedure calls for the meta-analyst to make at least some judgments about study methodological quality and to exclude studies with deficiencies judged serious enough to distort study outcomes. In reviewing experimental studies, for example, the experimental treatment must be at least similar to those judged by experts in the research area to be appropriate, or the study will be excluded. This procedure seeks to determine the effect of a particular treatment on a particular outcome (construct), rather than to paint a broad Glassian picture of a research area. Some of those instrumental in developing and using this procedure are Mansfield and Busse (1977), Kulik and his associates (Bangert-Drowns, Kulik, & Kulik, 1983; Kulik & Bangert-Drowns, 1983/1984), Landman and Dawes (1982), and Wortman and Bryant (1985).

Homogeneity Test-Based Meta-Analysis

This method was advanced primarily as an improvement in Glassian methods of attempting to find moderators. In Glassian meta-analysis, two methods are used to identify potential moderators. In the first method, the initial all-inclusive meta-analysis is broken down into separate meta-analyses for different features or variations in the independent variable; for example, separate meta-analyses for different types of psychotherapy.In the second method, coded study features, such as age of subjects, date of publication, and so on, are correlated with study outcomes and regression analyses are run predicting study outcomes from multiple study characteristics. Hedges (1982a) and Rosenthal and Rubin (1982a) proposed that statistical tests be used as an aid in deciding whether study outcomes are more variable than would be expected from sampling error alone. If they are not, then there is no basis for searching for moderators. The statistical tests they advocate are based on the chi-square distribution. (A similar test was presented but not recommended in Hunter et al. 1982; see also Chapters 3 and 7 of the present book.) Use of chi-square tests of homogeneity to determine whether findings in a set of studies differ more than would be produced by sampling error is not new; such tests were advanced by Snedecor (1946) over forty years ago.

Hedges (1982b) extended the concept of homogeneity tests to develop a more general procedure for moderator analysis based on significance testing. Essentially, it calls for breaking the overall chi-square statistic down into the sum of within- and between-group chi-squares. The original set of effect sizes in the meta-analysis is divided into successively smaller subgroups until the chi-square statistics within the subgroups are non-significant, indicating that sampling error can explain all the variation within the last set of subgroups.

This approach represents a return to the very practice that originally led to the great difficulties in making sense out of research literatures: over-reliance on statistical significance tests (see Chapters 1 and 2). Except for the method of cumulating p-values across studies, no other method of meta-analysis is built so squarely on the quicksand foundation of significance testing. The first problem is that the significance tests advocated allow only for sampling error; there are many other purely artifactual sources of variance between studies in effect sizes, as detailed in Chapters 2 and 6. These include computational, transcriptional, and other data errors, differences between studies in reliability of measurement, and in levels of range restriction, and many others. Thus, even when true study effect sizes are actually the same across studies, these sources of artifactual variance will create variance beyond sampling error, causing the chi-square test to be significant and to falsely indicate heterogeneity of effect sizes. This is especially likely to be true when the number of studies is large, creating high "power" to detect even small amounts of such artifactual variance. Second, even when the variance beyond sampling error is not artifactual, it often will be small in magnitude and of little or no theoretical or practical significance. Hedges and Olkin (1985) recognize this fact and caution that researchers should evaluate the actual size of the variance; unfortunately, however, once researchers are caught up in significance tests, the usual practice is to assume that if it is significant it is important, and act (or interpret) accordingly. Once the focus is on significance test results, there is a tendency to ignore effect size. Third, especially in its elaborated form as advanced by Hedges (1982b; Hedges & Olkin, 1985, Chapter 13), this method tends to encourage atheoretical, purely empirical quests for moderators (see Chapter 9). One is, in effect, invited to keep dividing the original effect sizes into smaller and smaller groups, on whatever bases are available, until the chi-square statistics are no longer significant within groupings. This is especially true in the case of the procedure described in Chapter 13 of Hedges and Olkin (1985).

The Schmidt-Hunter Meta-Analysis Methods: Validity Generalization

This procedure was developed concurrently with Glass's work for application to validity studies of employment tests (Pearlman et al. 1980; Schmidt, Gast-Rosenberg, & Hunter, 1980; Schmidt & Hunter, 1977; Schmidt, Hunter, Pearlman, & Shane, 1979); however, its principles are general and were quickly extended to other research areas (Hunter, 1979). Even though its developers were unaware of Glass's work at the time, this procedure can be regarded as an extension of Glassian meta-analysis to deal with problems such as sampling error, unreliability, restriction in range, and the like. The primary properties of this procedure are:

1. A strong emphasis on effect sizes rather than p-values. This emphasis is pretty much the same as that in Glassian meta-analysis, and for the same reasons. Effect sizes are expressed as correlations, but this is not an important distinction. Unlike Glassian meta-analysis, this meta-analysis procedure calls for correcting the mean effect size for attenuation due to instrument unreliability and range restriction (if any), yielding more accurate estimates of mean effect sizes.

2. Unlike Glassian meta-analysis, Schmidt-Hunter meta-analysis does not take the variance of observed effect sizes (S_{ES}^2) at face value. Instead, the step after determination of the mean effect size is to test the hypothesis that S_{ES}^2 is

entirely due to various statistical artifacts. These artifacts include (1) sampling error, (2) study differences in reliability of independent and dependent variable measures, (3) study differences in range restriction, (4) study differences in instrument validity, and (5) computational, typographical, and transcription errors. Schmidt and Hunter developed methods of estimating and subtracting variance due to the first three of these five artifacts. Generally, if these three artifacts account for 75% or more of the observed S_{ES}^2, they conclude that the residual S_{ES}^2 is probably due to the remaining two artifacts and that true $S_{ES}^2 = 0$. In over more than 500 such applications to employment test validities, the average amount of observed S_{ES}^2 accounted for my statistical artifacts, 1, 2, and 3 above has been over 85%.

3. If the hypothesis $S_{ES}^2 > 0$ is not rejected, S_{ES}^2 adjusted for the effects of the three artifacts is used (with appropriate correction) to place a credibility interval around the estimated true mean effect size. (Generally, only the lower bound of this interval is emphasized in practical applications involving employment testing; see Schmidt, Gast-Rosenberg & Hunter, 1980, for complete details.)

Pyschometric Meta-Analysis

As Hunter (1979) pointed out, there is no incompatibility between the Glass meta-analysis methods and the Schmidt-Hunter meta-analysis methods. The Schmidt-Hunter procedures can be viewed as an extension of Glassian meta-analysis to deal with variations in study effect sizes due to sampling error and other artifacts and with attenuations of effect-size estimates due to measurement unreliability and range restriction. Both of these meta-analysis methods, however, are incomplete. Hunter (1979) rewrote the Schmidt-Hunter formulas to be appropriate for use with experimental studies (where d rather than r is the effect-size statistic). These formulas are given in Chapter 7. These extensions, when combined with provisions for moderator analyses when observed S_{ES}^2 is not due completely to artifacts, yield the method presented in this and in our 1982 book. We refer to these methods as psychometric meta-analysis.

The primary properties of this meta-analysis procedure are as follows:

1. Primary focus is on effect sizes. All effect sizes are to be corrected for statistical and measurement artifacts (e.g., instrument unreliability) that attenuates them from their true score values.

2. After estimating mean true effect size, the hypothesis that observed S_{ES}^2 is due to statistical artifacts is tested, using methods developed by Schmidt and Hunter. This is the hypothesis that the variance of *actual* (true) effect sizes is zero, i.e., $S_{ESA}^2 > 0$. If this hypothesis is rejected, the reviewer concludes

that the true ES is constant across the many factors varying in the studies reviewed. Estimated $\overline{ESA}$ is then the final and only product of the review.

3. If the hypothesis that $S^2_{ESA} > 0$ cannot be rejected, then selected properties that vary across studies are coded and correlated with study ESs as suggested by Glass — except that one relies on theoretical, logical, statistical, and psychometric considerations when possible in deciding what study characteristics to code and how to code them. Study properties coded should not be the artifacts (or products of the artifacts) controlled for in step 2; otherwise, the effects of a given artifact may be partialed out twice. Alternatively, one can subgroup studies based on study characteristics and conduct separate meta-analyses.

4. Correlations between study characteristics and ESs are corrected for sampling error in ESs using the procedure developed by Hunter (1979). Corrections are also made for unreliability in the measure of the study characteristic if it is not perfectly assessed. If all these correlations are trivial in magnitude, go to step 8.

5. Correlations among study characteristics are computed and corrected for unreliability in the study characteristics.

6. The true score regression of ES on study characteristics is computed. The resulting beta weights should be interpreted as indicating potential causal effects of true study characteristics on true study ES.

7. The resulting true score multiple R should be corrected for shrinkage using the appropriate shrinkage formula (Cattin, 1980). This shrunken R^2 then gives the percentage of variance S^2_{ESA} (from step 2) accounted for by variation in study characteristics. (Unfortunately, however, this procedure will often not fully correct for capitalization on chance. See the discussion of capitalization on chance below and in Chapter 2.)

8. Three different kinds of distributions of ES can then be derived. These constitute the final products of the meta-analysis.

   a. $\overline{X} = \overline{ESA}$, with standard deviation corrected for effects of statistical artifacts only. This distribution describes true effect sizes to be expected when study characteristics are allowed to vary as in the studies reviewed. This would be the information needed if, for example, a given educational program were to be implemented in somewhat different ways in different parts of the country. Credibility intervals are derived for this distribution.

   b. $\overline{X} = \overline{ESA}$ with standard deviation corrected for effects of statistical artifacts *and for effects of deviations of study characteristics from their mean values*. This distribution describes true ES to be expected when study characteristics are held constant at their mean values. Coredibility intervals can be derived for this distribution.

   c. The value of $\overline{X} = \overline{ESA}$ and the standard deviation can be found for a distribution in which study characteristics are held constant at values other than their means. Under the usual assumption of homoscedasticity, all such alternative sets of study characteristics values should leave SD_{ESA}

unchanged from distribution b. However, $\overline{ESA}$ would change. Thus, a decision maker could specify in advance the conditions of implementation and compute the expected ES under that specific set of conditions. He or she could then construct a credibility interval for the $\overline{ESA}$. This procedure tailors effect size predictions to the specific set of circumstances under which an intervention or program is to be implemented.

In cases in which study characteristics do not correlate with ES, the distributions in a, b, and c will be identical. In such a case, the combination procedure reduces to the Schmidt-Hunter procedure. The combination procedure also reduces to the Schmidt-Hunter procedure for data sets in which it is concluded that artifacts fully account for observed S_{ES}^2.

In both Glass's meta-analysis and in psychometric meta-analysis, there are unresolved problems. First, when effect size estimates are regressed on multiple-study characteristics, capitalization on chance operates to increase the apparent number of significant associations for those study characteristics that have no actual associations with study outcomes. Since the sample size is the *number of studies* and many study properties may be coded, this problem is potentially severe (see discussion in Chapter 2). There is no purely statistical solution to this problem. The problem can be mitigated, however, by basing choice of study characteristics and final conclusions not only on the statistics at hand, but also on other theoretically relevant findings (which may be the result of other meta-analyses) and on theoretical considerations. Results should be examined closely for substantive and theoretical meaning. Capitalization on chance is a threat whenever the (unknown) correlation or regression weight is actually zero or near zero. Second, when there is in fact a relationship, there is another problem: Statistical power to detect the relation may be low (see discussion in Chapter 2). Thus, true moderators of study outcomes (to the extent that such exist) may have only a low probability of showing up as statistically significant. In short, this step in meta-analysis is often plagued with all the problems of small-sample studies. For a discussion of these problems, see Schmidt, Hunter, and Urry (1976) and Schmidt and Hunter (1978). Other things being equal, conducting separate meta-analyses on subsets of studies to identify a moderator does not avoid these problems and may lead to additional problems of confounding (see Chapter 13).

Summary

We have reviewed ten different methods for integrating research findings across studies. These methods form a rough continuum of efficacy in revealing hidden facts that can be proven by the cumulative weight of previous studies. The narrative method is unsystematic, haphazard, and imposes an impossible information-processing burden on the reviewer. The traditional voting method uses only part of the available information, provides no information about effect size, and, worst of all, logically leads to false conclusions under circumstances that are quite common. Cumulating p-values across studies does not logically lead to false conclusions, but has all the other disadvantages of the traditional voting method. Statistically correct vote-counting methods that yield only an overall statistical significance level (p-value) for the group of studies reviewed have all the disadvantages of cumulating p-values across studies. In particular, these methods provide no estimate of effect size. Other vote-counting procedures presented by Hedges and Olkin (1980, 1985) do provide estimates of effect size, but the uncertainty in such estimates is substantial because these methods are based on only a part of the information that individual studies should present. These methods require the assumption that effect sizes are equal across studies; if this assumption is not met, then these methods yield only an approximate estimate of *mean* effect size.

Glassian meta-analysis is a quantum improvement over these research integration methods. It uses more of the available information from the individual studies and provides a more accurate estimate of effect size or mean effect size; it does not require the assumption that effect sizes are constant across studies; and it provides an estimate of the variance of effect sizes. It also provides for correlating study effect sizes with study characteristics in an attempt to determine the causes of variation in study findings.

For most purposes of scientific research, Study Effects meta-analysis is an improvement over Glassian meta-analysis. It allows clearer conclusions about relationships between specific independent and dependent variable constructs, permitting finer tests of scientific hypothesis. Homogeneity test-based meta-analysis, however, is in our judgment *less* useful than Glassian methods. Thus, the order of their presentation in this chapter does not correspond to their relative efficacy; they appear late in the presentation sequence only because they were developed relatively late in time.

The Schmidt-Hunter meta-analysis procedure used in validity generalization studies extends and improves Glass's methods (and the Study Effects method) by (1) introducing a more accurate estimate of effect size (weighted estimates), (2) correcting effect-size estimates to remove the artifactual attenuating effects of instrument unreliability and range restriction, and (3) providing tests of the hypothesis that the variance in observed effect sizes (S_{ES}^2) is due solely to artifacts. It also includes the strengths of

Study Effects meta-analysis. However, it does not include the step of correlating study characteristics with study effect sizes when S_{ES}^2 cannot be accounted for solely by artifacts.

The final form of meta-analysis, psychometric meta-anlaysis (the Hunter-Schmidt procedure), provides for examination of these relationships when appropriate. This method extends the earlier Schmidt-Hunter method by providing formulas for using the method with d statistics as well as with r statistics, and provision is made for correcting for additional artifacts. Other refinements have also been added. Even this procedure, however, does not solve all problems. If effect sizes are regressed on study characteristics — which is often not necessary — there may be substantial problems of capitalization on chance and low statistical power. Conducting separate meta-analyses on study subsets to identify moderators does not avoid these problems and may lead to additional problems of confounding (see Chapter 13).

NOTE

1. In purely correlational studies, the r statistic should not, strictly speaking, be referred to as an estimate of "effect size." However, for the sake of brevity and convenience, the term "effect size" is used here to refer to both r and d. This convention is widely used.

12 Locating, Selecting, and Evaluating Studies

This chapter discusses problems and issues in locating, selecting and evaluating studies to be included in a meta-analysis. Our comments in this chapter are by no means intended to be comprehensive. Rather, they are intended to complement other published discussions of this topic. That is, we have included in this chapter mostly material that we have found to be absent from other treatments. Cooper (1984) devotes much of his book to questions related to locating and evaluating studies. We commend his treatment to the reader. Another useful book is Stewart (1984). Ostensibly devoted to secondary research, that book also contains much information that is useful in locating primary studies for meta-analysis.

Conducting a Thorough Literature Search

There are three major approaches to locating research studies on a given topic: examining indices to documents, searching existing bibliographies, and querying other scholars who might be familiar with appropriate studies. During the last fifteen years there have been tremendous changes in the nature of indices to documents. For example, the SOCIAL SCI-SEARCH system now permits a forward citation search, i.e., a search for the studies published *after* a key article that cite that key article. Most of the following discussion will focus on the use of these indices, but the use of bibliographies and personal queries will be briefly touched on.

Indices

Existing indices vary along several different dimensions. These include the following.

1. *Subjects covered.* Different indices cover different subjects, but there is a moderate degree of overlap among some indices of the social sciences. Ten

indices that might be useful for identifying research of interest to organizational psychologists will be briefly described below.

2. *Thoroughness of coverage.* This depends primarily on (1) the types of documents that are indexed (which could include books, monographs, journal articles, papers presented at regular professional meetings, reports of federally supported research, summaries of work in progress, and/or other "fugitive literature"); (2) the number of sources of each type of document that are indexed (such as 200 journals versus 500); (3) the starting date of coverage; and (4) whether or not all articles or reports from a given source (such as a specific journal or professional meeting) are indexed.

3. *Form of the index.* Some indices are only in printed form, some are only in machine-readable form, and some are in both printed and machine-readable form.

4. *The kinds of information provided in the index.* Some indices provide only the full source citation, but some provide the source citation, subject description, a substantial abstract, and other information.

5. *Availability.* Indices in printed form are available primarily in libraries or from the publisher. Indices in machine-readable form may be purchased or leased. More commonly they are searched by on-line access to the data files of several information retrieval systems. The most widely used are those of Bibliographic Retrieval Services, Inc., Lockheed Information systems (Dialog), and Systems Development Corporation (Orbit).

Because of the variation in different indices, the use of two or more of them will usually result in a larger number of appropriate citations than would the use of just one. The characteristics of ten indices that might be of use to organizational psychologists are shown in Table 12.1.

Organizational psychologists will usually identify a larger number of appropriate studies when using *Psychological Abstracts (PA)* than when using any other index. But the Smithsonian Science Information Exchange (SSIE) covers studies that are hardly ever in *PA* at the time of a given search. The National Technical Information Services (NTIS) covers a substantial number of studies not in *PA*. CURRENT CONTENTS lists many articles one to five months prior to their citation in most other indices. SOCIAL SCISEARCH allows a forward citation search, which is impossible with any of the other listed indices. And the five other indices listed in the table will often identify at least a few appropriate studies not found through the use of *Psychological Abstracts*.

When an index is available in both printed and machine-readable form, there are several points worth remembering when deciding which to use.

1. The biggest advantages of computerized searches of machine-readable files are speed and accuracy.

Table 12.1 The Variance Comparison Ratio for Meta-Analyses of a Treatment That Fails in 50% of Studies

Index Name	Subject Coverage	Types of Documents	Approximate Number of Publications Covered	Starting Date (printed/machine readable form)
ABI/INFORM	All aspects of management and administration.	Journals, business magazines, and newspapers.	400	X/1971
ERIC (Education Resources Information Center)	Education and topics relevant to it such as personnel services, education management, and tests and measurement.	Journals, most government-sponsored research on education, papers presented at meetings, and other fugitive materials.	700	1966/1966
Comprehensive Dissertation Abstracts	All subjects.	Doctoral dissertations, listed University Microfilm publications of Dissertation Abstract International, American Doctors Dissertations, and Comprehensive Dissertation Index.	–	1861/1861
Management (Management Contents)	All aspects of business and management.	U.S. and non-U.S. journals, proceedings and transactions related to business and management.	–	X/1974
NTIS (National Technical Information Service)	Physical, social engineering, life sciences, including administration, behavior and economics, and communication.	Government-sponsored research journal articles, and translations prepared by or for the federal government.	–	1964/1964
Psychological Abstracts	Psychology and topics relevant to it.	Journals, technical reports and monographs, books, Dissertation Abstracts International.	900	1927/1967
SOCIAL SCISEARCH (Social Science Citation Index)	Social, behavioral and related sciences.	Journals in the social, natural, physical, and biomedical sciences.	3,800	1972/1972
SSIE (Smithsonian Information Exchange)	Physical, social, engineering and life behavioral sciences and social sciences.	Project descriptors from 1,300 organizations that fund research (see comments).	–	X/last 24 months
Sociological Abstracts	Sociology and topics relevant to it, including social psychology, management, and complex organizations.	Journals, other serials, monographs and papers presented at meetings.	1,200	X/1963

Table 12.1 (Continued)

Approximate Number of New Citations Each Year	Kinds of Information in the Record [a]	Approx. On-Line Connect Charge, Assuming Moderate Quantity Discount	Availability	Comments
17,000	Title, authors, source, and abstract.	$55/hr	BRS, Lockheed	
36,000	Title, authors, source, descriptors, identifiers, abstract, and other.	$20/hr	BRS, Lockheed, SDC	
42,000	Title, author, date, university, and references if it is abstracted in Dissertation Abstracts International or American Doctoral Dissertations.	$40/hr	BRS, Lockheed, SDC	Has about 99% of American doctoral dissertations, and thousands of Canadian and other foreign ones.
12,000	Title, author, source, descriptors, identifiers, abstract, and other.	$55/hr	BRS, Lockheed, SDC	
60,000	Title, author, source, descriptors, identifiers, abstract, and other.	$30/hr	BRS, Lockheed, SDC	Has reports to or by 300 government agencies, but thoroughness of coverage varies among agencies and over years. Coverage of behavioral and social science research is poor for the years prior to the mid seventies.
30,000	Title, author, source, descriptors, identifiers, abstracts, and other.	$50/hr	APA, BRS, Lockheed, SDC	
108,000	Title, author, source, cited references, and other.	$55/hr	BRS, Lockheed, SDC	For each indexed article, the author and source (but not title) of each reference is given. In addition, for each author there is a list of any of his or her articles that have been referenced in other indexed articles, with the name(s) of the author(s) who referred to each particular article.
108,000	Title, author, source, descriptors, abstract, and other.	$65/hr	BRS, Lockheed	Has descriptions of research that is in process or recently completed. Includes most federal government contract and grant research; other covered funding resources include state and local governments, foundations, universities, and so on.
7,500	Title, author, source, descriptors, identifiers, abstract, and other.	$40/hr	Lockheed	

[a] Descriptors are subject terms specified in the Thesaurus; identifiers are subject terms usually chosen at the discretion of the indexer.

2. Usually both forms of the index will cover the same documents and have the same kinds of information about the documents.

3. The machine-readable forms seldom cover documents released prior to the mid-sixties. Because of this, but usually only because of it, the coverage of the machine-readable form is often less thorough than that of the printed form.

4. Some machine-readable index files are considerably cheaper to search than others. Generally, the government supported or maintained files are the cheapest, running $25 to $40 per connect hour, and the proprietary files are the most expensive, running $60 to $80 per hour.

5. It will take about two days to become fairly competent using any of the major computerized information retrieval systems that access the indices, and another day or two to acquire a good knowledge of each index you wish to search. Consequently, if you do searches infrequently, it may pay to have an experienced information specialist do them. You might find one at your university library or computer center. Most of the organizations (including the American Psychological Association) that produce the indices will conduct, on a fee-for-services basis, a search of their own index.

Bibliographies and Personal Queries

Searching bibliographies of previous reviews and documents on the topic is a time-honored approach for locating appropriate studies.

Querying scholars who might be familiar with appropriate studies is also a widely used approach. We suspect it is most effective when you include with your letter a copy of the bibliography that you have compiled to that date, and a self-addressed stamped envelope. A query of "Please inform me of all studies on topic X that you are aware of" usually requires substantially more effort to answer than listing a few studies that one notices are not on the enclosed bibliography. When a research topic is fairly new, this often is the most productive search approach.

Complexities of the Search for Studies

Many practical problems and complexities are encountered in conducting a thorough search for the studies to be included in a meta-analysis. This is perhaps especially true in an area where there is good reason to believe that many of the relevant studies are unpublished. In such a case, considerable time must be spent writing and calling individuals and organizations that are likely to have such studies. In two of our meta-analyses, for example, most of the necessary studies were unpublished. McDaniel, Schmidt and Hunter's (1988a) is a meta-analysis of the validity (for job performance prediction) of different methods of evaluating job applicants' education, training, and experience. McDaniel, Whetzel et al. (1988) is a meta-analysis of the validity of employment interviews. In both cases, a large percentage of studies had been conducted by state and city Civil Service organizations and had never been published. Months were spent locating and attempting to obtain these studies. When it appeared that all obtainable studies were in hand, the studies were coded and the meta-analyses were run. In both cases, additiona unpublished studies were later received, necessitating the rerunning of the meta-analysis. This happened repeatedly. The interview validity analysis, for example, was rerun five times over a period of three years. A situation of this sort can be frustrating, but reanalysis is necessary to ensure the completeness of the meta-analysis. Cooper (1984, Chapter 3) provides a thorough discussion of questions and issues in searching for studies.

What To Do About Studies with "Methodological Weaknesses"

Many reviewers wish to eliminate from their analyses studies that they perceive as having methodological inadequacies (Slavin, 1986). This often is not as reasonable and desirable as it may seem. The assertion of "methodological inadequacy" always depends on theoretical assumptions about what *might* be true in a study. These assumptions may well be false and are rarely tested in their own right. Those who believe the assumptions usually feel no need to test them. That is, the hypothesis of "methodological inadequacy" is rarely tested empirically. No research study can be defended against all possible counterhypotheses; hence, no study can be "without methodological inadequacy." However, methodological inadequacies do not always cause biased findings, and, prior to the analyses of the full set of studies on the topic, it is difficult to determine reliably when methodological inadequacies have caused biased findings and when they have not.

Some reviewers are inclined to use the simple strategy of eliminating all the studies with methodological inadequacies. Since most studies have some weaknesses, these reviewers often end up reporting inferences based on only a few studies. When there is good a priori evidence that the eliminated studies had substantially biased results, this strategy would be justified, but that seldom is the case.

The hypothesis of methodological inadequacy should be tested only after two prior hypotheses have been rejected. First, one should determine if the variation across all studies can be accounted for by sampling error and other artifacts such as differences in reliability. If the variation is due solely to artifacts, then there can be no variance due to methodological inadequacy. Second, if there is substantial variation across studies, then theoretically plausible moderator variables should be tested. If the moderator variables account for nonartifactual variance, then there can be no variance due to methodological inadequacy. If the theoretically plausible moderator variables do not explain the variance, then methodological inadequacies may be present. One can then rate the internal and external validity of the studies or code the characteristics that might produce inadequacy and test these characteristics as moderator variables.

It is important to recognize that the actual threat to the internal and external validity of a study is not determined exclusively or even primarily by the design of the study. Campbell and Stanley's monograph (1963) on experimental and quasi-experimental design shows which threats are controlled by various research designs if none of the controlled factors interact. But the monograph does not indicate which threats are likely to be trivial in a given study or which threats can be reasonably controlled by other means (see the discussion in Chapter 8):

Some have suggested that there is a counterexample to our argument: violations of construct validity across studies. The fact that the same variable name is used in different studies does not mean that the same variable is measured in those studies. We believe that construct validity is potentially an empirical question, as well as a theoretical question. Ideally, one would do an empirical study in which alternative instruments or methods are used to measure the independent and dependent variables. Confirmatory factor analysis could then be used to see if the alternate measures differ by more than random error of measurement. That is, do the different measures correlate approximately 1.00 after correcting for measurement error? A much inferior test of the construct invalidity hypothesis can be run within a meta-analysis. If several instruments are really measuring different things, then it would be unlikely that they would have the same correlation with the second variable of the meta-analysis (or that the treatment effect would be identical across the different variables). If the meta-analysis shows no variance across studies, then that would suggest that the alternate measures are substantially equivalent. On the other hand, if the meta-analysis does find variance across studies, then the hypothesized nonequivalence of variables can be used as a moderator variable. If this moderator variable does explain the variance across studies, then this finding is confirmation of the hypothesis of construct invalidity. In any case, it is our belief that the *assertion* of construct invalidity is not the same as the *fact* of construct invalidity. We believe that methodological hypotheses are less likely to be true than substantive hypotheses since they are usually based on a much weaker data base.

If meta-analysis shows that the studies evaluated as methodologically superior yield different results from the studies rated methodologically poorer, then final conclusions can be based on the "good" studies. If there is no difference in results, this finding disconfirms the methodological hypotheses. In such cases, all studies should be retained and included in the final meta-analysis to provide the largest possible data base.

Cooper (1984, pp. 63-65) points out another reason for caution in attempts to exclude methodologically weak studies. To make such decisions, evaluators must judge and rate each study on methodological quality. The research on interrater agreement for judgments of research quality shows that the average correlation between experienced evaluators is at best about .50, illustrating the subjectivity of assessments of methodological quality. Based on the Spearman-Brown formula, it would require use of 6 evaluators to yield a reliability of approximately .85. Most meta-analyses will not be able to draw on the considerable time and effort of six experienced judges. And use of fewer judges would usually result in the erroneous elimination of a prohibitive number of acceptable studies.

The question of methodological weaknesses must be separated from the question of relevant and irrelevant studies. Relevant studies are those that focus on the relationship of interest. For example, if one is interested in the relationship between role conflict and job satisfaction, a study that reports only correlations between measures of role conflict and organizational identification should be excluded because it is irrelevant. (If enough such studies are encountered, one can of course conduct a separate meta-analysis of the relation between role conflict and organizational identification.) Measures of different dependent variable constructs should ordinarily not be combined in the same meta-analysis (see Chapter 11), but if they are, separate meta-analyses should also be reported for each conceptually different dependent variable. This is the approach preferred by Glass and his associates, and he has been severely criticized on this account (e.g., see Chapter 11 and Mansfield & Busse, 1977). While it is true that meta-analyses that "mix apples and oranges" are difficult to interpret, no harm is done as long as separate meta-analyses are presented later for each dependent variable construct. In general, meta-analyses that do not mix different *independent* variables are also more likely to be informative. But the question is not a simple one. For example, in our meta-analyses of the relation between verbal ability and job performance, we excluded job performance correlations based on other abilities (e.g., quantitative ability measures). For our purposes, such correlations were irrelevant. However, we later found that the mean and standard deviation of correlations for verbal ability were very similar to the mean and standard deviation for quantitative ability (e.g., see Pearlman et al., 1980). We also found that the validity of both kinds of measures stemmed entirely from the fact that they were both measures of general mental ability (e.g., see Hunter, 1986).

Although we have not conducted such an analysis, these findings provide a rationale for a meta-analysis that includes both kinds of measures — a meta-analysis of the relationship between "g-loaded" tests and job performance. The point is that measures that assess different constructs from one theoretical perspective may assess the same construct from the perspective of another theory. And the second theory may represent an advance in understanding. Thus, the question of how varied the independent and dependent variable measures included in a meta-analysis should be is a more complex and subtle one than it appears to be at first glance. The answer depends on the specific hypotheses, theories, and purposes of the investigator. Glass has stated that there is nothing objectionable about mixing apples and oranges if the focus of the research interest is fruit. This statement is consistent with our position here. However, Glass goes beyond the theory-based rationale presented here in arguing that it may be appropriate to include in the same meta-analysis independent and dependent variable measures that appear to be different constructs. Specifically, he argues that such broad, mixed meta-analyses may be justified and useful in summarizing a research literature in broad strokes (see Chapter 11). But most researchers — ourselves included — do not usually find such broad brush research summaries as informative as more focused meta-analyses. At least initially, meta-analyses in a given research area should probably be narrow and focused enough to correspond to the major constructs recognized by researchers in that area. Then as understanding develops, later meta-analyses may become broader in scope.

What To Report in the Review

A widely held precept in all the sciences is that reports of research ought to include enough information about the study so that the reader can critically examine the evidence. As a minimum, it is held that the report ought to describe the sampling, measurement, analyses, and the findings. Where unusual procedures have been used, it is expected that they will be described in some detail.

Researchers are never more acutely aware of the importance of these reporting standards than when they are reviewing a set of studies. Inadequate reports of primary research add tremendously to the burden of doing any kind of review. But, ironically, reports of reviews probably violate these precepts more often than do reports of primary research. Jackson's (1978) analysis of 36 review articles in quality journals found that only four reported major aspects of the search for relevant studies; only seven indicated whether or not the full set of located studies on the topic was analyzed; just half of the 36 reported the direction and magnitude of the findings of *any* of the primary studies; and only three cited the mean, range, or another summary of the magnitude of the primary study's findings.

The consequences of such reporting omissions are serious. There are two reasons for carefully describing the literature search process in a review article. First, it helps the reader to judge the comprehensiveness and representativeness of the sources that are the subject of the review. Second, briefly detailing the literature search process in a review article allows future reviewers of the topic to extend the review without duplicating it. If it is known that most of the articles included in the review were those listed under certain descriptors of certain years of certain indices, or found in the bibliographies of specified sources, it is very easy for a subsequent reviewer to broaden or deepen the search for relevant sources without duplicating the earlier work.

Excluding some located studies on a given topic from the analysis of the review can seriously affect the inferences drawn from the review. Readers need to know whether or not there may be such an effect. And if some studies are excluded, the criteria for exclusion, the number of studies excluded, and the citations of the excluded studies are useful to the critical reader.

The direction and magnitude of each primary study finding or of the mean or variance of the set of findings is important information. Without it the reader often cannot make even a preliminary judgment about the validity of a review's conclusions unless he or she laboriously consults the original reports of each study. Many meta-analyses do not cover more than forty or fifty studies. In such cases it is often possible to provide substantial data on each study in a single-page table. The table should include the author and date of each study, the sample size, and the standardized effect score. If sources of spurious variance do not account for most of the variation in the standardized effect scores, other characteristics of each study should be included, such as the status characteristics of the subjects, subjects' average pretreatment scores on the criterion (when applicable), level and duration or scope conditions (such as region of the country, occupations of subjects, and the like), strength of the study design with respect to internal and external validity, and other study characteristics. If there is not enough space for this table in the publication, there should be a reference indicating where it can be obtained.

Information Needed in Reports of Primary Studies

Meta-analysis procedures require certain kinds of data from each primary study that is to be included in the cumulation. Unfortunately, some of those data are usually missing from at least a few of the studies being reviewed. This forces the reviewer to track down authors and try to secure the data from them, and when this fails, to "guesstimate" it. Often the missing data would lengthen the report of the study by only one-fourth to one-half a page, and in all cases this data would provide the readers important information about the study as well as provide a basis for valid accumulations. Large correlation matrices may be awkward to include in some reports, but this primary data should be preserved for later analysis and referenced in the report.

Correlational Studies

Consider first correlation studies. If reported study findings are to be usable in cumulative studies, then the mean, standard deviation, and reliability of each variable should be published. The mean is necessary for the cumulation of norms, for the cumulation of regression lines (or for the assessment of possible nonlinearity over extreme ranges), or for the identification of very special populations. The standard deviation is necessary for the same reasons and for a further one. If the relation between two variables is linear, then there is little variation in the correlation produced by variation in the mean from study to study. However, this is quite different for the standard deviation. Differences in variability from study to study can have dramatic effects on intercorrelations between variables. If a study is being done in a homogeneous population in which the standard deviation is only half the size of the standard deviation in other studies, then in that population the correlations for that variable would be only about half the size of correlations observed in other populations. Similarly, if the variance is inflated by observing only high and low extreme groups on a given variable, then correlations for that study would be higher than in a population with the middle range included. The reliability is needed for two reasons. First, variations in standard deviation produce differences in the reliability. Second, and more importantly, the variable used in the study may not be identical to that used in published norm studies. For example, a study might include a measure of "authoritarianism," but that scale might consist of a subset of eight items chosen by the investigator; the reliability of this subscale may be quite different from the reliability for the whole scale published in norm studies. In the case of new scales, reliabilities may not have been established on large norm populations; in such cases the reliabilities can be established by cumulating across studies.

It is imperative that the entire matrix of zero-order correlations between all variables be published (note that the means, standard deviations, and reliabilities can be easily appended as extra rows or columns of this matrix). Each entry in this table may be used in entirely unrelated cumulation studies. Correlations that are not statistically significant should still be included; one cannot average a "–" or an "ns" or a "..." or whatever. If only significant correlations were printed, then cumulation would necessarily be biased. This is even more the case for correlations that are not even mentioned because they are not significant.

Moreover, there is a prevalent misperception concerning "nonsignificant" correlations. Many believe that nonsignificant means that no statistically significant finding could be associated with those variables in that study. This is not in fact the case. The size of a correlation is relative to the context in which it is considered; partial correlations and beta weights may be much larger than zero-order correlations. For example, suppose that we find a nonsignificant correlation of .10 between performance of supervisor and subordinate performance. If cognitive ability of subordinates were correlated .70 with their performance but correlated zero with quality of supervision, then the partial correlation between quality of supervision and subordinate performance with subordinate ability held constant would rise to .14, which might then be statistically significant. If motivation of subordinates were correlated .70 with their performances but were uncorrelated with their abilities, then the double partial correlation of quality of supervision and subordinate performance with both ability and motivation controlled would be .71, which would be highly significant. Thus, although quality of supervision might not be significantly correlated with subordinate performance at a zero level, it might be highly correlated when extraneous variables are controlled. To say the same thing another way, even though an independent variable is not significantly correlated with a dependent variable, its beta weight in multiple regression might be large and highly statistically significant. This is another important reason why all zero-order correlations should be included in published studies.

Experimental Studies

What about experimental studies in which analysis of variance is used instead of correlation? In a two-group design, the F value that is conventionally computed is an exact transformation of the point-biserial correlation. The significance test on the point-biserial correlation is exactly equivalent to the F test. In a 2 by 2 by 2 by ... design, every effect in the analysis of variance is the comparison of two means and could thus be represented by a point-biserial correlation. In fact, the square of that point-biserial correlation is the "eta square" or percentage of variance accounted for by that effect. In designs with more than two categories for a facet, the categories are frequently ordered (indeed frequently quantitative). In such cases, there is rarely any significant effect beyond the linear trend. In any case, the eta squared (or better, the appropriate square root) can be used as a correlation between the corresponding variables. Thus, everything stated above, including considerations of restrictions in range and reliability, is just as true of experimental as of correlational studies.

Studies Using Multiple Regression

A multiple regression analysis of a primary study is based on the full zero-order correlation matrix for the set of predictor variables and the criterion variable. Similarly, a cumulation of multiple regression analyses must be based on a cumulative zero-order correlation matrix. But many reports of multiple regression fail to report the full correlation matrix, usually omitting the zero-order correlations among the predictors and sometimes even the zero-order correlations between each predictor and the criterion. Reporting practices may have become even worse recently. Some studies now report only the multiple regression weights for the predictors. But cumulation leading to optimal estimates of multiple regression weights requires cumulation of the predictor intercorrelations as well as of the predictor-dependent variable correlations. That is, the formula for each multiple regression weight uses all the correlations between the predictors, and, hence, they must be cumulatively estimated.

The practice of ignoring the predictor intercorrelations is extremely frustrating even if large samples are used. Given the predictor intercorrelations, path analysis can be used to test hypotheses about direct and indirect causes. If the predictor intercorrelations are not given, one cannot distinguish between a predictor that makes no contribution and a predictor that makes a strong but indirect contribution. In short, one cannot do the desired path analysis unless the predictor correlations are given as well as the predictor-criterion correlations.

Finally, it should be noted that regression weights are not suitable for cumulation. Suppose that y is to be predicted from $X_1, X_2, \ldots X_m$. The beta weights for X_1 depend not only on the variables X_1 and Y, but on all the other variables, $X_2, X_3, \ldots$ contained in the same regression equation. That is, beta weights are relative to the set of predictors considered and will only replicate across studies if the exact set of predictors is considered in each. If any predictor is added or subtracted from one study to the next, then the beta weights for all variables may change. While it may be worthwhile to calculate beta weights within a study, it is crucial for cumulation purposes that the zero-order correlations be included in the published study. *After* cumulation of zero-order correlations, a multiple regression can be run using a set of predictors that may never have occurred together in any one study.

For example, suppose that we wanted to predict job performance from three abilities, *a*, *b*, and *c*. To cumulate beta weights, we would have to find either (1) studies that computed beta weights for the *a*, *b*, and *c* combination, or (2) studies that contained *a*, *b*, and *c* as a subset and that published the full set of predictor intercorrelations. On the other hand, cumulation from zero-order correlations greatly expands the set of studies that can contribute estimates of one or more of the needed correlations. In fact, any predictive study using *a* or *b* or *c* would contain at least one correlation of interest. In order for r_{ab} to be estimated, there must be at least one study with both *a* and *b*; estimation of r_{ac} requires at least one study with both *a* and *c*; and estimation of r_{bc} requires at least one study with both *b* and *c*. However, there need be no study in which all three predictors occur together.

Studies Using Factor Analysis

Factor analyses are often published with the zero-order correlation matrix omitted, presumably to conserve journal space. But zero-order correlations can be cumulated across studies while factor loadings cannot be cumulated. First, the factors that appear in a given study are not determined by the single variables that appear, but by the sets or clusters of variables that occur. For example, suppose a study contains one good measure of motivation and ten cognitive ability measures. Then, it is likely that the communality of the motivation variable will be zero, and motivation will not appear in the factor analysis. Factors are defined by *redundant* measurement; no factor will appear unless it is measured by at least two redundant indicators (and preferably by three or more). Second, the factors in an exploratory factor analysis (such as principal axis factors followed by VARIMAX rotation) are not defined independently of one another. For example, suppose that in the initial output one cluster of variables defines G_1 and another cluster defines G_2 and the correlations between G_1 and G_2 is *r*. Then if factor scores are standardized, the VARIMAX factors will be defined by

$$F_1 = G_1 - \alpha G_2$$

$$F_2 = G_2 - \alpha G_1$$

where

$$\alpha = \frac{1 - \sqrt{1 - r^2}}{r}.$$

Thus, each orthogonal factor is defined as a discrepancy variable between natural clusters, and the loading of an indicator of G_1 on factor F_1 will depend not only on the other indicators of G_1 in its own set but also on what other factors appear in the same study. Cluster analysis results and confirmatory factor analysis results present a somewhat different picture. If a cluster analysis or confirmatory factor analysis model fits the data (Hunter, 1980a; Hunter & Gerbing, 1982), then the factor loading of an indicator onto its own factor is the square root of its reliability and is independent of the rest of the variables and is thus subject to cumulation. However, high-quality confirmatory factor analyses are still quite rare in the literature.

Studies Using Canonical Correlation

Canonical correlation begins with a set of predictor variables and a set of dependent measures, and is thus conceptually a situation suitable for multiple regression. But in canonical correlation, two *new* variables are formed: a weighted combination of the predictor variables and a weighted combination of the dependent measures. These combinations are formed in such a way as to maximize the correlation between them.

Canonical correlations are not subject to cumulation across studies. Neither are the canonical weights. In multiple regression, each beta weight depends on the dependent variable and on the specific set of predictors. Thus, it generalizes only to other studies in which exactly the same set of predictors is used (which is rare indeed). But each canonical regression weight depends not only on the exact set of predictors in the study, but on the exact set of dependent measures as well. Thus, it will be very rare that the results of canonical regression can be compared or cumulated. On the other hand, the zero-order correlation matrices of such studies can be cumulated across studies.

Studies Using Multivariate Analysis of Variance (MANOVA)

Statistically, MANOVA is a canonical regression, with the treatment contrast variables as "independent" variables and with measured variables as "dependent" measures. Consequently, the data needed for cumulation across studies are the set of zero-order correlations between contrasts, between contrasts and other measured variables, and between other measured variables.

General Comments on Reporting in Primary Studies

For multiple regression, factor analysis, and canonical correlation analyses, the zero-order correlation matrices are essential for cumulations across studies. And once these data are secured, the reviewer is able to analyze the cumulative correlation matrix using any appropriate statistical procedure. For example, data gathered for multiple regression can be used for path analysis.

If journals required the publication of confidence intervals in place of, or in addition to, levels of statistical significance, three benefits would ensue. First, researchers would be alerted to how much uncertainty there is in estimates derived from most individual social science studies. The common small-sample studies will generally have wide confidence intervals. Second, the results across studies would correctly appear to be in greater agreement than they usually do when focusing on the proportions of studies that are statistically significant. For instance, if there are five studies, each with a sample size of fifty, and with correlations of .05, .13, .24, .33, and .34, only two of the five are statistically significant at the .05 level, but the .05 level confidence intervals of all five correlations would overlap substantially. And third, in the case of two sample tests, reports of the confidence interval and sample sizes are all that is needed for computing standardized effect scores.

When measures of variables with less than perfect reliability are used, should the correlations between such measures be corrected for attenuation due to error of measurement? It is clear from measurement theory that the reduction of correlations due to the use of imperfect measurement is purely a matter of artifact. Reliability of measurement is a matter of feasibility and practicality independent of the theoretical and psychological meaning of the variables measured. Thus, it is correlations between perfectly measured variables that are of theoretical importance; i.e., it is the corrected correlations that should be used in multiple correlations or path analysis. If the reliability of each variable is published, those cumulating findings across studies can analyze the data using appropriate methods. Cumulation should ideally be done on corrected correlations (although, as shown in Chapter 4, this correction can be made when necessary after the cumulation, using artifact distribution meta-analysis methods). As noted earlier (see Chapter 3), correction increases the sampling error in the estimated correlation, and, therefore, the formulas for the correction of variance due to sampling error in uncorrected correlation coefficients are not appropriate for correlations corrected for attenuation. Instead, the modified formulas given in Chapter 3 should be used to compute the sampling error in corrected correlations.

13 General Criticisms of Meta-Analysis

Questions, issues, and criticisms of meta-analysis that are technical in nature were discussed in Chapter 5 for meta-analyses of correlations, and in Chapter 8 for meta-analyses of d values. Also, some criticisms of Glassian meta-analysis were discussed in Chapter 11. This chapter explores broader, more general criticisms that have been aimed at meta-analysis. These criticisms are conceptual in nature, and are sometimes related to philosophy of science issues. Many of them apply to all forms of meta-analysis, not merely the meta-analysis methods presented in this book. This chapter is not intended to be comprehensive; many criticisms of meta-analysis have been analyzed in some detail in earlier sources (e.g., Cooper, 1984; Glass, McGaw & Smith, 1981, Chapter 7; Rosenthal, 1984, Chapter 7; Schmidt, Hunter, Pearlman, & Hirsch, 1985). For the most part, we focus here on new criticisms that have come to our attention and on older criticisms that we believe have not been fully explicated in earlier published discussions.

Availability Bias

One of the most frequent criticisms leveled against meta-analysis is the argument that the studies available for analysis will typically be a biased sample of all available studies. In particular, it is often suspected that published studies will show results that are more often statistically significant and have larger effect sizes than unpublished studies (e.g., see McNemar, 1960). Thus, it is contended, effect size estimates from meta-analysis will be biased upward. The first thing to be borne in mind about this criticism is that it applies equally well to the narrative review, the usual alternative to meta-analysis. The fact that the narrative review is not quantitative in no way mitigates the effects of any bias in the sample of studies. Thus, to the extent that source or availability bias is a problem, it is a completely general one and is not limited to meta-analysis.

But there is evidence that the problem may be much less severe than some have believed, and, in fact, may not exist in many literatures. Also, apparent differences in mean effect sizes by source (e.g., journals, books, and unpublished reports) may be the artifactual side effects of differences in average methodological quality between sources. If so, then a meta-analysis that corrects for methodological weaknesses (such as measurement error) will correct for these differences. Finally, even where there may be good reason to suspect availability or reporting biases, statistical methods are now available to control for these effects. We now examine each of these points in turn.

Does Source Bias Exist?

The hypothesis of source bias is closely related to the hypothesis of availability bias. The availability bias hypothesis holds that unpublished studies have two important properties: (1) They have smaller effect sizes, and (2) they are less frequently available to be included in meta-analysis. If the first of these were not true, then even if the second were true, no bias would be introduced into meta-analysis results. The question of whether effect sizes are smaller in unpublished studies can be addressed empirically.

Based on data presented in Glass et al. (1981), Rosenthal (1984, pp. 41-45) examined the effect sizes from 12 meta-analyses on different topics to determine whether mean effect sizes differed depending on their sources. Based on hundreds of effect sizes, he found there was virtually no difference on the average between those published in journals and those from unpublished reports. The mean d value was .08 *larger* for the unpublished reports; the median d value was .05 larger for the published journal articles. Thus, the mean and median differences were in the opposite directions, and neither was statistically or practically significant. His overall conclusion was that the effect sizes from journal articles, unpublished reports, and books are "essentially indistinguishable from each other" (p. 44). On the other hand, Rosenthal did find that doctoral dissertations' and master's theses' yielded average d values that were 40% or more smaller than those from other sources. The problem created by this difference for theses and dissertations is mitigated by the fact that most dissertations are retrievable by meta-analysts through *Dissertation Abstracts*.

In our own meta-analytic research on the validity of employment tests, we have examined that vast literature to determine whether correlations (validities) from published and unpublished studies differ. The evidence indicates they do not. Where it was possible to compare data sets like that of Pearlman et al. (1980) to other large data sets, the two data sets were found to be very similar. For example, the Pearlman et al. data is very similar to the U.S. Department of Labor GATB data set used by Hunter (1983b) in terms of means and variances (controlling for sample sizes) of observed validity coefficients. The same is true when the comparison is with large-sample military data sets. Military researchers routinely report all data, and the reported means and variances correspond closely to those from other data sets for the same criterion measures. Also, mean observed validities in our data sets are virtually identical to Ghishelli's (1966) reported medians, based on decades of careful information gathering.

There are other indications of a lack of source bias in validity generalization data sets. For example, in the Pearlman et al. (1980) data set for measures of performance on the job, 349 of the 2,795 observed validities (12.5%) were zero or negative; 737 (26.4%) were .10 or less. Further, 56.1% of the 2,795 observed validities were nonsignificant at the .05 level. This figure is consistent with our estimate (Schmidt, Hunter, & Urry, 1976) that the average criterion-related validity study has statistical power no greater than .50. If selectivity or bias in reporting were operating, many of the nonsignificant validities would have been omitted, and the percent significant would have been much higher than 43.9%.

Even more striking was the close comparability of the percentage of observed validities that were nonsignificant in the published studies reviewed by Lent et al. (1971a, 1971b) — 57% — and the percent nonsignificant in the mostly unpublished data set (68% of the sources were unpublished) of Pearlman et al. (1980) — 56.1%. The Pearlman et al. data almost perfectly match the published data, an empirical indication that the unpublished data were not different from published data. (Note: To provide comparability with Lent et al. [1971b] all figures for Pearlman et al. [1980] are for two-tailed tests. Using one-tailed tests, 49.1% of the Pearlman et al. proficiency coefficients are nonsignificant at the .05 level.)

We have examined many hundreds of unpublished studies in the personnel selection research domain. We have found that it is not true that data were suppressed or omitted. It has been our experience that studies typically reported results for all tests tried out (even poorly constructed experimental instruments with well below average reliabilities). In the typical scenario, the study was an exploratory one designed to determine the optimal test battery. A multi-test battery was tried out on a variety of jobs and/or criteria. Full tables of validities against all criteria for all jobs were reported. We found no evidence that reporting the full set of results (usually including many low and nonsignificant validities) was viewed negatively by the sponsoring organization, or that it allowed or encouraged either in-house psychologists or outside consultants to partially or fully suppress the results. Thus, this evidence also indicates that the results of unpublished studies are essentially identical to those of published studies. Again, where the evidence indicates that this is the case, there is no problem of availability bias.

Effects of Methodological Quality on
Mean Effect Sizes from Different Sources

If published studies do have larger observed effect sizes than unpublished studies in a particular research literature, that fact need not indicate the existence of a publication bias in favor of large or significant effect sizes. Instead, the publication "bias" could be in favor of methodologically stronger research studies. Reviewers are often selected by journal editors based on their judged methodological expertise, and it is therefore to be expected that their evaluations will focus heavily on the methodological quality of the study. Many methodological weaknesses have the expected effect of artifactually reducing the expected study effect size. For example, unreliability of measurement reduces study effect sizes in both correlational and experimental studies. Thus, publication decisions based on methodological quality alone would be expected to produce, as a side effect, differences in mean study effect sizes between published and unpublished studies, given only that the null hypothesis of no relation is false, the usual case today. This would be expected to be the case even though the actual effect size is exactly the same in published and unpublished studies.

Table 13.1 shows the approximate mean observed d values found by Smith and Glass (1977) for books (.80), journals (.70), dissertations (.60), and unpublished reports (.50) in studies on the effectiveness of psychotherapy. The difference between the largest and smallest $\overline{d}$ is $.80 - .50 = .30$, a considerable difference. But suppose the mean reliabilities of the dependent variables were as indicated in the second column of numbers in Table 13.1. Then, the true effect sizes (effect sizes corrected for the attenuating effects of measurement error) would be the same in all sources, and the apparent "source effect" on study outcomes would be shown to be entirely artifactual. The point is that the effects of methodological quality on study outcomes should be carefully examined before accepting the conclusion that real study findings differ by study source. This example also clearly illustrates the importance and necessity of making the appropriate corrections for measurement error in conducting meta-analyses.

Table 13.1 Hypothetical Example of Observed and True Mean Effect
Sizes for Four Sources of Effect Sizes

Source	Observed Mean $(\bar{d})$	Mean Dependent Variable Reliability $(\bar{R}_{yy})$	True Mean d Value $\bar{\delta}$
Books	.8	.90	.84
Journals	.7	.70	.84
Dissertations	.6	.51	.84
Unpublished	.5	.35	.84

Statistical Methods For Handling Availability Bias

If there is reason to believe that availability bias is a problem for a set
of studies, methods are available for addressing this problem. Rosenthal
(1979) has advanced his "File Drawer Analysis" as one approach; while
useful, this method focuses only on statistical significance, ignoring effect
sizes. Other methods are available that are based on effect sizes. Finally,
Hedges and Olkin (1985) have presented a method that is applied only to
statistically significant effect sizes. We now examine each of these in turn.

File Drawer Analysis

Rosenthal's (1979) file drawer analysis estimates the number of un-
located ("file drawer") studies averaging null results (i.e., $\bar{d} = 0$ or $\bar{r} = 0$)
that would have to exist to bring the significance level for a set of studies
down to the "just significant" level, that is, to $p = .05$. The required number
of studies is often so large as to have very little likelihood of existing, thus
supporting the conclusion that the study findings taken as a whole are
indeed unlikely to have occurred by chance. The first step in applying file
drawer analysis is computation of the overall significance level for the set
of studies. One first converts the p-value for each of the k effect sizes to
their corresponding z values using ordinary normal curve tables, for
example,

Study	p Value	z Value
1	.05	1.1645
2	.01	2.3300
3	.50	.0000
.	.	.
.	.	.
.	.	.

This test is directional (one-tailed), so the researcher must determine the direction of the hypothesized difference. For example, if females are hypothesized to have higher average levels of perceptual speed than males, then a finding that favors *males* at the .05 level (one-tailed) would be entered with a p-value of $1.00 - .05 = .95$ and its z value would be -1.645.

When variables are uncorrelated, the variance of the sum is the sum of the variances. If the z values are from independent studies, then each has a variance of 1.00, and the variance of the sum of the zs across the k studies is $(1)(k) = k$. Since the variance of Σz_k is k, the SD $= \sqrt{k}$. The z_c, the z score corresponding to the significance level of the total set of studies, is then

$$z_c = \frac{\Sigma z_k}{\sqrt{k}} = \frac{k\,\bar{z}_k}{\sqrt{k}} = \sqrt{k}\ \bar{z}_k .$$

For example, if there were 10 studies ($k = 10$) and $\bar{z}_k = 1.35$, then $z_c = \sqrt{10}\ (1.35) = 4.27$, a highly significant z_c value ($p = .0000098$).

In the file drawer analysis, we want to compute the number of additional unlocated studies averaging $z = 0$ needed to bring z_c down to 1.645 (or $p = .05$). Let this additional number of studies $= x$. Since these studies have $\bar{z} = 0$, the $\Sigma z_{k+x} = \Sigma z_k$. However, the number of studies will increase from k to $k + x$. Thus, the new SD for Σz_{k+z} will be $\sqrt{k+x}$. If we set $z_c = 1.645$, the desired value, we can then solve the following equation for x.

$$1.645 = \frac{k\,\bar{z}_k}{\sqrt{k+x}}$$

Solving for x,

$$x = k\ /\ 2.706\,[\,k\,(\bar{z}_k)^2 - 2.706\,] .$$

This is the file drawer formula when the critical overall significance level is $p = .05$. Returning to our earlier example where $k = 10$ and $\bar{z}_k = 1.35$, we obtain

$$x = \frac{10}{2.706} [10 (1.35)^2 - 2.706] = 57 .$$

Thus, there would have to be 57 unlocated studies averaging null results to bring the combined probability level for the group of studies up to .05. If in this example there were originally 100 studies ($k = 100$) instead of 10, then $x = 6,635$! Over 6,000 studies would be required to raise the combined p-value to .05. In most research areas, it is inconceivable that there could be over 6,000 "lost" studies. Examples of use of this method in personnel selection research are given in Callender and Osburn (1981) and Schmidt, Hunter, and Caplan (1981b).

File Drawer Analysis Based on Effect Size

The file drawer analysis of Rosenthal (1979) makes it clear in many cases that there could not be enough missing studies to change the conclusion that the combined study results are not due to chance. But this is a very weak conclusion. The combined study results can be highly significant statistically even though the mean effect size is small or even tiny. Neither the combined probability method in general nor the file drawer analysis in particular provides any information on effect size. For many purposes it would be more informative to know how many missing studies averaging null findings would have to exist to bring $\bar{d}$ or $\bar{r}$ down to some specific level. The formulas given below for this calculation were derived by the authors in 1979 and used extensively by Pearlman (1982). Later we learned that Orwin (1983) had independently derived the same formulas.

If k is again the number of studies, then,

$$\bar{d}_k = \frac{\Sigma d_k}{k} .$$

We want to know how many "lost" studies (x) must exist to bring $\bar{d}_k$ down to $\bar{d}_c$, the critical value for mean d (which may be the smallest mean value that we would consider theoretically or practically significant). Thus, the new total number of studies will again be $k + x$. Σd_k will again remain unchanged, since $\Sigma d = 0$ for the x new studies. We again set $\bar{d}_k$ equal to $\bar{d}_c$ and solve for x.

$$\overline{d}_c = \frac{\Sigma d_k}{k + x}$$

$$x = k \, \overline{d}_k \, / \, \overline{d}_c - k$$

$$x = k \, (\overline{d}_k \, / \, \overline{d}_c - 1)$$

The corresponding formula for $\overline{r}$ is

$$x = k \, (\overline{r}_k \, / \, \overline{r}_c - 1) \, .$$

For example if $\overline{d}_k = 1.00$, $k = 10$, and $\overline{d}_c = .10$, then

$$x = 10 \, (1.00 \, / \, .10 - 1)$$

$$x = 90 \text{ studies.}$$

If $k = 100$ but the other numbers remain the same, then $x = 900$. The number of missing studies averaging null results needed to reduce the effect size to some specified level is usually much smaller than the number required to reduce the combined probability value to $p = .05$. Nevertheless, in many research areas it is unlikely that there are even 90 "lost" studies, and it is highly unlikely that there are 900.

Use of Significant Results Only

If, in a certain research literature, only published studies were available and only studies reporting significant results were published, then, if the null hypothesis were true, there would be approximately equal numbers of positive and negative d or r values, and $\overline{r}$ and $\overline{d}$ would on the average be zero. Significant and extreme results in either direction would be equally likely. However, if the null hypothesis were false (i.e., $\overline{\delta} > 0$), the mean effect size computed from such studies would not equal its true value, but instead it would be biased upward. The amount of this bias would depend on the underlying δ and on study sample size.

Hedges and Olkin (1985) have tabled the (maximum likelihood) estimate of δ for different study sample sizes and values of g^*, where g^* is the observed value of d from a study in a set of studies from which all nonsignificant ds have been eliminated (censored). In a set of studies that excludes all nonsignificant ds, there is a bias in each d value. These biased d values, symbolized g^* by Hedges and Olkin, can be converted to approximately unbiased estimates of δ by use of Hedges and Olkin's Table

2 (pp. 293-294). For example, if $N_E = N_C = 20$ and $g^* = .90$, this table shows that the maximum likelihood estimate of $\delta(\hat{\delta})$ is .631. This conversion from g^* to $\hat{\delta}$ can be made for each of the g^* values in the set of studies. The table is based on the assumption that $N_E = N_C$, but Hedges and Olkin (p. 292) note that when the experimental and control group sample sizes are unequal, one can use the average of the two to enter the table with minimal loss of accuracy. Once all observed d values have been corrected for the bias induced by the reporting of only significant results, Hedges and Olkin recommend that the resulting $\hat{\delta}$ values be weighted by study sample sizes and averaged to estimate the (almost) unbiased mean effect size ($\bar{\delta}$). Thus, it is possible to obtain an unbiased estimate of mean effect size even when only studies that report significant effect sizes are available for analysis. Note that this estimate, $\bar{\delta}$, will be considerably smaller than the observed mean effect size, $\bar{g}^*$. The formulas for this method were derived under the assumption that the population effect size δ does not vary across studies. If δ varies substantially across studies, this method yields only an approximate estimate of the mean effect size $(\bar{\delta})$.

What about the variances of these effect size estimates? Can we correct the variance of the $\hat{\delta}$ for the sampling error to estimate the true SD_δ? Unfortunately, the sampling error variance of the $\hat{\delta}$ values is considerably larger than that given for ordinary d values in the formula in Chapter 7. This is true unless the actual δ is less than about .25 or both sample size and δ are "large" (e.g., $N_E = N_C = 50$ and $\delta = 1.50$). For most data sets that occur in meta-analysis, the sampling error variance formulas in Chapter 7 would underestimate actual sampling error variance by about one-third to one-half. Thus, the resulting estimate of SD_δ would be too large. However, as noted above, the estimate of $\bar{\delta}$ should be approximately unbiased.

Ordinarily, the censoring of studies is not complete. Some nonsignificant studies will be found among the significant ones. Hedges and Olkin note that in these cases, the researcher can eliminate the nonsignificant studies and then proceed to use the methods described here. In fact, these methods can be used where one is uncertain whether publication or availability bias has distorted the sample of available studies. First, compute the mean effect size using the usual meta-analysis methods, based on all available studies. Then, estimate the mean effect size based only on the significant studies using the methods described here. If these two estimates are similar, this is evidence that the available sample of studies is an unbiased sample. If they differ greatly, that is evidence that publication or availability biases have affected the sample of studies. The mean effect size estimated from only the significant studies would then be the more unbiased.

Rejection of the Entire Social Science Research Base

In the preceding section, we have examined the *conventional* version of the availability bias criticism. We have seen that, to the extent that the problem exists, it is not a problem associated specifically with meta-analysis: Any availability bias will affect the narrative review and all other methods of interpreting research literatures in the same way as it affects meta-analysis. We have also seen that the false appearance of availability bias can be created by differences in methodological quality (e.g., reliability of measurement scales) between published and unpublished studies (or between any other specific sources of studies). Next, we presented evidence that there is probably little or no availability bias in certain research literatures. These findings point up the important fact that availability bias is a *hypothesis* that must be investigated empirically. The fact that availability bias can be *hypothesized* does not mean that it does in fact exist. Finally, we saw that there are statistical methods available to test for and control for availability bias.

All of these points are relevant to evaluating the conventional version of the availability bias hypothesis. However, there are more extreme versions of this hypothesis. These more extreme versions usually reject the entire social science research base as inherently incapable of yielding any cumulative knowledge. Hence, they are attacks on the scientific value of the social sciences in general, and from the viewpoint of philosophy of science, represent epistomological nihilism. Novick (1986) is an example. Novick maintained that meta-analyses based on published studies are deceptive and misleading because of source bias created by publication bias. He maintained that generally only studies with statistically significant findings can be published. However, he also contended that unpublished studies are usually methodologically inferior and, hence, should not be used in meta-analyses. Thus, the conclusion is that neither published nor unpublished studies can be used in meta-analysis, thereby rejecting the entire social science research base. This leads to the conclusion that social science research is generally useless, and this despairing conclusion holds whether meta-analysis, the narrative review, or any other method is used to make sense of the data base. When fully explicated, as done here, this position would probably be rejected immediately by virtually all social scientists. One problem is that such arguments are often cloaked in the mantle of scientific rigor and advanced under the guise of laudable efforts to maintain high standards of research design, control, and methodological quality, thus giving them the appearance of intellectual respectability. Who among us is opposed to high standards for research? Another problem is that the presentation of such arguments often obscures the inevitable nihilistic conclusions. For example, in Novick (1986) the argument that unpublished studies cannot be used or relied on appears in a different part of the paper from the argument against the use of published studies, and the logical conclusion that no studies can therefore be used is never explicitly stated. We feel it is appropriate to caution social scientists against nihilism masquerading as a defense of scientific rigor.

Mixing of Apples and Oranges

One of the most frequent arguments against meta-analysis is that it mixes apples and oranges; that is, meta-analysis combines studies that are so different that they are not comparable. This criticism has usually been directed against Glassian meta-analysis, and it usually makes two allegations: Glassian meta-analysis combines across studies with (1) different independent variables, and (2) different dependent variables. That is, it is charged that the independent and dependent variable *constructs* vary across studies in the same meta-analysis. These criticisms of Glassian meta-analysis were discussed in Chapter 11 and will not be repeated here.

However, the apples-and-oranges criticism is sometimes leveled at meta-analyses in which the independent and dependent variable constructs are the same in all studies. It is maintained that all studies are nevertheless unique and individual and therefore not comparable. To average across studies is thus to average across apples and oranges, which is meaningless. We will present two counterarguments, one logical and one methodological. They can be summarized as follows. First, meta-analysis does not analyze studies, it analyzes study results, i.e., numbers. Any set of numbers can be compared, averaged, or otherwise analyzed without logical contradiction. Second, the question of whether study results differ across settings is an *empirical* question rather than a *semantic* or *logical* question. The question of whether a potential moderator variable is an actual moderator variable is impossible to answer without a meta-analysis of some kind. In particular, we will critique the most extreme argument of this kind against meta-analysis: the article by Algera, Jansen, Roe, and Vijn (1984).

On the other hand, it is possible to spread the domain of a given meta-analysis so wide that the results become misleading. This issue in meta-analysis is analogous to the issue of the interaction in Analysis of Variance (ANOVA). If there is a large interaction, then separate interpretation of the corresponding main effects is often erroneous. The same is true of meta-analysis. If there is a very large moderator variable, then the mean result across all studies may not represent any finding. That is, if there is a very large moderator variable, then the overall meta-analysis may be best not given any substantive interpretation. It should be noted that this can occur even though the independent and dependent variables represent the same constructs in every study.

The Logical Argument

In most research domains, the studies differ from one another on many dimensions; there are rarely any perfect replications. Does this mean that meta-analysis analyzes apples and oranges? The numerical values studied in meta-analysis are not studies, but study results, usually some number derived from a study, such as a correlation or d value. No matter how different the studies might be from one another, there is no logical problem in comparing numbers derived from those studies. Consider an engineer who wants to design a scale to be used in customs work with agricultural products. He would like the scale to measure the weight of any given agricultural object. Consider objects ranging in weight from a caraway seed to a redwood tree trunk. On that scale, consider the weights of apples and the weights of oranges. On this scale there is virtually no error in regarding apples and oranges as equal. The construct in question is always weight, and in fact the weight of apples and oranges is very similar. In conclusion, it is true that it makes no sense to numerically analyze apples and oranges as such because they are not numbers. But if there is a meaningful way to associate numbers with apples and oranges, then there will be meaningful ways to compare those numbers. Means and variances of such numbers are often useful in such comparisons.

In exactly the same sense, consider two radically different studies that produce an effect size for an intervention such as goal setting; say, a lab study looking at twenty minutes of work on an extremely simple unfamiliar task versus a field study on the coordination of subprojects on the ten-year Apollo moon landing mission. Suppose that goal setting produced a 30% increase in performance in one study and a 5% increase in the other. Since 30%/5% = 6, we can say that the difference due to goal setting in percentage terms is six times greater in one study than in the other. The nature of differences between studies has no bearing on the logical meaning of this sentence. Thus, even though the settings are quite different, it is meaningful to say that goal setting has six times more impact on performance in one study than in the other. The differences between the studies would then be considered as possible explanations for the difference in results.

Consider the same example with different study results. Suppose that we had gathered 100 goal setting studies. Suppose that the percent increase due to goal setting was exactly 10% in every case. If the results are equal across different settings, then it means that the differences in studies were in fact irrelevant to the impact of goal setting. Consider the implications of differences across settings as widely different as the lab and Apollo studies above. Homogeneity of results across studies that different would suggest that the impact of goal setting is a universal constant.

Consider the hypothesis that the impact of some factor always takes on some given value. This hypothesis would be supported by a meta-analysis that found that all differences across studies are due to artifacts such as sampling error. Would that inference be weakened if the studies in the meta-analysis were quite heterogeneous in content? It would be just the opposite. The strength of such an inference would be proportional to the extent of differences between studies. The greater the differences between studies in the current set of studies, the more likely it is that new studies will show the same result.

The Methodological Argument

Study differences do not render meta-analysis illogical. How then are study differences to be treated in meta-analysis? Any difference between studies that can be semantically defined constitutes a potential moderator variable by definition. That is, if we can attach semantic label "A" to one study and semantic label "B" to another, then it is an unarguable logical fact that the studies are "different." However, the fact that the studies are "different" in this logical sense does not in any way imply that the studies are different in any way that is relevant to the variables studies in the meta-analysis. The "difference" may be entirely irrelevant.

Consider the criticism of validity generalization studies made by Algera et al. (1984). Algera et al. criticized a meta-analysis by Pearlman, Schmidt, and Hunter (1980) that analyzed the correlations between various predictors and the job performance of clerical workers. On page 199, Algera et al. noted that Pearlman et al. considered clerical worker groups as different as secretaries and mailing machine operators. On page 202, they claim that since the jobs differ, the correlation coefficients cannot "form a homogeneous collection of data." Thus, they reject the meta-analysis.

Consider instead the proper interpretation of the Pearlman et al. (1980) study: Job family is a potential moderator variable of validity. Many authors in the literature have postulated validity differences between clerks who work with words and clerks who work with numbers. They have predicted that verbal aptitude will best predict performance differences among clerks who work with words, while quantitative aptitude will best predict performance differences among clerks who work with numbers. According to this hypothesis, job family will be a moderator variable for the validity of both verbal and quantitative aptitudes. Note that these authors treat job family as a *potential* moderator variable. They *hypothesize* that there will be differences between the correlations found in studies where clerks work with numbers and studies where they work with words. This hypothesis can then be compared to the empirical findings, i.e., it can be tested. On the other hand, Algera et al. (1984) do not consider the possibility that they might be wrong. They simply assert that because the studies are different, the results are not comparable. For them it is not an empirical question.

Algera et al. (1984) present no empirical evidence to support their assertion. On the other hand, Pearlman et al. (1980) present analyses that test exactly this hypothesis. They found that validity did not differ across the job families. Thus, their evidence showed that the study difference variable stressed by Algera et al. is in fact irrelevant. Algera et al. did not present a reanalysis of the data to show that the Pearlman et al. analysis contained an error. They did not present data showing different results, which might suggest some bias in the Pearlman et al. study search procedure. In fact, Algera et al. did not even mention in their article that the moderator analysis had been conducted by Pearlman et al. They simply ignored the analysis showing that their main argument is factually false.

It is crucial to distinguish between logical and factual issues. Logic can establish only semantic questions. Mathematics has long since shown that virtually any statement can be made logically "true" if suitable premises are assumed. The logical labels "true" and "false" are better translated by the words "consistent" and "inconsistent." Semantic questions may be critical in their own right, usually under the rubrics "measurement" or "construct validity." However, factual issues are entirely separate and are subject to empirical rather than logical verification.

To assert that a meta-analysis across studies is not meaningful because the studies differ on some dimension is to reject the concept of empirically testing hypotheses. We will never know if some potential moderator variable is actually a moderator unless we do a meta-analysis comparing results across corresponding study types. Algera et al. (1984) have taken the most extreme position on this issue yet expressed in the literature. Their position is summed up in the question that they ask on page 200: "In other words, can these coefficients be considered as replications?" Their position is that meta-analysis is only legitimate if studies are replications in the narrow sense of the word.

Homogeneity

Algera et al. (1984) argue that meta-analysis is meaningful only if results are homogeneous across studies. They repeatedly stress the need for the hypothesis

$$\rho_1 = \rho_2 = \rho_3 = \cdots$$

But is homogeneity necessary to meta-analysis? Suppose that a meta-analysis of 100 studies shows that the mean of actual study correlations is .50 with a standard deviation of .03. Is it reasonable to throw out the meta-analysis just because the standard deviation is not 0? For a normal distribution, the 95% interval would be

$$.44 < \rho < .56 .$$

For applied or even for theoretical purposes, it might not matter that the correlation is not always .50. It may be enough to know that it is never as low as .30.

In passing, we note a curious error in Algera et al. On pages 203-204, they take the Schmidt and Hunter validity generalization approach to task for not formally testing the "situational specificity hypothesis," i.e., the hypothesis that correlations are homogeneous across studies, which they formulate as

$$\rho_1 = \rho_2 = \rho_3 = \cdots$$

But Schmidt and Hunter (1977) test exactly this hypothesis in slightly different notation. They present considerable discussion of the hypothesis

$$\sigma_\rho^2 = 0$$

along with extensive computational formulas for testing this hypothesis in a meta-analysis. They included a "75% rule" to allow for artifacts for which no corrections were made. Note that to say that the variance is 0 is to say that for every study

$$\rho_i = \text{Ave}\,(\rho) .$$

But if $\rho_1 = \text{Ave}\,(\rho)$ and $\rho_2 = \text{Ave}\,(\rho)$, then $\rho_1 = \rho_2$. That is, if the variance of correlations is 0, then the correlations are each separately equal to the mean correlation and, hence, necessarily equal to each other. Thus, contrary to the claims of Algera et al., Schmidt and Hunter (1977) did in fact present a test of the homogeneity hypothesis.

Sampling Error

Many other errors in the Algera et al. (1984) article stem from their failure to distinguish between study differences as a categorical imperative and study differences as potential moderator variables. The most glaring example is their discussion of sampling error on pages 207-208. Consider the concept of situational differences in study results. Situational differences are real differences in outcome, not differences due solely to study imperfections. For example, differences in the validity of verbal and quantitative aptitude in predicting the job performance of clerical workers have been hypothesized based on the assumption that there are differences in the abilities used in dealing with verbal versus numerical tasks in different kinds of clerical jobs. Differences in validity could have shown up in the Pearlman et al. (1980) moderator analysis, but they did not. In particular, Schmidt and Hunter (1977) argued that differences in study outcome due to sampling error are not to be interpreted as "situational specificity." As far as we know, everyone except Algera et al. has agreed that sampling error is not a part of "situational specificity". But Algera et al. (p. 208) explicitly include sample size as a parameter of the "situation" and include sampling error as a part of "situational specificity." Thus, when they say that meta-analysis should be reserved for the study of "replications," they not only require identity of the independent variable (versus psychometric equivalence or construct validity), identity of the dependent variable (versus psychometric equivalence or construct validity), identity of population correlations, identity of study procedures, identity of situational determinants, but even identity of sampling errors. This means, then, that they would require that all studies included in a meta-analysis have exactly the same results!

Real Apples and Oranges

This section will consider cases in which an overall meta-analysis may include real apples and oranges. There are two such cases. First, some meta-analyses focus on the mean effect size without adequate attention — or with no attention — to the standard deviation. If the standard deviation is large, the mean effect size may be a misleading number when interpreted in isolation. Second, there are cases in which there is an important discontinuous moderator variable. In such cases, the corresponding study subsets may be so different from each other that there is no substantive meaning in the overall mean effect size. In such cases, it may be very misleading to consider anything except the separate meta-analyses within subsets.

Focus on Mean Only

In the approach to meta-analysis taken in this book, the results of the meta-analysis are always taken to be *two* numbers: the mean and the standard deviation of the actual study effect size outcome. We do not interpret the mean without reference to the standard deviation. The credibility interval explicitly shows that the meaning of the average is blurred if there is a large standard deviation. Any meta-analysis with a large standard deviation should be resolved by a moderator analysis. All further interpretation is then devoted to the subsets within which the standard deviation is smaller.

However, this is not true of all meta-analyses. Some meta-analyses focus entirely on the mean. If the standard deviation is large, the mean may be very misleading. This is especially true if the moderator variable is not taken fully into account in the discussion. Any time there is a large moderator variable, it is difficult to make accurate summary statements that do not include the moderator variable in the corresponding sentence.

One of the best known meta-analyses is the meta-analysis of psychotherapy outcomes carried out by Smith and Glass (1977). They began their meta-analysis by computing an overall average effect size across all studies; studies of different forms of therapy, studies of different clinical problems, studies focusing on different dependent variables, and more. In the end, they claimed that this average was meaningful because the moderator variables they studied were not so strong as to produce apples and oranges differences. Furthermore, they made no mention of sampling error, much less any attempt to control its effects. Instead, they handled variation in results by breaking the data down into subsets and computing mean effect sizes within each subset.

Thus this study introduced two traditions that have caused some problems in meta-analysis: a focus on means without regard to standard deviations and a disregard for the effects of sampling error. The disregard for sampling error is seen less often in current meta-analyses, but an exclusive focus on the mean effect is still frequent. Sampling error is often considered only in the form of a homogeneity test (see Chapter 11). If the homogeneity test indicates homogeneity, then of course there is no variation in population correlations and the missing standard deviation is of little consequence. However, if the set is not homogeneous, and the authors cannot hypothesize a moderator variable that accounts for the variation, then the analysis is incomplete without an estimate of the standard deviation. One potential problem with ignoring the standard deviation is that the researcher may fail to detect and eliminate outlier studies that are distorting the estimate of the mean. A very large standard deviation draws one's attention to the possibility of outliers.

Another problem in studies that ignore the standard deviation is that they also ignore other artifacts. Studies that fail to compute the standard deviation also usually pretend implicitly that there is no error of measurement, or construct invalidity, or other artifacts. The explanation appears to lie in the meta-analysis book used by each author as their main source. Those who use our previous book focus typically on both the standard deviation and on other artifacts. Those who rely on other books often ignore both the standard deviation and other artifacts. Because other artifacts frequently reduce the mean effect size by 50% or more, ignoring other artifacts leads to serious errors.

The Discontinuous Moderator

There are instances of meta-analysis in which the mean and standard deviation are misleading, even taken together. Most people implicitly interpret the mean as a measure of central tendency and the standard deviation as a measure of spread. These interpretations are only correct for unimodal distributions. If the underlying distribution of effect sizes is discontinuous, the mean may not be near any actual value. In this case, the typical interpretation may be quite wrong.

The classic formal method used to consider the mean and standard deviation together is to compute the credibility interval. The credibility interval implicitly assumes that moderator variables produce a normal distribution of effect sizes. However, the qualitative reasoning rarely depends on the exact values of the endpoints, and, thus, departures from normality rarely cause problems so long as the distribution is unimodal. Thus, both formal and informal reasoning using the mean and standard deviation together will still be qualitatively accurate as long as the distribution is unimodal. But sometimes the moderator variable is discontinuous, as in the dichotomous cases: studies where A is true versus studies where A is not true. In such cases, the mean outcome may not represent any studies at all.

Consider an example from Guzzo et al. (1985). They begin their meta-analysis of the effects of organizational interventions by averaging the effect size across all interventions and across all measures of the effect of the intervention. The average effect size is $d = .44$. However, the mean effect size for effects on output was .63, while the mean effect size for effects on "withdrawal" — turnover and absenteeism — was only .13. Thus, it is quite misleading to include the studies of withdrawal with the studies of output. Guzzo et al. do make this point in the text, but their summary of their findings focussed considerable attention on the mean effect size of .44, a misleading statistic.

There is an even more striking example in a meta-analysis of the effects of participative decision making by Locke (1986). He used mean productivity across studies without reference to the standard deviation. He concluded that the effect size was exactly zero. His finding can be explained by a later meta-analysis by Miller and Monge (in press), which separated the studies by lab versus field (and other considerations). The effect size for lab studies was $r = -.33$, while the effect size for field studies was $r = +.27$. Thus, the average of zero represents the effect size for neither group of studies.

The Hierarchical Breakdown: Incomplete Analysis

In searching for moderator variables using meta-analysis, some authors have used a partially hierarchical breakdown. First, all studies are included in an overall meta-analysis. The studies are then broken out by one key moderator variable, then they are broken out by another key moderator variable, and so on. The Gaugler et al. (1987) meta-analysis of assessment center validities is an example of this approach. This type of analysis, however, is not fully hierarchical because the moderator variables are not considered in combination, which can result in major errors of interpretation. These errors are analogous to problems in analysis of variance due to confounding and interaction. Consider the case of two large moderator variables. An analysis of each moderator separately may lead to quite misleading results. In a meta-analysis of the effects of management by objectives (MBO) on productivity by Rodgers and Hunter (1986), the initial analysis suggested two moderator variables: top level management commitment and length of time horizon. Their initial analysis suggested that MBO programs with the strong support of top management increased productivity by an average of 40%, while programs without the strong support of top management had little effect. Their initial analysis also suggested that studies based on an assessment period of more than two years showed much larger effects than studies based on less than two years. But when the studies were broken down by the two moderator variables together, the effect of time period virtually vanished. Most of the long-term studies were studies with strong top management commitment, while most of the short-term studies were studies with weak top management commitment. Thus, the apparent impact of time horizon as a moderator variable was due to the fact that it was confounded with commitment. The difficulty in conducting full hierarchical moderator analyses in meta-analysis is that there are often too few studies to yield adequate numbers of studies in cells beyond the two-way breakout. This simply means that it is not possible to address all moderator hypotheses at that time. As more studies accumulate over time, more complete moderator analyses can be performed.

The MBO meta-analysis illustrates the potential problems of confounding between moderators, i.e., "spurious" (in the language of path analysis) mean differences for one potential moderator produced by real differences on another. Thus confounding results from the fact that the moderators are correlated. The second problem is potential interaction between moderator variables. Suppose that two moderator variables A and B have been found to moderate effect sizes when analyzed separately, and assume the moderator variables to be independent (uncorrelated) across studies. Can we then conclude that A and B always moderate effect size? We cannot. Consider a hypothesized example. Suppose the mean effect size is .30 when A is present versus .20 when A is absent; and suppose the mean effect size is .30 when B is present versus .20 when B is absent. Assume that the frequency of A is 50% and the frequency of B is 50% and that A and B are independent. Then each of the four cells obtained by considering A and B together will have a 25% frequency. Consider the mean effect sizes in the following joint breakdown table.

Moderator B

		Present	Absent	Ave.
Moderator	Present	.40	.20	.30
A	Absent	.20	.20	.20
	Ave.	.30	.20	.25

Consider the 50% of studies in which moderator B is absent. Within those studies, the presence or absence of A does not matter; the mean effect size is .20 in either case. Thus, A is a moderator variable only for the studies in which B is present. The statement that "A moderates the effect of X on Y" is false for the 50% of the studies where B is absent. Consider the 50% of studies in which moderator A is absent. Within those studies, the presence or absence of B does not matter; mean effect size is .20 in either case. Thus, B is a moderator variable only for the studies in which A is present. To say "B moderates the effect of X on Y" is false for the 50% of the studies where A is absent. This means that A and B are inextricably linked as moderator variables. Within the 75% of studies in which one or the other is absent, the mean effect size is .20, regardless of whether either variable is present or absent. The only moderating effect is that studies in which both *A* and *B* are present together differ from the other studies.

There is a rule in analysis of variance that states, "If there is an interaction between two or more factors in the design, then interpretation of lower order main effects or interactions may be quite erroneous." This same rule applies to interaction between moderators. If moderators have interacting effects, then the interpretation of separate effects may be erroneous.

Hierarchical Breakdown: Interpretation

If the hierarchical breakdown reveals moderator variables, then the overall analysis without moderator variables is likely to be misleading. If the hierarchical analysis shows that moderator variables are correlated and/or interact, then the analysis of moderator variables separately is likely to be misleading. Thus, if a hierarchical breakdown is presented, it is critical to focus the interpretation solely on the bottom level.

Consider the partially hierarchical analysis in the meta-analysis of personnel selection validities by Schmitt, Gooding, Noe, and Kirsch (1984). These researchers first pooled correlations across all predictors (biodata, tests, interviews, and more) and all criterion measures (performance ratings, tenure, advancement, and so on). They then broke the data down by predictor and criterion separately, and finally by the two together. The combinatorial breakdown showed a strong interaction between predictor and criterion variables as moderators—as had been found in past analyses. Had they based their conclusions solely on that last analysis, they would have made no error of interpretation. Unfortunately, they based some of their conclusions on the earlier global analyses. For example, they claimed that their meta-analysis yielded results at odds with the comparable meta-analysis done by Hunter and Hunter (1984). But Hunter and Hunter broke their data down by both predictor variable and criterion variable from the beginning. Thus, the only table in Schmitt et al. comparable to the analysis of Hunter and Hunter is their final table, the combinatorial breakdown. There is no contradiction between their results in that analysis and that of Hunter and Hunter (1984). This was brought out in a side-by-side presentation in Hunter and Hirsh (1987) that showed the analyses to be in good agreement.

Hierarchical Breakdown: Summary

We have no fundamental objection to a hierarchical presentation of a meta-analysis. However, it is important to avoid two common errors in this procedure. First, many studies do not complete the analysis. If there are two large moderator variables, then it is critical to consider them together and not just separately. Second, it is critical to focus the main interpretation of the data on the final breakdown and not on the earlier potentially confounded global averages.

The analysis of multiple moderator variables separately will be correct only if one makes two assumptions: One must assume (1) that the moderator variables are independent and (2) that the moderator variables are additive in their effects. In the MBO analysis of Rodgers and Hunter (1986), the commitment and time moderator variables were correlated across studies. Thus, the large difference due to the commitment variable produced a "spurious" mean difference between studies of different time lengths. If the two potential moderator variables had been independent, then there could have been no spurious effect for time produced by commitment. The *AB* combination example showed that interactive moderators must always be considered together to generate correct conclusions.

If a fully hierarchical analysis is presented, it is critical to base conclusions on the highest level of interaction. Schmitt et al. (1984) made an error of interpretation because they went back to an analysis with confounded interactions for one of their conclusions. Finally, it is important to recognize that one will often not have enough studies to conduct a fully hierarchical moderator analysis. If the number of studies in the cells of the fully hierarchical analysis is very small, the conclusions about moderators can only be tentative. Firmer conclusions must await the accumulation of a larger number of studies.

False Defense of the Narrative Review

Guzzo et al. (1986) argue that meta-analysis is often no better than a good narrative review. We will argue that there are two problems with their argument. The first is that their argument is largely circular. Their definition of a "good" narrative review differs only trivially from a meta-analysis. Second, their most cogent arguments are trivial because they have to do with theoretical speculation rather than with the review process itself. There are many other minor errors in their paper, but we do not have the room to enumerate them here.

Guzzo et al. (1986) offer a number of examples in which they claim to show that "good" narrative reviews provide just as much information as a meta-analysis. They do this by contrasting the ideal narrative review with the weakest possible meta-analysis. The positive aspect of their analysis is that it brings in focus the continuum of review, ranging from an axe grinding selective narrative review at one end to a meta-analysis that individually corrects studies for all possible artifacts at the other end. The purpose of this discussion is to remind readers that ideal narrative reviews are rare (Jackson, 1978, 1980) and that one can ask many important questions that the weakest meta-analysis will not answer.

Guzzo et al. (1986) do not explicitly define the "good" narrative review. However an analysis of their examples shows steps by which a narrative review approaches meta-analysis. The review should be comprehensive rather than selective. The review should be quantitative. Each study result should be converted to a common statistic such as r or d. Finally, the review should compute a median effect size across studies. But if this ideal review had computed a mean effect size rather than a median, they would have called the review a Glass (1976) meta-analysis. If the review had computed medians for subsets of studies to try to account for differences in study results (we use the subjunctive here because Guzzo et al. could not find such a narrative review), the "narrative review" would be a full Glass meta-analysis. Thus, to some extent, the Guzzo et al. argument is a matter of definition rather than substance; what they call a "good narrative review" is what most people would call a "meta-analysis." What Guzzo et al. do not do is to determine how many narrative reviews are "good" reviews. Jackson (1978, 1980) did just this and found them to be rare. Guzzo et al. did not consider narrative reviews that broke one or more of their rules. This will be considered here.

Narrative reviews are typically selective. For example, the often cited review of management by objectives (MBO) studies by Kondrasuk (1981) located 45 quantitative evaluation studies. For various methodological reasons of a hypothetical sort, he discarded 40 of the studies and based his conclusions on only 5 of the original 45 studies. That is, Kondrasuk discarded 40 out of 45 or 89% of the original studies. As it happens, all the studies that he selected were studies with low commitment on the part of top management. Rodgers and Hunter (1986) showed that management commitment is a critical moderator variable for MBO. With high commitment, there is a 55% increase in productivity. With low commitment there is only about a 4% increase. When Kondrasuk's methodological rules happened to eliminate all the high commitment studies, it caused a sharp bias in his results. Furthermore, Rodgers and Hunter (1989) presented empirical evidence showing that Kondrasuk's methodological rules were derived from false assumptions. Thus, selection of studies led the review to reach false conclusions. Every narrative review of the MBO literature has been selective, although different reviewers use different rejection rules. Rodgers and Hunter (1989) have compiled evidence showing that six of those rejection rules are based on false assumptions, assumptions that the reviewers never tested.

Every book on meta-analysis has argued for a comprehensive analysis of studies. Thus even weak meta-analyses have usually been comprehensive. When Guzzo et al. (1986) argue that a narrative review can be just as good as a meta-analysis, they are assuming that the narrative review was comprehensive. That is a big assumption; narrative reviews are rarely comprehensive.

Narrative reviewers often have difficulty in deciding how to use the information in the studies that they do not discard. For example, had Kondrasuk (1981) averaged the results in the five studies that he retained, he would have found an average increase in performance of about 7%. This is a substantial increase. He instead counted the number of findings that were statistically significant — one out of five studies — and concluded that the studies showed no effect for MBO. Guzzo et al. (1986) assume that the comprehensive review quantifies the results in each study using a common effect size statistic. But a sampling of narrative reviews shows that this is rarely done. Most narrative reviewers take the author's results as stated and usually record only information about statistical significance. Thus, there is no quantification of the results. If results are not quantified, the reviewer cannot average the results and, thus, cannot produce the "representative" estimate of effect size, which is the Guzzo et al. criterion for a "good" review.

By the Guzzo et al. (1986) definition, a Glass (1976) meta-analysis stands at the dividing line between a "good comprehensive narrative review" and a "meta-analysis." They would call it a "good comprehensive narrative review." By our definition, a Glass meta-analysis is a meta-analysis. Thus, we do not disagree with their statement that a good comprehensive narrative review can be as instructive as a meta-analysis. However, we believe that the Guzzo et al. definition of a "good" narrative review is far from the usual definition.

Finally, we note that there are important questions that can be asked within a meta-analysis that Glass (1976) does not ask. Glass sought only to describe research results. However, for most scientists, the goal of cumulative review is to reach conclusions that are better than those reached in individual studies. Individual studies have artifacts: imperfect measurement, dichotomization of quantitative results, range restriction, and the like. Given the right information about those artifacts, it is possible for a meta-analysis to go beyond simple description and correct for the impact of the artifacts. Guzzo et al. (1986) ignore this issue.

Guzzo et al. (1986) also raise several false issues contrasting narrative reviews and meta-analysis. They claim that narrative reviews are better for theory development than meta-analysis. They offer four such arguments.

First, they argue that narrative reviews are more likely to "advance theory" than is a meta-analysis. However, analysis of their argument shows that it can be rephrased as follows: Narrative reviewers have no objective criterion to restrain them from speculation. Meta-analysis will not venture a hypothesis unless there is supporting evidence. But this is a false contrast; they confuse "reviewers" with "reviews." Meta-analysis does not speculate because it is defined as a body of objective techniques. On the other hand, there is no rule that says that the *meta-analyst* cannot speculate. The same is true of narrative review. According to every text that discusses good review procedures, the reviewer is supposed to clearly distinguish between conclusions drawn from the review — narrowly defined — and speculations related to those results. It is probably true that narrative reviewers have offered more speculations than have meta-analysts, but it is probably also true that meta-analysts have made far fewer errors as a result. Furthermore, speculation offered in a report focused on meta-analysis will be clearly labeled as speculation. The speculations offered by narrative reviews are often labeled "conclusions."

A second criticism in regard to theory construction offered by Guzzo et al. (1986) is that meta-analysis cannot detect differences in results for homogeneous subpopulations. They cite as a reason the fact that current studies report results only for overall heterogeneous total samples. But if results for homogeneous groups are not reported, a narrative review cannot learn about differences, either. A narrative review cannot draw inferences about nonexistent results.

A third criticism offered by Guzzo et al. (1986) is the claim that meta-analysis is selective, while "good" narrative reviews are not. What they mean by this is that the typical meta-analysis uses only those studies that have results that can be quantified. On the other hand, they note that the narrative reviews can include qualitative findings as well. However, they overlook the fact that there are meta-analysis methods for non-quantitative results — counts of various kinds — that can be used to assess the nonquantitative studies. For example, Rodgers and Hunter (1986) analyze results for MBO productivity studies by using quantitative meta-analysis for those studies that report quantitative results and by counting the direction of effect in those studies that make only qualitative reports. Guzzo et al. offer no example of a review in which the poorer reports —

those that do not report their quantitative results — offer findings that differ in any significant way from the results reported by the better studies. We know of no such review.

Fourth, Guzzo et al. (1986) claim that there is such a high "cost" to meta-analysis that most people should stop with narrative review. But once a review is comprehensive, and once each study has been quantified, and once the studies have been coded to explore possible moderator variables, there is little work left to do in computing the meta-analysis. If the coding tables have been recorded on a spreadsheet program such as REFLEX, the tables needed for meta-analysis computer programs can be generated by the spreadsheet program. At that juncture, there is no extra work at all in computing a bare-bones meta-analysis. Thus, once a review has done what Guzzo et al. call a "good" narrative review, there is no significant cost to doing a bare-bones meta-analysis. Furthermore, if a narrative review is to overcome the problems of measurement error, dichotomization, imperfect construct validity, and so on, then these features of the study also have to be coded. Once they are coded, there is no further cost in conducting a complete meta-analysis.

In summary, we find no argument with Guzzo et al. (1986) to support their conclusion that the narrative review is just as good as meta-analysis. They define a "good" narrative review as one that is comprehensive, quantitative, and thoroughly documented. But with meta-analysis computer programs now readily available, their "good" narrative review can be converted to a bare-bones meta-analysis with no additional effort. Why stop with an inferior analysis? Those areas in review studies where the reviewer goes beyond the data to speculate and generate hypotheses are as open in a meta-analysis as in a narrative review. The only thing holding back the meta-analyst is that the speculative nature of the hypothesis is more obvious, both to the reviewer and to the reader. The question is whether reticence about speculation is desirable or not. If it is not, meta-analysts can quickly be taught to speculate. One needs only to include a section advocating speculation in each text on meta-analysis. The problem is that current article referees usually argue that journal space is too limited to allow speculation. Thus, a major change in publication process would be required to greatly increase the amount of published speculation. In this sense, the masked nature of speculation in narrative reviews is a road around narrow publication practice. Perhaps Guzzo et al. would be willing to consciously endorse narrative reviews for that reason. As it stands, they have implicitly endorsed that position in their current arguments.

Checklists of Rules for Meta-Analysis

Some commentators have accepted the basic methods and assumptions of meta-analysis, but have proposed that no meta-analysis should be considered acceptable unless it conforms to a checklist of detailed rules that they have presented. Such a rigid rule-oriented approach is inconsistent with the creative nature of scientific research and with the unique complexities that each individual meta-analysis encounters. In addition, the rules such commentators seek to impose can be contrary to empirical fact. An example of this orientation is Bullock and Svyantek's (1985), which proposes a list of 14 rules that meta-analysts must meet if their meta-analyses are to be considered to be "of acceptable quality" (p. 114). These include the following,

1. The meta-analyst must use a theoretical model and must test a hypothesis from that model.
2. The meta-analyst must explicitly discuss alternative explanations for the findings.
3. The meta-analyst must use multiple data codes and "provide a rigorous assessment of interrater reliability."

If any of these 14 rules are not followed, the meta-analysis would be rejected. Is this reasonable? Consider the use of a theoretical model in meta-analysis: While this may be desirable, other things being equal, what about a meta-analysis that merely seeks to determine the relation between two variables? Should such an analysis be deemed "unacceptable"? Or can it be a useful contribution? Also, why should every meta-analysis be required to discuss "alternative explanations" for its findings? The third "requirement" above has been shown empirically to be unnecessary for one type of meta-analysis: validity generalization studies. Whetzel and McDaniel (1988) showed that agreement between coders was perfect ($r = 1.00$) for the data coded. This illustrates the dangers of universally imposing detailed procedural rules on meta-analysts. It is essential to maintain room for responsible scientific judgment.

Ironically, the impetus for those rules was a straw man. Bullock and Svyantek (1985) imposed their 14 rules in response to difficulties they encountered in attempting to replicate "a previous meta-analysis study." The study they attempted to replicate, Terpstra's (1981), was *not* a meta-analysis. The term meta-analysis is not mentioned in the Terpstra study, nor does Terpstra reference any article or book on meta-analysis. Standard meta-analysis methods are not used. It was not Terpstra's intention to conduct a meta-analysis, and there is no language in the study expressing the need or desirability of quantitatively integrating research findings.

This study was merely a case of a reviewer using some crude ad hoc quantitative methods in his attempt to make sense of the studies being reviewed. Yet Bullock and Svyantek portrayed Terpstra as an example of the things that can go wrong in a meta-analysis and as a demonstration of the need to require all meta-analysis to abide by their set of 14 mandatory rules. This problem is more serious than it would otherwise be, because Bullock and Svyantek have been cited in *Principles for the Validities and Use of Personnel Selection Instruments* (Society for Industrial and Organizational Psychology, 1987), magnifying the potential for erroneous interpretations and outright harm.

Criticisms of Corrections for Attenuation

The need for corrections for the attenuating effects of measurement error was presented in detail in Chapters 3, 4, 6, and 7. Rosenthal (1984, p. 30) has criticized these corrections on grounds that they reduce the comparability of the meta-analysis results relative to "typical research." His position is that meta-analytic results must be comparable to findings typically observed by primary researchers, or the credibility of the meta-analysis results will be low. He is not opposed to the application of corrections for attenuation per se, and he offers no statistical or measurement arguments against them. He simply feels that the resulting corrected correlations, or d values, are not as useful as uncorrected values, because (he maintains) most studies do not make measurement error corrections and, therefore, corrected values cannot be directly compared to values from those studies. Thus, he argues that because most researchers do not do things correctly, meta-analysts should not do things correctly either. He ignores the fact (demonstrated in Chapter 3) that failure to correct for measurement error leads to systematic underestimation of actual relationships among constructs. This is in contrast to the high level of concern he showed about the much smaller upward bias in d values (Rosenthal & Rubin, 1982a, see Chapter 8). He also ignores the fact that because different measures of a variable have different levels of reliability, failure to correct leads to many different "population" values for the correlation between any two constructs: There is one such value for every level of reliability. This is, of course, inconsistent with the basic goal of meta-analysis to identify the simple structure underlying social science data. In contrast to Rosenthal (1984), Hedges and Olkin (1985, pp. 131-136) acknowledge the need for corrections for measurement error.

Another criticism sometimes heard is that since the measures actually used are never perfectly reliable, one should not be concerned with what relationships would be if measures *were* perfectly reliable. This amounts to the position that science is concerned not with the relations among constructs themselves, but with the relations among imperfect measures of constructs. That is, the key interest in science is held to be measures and not constructs. This is an epistomological (philosophy of science) position or theory that we do not share and that, we believe, most scientists do not share.

14   Summary of Psychometric Meta-Analysis

The goal of research in any area is the production of an integrated statement of the findings of the many pieces of research done in that area. In a broad sense, this means a theoretical analysis of how the many facts fit together. However, this broad theoretical integration cannot be put on a sound footing until a narrower integration of the literature has taken place. We must first establish the basic facts before those facts can be integrated. This narrow focus on single facts is the starting point for the literature on meta-analysis.

Consider a theoretical question such as, "Does job satisfaction increase organizational commitment?" Before we can answer such a question, we must consider the more mundane question, "Is there a correlation between satisfaction and commitment?" Such questions cannot be answered in any one empirical study. Few social scientists have the resources to do the large-sample studies required to obtain the necessary population statistics. Results must be pooled across studies to eliminate sampling error. Furthermore, the correlation between satisfaction and commitment might vary across studies. That is, we must compare the population correlations in different settings. If there is variation across settings that is large enough to be theoretically important, then we must identify the moderator variables that produce this variation. To compare correlations across settings, we must correct these correlations for other artifacts such as measurement error or range variation. If the necessary information is given for each study, then error of measurement can be eliminated with the formula for correction for attenuation, and all results could be expressed in terms of the same reference population or treatment strength using the range variation formula. Otherwise, these effects must be corrected for in the meta-analysis.

Consider error of measurement. Satisfaction can be measured in many ways. These different methods might differ in two ways: Different methods may not measure exactly the same thing, or they may differ in the extent of random error in each method. Differences in random error can

535

be assessed by differences in reliability coefficients. If the reliability of each measure is known in each study, then the effect of random error of measurement can be eliminated from each study by correcting the correlation or effect-size statistic for attenuation. If only the distribution or reliability coefficients across studies is known, then the effect of random error of measurement can be eliminated using special meta-analysis formulas.

Systematic differences between measures with the same name require examination of the construct validity of the different methods. If there are large systematic differences between measures, then these must be assessed in multimeasure studies using techniques such as confirmatory factor analysis or path analysis. These studies have replication of results within studies as well as across studies and require special treatment.

Range variation on the independent variable produces differences of an artifactual nature in correlations and in effect-size statistics. If the basic relationship between variables is the same across studies, then variation in the extent of variance on the independent variable will produce variation in the correlation with the dependent variable. The larger the variance on the independent variable, the higher the correlation. In experimental studies, range variation is produced by differences in the strength of the treatment. If the range size in each study is known (i.e., if standard deviations are published or if treatment strengths are measured), then all correlations or effect sizes could be corrected to some standard value. This would eliminate the impact of range variation across studies. If the distribution of range variation is known, then this effect can be eliminated using special meta-analysis formulas.

Meta-analysis begins with a set of all studies that an investigator has found that provide empirical evidence that bears on some particular fact such as the relationship between organizational commitment and job satisfaction. The key findings of each study are expressed in a common statistic, such as the correlation between commitment and satisfaction or such as the d statistic, which measures the difference between experimental and control groups for the treatment of interest. Each such statistic can be examined across studies. The mean value of the statistic across studies is a good estimate of the mean attenuated population value across studies. However, the variance across studies is greatly inflated by sampling error. Thus, the first task in meta-analysis is to correct the observed variance across studies to eliminate the effect of sampling error. Then, the mean and variance of population values are corrected for the effect of error of measurement and range variation. This mean and standard deviation have thus been corrected for three sources of artifactual variation across studies: sampling error, error of measurement, and range variation. The largest source of variation not corrected for is often reporting errors, such as incorrect computations, typographical errors, failure to reverse score, and the like. However, there are numerous other potential sources of artifactual variation.

In many studies we have found no variance in results across studies once artifacts such as sampling error have been eliminated. In such cases the theorist is provided with a very straightforward fact to weave into the overall picture. For example, one way to obtain theoretical implications is to review all the reasons that have been cited as explanations for the nonexistent variation across studies. Most such explanations are based on more general theoretical considerations. Hence, the disconfirmation of the explanation leads to disconfirmation of the more general propositions behind the explanation. For example, meta-analysis has shown that the correlation between cognitive ability factors and job performance does not very across settings for a given job. This means that it is a waste of time for people in personnel research to do massive, detailed behavioristic job analyses to equate jobs with the same job description in different organizations.

If there is variation across studies, it may not be large enough to warrant an immediate search for moderator variables. For example, suppose that meta-analysis had shown the mean effect of interpersonal skills training on supervisor performance to be $\bar{\delta} = .50$ with a standard deviation of .05. It would be wise for an employer to institute a program of training immediately rather than wait to find out which programs work best. On the other hand, if the mean effect were $\bar{\delta} = .10$ with a standard deviation of .10, then the arbitrary choice of program might incur loss. There is a 16% chance that the program would be counterproductive, and another 34% chance that the program would cause a positive but nearly trivial improvement.

If there are large differences between studies, then moderator variables are usually not hard to find. For example, by the time the first meta-analysis was done on the effects of incentives on work performance, there were already interactive studies available showing that incentives work only if the worker has or is given specific information about what aspects of performance will be rewarded.

Meta-analysis provides a method for establishing the relevance of a potential moderator variable. The moderator variable is used to split the studies into subsets, and meta-analysis is then applied to each subset separately. Mean differences will appear if a moderator is present. If there are large differences in subset means, then there will be a corresponding reduction in within-subset variation across studies. Meta-analysis shows how much of that residual variation is due to artifacts. Homogeneity tests have less power to detect moderators than the method of subsetted meta-analyses. However, the latter method requires that the potential moderator variables be specified in advance by theory or hypothesis, while omnibus homogeneity methods do not.

The extent of variation is in part a question of the scope of the research review. If we start with all studies on psychotherapy, it is no surprise to find moderator effects. However, if we consider only studies using desensitization on snake phobias, then we might expect to find no differences. For meta-analysis, scope is an empirical question. If we have the resources for a wide scope, then meta-analysis can be used to assess the scope of the results. If meta-analysis shows only small differences over a very wide set of studies, then we have found that many moderator hypotheses are at most of only minor importance. If the wide-scope study shows large differences, then meta-analysis can be applied to subsets of studies with smaller scope. Meta-analysis then shows which aspects of scope (i.e., moderators) are truly important and which were erroneously thought to be important. The general finding of meta-analysis studies is that true differences across studies are much smaller than researchers believe them to be. These beliefs derive from the cumulative effect of sampling error, i.e., exposure to large but spurious differences in the observed results from small-sample studies.

A key point of consensus in meta-analysis is that restriction of scope should be topical rather than methodological. The worst reviews are those in which the author cites only "key" studies. First, reviews that selectively ignore studies with contrary findings may falsely suggest that there are no moderator variables. Second, even if there are no real variations across studies, there are spurious variations due to sampling error. Studies with particularly "sharp" findings are probably studies that capitalize on between-study variation that meta-analysis shows to be due to chance. In particular, consideration of only studies with statistically significant findings leads to great bias in the estimate of correlations or effect sizes.

Many authors justify selective reviews on the basis of the "methodological deficiencies" in the studies not considered. However, the assertion of "deficiency" is usually based on a theory that is itself empirically untested. Two authors could select mutually exclusive sets of studies from the same literature on the basis of "methodological flaws." Meta-analysis provides an empirical procedure for the identification of methodological deficiencies if there are any. First, one should gather a comprehensive set of studies. Second, one should identify those believed to be "defective." Third, one should apply meta-analysis to all studies. If there is no variation across studies, then there is no difference between the "defective" studies and the "competent" studies. Fourth, if there is variation across all studies, then that variation may or may not be explained by separate meta-analyses of the "defective" and "nondefective" studies, the next analysis to be conducted.

It is our belief that many real methodological problems are captured by the rubrics "error of measurement" and "range variation." Error of measurement, in particular, is universal, although some studies may have much poorer measurement than others. The solution to these methodological problems is to *measure* the deficiency and correct for it rather than to throw away data.

Appendix
Meta-Analysis Computer Programs for the PC

The Appendix presents four interactive meta-analysis programs and a program for creating data files for use by the programs. The programs are written in BASIC and can be run on any IBM PC or clone.

The first program, called VG6, is for correlations, and corrects each correlation individually for unreliability in both measures and for range restriction, as described in Chapter 3. Reliability corrections can be made before or after range restriction corrections, depending on in which group the reliabilities were estimated. Input to the program is a single data file organized as follows: column 1 = the observed correlations; column 2 = the reliabilities of the dependent variable; column 3 = the reliabilities of the independent variable; column 4 = the range restriction ratios, s/S; column 5 = sample size. Each row in the input matrix represents one study. Meta-analysis results are given for both the fully corrected and the observed correlations.

The second program meta-analyzes correlations using artifact distributions, as described in Chapter 4. This program is based on the noninteractive formula for SD_p (see Chapter 4). Input to the program consists of four data files of two columns each. In the first file, column 1 = the observed correlations and column 2 = the sample sizes. The second and third files contain the reliability distributions for the dependent and independent variables, respectively. The third file contains the distribution of restricted standard deviations (S) of the independent variable; the unrestricted SD is assumed to be 1.00. In all three of these files, the second column is the frequency of the first column entry. Meta-analysis output is given for both fully corrected correlations and observed correlations. A variety of supplemental output is also given.

The third program (D VALUE) is for d values corrected individually, as described in Chapter 7. In addition to sampling error, it corrects for unreliability in the dependent variable measure. Input into the program is a single data file; column 1 = the d values; column 2 = Ns; column 3 = the reliabilities of the dependent variable. Each row represents the data from one study. Meta-analysis results are given for both corrected and uncorrected *d* values. The individual values of the corrected *d* values are also printed.

The final meta-analysis program (D VALUE2) is for *d* values using artifact distributions (see Chapter 7). Input consists of two files, each with two columns. The first contains the *d* values and *N*s in column 1 and column 2, respectively. The second contains the reliabilities of the dependent variable in col 1 and the associated frequencies in column 2. Output is similar to that from the D VALUE program, discussed above.

The last program, MAKEDATA.BAS, is an interactive program that can be used to create the data files needed for these meta-analysis programs. These files are stored on disk until the meta-analysis programs are run.

Meta-Analysis Correcting Correlations Individually

```
1 REM BY F. SCHMIDT JAN 1985; IMPROVED FEB 1987
5 REM THIS IS A TRANSLATION OF VG6 BY JEC, MARCH, 1988
6 REM FOR USE ON IBM COMPATIBLE PC'S USING GWBASIC VERSION
  2.0
7 REM TO CREATE A DATA FILE FOR THIS PROGRAM USE PROGRAM
  MAKE DATA.BAS
10 REM V.G. FOR R'S CORRECTED INDIVIDUALLY. THIS IS PROGRAM
   VG6
15 REM VG6 USES MEAN OBS R IN S.E. FORMULA
20 REM VG6 HAS MORE ACCURATE ALPHA VALUE
25 REM ALPHA VARIES WITH ORDER OF REL CORRECTIONS
30 DIM A(100,6)
50 INPUT "DISK/DATA FILE NAME";N$
70 INPUT "NUMBER OF ROWS";NR
90 INPUT "NUMBER OF COLUMNS";NC
110 OPEN "I",1,N$
130 REM READ IN DATA MATRIX
150 FOR I=1 TO NR: FOR J=1 TO NC
170 INPUT#1,A(I,J)
190 NEXT J:NEXT I
210 CLOSE 1
230 REM PRINT DATA MATRIX AS CHECK
250 FOR I=1 TO NR:PRINT I;
270 FOR J=1 TO NC:PRINT A(I,J); :NEXT J
290 PRINT :NEXT I
310 DIM R(100)
330 REM COMPUTE MEAN UNCORRECTED R
340 TN=0:SUM=0
350 FOR I=1 TO NR
360 SUM=SUM+A(I,5)*A(I,1)
370 TN=TN+A(I,5)
380 NEXT I
390 RM=SUM/TN
400 PRINT "WHAT ORDER OF CORRECTION FOR RELIABILITY?
410 INPUT "ENTER B FOR BEFORE RANGE RES, A FOR AFTER ";A$
420 F$=LEFT$(A$,1)
422 IF F$="B" GOTO 1630
423 IF F$="A" GOTO 1770
430 REM COMPUTING MEAN CORRECTED R
450 TN=0
```

```
470 SUM=0
490 FOR I=1 TO NR
510 SUM=SUM+A(I,5)*A(I,6)
530 TN=TN+A(I,5)
550 NEXT I
570 MR=SUM/TN
790 REM COMPUTING VAR OF CORRECTED R'S
810 ND=0
830 TD=0
850 FOR I=1 TO NR
870 ND=A(I,5)*(A(I,6)-MR)^2
890 TD=TD+ND
910 NEXT I
930 VAR=TD/TN
950 VC=(SF/VAR)*100
970 REM COMPUTING SD OF TRUE SCORE
990 VR=VAR-SF
1000 GOSUB 2000
1010 IF VR<0 THEN SD=0
1030 IF VR>0 THEN SD=SQR(VR)
1050 REM COMPUTING BEST AND WORST CASES
1070 BC=MR+1.28*SD
1090 WC=MR-1.28*SD
1110 REM PRINT OUT ON SCREEN
1130 PRINT "VALIDITY GENERALIZATION RESULTS":PRINT
1150 PRINT"MEAN TRUE SCORE R=";:PRINT MR
1170 PRINT"SD OF TRUE SCORE R=";:PRINT SD
1190 PRINT"BEST CASE=";:PRINT BC
1210 PRINT"WORST CASE=";:PRINT WC
1230 PRINT"PERCENT VAR ACC FOR=";:PRINT VC
1250 PRINT"TOTAL N=";:PRINT TN
1270 PRINT"TOTAL VAR=";:PRINT VAR
1290 PRINT"SAMPLING VAR=";:PRINT SF
1310 PRINT"NO. OF R'S=";:PRINT RS:PRINT:PRINT
1312 PRINT"RESULTS FOR UNCORRECTED R'S:PRINT
1314 PRINT'MEAN UNCOR. R=";:PRINT RM
1316 PRINT"CORRECTED SD=";:PRINT S
1318 PRINT"TOTAL VAR=";:PRINT V
1320 PRINT"SAMPLING VAR";:PRINT SE
1322 PRINT"PERCENT VAR ACC FOR";:PRINT X
1330 REM PRINT ON PRINTER
1340 INPUT "IS PRINTER ON (Y/N)";Y$
```

```
1345 IF Y$="Y" THEN 1350 ELSE 1590
1350 INPUT "WHAT TITLE SHOULD APPEAR ON THE REPORT";D$
1355 LPRINT "TITLE: ";D$:LPRINT
1370 LPRINT"VALIDITY GENERALIZATION RESULTS":LPRINT
1390 LPRINT"MEAN TRUE SCORE R=";MR
1410 LPRINT"SD OF TRUE SCORE R=";SD
1430 LPRINT"BEST CASE=";BC
1450 LPRINT"WORST CASE=";WC
1470 LPRINT"PERCENT VAR ACC FOR=";VC
1490 LPRINT"TOTAL N=";TN
1510 LPRINT"TOTAL VAR=";VAR
1550 LPRINT"NO. OF R'S=";RS:LPRINT:LPRINT
1552 LPRINT"RESULTS FOR UNCORRECTED R'S":LPRINT
1554 LPRINT"MEAN UNCOR. R=';RM
1556 LPRINT"CORRECTED SD=":S
1558 LPRINT"TOTAL VAR=";V
1560 LPRINT"SAMPLING VAR=":SE
1562 LPRINT"PERCENT VAR ACC FOR=";X
1590 END
1610 REM REL CORRECTION BEFORE RR COR(RESTRICTED RELS)
1630 FOR I=1 TO NR
1650 A=A(I,1)/SQR(A(I,2)*A(I,3))
1670 W=1/A(I,4)
1690 A(I,6)=(W*A)/SQR(W^2*A^2-A^2+1)
1710 NEXT I:NC=6
1730 GOTO 2300
1750 REM REL CORRECTION AFTER RR COR(UNRESTRICTED RELS)
1770 FOR I=1 TO NR
1790 W=1/A(I,4)
1810 B=(W*AS(I,1))/SQR(W^2*A(I,1)^2-A(I,1)^2+1)
1830 A(I,6)=B/SQR(A(I,2)*A(I,3))
1850 NEXT I:NC=6
1870 GOTO 2480
2000 REM COMPUTE MEAN UNCORRECTED R
2010 TN=0:SUM=0
2020 FOR I=1 TO NR
2030 SUM=SUM+A(I,5)*A(I,1)
2040 TN=TN+A(I,5)
2050 NEXT I
2060 RM=SUM/TN
2070 REM COMPUTE UNCOR. SAMPLE. ERROR VAR
2080 SS=0
```

```
2090 FOR I=1 TO NR
2100 S2=((1-RM^2)^2)/(A(I,5)-1)
2110 SC=A(I,5)*S2
2120 SS=SS+SC
2130 NEXT I
2140 SE=SS/TN
2150 REM COMPUTE VAR OF UNCORRECTED R'S
2160 ND=0:TD=0
2170 FOR I=1 TO NR
2180 ND=A(I,5)*(A(I,1)-RM)^2
2190 TD=TD+ND:NEXT I
2200 V=TD/TN
2210 X=(SE/V)*100
2220 REM COMPUTE SD SUB RHO FOR UNCORRECTED R'S
2230 V2=V-SE
2240 IF V2<0 THEN S=0
2250 IF V2>0 THEN S=SQR(V2)
2260 RETURN
2270 REM COMPUTING SAMPLING ERROR VAR OF CORRECTED RS
2280 REM REL CORRECTIONS BEFORE RR CORRECTION
2290 REM NEW MORE ACCURATE ALPHA VALUE
2300 RS=0
2310 FOR I=1 TO NR
2320 S2=((1-RM^2)^2)/(A(I,5)-1)
2330 U=1/A(I,4)
2340 Z=A(I,1)/SQR(A(I,2)*A(I,3))
2350 AC=1/((U^2-1)*Z^2+1)
2360 A=A(I,6)/A(I,1)
2370 A2=(AC*A)^2
2380 REM A2 IS IMPROVED ALPHA SQUARED;A IS OLD ALPHA;AC=NEW
     COR FACTOR
2390 SC=A(I,5)*A2*S2
2400 SS=SS+SC
2405 RS=RS+1
2410 NEXT I
2430 SF=SS/TN
2440 GOTO 450
2460 REM COMPUTING SAMPLING ERROR VAR FOR CORRECTED RS
2465 REM REL CORRECTIONS AFTER RR CORRECTION
2470 REM NEW MORE ACCURATE ALPHA VALUE
2480 RS=0
2490 FOR I=1 TO NR
```

```
2500 S2=((1-RM^2)^2)/(A(I,5)-1
2510 U=1/A(I,4)
2520 AC=1/((U^2-1)*A(I,1)^2+1)
2530 A=A(I,6)/A(I,1)
2540 A2=(AC*A)^2
2560 SC=A(I,5)*A2*S2
2570 SS=SS+SC
2580 RS=RS+1
2590 NEXT I
2600 SF=SS/TN
2610 GOTO 450
```

Artifact Distribution Meta-Analysis of Correlations

```
10 REM V.G. WITH ARTIFACT DISTRIBUTIONS; NONINTERACTIVE
   V.G. PROGRAM
20 REM THIS IS PROGRAM VG-NONINTERACTIVE; BY F. SCHMIDT
   JAN. 14, 1985
30 REM TRANSLATED BY JEC, MARCH 1988 (CALLED VGNON.BAS)
40 REM FOR IBM COMPATIBLE PC'S USING GW BASIC VERSION 2.0
50 REM PROGRAM ASSUMES UNRES. SD=1.00
60 DIM R(100,2),RC(15,2),RX(15,2),SD(15,2)
70 PRINT"YOU MUST ENTER 4 DISK FILE NAMES IN THIS ORDER"
80 PRINT"FIRST, THE FILE WITH R'S & N'S":PRINT
90 PRINT"SECOND, THE FILE WITH RCC'S & FREQ'S":PRINT
100 PRINT"THIRD, THE FILE WITH RXX'S & FREQ'S":PRINT
110 PRINT"FOURTH, THE FILE WITH RR'S & FREQ'S":PRINT
120 PRINT"KEEP TRACK OF THIS ORDER":PRINT
130 PRINT"R AND N FILE":PRINT
140 INPUT "DISK/DATA FILE NAME";N$
150 INPUT "NUMBER OF ROWS";NR
160 INPUT "NUMBER OF COLUMNS";NC
170 OPEN "I",2,N$
180 REM READ IN R AND N MATRIX
190 FOR I=1 TO NR:FOR J=1 TO NC
200 INPUT#2,R(I,J)
210 NEXT J:NEXT I
220 CLOSE 2
230 REM PRINT R & N MATRIX AS CHECK
240 FOR I=1 TO NR:PRINT I;
250 FOR J=1 TO NC:PRINT R(I,J);:NEXT J
260 PRINT:NEXT I
270 REM READ IN RCC MATRIX
280 PRINT "RCC AND FREQ'S FILE":PRINT
290 INPUT "DISK/DATA FILE NAME";M$
300 INPUT "NUMBER OF ROWS";N1
310 INPUT "NUMBER OF COLUMNS";N2
320 OPEN "I",3,M$
330 FOR I=1 TO N1:FOR J=1 TO N2
340 INPUT#3,RC(I,J)
350 NEXT J:NEXT I
360 CLOSE 3
370 REM PRINT RCC MATRIX AS CHECK
380 FOR I=1 TO N1:PRINT I;
```

```
390 FOR J=1 TO N2:PRINT RC(I,J);:NEXT J
400 PRINT:NEXT I
410 REM READ IN RXX MATRIX
420 PRINT"RXX AND FREQ'S FILE":PRINT
430 INPUT "DISK/DATA FILE NAME";P$
440 INPUT "NUMBER OF ROWS";N3
450 INPUT "NUMBER OF COLUMNS";N4
460 OPEN "I",4,P$
470 FOR I=1 TO N3:FOR J=1 TO N4
480 INPUT#4,RX(I,J)
490 NEXT J:NEXT I
500 CLOSE 4
510 REM PRINT RXX MATRIX AS CHECK
520 FOR I=1 TO N3:PRINT I;
530 FOR J=1 TO N4:PRINT RX(I,J);:NEXT J
540 PRINT:NEXT I
550 REM READ IN RES. SD MATRIX
560 PRINT"RR AND FREQ'S FILE":PRINT
570 INPUT "DISK/DATA FILE NAME";Q$
580 INPUT "NUMBER OF ROWS";N5
590 INPUT "NUMBER OF COLUMNS";N6
600 OPEN "I",5,Q$
610 FOR I=1 TO N5:FOR J=1 TO N6
620 INPUT#5,SD(I,J)
630 NEXT J:NEXT I
640 CLOSE 5
650 REM PRINT SD MATRIX AS CHECK
660 FOR I=1 TO N5:PRINT I;
670 FOR J=1 TO N6:PRINT SD(I,J);:NEXT J
680 PRINT:NEXT I
690 REM COMPUTING MEAN OBSERVED R
700 TN=0:SUM=0
710 FOR I=1 TO NR
720 SUM=SUM+R(I,2)*R(I,1)
730 TN=TN+R(I,2):NEXT I
740 MR=SUM/TN
750 REM COMPUTING SAMPLING ERROR VAR.
760 RN=0:SS=0
770 FOR I=1 TO NR
780 S2=((1-R(I,1)^2)^2)/(R(I,2)-1)
790 SC=S2*R(I,2)
800 SS=SS+SC:RN=RN+1
```

```
810 NEXT I
820 VS=SS/TN
830 REM COMPUTING VAR OF OBSERVED R'S
840 ND=0:TD=0
850 FOR I=1 TO NR
860 ND=R(I,2)*(R(I,1)-MR)^2
870 TD=TD+ND
880 NEXT I
890 VAR=TD/TN:SO=SQR(VAR)
900 VP=(VS/VAR)*100
910 REM COMPUTING MEAN OF SQR OF RCC
920 Y1=0:Z1=0
930 FOR I=1 TO N1
940 X1=SQR(RC(I,1))*RC(I,2)
950 Y1=Y1+X1
960 Z1=Z1+RC(I,2)
970 NEXT I
980 CM=Y1/Z1
990 REM COMPUTING MEAN OF SQR OF RXX
1000 Y2=0:X2=0:Z2=0
1010 FOR I=1 TO N3
1020 X2=SQR(RX(I,1))*RX(I,2)
1030 Y2=Y2+X2
1040 Z2=Z2+RX(I,2)
1050 NEXT I
1060 XM=Y2/Z2
1070 REM COMPUTING MEAN RESTRICTED SD
1080 Y3=0:X3=0:Z3=0
1090 FOR I=1 TO N5
1100 X3=SD(I,1)*SD(I,2)
1110 Y3=Y3+X3
1120 Z3=Z3+SD(I,2)
1130 NEXT I
1140 SM=Y3/Z3
1150 REM COMPUTING TRUE SCORE MEAN R
1160 REM ASSUMES RXX & RCC ARE UNRESTRICTED VALUES
1170 U=1/SM
1180 RR=MR*U/SQR(U^2)*(MR^2)-MR^2+1)
1190 RS=RR/(CM*XM)
1200 REM COMPUTING VAR DUE TO RCC DIFFS
1210 X4=0:Y4=0:Z4=0:F4=0
1220 FOR I=1 TO N1
```

```
1230 RA=RS*SQR(RC(I,1))
1240 X4=RA*RC(I,2)
1250 Y4=Y4+X4
1260 Z4=Z4+RA^2*RC(I,2)
1270 F4=F4+RC(I,2)
1280 NEXT I
1290 VC=(Z4/F4)-(Y4/F4)^2
1300 REM COMPUTING VAR DUE TO RXX DIFFS
1310 X5=0:Y5=0:Z5=0:F5=0
1320 RB=RS*SQR(CM)
1330 FOR I=1 TO N3
1340 RD=RB*SQR(RX(I,1))
1350 X5=RD*RX(I,2)
1360 Y5=Y5+X5
1370 Z5=Z5+RD^2*RX(I,2)
1380 F5=F5+RX(I,2)
1390 NEXT I
1400 VX=(Z5/F5)-(Y5/F5)^2
1410 REM COMPUTING VAR DUE TO RR DIFFS
1420 X6=0:Y6=0:Z6=0:F6=0
1430 FOR I=1 TO N5
1440 V=SD(I,1)/1
1445 REM UNRES. SD=1.00
1450 RE=RR*V/SQR(1-RR^2+(V^2)*RR^2)
1460 X6=RE*SD(I,2)
1470 Y6=Y6+X6
1480 Z6=Z6+RE^2*SD(I,2)
1490 F6=F6+SD(I,2)
1500 NEXT I
1510 VR=(Z6/F6)-(Y6/F6)^2
1520 REM COMPUTING RESIDUAL VAR & SD
1530 S3=VAR-VS-VC-VX-VR
1540 IF S3<0 THEN S4=0
1550 IF S3>0 THEN S4=SQR(S3)
1560 REM COMPUTING SD-PREDICTED
1570 S5=SQR(VS+VC+VX+VR)
1580 REM COMPUTING PERCENT VAR ACC FOR
1590 S6=(S5^2/VAR)*100
1600 REM COMPUTE SD OF TRUE SCORE R
1610 S7=(RS/MR)*S4
1620 REM COMPUTE SD OF TRUE VALIDITY
1630 S8=S7*SQR(XM)
```

```
1640 REM COMPUTE MEAN TRUE VALIDITY
1650 R8=RS*SQR(XM)
1660 REM BEST & WORST CASES--TRUE VAL.
1670 BC=R8+1.28*S8
1680 WC=R8-1.28*S8
1690 REM PRINT OUTPUT ON PRINTER
1700 INPUT "IS PRINTER READY (Y/N)";Y$:IF Y$="Y" THEN 1702
     ELSE 1990
1702 INPUT "REPORT NAME";J$
1704 LPRINT "REPORT FOR   ";J$:LPRINT
1710 LPRINT"VALIDITY GENERALIZATION RESULTS"
1720 LPRINT"NONINTERACTIVE PROGRAM":LPRINT
1730 LPRINT"MEAN OBSERVED R=";MR
1740 LPRINT"SD OF OBSERVED R'S=";SO
1750 LPRINT"PREDICTED SD=";S5
1760 LPRINT"% VAR ACC FOR=";S6
1770 LPRINT"RESIDUAL SD=";S4
1780 LPRINT"RESIDUAL VAR=";S3
1790 LPRINT"NUMBER OF R'S=";RN
1800 LPRINT"TOTAL N=";TN:LPRINT
1810 LPRINT"MEAN TRUE SCORE R=";RS
1820 LPRINT"SD OF TRUE SCORE R=";S7
1830 LPRINT"MEAN TRUE VALIDITY=";R8
1840 LPRINT"SD OF TRUE VALIDITY=";S8
1850 LPRINT"BEST CASE=";BC
1860 LPRINT"WORST CASE=";WC:LPRINT:LPRINT
1870 LPRINT"SUPPLEMENTARY RESULTS":LPRINT
1880 LPRINT"TOTAL VARIANCE=";VAR
1890 LPRINT"SAMPLING ERROR VAR=";VS
1900 LPRINT"% VAR DUE TO SAMPLING ERROR=";VP
1910 LPRINT"VAR DUE TO CRITERION REL DIFFS=";VC
1920 LPRINT"VAR DUE TO TEST REL DIFFS=";VX
1930 LPRINT"VAR DUE TO RANGE RES DIFFS=";VR
1940 LPRINT"MEAN OF SQR OF CRITERION REL=";CM
1950 LPRINT"MEAN OF SQR OF TEST REL=";XM
1960 LPRINT"MEAN RESTRICTED SD=";SM:LPRINT
1970 LPRINT"MEAN R CORRECTED FOR RANGE RES=";RR
1990 END
```

Meta-Analysis Correcting *d* Values Individually

```
10 REM META-ANALYSIS OF D VALUES CORRECTED INDIVIDUALLY,
   PROGRAM D VALUE
20 REM BY F SCHMIDT, JAN. 1985
30 REM TRANSLATED BY JEC, MARCH, 1988
35 REM FOR IBM COMPATIBLE PC'S USING GW BASIC VERSION 2.0
40 DIM A(100,4)
50 INPUT "DISK/DATA FILE NAME";N$
60 INPUT "NUMBER OF ROWS";NR
70 INPUT "NUMBER OF COLUMNS";NC
80 OPEN "I",2,N$
90 REM READ IN DATA MATRIX
100 FOR I=1 TO NR;FOR J=1 TO NC
110 INPUT#2,A(I,J)
120 NEXT J:NEXT I
130 CLOSE 2
140 REM PRINT DATA MATRIX AS CHECK
150 FOR I=1 TO NR:PRINT I;
160 FOR J=1 TO NC:PRINT A(I,J);:NEXT J
170 PRINT:NEXT I
175 STOP
180 REM COMPUTE CORRECTED D VALUES
190 FOR I=1 TO NR
200 A(I,4)=A(I,1)/SQR(A(I,3))
210 NEXT I
220 REM COMPUTE MEAN CORRECTED D VALUE
230 TN=0:SUM=0
240 FOR I=1 TO NR
250 SUM=SUM+A(I,2)*A(I,4)
260 TN=TN+A(I,2)
270 NEXT I
280 MD=SUM/TN
290 REM COMPUTE MEAN UNCORRECTED D VALUE
300 L=0
310 FOR I=1 TO NR
320 L=L+A(I,1)*A(I,2)
330 NEXT I
340 DM=L/TN
350 REM COMPUTE SAMPLING VAR OF UNCORRECTED D'S
360 S1=(4*(1+(DM^2)/8)*NR)/TN
370 REM COMPUTE SAMPLING VAR OF CORRECTED D'S
```

```
380 P=0
390 FOR I=1 TO NR
400 P=P+1/A(I,3)
410 NEXT I
420 S2=S1*P/NR
430 REM COMPUTE VAR OF UNCORRECTED D'S
440 ND=0
450 FOR I=1 TO NR
460 ND=ND+A(I,2)*(A(I,1)-DM)^2
470 NEXT I
480 V1=ND/TN
490 X1=(S1/V1)*100
500 REM COMPUTE SD SUB DELTA FOR UNCORRECTED D'S
510 VU=V1-S1
520 IF VU<0 THEN SU=0
530 IF VU>0 THEN SU=SQR(VU)
540 REM COMPUTE OBS VAR OF CORRECTED D'S
550 Z=0
560 FOR I=1 TO NR
570 Z=Z+A(I,2)*(A(I,4)-MD)^2
580 NEXT I
590 V2=Z/TN
600 X2=(S2/V2)*100
610 REM COMPUTE SD SUB DELTA FOR CORRECTED D'S
620 VC=V2-S2
630 IF VC<0 THEN SC=0
640 IF VC>0 THEN SC=SQR(VC)
650 REM COMPUTE BEST AND WORST CASES-UNCORRECTED D'S
660 B1=DM+1.28*SU
670 W1=DM-1.28*SU
680 REM COMPUTE BEST AND WORST CASES-CORRECTED D'S
690 B2=MD+1.28*SC
700 W2=MD-1.28*SC
710 REM PRINT OUT ON PRINTER
720 INPUT "IS PRINTER READY (Y/N)";Y$
725 IF Y$="Y" THEN 730 ELSE 990
730 LPRINT"META-ANALYSIS RESULTS":LPRINT:LPRINT
740 LPRINT"RESULTS FOR CORRECTED D VALUES":LPRINT
750 LPRINT"MEAN CORRECTED D=";MD
760 LPRINT"TRUE SD OF CORRECTED D=";SC
770 LPRINT"BEST CASE=";B2
780 LPRINT"WORST CASE=";W2
```

```
790 LPRINT"PERCENT VAR ACC FOR=";X2
800 LPRINT"TOTAL VAR=";V2
810 LPRINT"SAMPLING VAR=";S2
820 LPRINT"TOTAL N=";TN
830 LPRINT"NO. OF D'S=";NR:LPRINT:LPRINT
840 LPRINT"RESULTS FOR UNCORRECTED D VALUES":LPRINT
850 LPRINT"MEAN UNCORRECTED D=";DM
860 LPRINT"CORRECTED SD=";SU
870 LPRINT"BEST CASE=";B1
880 LPRINT"WORST CASE=";W1
890 LPRINT"PERCENT VAR ACC FOR=';X1
900 LPRINT"TOTAL VAR=";V1
910 LPRINT"SAMPLING VAR=";S1:LPRINT:LPRINT
920 LPRINT"INDIVIDUAL CORRECTED D'S":LPRINT
930 FOR I=1 TO NR:LPRINT I;
940 LPRINT A(I,4)
950 NEXT I
960 LPRINT:LPRINT"PROGRAM BY F. SCHMIDT"
970 LPRINT"JAN. 1985"
990 END
```

Artifact Distribution Meta-Analysis of *d* Values

```
10 REM D VALUE META-ANALYSIS WITH ARTIFACT DISTRIBUTION
20 REM RELIABILITIES OF DEPENDENT VAR ASSUMED UNMATCHED
30 REM THESE RELIABILITIES ARE READ FROM A SEPARATE FILE
32 REM PROGRAM BY F. SCHMIDT, JAN. 1985, CALLED DVALUE2
34 REM TRANSLATED BY JEC, MARCH 1988
36 REM FOR IBM COMPATIBLE PC'S USING GW BASIC VERSION 2.0
50 DIM D(100,2),RY(50,2)
60 PRINT"D VALUE META-ANALYSIS WITH"
70 PRINT"ARTIFACT DISTRIBUTION FOR"
75 PRINT"RELIABILITIES OF DEPENDENT VAR":PRINT
80 PRINT"FIRST, INPUT THE D & N FILE":PRINT
90 INPUT"DISK/DATA FILE NAME";N$
100 INPUT"NUMBER OF ROWS";NR
110 INPUT"NUMBER OF COLUMNS";NC
120 OPEN "I",2,N$
130 REM READ IN D AND N MATRIX
140 FOR I=1 TO NR:FOR J=1 TO NC
150 INPUT#2,D(I,J)
160 NEXT J:NEXT I
170 CLOSE 2
180 REM PRINT D & N MATRIX AS CHECK
190 FOR I=1 TO NR:PRINT I;
200 FOR J=1 TO NC:PRINT D(I,J);:NEXT J
210 PRINT:NEXT I
220 REM READ IN RYY MATRIX
230 PRINT"RYY AND FREQ'S FILE":PRINT
240 INPUT"DISK/DATA FILE NAME";M$
250 INPUT"NUMBER OF ROWS";N1
260 INPUT"NUMBER OF COLUMNS";N2
270 OPEN "I",3,M$
280 FOR I=1 TO N1:FOR J=1 TO N2
290 INPUT#3,RY(I,J)
300 NEXT J:NEXT I
310 CLOSE 3
320 REM PRINT RYY MATRIX AS CHECK
330 FOR I=1 TO N1:PRINT I;
340 FOR J=1 TO N2:PRINT RY(I,J);:NEXT J
350 PRINT:NEXT I
360 REM COMPUTE MEAN UNCORRECTED D
370 TN=0:SUM=0
```

```
380 FOR I=1 TO NR
390 SUM=SUM+D(I,2)*D(I,1)
400 TN=TN+D(I,2):NEXT I
410 DM=SUM/TN
420 REM COMPUTE SAMPLING VAR OF OBS D'S
430 S1=(4*(1+(DM^2)/8)*NR)/TN
440 REM COMPUTE VAR OF OBS D'S
450 ND=0
460 FOR I=1 TO NR
470 ND=ND+D(I,2)*(I,1)-DM)^2
480 NEXT I
490 V1=ND/TN:SO=SQR(V1)
500 REM COMPUTE PERCENT VAR DUE TO SAMPLING ERROR
510 X1=(S1/V1)*100
520 REM COMPUTE MEAN SQR OF RYY
530 Y=0:Z=0
540 FOR I=1 TO N1
550 Y=Y+SQR(RY(I,1))*RY(I,2)
560 Z=Z+RY(I,2)
570 NEXT I
580 YM=Y/Z
590 REM COMPUTE TRUE SCORE MEAN D
600 DT=DM/YM
610 REM COMPUTE VAR DUE TO RYY DIFFS
620 X4=0:Y4=0:Z4=0:F4=0
630 FOR I=1 TO N1
640 DA=DT*SQR(RY(I,1))
650 X4=DA*RY(I,2)
660 Y4=Y4+X4
670 Z4=Z4+DA^2*RY(I,2)
680 F4=F4+RY(I,2)
690 NEXT I
700 VY=(Z4/F4)-(Y4/F4)^2
710 REM COMPUTE RESIDUAL VAR AND SD
720 RV=V1-S1-VY
730 IF RV<0 THEN RS=0
740 IF RV>0 THEN RS=SQR(RV)
750 REM COMPUTE SD-PREDICTED
760 SP=SQR(S1+VY)
770 REM COMPUTE PERCENT VAR ACC FOR
780 PV=((S1+VY)/V1)*100
790 REM COMPUTE SD OF TRUE SCORE D'S
```

```
800 S7=(DT/DM)*RS
810 REM BEST & WORST CASES-CORRECTED D
820 BC=DT+1.28*S7
830 WC=DT-1.28*S7
840 REM BEST & WORST CASES-UNCORRECTED D
850 B1=DM+1.28*RS
860 W1=DM+1.28*RS
870 REM PRINT OUTPUT ON PRINTER
880 INPUT "IS PRINTER READY (Y/N)";Y$
885 IF Y$="Y" THEN 890 ELSE 1190
890 LPRINT"META-ANALYSIS RESULTS":LPRINT
900 LPRINT"D VALUES WITH ARTIFACT DISTRIBUTION":LPRINT
    :LPRINT
910 LPRINT"MEAN CORRECTED D=";DT
920 LPRINT"SD OF CORRECTED D=";S7
930 LPRINT"BEST CASE=";BC
940 LPRINT"WORST CASE=";WC
950 LPRINT"PERCENT VAR ACC FOR=";PV
960 LPRINT"TOTAL N=";TN
970 LPRINT"NO. OF D'S=";NR:LPRINT:LPRINT
980 LPRINT"SUPPLEMENTARY RESULTS":LPRINT
990 LPRINT"MEAN UNCORRECTED D=";DM
1000 LPRINT"MEAN SQR OF RYY=";YM
1010 LPRINT"RESIDUAL SD=";RS
1020 LPRINT"BEST CASE=";B1
1030 LPRINT"WORST CASE=";W1
1040 LPRINT"VAR OF OBSERVED D'S=";V1
1050 LPRINT"SAMPLING ERROR VAR OF OBS D'S=";S1
1060 LPRINT"VAR DUE TO RYY DIFFS=";VY
1070 LPRINT"RESIDUAL VAR=";RV
1080 LPRINT"RESIDUAL SD=";RS
1090 LPRINT"PERCENT VAR ACC FOR=";PV
1100 LPRINT"PERCENT VAR DUE TO SAMPLING ERROR=";X1
1110 LPRINT"SD OF OBSERVED D'S=";SO
1120 LPRINT"PREDICTED SD=";SP:LPRINT:LPRINT
1130 LPRINT"OBSERVED D VALUES":LPRINT
1140 FOR I=1 TO NR:LPRINT I;
1150 LPRINT D(I,1):NEXT I:LPRINT
1160 LPRINT"PROGRAM BY F. SCHMIDT"
1170 LPRINT"JAN. 1985":LPRINT
1190 END
```

Program to Create Data Files

```
5 REM PROGRAM BY JOHN HUNTER
10 REM THIS PROGRAM WILL MAKE, REMAKE OR ADD DATA TO
20 REM A SEQUENTIAL DATA FILE. IT IS CALLED MAKEDATA.BAS
30 REM IT CAN ALSO PRINT A DATA FILE AS A CHECK.
35 REM FOR IBM COMPATIBLE PC'S USING GW BASIC VERSION 2.0
40 DIM A(100,10)
50 PRINT "OPTIONS ARE:"
60 PRINT "1. NEW DATA FILE'
70 PRINT "2. REDO EXISTING FILE"
80 PRINT "3. ADD TO EXISTING FILE"
90 PRINT:PRINT "CHOOSE BY ANSWERING THE FOLLOWING QUESTIONS
   YES OR NO"
100 INPUT "1. DO YOU WANT A NEW DATA FILE (Y/N)";Y1$
110 IF Y1$="Y" THEN 160
120 INPUT "2. DO YOU WANT TO REDO A FILE (Y/N)";Y2$
130 IF Y2$="Y" THEN 160
140 INPUT "3. DO YOU WANT TO ADD TO A FILE (Y/N)";Y3$
150 IF Y3$="Y" THEN 300 ELSE 430
160 PRINT "YOU WILL CREATE A NEW FILE IF YOU NAME A
    NONEXISTENT FILE"
170 PRINT "YOU WILL ERASE DATA IF YOU NAME A FILE ON THE
    DISK":PRINT
180 INPUT "DISK/DATA FILE NAME";N$
190 INPUT "NUMBER OF ROWS";NR
200 INPUT "NUMBER OF COLUMNS";NC
210 OPEN "O",1,N$
220 FOR I=1 TO NR:PRINT"ROW:";I
230    FOR J=1 TO NC
240    INPUT "DATA:",A(I,J)
250    PRINT#1,A(I,J);
260    NEXT J
270 PRINT:NEXT I
280 CLOSE 1
290 GOTO 430
300 PRINT "YOU WILL ADD TO THE END OF A FILE IF YOU NAME
    AN EXISTING FILE"
310 PRINT "YOU WILL CREATE A NEW FILE IF YOU NAME A
    NONEXISTING FILE":PRINT
320 INPUT "DISK/DATA FILE NAME";F$
330 INPUT "NUMBER OF ROWS";FR
```

```
340 INPUT "NUMBER OF COLUMNS";FC
350 OPEN "A",2,F$
360 FOR I=1 TO FR:PRINT "ROW:";I
370    FOR J=1 TO FC
380    INPUT "DATA:",A(I,J)
390    PRINT#2,A(I,J);
400    NEXT J
410 PRINT:NEXT I
420 CLOSE 2
430 INPUT "DO YOU WANT TO CHECK YOUR DATA (Y/N)";Y4$
440 IF Y4$="Y" THEN 450 ELSE 580
450 INPUT "DISK/DATA FILE NAME";C$
460 INPUT "NUMBER OF ROWS";CR
470 INPUT "NUMBER OF COLUMNS";CC
480 OPEN "I",3,C$
490 FOR I=1 TO CR:FOR J=1 TO CC
500 INPUT#3,A(I,J)
510 NEXT J:NEXT I
520 CLOSE 3
530 FOR I=1 TO CR:PRINT I;
540 FOR J=1 TO CC:PRINT A(I,J);:NEXT J
550 PRINT:NEXT I
560 INPUT "DO YOU WANT TO RUN THE PROGRAM AGAIN (Y/N)";Y5$
570 IF Y5$="Y" THEN 100
580 END
```

References

AERA-APA-NCME. (1985). *Standards for educational and psychological testing*. Washington, D.C.: American Psychological Association.

Albright, L. E., Glennon, J. R., & Smith, W. J. (1963). *The use of psychological tests in industry*. Cleveland, OH: Howard Allen.

Alexander, R.A. (1988). Group homogeneity, range restriction, and range enhancement effects on correlations. *Personnel Psychology, 41*, 773-777.

Alexander, R. A., Carson, K. P., Alliger, G. M., & Carr, L. (1987). Correcting doubly truncated correlations: An improved approximation for correcting the bivariate normal correlation when truncation has occurred on both variables. *Educational and Psychological Measurement, 47*, 309-315.

Alexander, R. A., Carson, K. P., Alliger. G. M., & Cronshaw, S. F. (1989). Empirical distributions of range restricted SD_x in validity studies. *Journal of Applied Psychology, 74*, 253-258.

Allen, M., Hunter, J. E., & Donahue, W. A (1988). *Meta-analysis of self report data on the effectiveness of communication apprehension treatment techniques*. Unpublished manuscript, Department of Communication, Wake Forest University.

Allen, M., Hunter, J. E., & Donohue, W. A (1989). Meta-analysis of self-report data on the effectiveness of public speaking anxiety treatment techniques. *Communication Education, 38*, 54-76.

American Psychological Association, Division of Industrial and Organizational Psychology (Division 14). (1987). *Principles for the validation and use of personnel selection procedures* (3rd Ed.). College Park, MD: Author.

Anastasi, A. (1986). *Psychological testing* (6th Ed.). New York: Macmillan.

Baker, P. C. (1952). Combining tests of significance in cross validation. *Educational and Psychological Measurement, 12*, 300-306.

Bangert-Drowns, R. L. (1986). Review of developments in meta-analytic method. *Psychological Bulletin, 99*, 388-399.

Bangert-Drowns, R. L., Kulik, J. A., & Kulik, C.-L. C. (1983). Effects of coaching programs on achievement test performance. *Review of Educational Research, 53*, 571-585.

Bangert-Drowns, R. L., Kulik, J. A., & Kulik, C.-L. C. (1984, August). *The influence of study features on outcomes of educational research*. Paper presented at the 92nd annual meeting of the American Psychological Association, Toronto.

Barnett, V., & Lewis, T. (1978). *Outliers in statistical data*. New York: John Wiley.

Bartlett, C. J., Bobko, P., Mosier, S. B., & Hannan, R. (1978). Testing for fairness with a moderated multiple regression strategy: An alternative to differential analysis. *Personnel Psychology, 31*, 233-241.

Baum, M. L., Anish, D. S., Chalmers, T. C., Sacks, H. S., Smith, H., & Fagerstrom, R. M. (1981). A survey of clinical trials of antibiotic prophyloxis in colon surgery: Evidence against further use of no-treatment controls. *New England Journal of Medicine, 305*, 795-799.

Becker, B. J. (1987). Applying tests of combined significance in meta-analysis. *Psychological Bulletin, 102*, 164-171.

Bloom, B. S. (1964). *Stability and change in human characteristics*. New York: Wiley.

Bobko, P. (1983). An analysis of correlations corrected for attenuation and range restriction. *Journal of Applied Psychology, 68*, 584-589.

Boudreau, J. W. (1983). Economic considerations in estimating the utility of human resource productivity improvement programs. *Personnel Psychology, 36*, 551-576.

Boudreau, J. W. (1984). Decision theory contributions to human resource management research and practice. *Industrial Relations, 23*, 198-217.

Bradley, J. V. (1968). *Distribution free statistical tests*. Englewood Cliffs, NJ: Prentice-Hall.

Brozek, J., & Tiede, K. (1952). Reliable and questionable significance in a series of statistical tests. *Psychological Bulletin, 49*, 339-344.

Brennan, R. L. (1983). *Elements of generalizability theory*. Iowa City, IA: ACT Publications.

Brogden, H. E. (1946). On the interpretation of the correlation coefficient as a measure of predictive efficiency. *Journal of Educational Psychology, 37*, 65-76.

Brogden, H. E. (1949). When testing pays off. *Personnel Psychology, 2*, 171-183.

Brogden, H. E. (1972). Some observations on two methods in psychology. *Psychological Bulletin, 77*, 431-437.

Bullock, R. J., & Svyantek, D. J. (1985). Analyzing meta-analysis: Potential problems, an unsuccessful replication, and evaluation criteria. *Journal of Applied Psychology, 70*, 108-115.

Callender, J. C. (1978). *A Monte Carlo investigation of the accuracy of two models for validity generalization*. Unpublished doctoral dissertation, University of Houston.

Callender, J. C. (1983, March). *Conducting validity generalization research based on correlations, regression slopes, and covariances*. Paper presented at the I/O and OB Graduate Student Convention, Chicago.

Callender, J. C., & Osburn, H. G. (1980). Development and test of a new model for validity generalization. *Journal of Applied Psychology, 65*, 543-558.

Callender, J. C., & Osburn, H. G. (1981). Testing the constancy of validity with computer generated sampling distributions of the multiplicative model variance estimate: Results for petroleum industry validation research. *Journal of Applied Psychology, 66*, 274-281.

Callender, J. C., & Osburn, H. G. (1988). Unbiased estimation of the sampling variance of correlations. *Journal of Applied Psychology, 73*, 312-315.

Callender, J. C., Osburn, H. G., & Greener, J. M. (1979). *Small sample tests of two validity generalization models*. Paper presented at the meeting of the American Psychological Association, New York.

Callender, J. C., Osburn, H. G., Greener, J. M., & Ashworth, S. (1982). Multiplicative validity generalization model: Accuracy of estimates as a function of sample size and mean, variance, and shape of the distribution of true validities. *Journal of Applied Psychology, 67*, 859-867.

Campbell, D. T., & Stanley, J. C. (1963). *Experimental and quasi-experimental designs for research*. Chicago: Rand McNally.

Cattin, P. (1980). The estimation of the predictive power of a regression model. *Journal of Applied Psychology, 65*, 407-414.

Coggin, T. D., & Hunter, J. E. (1983). Problems in measuring the quality of investment information: The perils of the information coefficient. *Financial Analysts Journal, May/June*, 25-33.

Coggin, T. D., & Hunter, J. E. (1987). A meta-analysis of pricing of "risk" factors in APT. *The Journal of Portfolio Management, 14*, 35-38.

Cohen, J. (1977). *Statistical power analysis for the behavior sciences (Rev. Ed.)*. New York: Academic Press.

Cohen, J. (1983). The cost of dichotomization. *Applied Psychological Measurement, 7*, 249-253.

Coleman, J. S., et al. (1966). *Equality of educational opportunity.* Washington, DC: U.S. Government Printing Office.

Cook, T. D., & Leviton, L. C. (1980). Reviewing the literature: A comparison of traditional methods with meta-analysis. *Journal of Personality, 48,* 449-472.

Cooper, H. (1984). *The integrative research review: A systematic approach.* Beverly Hills, CA: Sage.

Cooper, H. M., & Rosenthal, R. (1980). Statistical versus traditional procedures for summarizing research findings. *Psychological Bulletin, 87,* 442-449.

Cooper, W. W., Ho, J. L. Y., Hunter, J. E., & Rodgers. R. C. (1985). The impact of the Foreign Corrupt Practices Act on internal control practices (a meta-analysis). *Journal of Accounting, Auditing, and Finance, 9,* 22-39.

Cronbach, L. J. (1947). Test "reliability": Its meaning and determination. *Psychometrika, 12,* 1-16.

Cronbach, L. J. (1951). Coefficient alpha and the internal structure of tests. *Psychometrika, 16,* 297-334.

Cronbach, L. J. (1975). Beyond the two disciplines of scientific psychology revisited. *American Psychologist, 30,* 116-127.

Cronbach, L. J., & Gleser, G. C. (1965). *Psychological tests and personnel decisions* (2nd Ed.). Urbana: University of Illinois Press.

Cronbach, L. J., Gleser, G. C., Nanda, H., & Rajaratnam, N. (1972). *The dependability of behavioral measurements: Theory of generalizability for scores and profiles.* New York: Wiley.

Cuts raise new social science query: Does anyone appreciate social science? (1981, March 27). *Wall Street Journal,* p. 54.

Dillard, J. P., Hunter, J. E., & Burgoon, M. (1984). Sequential requests, persuasive message strategies: A meta-analysis of foot-in-door and door-in-the-face. *Human Communication Research, 10,* 461-488.

Dimson, E., & Marsh, P. (1984). An analysis of brokers' and analysts' unpublished forecasts of UK stock returns. *Journal of Finance, 39* (5), 1257-1292.

Dunnette, M. D., & Borman, W. C. (1979). Personnel selection and classification. In M. R. Rosenzweig & L. W. Porter (Eds.), *Annual review of psychology* (Vol. 30). Palo Alto, CA: Annual Reviews.w

Dunnette, M. D., Houston, J. S., Hough, L. M., Touquam, J., Lamnstein, S., King, K., Bosshardt, M. J., & Keys, M. (1982). *Development and validation of an industry-wide electric power plant operator selection system.* Minneapolis, MN: Personnel Decisions Research Institute.

Dye, D. (1982). *Validity generalization analysis for data from 16 studies participating in a consortium study.* Unpublished manuscript, Department of Psychology, George Washington University, Washington, DC

Eagly, A. H. (1978). Sex differences in influenceability. *Psychological Bulletin, 85,* 86-116.

Erlenmeyer-Kimling, L., & Jarvik, L. F. (1963). Genetics and intelligence: A review. *Science, 142,* 1477-1479.

Eysenck, H. J. (1978). An exercise in mega-silliness. *American Psychologist, 33,* 517.

Fisher, C. D., & Gittelson, R. (1983). A meta-analysis of the correlates of role conflict and ambiguity. *Journal of Applied Psychology, 68,* 320-333.

Fisher, R. A. (1932). *Statistical methods for research workers* (4th ed.). London: Oliver & Boyd.

Fisher, R. A. (1938). *Statistical methods for research workers* (7th ed.). London: Oliver & Boyd.

Fiske, D. W. (1978). The several kinds of generalization. *The Behavioral and Brain Sciences, 3,* 393-394.

Fleishman, E. A. (1975). Toward a taxonomy of human performance. *American Psychologist, 30,* 1127-1149.

Fleishman, E. A., & Hempel, W. E., Jr. (1954). Changes in factor structure of a complex psychomotor test as a function of practice. *Psychometrika, 19*, 239-252.

Fleishman, E. A., & Hempel, W. E., Jr. (1955). The relation between abilities and improvement with practice in a visual discrimination reaction test. *Journal of Experimental Psychology, 49*, 301-312.

Foley, P. P., & Swanson, L. (1985). *An investigation of validity generalization of Navy selector composites* (Technical Report). Navy Personnel Research and Development Center, San Diego, CA.

Gaugler, B. B., Rosenthal, D. B., Thornton, G. C., & Bentson, C. (1987). Meta-analysis of assessment center validity. *Journal of Applied Psychology, 72*, 493-511.

Gergen, K. J. (1982). *Toward transformation in social knowledge.* New York: Springer-Verlag.

Ghiselli, E. E. (1949). The validity of commonly employed occupational tests. *University of California Publications in Psychology, 5*, 253-288.

Ghiselli, E. E. (1955). The measurement of occupational aptitude. *University of California Publications in Psychology, 8*, 101-216.

Ghiselli, E. E. (1966). *The validity of occupational aptitude tests.* New York: Wiley.

Ghiselli, E. E. (1973). The validity of aptitude tests in personnel selection. *Personnel Psychology, 26*, 461-477.

Glass, G. V. (1972). The wisdom of scientific inquiry on education. *Journal of research in science teaching, 9*, 3-18.

Glass, G. V. (1976). Primary, secondary and meta-analysis of research. *Educational Researcher, 5*, 3-8.

Glass, G. V. (1977). Integrating findings: The meta-analysis of research. *Review of Research in Education, 5*, 351-379.

Glass, G. V., Cahen, L. S., Smith, M. L., & Filby, N. N. (1982). *School class size: Research and policy.* Beverly Hills, CA: Sage.

Glass, G. V., & Kliegl, R. M. (1983). An apology for research integration in the study of psychotherapy. *Journal of Consulting and Clinical Psychology, 51*, 28-41.

Glass, G. V., McGaw, B., & Smith, M. L. (1981). *Meta-analysis in social research.* Beverly Hills, CA: Sage.

Glass, G. V., Peckham, P. D., & Sanders, J. R. (1972). Consequences of failure to meet assumptions underlying fixed effects analysis of variance and covariance. *Review of Educational Research, 42*, 237-288.

Gottfredson, L. S. (1985). Education as a valid but fallible signal of worker quality. *Research in Sociology of Education and Socialization, 5*, 123-169.

Green, B. F., & Hall, J. A. (1984). Quantitative methods for literature reviews. *Annual Review of Psychology, 35*, 37-53.

Gross, A. L., & McGanney, M. L. (1987). The range restriction problem and nonignorable selection processes. *Journal of Applied Psychology, 72*, 604-610.

Grubbs, F. E. (1969). Procedures for detecting outliers. *Technometrics, 11*, 1-21.

Gulliksen, H. (1986). The increasing importance of mathematics in psychological research (Part 3). *The Score, 9*, 1-5.

Guzzo, R. A., Jackson, S. E., & Katzell, R. A. (1986). Meta-analysis analysis. In L. L. Cummings & B. M. Staw (Eds.), *Research in Organizational Behavior* (Vol. 9). Greenwich, CT: JAI Press.

Guzzo, R. A., Jette, R. D., & Katzell, R. A. (1985). The effects of psychologically based intervention programs on worker productivity: A meta-analysis. *Personnel Psychology, 38*, 275-292.

Hackett, R. D., & Guion, R. M. (1985). A re-evaluation of the absenteeism-job satisfaction relationship. *Organizational Behavior and Human Decision Processes, 35*, 340-381.

Hackman, J. R., & Oldham, G. R. (1975). Development of the Job Diagnostic Survey. *Journal of Applied Psychology, 60*, 159-170.

Hall, J. A. (1978). Gender effects in decoding nonverbal clues. *Psychological Bulletin, 85,* 845-857.

Halvorsen, K. T. (1986). Combining results from independent investigations: Meta-analysis in medical research. In J. C. Bailar & F. Mosteller (Eds.), *Medical uses of statistics.* Waltham, MA: NEJM Books.

Hartigan, J. A., & Wigdor, A. K. (1989). Fairness in employment testing: Validity generalization, minority issues, and the General Aptitude Test Battery. Washington, DC: National Academy Press.

Hamilton, M. A., & Hunter, J. E. (1987). *Two accounts of language intensity effects.* Paper presented at International Communication Association Convention. (City?)

Hedges, L. V. (1980). *Combining the results of experiments using different scales of measurement.* Unpublished manuscript, Center for Educational Research, Stanford University.

Hedges, L. V. (1981). Distribution theory for Glass's estimator of effect size and related estimators. *Journal of Educational Statistics, 6,* 107-128.

Hedges, L. V. (1982). *Methodological problems in validity generalization.* Unpublished manuscript, School of Education, University of Chicago, IL.

Hedges, L. V. (1982a). Estimation of effect size from a series of independent experiments. *Psychological Bulletin, 92,* 490-499.

Hedges, L. V. (1982b). Fitting categorical models to effect sizes from a series of experiments. *Journal of Educational Statistics, 7,* 119-137.

Hedges, L. V. (1982c). Fitting continuous models to effect size data. *Journal of Educational Statistics, 7,* 245-270.

Hedges, L. V. (1983a). Combining independent estimators in research synthesis. *British Journal of Mathematical and Statistical Psychology, 36* (1), 123-131.

Hedges, L. V. (1983b). A random effects model for effect sizes. *Psychological Bulletin, 93,* 388-395.

Hedges, L. V. (1987). How hard is hard science, how soft is soft science: The empirical cumulativeness of research. *American Psychologist, 42,* 443-455.

Hedges, L. V. (1988). The meta-analysis of test validity studies. In H. Wainer & H.I. Braun (Eds.), *Test validity* (pp. 191-212). Hillsdale, NJ: Lawrence Erlbaum.

Hedges, L. V., & Olkin, I. (1980). Vote counting methods in research synthesis. *Psychological Bulletin, 88,* 359-369.

Hedges, L. V., & Olkin, I. (1982). Analyses, reanalyses, and meta-analyses. *Contemporary Education Review, 1,* 157-165.

Hedges, L. V., & Olkin, I. (1983a). Clustering estimates of effect magnitude from independent studies. *Psychological Bulletin, 93,* 563-573.

Hedges, L. V., & Olkin, I. (1983b). Regression models in research synthesis. *The American Statistician, 37,* 137-140.

Hedges, L. V., & Olkin, I. (1985). *Statistical methods for meta-analysis.* Orlando, FL: Academic Press.

Hedges, L. V., & Stock, W. (1983). The effects of class size: An examination of rival hypotheses. *American Educational Research Journal, 20,* 63-85.

Hembree, R. (1988). Correlates, causes, effects, and treatment of test anxiety. *Review of Educational Research, 58,* 44-77.

Hill, T. E. (1980, September). *Development of a clerical program in Sears.* Paper presented as part of the Symposium "Methodological Implications of Large Scale Validity Studies of Clerical Occupations." (V. J. Benz, Chair) American Psychological Association Convention, Montreal, Canada.

Hirsh, H. R., & McDaniel, M. A. (1987). *Decision rules in applications of the Schmidt-Hunter meta-analysis technique: Some critical considerations.* Unpublished paper, Baruch College, City University of New York.

Hirsh, H. R., Northrop, L. C., & Schmidt, F. L. (1986). Validity generalization results for law enforcement occupations. *Personnel Psychology, 39,* 399-420.

Hirsh, H. R., Schmidt, F. L., Pearlman, K., & Hunter, J. E. (1985). *Improvements and refinements in validity generalization methods: Implications for the situational specificity hypothesis.* Paper presented at the 93rd annual convention of the American Psychological Association, Los Angeles.

Hotelling, H. (1953). New light on the correlation coefficient and its transforms. *Journal of the Royal Statistical Society, B, 15,* 193-225.

Huber, P. J. (1980). *Robust statistics.* New York: John Wiley.

Hunter, J. E. (1977, August). *Path Analysis: Longitudinal studies and causal analysis in program evaluation.* Invited address presented at the 85th American Psychological Association Convention, San Francisco.

Hunter, J. E. (1979, September). *Cumulating results across studies: A critique of factor analysis, canonical correlation, MANOVA, and statistical significance testing.* Invited address presented to the 86th Annual Convention of the American Psychological Association, New York.

Hunter, J. E. (1980a). Factor analysis. In P. Monge (Ed.), *Multivariate techniques in human communication research.* New York: Academic Press.

Hunter, J. E. (1980b). Validity generalization and construct validity. In *Construct validity in psychological measurement: Proceedings of a colloquium on theory and application in education and measurement.* Educational Testing Service, Princeton, NJ

Hunter, J. E. (1983a). *The dimensionality of the general aptitude tests battery (GATB) and the dominance of the general factors over specific factors in the prediction of job performance for USES* (Test Research Report No. 44). U.S. Department of Labor, U.S. Employment Services, Washington, DC.

Hunter, J. E. (1983b). *Test validation for 12,000 jobs: An application of job classification and validity generalization analysis to the general aptitude test battery (GATB)* (Test Research Report No. 45). U.S. Employment Service, U.S. Department of Labor, Washington, DC.

Hunter, J. E. (1983c). *Fairness of the general aptitude test battery (GATB): Ability differences and their impact on minority hiring rates* (Test Research Report No. 46). U.S. Employment Service, U.S. Department of Labor, Washington, DC.

Hunter, J. E. (1983d). *The economic benefits of personnel selection using ability tests: A state of the art review including a detailed analysis of the dollar benefit of U.S. employment service placements and a critique of the low cut off method of test use* (Test Research Report No. 47). U.S. Employment Service, U.S. Department of Labor, Washington, DC.

Hunter, J. E. (1983e). *The prediction of job performance in the military using ability composites: The dominance of general cognitive ability over specific aptitudes.* Report for Research Applications, Inc., in partial fulfillment of DOD Contract No. F41689-83-C-0025.

Hunter, J. E. (1983f). A causal analysis of cognitive ability, job knowledge, job performance, and supervisory ratings. In F. Landy, S. Zedeck, & J. Cleveland (Eds.), *Performance measurement and theory* (pp. 257-266). Hillsdale, NJ: Lawrence Erlbaum.

Hunter, J. E. (1984). *The validity of the Armed Forces Vocational Aptitude Battery (ASVAB) High School Composites.* Report for Research Applications, Inc., in partial fulfillment of DOD Contract No. F41689-83-C-0025.

Hunter, J. E. (1985). *Differential validity across jobs in the military.* Report for Research Applications, Inc., in partial fulfillment of DOD Contract No. F41689-83-C-0025.

Hunter, J. E. (1986). *Multiple dependent variables in experimental design.* Monograph presented at a workshop at the University of Iowa.

Hunter, J. E. (1987). Multiple dependent variables in program evaluation. In M. M. Mark & R. L. Shotland (Eds.), *Multiple Methods in Program Evaluation.* San Francisco: Josey-Bass.

Hunter, J. E. (1988). *A path analytic approach to analysis of covariance*. Unpublished manuscript, Department of Psychology, Michigan State University.

Hunter, J. E., Crosson, J. J., & Friedman, D. H. (1985). *The validity of the Armed Services Vocational Aptitude Battery (ASVAB) for civilian and military job performance*. Final report by Research Applications, Inc., in fulfillment of Contract No. F41689-83-C-0025.

Hunter, J. E., & Gerbing, D. W. (1982). Unidimensional measurement, second order factor analysis and causal models. In B. M. Staw & L. L. Cummings (Eds.), *Research in organizational behavior* (Vol. 4). Greer wich, CT: JAI Press.

Hunter, J. E., Hamilton, M. A., & Allen, M. (in press). The design and analysis of language experiments. *Communication Monographs*.

Hunter, J. E., & Hirsh, H. R. (1987). Applications of meta-analysis. In C. L. Cooper & I. T. Robertson (Eds.) *International Review of Industrial and Organizational Psychology 1987*. London: John Wiley.

Hunter, J. E., & Hunter, R. F. (1984). Validity and utility of alternate predictors of job performance. *Psychological Bulletin, 96*, 72-98.

Hunter, J. E., & Schmidt, F. L. (1977). A critical analysis of the statistical and ethical implications of various definitions of test fairness. *Psychological Bulletin, 83*, 1053-1071.

Hunter, J. E., & Schmidt, F. L. (1978). Differential and single group validity of employment tests by race: A critical analysis of three recent studies. *Journal of Applied Psychology, 63*, 1-11.

Hunter, J. E., & Schmidt, F. L. (1982a). Fitting people to jobs; Implications of personnel selection for national productivity. In E. A. Fleishman & M. D. Dunnette (Eds.), *Human performance and productivity: Vol. 1. Human capability assessment* (pp. 233-284). Hillsdale, NJ: Lawrence Earlbaum.

Hunter, J. E., & Schmidt, F. L. (1982b). Ability tests: Economic benefits versus the issue of fairness. *Industrial Relations, 21* (3), 293-308.

Hunter, J. E., & Schmidt, F. L. (1983). Quantifying the effects of psychological interventions on employee job performance and work force productivity. *American Psychologist, 38*, 473-478.

Hunter, J. E., & Schmidt, F. L. (1987a). *Error in the meta-analysis of correlations: The mean correlation*. Unpublished manuscript, Dept. of Psychology, Michigan State University.

Hunter, J. E., & Schmidt, F. L. (1987b). *Error in the meta-analysis of correlations: The standard deviation*. Unpublished manuscript, Dept. of Psychology, Michigan State University.

Hunter, J. E., & Schmidt, F. L. (in press). Dichotomizing continuous variables: The implications for meta-analysis. *Journal of Applied Psychology*.

Hunter, J. E., Schmidt, F. L., & Coggin, T. D. (1988). *Meta-analysis of correlations: The issue of bias and misconceptions about the Fisher z transformation*. Manuscript under review, Dept. of Psychology, Michigan State University.

Hunter, J. E., Schmidt, F. L., & Hunter, R. (1979). Differential validity of employment tests by race: A comprehensive review and analysis. *Psychological Bulletin, 31*, 215-232.

Hunter, J. E., Schmidt, F. L., & Jackson, G. B. (1982). *Meta-analysis: Cumulating research findings across studies*. Beverly Hills, CA: Sage.

Hunter, J. E., Schmidt, F. L., & Raju, N. S. (1986). *Analysis of Hoben Thomas' critique of validity generalization*. Unpublished manuscript, Dept. of Psychology, Michigan State University.

Iaffaldono, M. T., & Muchinsky, P. M. (1985). Job satisfaction and job performance: A meta-analysis. *Psychological Bulletin, 97*, 251-273.

Jackson, G. B. (1978, April). *Methods for reviewing and integrating research in the social sciences*. Final Reports to the National Science Foundation for Grant #DIS 76-20398. Washington, DC: Social Research Group, George Washington University, (NTIS No. PB283 747/AS)

Jackson, G. B. (1980). Methods for integrative reviews. *Review of Educational Research, 50,* 438-460.

Jackson, S. E. (1984, August). *Can meta-analysis be used for theory development in organizational psychology?* Paper presented at the meeting of the American Psychological Association, Toronto, Canada.

Jackson, S. E., & Schuler, R. S. (1985). A meta-analysis and conceptual critique of research on role ambiguity and role conflict in work settings. *Organizational Behavioral and Human Decision Processes, 36,* 16-78.

James, L. R., Demaree, R. G., & Mulaik, S. A. (1986). A note on validity generalization procedures. *Journal of Applied Psychology, 71,* 440-450.

Jensen, A. R. (1980). *Bias in mental testing.* New York: Free Press.

Jones, L. V., & Fiske, D. W. (1953). Models for testing the significance of combined results. *Psychological Bulletin, 50,* 375-382.

Joreskog, K. G., & Sorbom, D. (1979). *Advances in factor analysis and structural equation models.* Cambridge, MA: Abt. Books.

Katzell, R. A., & Dyer, F. J. (1977). Differential validity revived. *Journal of Applied Psychology, 62,* 137-145.

Kemery, E. R., Dunlap, W. P., & Griffeth, R. W. (1988). Correction for unequal proportions in point biserial correlations. *Journal of Applied Psychology, 73,* 688-691.

Kemery, E. R., Mossholder, K. W., & Dunlap, W. P. (1989). Meta-analysis and moderator variables: A cautionary note on transportability. *Journal of Applied Psychology, 74,* 168-170.

Kemery, E. R., Mossholder, K. W., & Roth, L. (1987). The power of the Schmidt and Hunter additive model of validity generalization. *Journal of Applied Psychology, 72,* 30-37.

King, L. M., Hunter, J. E., & Schmidt, F. L. (1980). Halo in multidimensional forced choice performance evaluation scale. *Journal of Applied Psychology, 65,* 507-516.

Kondrasuk, J. N. (1981). Studies in MBO effectiveness. *Academy of Management Review, 6,* 419-430.

Kraiger, K., & Ford, J. K. (1985). A meta-analysis of race effects in performance ratings. *Journal of Applied Psychology, 70,* 56-65.

Kulik, J. A. (1984, April). *The uses and misuses of meta-analysis.* Paper presented at the meeting of the American Educational Research Association. New Orleans.

Kulik, J. A., & Bangert-Drowns, R. L. (1983/1984). Effectiveness of technology in precollege mathematics and science teaching. *Journal of Educational Technology Systems, 12,* 137-158.

Kulik, C. C., & Kulik, J. A. (1986). *Estimating effect sizes in quantitative research integration.* Manuscript submitted for publication.

Kulik, J. A., Kulik, C. C., & Cohen, P. A. (1979). A meta-analysis of outcome studies of Keller's personalized system of instruction. *American Psychologist, 34,* 307-318.

Ladd, R. T., & Cornwell, J. M. (1986, April). The accuracy of meta-analysis estimates. Paper presented at the First Annual Conference of the Society for Industrial and Organizational Psychology, Inc., Chicago.

Lamb, W. K., & Whitla, D. K. (1983). *Meta-analysis and the integration of research findings: A trend analysis and bibliography prior to 1983.* Unpublished manuscript, Harvard University, Cambridge, MA.

Landman, J. T., & Dawes, R. M. (1982). Psychotherapy outcome: Smith and Glass' conclusions stand up under scrutiny. *American Psychologist, 37,* 504-516.

Lawshe, C. H. (1948). *Principles of personnel selection.* New York: McGraw-Hill.

Lee, R., Miller, K. J., & Graham, W. K. (1982). Corrections for restriction of range and attenuation in criterion-related validation studies. *Journal of Applied Psychology, 67,* 637-639.

Lent, R. H., Auerbach, H. A., & Levin, L. S. (1971a). Research design and validity assessment. *Personnel Psychology, 24,* 247-274.

Lent, R. H., Auerbach, H. A., & Levin, L. S. (1971b). Predictors, criteria and significant results. *Personnel Psychology, 24*, 519-533.

Leone, F. C., & Nelson, L. S. (1966). Sampling distributions of variance components. I. Empirical studies of balanced nested designs. *Technometrics, 8*, 457-468.

Levine, J. M., Kramer, G. G., & Levine, E. N. (1975). Effects of alcohol on human performance: An integration of research findings based on an abilities classification. *Journal of Applied Psychology, 60*, 285-293.

Levine, J. M., Romashko, T., & Fleishman, E. A. (1973). Evaluation of an abilities classification system for integration and generalizing human performance research findings: An application to vigilance tasks. *Journal of Applied Psychology, 58*, 149-157.

Light, R. J. (Ed.). (1983). *Evaluation studies review cnnual* (Vol. 8). Beverly Hills, CA: Sage.

Light, R. J., & Pillemer, D. B. (1984). *Summing up: The science of reviewing research.* Harvard University Press.

Light, R. J., & Smith, P. V. (1971). Accumulating evidence: Procedures for resolving contradictions among different research studies. *Harvard Educational Review, 41*, 429-471.

Lilienthal, R. A., & Pearlman, K. (1983). *The validity of federal selection tests for aid/technicians in the health, science, and engineering fields.* Washington, DC: U.S. Office of Personnel Management, Office of Personnel Research and Development.

Linn, R. L. (1968). Range restriction problems in the use of self-selected groups for test validation. *Psychological Bulletin, 69*, 69-73.

Linn, R. L. (in press). The Pearson selection formulas: Implications for studies of predictive bias and estimates of educational effects in selected samples. *Journal of Educational Measurement.*

Linn, R. L., & Dunbar, S. B. (1985). Validity generalization and predictive bias. In R. A. Burk (Ed.), *Performance assessment: State of the art.* Baltimore, MD: John Hopkins Press.

Linn, R. L., Harnisch, D. L., Dunbar, S. B. (1981a). Validity generalization and situational specificity: An analysis of the prediction of first year grades in law school. *Applied Psychological Measurement, 5*, 281-289.

Linn, R. L., Harnisch, D. L., & Dunbar, S. B. (1981b). Corrections for range restriction: An empirical investigation of conditions resulting in conservative corrections. *Journal of Applied Psychology, 66*, 655-663.

Locke, E. A. (1986). Generalizing from laboratory to field: Ecological validity or abstraction of elements? In E. A. Locke (Ed.), *Generalizing from laboratory to field settings.* Lexington, MA: Lexington Books.

Loher, B. T., Noe, R. A., Moeller, N., & Fitzgerald, M. P. (1985). A meta-analysis of the relationship of job characteristics to job satisfaction. *Journal of Applied Psychology, 70*, 280-289.

Mabe, P. A., III, and West, S. G. (1982). Validity of self evaluations of ability: A review and meta-analysis. *Journal of Applied Psychology, 67*, 280-296.

Mackenzie, B. D. (1972). Behaviorism and positivism. *Journal of History of the Behavioral Sciences, 8*, 222-231.

Mackenzie, B. D. (1977). *Behaviorism and the limits of scientific method.* Atlantic Highlands, NJ: Humanities Press.

Maloley et al. v. Department of National Revenue. (1986, February). Canadian Civil Service Appeals Board, Ottawa, Canada.

Mansfield, R. S., & Busse, T. V. (1977). Meta-analysis of research: A rejoinder to Glass. *Educational Researcher, 6*, 3.

McDaniel, M. A. (1985). *The evaluation of a causal model of job performance: The interrelationships of general mental ability, job experience and job performance.* Unpublished doctoral dissertation, Department of Psychology, George Washington University.

McDaniel, M. A., & Hirsh, H. R. (1986, April). Methods of moderator detection in meta-analysis. In M. A. McDaniel (Chair), *An Overview and New Directions in the Hunter-*

Schmidt-Jackson Meta-Analysis Technique. Symposium presented at the Annual Conference of the Society for Industrial/Organizational Psychology, Chicago, IL.

McDaniel, M. A., Schmidt, F. L., & Hunter, J. E. (1988a). A meta-analysis of the validity of training and experience ratings in personnel selection. *Personnel Psychology, 41,* 283-314.

McDaniel, M. A., Schmidt, F. L., & Hunter, J. E. (1988b). Job experience correlates of job performance. *Journal of Applied Psychology, 73,* 327-330.

McDaniel, M. A., Whetzel, D. L., Schmidt, F. L., Hunter, J. E., Mauer, S., & Russell, J. (1988). *The validity of employment interviews: A review and meta-analysis.* Unpublished Manuscript.

McEvoy, G. M., & Cascio, W. F. (1985). Strategies for reducing employee turnover: A meta-analysis. *Journal of Applied Psychology, 70,* 342-353.

McEvoy, G. M., & Cascio, W. F. (1987). Do poor performers leave? A meta-analysis of the relation between performance and turnover. *Academy of Management Journal, 30,* 744-762.

McKinney, M. W. (1984). *Final report: Validity generalization pilot study.* Submitted to the U.S.E.S. Southern Test Development Field Center, Raleigh, NC.

McNemar, Q. (1960). At random: Sense and nonsense. *American Psychologist, 15,* 295-300.

Meehl, P. E. (1978). Theoretical risks and tabular asterisks: Sir Karl, Sir Ronald and the slow progress of soft psychology. *Journal of Consulting and Clinical Psychology, 46,* 806-834.

Miller, K., & Monge, P. (in press). Participation, satisfaction, and productivity: a meta-analysis. *Academy of Management Review.*

Milsap, R. (1988). Sampling variance in attenuated correlation coefficients: A Monte Carlo study. *Journal of Applied Psychology, 73,* 316-319.

Milsap, R. (1989). The sampling variance in the correlation under range restriction: A Monte Carlo study. *Journal of Applied Psychology 74,* 456-461.

Mosier, C. I. (1943). On the reliability of a weighted composite. *Psychometrika, 8,* 161-168.

Mosteller, F., & Moynihan, D. (1972). *On equality of educational opportunity.* New York: Vintage Books.

Mosteller, F., & Tukey, J. W. (1977). *Data analysis and regression: A second course in statistics.* Reading, MA: Addison-Wesley.

Nathan, B. R., & Alexander, R. A. (1988). A comparison of criteria for test validation: A meta-analytic investigation. *Personnel Psychology, 41,* 517-535.

Nicol, T. S., & Hunter, J. E. (1973). *Mathematical models of the reliability of the semantic differential.* Paper presented at the Psychometric Society, Chicago.

Novick, M. R. (1986, April). *The limits of validity generalization: The future of prediction generalization.* Paper presented at the First Annual Meeting of the Society for Industrial/Organizational Psychology. Chicago, IL.

Nunnally, J. (1978). *Psychometric theory.* New York: McGraw-Hill.

Oakes, M. (1986). *Statistical inference: A commentary for the social and behavioral sciences.* New York: John Wiley.

O'Connor, E. J., Wexley, K. N., & Alexander, R. A. (1975). Single group validity: Fact or fallacy? *Journal of Applied Psychology, 60,* 352-355.

Orwin, R. G. (1983). A fail-safe N for effect size. *Journal of Educational Statistics, 8,* 147-159.

Orwin, R. G., & Cordroy, D. S. (1985). Effects of deficient reporting on meta-analysis: A conceptual framework and reanalysis. *Journal of Applied Psychology, 97,* 134-147.

Osburn, H. G. (1978). Optimal sampling strategies for validation studies. *Journal of Applied Psychology, 63,* 602-608.

Osburn, H. G., Callender, J. C. (1989). Accuracy of the validity generalization sampling variance estimate: A reply to Hoben Thomas. Under review by *Journal of Applied Psychology.*

Osburn, H. G., Callender, J. C., Greener, J. M., & Ashworth, S. (1983). Statistical power of tests of the situational specificity hypothesis in validity generalization studies: A cautionary note. *Journal of Applied Psychology, 68*, 115-122.

Paese, P. W., & Switzer, F. S., III. (1988). Validity generalization and hypothetical reliability distributions: A test of the Schmidt-Hunter procedure. *Journal of Applied Psychology, 73*, 267-274.

Paese, P. W., & Switzer, F. S., III (1989). Validity generalization and hypothetical reliability distributions: A reexamination. Paper under review by *Journal of Applied Psychology.*

Pearlman, K. (1979). *The validity of tests used to select clerical personnel: A comprehensive summary and evaluation.* Washington, DC: U.S. Office of Personnel Management.

Pearlman, K. (1980a, September). Seeing the whole picture: Application of cumulated validity data to issues in clerical selection. In V. J. Benz (Chair), *Methodological implications of large-scale validity studies of clerical occupations.* Symposium presented at the meeting of the American Psychological Association, Montreal.

Pearlman, K. (1980b). Job families: A review and discussion of their implications for personnel selection. *Psychological Bulletin, 87*, 1-28.

Pearlman, K. (1982). *The Bayesian approach to validity generalization: A systematic examination of the robustness of procedures and conclusions.* Unpublished doctoral dissertation, Department of Psychology, George Washington University.

Pearlman, K., & Schmidt, F. L. (1981, August). Effects of alternate job grouping methods on selection procedure validity. In E. L. Levine (Chair), *Job analysis/job families: Current perspectives on research and application.* Symposium conducted at the meeting of the American Psychological Association, Los Angeles.

Pearlman, K., Schmidt, F. L., & Hunter, J. E. (1980). Validity generalization results for tests used to predict job proficiency and training success in clerical occupations. *Journal of Applied Psychology, 65*, 373-406.

Pearson, E. S. (1938). The probability integral transformation for testing goodness of fit and combining tests of significance. *Biometrika, 30*, 134-148.

Peters, L. H., Harthe, D., & Pohlman, J. (1985). Fiedler's contingency theory of leadership: An application of the meta-analysis procedures of Schmidt and Hunter. *Psychological Bulletin, 97*, 274-285.

Peterson, N. G. (1982, October). *Investigation of validity generalization in clerical and technical/professional occupations in the insurance industry.* Paper presented at the Conference on Validity Generalization, Personnel Testing Council of Southern California, Newport Beach, CA.

Petty, M. M., McGee, G. W., & Cavender, J. W. (1984). A meta-analysis of the relationship between individual job satisfaction and individual performance. *Academy of Management Review, 9*, 712-721.

Premack, S., & Wanous, J. P. (1985). Meta-analysis of realistic job preview experiments. *Journal of Applied Psychology, 70*, 706-719.

Raju, N. S., & Burke, M. J. (1983). Two New Procedures for Studying Validity Generalization. *Journal of Applied Psychology, 68*, 382-395

Raju, N. S., Burke, M. J., & Normand, J. (1988). *A new correlation model for assessing validity generalization.* Unpublished manuscript, Dept. of Psychology, Illinois Institute of Technology, Chicago.

Raju, N. S., Burke, M. J., & Normand, J. (1983). *The asymptotic sampling distribution of correlations corrected for attenuation and range restriction.* Unpublished manuscript, Dept. of Psychology, Illinois Institute of Technology, Chicago..

Raju, N. S., Fralicx, R., & Steinhaus, S. D. (1986). Covariance and regression slope models for studying validity generalization. *Applied Psychological Measurement, 10*, 195-211.

Ramamurti, A. S. (1989). A systematic approach to generating excess returns using a multiple variable model. In F. J. Fabozzi (Ed.), *Institutional Investor Focus on Investment Management.* Cambridge, MA: Ballinger.

Raudenbush, S. W., & Bryk, A. S. (1985). Empirical Bayes meta-analysis. *Journal of Educational Statistics, 10*, 75-98.

Rodgers, R. C., & Hunter, J. E. (1986). *The impact of management by objectives on organizational productivity*. Unpublished manuscript, Management Department, University of Texas at Austin.

Rodgers, R. C., & Hunter, J. E. (1989). *The impact of false methodological hypotheses in reviews of management research: The case of management by objectives*. Unpublished manuscript.

Rosenthal, R. (1961, September). On the social psychology of the psychological experiment: With particular reference to experimenter bias. In H. W. Riecken (Chair), *On the social psychology of the psychological experiment*. Symposium conducted at the meeting of the American Psychological Association, New York.

Rosenthal, R. (1963). On the social psychology of the psychological experiment: The experimenter's hypothesis as unintended determinant of experimental results. *American Scientist, 51*, 268-283.

Rosenthal, R. (1978a). Combining results of independent studies. *Psychological Bulletin, 85*, 185-193.

Rosenthal, R. (1978b). How often are our numbers wrong? *American Psychologist, 33*, 1005-1008.

Rosenthal, R. (1979). The "file drawer problem" and tolerance for null results. *Psychological Bulletin, 86*, 638-641.

Rosenthal, R. (1983). Assessing the statistical and social importance of the effects of psychotherapy. *Journal of Consulting and Clinical Psychology, 51*, 4-13.

Rosenthal, R. (1984). *Meta-analysis procedures for social research*. Beverly Hills, CA. Sage.

Rosenthal, R., & Rubin, D. B. (1978a). Interpersonal expectancy effects: The first 345 studies. *The Behavioral and Brain Sciences, 3*, 377-386.

Rosenthal, R., & Rubin, D. B. (1978b). Issues in summarizing the first 345 studies of interpersonal expectancy effects. *The Behavioral and Brain Sciences, 3*, 410-415.

Rosenthal, R., & Rubin, D. B. (1979a). Comparing significance levels of independent studies. *Psychological Bulletin, 86*, 1165-1168.

Rosenthal, R., & Rubin, D. B. (1979b). A note on percent variance explained as a measure of the importance of effects. *Journal of Applied Psychology, 9*, 395-396.

Rosenthal, R., & Rubin, D. B. (1980). Further issues in summarizing 345 studies of interpersonal expectancy effects. *The Behavioral and Brain Sciences, 3*, 475-476.

Rosenthal, R., & Rubin, D. B. (1982a). Comparing effect sizes of independent studies. *Psychological Bulletin, 92*, 500-504.

Rosenthal, R., & Rubin, D. B. (1982b). Further meta-analytic procedures for assessing cognitive gender differences. *Journal of Educational Psychology, 74*, 708-712.

Rosenthal, R., & Rubin, D. B. (1982c). A simple, general purpose display of magnitude of experiment effect. *Journal of Educational Psychology, 74*, 166-169.

Rosenthal, R., & Rubin, D. B. (1983). Ensemble-adjusted p values. *Psychological Bulletin, 94*, 540-541.

Rothstein, H. R., Schmidt, F. L., Erwin, F. W., Owens, W. A., & Sparks, P. P. (in press). Biographical data in employment selection: Can the validities be made generalizable? *Journal of Applied Psychology*.

Sackett, P. R., Harris, M. M., & Orr, J. M. (1986). On seeking moderator variables in the meta-analysis of correlational data: A Monte Carlo investigation of statistical power and resistance to Type I error. *Journal of Applied Psychology, 71*, 302-310.

Sackett, P. R., Schmitt, N., Tenopyr, M. L., Kehoe, J., & Zedeck, S. (1985). Commentary on forty questions about validity generalization and meta-analysis. *Personnel Psychology, 38*, 697-798.

Sackett, P. R., & Wade, B. E. (1983). On the feasibility of criterion related validity: The effects of range restriction assumptions on needed sample size. *Journal of Applied Psychology, 68*, 374-381.

Schlagel, R. H. (1979). *Revaluation in the philosophy of science: Implications for method and theory in psychology.* Invited address at the meeting of the American Psychological Association, New York.

Schmidt, F. L. (1984, August). *Meta-analysis: Implications for cumulative knowledge in the behavioral and social sciences.* Invited Division 5 Address, 92nd Annual Meeting of the American Psychological Association, Toronto.

Schmidt, F. L. (1985, April). From validity generalization to meta-analysis: The development and application of a new research procedure. In M. J. Burke (Chair), *Validity generalization as meta-analysis.* Symposium at AERA annual meeting, Chicago.

Schmidt, F. L. (1988). Validity generalization and the future of criterion-related validity. In H. Wainer & H. Braun (Eds.), *Test validity* (pp. 173-189). Hillsdale, NJ: Lawrence Erlbaum.

Schmidt, F. L., Berner, J. G., & Hunter. J. E. (1973). Racial differences in validity of employment tests: Reality or illusion? *Journal of Applied Psychology, 58*, 5-9.

Schmidt, F. L., Caplan, J. R., Bemis, S. E., Decuir, R., Dunn, L., & Antone, L. (1979). *The behavioral consistency method of unassembled examining* (Technical Publication 79-21). Washington, DC: U.S. Office of Personnel Management, Personnel Research and Development Center.

Schmidt, F. L., Gast-Rosenberg, I., & Hunter, J. E. (1980). Validity generalization results for computer programmers. *Journal of Applied Psychology, 65*, 643-661.

Schmidt, F. L., & Hunter, J. E. (1977). Development of a general solution to the problem of validity generalization. *Journal of Applied Psychology, 62*, 529-540.

Schmidt, F. L., & Hunter, J. E. (1978). Moderator research and the law of small numbers. *Personnel Psychology, 31*, 215-232.

Schmidt, F. L., & Hunter, J. E. (1980). The future of criterion related validity. *Personnel Psychology, 33*, 41-60.

Schmidt, F. L., & Hunter, J. E. (1981). Employment testing: Old theories and new research findings. *American Psychologist, 36*, 1128-1137.

Schmidt, F. L., & Hunter, J. E. (1983). Individual differences in productivity: An empirical test of estimates derived from studies of selection procedure utility. *Journal of Applied Psychology, 68*, 407-415.

Schmidt, F. L., & Hunter, J. E. (1984). A within setting test of the situational specificity hypothesis in personnel selection. *Personnel Psychology, 37*, 317-326.

Schmidt, F. L., Hunter, J. E., & Caplan, J. R. (1981a). Validity generalization results for two job groups in the petroleum industry. *Journal of Applied Psychology, 66*, 261-273.

Schmidt, F. L., Hunter, J. E., & Caplan, J. R. (1981b). *Selection procedure validity generalization (transportability) results for three job groups in the petroleum industry.* American Petroleum Institute, Washington, DC.

Schmidt, F. L., Hunter, J. E., McKenzie, R. C., & Muldrow, T. W. (1979). The impact of valid selection procedures on work-force productivity. *Journal of Applied Psychology, 64*, 609-626.

Schmidt, F. L., Hunter, J. E., & Outerbridge, A. N. (1986). Impact of job experience and ability on job knowledge, work sample performance, and supervisory ratings of job performance. *Journal of Applied Psychology, 71*, 432-439.

Schmidt, F. L., Hunter, J. E., Outerbridge. A. M., & Trattner, M. H. (1986). The economic impact of job selection methods on the size, productivity, and payroll costs of the federal workforce: An empirical demonstration. *Personnel Psychology, 39*, 1-29.

Schmidt, F. L., Hunter, J. E., Outerbridge, A. N., & Goff, S. (1988). Joint relation of experience and ability with job performance: Test of three hypotheses. *Journal of Applied Psychology, 73*, 46-57.

Schmidt, F. L., Hunter, J. E., & Pearlman, K. (1981). Task differences and validity of aptitude tests in selection: A red herring. *Journal of Applied Psychology, 66,* 166-185.

Schmidt, F. L., Hunter, J. E., & Pearlman, K. (1982). Progress in validity generalization: Comments on Callender and Osburn and further developments. *Journal of Applied Psychology, 67,* 835-845.

Schmidt, F. L., Hunter, J. E., Pearlman, K., & Caplan, J. R. (1981c). *Validity generalization results for three occupations in Sears, Roebuck and Company.* Sears, Roebuck and Company, Chicago, IL.

Schmidt, F. L., Hunter, J. E., Pearlman, K., & Hirsh, H. R. (1985). Forty questions about validity generalization and meta-analysis. *Personnel Psychology, 38,* 697-798.

Schmidt, F. L., Hunter, J. E., Pearlman, K., & Shane, G. S. (1979). Further tests of the Schmidt-Hunter Bayesian validity generalization procedure. *Personnel Psychology, 32,* 257-381.

Schmidt, F. L., Hunter, J. E., & Raju, N. S. (1988). Validity generalization and situational specificity: A second look at the 75% rule and the Fisher's z transformation. *Journal of Applied Psychology, 73,* 665-672.

Schmidt, F. L., Hunter, J. E., & Urry, V. E. (1976). Statistical power in criterion-related validation studies, *Journal of Applied Psychology, 61,* 473-485.

Schmidt, F. L., Law, K., Hunter, J. E., Rothstein, J. R., & Pearlman, K. (1989). Refinements in validity generalization procedures: Implications for the situational specificity hypothesis. Unpublished paper, University of Iowa, Dept. of Management and Organization.

Schmidt, F. L., Mack, M. J., & Hunter, J. E. (1984). Selection utility in the occupation of U.S. Park Ranger for three modes of test use. *Journal of Applied Psychology, 69,* 490-497.

Schmidt, F. L., Ocasio, B. P., Hillery, J. M., & Hunter, J. E. (1985). Further within-setting empirical tests of the situational specificity hypothesis in personnel selection. *Personnel Psychology, 38,* 509-524.

Schmidt, F. L., Pearlman, K., & Hunter, J. E. (1980). The validity and fairness of employment and educational tests for Hispanic Americans: A review and analysis. *Personnel Psychology, 33,* 705-724.

Schmitt, N., Gooding, R. Z., Noe, R. A., & Kirsch, M. (1984). Meta-analysis of validity studies published between 1964 and 1982 and the investigation of study characteristics. *Personnel Psychology, 37,* 407-422.

Schwab, D. P., Olian-Gottlieb, J. D., & Heneman, H. G., III. (1979). Between subject's expectancy theory research: A statistical review of studies predicting effort and performance. *Psychological Bulletin, 86,* 139-147.

Sechrest, L., & Yeaton, W. H. (1982). Magnitudes of experimental effects in social science research. *Evaluation Review, 6,* 579-600.

Sedlmeier, P., & Gigerenzer, G. (1989). Do studies of statistical power have an effect on the power of studies? *Psychological Bulletin, 105,* 309-316.

Shapiro, D. A., & Shapiro, D. (1982). Meta-analysis of comparative therapy outcome studies: A replication and refinement. *Psychological Bulletin, 92,* 581-604.

Shapiro, D. A., & Shapiro, D. (1983). Comparative therapy outcome research: Methodological implications of meta-analysis. *Journal of Consulting and Clinical Psychology, 51,* 42-53.

Slavin, R. (1984). Meta-analysis in education: How has it been used? *The Educational Researcher, 3* (18), 6-15.

Slavin, R. E. (1986, November). Best-evidence synthesis: An alternative to meta-analytic and traditional reviews. *The Educational Researcher, 15,* 5-11.

Smith, M., & Glass, G. (1980). Meta-analysis of research on class size and its relationship to attitudes and instruction. *American Educational Research Journal, 17,* 419-433.

Smith, M. L., & Glass, G. V. (1977). Meta-analysis of psychotherapy outcome studies. *American Psychologist, 32,* 752-760.

Smith, M. L., Glass, G. V., & Miller, T. I. (1980). *The benefits of psychotherapy*. Baltimore: Johns Hopkins University Press.

Snedecor, G. W. (1946). *Statistical methods* (4th ed.). Ames: Iowa State College Press.

Spector, P. E., & Levine, E. L. (1987). Meta-analysis for integrating study outcomes: A Monte Carlo study of its susceptibility to Type I and Type II errors. *Journal of Applied Psychology, 72*, 3-9.

Steele, R. P., & Ovalle, N. K. (1984). A review and meta-analysis of research on the relationship between behavioral intentions and employee turnover. *Journal of Applied Psychology, 69*, 673-686.

Stewart, D. W. (1984). *Secondary research*. Beverly Hills, CA: Sage.

Stoffelmeyr, B. E., Dillavou, D., & Hunter, J. E. (1983). Premorbid functioning and recidivism in schizophrenia: A cumulative analysis. *Journal of Consulting and Clinical Psychology, 51*, 338-352.

Taveggia, T. (1974). Resolving research controversy through empirical cumulation. *Sociological Methods and Research, 2*, 395-407.

Terborg, J. R., & Lee, T. W. (1982). Extension of the Schmidt-Hunter validity generalization procedure to the prediction of absenteeism behavior from knowledge of job satisfaction and organizational commitment. *Journal of Applied Psychology, 67*, 280-296.

Terpstra, D. E. (1981). Relationship between methodological rigor and reported outcomes in organization development evaluation research. *Journal of Applied Psychology, 66*, 541-543.

Thomas, H. (1988). What is the interpretation of the validity generalization estimate $S_\rho^2 = S_r^2 - S_e^2$? *Journal of Applied Psychology, 73*, 679-682.

Thorndike, R. L. (1933). The effect of the interval between test and retest on the constancy of the IQ. *Journal of Educational Psychology, 25*, 543-549.

Timmreck, C. W. (1981). *Moderating effect of tasks on the validity of selection tests*. Unpublished doctoral dissertation, Department of Psychology, University of Houston, TX.

Tukey, J. W. (1960). A survey of sampling from contaminated distributions. In I. Olkin, J. G. Ghurye, W. Hoeffding, W. G. Madoo, H. Mann. (Eds.), *Contributions to probability and statistics*. Stanford, CA: Stanford University Press.

Tukey, J. (1977). *Exploratory data analysis*. Reading, MA: Addison-Wesley.

U.S. Department of Labor. (1970). *Manual for the U.S.E.S. General Aptitude Test Battery. Section III: Development*. Washington, DC: U.S. Employment Service.

U.S. Equal Employment Opportunity Commission, U.S. Civil Service Commission, U.S. Department of Labor, and U.S. Department of Justice. Uniform guidelines on employee selection procedures. *Federal Register*, 1978, 43 (166), 38295-38309.

Whetzel, D. L., & McDaniel, M. A. (1988). Reliability of validity generalization data bases. *Psychological Reports, 63*, 131-134.

Whetzel, D. L., McDaniel, M. A., & Schmidt, F. L. (1985). The validity of employment interviews: A review and meta-analysis. In H. R. Hirsh (Chair), *Meta-analysis of alternative predictors of job performance*. Symposium conducted at 93rd annual convention of the American Psychological Association, Los Angeles.

Wolf, F. M. (1986). *Meta-analysis: Quantitative methods for research synthesis*. Beverly Hills, CA: Sage.

Wortman, P. M. (1983). Evaluation research: A methodological perspective. *Annotated Review of Psychology, 34*, 223-260.

Wortman, P. M., & Bryant, F. B. (1985). School desegregation and black achievement: An integrative review. *Sociological Methods and Research, 13*, 289-324.

Wolins, L. (1962). Responsibility for raw data. *American Psychologist, 17*, 657-658.

Wigdor, A. K., & Garner, W. R. (Eds.). (1982a). *Ability testing: Uses, consequences and controversies, Part I: Report of the committee*, Washington, DC: National Academy Press.

Wigdor, A. K., & Garner, W. R. (Eds.). (1982b). *Ability testing: Uses, consequences and controversies, Part II: Documentation section*, Washington, DC: National Academy Press.

Wunder, R. S., & Herring, J. W. (1980). *Interpretive guide for the API test validity generalization project*. Human Resources Series, American Petroleum Institute, Publication 755.

Wunder, R. S., Herring, J. W., & Carron, T. J. (1982). *Interpretive guide for the API test validity generalization project*. Human Resources Series, American Petroleum Institute, Publication 755.

Author Index

Subject Index

Alpha coefficient, 461
Analysis of covariance, 254
Analysis of variance (ANOVA); effect size statistic and, 271; error of measurement and, 360; error rate of, 237-238; generalizability theory, 413; higher order interactions, 341; information from, 501-502; interaction and, 516; negative variance, 412-414; treatment main effect, 355
ANOVA, *see* Analysis of variance
Apples and oranges effects, 516-527
Artifact(s): compound effect of, 197; correctable, 93-95, 144, 263; *d* statistic and, 319-320, 336; in individual studies, 143-146; independence assumptions for, 159-160, 162-163; information availability and, 156-160, 196-197, 292, 338; mathematical similarity of, 95; methodology and, 495-498; overestimation of variance from, 224-226; partial information, 187-190; residual variance and, 100; study subsets and, 293; systematic, 97; types of, 44, 45 table, 144; undercorrection for, 84-85; *See also* Construct validity; Measurement, error of; Moderators; Multiple artifacts; Sampling error
Artifact distribution meta-analysis, 158-160, 196-198, 311-316, 334-336; computer code for, 541, 548-552, 556-558; moderator search and, 293-295; personnel selection and, 182-187
Attenuated treatment effect, 325-332
Attenuation: average attenuation factor, 162-163; bias in correlation, 141; compound attenuation factor, 145; correction for error of measurement and, 318-319; dichotomization, 47, 133-

138, 156; double attenuation, 138; double dichotomization, 47; double-range restriction, 52; of effect size, 58; error of measurement, 137; extraneous factors, 69, 140; imperfect construct validity, 138-139; independence of artifacts and, 162-163; mean uncorrected correlation, 161-163; multiple artifacts, 142-143, 321-324; non-study correlations, 160; for range variation, 146; reliability of treatment variable and, 249; squaring, 149; study correlation, 161-162; by systematic errors, 321; weighting and, 149, 188; *See also* Attenuation, correction for; *specific artifacts, problems*
Attenuation, correction for; arguments against, 303-304; classic formula for, 119; composite score, 455; confidence interval and, 120-122; criticisms of, 533-534; cross-study correlations, 116; cumulation and, 505; dichotomization and, 133; effect sizes, 303-308; measurement error, 97, 111-122, 304; multiple artifacts, 321-324; sampling error and, 120-121, 324-325; study characteristic correlation and, 293; substantive vs. statistical, 122-123
Attrition artifacts, 49-52, 94t, 139-140
Availability bias, 506-515

Bare bone meta-analysis, 156;; bias of, 157; correction for measurement error, 303; of *d* values, 284-292; second-order sampling error, 422-435; subset studies, 337; uncorrected effect sizes, 303; mean treatment effect, 336
Best evidence synthesis, 480
Between-subjects design, 339-346. *See also* Independent groups design

580

About the Authors

John E. (Jack) Hunter is a Professor in the Department of Psychology at Michigan State University. He received his Ph.D. in psychology from the University of Illinois. He has co-authored two books, *Meta-analysis* and *Mathematical Models of Attitude Change*, and has published over 150 articles on a wide variety of topics. His current research in personnel focuses on the determinants of job performance, and in meta-analysis on the extension of meta-analytic methods to correct for artifacts not yet handled. He is also doing research in psychometric theory. Professor Hunter is a Fellow of the Society of Industrial and Organization Psychology, the American Psychological Society, and the American Psychological Association.

Frank L. Schmidt is the Ralph L. Sheets Professor of Human Resources at the University of Iowa. He received his Ph.D. in industrial/organizational psychology from Purdue University and has been on the faculties of Michigan State and George Washington universities. He headed a research program in personnel selection at the U.S. Office of Personnel Management for 11 years, during which time he published numerous studies in personnel psychology, primarily with John Hunter. It was their research on the generalizability of employment test validities that led to the development of the meta-analysis methods presented in this book. Professor Schmidt is a Fellow of the American Psychological Association, the American Psychological Society, and is on the Editorial Board of *Journal of Applied Psychology*.